CORE STATUTES ON
PUBLIC LAW AND HUMAN RIGHTS

CORE STATUTES ON PUBLIC LAW AND HUMAN RIGHTS

Greer Hogan and Rhona Smith

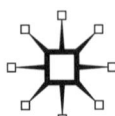 This selection © Greer Hogan and Rhona Smith 2008

All rights reserved. No reproduction, copy or transmission of this publication may be made without written permission.

Crown Copyright material is reproduced with the permission of the Controller of HMSO and the Queen's Printer for Scotland.

No paragraph of this publication may be reproduced, copied or transmitted save with written permission or in accordance with the provisions of the Copyright, Designs and Patents Act 1988, or under the terms of any licence permitting limited copying issued by the Copyright Licensing Agency, 90 Tottenham Court Road, London W1T 4LP.

Any person who does any unauthorized act in relation to this publication may be liable to criminal prosecution and civil claims for damages.

The authors have asserted their rights to be identified as the authors of this work in accordance with the Copyright, Designs and Patents Act 1988.

Published 2007, 2008 by
PALGRAVE MACMILLAN
Houndmills, Basingstoke, Hampshire RG21 6XS and
175 Fifth Avenue, New York, N.Y. 10010
Companies and representatives throughout the world

PALGRAVE MACMILLAN is the global academic imprint of the Palgrave Macmillan division of St. Martin's Press, LLC and of Palgrave Macmillan Ltd. Macmillan® is a registered trademark in the United States, United Kingdom and other countries. Palgrave is a registered trademark in the European Union and other countries.

ISBN-13: 978–0–230–21851–2 paperback
ISBN-10:   0–230–21851–2 paperback

This book is printed on paper suitable for recycling and made from fully managed and sustained forest sources. Logging, pulping and manufacturing processes are expected to conform to the environmental regulations of the country of origin.

A catalogue record for this book is available from the British Library.

A catalog record for this book is available from the Library of Congress.

10 9 8 7 6 5 4 3 2 1
17 16 15 14 13 12 11 10 09 08

Typeset by Style Photosetting Ltd, Mayfield, East Sussex
Printed and bound in Great Britain by
Cromwell Press Ltd, Trowbridge, Wiltshire

PREFACE

The enclosed materials represent the core statutes and additional instruments for undergraduate study of Public (Constitutional and Administrative) Law. We have edited the materials to focus on those aspects of the materials most commonly required for private study and examination. For the full text of the instruments, recourse should be had to the Office of Public Sector Information (formerly HMSO) or one of the paper or online consolidated version providers. Where possible, prospective amendments are marked in italics.

Due to restraints in the publishing schedule, we have been unable to include many bills being considered in the 2007/08 Parliamentary session. However, we have endeavoured to provide a snapshot of the law in force as of April 2008. Students should consult www.opsi.gov.uk for statutes enacted after that date.

Greer Hogan
Rhona Smith

CONTENTS

Preface v

Magna Carta (1215)	1
The Bill of Rights (1688)	2
The Act of Settlement (1700)	6
Union with Scotland Act 1706	8
Parliamentary Papers Act 1840	10
Official Secrets Act 1911	11
Parliament Act 1911	12
Official Secrets Act 1920	14
The Statute of Westminster 1931	15
Public Order Act 1936	16
Statutory Instruments Act 1946	17
Crown Proceedings Act 1947	19
Life Peerages Act 1958	22
Obscene Publications Act 1959	22
Parliamentary Commissioner Act 1967	24
European Communities Act 1972	31
Local Government Act 1972	33
Local Government Act 1974	38
House of Commons Disqualification Act 1975	45
Ministerial And Other Salaries Act 1975	47
Highways Act 1980	48
Supreme Court [Senior Courts] Act 1981	48
Police and Criminal Evidence Act 1984	53
Public Order Act 1986	94
Official Secrets Act 1989	105
Security Service Act 1989	112
Tribunals and Inquiries Act 1992	113
Intelligence Services Act 1994	115
Criminal Justice and Public Order Act 1994	119
Police Act 1996	126
Police Act 1997	146
Crime and Disorder Act 1998	151
Human Rights Act 1998	156
Scotland Act 1998	163
Northern Ireland Act 1998	181
House of Lords Act 1999	191
Freedom of Information Act 2000	192
Terrorism Act 2000	205
House of Commons (Removal of Clergy Disqualification) Act 2001	215
Criminal Justice and Police Act 2001	216
Anti-terrorism, Crime and Security Act 2001	223
Police Reform Act 2002	224
Anti-social Behaviour Act 2003	244
Criminal Justice Act 2003	246
Prevention of Terrorism Act 2005	248
Constitutional Reform Act 2005	258
Serious Organised Crime and Police Act 2005	265
Equality Act 2006	281
Terrorism Act 2006	284

Identity Cards Act 2006	294
Government of Wales Act 2006	314
Police and Justice Act 2006	331
Tribunals, Courts and Enforcement Act 2007	337
Serious Crime Act 2007	349
UK Borders Act 2007	354

PACE Codes

Police and Criminal Evidence Act 1984 Code A	355
Police and Criminal Evidence Act 1984 Code C	366
Police and Criminal Evidence Act 1984 Code G	379

Court rules

Civil Procedure Rules 1998, Part 54	383
Civil Procedure Rules 1998, PD 54	386

International convention

Convention for the Protection of Human Rights and Fundamental Freedoms	390

Index	399

ALPHABETICAL LIST OF CONTENTS

Act of Settlement (1700)	6
Anti-social Behaviour Act 2003	244
Anti-terrorism, Crime and Security Act 2001	223
Bill of Rights (1688)	2
Civil Procedure Rules 1998, Part 54	383
Civil Procedure Rules 1998, PD 54	386
Constitutional Reform Act 2005	258
Convention for the Protection of Human Rights and Fundamental Freedoms	390
Crime and Disorder Act 1998	151
Criminal Justice Act 2003	246
Criminal Justice and Police Act 2001	216
Criminal Justice and Public Order Act 1994	119
Crown Proceedings Act 1947	19
Equality Act 2006	281
European Communities Act 1972	31
Freedom of Information Act 2000	192
Government of Wales Act 2006	314
Highways Act 1980	48
House of Commons Disqualification Act 1975	45
House of Commons (Removal of Clergy Disqualification) Act 2001	215
House of Lords Act 1999	191
Human Rights Act 1998	156
Identity Cards Act 2006	294
Intelligence Services Act 1994	115
Life Peerages Act 1958	22
Local Government Act 1972	33
Local Government Act 1974	38
Magna Carta (1215)	1
Ministerial And Other Salaries Act 1975	47
Northern Ireland Act 1998	181
Obscene Publications Act 1959	22
Official Secrets Act 1911	11
Official Secrets Act 1920	14
Official Secrets Act 1989	105
Parliament Act 1911	12
Parliamentary Commissioner Act 1967	24
Parliamentary Papers Act 1840	10
Police Act 1996	126
Police Act 1997	146
Police and Criminal Evidence Act 1984	53
Police and Criminal Evidence Act 1984 Code A	355
Police and Criminal Evidence Act 1984 Code C	366
Police and Criminal Evidence Act 1984 Code G	379
Police and Justice Act 2006	331
Police Reform Act 2002	224
Prevention of Terrorism Act 2005	248
Public Order Act 1936	16
Public Order Act 1986	94
Scotland Act 1998	163
Security Service Act 1989	112
Serious Crime Act 2007	349
Serious Organised Crime and Police Act 2005	265
Statute of Westminster 1931	15

Statutory Instruments Act 1946	17
Supreme Court [Senior Courts] Act 1981	48
Terrorism Act 2000	205
Terrorism Act 2006	284
Tribunals and Inquiries Act 1992	113
Tribunals, Courts and Enforcement Act 2007	337
UK Borders Act 2007	354
Union with Scotland Act 1706	8

MAGNA CARTA (1215)

JOHN, by the grace of God King of England, Lord of Ireland, Duke of Normandy and Aquitaine, and Count of Anjou, to his archbishops, bishops, abbots, earls, barons, justices, foresters, sheriffs, stewards, servants, and to all his officials and loyal subjects, Greeting.

KNOW THAT BEFORE GOD, for the health of our soul and those of our ancestors and heirs, to the honour of God, the exaltation of the holy Church, and the better ordering of our kingdom, at the advice of our reverend fathers Stephen, archbishop of Canterbury, primate of all England, and cardinal of the holy Roman Church, Henry archbishop of Dublin, William bishop of London, Peter bishop of Winchester, Jocelin bishop of Bath and Glastonbury, Hugh bishop of Lincoln, Walter Bishop of Worcester, William bishop of Coventry, Benedict bishop of Rochester, Master Pandulf subdeacon and member of the papal household, Brother Aymeric master of the knighthood of the Temple in England, William Marshal earl of Pembroke, William earl of Salisbury, William earl of Warren, William earl of Arundel, Alan de Galloway constable of Scotland, Warin Fitz Gerald, Peter Fitz Herbert, Hubert de Burgh seneschal of Poitou, Hugh de Neville, Matthew Fitz Herbert, Thomas Basset, Alan Basset, Philip Daubeny, Robert de Roppeley, John Marshal, John Fitz Hugh, and other loyal subjects:

(1) FIRST, THAT WE HAVE GRANTED TO GOD, and by this present charter have confirmed for us and our heirs in perpetuity, that the English Church shall be free, and shall have its rights undiminished, and its liberties unimpaired. That we wish this so to be observed, appears from the fact that of our own free will, before the outbreak of the present dispute between us and our barons, we granted and confirmed by charter the freedom of the Church's elections – a right reckoned to be of the greatest necessity and importance to it – and caused this to be confirmed by Pope Innocent III. This freedom we shall observe ourselves, and desire to be observed in good faith by our heirs in perpetuity.

TO ALL FREE MEN OF OUR KINGDOM we have also granted, for us and our heirs for ever, all the liberties written out below, to have and to keep for them and their heirs,

(12) No "scutage" or "aid" may be levied in our kingdom without its general consent, unless it is for the ransom of our person, to make our eldest son a knight, and (once) to marry our eldest daughter. For these purposes only a reasonable "aid" may be levied. "Aids" from the city of London are to be treated similarly.

(13) The city of London shall enjoy all its ancient liberties and free customs, both by land and by water. We also will and grant that all other cities, boroughs, towns, and ports shall enjoy all their liberties and free customs.

(14) To obtain the general consent of the realm for the assessment of an "aid" – except in the three cases specified above – or a "scutage", we will cause the archbishops, bishops, abbots, earls, and greater barons to be summoned individually by letter. To those who hold lands directly of us we will cause a general summons to be issued, through the sheriffs and other officials, to come together on a fixed day (of which at least forty days notice shall be given) and at a fixed place. In all letters of summons, the cause of the summons will be stated. When a summons has been issued, the business appointed for the day shall go forward in accordance with the resolution of those present, even if not all those who were summoned have appeared.

(15) In future we will allow no one to levy an "aid" from his free men, except to ransom his person, to make his eldest son a knight, and (once) to marry his eldest daughter. For these purposes only a reasonable "aid" may be levied.

(16) No man shall be forced to perform more service for a knight's "fee", or other free holding of land, than is due from it.

(17) Ordinary lawsuits shall not follow the royal court around, but shall be held in a fixed place.

(20) For a trivial offence, a free man shall be fined only in proportion to the degree of his offence, and for a serious offence correspondingly, but not so heavily as to deprive him of his livelihood. In the same way, a merchant shall be spared his merchandise, and a villein the implements of his husbandry, if they fall upon the mercy of a royal court. None of these fines shall be imposed except by the assessment on oath of reputable men of the neighbourhood.

(21) Earls and barons shall be fined only by their equals, and in proportion to the gravity of their offence.

(23) No town or person shall be forced to build bridges over rivers except those with an ancient obligation to do so.
(24) No sheriff, constable, coroners, or other royal officials are to hold lawsuits that should be held by the royal justices.
(28) No constable or other royal official shall take corn or other movable goods from any man without immediate payment, unless the seller voluntarily offers postponement of this.
(30) No sheriff, royal official, or other person shall take horses or carts for transport from any free man, without his consent.
(31) Neither we nor any royal official will take wood for our castle, or for any other purpose, without the consent of the owner.
(35) There shall be standard measures of wine, ale, and corn (the London quarter), throughout the kingdom. There shall also be a standard width of dyed cloth, russet, and haberject, namely two ells within the selvedges. Weights are to be standardised similarly.
(38) In future no official shall place a man on trial upon his own unsupported statement, without producing credible witnesses to the truth of it.
(39) No free man shall be seized or imprisoned, or stripped of his rights or possessions, or outlawed or exiled, or deprived of his standing in any other way, nor will we proceed with force against him, or send others to do so, except by the lawful judgement of his equals or by the law of the land.
(40) To no one will we sell, to no one deny or delay right or justice.
(45) We will appoint as justices, constables, sheriffs, or other officials, only men that know the law of the realm and are minded to keep it well.
(54) No one shall be arrested or imprisoned on the appeal of a woman for the death of any person except her husband.

© British Library Board. All Rights Reserved (MS Cotton Augustus II 106)

THE BILL OF RIGHTS (1688)
(1 Will. & Mar. sess 2, c. 2)

An Act declaring the Rights and Liberties of the Subject and Setleing the Succession of the Crowne

Whereas the lords spirituall and temporall and comons assembled at Westminster lawfully fully and freely representing all estates of the people of this realme did upon the thirteenth day of February in the yeare of our Lord one thousand six hundred eighty eight present unto their Majesties then called and known by the names and stile of William and Mary Prince and Princesse of Orange being present in their proper persons a certaine declaration in writeing made by the said lords and comons in the words following viz

Whereas the late King James the Second by the assistance of diverse evill councillors judges and ministers imployed by him did endeavour to subvert and extirpate the Protestant religion and the lawes and liberties of this kingdome

By assumeing and exerciseing a power of dispensing with and suspending of lawes and the execution of lawes without consent of Parlyament.

By committing and prosecuting diverse worthy prelates for humbly petitioning to be excused from concurring to the said assumed power.

By issueing and causeing to be executed a commission under the great seale for erecting a court called the court of commissioners for ecclesiasticall causes.

By levying money for and to the use of the Crowne by pretence of prerogative for other time and in other manner then the same was granted by Parlyament.

By raising and keeping a standing army within this kingdome in time of peace without consent of Parlyament and quartering soldiers contrary to law.

By causing severall good subjects being protestants to be disarmed at the same time when papists were both armed and imployed contrary to law.

By violating the freedome of election of members to serve in Parlyament.

By prosecutions in the Court of King's Bench for matters and causes cognizable onely in Parlyament and by diverse other arbitrary and illegall courses.

And whereas of late yeares partiall corrupt and unqualifyed persons have beene returned and served on juryes in tryalls and particularly diverse jurors in tryalls for high treason which were not freeholders.

And excessive baile hath beene required of persons committed in criminall cases to elude the benefitt of the lawes made for the liberty of the subjects.

And excessive fines have beene imposed.

And illegall and cruell punishments inflicted.

And severall grants and promises made of fines and forfeitures before any conviction or judgement against the persons upon whome the same were to be levyed.

All which are uterly and directly contrary to the knowne lawes and statutes and freedome of the realme.

And whereas the said late King James the Second haveing abdicated the government and the throne being thereby vacant his Highnesse the Prince of Orange (whome it hath pleased Almighty God to make the glorious instrument of delivering this kingdome from popery and arbitrary power) did (by the advice of the lords spirituall and temporall and diverse principall persons of the commons) cause letters to be written to the lords spirituall and temporall being protestants and other letters to the severall countyes cityes universities boroughss and cinque ports for the choosing of such persons to represent them as were of right to be sent to Parlyament to meete and sitt at Westminster upon the two and twentyeth day of January in this yeare one thousand six hundred eighty and eight in order to such an establishment as that their religion lawes and liberties might not againe be in danger of being subverted, upon which letters elections haveing beene accordingly made.

And thereupon the said lords spirituall and temporall and commons pursuant to their respective letters and elections being now assembled in a full and free representative of this nation takeing into their most serious consideration the best meanes for attaining the ends aforesaid doe in the first place (as their auncestors in like case have usually done) for the vindicating and asserting their auntient rights and liberties, declare

That the pretended power of suspending of laws or the execution of laws by regall authority without consent of Parlyament is illegall.

That the pretended power of dispensing with laws or the execution of laws by regall authoritie as it hath beene assumed and exercised of late is illegall.

That the commission for erecting the late court of commissioners for ecclesiasticall causes and all other commissions and courts of like nature are illegal and pernicious.

That levying money for or to the use of the Crowne by pretence of prerogative without grant of Parlyament for longer time or in other manner than the same is or shall be granted is illegal.

That it is the right of the subjects to petition the King and all commitments and prosecutions for such petitioning are illegal.

That the raising or keeping a standing army within the kingdome in time of peace unlesse it be with consent of Parlyament is against law.

That the subjects which are protestants may have arms for their defence suitable to their conditions and as allowed by law.

That election of members of Parlyament ought to be free.

That the freedome of speech and debates or proceedings in Parlyament ought not to be impeached or questioned in any court or place out of Parlyament.

That excessive baile ought not to be required nor excessive fines imposed nor cruell and unusuall punishments inflicted.

That jurors ought to be duly impannelled and returned.

That all grants and promises of fines and forfeitures of particular persons before conviction are illegal and void.

And that for redresse of all grievances and for the amending strengthening and preserving of the lawes Parlyaments ought to be held frequently.

And they doe claime demand and insist upon all and singular the premises as their undoubted rights and liberties and that noe declarations judgements doeings or proceedings to the prejudice of the people in any of the said premisses ought in any wise to be drawne hereafter into consequence or example. To which demand of their rights they are particularly encouraged by the declaration of his Highnesse the Prince of Orange as being the only meanes for obtaining a full redresse and remedy therein. Haveing therefore an intire confidence that his said Highnesse the Prince of Orange will perfect the deliverance soe farr advanced by him and will still preserve them from the violation of their rights which they have here asserted and from all other attempts upon their religion rights and liberties.

The said lords spirituall and temporall and commons assembled at Westminster doe resolve that William and Mary Prince and Princesse of Orange be and be declared King and Queene of England France and Ireland and the dominions thereunto belonging to hold the crowne and royall dignity of the said kingdomes and dominions to them the said prince and princesse dureing their lives and the life of the survivour of them. And that the sole and full exercise of the regall power be onely in and executed by the said Prince of Orange in the names of the said prince and princesse dureing their joynt lives and after their deceases the said crowne and royall dignitie of the said kingdoms and dominions to be to the heires of the body of the said princesse and for default of such issue to the Princesse Anne of Denmarke and the heires of her body and for default of such issue to the heires of the body of the said Prince of Orange.

And the lords spirituall and temporall and commons doe pray the said prince and princesse to accept the same accordingly. And that the oathes hereafter mentioned be taken by all persons of whome the oathes of allegiance and supremacy might be required by law instead of them and that the said oathes of allegiance and supremacy be abrogated.

I A B doe sincerely promise and sweare that I will be faithfull and beare true allegiance to their Majestyes King William and Queen Mary

Soe helpe me God

I A B doe sweare that I doe from my heart abhorr, detest and abjure as impious and hereticall this damnable doctrine and position that princes excommunicated or deprived by the Pope or any authority of the see of Rome may be deposed or murdered by their subjects or any other whatsoever. And I doe declare that noe forreigne prince person prelate, state or potentate hath or ought to have any jurisdiction power superiority preeminence or authoritie ecclesiasticall or spirituall within this realme.

Soe help me God

Upon which their said Majestyes did accept the crowne and royall dignitie of the kingdoms of England France and Ireland and the dominions thereunto belonging according to the resolution and desire of the said lords and commons contained in the said declaration. And thereupon their Majestyes were pleased that the said lords spirituall and temporall and commons being the two Houses of Parlyament should continue to sitt and with their Majesties royall concurrence make effectuall provision for the settlement of the religion lawes and liberties of this kingdome soe that the same for the future might not be in danger againe of being subverted, to which the said lords spirituall and temporall and commons did agree and proceede to act accordingly.

Now in pursuance of the premises the said lords spirituall and temporall and commons in Parlyament assembled for the ratifying confirming and establishing the said declaration and the articles clauses matters and things therein contained by the force of a law made in due forme by authority of Parlyament doe pray that it may be declared and enacted that all and singular the rights and liberties asserted and claimed in the said declaration are the true auntient and indubitable rights and liberties of the people of this kingdome and soe shall be esteemed allowed adjudged deemed and taken to be and that all and every the pariticulars aforesaid shall be firmly and strictly holden and observed as they are expressed in the said declaration. And all officers and ministers whatsoever shall serve their Majestyes and their successors according to the same in all times to come. And the said lords spirituall and temporall and commons seriously considering how it hath pleased Almighty God in his marvellous providence and mercifull goodness to this nation to provide and preserve their said Majestyes royall persons most happily to raigne over us upon the throne of their auncestors for which they render unto him from the bottome of their hearts their humblest thanks and praises doe truely firmely assuredly and in the sincerity of their hearts thinke and doe hereby recognize acknowledge and declare that King James the Second haveing abdicated the government and their Majestyes having accepted the crowne and royall dignity as aforesaid their said Majestyes did become were are and of right ought to be by the lawes of the realme our soveraigne liege lord and lady King and Queene of England France and Ireland and the dominions thereunto belonging in and to whose princely persons the royall state crowne and dignity of the said realmes with all honours stiles titles regalities prerogatives powers jurisdictions and authorities to the same belonging and appertaining are most fully and rightfully and intirely invested and incorporated united and annexed.

And for preventing all questions and divisions in this realme by reason of any pretended titles to the crowne and for preserveing a certainty in the succession thereof in and upon which the unity peace tranquillity and safety of this nation doth under God wholly consist and depend the said lords spirituall and temporall and commons doe beseech their Majestyes that it may be enacted established and declared that the crowne and regall government of the said kingdoms and dominions with all and singular the premisses thereunto belonging and appertaining shall bee and continue to their said Majestyes and the survivour of them dureing their lives and the life of the survivour of them and that the entire perfect and full exercise of the regall power and government be onely in and executed by his Majestie in the names of both their Majestyes dureing their joynt lives and after their deceases the said crowne and premisses shall be and remaine to the heires of the body of her Majestie and for default of such issue to her royall Highnesse the Princess Anne of Denmarke and the heires of her body and for default of such issue to the heires of the body of his said Majestie And thereunto the said lords spirituall and temporall and commons doe in the name of all the people aforesaid most humbly and faithfully submitt themselves their heires and posterities for ever and doe faithfully promise that they will stand to maintaine and defend their said Majesties and alsoe the limitation and succession of the crowne herein specified and contained to the utmost of their powers with their lives and estates against all persons whatsoever that shall attempt any thing to the contrary.

And whereas it hath beene found by experience that it is inconsistent with the safety and welfare of this protestant kingdome to be governed by a popish prince or by any King or Queene marrying a papist the said lords spirtuall and temporall and commons doe further pray that it may be enacted that all and every person and persons that is are or shall be reconciled to or shall hold communion with the see or church of Rome or shall professe the popish religion or shall marry a papist shall be excluded and be for ever uncapeable to inherit possesse or enjoy the crowne and government of this realme and Ireland and the dominions thereunto belonging or any part of the same or to have use or exercise any regall power authoritie or jurisdiction within the same And in all and every such case or cases the people of these realmes shall be and are hereby absolved of their allegiance and the said crowne and government shall from time to time descend to and be enjoyed by such person or persons being protestants as should have inherited and enjoyed the same in case the said person or persons soe reconciled holding communion or professing or marrying as aforesaid were naturally dead.

And that every King and Queene of this realme who at any time hereafter shall come to and succeede in the imperiall crowne of this kingdome shall on the first day of the meeting of the first Parlyament next after his or her comeing to the crowne sitting in his or her throne in the House of Peeres in the presence of the lords and commons therein assembled or at his or her coronation before such person or persons who shall administer the coronation oath to him or her at the time of his or her takeing the said oath (which shall first happen) make subscribe and audibly repeate the declaration mentioned in the Statute made in the thirtyeth yeare of the raigne of King Charles the Second entituled An Act for the more effectuall preserveing the Kings person and government by disableing papists from sitting in either House of Parlyament.

But if it shall happen that such King or Queene upon his or her succession to the crowne of this realme shall be under the age of twelve yeares then every such King or Queene shall make subscribe and audibly repeate the said declaration at his or her coronation or the first day of the meeting of the first Parlyament as aforesaid which shall first happen after such King or Queene shall have attained the said age of twelve years. All which their Majestyes are contented and pleased shall be declared enacted and established by authoritie of this present Parliament and shall stand remaine and be the law of this realme for ever And the same are by their said Majesties by and with the advice and consent of the lords spirituall and temporall and commons in Parlyament assembled and by the authoritie of the same declared enacted and established accordingly.

2 Non obstantes made void

... noe dispensation by non obstante of or to any statute or any part thereof shall be allowed but ... the same shall be held void and of noe effect except a dispensation be allowed of in such statute ...

THE ACT OF SETTLEMENT (1700)
(12 & 13 Will. 3, c. 2)

An Act for the further Limitation of the Crown and better securing the Rights and Liberties of the Subject

Whereas in the first year of the reign of your Majesty and of our late most gracious soverign lady Queen Mary (of blessed memory) an Act of Parliament was made intituled (An Act for declaring the rights and liberties of the subject and for setling the succession of the crown) wherein it was (amongst other things) enacted established and declared that the crown and regall government of the kingdoms of England France and Ireland and the dominions thereunto belonging should be and continue to your Majestie and the said late Queen during the joynt lives of your Majesty and the said Queen and to the survivor and that after the decease of your Majesty and of the said Queen the said crown and regall government should be and remain to the heirs of the body of the said late Queen and for default of such issue to her royall Highness the Princess Ann of Denmark and the heirs of her body and for default of such issue to the heirs of the body of your Majesty And it was thereby further enacted that all and every person and persons that then were or afterwards should be reconciled to or shall hold communion with the see or church of Rome or should professe the popish religion or marry a papist should be excluded and are by that Act made for ever incapable to inherit possess or enjoy the crown and government of this realm and Ireland and the dominions thereunto belonging or any part of the same or to have use or exercise any regall power authority or jurisdiction within the same and in all and every such case and cases the people of these realms shall be and are thereby absolved of their allegiance and that the said crown and government shall from time to time descend to and be enjoyed by such person or persons being protestants as should have inherited and enjoyed the same in case the said person or persons so reconciled holding communion professing or marrying as aforesaid were naturally dead After the making of which Statute and the settlement therein contained your Majesties good subjects who were restored to the full and free possession and enjoyment of their religion rights and liberties by the providence of God giving success to your Majesties just undertakings and unwearied endeavours for that purpose had no greater temporall felicity to hope or wish for than to see a royall progeny descending from your Majesty to whom (under God) they owe their tranquility and whose ancestors have for many years been principall assertors of the reformed religion and the liberties of Europe and from our said most gracious sovereign lady whose memory will always be precious to the subjects of these realms And it having since pleased Almighty God to take away our said sovereign lady and also the most hopefull Prince William Duke of Gloucester (the only surviving issue of her royall Highness the Princess Ann of Denmark) to the unspeakable grief and sorrow of your Majesty and your said good subjects who under such losses being sensibly put in mind that it standeth wholly in the pleasure of Almighty God to prolong the lives of your Majesty and of her royall Highness and to grant to your Majesty or to her royall Highness such issue as may be inheritable to the crown and regall government aforesaid by the respective limitations in the said recited Act contained doe constantly implore the divine mercy for those blessings And your Majesties said subjects having daily experience of your royall care and concern for the present and future welfare of these kingdoms and particularly recommending from your throne a further provision to be made for the succession of the crown in the protestant line for the happiness of the nation and the security of our religion and it being absolutely necessary for the safety peace and quiet of this realm to obviate all doubts and contentions in the same by reason of any pretended titles to the crown and to maintain a certainty in the succession thereof to which your subjects may safely have recourse for their protection in case the limitations in the said recited Act should determine Therefore for a further provision of the succession of the crown in the protestant line we your Majesties most dutifull and loyal subjects the lords spirituall and temporall and commons in this present Parliament assembled do beseech your Majesty that it may be enacted and declared and be it enacted and declared by the Kings most excellent Majesty by and with the advice and consent of the lords spirituall and temporall and commons in this present Parliament assembled and by the authority of the same.

1   **The Princess Sophia, Electress and Duchess dowager of Hanover, daughter of the late Queen of Bohemia, daughter of King James the First, to inherit after the King and the Princess Anne, in default of issue of the said princess and his Majesty, respectively; and the heirs of her body, being protestants**

That the most excellent Princess Sophia Electress and Dutchess dowager of Hanover daughter of the most excellent Princess Elizabeth late Queen of Bohemia daughter of our late sovereign lord

King James the First of happy memory be and is hereby declared to be the next in succession in the protestant line to the imperiall crown and dignity of the said realms of England France and Ireland with the dominions and territories thereunto belonging after his Majesty and the Princess Ann of Denmark and in default of issue of the said Princess Ann and of his Majesty respectively and that from and after the deceases of his said Majesty our own soveriegn lord and of her royall Highness the Princess Ann of Denmark and for default of issue of the said Princess Ann and of his Majesty respectively the crown and regall government of the said kingdoms of England France and Ireland and of the dominions thereunto belonging with the royall state and dignity of the said realms and all honours stiles titles regalities prerogatives powers jurisdictions and authorities to the same belonging and appertaining shall be remain and continue to the said most excellent Princess Sophia and the heirs of her body being protestants And thereunto the said lords spirituall and temporall and commons shall and will in the name of all the people of this realm most humbly and faithfully submit themselves their heirs and posterities and do faithfully promise that after the deceases of his Majesty and her royall Highness and the failure of the heirs of their respective bodies to stand to maintain and defend the said Princess Sophia and the heirs of her body being protestants according to the limitation and succession of the crown in this Act specified and contained to the utmost of their powers with their lives and estates against all persons whatsoever that shall attempt any thing to the contrary.

2   The persons inheritable by this Act, holding communion with the church of Rome, incapacitated as by the former Act; to take the oath at their coronation, according to Stat 1 W & M c. 6

Provided always and it is hereby enacted that all and every person and persons who shall or may take or inherit the said crown by vertue of the limitation of this present Act and is are or shall be reconciled to or shall hold communion with the see or church of Rome or shall profess the popish religion or shall marry a papist shall be subject to such incapacities as in such case or cases are by the said recited Act provided enacted and established. And that every King and Queen of this realm who shall come to and succeed in the imperiall crown of this kingdom by vertue of this Act shall have the coronation oath administered to him her or them at their respective coronations according to the Act of Parliament made in the first year of the reign of his Majesty and the said late Queen Mary intituled An Act for establishing the coronation oath and shall make subscribe and repeat the declaration in the Act first above recited mentioned or referred to in the manner and form thereby prescribed.

3   Further provisions for securing the religions, laws, and liberties of these realms

And whereas it is requisite and necessary that some further provision be made for securing our religion laws and liberties from and after the death of his Majesty and the Princess Ann of Denmark and in default of issue of the body of the said princess and of his Majesty respectively Be it enacted by the Kings most excellent Majesty by and with the advice and consent of the lords spirituall and temporall and commons in Parliament and by the authority of the same

That whosoever shall hereafter come to the possession of this crown shall joyn in communion with the Church of England as by law established

That in case the crown and imperiall dignity of this realm shall hereafter come to any person not being a native of this kingdom of England this nation be not obliged to ingage in any warr for the defence of any dominions or territories which do not belong to the crown of England without the consent of Parliament

That after the said limitation shall take effect as aforesaid no person born out of the kingdoms of England Scotland or Ireland or the dominions thereunto belonging (although he be. . . made a denizen (except such as are born of English parents)) shall be capable to be of the privy council or a member of either House of Parliament or to enjoy any office or place of trust either civill or military or to have any grant of lands tenements or hereditaments from the Crown to himself or to any other or others in trust for him.

That no pardon under the great seal of England be pleadable to an impeachment by the commons in Parliament.

4   The laws and statutes of the realm confirmed

And whereas the laws of England are the birthright of the people thereof and all the Kings and Queens who shall ascend the throne of this realm ought to administer the government of the same according to the said laws and all their officers and ministers ought to serve them respectively according to the same The said lords spirituall and temporall and commons do therefore further humbly pray that all the laws and statutes of this realm for securing the established religion and the rights and liberties of the people thereof and all other laws and statutes of the same now in force may be ratified and confirmed And the same are by his Majesty by and with the advice and consent of the said lords spirituall and temporall and commons and by authority of the same ratified and confirmed accordingly.

UNION WITH SCOTLAND ACT 1706
(6 Anne, c. 11)

An Act for an Union of the Two Kingdoms of England and Scotland

Most Gracious Sovereign

Whereas articles of union were agreed on the twenty second day of July in the fifth year of your Majesties reign by the commissioners nominated on behalf of the kingdom of England under your Majesties great seal of England bearing date at Westminster the tenth day of April then last past in pursuance of an Act of Parliament made in England in the third year of your Majesties reign and the commissioners nominated on the behalf of the kingdom of Scotland under your Majesties great seal of Scotland bearing date the twenty-seventh day of February in the fourth year of your Majesties reign in pursuance of the fourth Act of the third session of the present Parliament of Scotland to treat of and concerning an union of the said kingdoms And whereas an Act hath passed in the Parliament of Scotland at Edinburgh the sixteenth day of January in the fifth year of your Majesties reign wherein 'tis mentioned that the estates of Parliament considering the said articles of union of the two kingdoms had agreed to and approved of the said articles of union with some additions and explanations and that your Majesty with advice and consent of the estates of Parliament for establishing the Protestant religion and Presbyterian Church government within the kingdom of Scotland had passed in the same session of Parliament an Act intituled Act for securing of the Protestant religion and Presbyterian Church government which by the tenor thereof was appointed to be inserted in any Act ratifying the treaty and expresly declared to be a fundamental and essential condition of the said treaty or union in all times coming the tenor of which articles as ratified and approved of with additions and explanations by the said Act of Parliament of Scotland follows.

Article I

That the two kingdoms of England and Scotland shall upon the first day of May which shall be in the year one thousand seven hundred and seven and for ever after be united into one kingdom by the name of Great Britain and that the ensigns armorial of the said United Kingdom be such as her Majesty shall appoint and the crosses of St. George and St. Andrew be conjoyned in such manner as Her Majesty shall think fit and used in all flags banners standards and ensigns both at sea and land.

Article II

That the succession to the monarchy of the United Kingdom of Great Britain and of the dominions thereto belonging after her most sacred Majesty and in default of issue of her Majesty be remain and continue to the most excellent Princess Sophia Electoress and Dutchess dowager of Hanover and the heirs of her body being protestants upon whom the crown of England is settled by an Act of Parliament made in England in the twelfth year of the reign of his late Majesty King William the Third intituled An Act for the further limitation of the crown and better securing the right and liberties of the subject And that all papists and persons marrying papists shall be excluded from and for ever incapable to inherit possess or enjoy the imperial crown of Great Britain and the dominions thereunto belonging or any part thereof and in every such case the crown and government shall from time to time descend to and be enjoyed by such person being a protestant as should have inherited and enjoyed the same in case such papist or person marrying a papist was naturally dead according to the provision for the descent of the crown of England made by another Act of Parliament in England in the first year of the reign of their late Majesties King William and Queen Mary intituled An Act declaring the rights and liberties of the subject and settling the succession of the crown.

Article III

That the United Kingdom of Great Britain be represented by one and the same Parliament to be stiled the Parliament of Great Britain.

Article IIII

That all the subjects of the United Kingdom of Great Britain shall from and after the union have full freedom and intercourse of trade and navigation to and from any port or place within the said United Kingdom and the dominions and plantations thereunto belonging and that there be a communication of all other rights privileges and advantages which do or may belong to the subjects of either kingdom except where it is otherwise expressly agreed in these articles.

Article VI

That all parts of the United Kingdom for ever from and after the union shall have the same allowances encouragements and drawbacks and be under the same prohibitions restrictions and regulations of trade and liable to the same customs and duties on import and export and that the allowances encouragements and drawbacks prohibitions restrictions and regulations of trade and the customs and duties on import and export settled in England when the union commences shall from and after the union take place throughout the whole United Kingdom . . .

Article XVIII

That the laws concerning regulation of trade customs and such excises to which Scotland is by virtue of this treaty to be liable be the same in Scotland from and after the union as in England and that all other laws in use within the kingdom of Scotland do after the union and notwithstanding thereof remain in the same force as before (except such as are contrary to or inconsistent with this treaty) but alterable by the Parliament of Great Britain with this difference betwixt the laws concerning publick right policy and civil government and those which concern private right that the laws which concern publick right policy and civil government may be made the same throughout the whole United Kingdom. But that no alteration be made in laws which concern private right except for evident utility of the subjects within Scotland

Article XXV

That all laws and statutes in either kingdom so far as they are contrary to or inconsistent with the terms of these articles or any of them shall from and after the union cease and become void and shall be so declared to be by the respective Parliaments of the said kingdoms.

As by the said articles of union ratified and approved by the said Act of Parliament of Scotland relation being thereunto had may appear.
And it is hereby further enacted by the authority aforesaid that the said Act passed in this present session of Parliament intituled An Act for securing the Church of England as by law established and all and every the matters and things therein contained and also the said Act of Parliament of Scotland intituled Act for securing the Protestant religion and Presbyterian Church government with the establishment in the said Act contained be and shall for ever be held and adjudged to be and observed as fundamental and essential conditions of the said union and shall in all times coming be taken to be and are hereby declared to be essential and fundamental parts of the said articles and union and the said articles of union so as aforesaid ratified approved and confirmed by Act of Parliament of Scotland and by this present Act and the said Act passed in this present session of Parliament intituled an Act for securing the Church of England as by law established and also the said Act passed in the Parliament of Scotland intituled Act for securing the Protestant religion and Presbyterian Church government are hereby enacted and ordained to be and continue in all times coming the complete and intire union of the two kingdoms of England and Scotland.

PARLIAMENTARY PAPERS ACT 1840
(3 & 4 Vict., c. 9)

An Act to give summary Protection to Persons employed in the Publication of Parliamentary Papers

1 **Proceedings, criminal or civil, against persons for publication of papers printed by order of Parliament to be stayed upon delivery of a certificte and affidavit to the effect that such publication is by order of either House of Parliament**

. . . It shall and may be lawful for any person or persons who now is or are, or hereafter shall be, a defendant or defendants in any civil or criminal proceedings commenced or prosecuted in any manner soever, for or on account or in respect of the publication of any such report, paper, votes, or proceedings by such person or persons, or by his, her, or their servant or servants, by or under the authority of either House of Parliament, to bring before the court in which such proceeding shall have been or shall be so commenced or prosecuted, or before any judge of the same (if one of the superior courts at Westminster), first giving twenty-four hours notice of his intention so to do to the prosecutor or plaintiff in such proceeding, a certificate under the hand of the . . . speaker of the House of Lords, . . . or of the clerk of the Parliaments, or of the speaker of the House of Commons, or of the clerk of the same house, stating that the report, paper, votes, or proceedings, as the case may be, in respect whereof such civil or criminal proceeding shall have been commenced or prosecuted, was published by such person or persons, or by his, her, or their servant or servants, by order or under the authority of the House of Lords or of the House of Commons, as the case may be, together with an affidavit verifying such certificate; and such court or judge shall thereupon immediately stay such civil or criminal proceeding, and the same, and every writ or process issued therein, shall be and shall be deemed and taken to be finally put an end to, determined, and superseded by virtue of this Act.

2 **Proceedings to be stayed when commenced in respect of a copy of an authenticated report, etc.**

. . . In case of any civil or criminal proceeding hereafter to be commenced or prosecuted for or on account or in respect of the publication of any copy of such report, paper, votes, or proceedings, it shall be lawful for the defendant or defendants at any stage of the proceedings to lay before the court or judge such report, paper, votes, or proceedings, and such copy, with an affidavit verifying such report, paper, votes, or proceedings, and the correctness of such copy, and the court or judge shall immediately stay such civil or criminal proceedings, and the same, and every writ or process issued therein, shall be and shall be deemed and taken to be finally put an end to, determined, and superseded by virtue of this Act.

3 **In proceedings for printing any extract or abstract of a paper, it may be shown that such extract was bona fide made**

. . . It shall be lawful in any civil or criminal proceeding to be commenced or prosecuted for printing any extract from or abstract of such report, paper, votes, or proceedings, to give in evidence . . . such report, paper, votes or proceedings, and to show that such extract or abstract was published bona fide and without malice; and if such shall be the opinion of the jury, a verdict of not guilty shall be entered for the defendant or defendants.

4 **Act not to affect the privileges of Parliament**

Provided always . . . that nothing herein contained shall be deemed or taken, or held or construed, directly or indirectly, by implication or otherwise, to affect the privileges of Parliament in any manner whatsoever.

OFFICIAL SECRETS ACT 1911
(1 & 2 Geo. 5, c. 28)

An Act to re-enact the Official Secrets Act 1889, with Amendments

1 **Penalties for spying**

(1) If any person for any purpose prejudicial to the safety or interests of the State—

    (a) approaches, inspects, passes over or is in the neighbourhood of, or enters any prohibited place within the meaning of this Act; or

    (b) makes any sketch, plan, model, or note which is calculated to be or might be or is intended to be directly or indirectly useful to an enemy; or

    (c) obtains, collects, records, or publishes, or communicates to any other person any secret official code word or pass word, or any sketch, plan, model, article, or note, or other document or information which is calculated to be or might be or is intended to be directly or indirectly useful to an enemy;

he shall be guilty of felony . . .

(2) On a prosecution under this section, it shall not be necessary to show that the accused person was guilty of any particular act tending to show a purpose prejudicial to the safety or interests of the State, and, notwithstanding that no such act is proved against him, he may be convicted if, from the circumstances of the case, or his conduct, or his known character as proved, it appears that his purpose was a purpose prejudicial to the safety or interests of the State; and if any sketch, plan, model, article, note, document, or information relating to or used in any prohibited place within the meaning of this Act, or anything in such a place or any secret official code word or pass word, is made, obtained, collected, recorded, published, or communicated by any person other than a person acting under lawful authority, it shall be deemed to have been made, obtained, collected, recorded, published or communicated for a purpose prejudicial to the safety or interests of the State unless the contrary is proved.

3 **Definition of prohibited place**

For the purposes of this Act, the expression "prohibited place" means—

    (a) any work of defence, arsenal, naval or air force establishment or station, factory, dockyard, mine, minefield, camp, ship, or aircraft belonging to or occupied by or on behalf of His Majesty, or any telegraph, telephone, wireless or signal station, or office so belonging or occupied, and any place belonging to or occupied by or on behalf of His Majesty and used for the purpose of building, repairing, making, or storing any munitions of war, or any sketches, plans, models, or documents relating thereto, or for the purpose of getting any metals, oil, or minerals of use in time of war;

    (b) any place not belonging to His Majesty where any munitions of war, or any sketches, models, plans or documents relating thereto, are being made, repaired, gotten or stored under contract with, or with any person on behalf of, His Majesty, or otherwise on behalf of His Majesty; and

    (c) any place belonging to or used for the purposes of His Majesty which is for the time being declared by order of a Secretary of State to be a prohibited place for the purposes of this section on the ground that information with respect thereto, or damage thereto, would be useful to an enemy; and

    (d) any railway, road, way, or channel, or other means of communication by land or water (including any works or structures being part thereof or connected therewith), or any place used for gas, water, or electricity works or other works for purposes of a public character, or any place where any munitions of war, or any sketches, models, plans or documents relating thereto, are being made, repaired, or stored otherwise than on behalf of His Majesty, which is for the time being declared by order or a Secretary of State to be a prohibited place for the purposes of this section, on the ground that information with respect thereto, or the destruction or obstruction thereof, or interference therewith, would be useful to an enemy.

8   Restriction on prosecution

A prosecution for an offence under this Act shall not be instituted except by or with the consent of the Attorney-General.

9   Search warrants

(1) If a justice of the peace is satisfied by information on oath that there is reasonable ground for suspecting that an offence under this Act has been or is about to be committed, he may grant a search warrant authorising any constable. . . to enter at any time any premises or place named in the warrant, if necessary, by force, and to search the premises or place and every person found therein, and to seize any sketch, plan, model, article, note, or document, or anything of a like nature or anything which is evidence of an offence under this Act having been or being about to be committed, which he may find on the premises or place or on any such person, and with regard to or in connexion with which he has reasonable ground for suspecting that an offence under this Act has been or is about to be committed.

(2) Where it appears to a superintendent of police that the case is one of great emergency and that in the interests of the State immediate action is necessary, he may by a written order under his hand give to any constable the like authority as may be given by the warrant of a justice under the section.

10   Extent of Act and place of trial of offence

(1) This Act shall apply to all acts which are offences under this Act when committed in any part of His Majesty's dominions, or when committed by British officers or subjects elsewhere.

. . .

PARLIAMENT ACT 1911
(1 & 2 Geo. 5, c. 13)

An Act to make provision with respect to the powers of the House of Lords in relation of the House of Commons, and to limit the duration of Parliament

Preamble

Whereas it is expedient that provision should be made for regulating the relations between the two Houses of Parliament:

And whereas it is intended to substitute for the House of Lords as it at present exists a Second Chamber constituted on a popular instead of hereditary basis, but such substitution cannot be immediately brought into operation:

And whereas provision will require hereafter to be made by Parliament in a measure effecting such substitution for limiting and defining the powers of the new Second Chamber, but it is expedient to make such provision as in this Act appears for restricting the existing powers of the House of Lords:

1   Powers of House of Lords as to Money Bills

(1) If a Money Bill, having been passed by the House of Commons, and sent up to the House of Lords at least one month before the end of the session, is not passed by the House of Lords without amendment within one month after it is so sent up to that House, the Bill shall, unless the House of Commons direct to the contrary, be presented to His Majesty and become an Act of Parliament on the Royal Assent being signified, notwithstanding that the House of Lords have not consented to the Bill.

(2) A Money Bill means a Public Bill which in the opinion of the Speaker of the House of Commons contains only provisions dealing with all or any of the following subjects, namely, the imposition, repeal, remission, alteration, or regulation of taxation; the imposition for the payment of debt or other financial purposes of charges on the Consolidated Fund, the National Loans Fund or on money provided by Parliament, or the variation or repeal of any such charges; supply; the appropriation, receipt, custody, issue or audit of accounts of public money; the raising or guarantee of any loan or the repayment

thereof; or subordinate matters incidental to those subjects or any of them. In this subsection the expressions "taxation", "public money" and "loan" respectively do not include any taxation, money, or loan raised by local authorities or bodies for local purposes.

(3) There shall be endorsed on every Money Bill when it is sent up to the House of Lords and when it is presented to His Majesty for assent the certificate of the Speaker of the House of Commons signed by him that it is a Money Bill. Before giving his certificate, the Speaker shall consult, if practicable, two members to be appointed from the Chairmen's Panel at the beginning of each Session by the Committee of Selection.

2 Restriction of the powers of the House of Lords as to Bills other than Money Bills

(1) If any Public Bill (other than a Money Bill or a Bill containing any provision to extend the maximum duration of Parliament beyond five years) is passed by the House of Commons in two successive sessions (whether of the same Parliament or not), and, having been sent up to the House of Lords at least one month before the end of the session, is rejected by the House of Lords in each of those sessions, that Bill shall, on its rejection for the second time by the House of Lords, unless the House of Commons direct to the contrary, be presented to His Majesty and become an Act of Parliament on the Royal Assent being signified thereto, notwithstanding that the House of Lords have not consented to the Bill:

Provided that this provision shall not take effect unless one year has elapsed between the date of the second reading in the first of those sessions of the Bill in the House of Commons and the date on which it passes the House of Commons in the second of those sessions.

(2) When a Bill is presented to His Majesty for assent in pursuance of the provisions of this section, there shall be endorsed on the Bill the certificate of the Speaker of the House of Commons signed by him that the provisions of this section have been duly complied with.

(3) A Bill shall be deemed to be rejected by the House of Lords if it is not passed by the House of Lords either without amendment or with such amendments only as may be agreed to by both Houses.

(4) A Bill shall be deemed to be the same Bill as a former Bill sent up to the House of Lords in the preceding session if, when it is sent up to the House of Lords, it is identical with the former Bill or contains only such alterations as are certified by the Speaker of the House of Commons to be necessary owing to the time which has elapsed since the date of the former Bill, or to represent any amendments which have been made by the House of Lords in the former Bill in the preceding sesion, and any amendments which are certified by the Speaker to have been made by the House of Lords in the second session and agreed to by the House of Commons shall be inserted in the Bill as presented for Royal Assent in pursuance of this section:

Provided that the House of Commons may, if they think fit, on the passage of such a Bill through the House in the second session, suggest any further amendments without inserting the amendments in the Bill, and any such suggested amendments shall be considered by the House of Lords, and, if agreed to by that House, shall be treated as amendments made by the House of Lords and agreed to by the House of Commons; but the exercise of this power by the House of Commons shall not affect the operation of this section in the event of the Bill being rejected by the House of Lords.

3 Certificate of Speaker

Any certificate of the Speaker of the House of Commons given under this Act shall be conclusive for all purposes, and shall not be questioned in any court of law.

4 Enacting words

(1) In every Bill presented to His Majesty under the preceding provisions of this Act, the words of enactment shall be as follows, that is to say:—

"Be it enacted by the King's most Excellent Majesty, by and with the advice and consent of the Commons in this present Parliament assembled, in accordance with the provisions of the Parliament Acts 1911 and 1949, and by authority of the same, as follows."

(2) Any alteration of a Bill necessary to give effect to this section shall not be deemed to be an amendment of the Bill.

5 **Provisional Order Bills excluded**
In this Act the expression "Public Bill" does not include any Bill for confirming a Provisional Order.

6 **Saving for existing rights and privileges of the House of Commons**
Nothing in this Act shall diminish or qualify the existing rights and privileges of the House of Commons.

7 **Duration of Parliament**
Five years shall be substituted for seven years as the time fixed for the maximum duration of Parliament under the Septennial Act, 1715.

OFFICIAL SECRETS ACT 1920
(10 & 11 Geo. 5, c. 75)

An Act to amend the Official Secrets Act 1911

1 **Unauthorised use of uniforms; falsification of reports, forgery, personation, and false documents**
(1) If any person for the purpose of gaining admission, or of assisting any other person to gain admission, to a prohibited place, within the meaning of the Official Secrets Act 1911 (hereinafter referred to as "the principal Act"), or for any other purpose prejudicial to the safety or interests of the State within the meaning of the said Act—
   (a) uses or wears, without lawful authority, any naval, military, air-force, police, or other official uniform, or any uniform so nearly resembling the same as to be calculated to deceive, or falsely represents himself to be a person who is or has been entitled to use or wear any such uniform; or
   (b) orally, or in writing in any declaration or application, or in any document signed by him or on his behalf, knowingly makes or connives at the making of any false statement or any omission; or
   (c) . . . tampers with any passport or any naval, military, air-force, police, or official pass, permit, certificate, licence, or other document of a similar character (hereinafter in this section referred to as an official document), . . . or has in his possession any . . . forged, altered, or irregular official document; or
   (d) personates, or falsely represents himself to be a person holding, or in the employment of a person holding office under His Majesty, or to be or not to be a person to whom an official document or secret official code word or pass word has been duly issued or communicated, or with intent to obtain an official document, secret official code word or pass word, whether for himself or any other person, knowingly makes any false statement; or
   (e) uses, or has in his possession or under his control, without the authority of the Government Department or the authority concerned, any die, seal, or stamp of or belonging to, or used, made or provided by any Government Department, or by any diplomatic, naval, military, or air force authority appointed by or acting under the authority of His Majesty, or any die, seal or stamp so nearly resembling any such die, seal or stamp as to be calculated to deceive, or counterfeits any such die, seal or stamp, or uses, or has in his possession, or under his control, any such counterfeited die, seal or stamp;
   he shall be guilty of a misdemeanour.
(2) If any person—
   (a) retains for any purpose prejudicial to the safety or interests of the State any official document, whether or not completed or issued for use, when he has no right to retain

it, or when it is contrary to his duty to retain it, or fails to comply with any directions issued by any Government Department or any person authorised by such department with regard to the return or disposal thereof; or
- (b) allows any other person to have possession of any official document issued for his use alone, or communicates any secret official code word or pass word so issued, or, without lawful authority or excuse, has in his possession any official document or secret official code word or pass word issued for the use of some person other than himself, or on obtaining possession of any official document by finding or otherwise, neglects or fails to restore it to the person or authority by whom or for whose use it was issued, or to a police constable; or
- (c) without lawful authority or excuse, manufactures or sells, or has in his possession for sale any such die, seal or stamp as aforesaid;

he shall be guilty of a misdemeanour.
- (3) In the case of any prosecution under this section involving the proof of a purpose prejudicial to the safety or interests of the State, subsection (2) of section one of the principal Act shall apply in like manner as it applies to prosecutions under that section.

6 Duty of giving information as to commission of offences

(1) Where a chief officer of police is satisfied that there is reasonable ground for suspecting that an offence under section one of the principal Act has been committed and for believing that any person is able to furnish information as to the offence or suspected offence, he may apply to a Secretary of State for permission to exercise the powers conferred by this subsection and, if such permission is granted, he may authorise a superintendent of police, or any police officer not below the rank of inspector, to require the person believed to be able to furnish information to give any information in his power relating to the offence or suspected offence, and, if so required and on tender of his reasonable expenses, to attend at such reasonable time and place as may be specified by the superintendent or other officer; and if a person required in pursuance of such an authorisation to give information, or to attend as aforesaid, fails to comply with any such requirement or knowingly gives false information, he shall be guilty of a misdemeanour.

(2) Where a chief officer of police has reasonable grounds to believe that the case is one of great emergency and that in the interest of the State immediate action is necessary, he may exercise the powers conferred by the last foregoing subsection without applying for or being granted the permission of a Secretary of State, but if he does so shall forthwith report the circumstances to the Secretary of State.

(3) References in this section to a chief officer of police shall be construed as including references to any other officer of police expressly authorised by a chief officer of police to act on his behalf for the purposes of this section when by reason of illness, absence or other cause he is unable to do so.

THE STATUTE OF WESTMINSTER 1931
(22 & 23 Geo. 5, c. 4)

An Act to give effect to certain resolutions passed by Imperial Conferences held in the years 1926 and 1930

Whereas the delegates of His Majesty's Governments in the United Kingdom, the Dominion of Canada, the Commonwealth of Australia, the Dominion of New Zealand, the Union of South Africa, the Irish Free State and Newfoundland, at Imperial Conferences holden at Westminster in the years of our Lord nineteen hundred and twenty-six and nineteen hundred and thirty did concur in making the declarations and resolutions set forth in the Reports of the said Conferences:

And whereas it is meet and proper to set out by way of preamble to this Act that, inasmuch as the Crown is the symbol of the free association of the members of the British Commonwealth of Nations, and as they are united by a common allegiance to the Crown, it would be in accord with the established constitutional position of all the members of the Commonwealth in relation to one another that any alteration in the law touching the Succession to the Throne or the Royal Style and Titles shall hereafter require the assent as well of the Parliaments of all the Dominions as of the Parliament of the United Kingdom:

And whereas it is in accord with the established constitutional position that no law hereafter made by the Parliament of the United Kingdom shall extend to any of the said Dominions as part of the law of that Dominion otherwise than at the request and with the consent of that Dominion:

And whereas it is necessary for the ratifying, confirming and establishing of certain of the said declarations and resolutions of the said Conferences that a law be made and enacted in due form by authority of the Parliament of the United Kingdom:

And whereas the Dominion of Canada, the Commonwealth of Australia, the Dominion of New Zealand, the Union of South Africa, the Irish Free State and Newfoundland have severally requested and consented to the submission of a measure to the Parliament of the United Kingdom for making such provision with regard to the matters aforesaid as is hereafter in this Act contained:

1   **Meaning of "Dominion" in this Act**
     In this Act the expression "Dominion" means any of the following Dominions, that is to say, the Dominion of Canada, the Commonwealth of Australia, the Dominion of New Zealand, . . . the Irish Free State and Newfoundland.

2   **Validity of laws made by Parliament of a Dominion**
     (1)   The Colonial Laws Validity Act 1865 shall not apply to any law made after the commencement of this Act by the Parliament of a Dominion.
     (2)   No law and no provision of any law made after the commencement of this Act by the Parliament of a Dominion shall be void or inoperative on the ground that it is repugnant to the law of England, or to the provisions of any existing or future Act of Parliament of the United Kingdom, or to any order, rule or regulation made under any such Act, and the powers of the Parliament of a Dominion shall include the power to repeal or amend any such Act, order, rule or regulation in so far as the same is part of the law of the Dominion.

3   **Power of Parliament of Dominion to legislate extra-territorally**
     It is hereby declared and enacted that the Parliament of a Dominion has full power to make laws having extra-territorial operation.

4   **Parliament of United Kingdom not to legislate for Dominion except by consent**
     No Act of Parliament of the United Kingdom passed after the commencement of this Act shall extend, or be deemed to extend, to a Dominion as part of the law of that Dominion unless it is expressly declared in that Act that that Dominion has requested, and consented to, the enactment thereof.

PUBLIC ORDER ACT 1936
(1 Edw. 8 & 1 Geo. 6, c. 6)

An Act to prohibit the wearing of uniforms in connection with political objects and the maintenance by private persons of associations of military or similar character; and to make further provision for the preservation of public order on the occasion of public processions and meetings and in public places

1   **Prohibition of uniforms in connection with political objects**
     (1)   Subject as hereinafter provided, any person who in any public place or at any public meeting wears uniform signifying his association with any political organisation or with the promotion of any political object shall be guilty of an offence:
            Provided that, if the chief officer of police is satisfied that the wearing of any such uniform as aforesaid on any ceremonial, anniversary, or other special occasion will not be likely to involve risk of public disorder, he may, with the consent of a Secretary of State, by order permit the wearing of such uniform on that occasion either absolutely or subject to such conditions as may be specified in the order.
     (2)   Where any person is charged before any court with an offence under this section, no further proceedings in respect thereof shall be taken against him without the consent of the

Attorney-General except such as are authorised by section 6 of the Prosecution of Offences Act 1979 so, however, that if that person is remanded in custody he shall, after the expiration of a period of eight days from the date on which he was so remanded, be entitled to be released on bail without sureties unless within that period the Attorney-General has consented to such further proceedings as aforesaid.

2 **Prohibition of quasi-military organisations**
  (1) If the members or adherents of any association of persons, whether incorporated or not, are—
    (a) organised or trained or equipped for the purpose of enabling them to be employed in usurping the functions of the police or of the armed forces of the Crown; or
    (b) organised and trained or organised and equipped either for the purpose of enabling them to be employed for the use or display of physical force in promoting any political object, or in such manner as to arouse reasonable apprehension that they are organised and either trained or equipped for that purpose;
  then any person who takes part in the control or management of the association, or in so organising or training as aforesaid any members or adherents thereof, shall be guilty of an offence under this section:
    Provided that in any proceedings against a person charged with the offence of taking part in the control or management of such an association as aforesaid it shall be a defence to that charge to prove that he neither consented to nor connived at the organisation, training, or equipment of members or adherents of the association in contravention of the provisions of this section.
  (2) No prosecution shall be instituted under this section without the consent of the Attorney-General.
  . . .
  (5) If a judge of the High Court is satisfied by information on oath that there is reasonable ground for suspecting that an offence under this section has been committed, and that evidence of the commission thereof is to be found at any premises or place specified in the information, he may, on an application made by an officer of police of a rank not lower than that of inspector, grant a search warrant authorising any such officer as aforesaid named in the warrant together with any other persons named in the warrant and any other officers of police to enter the premises or place at any time within three months from the date of the warrant, if necessary by force, and to search the premises or place and every person found therein, and to seize any-thing found on the premises or place or on any such person which the officer has reasonable ground for suspecting to be evidence of the commission of such an offence as aforesaid:
    Provided that no woman shall, in pursuance of a warrant issued under this subsection, be searched except by a woman.
  (6) Nothing in this section shall be construed as prohibiting the employment of a reasonable number of persons as stewards to assist in the preservation of order at any public meeting held upon private premises, or the making of arrangements for that purpose or the instruction of the persons to be so employed in their lawful duties as such stewards, or their being furnished with badges or other distinguishing signs.

STATUTORY INSTRUMENTS ACT 1946
(9 & 10 Geo. 6, c. 36)

An Act to repeal the Rules Publication Act, 1893, and to make further provision as to the instruments by which statutory powers to make orders, rules, regulations and other subordinate legislation are exercised

1 **Definition of "Statutory Instrument"**
  (1) Where by this Act or any Act passed after the commencement of this Act power to make, confirm or approve orders, rules, regulations or other subordinate legislation is conferred on His Majesty in Council or on any Minister of the Crown then, if the power is expressed—

(a) in the case of a power conferred on His Majesty, to be exercisable by Order in Council;
(b) in the case of a power conferred on a Minister of the Crown, to be exercisable by statutory instrument,

any document by which that power is exercised shall be known as a "statutory instrument" and the provisions of this Act shall apply thereto accordingly.

(1A) ... Where by any Act power to make, confirm or approve orders, rules, regulations or other subordinate legislation is conferred on the Welsh Ministers and the power is expressed to be exercisable by statutory instrument, any document by which that power is exercised shall be known as a "statutory instrument" and the provisions of this Act shall apply to it accordingly.

(2) Whereby any Act passed before the commencement of this Act power to make statutory rules within the meaning of the Rules Publication Act, 1893, was conferred on any rule-making authority within the meaning of that Act, any document by which that power is exercised after the commencement of this Act shall, save as is otherwise provided by regulations made under this Act, be known as a "statutory instrument" and the provisions of this Act shall apply thereto accordingly.

2 Numbering, printing, publication and citation

(1) Immediately after the making of any statutory instrument, it shall be sent to the King's printer of Acts of Parliament and numbered in accordance with regulations made under this Act, and except in such cases as may be provided by any Act passed after the commencement of this Act or prescribed by regulations made under this Act, copies thereof shall as soon as possible be printed and sold by or under the authority of the King's printer of Acts of Parliament.

(2) Any statutory instrument may, without prejudice to any other mode of citation, be cited by the number given to it in accordance with the provisions of this section, and the calendar year.

3 Supplementary provisions as to publication

(1) Regulations made for the purposes of this Act shall make provision for the publication by His Majesty's Stationery Office of lists showing the date upon which every statutory instrument printed and sold by or under the authority of the King's printer of Acts of Parliament was first issued by or under the authority of that office; and in any legal proceedings a copy of any list so published... shall be received in evidence as a true copy, and an entry therein shall be conclusive evidence of the date on which any statutory instrument was first issued by or under the authority of His Majesty's Stationery Office.

(2) In any proceedings against any person for an offence consisting of a contravention of any such statutory instrument, it shall be a defence to prove that the instrument had not been issued by or under the authority of His Majesty's Stationery Office at the date of the alleged contravention unless it is proved that at that date reasonable steps had been taken for the purpose of bringing the purport of the instrument to the notice of the public, or of persons likely to be affected by it, or of the person charged.

(3) Save as therein otherwise expressly provided, nothing in this section shall affect any enactment or rule of law relating to the time at which any statutory instrument comes into operation.

4 Statutory instruments which are required to be laid before Parliament

(1) Where by this Act or any Act passed after the commencement of this Act any statutory instrument is required to be laid before Parliament after being made, a copy of the instrument shall be laid before each House of Parliament and, subject as hereinafter provided, shall be so laid before the instrument comes into operation:

Provided that if it is essential that any such instrument should come into operation before copies thereof can be so laid as aforesaid, the instrument may be made so as to come into operation before it has been so laid; and where any statutory instrument comes into operation before it is laid before Parliament, notification shall forthwith be sent to the Speaker of the House of Lords and to the Speaker of the House of Commons drawing attention to the fact that copies of the instrument have yet to be laid before Parliament and explaining why such copies were not so laid before the instrument came into operation.

(2) Every copy of any such statutory instrument sold by or under the authority of the King's printer of Acts of Parliament shall bear on the face thereof—
   (a) a statement showing the date on which the statutory instrument came or will come into operation; and
   (b) either a statement showing the date on which copies thereof were laid before Parliament or a statement that such copies are to be laid before Parliament.

...

5 Statutory instruments which are subject to annulment by resolution of either House of Parliament

(1) Where by this Act or any Act passed after the commencement of this Act, it is provided that any statutory instrument shall be subject to annulment in pursuance of resolution of either House of Parliament, the instrument shall be laid before Parliament after being made and the provisions of the last foregoing section shall apply thereto accordingly, and if either House, within the period of forty days beginning with the day on which a copy thereof is laid before it, resolves that an Address be presented to His Majesty praying that the instrument be annulled, no further proceedings shall be taken thereunder after the date of the resolution, and His Majesty may by Order in Council revoke the instrument, so, however, that any such resolution and revocation shall be without prejudice to the validity of anything previously done under the instrument or to the making of a new statutory instrument.

...

6 Statutory instruments of which drafts are to be laid before Parliament

(1) Where by this Act or any Act passed after the commencement of this Act it is provided that a draft of any statutory instrument shall be laid before Parliament, but the Act does not prohibit the making of the instrument without the approval of Parliament, then, in the case of an Order in Council the draft shall not be submitted to His Majesty in Council, and in any other case the statutory instrument shall not be made, until after the expiration of a period of forty days beginning with the day on which a copy of the draft is laid before each House of Parliament, or, if such copies are laid on different days, with the later of the two days, and if within that period either House resolves that the draft be not submitted to His Majesty or that the statutory instrument be not made, as the case may be, no further proceedings shall be taken thereon, but without prejudice to the laying before Parliament of a new draft.

...

CROWN PROCEEDINGS ACT 1947
(10 & 11 Geo. 6, c. 44)

An Act to amend the law relating to the civil liabilities and rights of the Crown and to civil proceedings by and against the Crown, to amend the law relating to the civil liabilities of persons other than the Crown in certain cases involving the affairs or property of the Crown, and for purposes connected with the matters aforesaid [31 July 1947]

PART I
SUBSTANTIVE LAW

1 Right to sue the Crown

Where any person has a claim against the Crown after the commencement of this Act, and, if this Act had not been passed, the claim might have been enforced, subject to the grant of His Majesty's fiat, by petition of right, or might have been enforced by a proceeding provided by any stautory provision repealed by this Act, then, subject to the provisions of this Act, the claim may be enforced as of right, and without the fiat of His Majesty, by proceedings taken against the Crown for that purpose in accordance with the provisions of this Act.

2 Liability of the Crown in tort

(1) Subject to the provisions of this Act, the Crown shall be subject to all those liabilities in tort to which, if it were a private person of full age and capacity, it would be subject—
   (a) in respect of torts committed by its servants or agents;
   (b) in respect of any breach of those duties which a person owes to his servants or agents at common law by reason of being their employer; and
   (c) in respect of any breach of the duties attaching at common law to the ownership, occupation, possession or control of property:

   Provided that no proceedings shall lie against the Crown by virtue of paragraph (a) of this subsection in respect of any act or omission of a servant or agent of the Crown unless the act or omission would apart from the provisions of this Act have given rise to a cause of action in tort against that servant or agent or his estate.

(2) Where the Crown is bound by a statutory duty which is binding also upon persons other than the Crown and its officers, then, subject to the provisions of this Act, the Crown shall, in respect of a failure to comply with that duty, be subject to all those liabilities in tort (if any) to which it would be so subject if it were a private person of full age and capacity.

(3) Where any functions are conferred or imposed upon an officer of the Crown as such either by any rule of the common law or by statute, and that officer commits a tort while performing or purporting to perform those functions, the liabilities of the Crown in respect of the tort shall be such as they would have been if those functions had been conferred or imposed solely by virtue of instructions lawfully given by the Crown.

(4) Any enactment which negatives or limits the amount of the liability of any Government department, part of the Scottish Administration or officer of the Crown in respect of any tort committed by that department, part or officer shall, in the case of proceedings against the Crown under this section in respect of a tort committed by that department, part or officer, apply in relation to the Crown as it would have applied in relation to that department, part or officer if the proceedings against the Crown had been proceedings against that department, part or officer.

(5) No proceedings shall lie against the Crown by virtue of this section in respect of anything done or omitted to be done by any person while discharging or purporting to discharge any responsibilities of a judicial nature vested in him, or any responsibilities which he has in connection with the execution of judicial process.

(6) No proceedings shall lie against the Crown by virtue of this section in respect of any act, neglect or default of any officer of the Crown, unless that officer has been directly or indirectly appointed by the Crown and was at the material time paid in respect of his duties as an officer of the Crown wholly out of the Consolidated Fund of the United Kingdom, moneys provided by Parliament, the Scottish Consolidated Fund . . . or any other Fund certified by the Treasury for the purposes of this subsection or was at the material time holding an office in respect of which the Treasury certify that the holder thereof would normally be so paid.

4 Application of law as to indemnity, contribution, joint and several tort-feasors, and contributory negligence

(1) Where the Crown is subject to any liability by virtue of this Part of this Act, the law relating to indemnity and contribution shall be enforceable by or against the Crown in respect of the liability to which it is so subject as if the Crown were a private person of full age and capacity.

(2) . . .

(3) Without prejudice to the general effect of section one of this Act, the Law Reform (Contributory Negligence) Act 1945 (which amends the law relating to contributory negligence) shall bind the Crown.

11 Saving in respect of acts done under prerogative and statutory powers

(1) Nothing in Part I of this Act shall extinguish or abridge any powers or authorities which, if this Act had not been passed, would have been exercisable by virtue of the prerogative of the

Crown, or any powers or authorities conferred on the Crown by any statute, and, in particular, nothing in the said Part I shall extinguish or abridge any powers or authorities exercisable by the Crown, whether in time of peace or of war, for the purpose of the defence of the realm or of training, or maintaining the efficiency of, any of the armed forces of the Crown.

(2) Where in any proceedings under this Act it is material to determine whether anything was properly done or omitted to be done in the exercise of the prerogative of the Crown,. . . a Secretary of State may, if satisfied that the act or omission was necessary for any such purpose as is mentioned in the last preceding subsection, issue a certificate to the effect that the act or omission was necessary for that purpose; and the certificate shall, in those precedings, be conclusive as to the matter so certified.

PART II
JURISDICTION AND PROCEDURE

17 Parties to proceedings

(1) The Minister for the Civil Service shall publish a list specifying the several Government departments which are authorised departments for the purposes of this Act, and the name and address for service of the person who is, or is acting for the purposes of this Act as, the solicitor for each such department, and may from time to time amend or vary the said list.

Any document purporting to be a copy of a list published under this section and purporting to be printed under the superintendence or the authority of His Majesty's Stationery Office shall in any legal proceedings be received as evidence for the purpose of establishing what departments are authorised departments for the purposes of this Act, and what person is, or is acting for the purposes of this Act as, the solicitor for any such department.

(2) Civil proceedings by the Crown may be instituted either by an authorised Government department in its own name, whether that department was or was not at the commencement of this Act authorised to sue, or by the Attorney General.

(3) Civil proceedings against the Crown shall be instituted against the appropriate authorised Government department, or, if none of the authorised Government departments is appropriate or the person instituting the proceedings has any reasonable doubt whether any and if so which of those departments is appropriate, against the Attorney General.

. . .

21 Nature of relief

(1) In any civil proceedings by or against the Crown the court shall, subject to the provisions of this Act, have power to make all such orders as it has power to make in proceedings between subjects, and otherwise to give such appropriate relief as the case may require:
   Provided that:—
   (a) where in any proceedings against the Crown any such relief is sought as might in proceedings between subjects be granted by way of injunction or specific performance, the court shall not grant an injunction or make an order for specific performance, but may in lieu thereof make an order declaratory of the rights of the parties; and
   (b) in any proceedings against the Crown for the recovery of land or other property the court shall not make an order for the recovery of the land or the delivery of the property, but may in lieu thereof make an order declaring that the plaintiff is entitled as against the Crown to the land or property or to the possession thereof.

(2) The court shall not in any civil proceedings grant any injunction or make any order against an officer of the Crown if the effect of granting the injunction or making the order would be to give any relief against the Crown which could not have been obtained in proceedings against the Crown.

PART IV
MISCELLANEOUS AND SUPPLEMENTAL

40 Savings
(1) Nothing in this Act shall apply to proceedings by or against, or authorise proceedings in tort to be brought against, His Majesty in His private capacity.

. . .

LIFE PEERAGES ACT 1958
(6 & 7 Eliz. 2, c. 21)

An Act to make provision for the creation of life peerages carrying the right to sit and vote in the House of Lords [30 April 1958]

1 Power to create life peerages carrying right to sit in the House of Lords
(1) . . . Her Majesty shall have power by letters patent to confer on any person a peerage for life having the incidents specified in subsection (2) of this section.
(2) A peerage conferred under this section shall, during the life of the person on whom it is conferred, entitle him—
   (a) to rank as a baron under such style as may be appointed by the letters patent; and
   (b) subject to subsection (4) of this section, to receive writs of summons to attend the House of Lords and sit and vote therein accordingly,
   and shall expire on his death.
(3) A life peerage may be conferred under this section on a woman.
(4) Nothing in this section shall enable any person to receive a writ of summons to attend the House of Lords, or to sit and vote in that House, at any time when disqualified therefor by law.

OBSCENE PUBLICATIONS ACT 1959
(7 & 8 Eliz. 2, c. 66)

An Act to amend the law relating to the publication of obscene matter; to provide for the protection of literature; and to strengthen the law concerning pornography [29 July 1959]

1 Test of obscenity
(1) For the purposes of this Act an article shall be deemed to be obscene if its effect or (where the article comprises two or more distinct items) the effect of any one of its items is, if taken as a whole, such as to tend to deprave and corrupt persons who are likely, having regard to all relevant circumstances, to read, see or hear the matter contained or embodied in it.
(2) In this Act "article" means any description of article containing or embodying matter to be read or looked at or both, any sound record, and any film or other record of a picture or pictures.
(3) For the purposes of this Act a person publishes an article who—
   (a) distributes, circulates, sells, lets on hire, gives, or lends it, or who offers it for sale or for letting on hire; or
   (b) in the case of an article containing or embodying matter to be looked at or a record, shows, plays or projects it, or, where the matter is data stored electronically, transmits that data.
(4) For the purposes of this Act a person also publishes an article to the extent that any matter recorded on it is included by him in a programme included in a programme service.
(5) Where the inclusion of any matter in a programme so included would, if that matter were recorded matter, constitute the publication of an obscene article for the purposes of this Act by virtue of subsection (4) above, this Act shall have effect in relation to the inclusion of that matter in that programme as if it were recorded matter.

(6) In this section "programme" and "programme service" have the same meaning as in the Broadcasting Act 1990.

2 Prohibition of publication of obscene matter

(1) Subject as hereinafter provided, any person who, whether for gain or not, publishes an obscene article or who has an obscene article for publication for gain (whether gain to himself or gain to another) shall be liable—
   (a) on summary conviction to a fine not exceeding the prescribed sum or to imprisonment for a term not exceeding six months;
   (b) on conviction on indictment to a fine or to imprisonment for a term not exceeding three years or both.

(2) . . .

(3) A prosecution. . . for an offence against this section shall not be commenced more than two years after the commission of the offence.

(3A) Proceedings for an offence under this section shall not be instituted except by or with the consent of the Director of Public Prosecutions in any case where the article in question is a moving picture film of a width of not less than sixteen millimetres and the relevant publication or the only other publication which followed or could reasonably have been expected to follow from the relevant publication took place or (as the case may be) was to take place in the course of an exhibition of a film; and in this subsection "the relevant publication" means—
   (a) in the case any proceedings under this section for publishing an obscene article, the publication in respect of which the defendant would be charged if the proceedings were brought; and
   (b) in the case of any proceedings under this section for having an obscene article for publication for gain, the publication which, if the proceedings were brought, the defendant would be alleged to have had in contemplation.

(4) A person publishing an article shall not be proceeded against for an offence at common law consisting of the publication of any matter contained or embodied in the article where it is of the essence of the offence that the matter is obscene.

(4A) Without prejudice to subsection (4) above, a person shall not be proceeded against for an offence at common law—
   (a) in respect of an exhibition of a film or anything said or done in the course of an exhibition of a film, where it is of the essence of the common law offence that the exhibition or, as the case may be, what was said or done was obscene, indecent, offensive, disgusting or injurious to morality; or
   (b) in respect of an agreement to give an exhibition of a film or to cause anything to be said or done in the course of such an exhibition where the common law offence consists of conspiring to corrupt public morals or to do any act contrary to public morals or decency.

(5) A person shall not be convicted of an offence against this section if he proves that he had not examined the article in respect of which he is charged and had no reasonable cause to suspect that it was such that his publication of it would make him liable to be convicted of an offence against this section.

(6) In any proceedings against a person under this section the question whether an article is obscene shall be determined without regard to any publication by another person unless it could reasonably have been expected that the publication by the other person would follow from publication by the person charged.

(7) In this section "exhibition of a film" has the meaning given in paragraph 15 of Schedule 1 to the Licensing Act 2003.

3 Powers of search and seizure

(1) If a justice of the peace is satisfied by information on oath that there is reasonable ground for suspecting that, in any premises, or on any stall or vehicle in that area, being premises or a stall or vehicle specified in the information, obscene articles are, or are from time to time,

kept for publication for gain, the justice may issue a warrant under his hand empowering any constable to enter (if need be by force) and search the premises, or to search the stall or vehicle. . . and to seize and remove any articles found therein or thereon which the constable has reason to believe to be obscene articles and to be kept for publication for gain.

(2) A warrant under the foregoing subsection shall, if any obscene articles are seized under the warrant, also empower the seizure and removal of any documents found in the premises or, as the case may be, on the stall or vehicle which relate to a trade or business carried on at the premises or from the stall or vehicle.

. . .

4 Defence of public good

(1) Subject to subsection (1A) of this section a person shall not be convicted of an offence against section two of this Act, and an order for forfeiture shall not be made under the foregoing section, if it is proved that publication of the article in question is justified as being for the public good on the ground that it is in the interests of science, literature, art or learning, or of other objects of general concern.

(1A) Subsection (1) of this section shall not apply where the article in question is a moving picture film or soundtrack, but—
  (a) a person shall not be convicted of an offence against section 2 of this Act in relation to any such film or soundtrack, and
  (b) an order for forfeiture of any such film or soundtrack shall not be made under section 3 of this Act,
if it is proved that publication of the film or soundtrack is justified as being for the public good on the ground that it is in the interests of drama, opera, ballet or any other art, or of literature or learning.

(2) It is hereby declared that the opinion of experts as to the literary, artistic, scientific or other merits of an article may be admitted in any proceedings under this Act either to establish or to negative the said ground.

(3) In this section "moving picture soundtrack" means any sound record designed for playing with a moving picture film, whether incorporated with the film or not.

PARLIAMENTARY COMMISSIONER ACT 1967
(1967, c. 13)

An Act to make provision for the appointment and functions of a Parliamentary Commissioner for the investigation of administrative action taken on behalf of the Crown, and for purposes connected therewith
[22 March 1967]

The Parliamentary Commissioner for Administration

1 Appointment and tenure of office

(1) For the purpose of conducting investigations in accordance with the following provisions of this Act there shall be appointed a Commissioner, to be known as the Parliamentary Commissioner for Administration.

(2) Her Majesty may by Letters Patent from time to time appoint a person to be the Commissioner . . .

(2A) A person appointed to be the Commissioner shall hold office until the end of the period for which he is appointed.

(3) A person appointed to be the Commissioner may—
  (a) be relieved of office by Her Majesty at his own request, or
  (b) be removed from office by Her Majesty on the ground of misbehaviour, in consequence of Addresses from both Houses of Parliament . . .

(3A) Her Majesty may declare the office of Commissioner to have been vacated if satisfied that the person appointed to be the Commissioner is incapable for medical reasons—
  (a) of performing the duties of his office; and

(b) of requesting to be relieved of it.
(3B) A person appointed to be the Commissioner is not eligible for re-appointment.

3 **Administrative provisions**
(1) The Commissioner may appoint such officers as he may determine with the approval of the Treasury as to numbers and conditions of service.
. . .

4 **Departments etc. subject to investigation**
(1) Subject to the provisions of this section and to the notes contained in Schedule 2 to this Act, this Act applies to the government departments, corporations and unincorporated bodies listed in that Schedule; and references in this Act to an authority to which this Act applies are references to any such corporation or body.
(2) Her Majesty may by Order in Council amend Schedule 2 to this Act by the alteration of any entry or note, the removal of any entry or note or the insertion of any additional entry or note.
(3) An Order in Council may only insert an entry if—
   (a) it relates—
      (i) to a government department; or
      (ii) to a corporation or body whose functions are exercised on behalf of the Crown; or
   (b) it relates to a corporation or body—
      (i) which is established by virtue of Her Majesty's prerogative or by an Act of Parliament or an Order in Council or order made under an Act of Parliament or which is established in any other way by a Minister of the Crown in his capacity as a Minister or by a government department;
      (ii) at least half of whose revenues derive directly from money provided by Parliament, a levy authorised by an enactment, a fee or charge of any other description so authorised or more than one of those sources; and
      (iii) which is wholly or partly constituted by appointment made by Her Majesty or a Minister of the Crown or government department.
(3A) No entry shall be made if the result of making it would be that the Parliamentary Commissioner could investigate action which can be investigated by the Public Services Ombudsman for Wales under the Public Services Ombudsman (Wales) Act 2005.
(3B) No entry shall be made in respect of—
   (a) the Scottish Administration or any part of it;
   (b) any Scottish public authority with mixed functions or no reserved functions within the meaning of the Scotland Act 1998; or
   (c) the Scottish Parliamentary Corporate Body.
(4) No entry shall be made in respect of a corporation or body whose sole activity is, or whose main activities are, included among the activities specified in subsection (5) below.
(5) The activities mentioned in subsection (4) above are—
   (a) the provision of education, or the provision of training otherwise than under the Industrial Training Act 1982;
   (b) the development of curricula, the conduct of examinations or the validation of educational courses;
   (c) the control of entry to any profession or the regulation of the conduct of members of any profession;
   (d) the investigation of complaints by members of the public regarding the actions of any person or body, or the supervision or review of such investigations or of steps taken following them.
(6) No entry shall be made in respect of a corporation or body operating in an exclusively or predominantly commercial manner or a corporation carrying on under national ownership an industry or undertaking or part of an industry or undertaking.

(7) Any statutory instrument made by virtue of this section shall be subject to annulment in pursuance of a resolution of either House of Parliament.

...

5 Matters subject to investigation

(1) Subject to the provisions of this section, the Commissioner may investigate any action taken by or on behalf of a government department or other authority to which this Act applies, being action taken in the exercise of administrative functions of that department or authority, in any case where—
   (a) a written complaint is duly made to a member of the House of Commons by a member of the public who claims to have sustained injustice in consequence of maladministration in connection with the action so taken; and
   (b) the complaint is referred to the Commissioner, with the consent of the person who made it, by a member of that House with a request to conduct an investigation thereon.

(1A) Subsection (1C) of this section applies if—
   (a) a written complaint is duly made to a member of the House of Commons by a member of the public who claims that a person has failed to perform a relevant duty owed by him to the member of the public, and
   (b) the complaint is referred to the Commissioner, with the consent of the person who made it, by a member of the House of Commons with a request to conduct an investigation into it.

(1B) For the purposes of subsection (1A) of this section a relevant duty is a duty imposed by any of these—
   (a) a code of practice issued under section 32 of the Domestic Violence, Crime and Victims Act 2004 (code of practice for victims), or
   (b) sections 35 to 44 of that Act (duties of local probation boards in connection with victims of sexual or violent offences).

(1C) If this subsection applies, the Commissioner may investigate the complaint.

(2) Except as hereinafter provided, the Commissioner shall not conduct an investigation under this Act in respect of any of the following matters, that is to say—
   (a) any action in respect of which the person aggrieved has or had a right of appeal, reference or review to or before a tribunal constituted by or under any enactment or by virtue of Her Majesty's prerogative;
   (b) any action in respect of which the person aggrieved has or had a remedy by way of proceedings in any court of law:

Provided that the Commissioner may conduct an investigation notwithstanding that the person aggrieved has or had such a right or remedy if satisfied that in the particular circumstances it is not reasonable to expect him to resort or have resorted to it.

(2A) Subsection (2)(a) of this section shall have effect in relation to the right of a person to make a complaint of unlawful discrimination under the Fair Employment and Treatment (Northern Ireland) Order 1998 as if it were such a right of appeal, reference or review as is mentioned in that subsection.

(3) Without prejudice to subsection (2) of this section, the Commisioner shall not conduct an investigation under subsection (1) of this section in respect of any such action or matter as is described in Schedule 3 to this Act.

(4) Her Majesty may by Order in Council amend the said Schedule 3 so as to exclude from the provisions of that Schedule such actions or matters as may be described in the Order; and any statutory instrument made by virtue of this subsection shall be subject to annulment in pursuance of a resolution of either House of Parliament.

(4A) Without prejudice to subsection (2) of this section, the Commissioner shall not conduct an investigation pursuant to a complaint under subsection (1A) of this section in respect of—
   (a) action taken by or with the authority of the Secretary of State for the purposes of protecting the security of the State, including action so taken with respect to passports, or

(b) any action or matter described in any of paragraphs 1 to 4 and 6A to 11 of Schedule 3 to this Act.

...

(5) In determining whether to initiate, continue or discontinue an investigation under this Act, the Commissioner shall, subject to the foregoing provisions of this section, act in accordance with his own discretion; and any question whether a complaint is duly made under this Act shall be determined by the Commissioner.

(5A) For the purposes of this section, administrative functions of a government department to which this Act applies include functions exercised by the department on behalf of the Scottish Ministers by virtue of section 93 of the Scotland Act 1998.

(5B) The Commissioner shall not conduct an investigation under this Act in respect of any action concerning Scotland and not relating to reserved matters which is taken by or on behalf of a cross-border public authority within the meaning of the Scotland Act 1998.

(6) For the purposes of this section, administrative functions exercised by any person appointed by the Lord Chancellor as a member of the administrative staff of any court or tribunal shall be taken to be administrative functions of the Ministry of Justice or, in Northern Ireland, of the Northern Ireland Court Service.

...

6 Provisions relating to complaints

(1) A complaint under this Act may be made by any individual, or by any body of persons whether incorporated or not, not being—

(a) a local authority or other authority or body constituted for purposes of the public service or of local government or for the purposes of carrying on under national ownership any industry or undertaking or part of an industry or undertaking;

(b) any other authority or body whose members are appointed by Her Majesty or any Minister of the Crown or government department, or whose revenues consist wholly or mainly of moneys provided by Parliament.

...

(2) Where the person by whom a complaint might have been made under the foregoing provisions of this Act has died or is for any reason unable to act for himself, the complaint may be made by his personal representative or by a member of his family or other individual suitable to represent him; but except as aforesaid a complaint shall not be entertained under this Act unless made by the person aggrieved himself.

(3) A complaint shall not be entertained under this Act unless it is made to a member of the House of Commons not later than twelve months from the day on which the person aggrieved first had notice of the matters alleged in the complaint; but the Commissioner may conduct an investigation pursuant to a complaint not made within that period if he considers that there are special circumstances which make it proper to do so.

(4) Except as provided in subsection (5) below a complaint shall not be entertained under this Act unless the person aggrieved is resident in the United Kingdom (or, if he is dead, was so resident at the time of his death) or the complaint relates to action taken in relation to him while he was present in the United Kingdom or on an installation in a designated area within the meaning of the Continental Shelf Act 1964 or on a ship registered in the United Kingdom or an aircraft so registered, or in relation to rights or obligations which accrued or arose in the United Kingdom or on such an installation, ship or aircraft.

(5) A complaint may be entertained under this Act in circumstances not falling within subsection (4) above where—

(a) the complaint relates to action taken in any country or territory outside the United Kingdom by an officer (not being an honorary consular officer) in the exercise of a consular function on behalf of the Government of the United Kingdom; and

(b) the person aggrieved is a citizen of the United Kingdom and Colonies who, under section 2 of the Immigration Act 1971, has the right of abode in the United Kingdom.

7 Procedure in respect of investigations

(1) Where the Commissioner proposes to conduct an investigation pursuant to a complaint under section 5(1) of this Act, he shall afford to the principal officer of the department or authority concerned, and to any person who is alleged in the complaint to have taken or authorised the action complained of, an opportunity to comment on any allegations contained in the complaint.

(1A) Where the Commissioner proposes to conduct an investigation pursuant to a complaint under section 5(1A) of this Act, he shall give the person to whom the complaint relates an opportunity to comment on any allegations contained in the complaint.

(2) Every investigation under this Act shall be conducted in private, but except as aforesaid the procedure for conducting an investigation shall be such as the Commissioner considers appropriate in the circumstances of the case; and without prejudice to the generality of the foregoing provision the Commissioner may obtain information from such persons and in such manner, and make such inquiries, as he thinks fit, and may determine whether any person may be represented, by counsel or solicitor or otherwise, in the investigation.

...

8 Evidence

(1) For the purposes of an investigation under section 5(1) of this Act the Commissioner may require any Minister, officer or member of the department or authority concerned or any other person who in his opinion is able to furnish information or produce documents relevant to the investigation to furnish any such information or produce any such document.

(1A) For the purposes of an investigation pursuant to a complaint under section 5(1A) of this Act the Commissioner may require any person who in his opinion is able to furnish information or produce documents relevant to the investigation to furnish any such information or produce any such document.

(2) For the purposes of any investigation under this Act the Commissioner shall have the same powers as the Court in respect of the attendance and examination of witnesses (including the administration of oaths or affirmations and the examination of witnesses abroad) and in respect of the production of documents.

(3) No obligation to maintain secrecy or other restriction upon the disclosure of information obtained by or furnished to persons in Her Majesty's service, whether imposed by any enactment or by any rule of law, shall apply to the disclosure of information for the purposes of an investigation under this Act; and the Crown shall not be entitled in relation to any such investigation to any such privilege in respect of the production of documents or the giving of evidence as is allowed by law in legal proceedings.

(4) No person shall be required or authorised by virtue of this Act to furnish any information or answer any question relating to proceedings of the Cabinet or of any committee of the Cabinet or to produce so much of any document as relates to such proceedings; and for the purposes of this subsection a certificate issued by the Secretary of the Cabinet with the approval of the Prime Minister and certifying that any information, question, document or part of a document so relates shall be conclusive.

...

9 Obstruction and contempt

(1) If any person without lawful excuse obstructs the Commissioner or any officer of the Commissioner in the performance of his functions under this Act, or is guilty of any act or omission in relation to any investigation under this Act which, if that investigation were a proceeding in the Court, would constitute contempt of court, the Commissioner may certify the offence to the Court.

(2) Where an offence is certified under this section, the Court may inquire into the matter and, after hearing any witnesses who may be produced against or on behalf of the person charged with the offence, and after hearing any statement that may be offered in defence, deal with him in any manner in which the court could deal with him if he had committed the like offence in relation to the Court.

...

10 Reports by Commissioner

(1) In any case where the Commissioner conducts an investigation under this Act or decides not to conduct such an investigation, he shall send to the member of the House of Commons by whom the request for investigation was made (or if he is no longer a member of that House, to such member of that House as the Commissioner thinks appropriate) a report of the results of the investigation or, as the case may be, a statement of his reasons for not conducting an investigation.

(2) In any case where the Commissioner conducts an investigation under section 5(1) of this Act, he shall also send a report of the results of the investigation to the principal officer of the department or authority concerned and to any other person who is alleged in the relevant complaint to have taken or authorised the action complained of.

(2A) In any case where the Commissioner conducts an investigation pursuant to a complaint under section 5(1A) of this Act, he shall also send a report of the results of the investigation to the person to whom the complaint relates.

(3) If, after conducting an investigation under section 5(1) of this Act, it appears to the Commissioner that injustice has been caused to the person aggrieved in consequence of maladministration and that the injustice has not been, or will not be, remedied, he may, if he thinks fit, lay before each House of Parliament a special report upon the case.

(3A) If, after conducting an investigation pursuant to a complaint under section 5(1A) of this Act, it appears to the Commissioner that—
 (a) the person to whom the complaint relates has failed to perform a relevant duty owed by him to the person aggrieved, and
 (b) the failure has not been, or will not be, remedied,
 the Commissioner may, if he thinks fit, lay before each House of Parliament a special report upon the case.

(3B) For the purposes of subsection (3A) of this section "relevant duty" has the meaning given by section 5(1B) of this Act.

(4) The Commissioner shall annually lay before each House of Parliament a general report on the performance of his functions under this Act and may from time to time lay before each House of Parliament such other reports with respect to those functions as he thinks fit.

(5) For the purposes of the law of defamation, any such publication as is hereinafter mentioned shall be absolutely privileged, that is to say—
 (a) the publication of any matter by the Commissioner in making a report to either House of Parliament for the purposes of this Act;
 (b) the publication of any matter by a member of the House of Commons in communicating with the Commissioner or his officers for those purposes or by the Commissioner or his officers in communicating with such a member for those purposes;
 (c) the publication by such a member to the person by whom a complaint was made under this Act of a report or statement sent to the member in respect of the complaint in pursuance of section (1) of this section;
 (d) the publication by the Commissioner to such a person as is mentioned in subsection (2) or (2A) of this section of a report to that person in pursuance of that subsection.

Supplemental

12 Interpretation

...

(3) It is hereby declared that nothing in this Act authorises or requires the Commissioner to question the merits of a decision taken without maladministration by a government department or other authority in the exercise of a discretion vested in that department or authority.

SCHEDULE 3
MATTERS NOT SUBJECT TO INVESTIGATION

1. Action taken in matters certified by a Secretary of State or other Minister of the Crown to affect relations or dealings between the Government of the United Kingdom and any other Government or any international organisation of States or Governments.
2. (1) Action taken, in any country or territory outside the United Kingdom, by or on behalf of any officer representing or acting under the authority of Her Majesty in respect of the United Kingdom, or any other officer of the Government of the United Kingdom other than,
   (a) action which is taken by an officer (not being an honorary consular officer) in the exercise of a consular function on behalf of the Government of the United Kingdom;
   (b) action which is taken by an officer within a control zone or supplementary control zone; or
   (c) action which is taken by a British sea-fishery officer.
   . . .
3. Action taken in connection with the administration of the goverment of any country or territory outside the United Kingdom which forms part of Her Majesty's dominions or in which Her Majesty has jurisdiction.
4. Action taken by the Secretary of State under the Extradition Act 2003.
5. Action taken by or with the authority of the Secretary of State for the purposes of investigating crime or of protecting the security of the State, including action so taken with respect to passports.
6. The commencement or conduct of civil or criminal proceedings before any court of law in the United Kingdom, of proceedings at any place under the Naval Discipline Act 1957, the Army Act 1955 or the Air Force Act 1955 . . ., or of proceedings before any international court or tribunal.
6A. Action taken by any person appointed by the Lord Chancellor as a member of the administrative staff of any court or tribunal, so far as that action is taken at the direction, or on the authority (whether express or implied) of any person acting in a judicial capacity or as a member of the tribunal.
6B. (1) Action taken by any member of the administrative staff of a relevant tribunal so far as that action is taken at the direction, or on the authority (whether express or implied), of any person acting in his capacity as a member of the tribunal.
   (2) In this paragraph, "relevant tribunal" has the meaning given by section 5(8) of this Act.
6C. Action taken by any person appointed under section 5(3)(c) of the Criminal Injuries Compensation Act 1995, so far as that action is taken at the direction, or on the authority (whether express or implied) of any person acting as an adjudicator appointed under section 5 of that Act to determine appeals.
7. Any exercise of the prerogative of mercy or of the power of a Secretary of State to make a reference in respect of any person to the High Court of Justiciary or the Court Martial Appeal Court.
8. (1) Action taken on behalf of the Minister of Health or the Secretary of State by a Strategic Health Authority, a Health Authority, a Primary Care Trust, a Special Health Authority, except the Rampton Hospital Review Board, . . . the Rampton Hospital Board, the Broadmoor Hospital Board or the Moss Side and Park Lane Hospitals' Board, . . . a Health Board or the Common Services Agency for the Scottish Health Service, by the Dental Practice Board or the Scottish Dental Practice Board.
   (2) . . .
9. Action taken in matters relating to contractual or other commercial transactions, whether within the United Kingdom or elsewhere, being transactions of a government department or authority to which this Act applies or of any such authority or body as is mentioned in paragraph (a) or (b) of subsection (1) of section 6 of this Act and not being transactions for or relating to—
   (a) the acquisition of land compulsorily or in circumstances in which it could be acquired compulsorily;
   (b) the disposal as surplus of land acquired compulsorily or in such circumstances as aforesaid.
10. (1) Action taken in respect of appointments or removals, pay, discipline, superannuation or other personnel matters, in relation to—

(a) service in any of the armed forces of the Crown, including reserve and auxiliary and cadet forces;
(b) service in any office or employment under the Crown or under any authority (to which this Act applies); or
(c) service in any office or employment, or under any contract for services, in respect of which power to take action, or to determine or approve the action to be taken, in such matters is vested in Her Majesty, any Minister of the Crown or any such authority as aforesaid.

(2) Sub-paragraph (1)(c) above shall not apply to any action (not otherwise excluded from investigation by this Schedule) which is taken by the Secretary of State in connection with—
(a) the provision of information relating to the terms and conditions of any employment covered by an agreement entered into by him under section 12(1) of the Overseas Development and Cooperation Act 1980 or pursuant to the exercise of his powers under Part 1 of the International Development Act 2002; or
(b) the provision of any allowance, grant or supplement or any benefit (other than those relating to superannuation) arising from the designation of any person in accordance with such an agreement.

...

EUROPEAN COMMUNITIES ACT 1972
(1972, c. 68)

An Act to make provision in connection with the enlargement of the European Communities to include the United Kingdom, together with (for certain purposes) the Channel Islands, the Isle of Man and Gibraltar

[17 October 1972]

PART I
GENERAL PROVISIONS

1 **Short title and interpretation**
(1) This Act may be cited as the European Communities Act 1972.
(2) In this Act...
"the Communities" means the European Economic Community, the European Coal and Steel Community and the European Atomic Energy Community;
"the Treaties" or "the Community Treaties" means, subject to subsection (3) below, the pre-accession treaties, that is to say, those described in Part I of Schedule 1 to this Act, taken with—
...
and any expression defined in Schedule 1 to this Act has the meaning there given to it.
(3) If Her Majesty by Order in Council declares that a treaty specified in the Order is to be regarded as one of the Community Treaties as herein defined, the Order shall be conclusive that it is to be so regarded; but a treaty entered into by the United Kingdom after the 22nd January 1972, other than a pre-accession treaty to which the United Kingdom accedes on terms settled on or before that date, shall not be so regarded unless it is so specified, nor be so specified unless a draft of the Order in Council has been approved by resolution of each House of Parliament.
(4) For purposes of subsections (2) and (3) above, "treaty" includes any international agreement, and any protocol or annex to a treaty or international agreement.

2 **General implementation of Treaties**
(1) All such rights, powers, liabilities, obligations and restrictions from time to time created or arising by or under the Treaties, and all such remedies and procedures from time to time provided for by or under the Treaties, as in accordance with the Treaties are without further enactment to be given legal effect or used in the United Kingdom shall be recognised and

available in law, and be enforced, allowed and followed accordingly; and the expression "enforceable Community right" and similar expressions shall be read as referring to one to which this subsection applies.

(2) Subject to Schedule 2 to this Act, at any time after its passing Her Majesty may by Order in Council, and any designated Minister or department may by order, rules, regulations or schemes, make provision—
   (a) for the purpose of implementing any Community obligation of the United Kingdom, or enabling any such obligation to be implemented, or of enabling any rights enjoyed or to be enjoyed by the United Kingdom under or by virtue of the Treaties to be exercised; or
   (b) for the purpose of dealing with matters arising out of or related to any such obligation or rights or the coming into force, or the operation from time to time, of subsection (1) above;
and in the exercise of any statutory power or duty, including any power to give directions or to legislate by means of orders, rules, regulations or other subordinate instrument, the person entrusted with the power or duty may have regard to the objects of the Communities and to any such obligation or rights as aforesaid.

In this subsection "designated Minister or Department" means such Minister of the Crown or government department as may from time to time be designated by Order in Council in relation to any matter or for any purpose, but subject to such restrictions or conditions (if any) as may be specified by the Order in Council.

. . .

(4) The provision that may be made under subsection (2) above includes, subject to Schedule 2 to this Act, any such provision (of any such extent) as might be made by Act of Parliament, and any enactment passed or to be passed, other than one contained in this Part of this Act, shall be construed and have effect subject to the foregoing provisions of this section; but, except as may be provided by any Act passed after this Act, Schedule 2 shall have effect in connection with the powers conferred by this and the following sections of this Act to make Orders in Council or orders, rules, regulations or schemes.

. . .

3 **Decisions on, and proof of, Treaties and Community instruments, etc.**

(1) For the purposes of all legal proceedings any question as to the meaning or effect of any of the Treaties, or as to the validity, meaning or effect of any Community instrument, shall be treated as a question of law (and, if not referred to the European Court, be for determination as such in accordance with the principles laid down by and any relevant decision of the European Court).

(2) Judicial notice shall be taken of the Treaties, of the Official Journal of the Communities and of any decision of, or expression of opinion by, the European Court on any such question as aforesaid; and the Official Journal shall be admissible as evidence of any instrument or other act thereby communicated of any of the Communities or of any Community institution.

. . .

LOCAL GOVERNMENT ACT 1972
(1972, c. 70)

An Act to make provision with respect to local government and the functions of local authorities in England and Wales; to amend Part II of the Transport Act 1968; to confer rights of appeal in respect of decisions relating to licences under the Home Counties (Music and Dancing) Licensing Act 1926; to make further provision with respect to magistrates' courts committees; to abolish certain inferior courts of record; and for connected purposes [26 October 1972]

PART VA

ACCESS TO MEETINGS AND DOCUMENTS OF CERTAIN AUTHORITIES, COMMITTEES AND SUB-COMMITEES

100A Admission to meetings of principal councils

(1) A meeting of a principal council shall be open to the public except to the extent that they are excluded (whether during the whole or part of the proceedings) under subsection (2) below or by resolution under subsection (4) below.

(2) The public shall be excluded from a meeting of a principal council during an item of business whenever it is likely, in view of the nature of the business to be transacted or the nature of the proceedings, that, if members of the public were present during that item, confidential information would be disclosed to them in breach of the obligation of confidence; and nothing in this Part shall be taken to authorise or require the disclosure of confidential information in breach of the obligation of confidence.

(3) For the purposes of subsection (2) above, "confidential information" means—

(a) information furnished to the council by a Government department upon terms (however expressed) which forbid the disclosure of the information to the public; and

(b) information the disclosure of which to the public is prohibited by or under any enactment or by the order of a court;

and, in either case, the reference to the obligation of confidence is to be construed accordingly.

(4) A principal council may by resolution exclude the public from a meeting during an item of business whenever it is likely, in view of the nature of the business to be transacted or the nature of the proceedings, that if members of the public were present during that item there would be disclosure to them of exempt information, as defined in section 100I below.

. . .

(7) Nothing in this section shall require a principal council to permit the taking of photographs of any proceedings, or the use of any means to enable persons not present to see or hear any proceedings (whether at the time or later), or the making of any oral report on any proceedings as they take place.

(8) This section is without prejudice to any power of exclusion to suppress or prevent disorderly conduct or other misbehaviour at a meeting.

100B Access to agenda and connected reports

(1) Copies of the agenda for a meeting of a principal council and, subject to subsection (2) below, copies of any report for the meeting shall be open to inspection by members of the public at the offices of the council in accordance with subsection (3) below.

(2) If the proper officer thinks fit, there may be excluded from the copies of reports provided in pursuance of subsection (1) above the whole of any report which, or any part which, relates only to items during which, in his opinion, the meeting is likely not to be open to the public.

(3) Any document which is required by subsection (1) above to be open to inspection shall be so open at least five clear days before the meeting, except that—

(a) where the meeting is convened at shorter notice, the copies of the agenda and reports shall be open to inspection from the time the meeting is convened, and

(b) where an item is added to an agenda copies of which are open to inspection by the public, copies of the item (or of the revised agenda), and the copies of any report for the meeting relating to the item, shall be open to inspection from the time the item is added to the agenda;

but nothing in this subsection requires copies of any agenda, item or report to be open to inspection by the public until copies are available to members of the council.

(4) An item of business may not be considered at a meeting of a principal council unless either—
   (a) a copy of the agenda including the item (or a copy of the item) is open to inspection by members of the public in pursuance of subsection (1) above for at least five clear days before the meeting or, where the meeting is convened at shorter notice, from the time the meeting is convened; or
   (b) by reason of special circumstances, which shall be specified in the minutes, the chairman of the meeting is of the opinion that the item should be considered at the meeting as a matter of urgency.

...

100C Inspection of minutes and other documents after meetings
   (1) After a meeting of a principal council the following documents shall be open to inspection by members of the public at the offices of the council until the expiration of the period of six years beginning with the date of the meeting, namely—
   (a) the minutes, or a copy of the minutes, of the meeting, excluding so much of the minutes of proceedings during which the meeting was not open to the public as discloses exempt information;
   (b) where applicable, a summary under subsection (2) below;
   (c) a copy of the agenda for the meeting; and
   (d) a copy of so much of any report for the meeting as relates to any item during which the meeting was open to the public.

...

100D Inspection of background papers
   (1) Subject, in the case of section 100C(1), to subsection (2) below, if and so long as copies of the whole or part of a report for a meeting of a principal council are required by section 100B(1) or 100C(1) above to be open to inspection by members of the public—
   (a) those copies shall each include a copy of a list compiled by the proper officer, of the background papers for the report or the part of the report; and
   (b) at least one copy of each of the documents included in that list shall also be open to inspection at the offices of the council.
   (2) Subsection (1) above does not require a copy. . . of any document included in the list, to be open to inspection after the expiration of the period of four years beginning with the date of the meeting.

...

100E Application to committees and sub-committees
   (1) Sections 100A to 100D above shall apply in relation to a committee or sub-committee of a principal council as they apply in relation to a principal council.

...

100G Principal councils to publish additional information
   (1) A principal council shall maintain a register stating—
   (a) the name and address of every member of the council for the time being together with, in the case of a councillor, the ward or division which he represents; and
   (b) in respect of every committee or sub-committee of the council—
      (i) the members of the council who are members of the committee or sub-committee or who are entitled, in accordance with any standing orders relating to the committee or sub-committee, to speak at its meetings or any of them;
      (ii) the name and address of every other person who is a member of the committee or sub-committee or who is entitled, in accordance with any standing orders relat-

ing to the committee or sub-committee, to speak at its meetings or any of them otherwise than in the capacity of an officer of the council; and

(iii) the functions in relation to the committee or sub-committee of every person falling within sub-paragraph (i) above who is not a member of the committee or sub-committee and of every person falling within sub-paragraph (ii) above.

(2) A principal council shall maintain a list—

(a) specifying those powers of the council which, for the time being, are exercisable from time to time by officers of the council in pursuance of arrangements made under this Act or any other enactment for their discharge by those officers; and

(b) stating the title of the officer by whom each of the powers so specified is for the time being so exercisable;

but this subsection does not require a power to be specified in the list if the arrangements for its discharge by the officer are made for a specified period not exceeding six months.

. . .

PART VI
DISCHARGE OF FUNCTIONS

101 Arrangements for discharge of functions by local authorities

(1) Subject to any express provision contained in this Act or any Act passed after this Act, a local authority may arrange for the discharge of any of their functions—

(a) by a committee, a sub-committee or an officer of the authority; or

(b) by any other local authority.

(1A) A local authority may not under subsection (1)(b) above arrange for the discharge of any of their functions by another local authority if, or to the extent that, that function is also a function of the other local authority and is the responsibility of the other authority's executive.

(1B) Arrangements made under subsection (1)(b) above by a local authority ("the first authority") with respect to the discharge of any of their functions shall cease to have effect with respect to that function if, or to the extent that,—

(a) the first authority are operating or begin to operate executive arrangements, and that function becomes the responsibility of the executive of that authority; or

(b) the authority with whom the arrangements are made ("the second authority") are operating or begin to operate executive arrangements, that function is also a function of the second authority and that function becomes the responsibility of the second authority's executive.

(1C) Subsections (1A) and (1B) above do not affect arrangements made by virtue of section 19 of the Local Government Act 2000 (discharge of functions of and by another authority).

(2) Where by virtue of this section any functions of a local authority may be discharged by a committee of theirs, then, unless the local authority otherwise direct, the committee may arrange for the discharge of any of those functions by a sub-committee or an officer of the authority and where by virtue of this section any functions of a local authority may be discharged by a sub-committee of the authority, then, unless the local authority or the committee otherwise direct, the sub-committee may arrange for the discharge of any of those functions by an officer of the authority.

(3) Where arrangements are in force under this section for the discharge of any functions of a local authority by another local authority, then, subject to the terms of the arrangements, that other authority may arrange for the discharge of those functions by a committee, sub-committee or officer of theirs and subsection (2) above shall apply in relation to those functions as it applies in relation to the functions of that other authority.

(4) Any arrangements made by a local authority or committee under this section for the discharge of any functions by a committee, sub-committee, officer or local authority shall not prevent the authority or committee by whom the arrangements are made from exercising those functions.

(5) Two or more local authorities may discharge any of their functions jointly and, where arrangements are in force for them to do so,—
   (a) they may also arrange for the discharge of those functions by a joint committee of theirs or by an officer of one of them and subsection (2) above shall apply in relation to those functions as it applies in relation to the functions of the individual authorities; and
   (b) any enactment relating to those functions or the authorities by whom or the areas in respect of which they are to be discharged shall have effect subject to all necessary modifications in its application in relation to those functions and the authorities by whom and the areas in respect of which (whether in pursuance of the arrangements or otherwise) they are to be discharged.
(5A) Arrangements made under subsection (5) above by two or more local authorities with respect to the discharge of any of their functions shall cease to have effect with respect to that function if, or to the extent that, the function becomes the responsibility of an executive of any of the authorities.
(5B) Subsection (5A) above does not affect arrangements made by virtue of section 20 of the Local Government Act 2000 (joint exercise of functions).
(6) A local authority's functions with respect to levying, or issuing a precept for, a rate... shall be discharged only by the authority.

. . .

PART VII
MISCELLANEOUS POWERS OF LOCAL AUTHORITIES

111 Subsidiary powers of local authorities
(1) Without prejudice to any powers exercisable apart from this section but subject to the provisions of this Act and any other enactment passed before or after this Act, a local authority shall have power to do anything (whether or not involving the expenditure, borrowing or lending of money or the acquisition or disposal of any property or rights) which is calculated to facilitate, or is conducive or incidental to, the discharge of any of their functions.
(2) For the purposes of this section, transacting the business of a parish or community meeting or any other parish or community business shall be treated as a function of the parish or community council.
(3) A local authority shall not by virtue of this section raise money, whether by means of rates, precepts or borrowing, or lend money except in accordance with the enactments relating to those matters respectively.
(4) In this section "local authority" includes the Common Council.

112 Appointment of staff
(1) Without prejudice to section 111 above but subject to the provisions of this Act, a local authority shall appoint such officers as they think necessary for the proper discharge by the authority of such of their or another authority's functions as fall to be discharged by them and the carrying out of any obligations incurred by them in connection with an agreement made by them in pursuance of section 113 below.
(2) An officer appointed under subsection (1) above shall hold office on such reasonable terms and conditions, including conditions as to remuneration, as the authority appointing him think fit.
(3) Subject to subsection (4) below, any enactment or instrument made under an enactment which requires or empowers all local authorities or local authorities of any description or committees of local authorities to appoint a specified officer shall, to the extent that it makes any such provision, cease to have effect.

The reference in this section to committees of local authorities does not include a reference to any committee of which some members are required to be appointed by a body or person other than a local authority.

. . .

PART XI
GENERAL PROVISIONS AS TO LOCAL AUTHORITIES

Legal proceedings

222 Power of local authorities to prosecute or defend legal proceedings

(1) Where a local authority consider it expedient for the promotion or protection of the interests of the inhabitants of their area—
  (a) they may prosecute or defend or appear in any legal proceedings and, in the case of civil proceedings, may institute them in their own name, and
  (b) they may, in their own name, make representations in the interests of the inhabitants at any public inquiry held by or on behalf of any Minister or public body under any enactment.

(2) In this section "local authority" includes the Common Council and the London Fire and Emergency Planning Authority.

Byelaws

235 Power of councils to make byelaws for good rule and government and suppression of nuisances

(1) The council of a district, the council of a principal area in Wales and the council of a London borough may make byelaws for the good rule and government of the whole or any part of the district principal area or borough, as the case may be, and for the prevention and suppression of nuisances therein.

(2) The confirming authority in relation to byelaws made under this section shall be the Secretary of State.

(3) Byelaws shall not be made under this section for any purpose as respects any area if provision for that purpose as respects that area is made by, or is or may be made under, any other enactment.

SCHEDULE 12A

PART 1

DESCRIPTIONS OF EXEMPT INFORMATION: ENGLAND

1. Information relating to any individual.
2. Information which is likely to reveal the identity of an individual.
3. Information relating to the financial or business affairs of any particular person (including the authority holding that information).
4. Information relating to any consultations or negotiations, or contemplated consultations or negotiations, in connection with any labour relations matter arising between the authority or a Minister of the Crown and employees of, or office holders under, the authority.
5. Information in respect of which a claim to legal professional privilege could be maintained in legal proceedings.
6. Information which reveals that the authority proposes—
  (a) to give under any enactment a notice under or by virtue of which requirements are imposed on a person; or
  (b) to make an order or direction under any enactment.
7. Information relating to any action taken or to be taken in connection with the prevention, investigation or prosecution of crime.

PART 4

DESCRIPTIONS OF EXEMPT INFORMATION: WALES

12. Information relating to a particular individual.
13. Information which is likely to reveal the identity of an individual.
14. Information relating to the financial or business affairs of any particular person (including the authority holding that information).

15. Information relating to any consultations or negotiations, or contemplated consultations or negotiations, in connection with any labour relations matter arising between the authority or a Minister of the Crown and employees of, or office holders under, the authority.
16. Information in respect of which a claim to legal professional privilege could be maintained in legal proceedings.
17. Information which reveals that the authority proposes—
    (a) to give under any enactment a notice under or by virtue of which requirements are imposed on a person; or
    (b) to make an order or direction under any enactment.
18. Information relating to any action taken or to be taken in connection with the prevention, investigation or prosecution of crime

LOCAL GOVERNMENT ACT 1974
(1974, c. 7)

An Act to make further provision, in relation to England and Wales, with respect to the payment of grants to local authorities, rating and valuation, borrowing and lending by local authorities and the classification of highways; to extend the powers of the Countryside Commission to give financial assistance; to provide for the establishment of Commissions for the investigation of administrative action taken by or on behalf of local and other authorities; to restrict certain grants under the Transport Act 1968; to provide for the removal or relaxation of certain statutory controls affecting local government activities; to make provision in relation to the collection of sums by local authorities on behalf of water authorities; to amend section 259(3) of the Local Government Act 1972 and to make certain minor amendments of or consequential on that Act; and for connected purposes [8 February 1974]

PART III
LOCAL GOVERNMENT ADMINISTRATION

23 **The Commission for Local Administration**

(1) For the purpose of conducting investigations in accordance with this Part of this Act, there shall be—
   (a) a body of commissioners to be known as the Commission for Local Administration in England,
   (b) . . .
   but the Commission may include persons appointed to act as advisers, not exceeding the number appointed to conduct investigations.

(2) The Parliamentary Commissioner shall be a member of the Commission.
. . .

(3) In the following provisions of this Part of this Act the expression "Local Commissioner" means a person, other than the Parliamentary Commissioner, or an advisory member who is a member of the Commission.

(4) Appointments to the office of . . . Commissioner shall be made by Her Majesty on the recommendation of the Secretary of State . . .

(5) A Commissioner's appointment may be a full-time or part-time appointment and, with the Commissioner's consent, the terms of the appointment may be varied as to whether it is full-time or part-time.

(5A) A Commissioner must be appointed for a period of not more than 7 years.
. . .

(6) A Commissioner may be relieved of office by Her Majesty at his own request or may be removed from office by Her Majesty on grounds of incapacity or misbehaviour . . .

(6A) A person appointed to be a Commissioner is not eligible for re-appointment.

(7) The Secretary of State shall designate two of the Local Commissioners for England as chairman and vice-chairman respectively of the Commission for Local Administration in England.

(8) The Commission for Local Administration in England shall divide England into areas and shall provide, in relation to each area, for one or more of the Local Commissioners to be responsible for the area; ...

A Local Commissioner may, by virtue of this Subsection, be made responsible for more than one area.

...

(10) The Commission—
   (a) shall make arrangements for Local Commissioners to deal with matters for which they do not have responsibility pursuant to subsection 8A, and
   (b) shall publish information about the procedures for making complaints under this Part of this Act.

25 Authorities subject to investigation

(1) This Part of this Act applies to the following authorities—
   (a) any local authority;
   (aaa) the Greater London Authority;
   (ab) a National Park Authority for a National Park in England;
   (b) any joint board the constituent authorities of which are all local authorities;
   (ba) the Commission for the New Towns;
   (bb) any development corporation established for the purposes of a new town;
   (bbb) the London Development Agency;
   (bd) any urban development corporation established by an order under section 135 of the Local Government, Planning and Land Act 1980 for an urban development area in England or a designated area in England;
   (be) any housing action trust established under Part III of the Housing Act 1988,
   (bf) the Urban Regeneration Agency;
   (bg) a fire and rescue authority in England constituted by a scheme under section 2 of the Fire and Rescue Services Act 2004 or a scheme to which section 4 of that Act applies;
   (c) any joint authority established by Part IV of the Local Government Act 1985;
   (cza) the London Fire and Emergency Planning Authority;
   (ca) any police authority established under section 3 of the Police Act 1996 for a police area in England;
   (caa) the Metropolitan Police Authority;
   (cc) Transport for London;
   (d) in relation to the flood defence functions of the Environment Agency, within the meaning of the Water Resources Act 1991, the Environment Agency and any regional flood defence committee for an area wholy or partly in England; and
   (e) The London Transport Users' Committee.

(2) Her Majesty may by Order in Council provide that this Part of this Act shall also apply, subject to any modifications or exceptions specified in the Order, to any authority specified in the Order, being an authority which is established by or under an Act of Parliament, and which has power to levy a rate, or to issue a precept.

...

(4) Any reference to an authority to which this Part of this Act applies includes a reference—
   (a) to the members and officers of that authority, and
   (b) to a committee or sub-committee of that authority (including a joint committee or joint sub-committee on which the authority are represented),
   and (for the avoidance of doubt) subsections (4ZA) to (5) apply for the purposes of this subsection.

(4ZA) Any reference to an authority to which this Part of this Act applies also includes, in the case of a local authority operating executive arrangements, the executive.

(4A) Any reference to an authority to which this Part of this Act applies also includes, in the case of the Greater London Authority, a reference to each of the following—
   (a) the London Assembly;
   (b), (c) ...

(4B) ...
(5) Any reference to an authority to which this Part of this Act applies also includes a reference to—
  (a) a school organisation committee constituted in accordance with section 24 of the School Standards and Framework Act 1998,
  (b) ...
  (c) an admission appeal panel constituted in accordance with regulations under section 94(5) or 95(3) of that Act,
  (d) the governing body of any community, foundation or voluntary school so far as acting in connection with the admission of pupils to the school or otherwise performing any of their functions under Chapter I of Part III of that Act, and
  (e) an exclusion appeal panel constituted in accordance with regulations under section 52 of the Education Act 2002.
(6) Subsection (7) has effect where an authority to which this Part of this Act applies exercise a function entirely or partly by means of an arrangement with another person.
(7) For the purposes of this Part of this Act, action taken by or on behalf of the other person in carrying out the arrangement shall be treated as action taken—
  (a) on behalf of the authority, and
  (b) in the exercise of the authority's function.
(8) Subsection (7) does not have effect where, by virtue of another enactment, the action would be treated as action taken by the authority.

26 Matters subject to investigation

(1) For the purpose of section 24A(1)(b), in relation to an authority to which this part of this Act applies, the following matters are subject to investigation by a Local Commissioner under this Part of this Act—
  (a) alleged or apparent maladministration in connection with the exercise of the authority's administrative functions;
  (b) an alleged or apparent failure in a service which it was the authority's function to provide;
  (c) an alleged or apparent failure to provide such a service.
(1A)–(4) ...
(5) Before proceeding to investigate a matter, a Local Commissioner shall satisfy himself that—
  (a) the matter has been brought, by or on behalf of the person affected, to the notice of the authority to which it relates and that that authority has been afforded a reasonable opportunity to investigate the matter and to respond; or
  (b) in the particular circumstances, it is not reasonable to expect the matter to be brought to the notice of that authority or for that authority to be afforded a reasonable opportunity to investigate the matter and to respond.
(6) A Local Commissioner shall not conduct an investigation under this Part of this Act in respect of any of the following matters, that is to say,—
  (a) any action in respect of which the person affected has or had a right of appeal, reference or review to or before a tribunal constituted by or under any enactment;
  (b) any action in respect of which in the person affected has or had a right of appeal to a Minister of the Crown . . .; or
  (c) any action in respect of which the person affected has or had a remedy by way of proceedings in any court of law:
  Provided that a Local Commissioner may conduct an investigation notwithstanding the existence of such a right or remedy if satisfied that in the particular circumstances it is not reasonable to expect the person affected to resort or have resorted to it.
(6A) A Local Commissioner shall not conduct an investigation under this Part of this Act in respect of any action taken by or on behalf of an authority in the exercise of any of the authority's functions otherwise than in relation to England.

(7) A Local Commissioner shall not conduct an investigation in respect of any action which in his opinion affects all or most of the inhabitants of the following area:
- (aa) where the matter relates to a National Park Authority, the area of the Park for which it is such an authority;
- (a) where the matter relates to the Commission for the New Towns, the area of the new town or towns to which the complaint relates;
- (b) ...
- (ba) where the matter relates to the Urban Regeneration Agency, any designated area within the meaning of Part III of the Leasehold Reform, Housing and Urban Development Act 1993;
- (c) in any other case, the area of the authority concerned.

(8) Without prejudice to the preceding provisions of this section, a Local Commissioner shall not conduct an investigation under this Part of this Act in respect of any such action or matter as is described in Schedule 5 to this Act.

(9) Her Majesty may by Order in Council amend the said Schedule 5 so as to add to or to exclude from the provisions of that Schedule (as it has effect for the time being) such actions or matters as may be described in the Order; and any Order made by virtue of this subsection shall be subject to annulment in pursuance of a resolution of either House of Parliament.

...

26A   Who can complain

(1) Under this Part of this Act, a complaint about a matter may only be made—
- (a) by a member of the public who claims to have sustained injustice in consequence of the matter,
- (b) by a person authorised in writing by such a member of the public to act on his behalf, or
- (c) in accordance with subsection (2).

(2) Where a member of the public by whom a complaint about a matter might have been made under this Part of this Act has died or is otherwise unable to authorise a person to act on his behalf, the complaint may be made—
- (a) by a personal representative (if any), or
- (b) by a peron who appears to a Local Commissioner to be suitable to represent him.

28   Procedure in respect of investigations

(1) Where a Local Commissioner proposes to investigate a matter under this Part of this Act, he shall afford to the authority concerned, and to any person who is alleged in the complaint (if any) or who otherwise appears to the Local Commissioner, to have taken or authorised the action which would be the subject of the investigation, an opportunity to comment on any allegations contained in the matter.

(2) Every ... investigation under this Part of the Act shall be conducted in private, but except as aforesaid the procedure for conducting an investigation shall be such as the Local Commissioner considers appropriate in the circumstances of the case; and without prejudice to the generality of the preceding provision the Local Commissioner may obtain information from such persons and in such manner, and make such inquiries as he thinks fit, and may determine whether any person may be represented (by counsel or solicitor or otherwise) in the investigation.

...

(4) The conduct of an investigation under this Part of this Act shall not affect any action taken by the authority concerned or any other person, or any power or duty of the authority concerned or any other person to take further action with respect to any matters subject to the investigation.

29   Investigations: further provisions

(1) For the purposes of an investigation under this Part of this Act a Local Commissioner may require any member or officer of the authority concerned, or any other person who in his

opinion is able to furnish information or produce documents relevant to the investigation, to furnish any such information or produce any such documents.

(2) For the purposes of any such investigation a Local Commissioner shall have the same powers as the High Court in respect of the attendance and examination of witnesses, and in respect of the production of documents.

(3) A Local Commissioner may, under subsection (1) above, require any person to furnish information concerning communications between the authority concerned and any Government department . . ., or to produce any correspondence or other documents forming part of any such written communications.

(4) No obligation to maintain secrecy or other restriction upon the disclosure of information obtained by or furnished to persons in Her Majesty's service, whether imposed by any enactment or by any rule of law, shall apply to the disclosure of information in accordance with subsection (3) above; and where that subsection applies the Crown shall not be entitled to any such privilege in respect of the production of documents or the giving of evidence as is allowed by law in legal proceedings.

. . .

30 Reports on investigations

(1) If a Local Commissioner completes an investigation of a matter, he shall prepare a report of the results of the investigation and send a copy to each of the persons concerned (subject to subsection (1B)).

(1A) A Local Commissioner may include in a report on a matter under subsection (1) any recommendations that he could include in a further report on the matter by virtue of section 31(2A) to (2BA).

(1B) If, after the investigation of a matter is completed, the Local Commissioner decides—
   (a) that he is satisfied with action which the authority concerned have taken or propose to take, and
   (b) that it is not appropriate to prepare and send a copy of a report under subsection (1),
he may instead prepare a statement of his reasons for the decision and send a copy to each of the persons concerned.

. . .

(4) Subject to the provisions of subsection (7) below, the authority concerned shall for a period of three weeks make copies of the report available for inspection by the public without charge at all reasonable hours at one or more of their offices; and any person shall be entitled to take copies of, or extracts from, the report when so made available.

(4A) Subject to subsection (7) below, the authority concerned shall supply a copy of the report to any person on request if he pays such charge as the authority may reasonably require.

(5) Not later than two weeks after the report is received by the authority concerned, the proper officer of the authority shall give public notice, by advertisement in the newspapers and such other ways as appear to him appropriate, that copies of the report will be available as provided by subsections (4) and (4A) above, and shall specify the date, being a date not more than one week after the public notice is first given from which the period of three weeks will begin.

. . .

(7) The Local Commissioner may, if he thinks fit after taking into account the public interest as well as the interests of the complainant (if any) and of other persons, direct that a report specified in the direction shall not be subject to the provisions of subsections (4), (4A) and (5) above.

31 Reports on investigations: further provisions

(1) This section applies where a Local Commissioner reports that there has been—
   (a) maladministration in connection with the exercise of the authority's administrative functions,
   (b) a failure in a service which it was the function of an authority to provide, or
   (c) a failure to provide such a service.

(2) The report shall be laid before the authority concerned and it shall be the duty of that authority to consider the report and, within the period of three months beginning with the date on which they received the report, or such longer period as the Local Commissioner may agree in writing, to notify the Local Commissioner of the action which the authority have taken or propose to take.

(2A) If the Local Commissioner—
- (a) does not receive the notification required by subsection (2) above within the period allowed by or under that subsection; or
- (b) is not satisfied with the action which the authority concerned have taken; or
- (c) does not within a period of three months beginning with the end of the period so allowed or such longer period as the Local Commissioners may agree in writing, receive confirmation from the authority concerned that they have taken action, as proposed, to the satisfaction of the Local Commissioner,

he shall make a further report setting out those facts and making recommendations.

...

(2B) Where the report relates to maladministration, those recommendations are recommendations with respect to action which, in the Local Commissioner's opinion, the authority concerned should take—
- (a) to remedy any injustice sustained by the person affected in consequence of the maladministration, and
- (b) to prevent injustice being caused in the future in consequence of similar maladministration in connection with the exercise of the authority's administrative functions.

...

(2C) Section 30 above, with any necessary modifications, and subsection (2) above shall apply to a report under subsection (2A) above as they apply to a report under that section.

(2D) If the Local Commissioner—
- (a) does not receive the notification required by subsection (2) above as applied by subsection (2C) above within the period allowed by or under that subsection or is satisfied before the period allowed by that subsection has expired that the authority concerned have decided to take no action, or
- (b) is not satisfied with the action which the authority concerned have taken or propose to take, or
- (c) does not within a period of three months beginning with the end of the period allowed by or under subsection (2) above as applied by subsection (2C) above, or such longer period as the Local Commissioner may agree in writing, receive confirmation from the authority concerned that they have taken action, as proposed, to the satisfaction of the Local Commissioner,

he may, by notice to the authority, require them to arrange for a statement to be published in accordance with subsections (2E) and (2F) below.

(2E) The statement referred to in subsection (2D) above is a statement, in such form as the authority concerned and the Local Commissioner may agree, consisting of—
- (a) details of any action recommended by the Local Commissioner in his further report which the authority have not taken;
- (b) such supporting material as the Local Commissioner may require; and
- (c) if the authority so require, a statement of the reasons for their having taken no action on, or not the action recommended in, the report.

(2F) The requirements for the publication of the statement are that—
- (a) publication shall be in any two editions within a fortnight of a newspaper circulating in the area of the authority agreed with the Local Commissioner or, in default of agreement, nominated by him; and
- (b) publication in the first such edition shall be arranged for the earliest practicable date.

(2G) If the authority concerned—

(a) fail to arrange for the publication of the statement in accordance with subsections (2E) and (2F) above, or
(b) are unable, within the period of one month beginning with the date on which they received the notice under subsection (2D) above, or such longer period as the Local Commissioner may agree in writing, to agree with the Local Commissioner the form of the statement to be published,

the Local Commissioner shall arrange for such a statement as is mentioned in subsection (2E) above to be published in any two editions within a fortnight of a newspaper circulating within the authority's area.

(2H) The authority concerned shall reimburse the Commission on demand any reasonable expenses incurred by the Local Commissioner in performing his duty under subsection (2G) above.

(3) In any case where—
(a) a report is laid before an authority under subsection (2) or (2C) above, and
(b) on consideration of the report, it appears to the authority that a payment should be made to, or some other benefit should be provided for, a person who has suffered injustice in consequence of the maladministration or failure to which the report relates,

the authority may incur such expenditure as appears to them to be appropriate in making such a payment or providing such a benefit.

(4) Where the authority concerned is the Greater London Authority, any functions exercisable under this section by or in relation to the Authority shall be exercisable by or in relation to the Mayor and the Assembly acting jointly on behalf of the Authority, and references to the authority concerned (other than references to a member of the authority concerned) shall be construed accordingly.

34 Interpretation of Part III

. . .

(3) It is hereby declared that nothing in this Part of this Act authorises or requires a Local Commissioner to question the merits of a decision taken without maladministration by an authority in the exercise of a discretion vested in that authority.

SCHEDULE 5
MATTERS NOT SUBJECT TO INVESTIGATION

1. The commencement or conduct of civil or criminal proceedings before any court of law.
2. Action taken by any police authority in connection with the investigation or prevention of crime.
3. (1) Action taken in matters relating to contractual or other commercial transactions of any authority to which Part 3 of this Act applies relating to—
    (a) the operation of public passenger transport;
    (b) the carrying on of a dock or harbour undertaking;
    (c) the provision of entertainment;
    (d) the provision and operation of industrial establishments;
    (e) the provision and operation of markets.
   (2) Sub-paragraph (1) does not include transactions for or relating to—
    (a) the acquisition or disposal of land;
    (b) the acquisition or disposal of moorings which are not moorings provided in connection with a dock or harbour undertaking.
   (3) Sub-paragraph (1)(a) does not include action taken by or on behalf of the London Transport Users Committee in operating a procedure for examining complaints or reviewing decisions.
   (4) Sub-paragraph (1)(e) does not include transactions relating to—
    (a) the grant, renewal or revocation of a licence to occupy a pitch or stall in a fair or market, or
    (b) the attachment of any condition to such a licence.

4. Action taken in respect of appointments or removals, pay, discipline, superannuation or other personnel matters.
5. (1) ...
   (2) Any action concerning—
       (a) the giving of instruction, whether secular or religious, or
       (b) conduct, curriculum, internal organisation, management or discipline in any school or other educational establishment maintained by the authority.
6. Any action taken by or on behalf of an authority mentioned in section 25(1)(ba) or (bb) of this Act which is not action in connection with functions in relation to housing.
7. Action taken by or on behalf of an authority mentioned in section 25(1)(bd) of this Act which is not action in connection with functions in relation to town and country planning.
8. Action taken by or on behalf of the Urban Regeneration Agency which is not action in connection with functions in relation to town and country planning.

HOUSE OF COMMONS DISQUALIFICATION ACT 1975
(1975, c. 24)

An Act to consolidate certain enactments relating to disqualification for membership of the House of Commons [8 May 1975]

1 Disqualification of holders of certain offices and places
   (1) Subject to the provisions of this Act, a person is disqualified for membership of the House of Commons who for the time being—
   (za) is a Lord Spiritual;
   (a) holds any of the judicial offices specified in Part I of Schedule 1 to this Act;
   (b) is employed in the civil service of the Crown, whether in an established capacity or not, and whether for the whole or part of his time;
   (c) is a member of any of the regular armed forces of the Crown or the *Ulster Defence Regiment*;
   (d) is a member of any police force maintained by a police authority;
   (e) is a member of the legislature of any country or territory outside the Commonwealth (other than Ireland); or
   (f) holds any office described in Part II or Part III of Schedule 1.
   ...
   (4) Except as provided by this Act, a person shall not be disqualified for membership of the House of Commons by reason of his holding an office or place of profit under the Crown or any other office or place; and a person shall not be disqualified for appointment to or for holding any office or place by reason of his being a member of that House.

2 Ministerial offices
   (1) Not more than ninety-five persons being the holders of offices specified in Schedule 2 to this Act (in this section referred to as Ministerial offices) shall be entitled to sit and vote in the House of Commons at any one time.
   (2) If at any time the number of members of the House of Commons who are holders of Ministerial offices exceeds the number entitled to sit and vote in that House under subsection (1) above, none except any who were both members of that House and holders of Ministerial offices before the excess occurred shall sit or vote therein until the number has been reduced, by death, resignation or otherwise, to the number entitled to sit and vote as aforesaid.
   (3) A person holding a Ministerial office is not disqualified by this Act by reason of any office held by him ex officio as the holder of that Ministerial office.

5 Power to amend Schedule 1
   (1) If at any time it is resolved by the House of Commons that Schedule 1 to this Act be amended, whether by the addition or omission of any office or the removal of any office

from one Part of the Schedule to another, or by altering the description of any office specified therein, Her Majesty may by Order in Council amend that Schedule accordingly.

...

6 Effects of disqualification and provision for relief

(1) Subject to any order made by the House of Commons under this section,—
   (a) if any person disqualified by this Act for membership of that House, or for membership for a particular constituency, is elected as a member of that House, or as a member for that constituency, as the case may be, his election shall be void; and
   (b) if any person being a member of that House becomes disqualified by this Act for membership for the constituency for which he is sitting, his seat shall be vacated.

(2) If, in a case falling or alleged to fall within subsection (1) above, it appears to the House of Commons that the grounds of disqualification or alleged disqualification under this Act which subsisted or arose at the material time have been removed, and that it is otherwise proper so to do, that House may by order direct that any such disqualification incurred on those grounds at that time shall be disregarded for the purposes of this section.

...

7 Jurisdiction of Privy Council as to disqualification

(1) Any person who claims that a person purporting to be a member of the House of Commons is disqualified by this Act, or has been so disqualified at any time since his (election, may apply to Her Majesty in Council, in accordance with such rules as Her Majesty in Council may prescribe, for a declaration to that effect.

(2) Section 3 of the Judicial Committee Act 1833 (reference to the Judicial Committee of the Privy Council of appeals to Her Majesty in Council) shall apply to any application under this section as it applies to an appeal to Her Majesty in Council from a court.

...

8 Relaxation of obligation to accept office

(1) No person being a member of the House of Commons, or for the time being nominated as a candidate for election to that House, shall be required to accept any office or place by virtue of which he would be disqualified by this Act for membership of that House, or for membership of that House for the constituency for which he is sitting or is a candidate.

(2) This section does not affect any obligation to serve in the armed forces of the Crown, whether imposed by an enactment or otherwise.

SCHEDULE 2
MINISTERIAL OFFICE

Prime Minister and First Lord of the Treasury.
Lord President of the Council.
Lord Privy Seal.
Chancellor of the Duchy of Lancaster.
Paymaster General.
President of the Board of Trade.
Secretary of State.
Chancellor of the Exchequer.

...

President of the Board of Trade.
Minister of State.
Chief Secretary to the Treasury.
Minister in charge of a public department of Her Majesty's Government in the United Kingdom (if not within the other provisions of this Schedule).
Attorney General.

...

Solicitor General.

Advocate General for Scotland.
...
Parliamentary Secretary to the Treasury.
Financial Secretary to the Treasury.
Parliamentary Secretary in a Government Department other than the Treasury, or not in a department.
Junior Lord of the Treasury.
Treasurer of Her Majesty's Household.
Comptroller of Her Majesty's Household.
Vice-Chamberlain of Her Majesty's Household.
Assistant Government Whip.

MINISTERIAL AND OTHER SALARIES ACT 1975
(1975, c. 27)

An Act to consolidate the enactments relating to the salaries of Ministers and Opposition Leaders and Chief Whips and to other matters connected therewith [8 May 1975]

1 **Salaries**
  (1) Subject to the provisions of this Act—
    (a) there shall be paid to the holder of any Ministerial office specified in Schedule 1 to this Act such salary as is provided for by that Schedule; and
    (b) there shall be paid to the Leaders and Whips of the Opposition such salaries as are provided for by Schedule 2 to this Act.
  (2) There shall be paid to the Lord Chancellor a salary (which shall be charged on and paid out of the Consolidated Fund of the United Kingdom) at such rate as together with the salary payable to him as Speaker of the House of Lords will amount to £2,500 a year more than the salary payable to the Lord Chief Justice, . . .
  (3) There shall be paid to the Speaker of the House of Commons a salary (which shall be charged on and paid out of the Consolidated Fund of the United Kingdom) of £60,000 a year; and on a dissolution of Parliament the Speaker of the House of Commons at the time of the dissolution shall for this purpose be deemed to remain Speaker until a Speaker is chosen by the New Parliament.
  (3A) There shall be paid to the Speaker of the House of Lords a salary (which shall be paid out of money provided by Parliament) of £103,701 a year.
    . . .

2 **Opposition Leaders and Whips**
  (1) In this Act "Leader of the Opposition" means, in relation to either House of Parliament, that Member of that House who is for the time being the Leader in that House of the party in opposition to Her Majesty's Government having the greatest numerical strength in the House of Commons; and "Chief Opposition Whip" means, in relation to either House of Parliament, the person for the time being nominated as such by the Leader of the Opposition in that House; and "Assistant Opposition Whip", in relation to the House of Commons, means a person for the time being nominated as such, and to be paid as such, by the Leader of the Opposition in the House of Commons.
  (2) If any doubt arises as to which is or was at any material time the party in opposition to Her Majesty's Government having the greatest numerical strength in the House of Commons, or as to who is or was at any material time the leader in that House of such a party, the question shall be decided for the purposes of this Act by the Speaker of the House of Commons, and his decision, certified in writing under his hand, shall be final and conclusive.
  (3) If any doubt arises as to who is or was at any material time the Leader in the House of Lords of the said party, the question shall be decided for the purposes of this Act by the Speaker of the House of Lords, and his decision, certified in writing under his hand, shall be final and conclusive.

4 Interpretation

(1) In this Act—

"Junior Lord of the Treasury" means any Lord Commissioner of the Treasury other than the First Lord and the Chancellor of the Exchequer;

"Minister of State" and "Parliamentary Secretary" have the same meanings as in the House of Commons Disqualification Act 1975.

. . .

HIGHWAYS ACT 1980
(1980, c. 66)

An Act to consolidate the Highways Acts 1959 to 1971 and related enactments with amendments to give effect to recommendations of the Law Commission [13 November 1980]

Obstruction of highways and streets

137 Penalty for wilful obstruction

(1) If a person, without lawful authority or excuse, in any way wilfully obstructs the free passage along a highway he is guilty of an offence and liable to a fine not exceeding level 3 on the standard scale.

. . .

SUPREME COURT [SENIOR COURTS] ACT 1981
(1981, c. 54)

An Act to consolidate with amendments the Supreme Court of Judicature (Consolidation) Act 1925 and other enactments relating to the Supreme Court in England and Wales and the administration of justice therein; to repeal certain obsolete or unnecessary enactments so relating; to amend Part VIII of the Mental Health Act 1959, the Courts-Martial (Appeals) Act 1968, the Arbitration Act 1979 and the law relating to county courts; and for connected purposes [28 July 1981]

PART I

CONSTITUTION OF SUPREME COURT *[SENIOR COURTS]*

The Supreme Court [Senior Courts]

1 The Supreme Court *[Senior Courts]*

(1) The Supreme Court *[Senior Courts]* of England and Wales shall consist of the Court of Appeal, the High Court of Justice and the Crown Court, each having such jurisdiction as is conferred on it by or under this or any other Act.

(2) . . .

The Court of Appeal

2 The Court of Appeal

(1) The Court of Appeal shall consist of ex-officio judges and not more than thirty-seven ordinary judges.

(2) The following shall be ex-officio judges of the Court of Appeal—

(a) . . .

(b) any person who was Lord Chancellor before 12 June 2003;

(c) any judge of the Supreme Court *[Senior Courts]* who at the date of his appointment was, or was qualified for appointment as, an ordinary judge of the Court of Appeal or held an office within paragraphs (d) to (g);

(d) the Lord Chief Justice;

(e) the Master of the Rolls;

(f) the President of the Family Division; and

(g) the Vice-Chancellor;
but a person within paragraph (b) or (c) shall not be required to sit and act as a judge of the Court of Appeal unless at the request of the Lord Chief Justice he consents to do so.
(2A) The Lord Chief Justice may nominate a judicial officer holder (as defined in section 109(4) of the Constitutional Reform Act 2005) to exercise his function under subsection (2) of making requests to persons within paragraphs (b) and (c) of that subsection.
(3) An ordinary judge of the Court of Appeal (including the vice-president, if any, of either division) shall be styled "Lord Justice of Appeal" or "Lady Justice of Appeal".
(4) Her Majesty may by Order in Council from time to time amend subsection (1) so as to increase or further increase the maximum number of ordinary judges of the Court of Appeal.
. . .
(5) No recommendation shall be made to Her Majesty in Council to make an Order under subsection (4) unless a draft of the Order has been laid before Parliament and approved by resolution of each House of Parliament.
(6) The Court of Appeal shall be taken to be duly constituted notwithstanding any vacancy in the office of . . . Lord Chief Justice, Master of the Rolls, President of the Queen's Bench Division, President of the Family Division or Chancellor of the High Court.

3 Divisions of Court of Appeal
(1) There shall be two divisions of the Court of Appeal, namely the criminal division and the civil division.
(2) The Lord Chief Justice shall be president of the criminal division of the Court of Appeal and the Master of the Rolls shall be president of the civil division of that Court.
. . .

The High Court

4 The High Court
(1) The High Court shall consist of—
   (a) . . .
   (b) the Lord Chief Justice;
   (c) the President of the Family Division;
   (d) the Vice-Chancellor;
   (dd) the Senior Presiding Judge;
   (ddd) the vice-president of the Queen's Bench Division; and
   (e) not more than 108 puisne judges of that court.
(2) The puisne judges of the High Court shall be styled "Justices of the High Court".
(3) All the judges of the High Court shall, except where this Act expressly provides otherwise, have in all respects equal power, authority and jurisdiction.
. . .

The Crown Court

8 The Crown Court
(1) The jurisdiction of the Crown Court shall be exercisable by—
   (a) any judge of the High Court; or
   (b) any Circuit judge, Recorder or District Judge (Magistrates' Courts); or
   (c) subject to and in accordance with the provisions of sections 74 and 75(2), a judge of the High Court, Circuit judge or Recorder sitting with not more than four justices of the peace,
and any such persons when exercising the jurisdiction of the Crown Court shall be judges of the Crown Court.
(2) A justice of the peace is not disqualified from acting as a judge of the Crown Court merely because the proceedings are not at a place within the local justice area to which he is assigned or because the proceedings are not related to that area in any other way.

(3) When the Crown Court sits in the City of London it shall be known as the Central Criminal Court; and the Lord Mayor of the City and any Alderman of the City shall be entitled to sit as judges of the Central Criminal Court with any judge of the High Court or any Circuit judge or Recorder, Circuit judge, Recorder or District Judge (Magistrates' Courts).

10 Appointment of judges of Supreme Court *[Senior Courts]*

(1) Whenever the office of Lord Chief Justice, Master of the Rolls, President of the Queen's Bench Division, President of the Family Division or Chancellor of the High Court is vacant, Her Majesty may on the recommendation of the Lord Chancellor by letters patent appoint a qualified person to that office.

(2) Subject to the limits on numbers for the time being imposed by sections 2(1) and 4(1), Her Majesty may on the recommendation of the Lord Chancellor from time to time by letters patent appoint qualified persons as Lords Justices of Appeal or as puisne judges of the High Court.

(3) No person shall be qualified for appointment—
 (a) as Lord Chief Justice, Master of the Rolls, President of the Queen's Bench Division, President of the Family Division or Chancellor of the High Court, unless he is qualified for appointment as a Lord Justice of Appeal or is a judge of the Court of Appeal;
 (b) as a Lord Justice of Appeal, unless—
  (i) he has a 10 year High Court qualification within the meaning of section 71 of the Courts and Legal Services Act 1990; or
  [(i) *he satisfies the judicial appointment eligibility condition on a seven year basis; or*]
  (ii) he is a judge of the High Court; or
 (c) as a puisne judge of the High Court, unless—
  (i) he has a 10 year High Court qualification within the meaning of section 71 of the Courts and Legal Services Act 1990; or
  [(i) *he satisfies the judicial appointment eligibility condition on a seven year basis; or*]
  (ii) he is a Circuit Judge who has held that office for at least 2 years.

(4) A person appointed—
 (a) to any of the offices mentioned in subsection (1);
 (b) as a Lord Justice of Appeal;
 (c) as a puisne judge of the High Court;
 shall take the required oaths as soon as may be after accepting office . . .

11 Tenure of office of judges of Supreme Court *[Senior Courts]*

(1) This section applies to the office of any judge of the Supreme Court *[Senior Courts]* . . .

(2) A person appointed to an office to which this section applies shall vacate it on the day on which he attains the age of seventy years unless by virtue of this section he has ceased to hold it before then.

(3) A person appointed to an office to which this section applies shall hold that office during good behaviour, subject to a power of removal by Her Majesty on an address presented to Her by both Houses of Parliament.

. . .

(7) A person who holds an office to which this section applies may at any time resign it by giving the Lord Chancellor notice in writing to that effect.

(8) The Lord Chancellor, if satisfied by means of a medical certificate that a person holding an office to which this section applies—
 (a) is disabled by permanent infirmity from the performance of the duties of his office; and
 (b) is for the time being incapacitated from resigning his office,

may, subject to subsection (9), by instrument under his hand declare that person's office to have been vacated; and the instrument shall have the like effect for all purposes as if that person had on the date of the instrument resigned his office.

(9) A declaration under subsection (8) with respect to a person shall be of no effect unless it is made—
  (a) in the case of any of the Lord Chief Justice, the Master of the Rolls, the President of the Queen's Bench Division, the President of the Family Division and the Chancellor of the High Court, with the concurrence of two others of them;
  (b) in the case of a Lord Justice of Appeal, with the concurrence of the Master of the Rolls;
  (c) in the case of a puisne judge of any Division of the High Court, with the concurrence of the senior judge of that Division.

...

12 Salaries etc. of judges of Supreme Court *[Senior Courts]*

(1) Subject to subsections (2) and (3), there shall be paid to judges of the Supreme Court *[Senior Courts]* ... such salaries as may be determined by the Lord Chancellor with the concurrence of the Minister for the Civil Service.
(2) Until otherwise determined under this section, there shall be paid to the judges mentioned in subsection (1) the same salaries as at the commencement of this Act.
(3) Any salary payable under this section may be increased, but not reduced, by a determination or further determination under this section.
(4) ...

...

PART II
JURISDICTION
THE HIGH COURT

General jurisdiction

19 General jurisdiction

(1) The High Court shall be a superior court of record.
(2) Subject to the provisions of this Act, there shall be exercisable by the High Court—
  (a) all such jurisdiction (whether civil or criminal) as is conferred on it by this or any other Act; and
  (b) all such other jurisdiction (whether civil or criminal) as was exercisable by it immediately before the commencement of this Act (including jurisdiction conferred on a judge of the High Court by any statutory provision).

...

Other particular fields of jurisdiction

29 Mandatory, prohibiting and quashing orders

(1) The orders of mandamus, prohibition and certiorari shall be known instead as mandatory, prohibiting and quashing orders respectively.
(1A) The High Court shall have jurisdiction to make mandatory, prohibiting and quashing orders in those classes of case in which, immediately before 1st May 2004, it had jurisdiction to make orders of mandamus, prohibition and certiorari respectively.
(2) Every such order shall be final, subject to any right of appeal therefrom.
(3) In relation to the jurisdiction of the Crown Court, other than its jurisdiction in matters relating to trial on indictment, the High Court shall have all such jurisdiction to make mandatory, prohibiting or quashing orders as the High Court possesses in relation to the jurisdiction of an inferior court.
(3A) The High Court shall have no jurisdiction to make mandatory, prohibiting or quashing orders in relation to the jurisdiction of a court-martial in matters relating to—
  (a) trial by the Court Martial for an offence, or

(b) appeals from the Service Civilian Court;

...

(4) The power of the High Court under any enactment to require justices of the peace or a judge or officer of a county court to do any act relating to the duties of their respective offices, or to require a magistrates' court to state a case for the opinion of the High Court, in any case where the High Court formerly had by virtue of any enactment jurisdiction to make a rule absolute, or an order, for any of those purposes, shall be exercisable by mandatory order.

(5) In any statutory provision—
   (a) references to mandamus or to a writ or order of mandamus shall be read as references to a mandatory order;
   (b) references to prohibition or to a writ or order of prohibition shall be read as references to a prohibiting order;
   (c) references to certiorari or to a writ or order of certiorari shall be read as references to a quashing order; and
   (d) references to the issue or award of a writ of mandamus, prohibition or certiorari shall be read as references to the making of the corresponding mandatory, prohibiting or quashing order.

(6) In subsection (3) the reference to the Crown Court's jurisdiction in matters relating to trial on indictment does not include its jurisdiction relating to orders under section 17 of the Access to Justice Act 1999.

31 Application for judicial review

(1) An application to the High Court for one or more of the following forms of relief, namely—
   (a) a mandatory, prohibiting or quashing order;
   (b) a declaration or injunction under subsection (2); or
   (c) an injunction under section 30 restraining a person not entitled to do so from acting in an office to which that section applies,

shall be made in accordance with rules of court by a procedure to be known as an application for judicial review.

(2) A declaration may be made or an injunction granted under this subsection in any case where an application for judicial review, seeking that relief, has been made and the High Court considers that, having regard to—
   (a) the nature of the matters in respect of which relief may be granted by mandatory, prohibiting or quashing orders;
   (b) the nature of the persons and bodies against whom relief may be granted by such orders; and
   (c) all the circumstances of the case,

it would be just and convenient for the declaration to be made or for the injunction to be granted, as the case may be.

(3) No application for judicial review shall be made unless the leave of the High Court has been obtained in accordance with rules of court; and the court shall not grant leave to make such an application unless it considers that the applicant has a sufficient interest in the matter to which the application relates.

(4) On an application for judicial review the High Court may award . . . to the applicant damages, restitution or the recovery of a sum due if—
   (a) the application includes a claim for such an award arising from any matter to which the application relates; and
   (b) the court is satisfied that such an award would have been made if the claim had been made in an action begun by the applicant at the time of making the application.

(5) If, on an application for judicial review, the High Court quashes the decision to which the application relates, it may in addition—
   (a) remit the matter to the court, tribunal or authority which made the decision, with a direction to reconsider the matter and reach a decision in accordance with the findings of the High Court, or
   (b) substitute its own decision for the decision in question.

(5A) But the power conferred by subsection (5)(b) is exercisable only if—
    (a) the decision in question was made by a court or tribunal,
    (b) the decision is quashed on the ground that there has been an error of law, and
    (c) without the error, there would have been only one decision which the court or tribunal could have reached.
(5B) Unless the High Court otherwise directs, a decision substituted by it under subsection (5)(b) has effect as if it were a decision of the relevant court or tribunal.
(6) Where the High Court considers that there has been undue delay in making an application for judicial review, the court may refuse to grant—
    (a) leave for the making of the application; or
    (b) any relief sought on the application,
if it considers that the granting of the relief sought would be likely to cause substantial hardship to, or substantially prejudice the rights of, any person or would be detrimental to good administration.
(7) Subsection (6) is without prejudice to any enactment or rule of court which has the effect of limiting the time within which an application for judicial review may be made.

POLICE AND CRIMINAL EVIDENCE ACT 1984
(1984, c. 60)

An Act to make further provision in relation to the powers and duties of the police, persons in police detention, criminal evidence, police discipline and complaints against the police; to provide for arrangements for obtaining the views of the community on policing and for a rank of deputy chief constable; to amend the law relating to the Police Federations and Police Forces and Police Cadets in Scotland; and for connected purposes [31 October 1984]

PART I
POWERS TO STOP AND SEARCH

1 Power of constable to stop and search persons, vehicles etc
(1) A constable may exercise any power conferred by this section—
    (a) in any place to which at the time when he proposes to exercise the power the public or any section of the public has access, on payment or otherwise, as of right or by virtue of express or implied permission; or
    (b) in any other place to which people have ready access at the time when he proposes to exercise the power but which is not a dwelling.
(2) Subject to subsection (3) to (5) below, a constable—
    (a) may search—
        (i) any person or vehicle;
        (ii) anything which is in or on a vehicle,
for stolen or prohibited articles, any article to which subsection (8A) below applies or any firework to which subsection (8B) below applies; and
    (b) may detain a person or vehicle for the purpose of such a search.
(3) This section does not give a constable power to search a person or vehicle or anything in or on a vehicle unless he has reasonable grounds for suspecting that he will find stolen or prohibited articles, any article to which subsection (8A) below applies, or any firework to which subsection (8B) below applies.
(4) If a person is in a garden or yard occupied with and used for the purposes of a dwelling or on other land so occupied and used, a constable may not search him in the exercise of the power conferred by this section unless the constable has reasonable grounds for believing—
    (a) that he does not reside in the dwelling; and
    (b) that he is not in the place in question with the express or implied permission of a person who resides in the dwelling.
(5) If a vehicle is in a garden or yard occupied with and used for the purposes of a dwelling or on other land so occupied and used, a constable may not search the vehicle or anything in or

on it in the exercise of the power conferred by this section unless he has reasonable grounds for believing—
   (a) that the person in charge of the vehicle does not reside in the dwelling; and
   (b) that the vehicle is not in the place in question with the express or implied permission of a person who resides in the dwelling.
(6) If in the course of such a search a constable discovers an article which he has reasonable grounds for suspecting to be a stolen or prohibited article, an article to which subsection (8A) below applies or a firework to which subsection (8B) below applies, he may seize it.
(7) An article is prohibited for the purposes of this Part of this Act if it is—
   (a) an offensive weapon; or
   (b) an article—
      (i) made or adapted for use in the course of or in connection with an offence to which this sub-paragraph applies; or
      (ii) intended by the person having it with him for such use by him or by some other person.
(8) The offences to which subsection (7)(b)(i) above applies are—
   (a) burglary;
   (b) theft;
   (c) offences under section 12 of the Theft Act 1968 (taking motor vehicle or other conveyance without authority);
   (d) fraud (contrary to section 1 of the Fraud Act 2006); and
   (e) offences under section 1 of the Criminal Damage Act 1971 (destroying or damaging property).
(8A) This subsection applies to any article in relation to which a person has committed, or is committing or is going to commit an offence under section 139 of the Criminal Justice Act 1988.
(8B) This subsection applies to any firework which a person possesses in contravention of a prohibition imposed by fireworks regulations.
(8C) In this section—
   (a) "firework" shall be construed in accordance with the definition of "fireworks" in section 1(1) of the Fireworks Act 2003; and
   (b) "fireworks regulations" has the same meaning as in that Act.
(9) In this Part of this Act "offensive weapon" means any article—
   (a) made or adapted for use for causing injury to persons; or
   (b) intended by the person having it with him for such use by him or by some other person.

2 **Provisions relating to search under section 1 and other powers**
(1) A constable who detains a person or vehicle in the exercise—
   (a) of the power conferred by section 1 above; or
   (b) of any other power—
      (i) to search a person without first arresting him; or
      (ii) to search a vehicle without making an arrest,
   need not conduct a search if it appears to him subsequently—
      (i) that no search is required; or
      (ii) that a search is impracticable.
(2) If a constable contemplates a search, other than a search of an unattended vehicle, in the exercise—
   (a) of the power conferred by section 1 above; or
   (b) of any other power, except the power conferred by section 6 below and the power conferred by section 27(2) of the Aviation Security Act 1982—
      (i) to search a person without first arresting him; or
      (ii) to search a vehicle without making an arrest,
   it shall be his duty, subject to subsection (4) below, to take reasonable steps before he commences the search to bring to the attention of the appropriate person—

(i) if the constable is not in uniform, documentary evidence that he is a constable; and
(ii) whether he is in uniform or not, the matters specified in subsection (3) below;
and the constable shall not commence the search until he has performed that duty.
(3) The matters referred to in subsection (2)(ii) above are—
   (a) the constable's name and the name of the police station to which he is attached;
   (b) the object of the proposed search;
   (c) the constable's grounds for proposing to make it; and
   (d) the effect of section 3(7) or (8) below, as may be appropriate.
(4) A constable need not bring the effect of section 3(7) or (8) below to the attention of the appropriate person if it appears to the constable that it will not be practicable to make the record in section 3(1) below.
(5) In this section "the appropriate person" means—
   (a) if the constable proposes to search a person, that person; and
   (b) if he proposes to search a vehicle, or anything in or on a vehicle, the person in charge of the vehicle.
(6) On completing a search of an unattended vehicle or anything in or on such a vehicle in the exercise of any such power as is mentioned in subsection (2) above a constable shall leave a notice—
   (a) stating that he has searched it;
   (b) giving the name of the police station to which he is attached;
   (c) stating that an application for compensation for any damage caused by the search may be made to that police station; and
   (d) stating the effect of section 3(8) below.
(7) The constable shall leave the notice inside the vehicle unless it is not reasonably practicable to do so without damaging the vehicle.
(8) The time for which a person or vehicle may be detained for the purposes of such a search is such time as is reasonably required to permit a search to be carried out either at the place where the person or vehicle was first detained or nearby.
(9) Neither the power conferred by section 1 above nor any other power to detain and search a person without first arresting him or to detain and search a vehicle without making an arrest is to be construed—
   (a) as authorising a constable to require a person to remove any of his clothing in public other than an outer coat, jacket or gloves; or
   (b) as authorising a constable not in uniform to stop a vehicle.
. . .

3 Duty to make records concerning searches

(1) Where a constable has carried out a search in the exercise of any such power as is mentioned in section 2(1) above, other than a search—
   (a) under section 6 below; or
   (b) under section 27(2) of the Aviation Security Act 1982,
   he shall make a record of it in writing unless it is not practicable to do so.
(2) If—
   (a) a constable is required by subsection (1) above to make a record of a search; but
   (b) it is not practicable to make the record on the spot,
   he shall make it as soon as practicable after the completion of the search.
(3) The record of a search of a person shall include a note of his name, if the constable knows it, but a constable may not detain a person to find out his name.
(4) If a constable does not know the name of the person whom he has searched, the record of the search shall include a note otherwise describing that person.
(5) The record of a search of a vehicle shall include a note describing the vehicle.
(6) The record of a search of a person or a vehicle—
   (a) shall state—
      (i) the object of the search;

(ii) the grounds for making it;
(iii) the date and time when it was made;
(iv) the place where it was made;
(v) whether anything, and if so what, was found;
(vi) whether any, and if so what, injury to a person or damage to property appears to the constable to have resulted from the search; and
(b) shall identify the constable making it.
(7) If a constable who conducted a search of a person made a record of it, the person who was searched shall be entitled to a copy of the record if he asks for one before the end of the period specified in subsection (9) below.
(8) If—
(a) the owner of a vehicle which has been searched or the person who was in charge of the vehicle at the time when it was searched asks for a copy of the record of the search before the end of the period specified in subsection (9) below; and
(b) the constable who conducted the search made a record of it,
the person who made the request shall be entitled to a copy.

...

4 Road checks

(1) This section shall have effect in relation to the conduct of road checks by police officers for the purpose of ascertaining whether a vehicle is carrying—
(a) a person who has committed an offence other than a road traffic offence or a vehicle excise offence;
(b) a person who is a witness to such an offence;
(c) a person intending to commit such an offence; or
(d) a person who is unlawfully at large.
(2) For the purposes of this section a road check consists of the exercise in a locality of the power conferred by section 163 of the Road Traffic Act 1988 in such a way as to stop during the period for which its exercise in that way in that locality continues all vehicles or vehicles selected by any criterion.
(3) Subject to subsection (5) below, there may only be such a road check if a police officer of the rank of superintendent or above authorises it in writing.
(4) An officer may only authorise a road check under subsection (3) above—
(a) for the purpose specified in subsection (1)(a) above, if he has reasonable grounds—
(i) for believing that the offence is an indictable offence; and
(ii) for suspecting that the person is, or is about to be, in the locality in which vehicles would be stopped if the road check were authorised;
(b) for the purpose specified in subsection (1)(b) above, if he has reasonable grounds for believing that the offence is an indictable offence;
(c) for the purpose specified in subsection (1)(c) above, if he has reasonable grounds—
(i) for believing that the offence would be an indictable offence; and
(ii) for suspecting that the person is, or is about to be, in the locality in which vehicles would be stopped if the road check were authorised;
(d) for the purpose specified in subsection (1)(d) above, if he has reasonable grounds for suspecting that the person is, or is about to be, in that locality.
(5) An officer below the rank of superintendent may authorise such a road check if it appears to him that it is required as a matter of urgency for one of the purposes specified in subsection (1) above.
(6) If an authorisation is given under subsection (5) above, it shall be the duty of the officer who gives it—
(a) to make a written record of the time at which he gives it; and
(b) to cause an officer of the rank of superintendent or above to be informed that it has been given.

...

(15) Where a vehicle is stopped in a road check, the person in charge of the vehicle at the time when it is stopped shall be entitled to obtain a written statement of the purpose of the road check if he applies for such a statement not later than the end of the period of twelve months from the day on which the vehicle was stopped.

(16) Nothing in this section affects the exercise by police officers of any power to stop vehicles for purposes other than those specified in subsection (1) above.

PART II
POWERS OF ENTRY, SEARCH AND SEIZURE

Search warrants

8 Power of justice of the peace to authorise entry and search of premises

(1) If on an application made by a constable a justice of the peace is satisfied that there are reasonable grounds for believing—
  (a) that an indictable offence has been committed; and
  (b) that there is material on premises mentioned in subsection (1A) below which is likely to be of substantial value (whether by itself or together with other material) to the investigation of the offence; and
  (c) that the material is likely to be relevant evidence; and
  (d) that it does not consist of or include items subject to legal privilege, excluded material or special procedure material; and
  (e) that any of the conditions specified in subsection (3) below applies,

he may issue a warrant authorising a constable to enter and search the premises in relation to each set of premises specified in the application.

(1A) The premises referred to in subsection (1)(b) above are—
  (a) one or more sets of premises specified in the application (in which case the application is for a "specific premises warrant"); or
  (b) any premises occupied or controlled by a person specified in the application, including such sets of premises as are so specified (in which case the application is for an "all premises warrant").

(1B) If the application is for an all premises warrant, the justice of the peace must also be satisfied—
  (a) that because of the particulars of the offence referred to in paragraph (a) of subsection (1) above, there are reasonable grounds for believing that it is necessary to search premises occupied or controlled by the person in question which are not specified in the application in order to find the material referred to in paragraph (b) of that subsection; and
  (b) that it is not reasonably practicable to specify in the application all the premises which he occupies or controls and which might need to be searched.

(1C) The warrant may authorise entry to and search of premises on more than one occasion if, on the application, the justice of the peace is satisfied that it is necessary to authorise multiple entries in order to achieve the purpose for which he issues the warrant.

(1D) If it authorises multiple entries, the number of entries authorised may be unlimited, or limited to a maximum.

(2) A constable may seize and retain anything for which a search has been authorised under subsection (1) above.

(3) The conditions mentioned in subsection (1)(e) above are—
  (a) that it is not practicable to communicate with any person entitled to grant entry to the premises;
  (b) that it is practicable to communicate with a person entitled to grant entry to the premises but it is not practicable to communicate with any person entitled to grant access to the evidence;
  (c) that entry to the premises will not be granted unless a warrant is produced;
  (d) that the purpose of a search may be frustrated or seriously prejudiced unless a constable arriving at the premises can secure immediate entry to them.

(4) In this Act "relevant evidence", in relation to an offence, means anything that would be admissible in evidence at a trial for the offence.
(5) The power to issue a warrant conferred by this section is in addition to any such power otherwise conferred.
...

9 **Special provisions as to access**
(1) A constable may obtain access to excluded material or special procedure material for the purposes of a criminal investigation by making an application under Schedule 1 below and in accordance with that Schedule.
(2) Any Act (including a local Act) passed before this Act under which a search of premises for the purposes of a criminal investigation could be authorised by the issue of a warrant to a constable shall cease to have effect so far as it relates to the authorisation of searches—
    (a) for items subject to legal privilege; or
    (b) for excluded material; or
    (c) for special procedure material consisting of documents or records other than documents.
...

10 **Meaning of "items subject to legal privilege"**
(1) Subject to subsection (2) below, in this Act "items subject to legal privilege"means—
    (a) communications between a professional legal adviser and his client or any person representing his client made in connection with the giving of legal advice to the client;
    (b) communications between a professional legal adviser and his client or any person representing his client or between such an adviser or his client or any such representative and any other person made in connection with or in contemplation of legal proceedings and for the purposes of such proceedings; and
    (c) items enclosed with or referred to in such communications and made—
        (i) in connection with the giving of legal advice; or
        (ii) in connection with or in contemplation of legal proceedings and for the purposes of such proceedings,
    when they are in the possession of a person who is entitled to possession of them.
(2) Items held with the intention of furthering a criminal purpose are not items subject to legal privilege.

11 **Meaning of "excluded material"**
(1) Subject to the following provisions of this section, in this Act "excluded material" means—
    (a) personal records which a person has acquired or created in the course of any trade, business, profession or other occupation or for the purposes of any paid or unpaid office and which he holds in confidence;
    (b) human tissue or tissue fluid which has been taken for the purposes of diagnosis or medical treatment and which a person holds in confidence;
    (c) journalistic material which a person holds in confidence and which consists—
        (i) of documents; or
        (ii) of records other than documents.
(2) A person holds material other than journalistic material in confidence for the purposes of this section if he holds it subject—
    (a) to an express or implied undertaking to hold it in confidence; or
    (b) to a restriction on disclosure or an obligation of secrecy contained in any enactment, including an enactment contained in an Act passed after this Act.
(3) A person holds journalistic material in confidence for the purposes of this section if—
    (a) he holds it subject to such an undertaking, restriction or obligation; and
    (b) it has been continuously held (by one or more persons) subject to such an undertaking, restriction or obligation since it was first acquired or created for the purposes of journalism.

12 Meaning of "personal records"
In this Part of this Act "personal records" means documentary and other records concerning an individual (whether living or dead) who can be identified from them and relating—
(a) to his physical or mental health;
(b) to spiritual counselling or assistance given or to be given to him; or
(c) to counselling or assistance given or to be given to him, for the purposes of his personal welfare, by any voluntary organisation or by any individual who—
 (i) by reason of his office or occupation has responsibilities for his personal welfare; or
 (ii) by reason of an order of a court has responsibilities for his supervision.

13 Meaning of "journalistic material"
(1) Subject to subsection (2) below, in this Act "journalistic material" means material acquired or created for the purposes of journalism.
(2) Material is only journalistic material for the purposes of this Act if it is in the possession of a person who acquired or created it for the purposes of journalism.
(3) A person who receives material from someone who intends that the recipient shall use it for the purposes of journalism is to be taken to have acquired it for those purposes.

14 Meaning of "special procedure material"
(1) In this Act "special procedure material" means—
(a) material to which subsection (2) below applies; and
(b) journalistic material, other than excluded material.
(2) Subject to the following provisions of this section, this subsection applies to material, other than items subject to legal privilege and excluded material, in the possession of a person who—
(a) acquired or created it in the course of any trade, business, profession or other occupation or for the purposes of any paid or unpaid office; and
(b) holds it subject—
 (i) to an express or implied undertaking to hold it in confidence; or
 (ii) to a restriction or obligation such as is mentioned in section 11(2)(b) above.
...

15 Search warrants — safeguards
(1) This section and section 16 below have effect in relation to the issue to constables under any enactment, including an enactment contained in an Act passed after this Act, of warrants to enter and search premises; and an entry on or search of premises under a warrant is unlawful unless it complies with this section and section 16 below.
(2) Where a constable applies for any such warrant, it shall be his duty—
(a) to state—
 (i) the ground on which he makes the application; and
 (ii) the enactment under which the warrant would be issued; and
 (iii) if the application is for a warrant authorising entry and search on more than one occasion, the ground on which he applies for such a warrant, and whether he seeks a warrant authorising an unlimited number of entries, or (if not) the maximum number of entries desired;
(b) to specify the matters set out in subsection 2A below; and
(c) to identify, so far as is practicable, the articles or persons to be sought.
(2A) The matters which must be specified pursuant to subsection (2)(b) above are—
(a) if the application relates to one or more sets of premises specified in the application, each set of premises which it is desired to enter and search;
(b) if the application relates to any premises occupied or controlled by a person specified in the application—
 (i) as many sets of premises which it is desired to enter and search as it is reasonably practicable to specify;
 (ii) the person who is in occupation or control of those premises and any others which it is desired to enter and search;

(iii) why it is necessary to search more premises than those specified under sub-paragraph (i); and
(iv) why it is not reasonably practicable to specify all the premises which it is desired to enter and search.
(3) An application for such a warrant shall be made ex parte and supported by an information in writing.
(4) The constable shall answer on oath any question that the justice of the peace or judge hearing the application asks him.
(5) A warrant shall authorise an entry on one occasion only unless specified that it authorises multiple entries.
(5A) If it specifies that it authorises multiple entries, it must also specify whether the number of entries authorised is unlimited, or limited to a specified maximum.
(6) A warrant—
(a) shall specify—
(i) the name of the person who applies for it;
(ii) the date on which it is issued;
(iii) the enactment under which it is issued; and
(iv) each set of premises to be searched, or (in the case of an all premises warrant) the person who is in occupation or control of premises to be searched, together with any premises under his occupation or control which can be specified and which are to be searched; and.
(b) shall identify, so far as is practicable, the articles or persons to be sought.
...

16 Execution of warrants

(1) A warrant to enter and search premises may be executed by any constable.
(2) Such a warrant may authorise persons to accompany any constable who is executing it.
(2A) A person so authorised has the same powers as the constable whom he accompanies in respect of—
(a) the execution of the warrant, and
(b) the seizure of anything to which the warrant relates.
(2B) But he may exercise those powers only in the company, and under the supervision, of a constable.
(3) Entry and search under a warrant must be within three months from the date of its issue.
(3A) If the warrant is an all premises warrant, no premises which are not specified in it may be entered or searched unless a police officer of at least the rank of inspector has in writing authorised them to be entered.
(3B) No premises may be entered or searched for the second or any subsequent time under a warrant which authorises multiple entries unless a police officer of at least the rank of inspector has in writing authorised that entry to those premises.
(4) Entry and search under a warrant must be at a reasonable hour unless it appears to the constable executing it that the purpose of a search may be frustrated on an entry at a reasonable hour.
(5) Where the occupier of premises which are to be entered and searched is present at the time when a constable seeks to execute a warrant to enter and search them, the constable—
(a) shall identify himself to the occupier and, if not in uniform, shall produce to him documentary evidence that he is a constable;
(b) shall produce the warrant to him; and
(c) shall supply him with a copy of it.
(6) Where—
(a) the occupier of such premises is not present at the time when a constable seeks to execute such a warrant; but
(b) some other person who appears to the constable to be in charge of the premises is present,

subsection (5) above shall have effect as if any reference to the occupier were a reference to that other person.

(7) If there is no person present who appears to the constable to be in charge of the premises, he shall leave a copy of the warrant in a prominent place on the premises.

(8) A search under a warrant may only be a search to the extent required for the purpose for which the warrant was issued.

(9) A constable executing a warrant shall make an endorsement on it stating—
   (a) whether the articles or persons sought were found; and
   (b) whether any articles were seized, other than articles which were sought.

. . .

Entry and search without search warrant

17   Entry for purpose of arrest etc.

(1) Subject to the following provisions of this section, and without prejudice to any other enactment, a constable may enter and search any premises for the purpose—
   (a) of executing—
      (i) a warrant of arrest issued in connection with or arising out of criminal proceedings; or
      (ii) a warrant of commitment issued under section 76 of the Magistrates' Courts Act 1980;
   (b) of arresting a person for an indictable offence;
   (c) of arresting a person for an offence under—
      (i) section 1 (prohibition of uniforms in connection with political objects)... of the Public Order Act 1936;
      (ii) any enactment contained in sections 6 to 8 or 10 of the Criminal Law Act 1977 (offences relating to entering and remaining on property);
      (iii) section 4 of the Public Order Act 1986 (fear or provocation of violence); or
      (iiia) section 4 (driving etc. when under influence of drink or drugs) or 163 (failure to stop when required to do so by constable in uniform) of the Road Traffic Act 1988;
      (iiib) section 27 of the Transport and Works Act 1992 (which relates to offences involving drink or drugs);
      (iv) section 76 of the Criminal Justice and Public Order Act 1994 (failure to comply with an interim possession order);
      (v) any of sections 4, 5, 6(1) and (2), 7 and 8(1) and (2) of the Animal Welfare Act 2006 (offences relating to the prevention of harm to animals);
   (ca) of arresting, in pursuance of section 32(1A) of the Children and Young Persons Act 1969, any child or young person who has been remanded or committed to local authority accommodation under section 23(1) of that Act;
   (caa) of arresting a person for an offence to which section 61 of the Animal Health Act 1981 applies;
   (cb) of recapturing any person who is, or is deemed for any purpose to be, unlawfully at large while liable to be detained—
      (i) in a prison, remand centre, young offender institution or secure training centre, or
      (ii) in pursuance of section 92 of the Powers of Criminal Courts (Sentencing) Act 2000 (dealing with children and young persons guilty of grave crimes), in any other place;
   (d) of recapturing any person whatever who is unlawfully at large and whom he is pursuing; or
   (e) of saving life or limb or preventing serious damage to property.

(2) Except for the purpose specified in paragraph (e) of subsection (1) above, the powers of entry and search conferred by this section—

(a) are only exercisable if the constable has reasonable grounds for believing that the person whom he is seeking is on the premises; and
(b) are limited, in relation to premises consisting of two or more separate dwellings, to powers to enter and search—
    (i) any parts of the premises which the occupiers of any dwelling comprised in the premises use in common with the occupiers of any other such dwelling; and
    (ii) any such dwelling in which the constable has reasonable grounds for believing that the person whom he is seeking may be.
(3) The powers of entry and search conferred by this section are only exercisable for the purposes specified in subsection (1)(c)(ii) or (iv) above by a constable in uniform.
(4) The power of search conferred by this section is only a power to search to the extent that is reasonably required for the purpose for which the power of entry is exercised.
(5) Subject to subsection (6) below, all the rules of common law under which a constable has power to enter premises without a warrant are hereby abolished.
(6) Nothing in subsection (5) above affects any power of entry to deal with or prevent a breach of the peace.

18 Entry and search after arrest
(1) Subject to the following provisions of this section, a constable may enter and search any premises occupied or controlled by a person who is under arrest for an *indictable* offence, if he has reasonable grounds for suspecting that there is on the premises evidence, other than items subject to legal privilege, that relates—
    (a) to that offence; or
    (b) to some other indictable offence which is connected with or similar to that offence.
(2) A constable may seize and retain anything for which he may search under subsection (1) above.
(3) The power to search conferred by subsection (1) above is only a power to search to the extent that is reasonably required for the purpose of discovering such evidence.
(4) Subject to subsection (5) below, the powers conferred by this section may not be exercised unless an officer of the rank of inspector or above has authorised them in writing.
(5) A constable may conduct a search under subsection (1)—
    (a) before the person is taken to a police station or released on bail under section 30A, and
    (b) without obtaining an authorisation under subsection (4),
    if the condition in subsection (5A) is satisfied.
(5A) The condition is that the presence of the person at a place (other than a police station) is necessary for the effective investigation of the offence.
(6) If a constable conducts a search by virtue of subsection (5) above, he shall inform an officer of the rank of inspector or above that he has made the search as soon as practicable after he has made it.
(7) An officer who—
    (a) authorises a search; or
    (b) is informed of a search under subsection (6) above, shall make a record in writing—
        (i) of the ground for the search; and
        (ii) of the nature of the evidence that was sought.
(8) If the person who was in occupation or control of the premises at the time of the search is in police detention at the time the record is to be made, the officer shall make the record as part of his custody record.

Seizure etc.

19 General power of seizure etc.
(1) The powers conferred by subsections (2), (3) and (4) below are exercisable by a constable who is lawfully on any premises.
(2) The constable may seize anything which is on the premises if he has reasonable grounds for believing—
    (a) that it has been obtained in consequence of the commission of an offence; and

(b) that it is necessary to seize it in order to prevent it being concealed, lost, damaged, altered or destroyed.
(3) The constable may seize anything which is on the premises if he has reasonable grounds for believing—
   (a) that it is evidence in relation to an offence which he is investigating or any other offence; and
   (b) that it is necessary to seize it in order to prevent the evidence being concealed, lost, altered or destroyed.
(4) The constable may require any information which is stored in any electronic form and is accessible from the premises to be produced in a form in which it can be taken away and in which it is visible and legible or which can readily be produced in a visible and legible form if he has reasonable grounds for believing—
   (a) that—
      (i) it is evidence in relation to an offence which he is investigating or any other offence; or
      (ii) it has been obtained in consequence of the commission of an offence; and
   (b) that it is necessary to do so in order to prevent it being concealed, lost, tampered with or destroyed.
(5) The powers conferred by this section are in addition to any power otherwise conferred.
(6) No power of seizure conferred on a constable under any enactment (including an enactment contained in an Act passed after this Act) is to be taken to authorise the seizure of an item which the constable exercising the power has reasonable grounds for believing to be subject to legal privilege.

20   Extension of powers of seizure to computerised information
(1) Every power of seizure which is conferred by an enactment to which this section applies on a constable who has entered premises in the exercise of a power conferred by an enactment shall be construed as including a power to require any information stored in any electronic form and accessible from the premises to be produced in a form in which it can be taken away and in which it is visible and legible or from which it can readily be produced in a visible and legible form.
(2) This section applies—
   (a) to any enactment contained in an Act passed before this Act;
   (b) to sections 8 and 18 above;
   (c) to paragraph 13 of Schedule 1 to this Act; and
   (d) to any enactment contained in an Act passed after this Act.

21   Access and copying
(1) A constable who seizes anything in the exercise of a power conferred by any enactment, including an enactment contained in an Act passed after this Act, shall, if so requested by a person showing himself—
   (a) to be the occupier of premises on which it was seized; or
   (b) to have had custody or control of it immediately before the seizure,
   provide that person with a record of what he seized.
(2) The officer shall provide the record within a reasonable time from the making of the request for it.
(3) Subject to subsection (8) below, if a request for permission to be granted access to anything which—
   (a) has been seized by a constable; and
   (b) is retained by the police for the purpose of investigating an offence,
   is made to the officer in charge of the investigation by a person who had custody or control of the thing immediately before it was so seized or by someone acting on behalf of such a person the officer shall allow the person who made the request access to it under the supervision of a constable.

(4) Subject to subsection (8) below, if a request for a photograph or copy of any such thing is made to the officer in charge of the investigation by a person who had custody or control of the thing immediately before it was so seized, or by someone acting on behalf of such a person, the officer shall—
   (a) allow the person who made the rquest access to it under the supervision of a constable for the purpose of photographing or copying it; or
   (b) photograph or copy it, or cause it to be photographed or copied.
(5) A constable may also photograph or copy, or have photographed or copied, anything which he has power to seize, without a request being made under subsection (4) above.
(6) Where anything is photographed or copied under subsection (4)(b) above, the photograph or copy shall be supplied to the person who made the request.
(7) The photograph or copy shall be so supplied within a reasonable time from the making of the request.
(8) There is no duty under this section to grant access to, or to supply a photo-graph or copy of, anything if the officer in charge of the investigation for the purposes of which it was seized has reasonable grounds for believing that to do so would prejudice—
   (a) that investigation;
   (b) the investigation of an offence other than the offence for the purposes of investigating which the thing was seized; or
   (c) any criminal proceedings which may be brought as a result of—
      (i) the investigation of which he is in charge; or
      (ii) any such investigation as is mentioned in paragraph (b) above.
(9) The references to a constable in subsections (1), (2), (3)(a) and (5) include a person authorised under section 16(2) to accompany a constable executing a warrant.

22 Retention

(1) Subject to subsection (4) below, anything which has been seized by a constable or taken away by a constable following a requirement made by virtue of section 19 or 20 above may be retained so long as is necessary in all the circumstances.
(2) Without prejudice to the generality of subsection (1) above—
   (a) anything seized for the purposes of a criminal investigation may be retained, except as provided by subsection (4) below—
      (i) for use as evidence at a trial for an offence; or
      (ii) for forensic examination or for investigation in connection with an offence; and
   (b) anything may be retained in order to establish its lawful owner, where there are reasonable grounds for believing that it has been obtained in consequence of the commission of an offence.
(3) Nothing seized on the ground that it may be used—
   (a) to cause physical injury to any person;
   (b) to damage property;
   (c) to interfere with evidence; or
   (d) to assist in escape from police detention or lawful custody,
may be retained when the person from whom it was seized is no longer in police detention or the custody of a court or is in the custody of a court but has been released on bail.
(4) Nothing may be retained for either of the purposes mentioned in subsection (2)(a) above if a photograph or copy would be sufficient for that purpose.
...

23

In this Act—
"premises" includes any place and, in particular, includes—
   (a) any vehicle, vessel, aircraft or hovercraft;
   (b) any offshore installation;
   (ba) any renewable energy installation;
   (c) any tent or moveable structure.

PART III
ARREST

24 Arrest without warrant: constables

(1) A constable may arrest without a warrant—
- (a) anyone who is about to commit an offence;
- (b) anyone who is in the act of committing an offence;
- (c) anyone whom he has reasonable grounds for suspecting to be about to commit an offence;
- (d) anyone whom he has reasonable grounds for suspecting to be committing an offence.

(2) If a constable has reasonable grounds for suspecting that an offence has been committed, he may arrest without a warrant anyone whom he has reasonable grounds to suspect of being guilty of it.

(3) If an offence has been committed, a constable may arrest without a warrant—
- (a) anyone who is guilty of the offence;
- (b) anyone whom he has reasonable grounds for suspecting to be guilty of it.

(4) But the power of summary arrest conferred by subsection (1), (2) or (3) is exercisable only if the constable has reasonable grounds for believing that for any of the reasons mentioned in subsection (5) it is necessary to arrest the person in question.

(5) The reasons are—
- (a) to enable the name of the person in question to be ascertained (in the case where the constable does not know, and cannot readily ascertain, the person's name, or has reasonable grounds for doubting whether a name given by the person as his name is his real name);
- (b) correspondingly as regards the person's address;
- (c) to prevent the person in question—
  - (i) causing physical injury to himself or any other person;
  - (ii) suffering physical injury;
  - (iii) causing loss of or damage to property;
  - (iv) committing an offence against public decency (subject to subsection (6)); or
  - (v) causing an unlawful obstruction of the highway;
- (d) to protect a child or other vulnerable person from the person in question;
- (e) to allow the prompt and effective investigation of the offence or of the conduct of the person in question;
- (f) to prevent any prosecution for the offence from being hindered by the disappearance of the person in question.

(6) Subsection (5)(c)(iv) applies only where members of the public going about their normal business cannot reasonably be expected to avoid the person in question.

24A Arrest without warrant: other persons

(1) A person other than a constable may arrest without a warrant—
- (a) anyone who is in the act of committing an indictable offence;
- (b) anyone whom he has reasonable grounds for suspecting to be committing an indictable offence.

(2) Where an indictable offence has been committed, a person other than a constable may arrest without a warrant—
- (a) anyone who is guilty of the offence;
- (b) anyone whom he has reasonable grounds for suspecting to be guilty of it.

(3) But the power of summary arrest conferred by subsection (1) or (2) is exercisable only if—
- (a) the person making the arrest has reasonable grounds for believing that for any of the reasons mentioned in subsection (4) it is necessary to arrest the person in question; and
- (b) it appears to the person making the arrest that it is not reasonably practicable for a constable to make it instead.

(4) The reasons are to prevent the person in question—
- (a) causing physical injury to himself or any other person;

(b) suffering physical injury;
(c) causing loss of or damage to property; or
(d) making off before a constable can assume responsibility for him.
(5) This section does not apply in relation to an offence under Part 3 or 3A of the Public Order Act 1986

26 Repeal of statutory powers of arrest without warrant or order
(1) Subject to subsection (2) below, so much of any Act (including a local Act) passed before this Act as enables a constable—
(a) to arrest a person for an offence without a warrant; or
(b) to arrest a person otherwise than for an offence without a warrant or an order of a court,
shall cease to have effect.
(2) Nothing in subsection (1) above affects the enactments specified in Schedule 2 to this Act.

28 Information to be given on arrest
(1) Subject to subsection (5) below, where a person is arrested, otherwise than by being informed that he is under arrest, the arrest is not lawful unless the person arrested is informed that he is under arrest as soon as is practicable after his arrest.
(2) Where a person is arrested by a constable, subsection (1) above applies regardless of whether the fact of the arrest is obvious.
(3) Subject to subsection (5) below, no arrest is lawful unless the person arrested is informed of the ground for the arrest at the time of, or as soon as is practicable after, the arrest.
(4) Where a person is arrested by a constable, subsection (3) above applies regardless of whether the ground for the arrest is obvious.
(5) Nothing in this section is to be taken to require a person to be informed—
(a) that he is under arrest; or
(b) of the ground for the arrest,
if it was not reasonably practicable for him to be so informed by reason of his having escaped from arrest before the information could be given.

29 Voluntary attendance at police station etc.
Where for the purpose of assisting with an investigation a person attends voluntarily at a police station, SOCA office, or at any other place where a constable is present or accompanies a constable to a police station, SOCA office or any such other place without having been arrested—
(a) he shall be entitled to leave at will unless he is placed under arrest;
(b) he shall be informed at once that he is under arrest if a decision is taken by a constable to prevent him from leaving at will.

30 Arrest elsewhere than at police station
(1) Subsection (1A) applies where a person is, at any place other than a police station—
(a) arrested by a constable for an offence, or
(b) taken into custody by a constable after being arrested for an offence by a person other than a constable.
(1A) The person must be taken by a constable to a police station as soon as practicable after the arrest.
(1B) Subsection (1A) has effect subject to section 30A (release on bail) and subsection (7) (release without bail).
(2) Subject to subsections (3) and (5) below, the police station to which an arrested person is taken under subsection (1A) above shall be a designated police station.
. . .
(6) If the first police station to which an arrested person is taken after his arrest is not a designated police station, he shall be taken to a designated police station not more than six hours after his arrival at the first police station unless he is released previously.
(7) A person arrested by a constable at any place other than a police station must be released without bail if the condition in subsection (7A) is satisfied.

(7A) The condition is that, at any time before the person arrested reaches a police station, a constable is satisfied that there are no grounds for keeping him under arrest or releasing him on bail under section 30A.

...

(10) Nothing in subsection (1A) or in section 30A prevents a constable delaying taking a person to a police station or releasing him on bail if the condition in subsection (10A) is satisfied.

(10A) The condition is that the presence of the person at a place (other than a police station) is necessary in order to carry out such investigations as it is reasonable to carry out immediately.

(11) Where there is any such delay the reasons for the delay must be recorded when the person first arrives at the police station or (as the case may be) is released on bail.

30A Bail elsewhere than at police station

(1) A constable may release on bail a person who is arrested or taken into custody in the circumstances mentioned in section 30(1).

(2) A person may be released on bail under subsection (1) at any time before he arrives at a police station.

(3) A person released on bail under subsection (1) must be required to attend a police station.

(3A) Where a constable releases a person on bail under subsection (1)—
  (a) no recognizance for the person's surrender to custody shall be taken from the person,
  (b) no security for the person's surrender to custody shall be taken from the person or from anyone else on the person's behalf,
  (c) the person shall not be required to provide a surety or sureties for his surrender to custody, and
  (d) no requirement to reside in a bail hostel may be imposed as a condition of bail.

(3B) Subject to subsection (3A), where a constable releases a person on bail under subsection (1) the constable may impose, as conditions of the bail, such requirements as appear to the constable to be necessary—
  (a) to secure that the person surrenders to custody,
  (b) to secure that the person does not commit an offence while on bail,
  (c) to secure that the person does not interfere with witnesses or otherwise obstruct the course of justice, whether in relation to himself or any other person, or
  (d) for the person's own protection or, if the person is under the age of 17, for the person's own welfare or in the person's own interests.

(4) Where a person is released on bail under subsection (1), a requirement may be imposed on the person as a condition of bail only under the preceding provisions of this section.

(5) The police station which the person is required to attend may be any police station.

30B Bail under section 30A: notices

(1) Where a constable grants bail to a person under section 30A, he must give that person a notice in writing before he is released.

(2) The notice must state—
  (a) the offence for which he was arrested, and
  (b) the ground on which he was arrested.

(3) The notice must inform him that he is required to attend a police station.

(4) It may also specify the police station which he is required to attend and the time when he is required to attend.

(4A) If the person is granted bail subject to conditions under section 30A(3B), the notice also—
  (a) must specify the requirements imposed by those conditions,
  (b) must explain the opportunities under sections 30CA(1) and 30CB(1) for variation of those conditions, and
  (c) if it does not specify the police station at which the person is required to attend, must specify a police station at which the person may make a request under section 30CA(1)(b).

(5) If the notice does not include the information mentioned in subsection (4), the person must subsequently be given a further notice in writing which contains that information.
(6) The person may be required to attend a different police station from that specified in the notice under subsection (1) or (5) or to attend at a different time.
(7) He must be given notice in writing of any such change as is mentioned in subsection (6) but more than one such notice may be given to him.

30CA Bail under section 30A: variation of conditions by police
(1) Where a person released on bail under section 30A(1) is on bail subject to conditions—
    (a) a relevant officer at the police station at which the person is required to attend, or
    (b) where no notice under section 30B specifying that police station has been given to the person, a relevant officer at the police station specified under section 30B(4A)(c),
    may, at the request of the person but subject to subsection (2), vary the conditions.
(2) On any subsequent request made in respect of the same grant of bail, subsection (1) confers power to vary the conditions of the bail only if the request is based on information that, in the case of the previous request or each previous request, was not available to the relevant officer considering that previous request when he was considering it.
(3) Where conditions of bail granted to a person under section 30A(1) are varied under subsection (1)—
    (a) paragraphs (a) to (d) of section 30A(3A) apply,
    (b) requirements imposed by the conditions as so varied must be requirements that appear to the relevant officer varying the conditions to be necessary for any of the purposes mentioned in paragraphs (a) to (d) of section 30A(3B), and
    (c) the relevant officer who varies the conditions must give the person notice in writing of the variation.
(4) Power under subsection (1) to vary conditions is, subject to subsection (3)(a) and (b), power—
    (a) to vary or rescind any of the conditions, and
    (b) to impose further conditions.
(5) In this section "relevant officer", in relation to a designated police station, means a custody officer but, in relation to any other police station—
    (a) means a constable, or a person designated as a staff custody officer under section 38 of the Police Reform Act 2002, who is not involved in the investigation of the offence for which the person making the request under subsection (1) was under arrest when granted bail under section 30A(1), if such a constable or officer is readily available, and
    (b) if no such constable or officer is readily available—
        (i) means a constable other than the one who granted bail to the person, if such a constable is readily available, and
        (ii) if no such constable is readily available, means the constable who granted bail.

30D Failure to answer to bail under section 30A
(1) A constable may arrest without a warrant a person who—
    (a) has been released on bail under section 30A subject to a requirement to attend a specified police station, but
    (b) fails to attend the police station at the specified time.
...
(2A) A person who has been released on bail under section 30A may be arrested without a warrant by a constable if the constable has reasonable grounds for suspecting that a person has broken any of the conditions of bail.

31 Arrest for further offence
Where—
(a) a person—
    (i) has been arrested for an offence; and
    (ii) is at a police station in consequence of that arrest; and

(b) it appears to a constable that, if he were released from that arrest, he would be liable to arrest for some other offence,

he shall be arrested for that other offence.

32 Search upon arrest

(1) A constable may search an arrested person, in any case where the person to be searched has been arrested at a place other than a police station, if the constable has reasonable grounds for believing that the arrested person may present a danger to himself or others.

(2) Subject to subsections (3) to (5) below, a constable shall also have power in any such case—
   (a) to search the arrested person for anything—
      (i) which he might use to assist him to escape from lawful custody; or
      (ii) which might be evidence relating to an offence; and
   (b) if the offence for which he has been arrested is an indictable offence, to enter and search any premises in which he was when arrested or immediately before he was arrested for evidence relating to the offence.

(3) The power to search conferred by subsection (2) above is only a power to search to the extent that is reasonably required for the purpose of discovering any such thing or any such evidence.

(4) The powers conferred by this section to search a person are not to be construed as authorising a constable to require a person to remove any of his clothing in public other than an outer coat, jacket or gloves but they do authorise a search of a person's mouth.

(5) A constable may not search a person in the exercise of the power conferred by subsection (2)(a) above unless he has reasonable grounds for believing that the person to be searched may have concealed on him anything for which a search is permitted under that paragraph.

(6) A constable may not search premises in the exercise of the power conferred by subsection (2)(b) above unless he has reasonable grounds for believing that there is evidence for which a search is permitted under that paragraph on the premises.

(7) In so far as the power of search conferred by subsection (2)(b) above relates to premises consisting of two or more separate dwellings, it is limited to a power to search—
   (a) any dwelling in which the arrest took place or in which the person arrested was immediately before his arrest; and
   (b) any parts of the premises which the occupier of any such dwelling uses in common with the occupiers of any other dwellings comprised in the premises.

(8) A constable searching a person in the exercise of the power conferred by subsection (1) above may seize and retain anything he finds, if he has reasonable grounds for believing that the person searched might use it to cause physical injury to himself or to any other person.

(9) A constable searching a person in the exercise of the power conferred by subsection (2)(a) above may seize and retain anything he finds, other than an item subject to legal privilege, if he has reasonable grounds for believing—
   (a) that he might use it to assist him to escape from lawful custody; or
   (b) that it is evidence of an offence or has been obtained in consequence of the commission of an offence.

(10) Nothing in this section shall be taken to affect the power conferred by section 43 of the Terrorism Act 2000.

PART IV
DETENTION

Detention — conditions and duration

34 Limitations on police detention

(1) A person arrested for an offence shall not be kept in police detention except in accordance with the provisions of this Part of this Act.

(2) Subject to subsection (3) below, if at any time a custody officer—
   (a) becomes aware, in relation to any person in police detention, that the grounds for the detention of that person have ceased to apply; and

(b) is not aware of any other grounds on which the continued detention of that person could be justified under the provisions of this Part of this Act,
it shall be the duty of the custody officer, subject to subsection (4) below, to order his immediate release from custody.
(3) No person in police detention shall be released except on the authority of a custody officer at the police station where his detention was authorised or, if it was authorised at more than one station, a custody officer at the station where it was last authorised.
(4) A person who appears to the custody officer to have been unlawfully at large when he was arrested is not to be released under subsection (2) above.
...

35 Designated police stations

(1) The chief officer of police for each police area shall designate the police stations in his area which, subject to sections 30(3) and (5), 30A(5) and 30D(2) above, are to be the stations in that area to be used for the purpose of detention arrested persons.
(2) A chief officer's duty under subsection (1) above is to designate police stations appearing to him to provide enough accommodation for that purpose.
(3) Without prejudice to section 12 of the Interpretation Act 1978 (continuity of duties) a chief officer—
   (a) may designate a station which was not previously designated;
   ...

36 Custody officers at police stations

(1) One or more custody officers shall be appointed for each designated police station.
(2) A custody officer for a police station designated under section 35(1) above shall be appointed—
   (a) by the chief officer of police for the area in which the designated police station is situated; or
   (b) by such other police officer as the chief officer of police for that area may direct.
   ...
(3) No officer may be appointed a custody officer unless—
   (a) he is a police officer of at least the rank of sergeant; or
   (b) he is a staff custody officer.
(4) An officer of any rank may perform the functions of a custody officer at a designated police station if a custody officer is not readily available to perform them.
(5) Subject to the following provisions of this section and to section 39(2) below, none of the functions of a custody officer in relation to a person shall be performed by *an individual* who at the time when the function falls to be performed is involved in the investigation of an offence for which that person is in police detention at that time.
...

37 Duties of custody officer before charge

(1) Where—
   (a) a person is arrested for an offence—
      (i) without a warrant; or
      (ii) under a warrant not endorsed for bail,
   the custody officer at each police station where he is detained after his arrest shall determine whether he has before him sufficient evidence to charge that person with the offence for which he was arrested and may detain him at the police station for such period as is necessary to enable him to do so.
(2) If the custody officer determines that he does not have such evidence before him, the person arrested shall be released either on bail or without bail, unless the custody officer has reasonable grounds for believing that his detention without being charged is necessary to secure or preserve evidence relating to an offence for which he is under arrest or to obtain such evidence by questioning him.

(3) If the custody officer has reasonable grounds for so believing, he may authorise the person arrested to be kept in police detention.

(4) Where a custody officer authorises a person who has not been charged to be kept in police detention, he shall, as soon as is practicable, make a written record of the grounds for the detention.

(5) Subject to subsection (6) below, the written record shall be made in the presence of the person arrested who shall at that time be informed by the custody officer of the grounds for his detention.

(6) Subsection (5) above shall not apply where the person arrested is, at the time when the written record is made—
   (a) incapable of understanding what is said to him;
   (b) violent or likely to become violent; or
   (c) in urgent need of medical attention.

(7) Subject to section 41(7) below, if the custody officer determines that he has before him sufficient evidence to charge the person arrested with the offence for which he was arrested, the person arrested—
   (a) shall be (i) released without charge and on bail or (ii) kept in police detention for the purpose of enabling the Director of Public Prosecutions to make a decision under section 37B below,
   (b) shall be released without charge and on bail but not for that purpose,
   (c) shall be released without charge and without bail, or
   (d) shall be charged.

(7A) The decision as to how a person is to be dealt with under subsection (7) above shall be that of the custody officer.

(7B) Where a person is dealt with under subsection (7)(a) above, it shall be the duty of the custody officer to inform him that he is being released (or as the case may be) detained to enable the Director of Public Prosecutions to make a decision under section 37B below.

. . .

(9) If the person arrested is not in a fit state to be dealt with under subsection (7) above, he may be kept in police detention until he is.

(10) The duty imposed on the custody officer under subsection (1) above shall be carried out by him as soon as practicable after the person arrested arrives at the police station or, in the case of a person arrested at the police station, as soon as practicable after the arrest.

. . .

37A Guidance

(1) The Director of Public Prosecutions may issue guidance—
   (a) for the purpose of enabling custody officers to decide how persons should be dealt with under section 37(7) above or 37C(2) or 37CA(2) below, and
   (b) as to the information to be sent to the Director of Public Prosecutions under section 37B(1) below.

(2) The Director of Public Prosecutions may from time to time revise guidance issued under this section.

(3) Custody officers are to have regard to guidance under this section in deciding how persons should be dealt with under section 37(7) above or 37C(2) or 37CA(2) below.

. . .

(5) The Director of Public Prosecutions must publish in such manner as he thinks fit—
   (a) any guidance issued under this section, and
   (b) any revisions made to such guidance.
   (6) Guidance under this section may make different provision for different cases, circumstances or areas.

37B Consultation with the Director of Public Prosecutions

(1) Where a person is dealt with under section 37(7)(a) above, an officer involved in the investigation of the offence shall, as soon as is practicable, send to the Director of Public Prosecutions such information as may be specified in guidance under section 37A above.

(2) The Director of Public Prosecutions shall decide whether there is sufficient evidence to charge the person with an offence.
(3) If he decides that there is sufficient evidence to charge the person with an offence, he shall decide—
    (a) whether or not the person should be charged and, if so, the offence with which he should be charged, and
    (b) whether or not the person should be given a caution and, if so, the offence in respect of which he should be given a caution.
(4) The Director of Public Prosecutions shall give written notice of his decision to an officer involved in the investigation of the offence.
(4A) A notice under subsection (4) above shall be in writing, but in the case of a person kept in police detention under section 37(7)(a) above it may be given orally in the first instance and confirmed in writing subsequently.
(5) If his decision is—
    (a) that there is not sufficient evidence to charge the person with an offence, or
    (b) that there is sufficient evidence to charge the person with an offence but that the person should not be charged with an offence or given a caution in respect of an offence,
    a custody officer shall give the person notice in writing that he is not to be prosecuted.
(6) If the decision of the Director of Public Prosecutions is that the person should be charged with an offence, or given a caution in respect of an offence, the person shall be charged or cautioned accordingly.
(7) But if his decision is that the person should be given a caution in respect of the offence and it proves not to be possible to give the person such a caution, he shall instead be charged with the offence.

. . .

38 Duties of custody officer after charge
(1) Where a person arrested for an offence otherwise than under a warrant endorsed for bail is charged with an offence, the custody officer shall subject to section 25 of the Criminal Justice and Public Order Act 1994 order his release from police detention, either on bail or without bail, unless—
    (a) if the person arrested is not an arrested juvenile—
        (i) his name or address cannot be ascertained or the custody officer has reasonable grounds for doubting whether a name or address furnished by him as his name or address is his real name or address;
        (ii) the custody officer has reasonable grounds for believing that the person arrested will fail to appear in court to answer to bail;
        (iii) in the case of a person arrested for an imprisonable offence, the custody officer has reasonable grounds for believing that the detention of the person arrested is necessary to prevent him from committing an offence;
        (iiia) in a case of where a sample may be taken from the person under section 63B below, the custody officer has reasonable grounds for believing that the detention of the person is necessary to enable the sample to be taken from him.
        (iv) in the case of a person arrested for an offence which is not an imprisonable offence, the custody officer has reasonable grounds for believing that the detention of the person arrested is necessary to prevent him from causing physical injury to any other person or from causing loss of or damage to property;
        (v) the custody officer has reasonable grounds for believing that the detention of the person arrested is necessary to prevent him from interfering with the administration of justice or with the investigation of offences or of a particular offence; or
        (vi) the custody officer has reasonable grounds for believing that the detention of the person arrested is necessary for his own protection;
    (b) if he is an arrested juvenile—

(i) any of the requirements of paragraph (a) above is satisfied but in the case of paragraph (a)(iiia) above, only if the arrested juvenile has attained the minimum age of 21; or
(ii) the custody officer has reasonable grounds for believing that he ought to be detained in his own interests.

(2) If the release of a person arrested is not required by subsection (1) above, the custody officer may authorise him to be kept in police detention but may not authorise a person to be kept in police detention by virtue of subsection (1)(a)(iiia) after the end of the period of six hours beginning when he was charged with the offence.

. . .

(3) Where a custody officer authorises a person who has been charged to be kept in police detention, he shall, as soon as practicable, make a written record of the grounds for the detention.

(4) Subject to subsection (5) below, the written record shall be made in the presence of the person charged who shall at that time be informed by the custody officer of the grounds for his detention.

(5) Subsection (4) above shall not apply where the person charged is, at the time when the written record is made—
(a) incapable of understanding what is said to him;
(b) violent or likely to become violent; or
(c) in urgent need of medical attention.

(6) Where a custody officer authorises an arrested juvenile to be kept in police detention under subsection (1) above, the custody officer shall, unless he certifies—
(a) that by reason of such circumstances as are specified in the certificate, it is impracticable for him to do so; or
(b) in the case of an arrested juvenile who has attained the age of 12 years, that no secure accommodation is available and that keeping him in other local authority accommodation would not be adequate to protect the public from serious harm from him,
secure that the arrested juvenile is moved to local authority accommodation.

. . .

(6B) Where an arrested juvenile is moved to local authority accommodation under subsection 6 above, it shall be lawful for any person acting on behalf of the authority to detain him.

. . .

39 Responsibilities in relation to persons detained

(1) Subject to subsection (2) and (4) below, it shall be the duty of the custody officer at a police station to ensure—
(a) that all persons in police detention at that station are treated in accordance with this Act and any code of practice issued under it and relating to the treatment of persons in police detention; and
(b) that all matters relating to such persons which are required by this Act or by such codes of practice to be recorded are recorded in the custody records relating to such persons.

. . .

(6) Where—
(a) an officer of higher rank than the custody officer *or, if the custody officer is a staff custody officer, any police officer or any police employee* gives directions relating to a person in police detention; and
(b) the directions are at variance—
(i) with any decision made or action taken by the custody officer in the performance of a duty imposed on him under this Part of this Act; or
(ii) with any decision or action which would be for the directions have been made or taken by him in the performance of such a duty,

the custody officer shall refer the matter at once to an officer of the rank of superintendent or above who is responsible for the police station for which the custody officer is acting as custody officer.

...

40 Review of police detention

(1) Reviews of the detention of each person in police detention in connection with the investigation of an offence shall be carried out periodically in accordance with the following provisions of this section—
   (a) in the case of a person who has been arrested and charged, by the custody officer; and
   (b) in the case of a person who has been arrested but not charged, by an officer of at least the rank of inspector who has not been directly involved in the investigation.
(2) The officer to whom it falls to carry out a review is referred to in this section as a "review officer".
(3) Subject to subsection (4) below—
   (a) the first review shall be not later than six hours after the detention was first authorised;
   (b) the second review shall be not later than nine hours after the first;
   (c) subsequent reviews shall be at intervals of not more than nine hours.
(4) A review may be postponed—
   (a) if, having regard to all the circumstances prevailing at the latest time for it specified in subsection (3) above, it is not practicable to carry out the review at that time;
   (b) without prejudice to the generality of paragraph (a) above—
      (i) if at that time the person in detention is being questioned by a police officer and the review officer is satisfied that an interruption of the questioning for the purpose of carrying out the review would prejudice the investigation in connection with which he is being questioned; or
      (ii) if at that time no review officer is readily available.
(5) If a review is postponed under subsection (4) above it shall be carried out as soon as practicable after the latest time specified for it in subsection (3) above.
(6) If a review is carried out after postponement under subsection (4) above, the fact that it was so carried out shall not affect any requirement of this section as to the time at which any subsequent review is to be carried out.
(7) The review officer shall record the reasons for any postponement of a review in the custody record.
(8) Subject to subsection (9) below, where the person whose detention is under review has not been charged before the time of the review, section 37(1) to (6) above shall have effect in relation to him, but with the modifications specified in subsection (8A).
(8A) The modifications are—
   (a) the substitution of references to the person whose detention is under review for references to the person arrested;
   (b) the substitution of references to the review officer for references to the custody officer; and
   (c) in subsection (6), the insertion of the following paragraph after paragraph (a)—
      "(aa) asleep;"
(9) Where a person has been kept in police detention by virtue of section 37(9) or 37D(5) above, section 37(1) to (6) shall not have effect in relation to him but it shall be the duty of the review officer to determine whether he is yet in a fit state.
(10) Where the person whose detention is under review has been charged before the time of the review, section 38(1) to (6B) above shall have effect in relation to him, with the modifications specified in subsection 10A.
(10A)The modifications are—
   (a) the substitution of a reference to the person whose detention is under review for any reference to the person arrested or to the person charged; and
   (b) in subsection (5), the insertion of the following paragraph after paragraph (a)—
      "(aa) asleep;".

(11) Where—
   (a) an officer of higher rank than the review officer gives directions relating to a person in police detention; and
   (b) the directions are at variance—
      (i) with any decision made or action taken by the review officer in the performance of a duty imposed on him under this Part of this Act; or
      (ii) with any decision or action which would but for the directions have been made or taken by him in the performance of such a duty,
   the review officer shall refer the matter at once to an officer of the rank of superintendent or above who is responsible for the police station for which the review officer is acting as review officer in connection with the detention.
(12) Before determining whether to authorise a person's continued detention the review officer shall give—
   (a) that person (unless he is asleep); or
   (b) any solicitor representing him who is available at the time of the review,
   an opportunity to make representations to him about the detention.
...

40A Use of telephone for review under s. 40
(1) This section applies, notwithstanding anything in section 40 above, where in the case of a person who has been arrested but not charged—
   (a) it is not reasonably practicable for an officer of at least the rank of inspector to be present in the police station where that person is held to carry out any review of that person's detention that is required by subsection (1)(b) of that section; and
   (b) the review is not one which regulations under section 45A below authorise to be carried out using video-conferencing facilities, or is one which it is not reasonably practicable, in the circumstances, to carry out using any such facilities.
(2) The review may be carried out by an officer of at least the rank of inspector who has access to a means of communication by telephone to persons in the police station where the arrested person is held.
...

41 Limits on period of detention without charge
(1) Subject to the following provisions of this section and to sections 42 and 43 below, a person shall not be kept in police detention for more than 24 hours without being charged.
(2) The time from which the period of detention of a person is to be calculated (in this Act referred to as "the relevant time")—
   (a) in the case of a person to whom this paragraph applies, shall be—
      (i) the time at which that person arrives at the relevant police station; or
      (ii) the time 24 hours after the time of that person's arrest,
   whichever is the earlier;
   (b) in the case of a person arrested outside England and Wales, shall be—
      (i) the time at which that person arrives at the first police station to which he is taken in the police area in England or Wales in which the offence for which he was arrested is being investigated; or
      (ii) the time 24 hours after the time of that person's entry into England and Wales,
   whichever is the earlier;
   (c) in the case of a person who—
      (i) attends voluntarily at a police station; or
      (ii) accompanies a constable to a police station without having been arrested,
   and is arrested at the police station, the time of his arrest;
   (ca) in the case of a person who attends a police station to answer to bail granted under section 30A, the time when he arrives at the police station;
   (d) in any other case ... shall be the time at which the person arrested arrives at the first police station to which he is taken after his arrest.

...

(7) Subject to subsection (8) below, a person who at the expiry of 24 hours after the relevant time is in police detention and has not been charged shall be released at that time either on bail or without bail.

(8) Subsection (7) above does not apply to a person whose detention for more than 24 hours after the relevant time has been authorised or is otherwise permitted in accordance with section 42 or 43 below.

...

42   Authorisation of continued detention

(1) Where a police officer of the rank of superintendent or above who is responsible for the police station at which a person is detained has reasonable grounds for believing that—
   (a) the detention of that person without charge is necessary to secure or preserve evidence relating to an offence for which he is under arrest or to obtain such evidence by questioning him;
   (b) an offence for which he is under arrest is an indictable offence; and
   (c) the investigation is being conducted diligently and expeditiously,
   he may authorise the keeping of that person in police detention for a period expiring at or before 36 hours after the relevant time.

(2) Where an officer such as is mentioned in subsection (1) above has authorised the keeping of a person in police detention for a period expiring less than 36 hours after the relevant time, such an officer may authorise the keeping of that person in police detention for a further period expiring not more than 36 hours after that time if the conditions specified in subsection (1) above are still satisfied when he gives the authorisation.

(3) If it is proposed to transfer a person in police detention to another police area, the officer determining whether or not to authorise keeping him in detention under subsection (1) above shall have regard to the distance and the time the journey would take.

(4) No authorisation under subsection (1) above shall be given in respect of any person—
   (a) more than 24 hours after the relevant time; or
   (b) before the second review of his detention under section 40 above has been carried out.

(5) Where an officer authorises the keeping of a person in police detention under subsection (1) above, it shall be his duty—
   (a) to inform that person of the grounds for his continued detention; and
   (b) to record the grounds in that person's custody record.

(6) Before determining whether to authorise the keeping of a person in detention under subsection (1) or (2) above, an officer shall give—
   (a) that person; or
   (b) any solicitor representing him who is available at the time when it falls to the officer to determine whether to give the authorisation,
   an opportunity to make representations to him about the detention.

...

(9) Where—
   (a) an officer authorises the keeping of a person in detention under subsection (1) above; and
   (b) at the time of the authorisation he has not yet exercised a right conferred on him by section 56 or 58 below,
   the officer—
      (i) shall inform him of that right;
      (ii) shall decide whether he should be permitted to exercise it;
      (iii) shall record the decision in his custody record; and
      (iv) if the decision is to refuse to permit the exercise of the right, shall also record the grounds for the decision in that record.

(10) Where an officer has authorised the keeping of a person who has not been charged in detention under subsection (1) or (2) above, he shall be released from detention, either on bail or without bail, not later than 36 hours after the relevant time, unless—

(a) he has been charged with an offence; or
(b) his continued detention is authorised or otherwise permitted in accordance with section 43 below.
(11) A person released under subsection (10) above shall not be re-arrested without a warrant for the offence for which he was previously arrested unless new evidence justifying a further arrest has come to light since his release; but this subsection does not prevent an arrest under section 46A below.

43 Warrants of further detention

(1) Where, on an application on oath made by a constable and supported by an information, a magistrate's court is satisfied that there are reasonable grounds for believing that the further detention of the person to whom the application relates is justified, it may issue a warrant of further detention authorising the keeping of that person in police detention.

(2) A court may not hear an application for a warrant of further detention unless the person to whom the application relates—
(a) has been furnished with a copy of the information; and
(b) has been brought before the court for the hearing.

(3) The person to whom the application relates shall be entitled to be legally represented at the hearing and, if he is not so represented but wishes to be so represented—
(a) the court shall adjourn the hearing to enable him to obtain representation; and
(b) he may be kept in police detention during the adjournment.

(4) A person's further detention is only justified for the purposes of this section or section 44 below if—
(a) his detention without charge is necessary to secure or preserve evidence relating to an offence for which he is under arrest or to obtain such evidence by questioning him;
(b) an offence for which he is under arrest is an indictable offence; and
(c) the investigation is being conducted diligently and expeditiously.

(5) Subject to subsection (7) below, an application for a warrant of further detention may be made—
(a) at any time before the expiry of 36 hours after the relevant time; or
(b) in a case where—
(i) it is not practicable for the magistrates' court to which the application will be made to sit at the expiry of 36 hours after the relevant time; but
(ii) the court will sit during the 6 hours following the end of that period, at any time before the expiry of the said 6 hours.

(6) In a case to which subsection (5)(b) above applies—
(a) the person to whom the application relates may be kept in police detention until the application is heard; and
(b) the custody officer shall make a note in that person's custody record—
(i) of the fact that he was kept in police detention for more than 36 hours after the relevant time; and
(ii) of the reason why he was so kept.

(7) If—
(a) an application for a warrant of further detention is made after the expiry of 36 hours after the relevant time; and
(b) it appears to the magistrates' court that it would have been reasonable for the police to make it before the expiry of that period,
the court shall dismiss the application.

(8) Where on an application such as is mentioned in subsection (1) above a magistrates' court is not satisfied that there are reasonable grounds for believing that the further detention of the person to whom the application relates is justified, it shall be its duty—
(a) to refuse the application; or
(b) to adjourn the hearing of it until a time not later than 36 hours after the relevant time.

(9) The person to whom the application relates may be kept in police detention during the adjournment.

(10) A warrant of further detention shall—
   (a) state the time at which it is issued;
   (b) authorise the keeping in police detention of the person to whom it relates for the period stated in it.
(11) Subject to subsection (12) below, the period stated in a warrant of further detention shall be such period as the magistrates' court thinks fit, having regard to the evidence before it.
(12) The period shall not be longer than 36 hours.
...
(14) Any information submitted in support of an application under this section shall state—
   (a) the nature of the offence for which the person to whom the application relates has been arrested;
   (b) the general nature of the evidence on which that person was arrested;
   (c) what inquiries relating to the offence have been made by the police and what further inquiries are proposed by them;
   (d) the reasons for believing the continued detention of that person to be necessary for the purposes of such further inquiries.
(15) Where an application under this section is refused, the person to whom the application relates shall forthwith be charged or, subject to subsection (16) below, released, either on bail or without bail.
(16) A person need not be released under subsection (15) above—
   (a) before the expiry of 24 hours after the relevant time; or
   (b) before the expiry of any longer period for which his continued detention is or has been authorised under section 42 above.
(17) Where an application under this section is refused, no further application shall be made under this section in repect of the person to whom the refusal relates, unless supported by evidence which has come to light since the refusal.
(18) Where a warrant of further detention is issued, the person to whom it relates shall be released from police detention, either on bail or without bail, upon or before the expiry of the warrant unless he is charged.
(19) A person released under subsection (18) above shall not be re-arrested without a warrant for the offence for which he was previously arrested unless new evidence justifying a further arrest has come to light since his release; but this subsection does not prevent an arrest under section 46A below.

44 Extension of warrants of further detention

(1) On an application on oath made by a constable and supported by an information a magistrates' court may extend a warrant of further detention issued under section 43 above if it is satisfied that there are reasonable grounds for believing that the further detention of the person to whom the application relates is justified.
(2) Subject to subsection (3) below, the period for which a warrant of further detention may be extended shall be such period as the court thinks fit, having regard to the evidence before it.
(3) The period shall not—
   (a) be longer than 36 hours; or
   (b) end later than 96 hours after the relevant time.
(4) Where a warrant of further detention has been extended under subsection (1) above, or further extended under this subsection, for a period ending before 96 hours after the relevant time, on an application such as is mentioned in that subsection a magistrates' court may further extend the warrant if it is satisfied as there mentioned; and subsections (2) and (3) above apply to such further extensions as they apply to extensions under subsection (1) above.
(5) A warrant of further detention shall, if extended or further extended under this section, be endorsed with a note of the period of the extension.
(6) Subsections (2), (3), and (14) of section 43 above shall apply to an application made under this section as they apply to an application made under that section.
...

45 Detention before charge — supplementary

...

(2) Any reference in this Part of this Act to a period of time or a time of day is to be treated as approximate only.

Detention — miscellaneous

45A Use of video-conferencing facilities for decisions about detention

(1) Subject to the following provisions of this section, the Secretary of State may by regulations provide that, in the case of an arrested person who is held in a police station, some or all of the functions mentioned in subsection (2) may be performed (notwithstanding anything in the preceding provisions of this Part) by an officer who—
   (a) is not present in that police station; but
   (b) has access to the use of video-conferencing facilities that enable him to communicate with persons in that station.

(2) Those functions are—
   (a) the functions in relation to an arrested person taken to, or answering to bail at, a police station that is not a designated police station which, in the case of an arrested person taken to a station that is a designated police station, are functions of a custody officer under section 37, 38 or 40 above; and
   (b) the function of carrying out a review under section 40(1)(b) above (review, by an officer of at least the rank of inspector, of the detention of person arrested but not charged).

(3) Regulations under this section shall specify the use to be made in the performance of the functions mentioned in subsection (2) above of the facilities mentioned in subsection (1) above.

...

46 Detention after charge

(1) Where a person—
   (a) is charged with an offence; and
   (b) after being charged—
      (i) is kept in police detention; or
      (ii) is detained by a local authority in pursuance of arrangements made under section 38(6) above,

   he shall be brought before a magistrates' court in accordance with the provisions of this section.

(2) If he is to be brought before a magistrates' court in the local justice area in which the police station at which he was charged is situated, he shall be brought before such a court as soon as is practicable and in any event not later than the first sitting after he is charged with the offence.

(3) If no magistrates' court in that area is due to sit either on the day on which he is charged or on the next day, the custody officer for the police station at which he was charged shall inform the designated officer for the area that there is a person in the area to whom subsection (2) above applies.

(4) If the person charged is to be brought before a magistrates' court in a local justice area other than that in which the police station at which he was charged is situated, he shall be removed to that area as soon as is practicable and brought before such a court as soon as is practicable after this arrival in the area and in any event not later than the first sitting of a magistrates' court in that area after this arrival in the area.

(5) If no magistrates' court in that area is due to sit either on the day on which he arrives in the area or on the next day—
   (a) he shall be taken to a police station in the area; and
   (b) the custody officer at that station shall inform the designated officer for the area that there is a person in the area to whom subsection (4) applies.

(6) Subject to subsection (8) below, where the designated officer for a local justice area has been informed—

(a) under subsection (3) above that there is a person in the area to whom subsection (2) above applies; or
(b) under subsection (5) above that there is a person in the area to whom subsection (4) above applies,
the designated officer shall arrange for a magistrates' court to sit not later than the day next following the relevant day.
(7) In this section "the relevant day" —
(a) in relation to a person who is to be brought before a magistrates' court in the local justice area in which the police station at which he was charged is situated, means the day on which he was charged; and
(b) in relation to a person who is to be brought before a magistrates' court in any other local justice area, means the day on which he arrives in the area.
(8) Where the day next following the relevant day is Christmas Day, Good Friday or a Sunday, the duty of the designated officer under subsection (6) above is a duty to arrange for a magistrates' court to sit not later than the first day after the relevant day which is not one of those days.

. . .

46A Power of arrest for failure to answer to police bail
(1) A constable may arrest without a warrant any person who, having been released on bail under this Part of this Act subject to a duty to attend at a police station, fails to attend at that police station at the time appointed for him to do so.
(1ZA). . .
(1A) A person who has been released on bail under section 37, 37C(2)(b) or 37(CA)(2)(b) above may be arrested without warrant by a constable if the constable has reasonable grounds for suspecting that the person has broken any of the conditions of bail.
(2) A person who is arrested under this section shall be taken to the police station appointed as the place at which he is to surrender to custody as soon as practicable after the arrest.
(3) For the purpose of—
(a) section 30 above (subject to the obligation in subsection (2) above), and
(b) section 31 above,
an arrest under the section shall be treated as an arrest for an offence.

47 Bail after arrest
(1) Subject to the following provisions of this section, a release on bail of a person under this Part of this Act shall be a release on bail granted in accordance with sections 3, 3A, 5 and 5A of the Bail Act 1976 as they apply to bail granted by a constable.
(1A) The normal powers to impose conditions of bail shall be available to him where a custody officer releases a person on bail under section 37 above or section 38(1) above (including that subsection as applied by section 40(10) above) but not in any other cases.
In this subsection "the normal powers to impose conditions of bail" has the meaning given in section 3(6) of the Bail Act 1976.
(2) Nothing in the Bail Act 1976 shall prevent the re-arrest without warrant of a person released on bail subject to a duty to attend at a police station if new evidence justifying a further arrest has come to light since his release.

. . .

PART V
QUESTIONING AND TREATMENT OF PERSONS BY POLICE

53 Abolition of certain powers of constables to search persons
(1) Subject to subsection (2) below, there shall cease to have effect any Act (including a local Act) passed before this Act in so far as it authorises—
(a) any search by a constable of a person in police detention at a police station; or
(b) an intimate search of a person by a constable;

and any rule of common law which authorises a search such as is mentioned in paragraph (a) or (b) above is abolished.

(2) ...

54 Search of detained persons

(1) The custody officer at a police station shall ascertain everything which a person has with him when he is—
   (a) brought to the station after being arrested elsewhere or after being committed to custody by an order or sentence of a court; or
   (b) arrested at the station or detained there as a person falling within section 34(7), under section 37 above or as a person to whom section 46ZA(4) or (5) applies.
(2) The custody officer may record or cause to be recorded all or any of the things which he ascertains under subsection (1).
(2A) In the case of an arrested person, any such record may be made as part of his custody record.
(3) Subject to subsection (4) below, a custody officer may seize and retain any such thing or cause any such thing to be seized and retained.
(4) Clothes and personal effects may only be seized if the custody officer—
   (a) believes that the person from whom they are seized may use them—
      (i) to cause physical injury to himself or any other person;
      (ii) to damage property;
      (iii) to interfere with evidence; or
      (iv) to assist him to escape; or
   (b) has reasonable grounds for believing that they may be evidence relating to an offence.
(5) Where anything is seized, the person from whom it is seized shall be told the reason for the seizure unless he is—
   (a) violent or likely to become violent; or
   (b) incapable of understanding what is said to him.
(6) Subject to subsection (7) below, a person may be searched if the custody officer considers it necessary to enable him to carry out his duty under subsection (1) above and to the extent that the custody officer considers necessary for that purpose.
(6A) A person who is in custody at a police station or is in police detention otherwise than at a police station may at any time be searched in order to ascertain whether he has with him anything which he could use for any of the purposes specified in subsection (4)(a) above.
(6B) Subject to subsection (6C) below, a constable may seize and retain, or cause to be seized and retained, anything found on such a search.
(6C) A constable may only seize clothes and personal effects in the circumstances specified in subsection (4) above.
(7) An intimate search may not be conducted under this section.
(8) A search under this section shall be carried out by a constable.
(9) The constable carrying out a search shall be of the same sex as the person searched.

55 Intimate searches

(1) Subject to the following provisions of this section, if an officer of at least the rank of inspector has reasonable grounds for believing—
   (a) that a person who has been arrested and is in police detention may have concealed on him anything which—
      (i) he could use to cause physical injury to himself or others; and
      (ii) he might so use while he is in police detention or in the custody of a court; or
   (b) that such a person—
      (i) may have a Class A drug concealed on him; and
      (ii) was in possession of it with the appropriate criminal intention before his arrest,
   he may authorise an intimate search of that person.

...

(3A) A drug offence search shall not be carried out unless the appropriate consent is given in writing.

...

(4) An intimate search which is only a drug offence search shall be by way of examination by a suitably qualified person.

(5) Except as provided by subsection (4) above, an intimate search shall be by way of examination by a suitably qualified person unless an officer of at least the rank of inspector considers that this is not practicable.

(6) An intimate search which is not carried out as mentioned in subsection (5) above shall be carried out by a constable.

(7) A constable may not carry out an intimate search of a person of the opposite sex.

(8) No intimate search may be carried out except—
   (a) at a police station;
   (b) at a hospital;
   (c) at a registered medical practitioner's surgery; or
   (d) at some other place used for medical purposes.

(9) An intimate search which is only a drug offence search may not be carried out at a police station.

(10) If an intimate search of a person is carried out, the custody record relating to him shall state—
   (a) which parts of his body were searched; and
   (b) why they were searched.

...

(12) This custody officer at a police station may seize and retain anything which is found on an intimate search of a person, or cause any such thing to be seized and retained—
   (a) if he believes that the person from whom it is seized may use it—
      (i) to cause physical injury to himself or any other person;
      (ii) to damage property;
      (iii) to interfere with evidence; or
      (iv) to assist him to escape; or
   (b) if he has reasonable grounds for believing that it may be evidence relating to an offence.

(13) Where anything is seized under this section, the person from whom it is seized shall be told the reason for the seizure unless he is—
   (a) violent or likely to become violent; or
   (b) incapable of understanding what is said to him.

...

56 Right to have someone informed when arrested

(1) Where a person has been arrested and is being held in custody in a police station or other premises, he shall be entitled, if he so requests, to have one friend or relative or other person who is known to him or who is likely to take an interest in his welfare told, as soon as is practicable except to the extent that delay is permitted by this section, that he has been arrested and is being detained there.

(2) Delay is only permitted—
   (a) in the case of a person who is in police detention for an indictable offence; and
   (b) if an officer of at least the rank of inspector authorises it.

(3) In any case the person in custody must be permitted to exercise the right conferred by subsection (1) above within 36 hours from the relevant time as defined in section 41(2) above.

...

(5) Subject to subsection (5A) below an officer may only authorise delay where he has reasonable grounds for believing that telling the named person of the arrest—
   (a) will lead to interference with or harm to evidence connected with an indictable offence or interference with or physical injury to other persons; or
   (b) will lead to the alerting of other persons suspected of having committed such an offence but not yet arrested for it; or

(c) will hinder the recovery of any property obtained as a result of such an offence.
(5A) An officer may also authorise delay where he has reasonable grounds for believing that—
  (a) the person detained for the indictable offence has benefited from his criminal conduct, and
  (b) the recovery of the value of the property constituting the benefit will be hindered by telling the named person of the arrest.
(5B) For the purposes of subsection (5A) above the question whether a person has benefited from his criminal conduct is to be decided in accordance with Part 2 of the Proceeds of Crime Act 2002.
(6) If a delay is authorised—
  (a) the detained person shall be told the reason for it; and
  (b) the reason shall be noted on his custody record.
(7) The duties imposed by subsection (6) above shall be performed as soon as is practicable.
(8) The rights conferred by this section on a person detained at a police station or other premises are exercisable whenever he is transferred from one place to another; and this section applies to each subsequent occasion on which they are exercisable as it applies to the first such occasion.
(9) There may be no further delay in permitting the exercise of the right conferred by subsection (1) above once the reason for authorising delay ceases to subsist.
(10) Nothing in this section applies to a person arrested or detained under the terrorism provisions.

58 Access to legal advice

(1) A person arrested and held in custody in a police station or other premises shall be entitled, if he so requests, to consult a solicitor privately at any time.
(2) Subject to subsection (3) below, a request under subsection (1) above and the time at which it was made shall be recorded in the custody record.
(3) Such a request need not be recorded in the custody record of a person who makes it at a time while he is at a court after being charged with an offence.
(4) If a person makes such a request, he must be permitted to consult a solicitor as soon as is practicable except to the extent that delay is permitted by this section.
(5) In any case he must be permitted to consult a solicitor within 36 hours from the relevant time, as defined in section 41(2) above.
(6) Delay in compliance with a request is only permitted—
  (a) in the case of a person who is in police detention for an indictable offence; and
  (b) if an officer of at least the rank of superintendent authorises it.
(7) An officer may give an authorisation under subsection (6) above orally or in writing but, if he gives it orally, he shall confirm it in writing as soon as is practicable.
(8) Subject to subsection (8A) below an officer may only authorise delay where he has reasonable grounds for believing that the exercise of the right conferred by subsection (1) above at the time when the person detained desires to exercise it—
  (a) will lead to interference with or harm to evidence connected with an indictable offence or interference with or physical injury to other persons; or
  (b) will lead to the alerting of other persons suspected of having committed such an offence but not yet arrested for it; or
  (c) will hinder the recovery of any property obtained as a result of such an offence.
(8A) An officer may also authorise delay where he has reasonable grounds for believing that—
  (a) the person detained for the indictable offence has benefited from his criminal conduct, and
  (b) the recovery of the value of the property constituting the benefit will be hindered by the exercise of the right conferred by subsection (1) above.
(8B) For the purposes of subsection (8A) above the question whether a person has benefited from his criminal conduct is to be decided in accordance with Part 2 of the Proceeds of Crime Act 2002.
(9) If delay is authorised—

(a) the detained person shall be told the reason for it; and
(b) the reason shall be noted on his custody record.
(10) The duties imposed by subsection (9) above shall be performed as soon as is practicable.
(11) There may be no further delay in permitting the exercise of the right conferred by subsection (1) above once the reason for authorising delay ceases to subsist.
(12) Nothing in this section applies to a person arrested or detained under the terrorism provisions.

60   Tape-recording of interviews
(1) It shall be the duty of the Secretary of State—
   (a) to issue a code of practice in connection with the tape-recording of interviews of persons suspected of the commission of criminal offences which are held by police officers at police stations; and
   (b) to make an order requiring the tape-recording of interviews of persons suspected of the commission of criminal offences, or of such descriptions of criminal offences as may be specified in the order, which are so held, in accordance with the code as it has effect for the time being.
(2) An order under subsection (1) above shall be made by statutory instrument and shall be subject to annulment in pursuance of a resolution of either House of Parliament.

60A   Visual recording of interviews
(1) The Secretary of State shall have power—
   (a) to issue a code of practice for the visual recording of interviews held by police officers at police stations; and
   (b) to make an order requiring the visual recording of interviews so held, and requiring the visual recording to be in accordance with the code for the time being in force under this section.
(2) A requirement imposed by an order under this section may be imposed in relation to such cases or police stations in such areas, or both, as may be specified or described in the order.
(3) An order under subsection (1) above shall be made by statutory instrument and shall be subject to annulment in pursuance of a resolution of either House of Parliament.
. . .

61   Fingerprinting
(1) Except as provided by this section no person's fingerprints may be taken without the appropriate consent.
(2) Consent to the taking of a person's fingerprints must be in writing if it is given at a time when he is at a police station.
(3) The fingerprints of a person detained at a police station may be taken without the appropriate consent if—
   (a) he is detained in consequence of his arrest for a recordable offence; and
   (b) he has not had his fingerprints taken in the course of the investigation of the offence by the police.
(3A) Where a person charged with a recordable offence or informed that he will be reported for such an offence has already had his fingerprints taken as mentioned in paragraph (b)(ii) of subsection (3) above, that fact shall be disregarded for the purposes of that subsection if—
   (a) the fingerprints taken on the previous occasion do not constitute a complete set of his fingerprints; or
   (b) some or all of the fingerprints taken on the previous occasion are not of sufficient quality to allow satisfactory analysis, comparison or matching (whether in the case in question or generally).
(4) The fingerprints of a person detained at a police station may be taken without the appropriate consent if—
   (a) he has been charged with a recordable offence or informed that he will be reported for such an offence; and

(b) he has not had his fingerprints taken in the course of the investigation of the offence by the police.
(4A) The fingerprints of a person who has answered to bail at a court or police station may be taken without the appropriate consent at the court or station if—
  (a) the court, or
  (b) an officer of at least the rank of inspector,
  authorises them to be taken.
(4B) A court or officer may only give an authorisation under subsection (4A) if—
  (a) the person who has answered to bail has answered to it for a person whose fingerprints were taken on a previous occasion and there are reasonable grounds for believing that he is not the same person; or
  (b) the person who has answered to bail claims to be a different person from a person whose fingerprints were taken on a previous occasion.
(5) An officer may give an authorisation under subsection . . . (4A) above orally or in writing but, if he gives it orally, he will confirm it in writing as soon as is practicable.
(6) Any person's fingerprints may be taken without the appropriate consent if—
  (a) he has been convicted of a recordable offence;
  (b) he has been given a caution in respect of a recordable offence which, at the time of the caution, he has admitted; or
  (c) he has been warned or reprimanded under section 65 of the Crime and Disorder Act 1998 for a recordable offence.
(6A) A constable may take a person's fingerprints without the appropriate consent if—
  (a) the constable reasonably suspects that the person is committing or attempting to commit an offence, or has committed or attempted to commit an offence; and
  (b) either of the two conditions mentioned in subsection (6B) is met.
(6B) The conditions are that—
  (a) the name of the person is unknown to, and cannot be readily ascertained by, the constable;
  (b) the constable has reasonable grounds for doubting whether a name furnished by the person as his name is his real name.
(6C) The taking of fingerprints by virtue of subsection (6A) does not count for any of the purposes of this Act as taking them in the course of the investigation of an offence by the police.
(7) In a case where by virtue of subsection (3), (4), (6) *or (6A)* above a person's fingerprints are taken without the appropriate consent—
  (a) he shall be told the reason before his fingerprints are taken; and
  (b) the reason shall be recorded as soon as is practicable after the fingerprints are taken.
(7A) If a person's fingerprints are taken at a police station *or by virtue of subsection 6A at a place other than a police station*, whether with or without the appropriate consent—
  (a) before the fingerprints are taken, an officer or, in a subsection (6A) case, the constable shall inform him that they may be the subject of a speculative search; and
  (b) the fact that the person has been informed of this possibility shall be recorded as soon as is practicable after the fingerprints have been taken.
(8) If he is detained at a police station when the fingerprints are taken, the reason for taking them shall be recorded on his custody record *and, in the case falling within subsection (7A) above, the fact referred to in paragraph (b) of that subsection*.
. . .
(9) Nothing in this section—
  (a) affects any power conferred by paragraph 18(2) of Schedule 2 to the Immigration Act 1971, *section 141 of the Immigration and Asylum Act 1999 or regulations made under section 144 of that Act*; or
  (b) applies to a person arrested or detained under the terrorism provisions.

61A Impressions of footwear
(1) Except as provided by this section, no impression of a person's footwear may be taken without the appropriate consent.

(2) Consent to the taking of an impression of a person's footwear must be in writing if it is given at a time when he is at a police station.
(3) Where a person is detained at a police station, an impression of his footwear may be taken without the appropriate consent if—
  (a) he is detained in consequence of his arrest for a recordable offence, or has been charged with a recordable offence, or informed that he will be reported for a recordable offence; and
  (b) he has not had an impression taken of his footwear in the course of the investigation of the offence by the police.
(4) Where a person mentioned in paragraph (a) of subsection (3) above has already had an impression taken of his footwear in the course of the investigation of the offence by the police, that fact shall be disregarded for the purposes of that subsection if the impression of his footwear taken previously is—
  (a) incomplete; or
  (b) is not of sufficient quality to allow satisfactory analysis, comparison or matching (whether in the case in question or generally).
(5) If an impression of a person's footwear is taken at a police station, whether with or without the appropriate consent—
  (a) before it is taken, an officer shall inform him that it may be the subject of a speculative search; and
  (b) the fact that the person has been informed of this possibility shall be recorded as soon as is practicable after the impression has been taken, and if he is detained at a police station, the record shall be made on his custody record.
(6) In a case where, by virtue of subsection (3) above, an impression of a person's footwear is taken without the appropriate consent—
  (a) he shall be told the reason before it is taken; and
  (b) the reason shall be recorded on his custody record as soon as is practicable after the impression is taken.
(7) The power to take an impression of the footwear of a person detained at a police station without the appropriate consent shall be exercisable by any constable.
(8) Nothing in this section applies to any person—
  (a) arrested or detained under the terrorism provisions;
  (b) arrested under an extradition arrest power.

62 Intimate samples

(1) Subject to section 63B below, an intimate sample may be taken from a person in police detention only—
  (a) if a police officer of at least the rank of inspector authorises it to be taken; and
  (b) if the appropriate consent is given.
(1A) An intimate sample may be taken from a person who is not in police detention but from whom, in the course of the investigation of an offence, two or more non-intimate samples suitable for the same means of analysis have been taken which have proved insufficient—
  (a) if a police officer of at least the rank of inspector authorises it to be taken; and
  (b) if the appropriate consent is given.
(2) An officer may only give an authorisation under subsection (1) or (1A) above if he has reasonable grounds—
  (a) for suspecting the involvement of the person from whom the sample is to be taken in a recordable offence; and
  (b) for believing that the sample will tend to confirm or disprove his involvement.
(3) An officer may give an authorisation under subsection (1) or (1A) above orally or in writing but, if he gives it orally, he shall confirm it in writing as soon as is practicable.
(4) The appropriate consent must be given in writing.
(5) Where—
  (a) an authorisation has been given; and
  (b) it is proposed that an intimate sample shall be taken in pursuance of the authorisation,

an officer shall inform the person from whom the sample is to be taken—
(i) of the giving of the authorisation; and
(ii) of the grounds for giving it.
(6) The duty imposed by subsection (5)(ii) above includes a duty to state the nature of the offence in which it is suspected that the person from whom the sample is to be taken has been involved.
(7) If an intimate sample is taken from a person—
(a) the authorisation by virtue of which it was taken;
(b) the grounds for giving the authorisation; and
(c) the fact that the appropriate consent was given,
shall be recorded as soon as is practicable after the sample is taken.
(7A) If an intimate sample is taken from a person at a police station—
(a) before the sample is taken, an officer shall inform him that it may be the subject of a speculative search; and
(b) the fact that the person has been informed of this possibility shall be recorded as soon as practicable after the sample has been taken.
(8) If an intimate sample is taken from a person detained at a police station, the matters required to be recorded by subsection (7) or (7A) above shall be recorded in his custody record.
(9) In the case of an intimate sample which is a dental impression, the sample may be taken from a person only by a registered dentist.
(9A) In the case of any other form of intimate sample, except in the case of a sample of urine, the sample may be taken from a person only by—
(a) a registered medical practitioner; or
(b) a registered health care professional.

. . .

63 Other samples

(1) Except as provided by this section, a non-intimate sample may not be taken from a person without the appropriate consent.
(2) Consent to the taking of a non-intimate sample must be given in writing.
(2A) A non-intimate sample may be taken from a person without the appropriate consent if two conditions are satisfied.
(2B) The first is that the person is in police detention in consequence of his arrest for a recordable offence.
(2C) The second is that—
(a) he has not had a non-intimate sample of the same type and from the same part of the body taken in the course of the investigation of the offence by the police, or
(b) he has had such a sample taken but it proved insufficient.
(3) A non-intimate sample may be taken from a person without the appropriate consent if—
(a) he is being held in custody by the police on the authority of a court; and
(b) an officer of at least the rank of inspector authorises it to be taken without the appropriate consent.
(3A) A non-intimate sample may be taken from a person (whether or not he is in police detention or held in custody by the police on the authority of a court) without the appropriate consent if—
(a) he has been charged with a recordable offence or informed that he will be reported for such an offence; and
(b) either he has not had a non-intimate sample taken from him in the course of the investigation of the offence by the police or he has had a non-intimate sample taken from him but either it was not suitable for the same means of analysis or, though so suitable, the sample proved insufficient.
(3B) A non-intimate sample may be taken from a person without the appropriate consent if he has been convicted of a recordable offence.

(3C) A non-intimate sample may also be taken without the appropriate consent if he is a person to whom section 2 of the Criminal Evidence (Amendment) Act 1997 applies (persons detained following acquittal on grounds of insanity or finding of unfitness to plead).

(4) An officer may only give an authorisation under subsection (3) above if he has reasonable grounds—
    (a) for suspecting the involvement of the person from whom the sample is to be taken in a recordable offence; and
    (b) for believing that the sample will tend to confirm or disprove his involvement.

(5) An officer may give an authorisation under subsection (3) above orally or in writing but, if he gives it orally, he shall confirm it in writing as soon as is practicable.

...

(6) Where—
    (a) an authorisation has been given; and
    (b) it is proposed that a non-intimate sample shall be taken in pursuance of the authorisation,
    an officer shall inform the person from whom the sample is to be taken—
        (i) of the giving of the authorisation; and
        (ii) of the grounds for giving it.

(7) the duty imposed by subsection (6)(ii) above includes a duty to state the nature of the offence in which it is suspected that the person from whom the sample is to be taken has been involved.

...

63B Testing for presence of Class A drugs

(1) A sample of urine or a non-intimate sample may be taken trom a person in police detention for the purpose of ascertaining whether he has any specified Class A drug in his body if—
    (a) either the arrest condition or the charge condition is met;
    (b) both the age condition and the request condition are met; and
    (c) the notification condition is met in relation to the arrest condition, the charge condition or the age condition (as the case may be).

(1A) The arrest condition is that the person concerned has been arrested for an offence but has not been charged with that offence and either—
    (a) the offence is a trigger offence; or
    (b) a police officer of at least the rank of inspector has reasonable grounds for suspecting that the misuse by that person of a specified Class A drug caused or contributed to the offence and has authorised the sample to be taken.

(2) The charge condition is either—
    (a) that the person concerned has been charged with a trigger offence; or
    (b) that the person concerned has been charged with an offence and a police officer of at least the rank of inspector, who has reasonable grounds for suspecting that the misuse by that person of any specified Class A drug caused or contributed to the offence, has authorised the sample to be taken.

(3) The age condition is—
    (a) if the arrest condition is met, that the person concerned has attained the age of 18;
    (b) if the charge condition is met, that he has attained the age of 14.

(4) The request condition is that a police officer has requested the person concerned to give the sample.

(4A) The notification condition is that—
    (a) the relevant chief officer has been notified by the Secretary of State that appropriate arrangements have been made for the police area as a whole, or for the particular police station, in which the person is in police detention, and
    (b) the notice has not been withdrawn.

(4B) For the purposes of subsection (4A) above, appropriate arrangements are arrangements for the taking of samples under this section from whichever of the following is specified in the notification—

(a) persons in respect of whom the arrest condition is met;
(b) persons in respect of whom the charge condition is met;
(c) persons who have not attained the age of 18.
(5) Before requesting the person concerned to give a sample, an officer must—
   (a) warn him that if, when so requested, he fails without good cause to do so he may be liable to prosecution, and
   (b) in a case within subsection (1A)(b) or (2)(b) above, inform him of the giving of the authorisation and of the grounds in question.

...

64 Destruction of fingerprints and samples

(1A) Where—
   (a) fingerprints, impressions of footwear or samples are taken from a person in connection with the investigation of an offence, and
   (b) subsection (3) below does not require them to be destroyed,
   the fingerprints, impressions of footwear or samples may be retained after they have fulfilled the purposes for which they were taken but shall not be used by any person except for purposes related to the prevention or detection of crime, the investigation of an offence or the conduct of a prosecution or the identification of a deceased person or of the person from whom a body part came.

(1BA)*Fingerprints taken from a person by virtue of section 61(6A) above must be destroyed as soon as they have fulfilled the purpose for which they were taken.*

(2) ...

(3) If—
   (a) fingerprints, impressions of footwear or samples are taken from a person in connection with the investigation of an offence; and
   (b) that person is not suspected of having committed the offence,
   they must except as provided in the following subsections of this section be destroyed as soon as they have fulfilled the purpose for which they were taken.

(3AA) Samples, fingerprints and impressions of footwear are not required to be destroyed under subsection (3) above if—
   (a) they were taken for the purposes of the investigation of an offence of which a person has been convicted; and
   (b) a sample, fingerprints or, as the case may be, an impression of footwear was also taken from the convicted person for the purposes of that investigation.

(3AB) Subject to subsection (3AC) below, where a person is entitled under subsection (1BA) or (3) above to the destruction of any fingerprint or sample taken from him (or would be but for subsection (3AA) above), neither the fingerprint, not the impressions of footwear nor the sample, nor any information derived from the sample, shall be used—
   (a) in evidence against the person who is or would be entitled to the destruction of that fingerprint or sample; or
   (b) for the purposes of the investigation of any offence;
   and subsection (1B) above applies for the purposes of this subsection as it applies for the purposes of subsection (1A) above.

(3AC) Where a person from whom a fingerprint, impression of footwear or sample has been taken consents in writing to its retention—
   (a) that fingerprint, impression of footwear or sample need not be destroyed under subsection (3) above;
   (b) subsection (3AB) above shall not restrict the use that may be made of the fingerprint, impression of footwear or sample or, in the case of a sample, of any information derived from it; and
   (c) that consent shall be treated as comprising a consent for the purposes of section 63A(1C) above;
   and a consent given for the purpose of this subsection shall not be capable of being withdrawn.

The subsection does not apply to fingerprints taken from a person by virtue of section 61(6A) above.

(3AD) For the purposes of subsection (3AC) above it shall be immaterial whether the consent is given at, before or after the time when the entitlement to the destruction, of the fingerprint, impression of footwear or sample arises.

(4) ...

...

64A Photographing of suspects etc.

(1) A person who is detained at a police station may be photographed—
   (a) with the appropriate consent; or
   (b) if the appropriate consent is withheld or it is not practicable to obtain it, without it.

...

(2) A person proposing to take a photograph of any person under this section—
   (a) may, for the purpose of doing so, require the removal of any item or substance worn on or over the whole or any part of the head or face of the person to be photographed; and
   (b) if the requirement is not complied with, may remove the item or substance himself.

...

(4) A photograph taken under this section—
   (a) may be used by, or disclosed to, any person for any purpose related to the prevention or detection of crime, the investigation of an offence or the conduct of a prosecution or the enforcement of a sentence; and
   (b) after being so used or disclosed, may be retained but may not be used or disclosed except for a purpose so related.

65 Part V — supplementary

(1) In this Part of this Act—
   ...
   "intimate sample" means—
   (a) a sample of blood, semen or any other tissue fluid, urine or pubic hair;
   (b) a dental impression;
   (c) a swab taken from a person's genitals (including pubic hair) or from a person's body orifice other than the mouth;
   "intimate search" means a search which consists of the physical examination of a person's body orifices other than the mouth;
   "non-intimate sample" means—
   (a) a sample of hair other than pubic hair;
   (b) a sample taken from a nail or from under a nail;
   (c) a swab taken from any part of a person's body other than a part from which a swab taken would be an intimate sample;
   (d) saliva;
   (e) a skin impression;
   ...

...

PART VI
CODES OF PRACTICE — GENERAL

66 Codes of practice

(1) The Secretary of State shall issue codes of practice in connection with—
   (a) the exercise by police officers of statutory powers—
      (i) to search a person without first arresting him;
      (ii) to search a vehicle without making an arrest; or
      (iii) to arrest a person;
   (b) the detention, treatment, questioning and indication of persons by police officers;
   (c) searches of premises by police officers; and

(d) the seizure of property found by police officers on persons or premises.

(2) Codes shall (in particular) include provisions in connection with the exercise by police officers of powers under section 63B, above.

67 Codes of practice — supplementary

(1) In this section, "code" means a code of practice under section 60, 60A or 66.

(2) The Secretary of State may at any time revise the whole or any part of a code.

(3) A code may be made, or revised, so as to—
   (a) apply only in relation to one or more specified areas,
   (b) have effect only for a specified period,
   (c) apply only in relation to specified offences or descriptions of offender.

(4) Before issuing a code, or any revision of a code, the Secretary of State must consult—
   (a) the Association of Police Authorities,
   (b) the Association of Chief Police Officers of England, Wales and Northern Ireland,
   (c) the General Council of the Bar,
   (d) the Law Society of England and Wales,
   (e) the Institute of Legal Executives, and
   (f) such other persons as he thinks fit.

(5) A code, or a revision of a code, does not come into operation until the Secretary of State by order so provides.

(6) The power conferred by subsection (5) is exercisable by statutory instrument.

(7) An order bringing a code into operation may not be made unless a draft of the order has been laid before Parliament and approved by a resolution of each House.

(7A) An order bringing a revision of a code into operation must be laid before Parliament if the order has been made without a draft having been so laid and approved by a resolution of each House.

(7B) When an order or draft of an order is laid, the code or revision of a code to which it relates must also be laid.

. . .

(8) . . .

(9) . . .

(10) A failure on the part—
   (a) of a police officer to comply with any provision of a code;
   (b) of any person other than a police officer who is charged with the duty of investigating offences or charging offenders to have regard to any relevant provision of a code in the discharge of the duty, or
   (c) of a person designated under section 38 or 39 or accredited under section 41 of the Police Reform Act 2002 to have regard to any relevant provision of such a code in the exercise or performance of the powers and duties conferred or imposed on him by that designation or accreditation,
   shall not of itself render him liable to any criminal or civil proceedings.

(11) In all criminal and civil proceedings any such code shall be admissible in evidence; and if any provision of a code appears to the court or tribunal conducting the proceedings to be relevant to any question arising in the proceedings it shall be taken into account in determining that question.

. . .

PART VIII
EVIDENCE IN CRIMINAL PROCEEDINGS — GENERAL

Confessions

76 Confessions

(1) In any proceedings a confession made by an accused person may be given in evidence against him in so far as it is relevant to any matter in issue in the proceedings and is not excluded by the court in pursuance of this section.

(2) If, in any proceedings where the prosecution proposes to give in evidence a confession made by an accused person, it is represented to the court that the confession was or may have been obtained—
   (a) by oppression of the person who made it; or
   (b) in consequence of anything said or done which was likely, in the circumstances existing at the time, to render unreliable any confession which might be made by him in consequence thereof,
   the court shall not allow the confession to be given in evidence against him except in so far as the prosecution proves to the court beyond reasonable doubt that the confession (notwithstanding that it may be true) was not obtained as aforesaid.
(3) In any proceedings where the prosecution proposes to give in evidence a confession made by an accused person, the court may of its own motion require the prosecution, as a condition of allowing it to do so, to prove that the confession was not obtained as mentioned in subsection (2) above.
(4) The fact that a confession is wholly or partly excluded in pursuance of this section shall not affect the admissibility in evidence—
   (a) of any facts discovered as a result of the confession; or
   (b) where the confession is relevant as showing that the accused speaks, writes or expresses himself in a particular way, of so much of the confession as is necessary to show that he does so.
(5) Evidence that a fact to which this subsection applies was discovered as a result of a statement made by an accused person shall not be admissible unless evidence of how it was discovered is given by him or on his behalf.
(6) Subsection (5) above applies—
   (a) to any fact discovered as a result of a confession which is wholly excluded in pursuance of this section; and
   (b) to any fact discovered as a result of a confession which is partly so excluded, if that fact is discovered as a result of the excluded part of the confession.
(7) Nothing in Part VII of this Act shall prejudice the admissibility of a confession made by an accused person.
(8) In this section "oppression" includes torture, inhuman or degrading treatment, and the use or threat of violence (whether or not amounting to torture).
...

76A Confessions may be given in evidence for co-accused

(1) In any proceedings a confession made by an accused person may be given in evidence for another person charged in the same proceedings (a co-accused) in so far as it is relevant to any matter in issue in the proceedings and is not excluded by the court in pursuance of this section.
(2) If, in any proceedings where a co-accused proposes to give in evidence a confession made by an accused person, it is represented to the court that the confession was or may have been obtained—
   (a) by oppression of the person who made it; or
   (b) in consequence of anything said or done which was likely, in the circumstances existing at the time, to render unreliable any confession which might be made by him in consequence thereof,
   the court shall not allow the confession to be given in evidence for the co-accused except in so far as it is proved to the court on the balance of probabilities that the confession (notwithstanding that it may be true) was not so obtained.
(3) Before allowing a confession made by an accused person to be given in evidence for a co-accused in any proceedings, the court may of its own motion require the fact that the confession was not obtained as mentioned in subsection (2) above to be proved in the proceedings on the balance of probabilities.
(4) The fact that a confession is wholly or partly excluded in pursuance of this section shall not affect the admissibility in evidence—

(a) of any facts discovered as a result of the confession; or
(b) where the confession is relevant as showing that the accused speaks, writes or expresses himself in a particular way, of so much of the confession as is necessary to show that he does so.

77 Confessions by mentally handicapped persons

(1) Without prejudice to the general duty of the court at a trial on indictment *with a jury* to direct the jury on any matter on which it appears to the court appropriate to do so, where at such a trial—
   (a) the case against the accused depends wholly or substantially on a confession by him; and
   (b) the court is satisfied—
      (i) that he is mentally handicapped; and
      (ii) that the confession was not made in the presence of an independent person,
   the court shall warn the jury that there is special need for caution before convicting the accused in reliance on the confession, and shall explain that the need arises because of the circumstances mentioned in paragraphs (a) and (b) above, but in doing so shall not be required to use any particular form of words.
(2) In any case where at the summary trial of a person for an offence it appears to the court that a warning under subsection (1) above would be required if the trial were on indictment *with a jury*, the court shall treat the case as one in which there is a special need for caution before convicting the accused on his confession.

...

Miscellaneous

78 Exclusion of unfair evidence

(1) In any proceedings the court may refuse to allow evidence on which the prosecution proposes to rely to be given if it appears to the court that, having regard to all the circumstances, including the circumstances in which the evidence was obtained, the admission of the evidence would have such an adverse effect on the fairness of the proceedings that the court ought not to admit it.
(2) Nothing in this section shall prejudice any rule of law requiring a court to exclude evidence.
(3) This section shall not apply in the case of proceedings before a magistrates' court inquiring into an offence as examining justices.

PART VIII
SUPPLEMENTARY

82 Part VIII — interpretation

(1) In this Part of this Act—
   "confession" includes any statement wholly or partly adverse to the person who made it, whether made to a person in authority or not and whether made in words or otherwise;
   ...

...

(3) Nothing in this Part of this Act shall prejudice any power of a court to exclude evidence (whether by preventing questions from being put or otherwise) at its discretion.

PART XI
MISCELLANEOUS AND SUPPLEMENTARY

117 Power of constable to use reasonable force

Where any provision of this Act—
(a) confers a power on a constable; and
(b) does not provide that the power may only be exercised with the consent of some person, other than a police officer,
the officer may use reasonable force, if necessary, in the exercise of the power.

SCHEDULE 1
SPECIAL PROCEDURE

Making of orders by circuit judge

1. If on an application made by a constable a circuit judge [*judge*] is satisfied that one or other of the sets of access conditions is fulfilled, he may make an order under paragraph 4 below.
2. The first set of access conditions is fulfilled if—
   (a) there are reasonable grounds for believing—
      (i) that an indictable offence has been committed;
      (ii) that there is material which consists of special procedure material or includes special procedure material and does not also include excluded material on premises specified in the application;
      (iii) that the material is likely to be of substantial value (whether by itself or together with other material) to the investigation in connection with which the application is made; and
      (iv) that the material is likely to be relevant evidence;
   (b) other methods of obtaining the material—
      (i) have been tried without success; or
      (ii) have not been tried because it appeared that they were bound to fail; and
   (c) it is in the public interest, having regard—
      (i) to the benefit likely to accrue to the investigation if the material is obtained; and
      (ii) to the circumstances under which the person in possession of the material holds it,
   that the material should be produced or that access to it should be given.
3. The second set of access conditions is fulfilled if—
   (a) there are reasonable grounds for believing that there is material which consists of or includes excluded material or special procedure material on premises specified in the application;
   (b) but for section 9(2) above a search of the premises for that material could have been authorised by the issue of a warrant to a constable under an enactment other than this Schedule; and
   (c) the issue of such a warrant would have been appropriate.

...

PUBLIC ORDER ACT 1986
(1986, c. 64)

An Act to abolish the common law offences of riot, rout, unlawful assembly and affray and certain statutory offences relating to public order; to create new offences relating to public order; to control public processions and assemblies; to control the stirring up of racial hatred; to provide for the exclusion of certain offenders from sporting events; to create a new offence relating to the contamination of or interference with goods; to confer power to direct certain trespassers to leave land; to amend section 7 of the Conspiracy and Protection of Property Act 1875, section 1 of the Prevention of Crime Act 1953, Part V of the Criminal Justice (Scotland) Act 1980 and the Sporting Events (Control of Alcohol etc.) Act 1985; to repeal certain obsolete or unnecessary enactments; and for connected purposes [7 November 1986]

PART I
NEW OFFENCES

1   Riot
   (1) Where 12 or more persons who are present together use or threaten unlawful violence for a common purpose and the conduct of them (taken together) is such as would cause a person of reasonable firmness present at the scene to fear for his personal safety, each of the persons using unlawful violence for the common purpose is guilty of riot.
   (2) It is immaterial whether or not the 12 or more use or threaten unlawful violence simultaneously.

(3) The common purpose may be inferred from conduct.
(4) No person of reasonable firmness need actually be, or be likely to be, present at the scene.
(5) Riot may be committed in private as well as in public places.
(6) A person guilty of riot is liable on conviction on indictment to imprisonment for a term not exceeding ten years or a fine or both.

2 **Violent disorder**
(1) Where 3 or more persons who are present together use or threaten unlawful violence and the conduct of them (taken together) is such as would cause a person of reasonable firmness present at the scene to fear for his personal safety, each of the persons using or threatening unlawful violence is guilty of violent disorder.
(2) It is immaterial whether or not the 3 or more use or threaten unlawful violence simultaneously.
(3) No person of reasonable firmness need actually be, or be likely to be, present at the scene.
(4) Violent disorder may be committed in private as well as in public places.
(5) A person guilty of violent disorder is liable on conviction on indictment to imprisonment for a term not exceeding 5 years or a fine or both, or on summary conviction to imprisonment for a term not exceeding 6 months or a fine not exceeding the statutory maximum or both.

3 **Affray**
(1) A person is guilty of affray if he uses or threatens unlawful violence towards another and his conduct is such as would cause a person of reasonable firmness present at the scene to fear for his personal safety.
(2) Where 2 or more persons use or threaten the unlawful violence, it is the conduct of them taken together that must be considered for the purposes of subsection (1).
(3) For the purposes of this section a threat cannot be made by the use of words alone.
(4) No person of reasonable firmness need actually be, or be likely to be, present at the scene.
(5) Affray may be committed in private as well as in public places.
(6) . . .
(7) A person guilty of affray is liable on conviction on indictment to imprisonment for a term not exceeding 3 years or a fine or both, or on summary conviction to imprisonment for a term not exceeding 6 months or a fine not exceeding the statutory maximum or both.

4 **Fear or provocation of violence**
(1) A person is guilty of an offence if he—
  (a) uses towards another person threatening, abusive or insulting words or behaviour, or
  (b) distributes or displays to another person any writing, sign or other visible representation which is threatening, abusive or insulting,
with intent to cause that person to believe that immediate unlawful violence will be used against him or another by any person, or to provoke the immediate use of unlawful violence by that person or another, or whereby that person is likely to believe that such violence will be used or it is likely that such violence will be provoked.
(2) An offence under this section may be committed in a public or a private place, except that no offence is committed where the words or behaviour are used, or the writing, sign or other visible representation is distributed or displayed, by a person inside a dwelling and the other person is also inside that or another dwelling.
(3) . . .
(4) A person guilty of an offence under this section is liable on summary conviction to imprisonment for a term not exceeding 6 months or a fine not exceeding level 5 on the standard scale or both.

4A **Intentional harassment, alarm or distress**
(1) A person is guilty of an offence if, with intent to cause a person harassment, alarm or distress, he—
  (a) uses threatening, abusive or insulting words or behaviour, or disorderly behaviour, or

    (b) displays any writing, sign or other visible representation which is threatening, abusive or insulting,

thereby causing that or another person harassment, alarm or distress.

(2) An offence under this section may be committed in a public or a private place, except that no offence is committed where the words or behaviour are used, or the writing, sign or other visible representation is displayed, by a person inside a dwelling and the person who is harassed, alarmed or distressed is also inside that or another dwelling.

(3) It is a defence for the accused to prove—
    (a) that he was inside a dwelling and had no reason to believe that the words or behaviour used, or the writing, sign or other visible representation displayed, would be heard or seen by a person outside that or any other dwelling, or
    (b) that his conduct was reasonable.

(4), (5) . . .

(6) A person guilty of an offence under this section is liable on summary conviction to imprisonment for a term not exceeding 6 months or a fine not exceeding level 5 on the standard scale or both.

5   Harassment, alarm or distress

(1) A person is guilty of an offence if he—
    (a) uses threatening, abusive or insulting words or behaviour, or disorderly behaviour, or
    (b) displays any writing, sign or other visible representation which is threatening, abusive or insulting,

within the hearing or sight of a person likely to be caused harassment, alarm or distress thereby.

(2) An offence under this section may be committed in a public or a private place, except that no offence is committed where the words or behaviour are used, or the writing, sign or other visible representation is displayed, by a person inside a dwelling and the other person is also inside that or another dwelling.

(3) It is a defence for the accused to prove—
    (a) that he had no reason to believe that there was any person within hearing or sight who was likely to be caused harassment, alarm or distress, or
    (b) that he was inside a dwelling and had no reason to believe that the words or behaviour used, or the writing, sign or other visible representation displayed, would be heard or seen by a person outside that or any other dwelling, or
    (c) that his conduct was reasonable.

(4) . . .

(6) A person guilty of an offence under this section is liable on summary conviction to a fine not exceeding level 3 on the standard scale.

6   Mental element: miscellaneous

(1) A person is guilty of riot only if he intends to use violence or is aware that his conduct may be violent.

(2) A person is guilty of violent disorder or affray only if he intends to use or threaten violence or is aware that his conduct may be violent or threaten violence.

(3) A person is guilty of an offence under section 4 only if he intends his words or behaviour, or the writing, sign or other visible representation, to be threatening, abusive or insulting, or is aware that it may be threatening, abusive or insulting.

(4), (5) A person is guilty of an offence under section 5 only if he intends his words or behaviour, or the writing, sign or other visible representation, to be threatening, abusive or insulting, or is aware that it may be threatening, abusive or insulting or (as the case may be) he intends his behaviour to be or is aware that it may be disorderly.

(5) For the purposes of this section a person whose awareness is impaired by intoxication shall be taken to be aware of that of which he would be aware if not intoxicated, unless he shows either that his intoxication was not self-induced or that it was caused solely by the taking or administration of a substance in the course of medical treatment.

(6) In subsection (5) "intoxication" means any intoxication, whether caused by drink, drugs or other means, or by a combination of means.
(7) Subsections (1) and (2) do not affect the determination for the purposes of riot or violent disorder of the number of persons who use or threaten violence.

7 Procedure: miscellaneous
(1) No prosecution for an offence of riot or incitement to riot may be instituted except by or with the consent of the Director of Public Prosecutions.
...

8 Interpretation
In this Part—
"dwelling" means any structure or part of a structure occupied as a person's home or as other living accommodation (whether the occupation is separate or shared with others) but does not include any part not so occupied, and for this purpose "structure" includes a tent, caravan, vehicle, vessel or other temporary or movable structure;
"violence" means any violent conduct, so that—
(a) except in the context of affray, it includes violent conduct towards property as well as violent conduct towards persons, and
(b) it is not restricted to conduct causing or intended to cause injury or damage but includes any other violent conduct (for example, throwing at or towards a person a missile of a kind capable of causing injury which does not hit or falls short).

9 Offences abolished
(1) The Common Law offences of riot, rout, unlawful assembly and affray are abolished.
...

PART II
PROCESSIONS AND ASSEMBLIES

11 Advance notice of public processions
(1) Written notice shall be given in accordance with this section of any proposal to hold a public procession intended—
(a) to demonstrate support for or opposition to the views or actions of any person or body of persons,
(b) to publicise a cause or campaign, or
(c) to mark or commemorate an event,
unless it is not reasonably practicable to give any advance notice of the procession.
(2) Subsection (1) does not apply where the procession is one commonly or customarily held in the police area (or areas) in which it is proposed to be held or is a funeral procession organised by a funeral director acting in the normal course of his business.
(3) The notice must specify the date when it is intended to hold the procession, the time when it is intended to start it, its proposed route, and the name and address of the person (or of one of the persons) proposing to organise it.
(4) Notice must be delivered to a police station—
(a) in the police area in which it is proposed the procession will start, or
(b) where it is proposed the procession will start in Scotland and cross into England, in the first police area in England on the proposed route.
(5) If delivered not less than 6 clear days before the date when the procession is intended to be held, the notice may be deliverd by post by the recorded delivery service; but section 7 of the Interpretation Act 1978 (under which a document sent by post is deemed to have been served when posted and to have been delivered in the ordinary course of post) does not apply.
(6) If not delivered in accordance with subsection (5), the notice must be delivered by hand not less than 6 clear days before the date when the procession is intended to be held or, if that is not reasonably practicable, as soon as delivery is reasonably practicable.

(7) Where a public procession is held, each of the persons organising it is guilty of an offence if—
  (a) the requirements of this section as to notice have not been satisfied, or
  (b) the date when it is held, the time when it starts, or its route, differs from the date, time or route specified in the notice.
(8) It is a defence for the accused to prove that he did not know of, and neither suspected nor had reason to suspect, the failure to satisfy the requirements or (as the case may be) the difference of date, time or route.
(9) To the extent that an alleged offence turns on a difference of date, time or route, it is a defence for the accused to prove that the difference arose from circumstances beyond his control or from something done with the agreement of a police officer or by his direction.
(10) A person guilty of an offence under subsection (7) is liable on summary conviction to a fine not exceeding level 3 on the standard scale.

12 Imposing conditions on public processions

(1) If the senior police officer, having regard to the time or place at which and the circumstances in which any public procession is being held or is intended to be held and to its route or proposed route, reasonably believes that—
  (a) it may result in serious public disorder, serious damage to property or serious disruption to the life of the community, or
  (b) the purpose of the persons organising it is the intimidation of others with a view to compelling them not to do an act they have a right to do, or to do an act they have a right not to do,
he may give directions imposing on the persons organising or taking part in the procession such conditions as appear to him necessary to prevent such disorder, damage, disruption or intimidation, including conditions as to the route of the procession or prohibiting it from entering any public place specified in the directions.
(2) In subsection (1) "the senior police officer" means—
  (a) in relation to a procession being held, or to a procession intended to be held in a case where persons are assembling with a view to taking part in it, the most senior in rank of the police officers present at the scene, and
  (b) in relation to a procession intended to be held in a case where paragraph (a) does not apply, the chief officer of police.
(3) A direction given by a chief officer of police by virtue of subsection (2)(b) shall be given in writing.
(4) A person who organises a public procession and knowingly fails to comply with a condition imposed under this section is guilty of an offence, but it is a defence for him to prove that the failure arose from circumstances beyond his control.
(5) A person who takes part in a public procession and knowingly fails to comply with a condition imposed under this section is guilty of an offence, but it is a defence for him to prove that the failure arose from circumstances beyond his control.
(6) a person who incites another to commit an offence under subsection (5) is guilty of an offence.
(7) ...
(8) A person guilty of an offence under subsection (4) is liable on summary conviction to imprisonment for a term not exceeding 3 months [*51 weeks*] or a fine not exceeding level 4 on the standard scale or both.
(9) A person guilty of an offence under subsection (5) is liable on summary conviction to a fine not exceeding level 3 on the standard scale.
(10) A person guilty of an offence under subsection (6) is liable on summary conviction to imprisonment for a term not exceeding 3 months [*51 weeks*] or a fine not exceeding level 4 on the standard scale or both, notwithstanding section 45(3) of the Magistrates' Courts Act 1980 (inciter liable to same penalty as incited).

...

13 Prohibiting public processions

(1) If at any time the chief officer of police reasonably believes that, because of particular circumstances existing in any district or part of a district, the powers under section 12 will not be sufficient to prevent the holding of public processions in that district or part from resulting in serious public disorder, he shall apply to the council of the district for an order prohibiting for such period not exceeding 3 months as may be specified in the application the holding of all public processions (or of any class of public procession so specified) in the district or part concerned.

(2) On receiving such an application, a council may with the consent of the Secretary of State make an order either in the terms of the application or with such modifications as may be approved by the Secretary of State.

(3) Subsection (1) does not apply in the City of London or the metropolitan police district.

(4) If at any time the Commissioner of Police for the City of London or the Commissioner of Police of the Metropolis reasonably believes that, because of particular circumstances existing in his police area or part of it, the powers under section 12 will not be sufficient to prevent the holding of public processions in that area or part from resulting in serious public disorder, he may with the consent of the Secretary of State make an order prohibiting for such period not exceeding 3 months as may be specified in the order the holding of all public processions (or of any class of public procession so specified) in the area or part concerned.

(5) An order made under this section may be revoked or varied by a subsequent order made in the same way, that is, in accordance with subsections (1) and (2) or subsection (4), as the case may be.

(6) An order under this section shall, if not made in writing, be recorded in writing as soon as practicable after being made.

(7) A person who organises a public procession the holding of which he knows is prohibited by virtue of an order under this section is guilty of an offence.

(8) A person who takes part in a public procession the holding of which he knows is prohibited by virtue of an order under this section is guilty of an offence.

(9) A person who incites another to commit an offence under subsection (8) is guilty of an offence.

(10) ...

(11) A person guilty of an offence under subsection (7) is liable on summary conviction to imprisonment for a term not exceeding 3 months [*51 weeks*] or a fine not exceeding level 4 on the standard scale or both.

(12) A person guilty of an offence under subsection (8) is liable on summary conviction to a fine not exceeding level 3 on the standard scale.

(13) A person guilty of an offence under subsection (9) is liable on summary conviction to imprisonment for a term not exceeding 3 months [*51 weeks*] or a fine not exceeding level 4 on the standard scale or both, *notwithstanding section 45(3) of the Magistrates' Courts Act 1980.*

14 Imposing conditions on public assemblies

(1) If the senior police officer, having regard to the time or place at which and the circumstances in which any public assembly is being held or is intended to be held, reasonably believes that—

   (a) it may result in serious public disorder, serious damage to property or serious disruption to the life of the community, or

   (b) the purpose of the persons organising it is the intimidation of others with a view to compelling them not to do an act they have a right to do, or to do an act they have a right not to do,

he may give directions imposing on the persons organising or taking part in the assembly such conditions as to the place at which the assembly may be (or continue to be) held, its maximum duration, or the maximum number of persons who may constitute it, as appear to him necessary to prevent such disorder, damage, disruption or intimidation.

(2) In subsection (1) "the senior police officer" means—
   (a) in relation to an assembly being held, the most senior in rank of the police officers present at the scene, and
   (b) in relation to an assembly intended to be held, the chief officer of police.
(3) A direction given by a chief officer of police by virtue of subsection (2)(b) shall be given in writing.
(4) A person who organises a public assembly and knowingly fails to comply with a condition imposed under this section is guilty of an offence, but it is a defence for him to prove that the failure arose from circumstances beyond his control.
(5) A person who takes part in a public assembly and knowingly fails to comply with a condition imposed under this section is guilty of an offence, but it is a defence for him to prove that the failure arose from circumstances beyond his control.
(6) A person who incites another to commit an offence under subsection (5) is guilty of an offence.
(7) ...
(8) A person guilty of an offence under subsection (4) is liable on summary conviction to imprisonment for a term not exceeding 3 months [*51 weeks*] or a fine not exceeding level 4 on the standard scale or both.
(9) A person guilty of an offence under subsection (5) is liable on summary conviction to a fine not exceeding level 3 on the standard scale.
(10) A person guilty of an offence under subsection (6) is liable on summary conviction to imprisonment for a term not exceeding 3 months [*51 weeks*] or a fine not exceeding level 4 on the standard scale or both, notwithstanding section 45(3) of the Magistrates' Courts Act 1980.

14A Prohibiting trespassory assemblies

(1) If at any time the chief officer of police reasonably believes that an assembly is intended to be held in any district at a place on land to which the public has no right of access or only a limited right of access and that the assembly—
   (a) is likely to be held without the permission of the occupier of the land or to conduct itself in such a way as to exceed the limits of any permission of his or the limits of the public's right of access, and
   (b) may result—
      (i) in serious disruption to the life of the community, or
      (ii) where the land, or a building or monument on it, is of historical, architectural, archaeological or scientific importance, in significant damage to the land, building or monument,
   he may apply to the council of the district for an order prohibiting for a specified period the holding of all trespassory assemblies in the district or a part of it, as specified.
(2) On receiving such an application, a council may—
   (a) in England and Wales, with the consent of the Secretary of State make an order either in the terms of the application or with such modifications as may be approved by the Secretary of State; or
   (b) in Scotland, make an order in the terms of the application.
(3) Subsection (1) does not apply in the City of London or the metropolitan police district.
(4) If at any time the Commissioner of Police for the City of London or the Commissioner of Police of the Metropolis reasonably believes that an assembly is intended to be held at a place on land to which the public has no right of access or only a limited right of access in his police area and that the assembly—
   (a) is likely to be held without the permission of the occupier of the land or to conduct itself in such a way as to exceed the limits of any permission of his or the limits of the public's right of access, and
   (b) may result—
      (i) in serious disruption to the life of the community, or

(ii) where the land, or a building or monument on it, is of historical, architectural, archaeological or scientific importance, in significant damage to the land, building or monument,

he may with the consent of the Secretary of State make an order prohibiting for a specified period the holding of all trespassory assemblies in this area or a part of it, as specified.

(5) An order prohibiting the holding of trespassory assemblies operates to prohibit any assembly which—
   (a) is held on land to which the public has no right of access or only a limited right of access, and
   (b) takes place in the prohibited circumstances, that is to say, without the permission of the occupier of the land or so as to exceed the limits of any permission of his or the limits of the public as right of access.

(6) No order under this section shall prohibit the holding of assemblies for a period exceeding 4 days or in an area exceeding an area represented by a circle with a radius of 5 miles from a specified centre.

(7) An order made under this section may be revoked or varied by a subsequent order made in the same way, that is, in accordance with subsection (1) and (2) or subsection (4), as the case may be.

(8) Any order under this section shall, if not made in writing, be recorded in writing as soon as practicable after being made.

(9) In this section and sections 14B and 14C—
"assembly" means an assembly of 20 or more persons;
"land", means land in the open air;
"limited", in relation to a right of access by the public to land, means that their use of it is restricted to use for a particular purpose (as in the case of a highway or road) or is subject to other restrictions;
"occupier" means—
   (a) in England and Wales, the person entitled to possession of the land by virtue of an estate or interest held by him; or
   (b) in Scotland, the person lawfully entitled to natural possession of the land,
and in subsection (1) and (4) includes the person reasonably believed by the authority applying for or making the order to be the occupier;
"public" includes a section of the public; and
"specified" means specified in an order under this section.

...

14B Offences in connection with trespassory assemblies and arrest therefor

(1) A person who organises an assembly the holding of which he knows is prohibited by an order under section 14A is guilty of an offence.

(2) A person who takes part in an assembly which he knows is prohibited by an order under section 14A is guilty of an offence.

(3) In England and Wales, a person who incites another to commit an offence under subsection (2) is guilty of an offence.

(4) ...

...

14C Stopping persons from proceeding to trespassory assemblies

(1) If a constable in uniform reasonably believes that a person is on his way to an assembly within the area to which an order under section 14A applies which the constable reasonably believes is likely to be an assembly which is prohibited by that order, he may, subject to subsection (2) below—
   (a) stop that person, and
   (b) direct him not to proceed in the direction of the assembly.

(2) The power conferred by subsection (1) may only be exercised within the area to which the order applies.

(3) A person who fails to comply with a direction under subsection (1) which he knows has been given to him is guilty of an offence.
(4) ...
(5) A person guilty of an offence under subsection (3) is liable on summary conviction to a fine not exceeding level 3 on the standard scale.

15 Delegation
(1) The chief officer of police may delegate, to such extent and subject to such conditions as he may specify, any of his functions under sections 12 to 14A to an assistant chief constable; and references in those subsections to the person delegating shall be construed accordingly.
(2) Subsection (1) shall have effect in the City of London and the metropolitan police district as if "an assistant chief constable" read "an assistant commissioner of police".

16 Interpretation
In this Part—
...
"public assembly" means an assembly of 2 or more persons in a public place which is wholly or partly open to the air;
"public place" means—
(a) any highway, or in Scotland any road within the meaning of the Roads (Scotland) Act 1984, and
(b) any place to which at the material time the public or any section of the public has access, on payment or otherwise, as of right or by virtue of express or implied permission;
"public procession" means a procession in a public place.

PART III
RACIAL HATRED

Meaning of "racial hatred"

17 Meaning of "racial hatred"
In this Part "racial hatred" means hatred against a group of persons defined by reference to colour, race, nationality (including citizenship) or ethnic or national origins.

Acts intended or likely to stir up racial hatred

18 Use of words or behaviour or display of written material
(1) A person who uses threatening, abusive or insulting words or behaviour, or displays any written material which is threatening, abusive or insulting, is guilty of an offence if—
(a) he intends thereby to stir up racial hatred, or
(b) having regard to all the circumstances racial hatred is likely to be stirred up thereby.
(2) An offence under this section may be committed in a public or a private place, except that no offence is committed where the words or behaviour are used, or the written material is displayed, by a person inside a dwelling and are not heard or seen except by other persons in that or another dwelling.
(3) ...
(4) In proceedings for an offence under this section it is a defence for the accused to prove that he was inside a dwelling and had no reason to believe that the words or behaviour used, or the written material displayed, would be heard or seen by a person outside that or any other dwelling.
(5) A person who is not shown to have intended to stir up racial hatred is not guilty of an offence under this section if he did not intend his words or behaviour, or the written material, to be, and was not aware that it might be, threatening, abusive or insulting.
(6) This section does not apply to words or behaviour used, or written material displayed, solely for the purpose of being included in a programme service.

19 Publishing or distributing written material

(1) A person who publishes or distributes written material which is threatening, abusive or insulting is guilty of an offence if—
  (a) he intends thereby to stir up racial hatred, or
  (b) having regard to all the circumstances racial hatred is likely to be stirred up thereby.
(2) In proceedings for an offence under this section it is a defence for an accused who is not shown to have intended to stir up racial hatred to prove that he was not aware of the content of the material and did not suspect, and had no reason to suspect, that it was threatening, abusive or insulting.
(3) References in this Part to the publication or distribution of written material are to its publication or distribution to the public or a section of the public.

20 Public performance of play

(1) If a public performance of a play is given which involves the use of threatening, abusive or insulting words or behaviour, any person who presents or directs the performance is guilty of an offence if—
  (a) he intends thereby to stir up racial hatred, or
  (b) having regard to all the circumstances (and, in particular, taking the performance as a whole) racial hatred is likely to be stirred up thereby.

...

21 Distributing, showing or playing a recording

(1) A person who distributes, or shows or plays, a recording of visual images or sounds which are threatening, abusive or insulting is guilty of an offence if—
  (a) he intends thereby to stir up racial hatred, or
  (b) having regard to all the circumstances racial hatred is likely to be stirred up thereby.
(2) In this Part "recording" means any record from which visual images or sounds may, by any means, be reproduced; and references to the distribution, showing or playing of a recording are to its distribution, showing or playing to the public or a section of the public.
(3) In proceedings for an offence under this section it is a defence for an accused who is not shown to have intended to stir up racial hatred to prove that he was not aware of the content of the recording and did not suspect, and had no reason to suspect, that it was threatening, abusive or insulting.
(4) This section does not apply to the showing or playing of a recording solely for the purpose of enabling the recording to be included in a programme service.

22 Broadcasting or including programme in cable programme service

(1) If a programme involving threatening, abusive or insulting visual images or sounds is included in a programme service, each of the persons mentioned in subsection (2) is guilty of an offence if—
  (a) he intends thereby to stir up racial hatred, or
  (b) having regard to all the circumstances racial hatred is likely to be stirred up thereby.
(2) The persons are—
  (a) the person providing the... programme service,
  (b) any person by whom the programme is produced or directed, and
  (c) any person by whom offending words or behaviour are used.

...

Racially inflammatory material

23 Possession of racially inflammatory material

(1) A person who has in his possession written material which is threatening, abusive or insulting, or a recording of visual images or sounds which are threatening, abusive or insulting, with a view to—
  (a) in the case of written material, its being displayed, published, distributed, broadcast or included in a cable programme service, whether by himself or another, or

(b) in the case of a recording, its being distributed, shown, played, or included in a programme service, whether by himself or another,

is guilty of an offence if he intends racial hatred to be stirred up thereby or, having regard to all the circumstances, racial hatred is likely to be stirred up thereby.

(2) For this purpose regard shall be had to such display, publication, distribution, showing, playing, or inclusion in a programme service as he has, or it may reasonably be inferred that he has, in view.

(3) In proceedings for an offence under this section it is a defence for an accused who is not shown to have intended to stir up racial hatred to prove that he was not aware of the content of the written material or recording and did not suspect, and had no reason to suspect, that it was threatening, abusive or insulting.

(4) ...

24 Powers of entry and search

(1) If in England and Wales a justice of the peace is satisfied by information on oath laid by a constable that there are reasonable grounds for suspecting that a person has possession of written material or a recording in contravention of section 23, the justice may issue a warrant under his hand authorising any constable to enter and search the premises where it is suspected the material or recording is situated.

(2) If in Scotland a sheriff or justice of the peace is satisfied by evidence on oath that there are reasonable grounds for suspecting that a person has possession of written material or a recording in contravention of section 23, the sheriff or justice may issue a warrant authorising any constable to enter and search the premises where it is suspected the material or recording is situated.

(3) A constable entering or searching premises in pursuance of a warrant issued under this section may use reasonable force if necessary.

...

Supplementary provisions

26 Savings for reports of parliamentary or judicial proceedings

(1) Nothing in this Part applies to a fair and accurate report of proceedings in Parliament or the Scottish Parliament.

(2) Nothing in this Part applies to a fair and accurate report of proceedings publicly heard before a court or tribunal exercising judicial authority where the report is published contemporaneously with the proceedings or, if it is not reasonably practicable or would be unlawful to publish a report of them contemporaneously, as soon as publication is reasonably practicable and lawful.

27 Procedure and punishment

(1) No proceedings for an offence under this Part may be instituted in England and Wales except by or with the consent of the Attorney General.

(2) For the purposes of the rules in England and Wales against charging more than one offence in the same count or information, each of sections 18 to 23 creates one offence.

(3) A person guilty of an offence under this Part is liable—
    (a) on conviction on indictment to imprisonment for a term not exceeding seven years or a fine or both;
    (b) on summary conviction to imprisonment for a term not exceeding six months or a fine not exceeding the statutory maximum or both.

40 Amendments repeals and savings

...

(4) Nothing in this Act affects the common law powers in England and Wales to deal with or prevent a breach of the peace.

(5) As respects Scotland, nothing in this Act affects any power of a constable under any rule of law.

OFFICIAL SECRETS ACT 1989
(1989, c. 6)

An Act to replace section 2 of the Official Secrets Act 1911 by provisions protecting more limited classes of official information. [11 May 1989]

1 Security and intelligence

(1) A person who is or has been—
  (a) a member of the security and intelligence services; or
  (b) a person notified that he is subject to the provisions of this subsection,
  is guilty of an offence if without lawful authority he discloses any information, document or other article relating to security or intelligence which is or has been in his possession by virtue of his position as a member of any of those services or in the course of his work while the notification is or was in force.

(2) The reference in subsection (1) above to disclosing information relating to security or intelligence includes a reference to making any statement which purports to be a disclosure of such information or is intended to be taken by those to whom it is addressed as being such a disclosure.

(3) A person who is or has been a Crown servant or government contractor is guilty of an offence if without lawful authority he makes a damaging disclosure of any information, document or other article relating to security or intelligence which is or has been in his possession by virtue of his position as such but otherwise than as mentioned in subsection (1) above.

(4) For the purposes of subsection (3) above a disclosure is damaging if—
  (a) it causes damage to the work of, or of any part of, the security and intelligence services; or
  (b) it is of information or a document or other article which is such that its unauthorised disclosure would be likely to cause such damage or which falls within a class or description of information, documents or articles the unauthorised disclosure of which would be likely to have that effect.

(5) It is a defence for a person charged with an offence under this section to prove that at the time of the alleged offence he did not know, and had no reasonable cause to believe, that the information, document or article in question related to security or intelligence or, in the case of an offence under subsection (3), that the disclosure would be damaging within the meaning of that subsection.

(6) Notification that a person is subject to subsection (1) above shall be effected by a notice in writing served on him by a Minister of the Crown; and such a notice may be served if, in the Minister's opinion, the work undertaken by the person in question is or includes work connected with the security and intelligence services and its nature is such that the interests of national security require that he should be subject to the provisions of that subsection.

(7) Subject to subsection (8) below, a notification for the purposes of subsection (1) above shall be in force for the period of five years beginning with the day on which it is served but may be renewed by further notices under subsection (6) above for periods of five years at a time.

(8) A notification for the purposes of subsection (1) above may at any time be revoked by a further notice in writing served by the Minister on the person concerned; and the Minister shall serve such a further notice as soon as, in his opinion, the work undertaken by that person ceases to be such as is mentioned in subsection (6) above.

(9) In this section "security or intelligence" means the work of, or in support of, the security and intelligence services or any part of them, and references to information relating to security or intelligence include references to information held or transmitted by those services or by persons in support of, or of any part of, them.

2 Defence

(1) A person who is or has been a Crown servant or government contractor is guilty of an offence if without lawful authority he makes a damaging disclosure of any information,

document or other article relating to defence which is or has been in his possession by virtue of his position as such.
(2) For the purposes of subsection (1) above a disclosure is damaging if—
(a) it damages the capability of, or of any part of, the armed forces of the Crown to carry out their tasks or leads to loss of life or injury to members of those forces or serious damage to the equipment or installations of those forces; or
(b) otherwise than as mentioned in paragraph (a) above, it endangers the interests of the United Kingdom abroad, seriously obstructs the promotion or protection by the United Kingdom of those interests or endangers the safety of British citizens abroad; or
(c) it is of information or of a document or article which is such that its unauthorised disclosure would be likely to have any of those effects.
(3) It is a defence for a person charged with an offence under this section to prove that at the time of the alleged offence he did not know, and had no reasonable cause to believe, that the information, document or article in question related to defence or that its disclosure would be damaging within the meaning of subsection (1) above.
(4) In this section "defence" means—
(a) the size, shape, organisation, logistics, order of battle, deployment, operations, state of readiness and training of the armed forces of the Crown;
(b) the weapons, stores or other equipment of those forces and the invention, development, production and operation of such equipment and research relating to it;
(c) defence policy and strategy and military planning and intelligence;
(d) plans and measures for the maintenance of essential supplies and services that are or would be needed in time of war.

3 **International relations**
(1) A person who is or has been a Crown servant or government contractor is guilty of an offence if without lawful authority he makes a damaging disclosure of—
(a) any information, document or other article relating to international relations; or
(b) any confidential information, document or other article which was obtained from a State other than the United Kingdom or an international organisation,
being information or a document or article which is or has been in his possession by virtue of his position as a Crown servant or government contractor.
(2) For the purposes of subsection (1) above a disclosure is damaging if—
(a) it endangers the interests of the United Kingdom abroad, seriously obstructs the promotion or protection by the United Kingdom of those interests or endangers the safety of British citizens abroad; or
(b) it is of information or of a document or article which is such that its unauthorised disclosure would be likely to have any of those effects.
(3) In the case of information or a document or article within subsection (1)(b) above—
(a) the fact that it is confidential, or
(b) its nature or contents,
may be sufficient to establish for the purposes of subsection (2)(b) above that the information, document or article is such that its unauthorised disclosure would be likely to have any of the effects there mentioned.
(4) It is a defence for a person charged with an offence under this section to prove that at the time of the alleged offence he did not know, and had no reasonable cause to believe, that the information, document or article in question was such as is mentioned in subsection (1) above or that its disclosure would be damaging within the meaning of that subsection.
(5) In this section "international relations" means the relations between States, between international organisations or between one or more States and one or more such organisations and includes any matter relating to a State other than the United Kingdom or to an international organisation which is capable of affecting the relations of the United Kingdom with another State or with an international organisation.
(6) For the purposes of this section any information, document or article obtained from a State or organisation is confidential at any time while the terms on which it was obtained require

it to be held in confidence or while the circumstances in which it was obtained make it reasonable for the State or organisation to expect that it would be so held.

4 **Crime and special investigation powers**
  (1) A person who is or has been a Crown servant or government contractor is guilty of an offence if without lawful authority he discloses any information, document or other article to which this section applies and which is or has been in his possession by virtue of his position as such.
  (2) This section applies to any information, document or other article—
    (a) the disclosure of which—
      (i) results in the commission of an offence; or
      (ii) facilitates an escape from legal custody or the doing of any other act prejudicial to the safekeeping of persons in legal custody; or
      (iii) impedes the prevention or detection of offences or the apprehension or prosecution of suspected offenders; or
    (b) which is such that its unauthorised disclosure would be likely to have any of those effects.
  (3) This section also applies to—
    (a) any information obtained by reason of the interception of any communication in obedience to a warrant issued under section 2 of the Interception of Communications Act 1985, or under the authority of an interception warrant under Section 5 of the Regulation of Investigatory Powers Act 2000, any information relating to the obtaining of information by reason of any such interception and any document or other article which is or has been used or held for use in, or has been obtained by reason of, any such interception; and
    (b) any information obtained by reason of action authorised by a warrant issued under section 3 of the Security Service Act 1989 or under section 5 of the Intelligence Services Act 1994 or by an authorisation given under section 7 of that Act, any information relating to the obtaining of information by reason of any such action and any document or other article which is or has been used or held for use in, or has been obtained by reason of, any such action.
  (4) It is a defence for a person charged with an offence under this section in respect of a disclosure falling within subsection (2)(a) above to prove that at the time of the alleged offence he did not know, and had no reasonable cause to believe, that the disclosure would have any of the effects there mentioned.
  (5) It is a defence for a person charged with an offence under this section in respect of any other disclosure to prove that at the time of the alleged offence he did not know, and had no reasonable cause to believe, that the information, document or article in question was information or a document or article to which this section applies.
  (6) In this section "legal custody" includes detention in pursuance of any enactment or any instrument made under an enactment.

5 **Information resulting from unauthorised disclosures or entrusted in confidence**
  (1) Subsection (2) below applies where—
    (a) any information, document or other article protected against disclosure by the foregoing provisions of this Act has come into a person's possession as a result of having been—
      (i) disclosed (whether to him or another) by a Crown servant or government contractor without lawful authority; or
      (ii) entrusted to him by a Crown servant or government contractor on terms requiring it to be held in confidence or in circumstances in which the Crown servant or government contractor could reasonably expect that it would be so held; or
      (iii) disclosed (whether to him or another) without lawful authority by a person to whom it was entrusted as mentioned in sub-paragraph (ii) above; and

(b) the disclosure without lawful authority of the information, document or article by the person into whose possession it has come is not an offence under any of those provisions.

(2) Subject to subsections (3) and (4) below, the person into whose possession the information, document or article has come is guilty of an offence if he discloses it without lawful authority knowing, or having reasonable cause to believe, that it is protected against disclosure by the foregoing provisions of this Act and that it has come into his possession as mentioned in subsection (1) above.

(3) In the case of information or a document or article protected against disclosure by sections 1 to 3 above, a person does not commit an offence under subsection (2) above unless—
  (a) the disclosure by him is damaging; and
  (b) he makes it knowing, or having reasonable cause to believe, that it would be damaging;
and the question whether a disclosure is damaging shall be determined for the purposes of this subsection as it would be in relation to a disclosure of that information, document or article by a Crown servant in contravention of section 1(3), 2(1) or 3(1) above.

(4) A person does not commit an offence under subsection (2) above in respect of information or a document or other article which has come into his possession as a result of having been disclosed—
  (a) as mentioned in subsection (1)(a)(i) above by a government contractor; or
  (b) as mentioned in subsection (1)(a)(iii) above,
unless that disclosure was by a British citizen or took place in the United Kingdom, in any of the Channel Islands or in the Isle of Man or a colony.

(5) For the purposes of this section information or a document or article is protected against disclosure by the foregoing provisions of this Act if—
  (a) it relates to security or intelligence, defence or international relations within the meaning of section 1, 2 or 3 above or is such as is mentioned in section 3(1)(b) above; or
  (b) it is information or a document or article to which section 4 above applies;
and information or a document or article is protected against disclosure by sections 1 to 3 above if it falls within paragraph (a) above.

(6) A person is guilty of an offence if without lawful authority he discloses any information, document or other article which he knows, or has reasonable cause to believe, to have come into his possession as a result of a contravention of section 1 of the Official Secrets Act 1911.

6 Information entrusted in confidence to other States or international organisations

(1) This section applies where—
  (a) any information, document or other article which—
    (i) relates to security or intelligence, defence or international relations; and
    (ii) has been communicated in confidence by or on behalf of the United Kingdom to another State or to an international organisation,
    has come into a person's possession as a result of having been disclosed (whether to him or another) without the authority of that State or organisation or, in the case of an organisation, of a member of it; and
  (b) the disclosure without lawful authority of the information, document or article by the person into whose possession it has come is not an offence under any of the foregoing provisions of this Act.

(2) Subject to subsection (3) below, the person into whose possession the information, document or article has come is guilty of an offence if he makes a damaging disclosure of it knowing, or having reasonable cause to believe, that it is such as is mentioned in subsection (1) above, that it has come into his possession as there mentioned and that its disclosure would be damaging.

(3) A person does not commit an offence under subsection (2) above if the information, document or article is disclosed by him with lawful authority or has previously been made

available to the public with the authority of the State or organisation concerned or, in the case of an organisation, of a member of it.

(4) For the purposes of this section "security or intelligence", "defence" and "international relations" have the same meaning as in sections 1, 2 and 3 above and the question whether a disclosure is damaging shall be determined as it would be in relation to a disclosure of the information, document or article in question by a Crown servant in contravention of section 1(3), 2(1) and 3(1) above.

(5) For the purposes of this section information or a document or article is communicated in confidence if it is communicated on terms requiring it to be held in confidence or in circumstances in which the person communicating it could reasonably expect that it would be so held.

7 Authorised disclosures

(1) For the purposes of this Act a disclosure by—
   (a) a Crown servant; or
   (b) a person, not being a Crown servant or government contractor, in whose case a notification for the purposes of section 1(1) above is in force,
   is made with lawful authority if, and only if, it is made in accordance with his official duty.

(2) For the purposes of this Act a disclosure by a government contractor is made with lawful authority if, and only if, it is made—
   (a) in accordance with an official authorisation; or
   (b) for the purposes of the functions by virtue of which he is a government contractor and without contravening an official restriction.

(3) For the purposes of this Act a disclosure made by any other person is made with lawful authority if, and only if, it is made—
   (a) to a Crown servant for the purposes of his functions as such; or
   (b) in accordance with an official authorisation.

(4) It is a defence for a person charged with an offence under any of the foregoing provisions of this Act to prove that at the time of the alleged offence he believed that he had lawful authority to make the disclosure in question and had no reasonable cause to believe otherwise.

(5) In this section "official authorisation" and "official restriction" mean, subject to subsection (6) below, an authorisation or restriction duly given or imposed by a Crown servant or government contractor or by or on behalf of a prescribed body or a body of a prescribed class.

(6) In relation to section 6 above "official authorisation" includes an authorisation duly given by or on behalf of the State or organisation concerned or, in the case of an organisation, a member of it.

8 Safeguarding of information

(1) Where a Crown servant or government contractor, by virtue of his position as such, has in his possession or under his control any document or other article which it would be an offence under any of the foregoing provisions of this Act for him to disclose without lawful authority he is guilty of an offence if—
   (a) being a Crown servant, he retains the document or article contrary to his official duty; or
   (b) being a government contractor, he fails to comply with an official direction for the return or disposal of the document or article,
   or if he fails to take such care to prevent the unauthorised disclosure of the document or article as a person in his position may reasonably be expected to take.

(2) It is a defence for a Crown servant charged with an offence under subsection (1)(a) above to prove that at the time of the alleged offence he believed that he was acting in accordance with his official duty and had no reasonable cause to believe otherwise.

(3) In subsections (1) and (2) above references to a Crown servant include any person, not being a Crown servant or government contractor, in whose case a notification for the purposes of section 1(1) above is in force.

(4) Where a person has in his possession or under his control any document or other article which it would be an offence under section 5 above for him to disclose without lawful authority, he is guilty of an offence if—
   (a) he fails to comply with an official direction for its return or disposal; or
   (b) where he obtained it from a Crown servant or government contractor on terms requiring it to be held in confidence or in circumstances in which that servant or contractor could reasonably expect that it would be so held, he fails to take such care to prevent its unauthorised disclosure as a person in his position may reasonably be expected to take.

(5) Where a person has in his possession or under his control any document or other article which it would be an offence under section 6 above for him to disclose without lawful authority, he is guilty of an offence if he fails to comply with an official direction for its return or disposal.

(6) A person is guilty of an offence if he discloses any official information, document or other article which can be used for the purpose of obtaining access to any information, document or other article protected against disclosure by the foregoing provisions of this Act and the circumstances in which it is disclosed are such that it would be reasonable to expect that it might be used for that purpose without authority.

(7) For the purposes of subsection (6) above a person discloses information or a document or article which is official if—
   (a) he has or has had it in his possession by virtue of his position as a Crown servant or government contractor; or
   (b) he knows or has reasonable cause to believe that a Crown servant or government contractor has or has had it in his possession by virtue of his position as such.

(8) Subsection (5) of section 5 above applies for the purposes of subsection (6) above as it applies for the purposes of that section.

(9) In this section "official direction" means a direction duly given by a Crown servant or government contractor or by or on behalf of a prescribed body or a body of a prescribed class.

9 Prosecutions

(1) Subject to subsection (2) below, no prosecution for an offence under this Act shall be instituted in England and Wales or in Northern Ireland except by or with the consent of the Attorney General or, as the case may be, the Advocate General for Northern Ireland.

(2) Subsection (1) above does not apply to an offence in respect of any such information, document or article as is mentioned in section 4(2) above but no prosecution for such an offence shall be instituted in England and Wales or in Northern Ireland except by or with the consent of the Director of Public Prosecutions or, as the case may be, the Director of Public Prosecutions for Northern Ireland.

10 Penalties

(1) A person guilty of an offence under any provision of this Act other than section 8(1), (4) or (5) shall be liable—
   (a) on conviction on indictment, to imprisonment for a term not exceeding two years or a fine or both;
   (b) on summary conviction, to imprisonment for a term not exceeding six months or a fine not exceeding the statutory maximum or both.

(2) A person guilty of an offence under section 8(1), (4) or (5) above shall be liable on summary conviction to imprisonment for a term not exceeding *three months [51 weeks]* or a fine not exceeding level 5 on the standard scale or both.

12 "Crown servant" and "government contractor"

(1) In this Act "Crown servant" means—

(a) a Minister of the Crown;
(aa) a member of the Scottish Executive or a junior Scottish Minister;
(ab) The First Minister for Wales, a Welsh Minister appointed under section 48 of the Government of Wales Act 2006, the Counsel General to the Welsh Assembly Government or a Deputy Welsh Minister;
(c) any person employed in the civil service of the Crown, including Her Majesty's Diplomatic Service, Her Majesty's Overseas Civil Service, the civil service of Northern Ireland and the Northern Ireland Court Service;
(d) any member of the naval, military or air forces of the Crown, including any person employed by an association established for the purposes of the Reserve Forces Act 1980;
(e) any constable and any other person employed or appointed in or for the purposes of any police force (including the Police Service of Northern Ireland and the Police Service of Northern Ireland Reserve or the Serious Organised Crime Agency);
(f) any person who is a member or employee of a prescribed body or a body of a prescribed class and either is prescribed for the purposes of this paragraph or belongs to a prescribed class of members or employees of any such body;
(g) any person who is the holder of a prescribed office or who is an employee of such a holder and either is prescribed for the purposes of this paragraph or belongs to a prescribed class of such employees.

(2) In this Act "government contractor" means, subject to subsection (3) below, any person who is not a Crown servant but who provides, or is employed in the provision of, goods or services—
(a) for the purposes of any Minister or person mentioned in paragraph (a) or (b) of subsection (1) above, or any office-holder in the Scottish Administration, of any of the services, forces or bodies mentioned in that subsection or of the holder of any office prescribed under that subsection; or
(b) under an agreement or arrangement certified by the Secretary of State as being one to which the government of a State other than the United Kingdom or an international organisation is a party or which is subordinate to, or made for the purposes of implementing, any such agreement or arrangement.

...

13 Other interpretation provisions

(1) In this Act—

"disclose" and "disclosure", in relation to a document or other article, include parting with possession of it;

"international organisation" means, subject to subsections (2) and (3) below, an organisation of which only States are members and includes a reference to any organ of such an organisation;

"prescribed" means prescribed by an order made by the Secretary of State;

"State" includes the government of a State and any organ of its government and references to a State other than the United Kingdom include references to any territory outside the United Kingdom.

(2) In section 12(2)(b) above the reference to an international organisation includes a reference to any such organisation whether or not one of which only States are members and includes a commercial organisation.

(3) In determining for the purposes of subsection (1) above whether only States are members of an organisation, any member which is itself an organisation of which only States are members, or which is an organ of such an organisation, shall be treated as a State.

SECURITY SERVICE ACT 1989
(1989, c. 5)

An Act to place the Security Service on a statutory basis; to enable certain actions to be taken on the authority of warrants issued by the Secretary of State, with provision for the issue of such warrants to be kept under review by a Commissioner; to establish a procedure for the investigation by a Tribunal or, in some cases, by the Commissioner of complaints about the Service; and for connected purposes

[27 April 1989]

1 The Security Service

(1) There shall continue to be a Security Service (in this Act referred to as "the Service") under the authority of the Secretary of State.

(2) The function of the Service shall be the protection of national security and, in particular, its protection against threats from espionage, terrorism and sabotage, from the activities of agents of foreign powers and from actions intended to overthrow or undermine parliamentary democracy by political, industrial or violent means.

(3) It shall also be the function of the Service to safeguard the economic well-being of the United Kingdom against threats posed by the actions or intentions of persons outside the British Islands.

(4) It shall also be the function of the Service to act in support of the activities of police forces, the Serious Organised Crime Agency and other law enforcement agencies in the prevention and detection of serious crime.

. . .

2 The Director-General

(1) The operations of the Service shall continue to be under the control of a Director-General appointed by the Secretary of State.

(2) The Director-General shall be responsible for the efficiency of the Service and it shall be his duty to ensure—

    (a) that there are arrangements for securing that no information is obtained by the Service except so far as necessary for the proper discharge of its functions or disclosed by it except so far as necessary for that purpose or for the purpose of the prevention or detection of serious crime or for the purpose of any criminal proceedings; and

    (b) that the Service does not take any action to further the interests of any political party; and

    (c) that there are arrangements, agreed with the Director General of the Serious Organised Crime Agency, for co-ordinating the activities of the Service in pursuance of section 1(4) of this Act with the activities of police forces, the Serious Organised Crime Agency and other law enforcement agencies.

(3) The arrangements mentioned in subsection (2)(a) above shall be such as to ensure that information in the possession of the Service is not disclosed for use in determining whether a person should be employed, or continue to be employed, by any person, or in any office or capacity, except in accordance with provisions in that behalf approved by the Secretary of State.

. . .

(4) The Director-General shall make an annual report on the work of the Service to the Prime Minister and the Secretary of State and may at any time report to either of them on any matter relating to its work.

TRIBUNALS AND INQUIRIES ACT 1992
(1992, c. 53)

An Act to consolidate the Tribunals and Inquiries Act 1971 and certain other enactments relating to tribunals and inquiries. [16th July 1992]

The Council on Tribunals and their functions

10 Reasons to be given for decisions of tribunals and Ministers

(1) Subject to the provisions of this section and of section 14, where—
   (a) any tribunal specified in Schedule 1 gives any decision, or
   (b) any Minister notifies any decision taken by him—
      (i) after a statutory inquiry has been held by him or on his behalf, or
      (ii) in a case in which a person concerned could (whether by objecting or otherwise) have required a statutory inquiry to be so held,

   it shall be the duty of the tribunal or Minister to furnish a statement, either written or oral, of the reasons for the decision if requested, on or before the giving or notification of the decision, to state the reasons.

(2) The statement referred to in subsection (1) may be refused, or the specification of the reasons restricted, on grounds of national security.

(3) A tribunal or Minister may refuse to furnish a statement under subsection (1) to a person not primarily concerned with the decision if of the opinion that to furnish it would be contrary to the interests of any person primarily concerned.

(4) Subsection (1) does not apply to any decision taken by a Minister after the holding by him or on his behalf of an inquiry or hearing which is a statutory inquiry by virtue only of an order made under section 16(2) unless the order contains a direction that this section is to apply in relation to any inquiry or hearing to which the order applies.

(5) Subsection (1) does not apply—
   (a) to decisions in respect of which any statutory provision has effect, apart from this section, as to the giving of reasons,
   (b) to decisions of a Minister in connection with the preparation, making, approval, confirmation, or concurrence in regulations, rules or byelaws, or orders or schemes of a legislative and not executive character, or
   . . .

(6) Any statement of the reasons for a decision referred to in paragraph (a) or (b) of subsection (1), whether given in pursuance of that subsection or of any other statutory provision, shall be taken to form part of the decision and accordingly to be incorporated in the record.

(7) If, after consultation with the Council, it appears to the Lord Chancellor and the Secretary of State that it is expedient that—
   (a) decisions of any particular tribunal or any description of such decisions, or
   (b) any description of decisions of a Minister,

   should be excluded from the operation of subsection (1) on the ground that the subject-matter of such decisions, or the circumstances in which they are made, make the giving of reasons unnecessary or impracticable, the Lord Chancellor and the Secretary of State may by order direct that subsection (1) shall not apply to such decisions.

(8) Where an order relating to any decisions has been made under subsection (7), the Lord Chancellor and the Secretary of State may, by a subsequent order made after consultation with the Council, revoke or vary the earlier order so that subsection (1) applies to any of those decisions.

11 Appeals from certain tribunals

(1) Subject to subsection (2), if any party to proceedings before any tribunal specified in paragraph 8, 15(a) or (d), 16, 24, 26, 31, 33(b), 37, 40A, 40B, 44 or 45 of Schedule 1 is dissatisfied in point of law with a decision of the tribunal he may, according as rules of court may provide, either appeal from the tribunal to the High Court or require the tribunal to state and sign a case for the opinion of the High Court.

(2) This section shall not apply in relation to—
  (a) proceedings before employment tribunals which arise under or by virtue of any of the enactments mentioned in section 21(1) of the Employment Tribunals Act 1996; or
  (b) proceedings under section 20 of the Abolition of Feudal Teure (Scotland) Act 2000.
(3) Rules of court made with respect to all or any of the tribunals referred to in subsection (1) may provide for authorising or requiring a tribunal, in the course of proceedings before it, to state, in the form of a special case for the decision of the High Court, any question of law arising in the proceedings; and a decision of the High Court on a case stated by virtue of this subsection shall be deemed to be a judgment of the Court within the meaning of section 16 of the Supreme Court *[Superior Courts]* Act 1981 (jurisdiction of Court of Appeal to hear and determine appeals from judgments of the High Court).
(4) In relation to proceedings in the High Court or the Court of Appeal brought by virtue of this section, the power to make rules of court shall include power to make rules prescribing the powers of the High Court or the Court of Appeal with respect to—
  (a) the giving of any decision which might have been given by the tribunal;
  (b) the remitting of the matter with the opinion or direction of the court for re-hearing and determination by the tribunal;
  (c) the giving of directions to the tribunal; and different provisions may be made for different tribunals.
(5) An appeal to the Court of Appeal shall not be brought by virtue of this section except with the leave of the High Court or the Court of Appeal.
(6) ...
...
(10) In this section "decision" includes any direction or order, and references to the giving of a decision shall be construed accordingly.

12 Supervisory functions of superior courts not excluded by Acts passed before 1st August 1958

(1) As respects England and Wales—
  (a) any provision in an Act passed before 1st August 1958 that any order or determination shall not be called into question in any court, or
  (b) any provision in such an Act which by similar words excludes any of the powers of the High Court,
shall not have effect so as to prevent the removal of the proceedings into the High Court by order of certiorari or to prejudice the powers of the High Court to make orders of mandamus.
...
(3) Nothing in this section shall apply—
  (a) to any order or determination of a court of law, or
  (b) where an Act makes special provision for application to the High Court or the Court of Session within a time limited by the Act.

INTELLIGENCE SERVICES ACT 1994
(1994, c. 33)

An Act to make provision about the Secret Intelligence Service and the Government Communications Headquarters, including provision for the issue of warrants and authorisations enabling certain actions to be taken and for the issue of such warrants and authorisations to be kept under review; to make further provision about warrants issued on applications by the Security Service; to establish a procedure for the investigation of complaints about the Secret Intelligence Service and the Government Communications Headquarters; to make provision for the establishment of an Intelligence and Security Committee to scrutinise all three of those bodies; and for connected purposes. [26 May 1994]

The Secret Intelligence Service

1   **The Secret Intelligence Service**

(1) There shall continue to be a Secret Intelligence Service (in this Act referred to as "the Intelligence Service") under the authority of the Secretary of State; and, subject to subsection (2) below, its functions shall be—

(a) to obtain and provide information relating to the actions or intentions of persons outside the British Islands; and

(b) to perform other tasks relating to the actions or intentions of such persons.

(2) The functions of the Intelligence Service shall be exercisable only—

(a) in the interests of national security, with particular reference to the defence and foreign policies of Her Majesty's Government in the United Kingdom; or

(b) in the interests of the economic well-being of the United Kingdom; or

(c) in support of the prevention or detection of serious crime.

2   **The Chief of the Intelligence Service**

(1) The operations of the Intelligence Service shall continue to be under the control of a Chief of that Service appointed by the Secretary of State.

(2) The Chief of the Intelligence Service shall be responsible for the efficiency of that Service and it shall be his duty to ensure—

(a) that there are arrangements for securing that no information is obtained by the Intelligence Service except so far as necessary for the proper discharge of its functions and that no information is disclosed by it except so far as necessary—

(i) for that purpose;

(ii) in the interests of national security;

(iii) for the purpose of the prevention or detection of serious crime; or

(iv) for the purpose of any criminal proceedings; and

(b) that the Intelligence Service does not take any action to further the interests of any United Kingdom political party.

(3) Without prejudice to the generality of subsection (2)(a) above, the disclosure of information shall be regarded as necessary for the proper discharge of the functions of the Intelligence Service if it consists of—

(a) the disclosure of records subject to and in accordance with the Public Records Act 1958; or

(b) the disclosure, subject to and in accordance with arrangements approved by the Secretary of State, of information to the Comptroller and Auditor General for the purposes of his functions.

(4) The Chief of the Intelligence Service shall make an annual report on the work of the Intelligence Service to the Prime Minister and the Secretary of State and may at any time report to either of them on any matter relating to its work.

GCHQ

3   **The Government Communications Headquarters**

(1) There shall continue to be a Government Communications Headquarters under the authority of the Secretary of State; and, subject to subsection (2) below, its functions shall be—

(a) to monitor or interfere with electromagnetic, acoustic and other emissions and any equipment producing such emissions and to obtain and provide information derived from or related to such emissions or equipment and from encrypted material; and
(b) to provide advice and assistance about—
   (i) languages, including terminology used for technical matters, and
   (ii) cryptography and other matters relating to the protection of information and other material,
   to the armed forces of the Crown, to Her Majesty's Government in the United Kingdom or to a Northern Ireland Department or to any other organisation which is determined for the purposes of this section in such manner as may be specified by the Prime Minister.

(2) The functions referred to in subsection (1)(a) above shall be exercisable only—
   (a) in the interests of national security, with particular reference to the defence and foreign policies of Her Majesty's Government in the United Kingdom; or
   (b) in the interests of the economic well-being of the United Kingdom in relation to the actions or intentions of persons outside the British Islands; or
   (c) in support of the prevention or detection of serious crime.

(3) In this Act the expression "GCHQ" refers to the Government Communications Headquarters and to any unit or part of a unit of the armed forces of the Crown which is for the time being required by the Secretary of State to assist the Government Communications Headquarters in carrying out its functions.

4 The Director of GCHQ

(1) The operations of GCHQ shall continue to be under the control of a Director appointed by the Secretary of State.

(2) The Director shall be responsible for the efficiency of GCHQ and it shall be his duty to ensure—
   (a) that there are arrangements for securing that no information is obtained by GCHQ except so far as necessary for the proper discharge of its functions and that no information is disclosed by it except so far as necessary for that purpose or for the purpose of any criminal proceedings; and
   (b) that GCHQ does not take any action to further the interests of any United Kingdom political party.

(3) Without prejudice to the generality of subsection (2)(a) above, the disclosure of information shall be regarded as necessary for the proper discharge of the functions of GCHQ if it consists of—
   (a) the disclosure of records subject to and in accordance with the Public Records Act 1958; or
   (b) the disclosure, subject to and in accordance with arrangements approved by the Secretary of State, of information to the Comptroller and Auditor General for the purposes of his functions.

(4) The Director shall make an annual report on the work of GCHQ to the Prime Minister and the Secretary of State and may at any time report to either of them on any matter relating to its work.

Authorisation of certain actions

5 Warrants: general

(1) No entry on or interference with property or with wireless telegraphy shall be unlawful if it is authorised by a warrant issued by the Secretary of State under this section.

(2) The Secretary of State may, on an application made by the Security Service, the Intelligence Service or GCHQ, issue a warrant under this section authorising the taking, subject to subsection (3) below, of such action as is specified in the warrant in respect of any property so specified or in respect of wireless telegraphy so specified if the Secretary of State—
   (a) thinks it necessary for the action to be taken for the purpose of assisting, as the case may be,—

(i) the Security Service in carrying out any of its functions under the 1989 Act; or
(ii) the Intelligence Service in carrying out any of its functions under section 1 above; or
(iii) GCHQ in carrying out any function which falls within section 3(1)(a) above; and
(b) is satisfied that the taking of the action is proportionate to what the action seeks to achieve;
(c) is satisfied that satisfactory arrangements are in force under section 2(2)(a) of the 1989 Act (duties of the Director-General of the Security Service), section 2(2)(a) above or section 4(2)(a) above with respect to the disclosure of information obtained by virtue of this section and that any information obtained under the warrant will be subject to those arrangements.

(2A) The matters to be taken into account in considering whether the requirements of subsection (2)(a) and (b) are satisfied in the case of any warrant shall include whether what it is thought necessary to achieve by the conduct authorised by the warrant could reasonably be achieved by other means.

(3) A warrant issued on the application of the Intelligence Service or GCHQ for the purposes of the exercise of their functions by virtue of section 1(2)(c) or 3(2)(c) above may not relate to property in the British Islands.

(3A) A warrant issued on the application of the Security Service for the purposes of the exercise of their function under section 1(4) of the Security Service Act 1989 may not relate to property in the British Islands unless it authorises the taking of action in relation to conduct within subsection (3B) below.

(3B) Conduct is within this subsection if it constitutes (or, if it took place in the United Kingdom, would constitute) one or more offences, and either—
(a) it involves the use of violence, results in substantial financial gain or is conduct by a large number of persons in pursuit of a common purpose; or
(b) the offence or one of the offences is an offence for which a person who has attained the age of twenty-one [*(eighteen in relation to England and Wales)*] and has no previous convictions could reasonably be expected to be sentenced to imprisonment for a term of three years or more.

(4) Subject to subsection (5) below, the Security Service may make an application under subsection (2) above for a warrant to be issued authorising that Service (or a person acting on its behalf) to take such action as is specified in the warrant on behalf of the Intelligence Service or GCHQ and, where such a warrant is issued, the functions of the Security Service shall include the carrying out of the action so specified, whether or not it would otherwise be within its functions.

(5) The Security Service may not make an application for a warrant by virtue of subsection (4) above except where the action proposed to be authorised by the warrant—
(a) is action in respect of which the Intelligence Service or, as the case may be, GCHQ could make such an application; and
(b) is to be taken otherwise than in support of the prevention or detection of serious crime.

6 Warrants: procedure and duration, etc

(1) A warrant shall not be issued except—
(a) under the hand of the Secretary of State or, in the case of a warrant by the Scottish Ministers (by virtue of provision made under section 63 of the Scotland Act 1998), a member of the Scottish Executive; or
(b) in an urgent case where the Secretary of State has expressly authorised its issue and a statement of that fact is endorsed on it, under the hand of a senior official; or
. . .

The Intelligence and Security Committee

10 The Intelligence and Security Committee

(1) There shall be a Committee, to be known as the Intelligence and Security Committee and in this section referred to as "the Committee", to examine the expenditure, administration and policy of—
   (a) the Security Service;
   (b) the Intelligence Service; and
   (c) GCHQ.

(2) The Committee shall consist of nine members—
   (a) who shall be drawn both from the members of the House of Commons and from the members of the House of Lords; and
   (b) none of whom shall be a Minister of the Crown.

(3) The members of the Committee shall be appointed by the Prime Minister after consultation with the Leader of the Opposition, within the meaning of the Ministerial and other Salaries Act 1975; and one of those members shall be so appointed as Chairman of the Committee.

(4) Schedule 3 to this Act shall have effect with respect to the tenure of office of members of, the procedure of and other matters relating to, the Committee; and in that Schedule "the Committee" has the same meaning as in this section.

(5) The Committee shall make an annual report on the discharge of their functions to the Prime Minister and may at any time report to him on any matter relating to the discharge of those functions.

(6) The Prime Minister shall lay before each House of Parliament a copy of each annual report made by the Committee under subsection (5) above together with a statement as to whether any matter has been excluded from that copy in pursuance of subsection (7) below.

(7) If it appears to the Prime Minister, after consultation with the Committee, that the publication of any matter in a report would be prejudicial to the continued discharge of the functions of either of the Services or, as the case may be, GCHQ, the Prime Minister may exclude that matter from the copy of the report as laid before each House of Parliament.

Supplementary

11 Interpretation and consequential amendments

(1) In this Act—
   (a) "the 1989 Act" means the Security Service Act 1989;
   (b) . . .
   (c) "Minister of the Crown" has the same meaning as in the Ministers of the Crown Act 1975;
   (d) "senior official" has the same meaning as in the Regulation of Investigatory Powers Act 2000;
   (e) "wireless telegraphy" has the same meaning as in the Wireless Telegraphy Act 1949 and, in relation to wireless telegraphy, "interfere" has the same meaning as in that Act;
   (f) "working day" means any day other than a Saturday, a Sunday, Christmas Day, Good Friday or a day which is a bank holiday under the Banking and Financial Dealings Act 1971 in any part of the United Kingdom.

(1A), (2) . . .

CRIMINAL JUSTICE AND PUBLIC ORDER ACT 1994
(1994, c. 33)

An Act to make further provision in relation to criminal justice (including employment in the prison service); to amend or extend the criminal law and powers for preventing crime and enforcing that law; to amend the Video Recordings Act 1984; and for purposes connected with those purposes.

[3 November 1994]

Note: Sections 34(2)(a), (b)(i) and (ii), 36(2)(a) and 37(2)(a) will be repealed when Sch. 3 of the Criminal Justice Act 2003 is brought fully into force and replaced by the words in square brackets.

PART III
COURSE OF JUSTICE: EVIDENCE, PROCEDURE, ETC.

Inferences from accused's silence

34 Effect of accused's failure to mention facts when questioned or charged

(1) Where, in any proceedings against a person for an offence, evidence is given that the accused—

    (a) at any time before he was charged with the offence, on being questioned under caution by a constable trying to discover whether or by whom the offence had been committed, failed to mention any fact relied on in his defence in those proceedings; or

    (b) on being charged with the offence or officially informed that he might be prosecuted for it, failed to mention any such fact,

being a fact which in the circumstances existing at the time the accused could reasonably have been expected to mention when so questioned, charged or informed, as the case may be, subsection (2) below applies.

(2) Where this subsection applies—

    (a) a magistrates' court, inquiring into the offence as examining justices;

    (b) a judge, in deciding whether to grant an application made by the accused under—

        (i) section 6 of the Criminal Justice Act 1987 (application for dismissal of charge of serious fraud in respect of which notice of transfer has been given under section 4 of that Act); or

        (ii) paragraph 5 of Schedule 6 to the Criminal Justice Act 1991 (application for dismissal of charge of violent or sexual offence involving child in respect of which notice of transfer has been given under section 53 of that Act);

    [paragraph 2 of Schedule 3 to the Crime and Disorder Act 1998]

    (c) the court, in determining whether there is a case to answer; and

    (d) the court or jury, in determining whether the accused is guilty of the offence charged,

may draw such inferences from the failure as appear proper.

(2A) Where the accused was at an authorised place of detention at the time of the failure, subsection (1) and (2) above do not apply if he had not been allowed an opportunity to consult a solicitor prior to being questioned, charged or informed as mentioned in subsection (1) above.

(3) Subject to any directions by the court, evidence tending to establish the failure may be given before or after evidence tending to establish the fact which the accused is alleged to have failed to mention.

(4) This section applies in relation to questioning by persons (other than constables) charged with the duty of investigating offences or charging offenders as it applies in relation to questioning by constables; and in subsection (1) above "officially informed" means informed by a constable or any such person.

(5) This section does not—

    (a) prejudice the admissibility in evidence of the silence or other reaction of the accused in the face of anything said in his presence relating to the conduct in respect of which he is charged, in so far as evidence thereof would be admissible apart from this section; or

(b) preclude the drawing of any inference from any such silence or other reaction of the accused which could properly be drawn apart from this section.

(6) This section does not apply in relation to a failure to mention a fact if the failure occurred before the commencement of this section.

...

35 Effect of accused's silence at trial

(1) At the trial of any person ... for an offence, subsections (2) and (3) below apply unless—
   (a) the accused's guilt is not in issue; or
   (b) it appears to the court that the physical or mental condition of the accused makes it undesirable for him to give evidence;
   but subsection (2) below does not apply if, at the conclusion of the evidence for the prosecution, his legal representative informs the court that the accused will give evidence or, where he is unrepresented, the court ascertains from him that he will give evidence.

(2) Where this subsection applies, the court shall, at the conclusion of the evidence for the prosecution, satisfy itself (in the case of proceedings on indictment with a jury, in the presence of the jury) that the accused is aware that the stage has been reached at which evidence can be given for the defence and that he can, if he wishes, give evidence and that, if he chooses not to give evidence, or having been sworn, without good cause refuses to answer any question, it will be permissible for the court or jury to draw such inferences as appear proper from his failure to give evidence or his refusal, without good cause, to answer any question.

(3) Where this subsection applies, the court or jury, in determining whether the accused is guilty of the offence charged, may draw such inferences as appear proper from the failure of the accused to give evidence or his refusal, without good cause, to answer any question.

(4) This section does not render the accused compellable to give evidence on his own behalf, and he shall accordingly not be guilty of contempt of court by reason of a failure to do so.

(5) For the purposes of this section a person who, having been sworn, refuses to answer any question shall be taken to do so without good cause unless—
   (a) he is entitled to refuse to answer the question by virtue of any enactment, whenever passed or made, or on the ground of privilege; or
   (b) the court in the exercise of its general discretion excuses him from answering it.

(6) ...

(7) This section applies—
   (a) in relation to proceedings on indictment for an offence, only if the person charged with the offence is arraigned on or after the commencement of this section;
   (b) in relation to proceedings in a magistrates' court, only if the time when the court begins to receive evidence in the proceedings falls after the commencement of this section.

36 Effect of accused's failure or refusal to account for objects, substances or marks

(1) Where—
   (a) a person is arrested by a constable, and there is—
       (i) on his person; or
       (ii) in or on his clothing or footwear; or
       (iii) otherwise in his possession; or
       (iv) in any place in which he is at the time of his arrest,
       any object, substance or mark, or there is any mark on any such object; and
   (b) that or another constable investigating the case reasonably believes that the presence of the object, substance or mark may be attributable to the participation of the person arrested in the commission of an offence specified by the constable; and
   (c) the constable informs the person arrested that he so believes, and requests him to account for the presence of the object, substance or mark; and
   (d) the person fails or refuses to do so,

then if, in any proceedings against the person for the offence so specified, evidence of those matters is given, subsection (2) below applies.

(2) Where this subsection applies—
   (a) a magistrates' court, inquiring into the offence as examining justices;
   (b) a judge, in deciding whether to grant an application made by the accused under—
      (i) section 6 of the Criminal Justice Act 1987 (application for dismissal of charge of serious fraud in respect of which notice of transfer has been given under section 4 of that Act); or
      (ii) paragraph 5 of Schedule 6 to the Criminal Justice Act 1991 (application for dismissal of charge of violent or sexual offence involving child in respect of which notice of transfer has been given under section 53 of that Act);
      [paragraph 2 of Schedule 3 to the Crime and Disorder Act 1998]
   (c) the court, in determining whether there is a case to answer; and
   (d) the court or jury, in determining whether the accused is guilty of the offence charged, may draw such inferences from the failure or refusal as appear proper.

(3) Subsections (1) and (2) above apply to the condition of clothing or footwear as they apply to a substance or mark thereon.

(4) Subsections (1) and (2) above do not apply unless the accused was told in ordinary language by the constable when making the request mentioned in subsection (1)(c) above what the effect of this section would be if he failed or refused to comply with the request.

(4A) Where the accused was at an authorised place of detention at the time of the failure or refusal, subsections (1) and (2) above do not apply if he had not been allowed an opportunity to consult a solicitor prior to the request being made.

(5) This section applies in relation to officers of customs and excise as it applies in relation to constables.

(6) This section does not preclude the drawing of any inference from a failure or refusal of the accused to account for the presence of an object, substance or mark or from the condition of clothing or footwear which could properly be drawn apart from this section.

(7) This section does not apply in relation to a failure or refusal which occurred before the commencement of this section.

(8) ...

37 Effect of accused's failure or refusal to account for presence at a particular place

(1) Where—
   (a) a person arrested by a constable was found by him at a place at or about the time the offence for which he was arrested is alleged to have been committed; and
   (b) that or another constable investigating the offence reasonably believes that the presence of the person at that place and at that time may be attributable to his participation in the commission of the offence; and
   (c) the constable informs the person that he so believes, and requests him to account for that presence; and
   (d) the person fails or refuses to do so,
   then if, in any proceedings against the person for the offence, evidence of those matters is given, subsection (2) below applies.

(2) Where this subsection applies—
   (a) a magistrates' court, inquiring into the offence as examining justices;
   (b) a judge, in deciding whether to grant an application made by the accused under—
      (i) section 6 of the Criminal Justice Act 1987 (application for dismissal of charge of serious fraud in respect of which notice of transfer has been given under section 4 of that Act); or
      (ii) paragraph 5 of Schedule 6 to the Criminal Justice Act 1991 (application for dismissal of charge of violent or sexual offence involving child in respect of which notice of transfer has been given under section 53 of that Act);
      [paragraph 2 of Schedule 3 to the Crime and Disorder Act 1998]
   (c) the court, in determining whether there is a case to answer; and

(d) the court or jury, in determining whether the accused is guilty of the offence charged, may draw such inferences from the failure or refusal as appear proper.

(3) Subsections (1) and (2) do not apply unless the accused was told in ordinary language by the constable when making the request mentioned in subsection (1)(c) above what the effect of this section would be if he failed or refused to comply with the request.

(3A) Where the accused was in an authorised place of detention at the time of the failure or refusal, subsections (1) and (2) do not apply if he had not been allowed an opportunity to consult a solicitor prior to the request being made.

(4) This section applies in relation to officers of customs and excise as it applies in relation to constables.

(5) This section does not preclude the drawing of any inference from a failure or refusal of the accused to account for his presence at a place which could properly be drawn apart from this section.

(6) This section does not apply in relation to a failure or refusal which occurred before the commencement of this section.

(7) . . .

PART IV
POLICE POWERS

Powers of police to stop and search

60 Powers to stop and search in anticipation of, or after, violence

(1) If a police officer of or above the rank of inspector reasonably believes—
   (a) that incidents involving serious violence may take place in any locality in his police area, and that it is expedient to give an authorisation under this section to prevent their occurrence, or
   (b) that persons are carrying dangerous instruments or offensive weapons in any locality in his police area without good reason,
   he may give an authorisation that the powers conferred by this section are to be exercisable at any place within that locality for a specified period not exceeding 24 hours.

(2) . . .

(3) If it appears to an officer of or above the rank of superintendent that it is expedient to do so, having regard to offences which have, or are reasonably suspected to have, been committed in connection with any activity falling within the authorisation, he may direct that the authorisation shall continue in being for a further 24 hours.

(3A) If an inspector gives an authorisation under subsection (1) he must, as soon as it is practicable to do so, cause an officer of or above the rank of superintendent to be informed.

(4) This section confers on any constable in uniform power—
   (a) to stop any pedestrian and search him or anything carried by him for offensive weapons or dangerous instruments;
   (b) to stop any vehicle and search the vehicle, its driver and any passenger for offensive weapons or dangerous instruments.

(5) A constable may, in the exercise of the powers conferred by subsection (4) above, stop any person or vehicle and make any search he thinks fit whether or not he has any grounds for suspecting that the person or vehicle is carrying weapons or articles of that kind.

(6) If in the course of a search under this section a constable discovers a dangerous instrument or an article which he has reasonable grounds for suspecting to be an offensive weapon, he may seize it.

(7) This section applies (with the necessary modifications) to ships, aircraft and hovercraft as it applies to vehicles.

(8) A person who fails—
   (a) to stop, or to stop a vehicle; *or*
   (b) to remove an item worn by him,

when required to do so by a constable in the exercise of his powers under this section shall be liable on summary conviction to imprisonment for a term not exceeding *one month* [*51 weeks*] or to a fine not exceeding level 3 on the standard scale or both.

(9) Any authorisation under this section shall be in writing signed by the officer giving it and shall specify the grounds on which it is given and the locality in which and the period during which the powers conferred by this section are exercisable and a direction under subsection (3) above shall also be given in writing or, where that is not practicable, recorded in writing as soon as it is practicable to do so.

. . .

(10) Where a vehicle is stopped by a constable under this section, the driver shall be entitled to obtain a written statement that the vehicle was stopped under the powers conferred by this section if he applies for such a statement not later than the end of the period of twelve months from the day on which the vehicle was stopped and similarly as respects a pedestrian who is stopped and searched under this section.

(10A) A person who is searched by a constable under this section shall be entitled to obtain a written statement that he was searched under the powers conferred by this section if he applies for such a statement not later than the end of the period of twelve months from the day on which he was searched.

(11) In this section—

"dangerous instruments" means instruments which have a blade or are sharply pointed;

"offensive weapon" has the meaning given by section 1(9) of the Police and Criminal Evidence Act 1984; and

"vehicle" includes a caravan as defined in section 29(1) of the Caravan Sites and Control of Development Act 1960.

(11A) For the purpose of this section, a person carries a dangerous instrument or an offensive weapon if he has it in his possession

(12) The powers conferred by this section are in addition to and not in derogation of, any power otherwise conferred.

PART V
PUBLIC ORDER: COLLECTIVE TRESPASS OR NUISANCE ON LAND

Powers to remove trespassers on land

61 Power to remove trespassers on land

(1) If the senior police officer present at the scene reasonably believes that two or more persons are trespassing on land and are present there with the common purpose of residing there for any period, that reasonable steps have been taken by or on behalf of the occupier to ask them to leave and—
   (a) that any of those persons has caused damage to the land or to property on the land or used threatening, abusive or insulting words or behaviour towards the occupier, a member of his family or an employee or agent of his, or
   (b) that those persons have between them six or more vehicles on the land, he may direct those persons, or any of them, to leave the land and to remove any vehicles or other property they have with them on the land.

(2) Where the persons in question are reasonably believed by the senior police officer to be persons who were not originally trespassers but have become trespassers on the land, the officer must reasonably believe that the other conditions specified in subsection (1) are satisfied after those persons became trespassers before he can exercise the power conferred by that subsection.

(3) A direction under subsection (1) above, if not communicated to the persons referred to in subsection (1) by the police officer giving the direction, may be communicated to them by any constable at the scene.

(4) If a person knowing that a direction under subsection (1) above has been given which applies to him—
   (a) fails to leave the land as soon as reasonably practicable, or

(b) having left again enters the land as a trespasser within the period of three months beginning with the day on which the direction was given,

he commits an offence and is liable on summary conviction to imprisonment for a term not exceeding three months [*51 weeks*] or a fine not exceeding level 4 on the standard scale, or both.

...

(5) ...

(6) In proceedings for an offence under this section it is a defence for the accused to show—
   (a) that he was not trespassing on the land, or
   (b) that he had a reasonable excuse for failing to leave the land as soon as reasonably practicable or, as the case may be, for again entering the land as a trespasser.

(7) In its application in England and Wales to common land this section has effect as if in the preceding subsections of it—
   (a) references to trespassing or trespassers were references to acts and persons doing acts which constitute either a trespass as against the occupier or an infringement of the commoners' rights; and
   (b) references to "the occupier" included the commoners or any of them or, in the case of common land to which the public has access, the local authority as well as any commoner.

(8) Subsection (7) above does not—
   (a) require action by more than one occupier; or
   (b) constitute persons trespassers as against any commoner or the local authority if they are permitted to be there by the other occupier.

...

62 Supplementary powers of seizure

(1) If a direction has been given under section 61 and a constable reasonably suspects that any person to whom the direction applies has, without reasonable excuse—
   (a) failed to remove any vehicle on the land which appears to the constable to belong to him or to be in his possession or under his control; or
   (b) entered the land as a trespasser with a vehicle within the period of three months beginning with the day on which the direction was given, the constable may seize and remove that vehicle.

(2) In this section, "trespasser" and "vehicle" have the same meaning as in section 61.

Powers in relation to raves

63 Powers to remove persons attending or preparing for a rave

(1) This section applies to a gathering on land in the open air of 20 or more persons (whether or not trespassers) at which amplified music is played during the night (with or without intermissions) and is such as, by reason of its loudness and duration and the time at which it is played, is likely to cause serious distress to the inhabitants of the locality; and for this purpose—
   (a) such a gathering continues during intermissions in the music and, where the gathering extends over several days, throughout the period during which amplified music is played at night (with or without intermissions); and
   (b) "music" includes sounds wholly or predominantly characterised by the emission of a succession of repetitive beats.

(1A) This section also applies to a gathering if—
   (a) it is a gathering on land of 20 or more persons who are trespassing on the land; and
   (b) it would be a gathering of a kind mentioned in subsection (1) above if it took place on land in the open air.

(2) If, as respects any land, a police officer of at least the rank of superintendent reasonably believes that—
   (a) two or more persons are making preparations for the holding there of a gathering to which this section applies,

(b) ten or more persons are waiting for such a gathering to begin there, or
(c) ten or more persons are attending such a gathering which is in progress,
he may give a direction that those persons and any other persons who come to prepare or wait for or to attend the gathering are to leave the land and remove any vehicles or other property which they have with them on the land.

(3) A direction under subsection (2) above, if not communicated to the persons referred to in subsection (2) by the police officer giving the direction, may be communicated to them by any constable at the scene.

(4) Persons shall be treated as having had a direction under subsection (2) above communicated to them if reasonable steps have been taken to bring it to their attention.

(5) A direction under subsection (2) above does not apply to an exempt person.

(6) If a person knowing that a direction has been given which applies to him—
  (a) fails to leave the land as soon as reasonably practicable, or
  (b) having left again enters the land within the period of 7 days beginning with the day on which the direction was given,
he commits an offence and is liable on summary conviction to imprisonment for a term not exceeding three months [*51 weeks*] or a fine not exceeding level 4 on the standard scale, or both.

(7) In proceedings for an offence under subsection 6 above it is a defence for the accused to show that he had a reasonable excuse for failing to leave the land as soon as reasonably practicable or, as the case may be, for again entering the land.

(7A) A person commits an offence if—
  (a) he knows that a direction under subsection (2) above has been given which applies to him, and
  (b) he makes preparations for or attends a gathering to which this section applies within the period of 24 hours starting when the direction was given.

(7B) A person guilty of an offence under subsection (7A) above is liable on summary conviction to imprisonment for a term not exceeding three months [*51 weeks*] or a fine not exceeding level 4 on the standard scale, or both.

(8) ...

...

64 Supplementary powers of entry and seizure

(1) If a police officer of at least the rank of superintendent reasonably believes that circumstances exist in relation to any land which would justify the giving of a direction under section 63 in relation to a gathering to which that section applies he may authorise any constable to enter the land for any of the purposes specified in subsection (2) below.

(2) Those purposes are—
  (a) to ascertain whether such circumstances exist; and
  (b) to exercise any power conferred on a constable by section 63 or subsection (4) below.

(3) A constable who is so authorised to enter land for any purpose may enter the land without a warrant.

(4) If a direction has been given under section 63 and a constable reasonably suspects that any person to whom the direction applies has, without reasonable excuse—
  (a) failed to remove any vehicle or sound equipment on the land which appears to the constable to belong to him or to be in his possession or under his control; or
  (b) entered the land as a trespasser with a vehicle or sound equipment within the period of 7 days beginning with the day on which the direction was given,
the constable may seize and remove that vehicle or sound equipment.

(5) Subsection (4) above does not authorise the seizure of any vehicle or sound equipment of an exempt person.

...

POLICE ACT 1996
(1996, c. 16)

An Act to consolidate the Police Act 1964, Part IX of the Police and Criminal Evidence Act 1984, Chapter I of Part I of the Police and Magistrates' Courts Act 1994 and certain other enactments relating to the police. [22 May 1996]

PART I
ORGANISATION OF POLICE FORCES

Police areas

1 **Police areas**
  (1) England and Wales shall be divided into police areas.
  (2) The police areas referred to in subsection (1) shall be—
   (a) those listed in Schedule 1 (subject to any amendment made to that Schedule by an order under section 32 below, section 58 of the Local Government Act 1972, or section 17 of the Local Government Act 1992 or Part 1 of the Local Government and Public Investment in Health Act 2007),
   (b) the metropolitan police district, and
   (c) the City of London police area.
  (3) References in Schedule 1 to any local government area are to that area as it is for the time being . . .

Forces outside London

2 **Maintenance of police forces**
  A police force shall be maintained for every police area for the time being listed in Schedule 1.

3 **Establishment of police authorities**
  (1) There shall be a police authority for every police area for the time being listed in Schedule 1.
  (2) A police authority established under this section for any area shall be a body corporate to be known by the name of the area with the adddition of the words "Police Authority".

4 **Membership of police authorities etc.**
  (1) Subject to subsection (2), each police authority established under section 3 shall consist of seventeen members.
  (2) The Secretary of State may by order provide in relation to a police authority specified in the order that the number of its members shall be a specified odd number greater than seventeen.
  (3) A statutory instrument containing an order under subsection (2) shall be laid before Parliament after being made.
  (4) Schedule 2 shall have effect in relation to police authorities established under section 3 and the appointment of their members.

5 **Reduction in size of police authorities**
  (1) This section applies to any order under section 4(2) which varies or revokes an earlier order so as to reduce the number of a police authority's members.
  (2) Before making an order to which this section applies, the Secretary of State shall consult—
   (a) the authority,
   (b) the councils which are relevant councils in relation to the authority for the purposes of Schedule 2, and
   (c) . . .
  (3) An order to which this section applies may include provision as to the termination of the appointment of the existing members of the authority and the making of new appointments or re-appointments.

The metropolitan police force

5A Maintenance of the metropolitan police force

A police force shall be maintained for the metropolitan police district.

5B Establishment of the Metropolitan Police Authority

(1) There shall be a police authority for the metropolitan police district.

(2) The police authority established under this section shall be a body corporate to be known as the Metropolitan Police Authority.

5C Membership etc. of the Metropolitan Police Authority

(1) The Metropolitan Police Authority shall consist of twenty three members (subject to subsection (2)).

(2) The Secretary of State may by order provide that the number of members of the Metropolitan Police Authority shall be a specified odd number not less than seventeen.

(3) Before making an order under subsection (2) which reduces the number of members of the Metropolitan Police Authority, the Secretary of State shall consult—
  (a) the Greater London Authority; and
  (b) the Metropolitan Police Authority;
  (c) . . .

(4) An order under subsection (2) which reduces the number of members of the Metropolitan Police Authority may include provision as to the termination of the appointment of the existing members of the Metropolitan Police Authority and the making of new appointments or re-appointments.

(5) A statutory instrument containing an order under subsection (2) shall be laid before Parliament after being made.

(6) Schedule 2A shall have effect in relation to the Metropolitan Police Authority and the appointment of its members.

The metropolitan police and forces outside London

6 General functions of police authorities

(1) Every police authority established under section 3—
  (a) shall secure the maintenance of an efficient and effective police force for its area, and
  (b) shall hold the chief officer of police of that force to account for the exercise of his functions and those of persons under his direction and control.

(2) In discharging its functions, every police authority established under section 3 shall have regard to—
  (a) any strategic priorities determined by the Secretary of State under section 37A,
  (b) any objectives determined by the authority by virtue of section 6ZB,
  (c) any performance targets established by the authority, whether in compliance with a direction under section 38 or otherwise, and
  (d) any . . . plan issued by the authority by virtue of section 6ZB.

(3) In discharging any function to which a code of practice issued under section 39 relates, a police authority established under section 3 shall have regard to the code.

(4) . . .

(5) This section shall apply in relation to the Metropolitan Police Authority as it applies in relation to a police authority established under section 3.

6ZA Power to confer particular functions on police authorities

(1) The Secretary of State may by order confer particular functions on police authorities.

(2) Without prejudice to the generality of subsection (1), an order under this section may contain provision requiring a police authority—
  (a) to monitor the performance of the police force maintained for its area in—
    (i) complying with any duty imposed on the force by or under this Act, the Human Rights Act 1998 or any other enactment;
    (ii) carrying out any plan issued by virtue of section 6ZB;

6ZB Plans by police authorities

(1) Before the beginning of each financial year every police authority shall issue a plan (a "policing plan") setting out—
   (a) the authority's objectives ("policing objectives") for the policing of its area during that year; and
   (b) the proposed arrangements for the policing of that area for the period of three years beginning with that year.
(2) Policing objectives shall be so framed as to be consistent with any strategic priorities determined under section 37A.
(3) Before determining policing objectives, a police authority shall—
   (a) consult the relevant chief officer of police, and
   (b) consider any views obtained by the authority in accordance with arrangements made under section 96.
(4) A draft of a policing plan required to be issued by a police authority under this section shall be prepared by the relevant chief officer of police and submitted by him to the authority for it to consider.
The authority shall consult the relevant chief officer of police before issuing a policing plan which differs from the draft submitted by him under this subsection.
(5) The Secretary of State may by regulations make provision supplementing that made by this section.
(6) The regulations may make provision (further to that made by subsection (3)) as to persons who are to be consulted, and matters that are to be considered, before determining policing objectives.
(7) The regulations may contain provision as to—
   (a) matters to be dealt with in policing plans (in addition to those mentioned in subsection (1));
   (b) persons who are to be consulted, and matters that are to be considered, in preparing policing plans;
   (c) modification of policing plans;
   (d) persons to whom copies of policing plans are to be sent.
...
(10) A statutory instrument containing regulations under this section shall be subject to annulment in pursuance of a resolution of either House of Parliament.
...

6ZC Reports by police authorities

(1) The Secretary of State may by order require police authorities to issue reports concerning the policing of their areas.
...

9A General functions of the Commissioner of Police of the Metropolis

(1) The metropolitan police force shall be under the direction and control of the Commissioner of Police of the Metropolis appointed under section 9B.
(2) In discharging his functions, the Commissioner of Police of the Metropolis shall have regard to—
   (a) any arrangements involving the metropolitan police force that are made by virtue of section 6ZA(2)(b);
   (b) the policing plan issued by the metropolitan police authority under section 6ZB.

9B Appointment of Commissioner of Police of the Metropolis

(1) There shall be a Commissioner of Police of the Metropolis.
(2) Any appointment of a Commissioner of Police of the Metropolis shall be made by Her Majesty by warrant under Her sign manual.

(3) A person appointed as Commissioner of Police of the Metropolis shall hold office at Her Majesty's pleasure.

(4) Any appointment of a Commissioner of Police of the Metropolis shall be subject to regulations under section 50.

(5) Before recommending to Her Majesty that She appoint a person as the Commissioner of Police of the Metropolis, the Secretary of State shall have regard to—
   (a) any recommendations made to him by the Metropolitan Police Authority; and
   (b) any representations made to him by the Mayor of London.

(6) Any functions exercisable by the Mayor of London under subsection (5) may only be exercised by him personally.

9C Functions of Deputy Commissioner of Police of the Metropolis

(1) The Deputy Commissioner of Police of the Metropolis may exercise any or all of the powers and duties of the Commissioner of Police of the Metropolis—
   (a) during any absence, incapacity or suspension from duty of the Commissioner,
   (b) during any vacancy in the office of the Commissioner, or
   (c) at any other time, with the consent of the Commissioner.

(2) The Deputy Commissioner of Police of the Metropolis shall not have power to act by virtue of subsection (1)(a) or (b) for a continuous period exceeding three months, except with the consent of the Secretary of State.

(3) The Deputy Commissioner of Police of the Metropolis shall also have all the powers and duties of an Assistant Commissioner of Police of the Metropolis.

9D Appointment of Deputy Commissioner of Police of the Metropolis

(1) There shall be a Deputy Commissioner of Police of the Metropolis.

(2) Any appointment of a Deputy Commissioner shall be made by Her Majesty by warrant under Her sign manual.

(3) A person appointed as the Deputy Commissioner shall hold office at Her Majesty's pleasure.

(4) Any appointment of a Deputy Commissioner shall be subject to regulations under section 50.

(5) Before recommending to Her Majesty that She appoint a person as the Deputy Commissioner, the Secretary of State shall have regard to—
   (a) any recommendations made to him by the Metropolitan Police Authority; and
   (b) any representations made to him by the Commissioner.

(6) In this section—
"the Commissioner" means the Commissioner of Police of the Metropolis;
"Deputy Commissioner" means Deputy Commissioner of Police of the Metropolis.

9E Removal of Commissioner or Deputy Commissioner

(1) The Metropolitan Police Authority, acting with the approval of the Secretary of State, may call upon the Commissioner of Police of the Metropolis to retire in the interests of efficiency or effectiveness.

(2) Before seeking the approval of the Secretary of State under subsection (1), the Metropolitan Police Authority shall give the Commissioner of Police of the Metropolis an opportunity to make representations and shall consider any representations that he makes.

(3) Where the Commissioner of Police of the Metropolis is called upon to retire under subsection (1), he shall retire on such date as the Metropolitan Police Authority may specify or on such earlier date as may be agreed upon between him and the Authority.

(4) This section shall apply in relation to the Deputy Commissioner of Police of the Metropolis as it applies to the Commissioner of Police of the Metropolis.

(5) This section is without prejudice to—
   (a) section 9B(3),
   (b) section 9D(3),
   (c) any regulations under section 50, or
   (d) any regulations under the Police Pensions Act 1976.

9F **Assistant Commissioners of Police of the Metropolis**
(1) The ranks that may be held in the metropolitan police force shall include that of Assistant Commissioner of Police of the Metropolis ("Assistant Commissioner").
(2) Any appointment of an Assistant Commissioner shall be made by the Metropolitan Police Authority, but subject to the approval of the Secretary of State and to regulations under section 50.
(3) Subsections (1) to (3) of section 9E shall apply in relation to an Assistant Commissioner as they apply to the Commissioner of Police of the Metropolis.
(4) Subsection (3) is without prejudice to—
  (a) any regulations under section 50, or
  (b) any regulations under the Police Pensions Act 1976.
(5) An Assistant Commissioner may exercise any of the powers and duties of the Commissioner of Police of the Metropolis with the consent of the Commissioner.
(6) Subsection (5) is without prejudice to any regulations under section 50.

9G **Commanders**
(1) The ranks that may be held in the metropolitan police force shall include that of Commander.
(2) Any appointment of a Commander in the metropolitan police force shall be made by the Metropolitan Police Authority, but subject to the approval of the Secretary of State and to regulations under section 50.
(3) Subsections (1) to (3) of section 9E shall apply in relation to a Commander in the metropolitan police force as they apply to the Commissioner of Police of the Metropolis.
(4) Subsection (3) is without prejudice to—
  (a) any regulations under section 50, or
  (b) any regulations under the Police Pensions Act 1976.

9H **Other members of the metropolitan police force**
(1) The ranks that may be held in the metropolitan police force shall be such as may be prescribed by regulations under section 50.
(2) The ranks so prescribed in the case of the metropolitan police force shall include, in addition to the ranks of—
  (a) Commissioner of Police of the Metropolis,
  (b) Deputy Commissioner of Police of the Metropolis,
  (c) Assistant Commissioner of Police of the Metropolis,
  (d) Deputy Assistant Commissioner of Police of the Metropolis, and
  (e) Commander,
  those of chief superintendent, superintendent, chief inspector, inspector, sergeant and constable.
(3) In the metropolitan police force, appointments and promotions to any rank below that of Commander shall be made in accordance with regulations under section 50 by the Commissioner of Police of the Metropolis.

10 **General functions of chief constables**
(1) A police force maintained under section 2 shall be under the direction and control of the chief constable appointed under section 11.
(2) In discharging his functions, every chief constable shall have regard to—
  (a) any arrangements involving his force that are made by virtue of section 6ZA(2)(b);
  (b) the policing plan issued by the police authority under section 6ZB.

11 **Appointment and removal of chief constables**
(1) The chief constable of a police force maintained under section 2 shall be appointed by the police authority responsible for maintaining the force, but subject to the approval of the Secretary of State and to regulations under section 50.

(2) Without prejudice to any regulations under section 50 or under the Police Pensions Act 1976, the police authority, acting with the approval of the Secretary of State, may call upon the chief constable in the interests of efficiency or effectiveness to retire or resign.

(3) Before seeking the approval of the Secretary of State under subsection (2), the police authority shall give the chief constable—
   (a) an explanation in writing of the authority's grounds for calling upon him, in the interests of efficiency or effectiveness, to retire or resign, and
   (b) an opportunity to make representations and the authority shall consider any representations made by or on behalf of the chief constable.
The opportunity given to the chief constable to make representations must include the opportunity to make them in person.
. . .
(4) A chief constable who is called upon to retire under subsection (2) shall retire or resign with effect from such date as the police authority may specify or with effect from such earlier date as may be agreed upon between him and the authority.

11A Appointment and removal of deputy chief constables
(1) Every police force maintained under section 2 shall have one or more deputy chief constables.
(2) The appointment of a person to be a deputy chief constable of a police force shall be made, in accordance with regulations under section 50, by the police authority responsible for maintaining that force . . .
(3) . . .

12 Assistant chief constables
(1) The ranks that may be held in a police force maintained under section 2 shall include that of assistant chief constable; and in every such police force there shall be at least one person holding that rank.
(2) Appointments and promotions to the rank of assistant chief constable shall be made, in accordance with regulations under section 50, by the police authority after consultation with the chief constable and subject to the approval of the Secretary of State.
(3) Subsections (2) to (4) of section 11 shall apply to an assistant chief constable as they apply to a chief constable but with the omission in subsection (3A) . . .
. . .

12A Power of deputy to exercise functions of chief constable
(1) The appropriate deputy chief constable of a police force may exercise or perform any or all of the powers or duties of the chief constable of that force—
   (a) during any absence, incapacity or suspension from duty of the chief constable,
   (b) during any vacancy in the office of the chief constable, or
   (c) at any other time, with the consent of the chief constable.
(2)–(5). . .

13 Other members of police forces
(1) The ranks that may be held in a police force maintained under section 2 shall be such as may be prescribed by regulations under section 50 and the ranks so prescribed shall include, in addition to chief constable, deputy chief constable and assistant chief constable, the ranks of chief superintendent, superintendent, chief inspector, inspector, sergeant and constable.
(2) . . .
(3) Appointments and promotions to any rank below that of assistant chief constable in any police force maintained under section 2 shall be made, in accordance with regulations under section 50, by the chief constable.

14 Police fund
(1) Each police authority established under section 3 shall keep a fund to be known as the police fund.

(2) Subject to any regulations under the Police Pensions Act 1976, all receipts of the police authority shall be paid into the police fund and all expenditure of the authority shall be paid out of that fund.

(3) Accounts shall be kept by each police authority of payments made into or out of the police fund.

20 **Questions on police matters at council meetings**

(1) Every relevant council shall make arrangements (whether by standing orders or otherwise) for enabling questions on the discharge of the functions of a police authority established under section 3 to be put by members of the council at a meeting of the council for answer by a person nominated by the authority for that purpose.

(2) On being given reasonable notice by a relevant council of a meeting of that council at which questions on the discharge of the police authority's functions are to be put, the police authority shall nominate one or more of its members to attend the meeting to answer those questions.

(3) In this section "relevant council" has the same meaning as in Schedule 2.

General provisions

22 **Reports by chief officers to police authorities**

(1) Every chief officer of police of a police force shall, as soon as possible after the end of each financial year, submit to the police authority a general report on the policing during that year of the area for which his force is maintained.

(2) A chief officer shall arrange for a report submitted by him under subsection (1) to be published in such manner as appears to him to be appropriate.

(3) The chief officer of police of a police force shall, whenever so required by the police authority, submit to that authority a report on such matters as may be specified in the requirement, being matters connected with the policing of the area for which the force is maintained.

(4) A report submitted under subsection (3) shall be in such form as the police authority may specify.

(5) If it appears to the chief officer that a report in compliance with subsection (3) would contain information which in the public interest ought not to be disclosed, or is not needed for the discharge of the functions of the police authority, he may request that authority to refer the requirement to submit the report to the Secretary of State; and in any such case the requirement shall be of no effect unless it is confirmed by the Secretary of State.

(6) The police authority may arrange, or require the chief officer to arrange, for a report submitted under subsection (3) to be published in such manner as appears to the authority to be appropriate.

25 **Provision of special services**

(1) The chief officer of police of a police force may provide, at the request of any person, special police services at any premises or in any locality in the police area for which the force is maintained, subject to the payment to the police authority of charges on such scales as may be determined by the authority.

. . .

29 **Attestation of constables**

Every member of a police force maintained for a police area and every special constable appointed for a police area shall, on appointment, be attested as a constable by making a declaration in the form set out in Schedule 4—

(a) . . .

(b) . . . before a justice of the peace having jurisdiction within the police area.

30 **Jurisdiction of constables**

(1) A member of a police force shall have all the powers and privileges of a constable throughout England and Wales and the adjacent United Kingdom waters.

(2) A special constable shall have all the powers and privileges of a constable throughout England and Wales and the adjacent United Kingdom waters.

. . .

Alteration of police areas

32 Power to alter police areas by order
(1) The Secretary of State may by order make alterations in police areas in England and Wales other than the City of London police area.
(2) The alterations that may be made by an order under this section include alterations that result in a reduction or an increase in the number of police areas, but not alterations that result in the abolition of the metropolitan police district.
(3) The Secretary of State shall not exercise his power under this section to make alterations unless either—
  (a) he has received a request to make the alterations from the police authority for each of the areas . . . affected by them, or
  (b) it appears to him to be expedient to make the alterations in the interests of efficiency or effectiveness.

. . .

PART II
CENTRAL SUPERVISION, DIRECTION AND FACILITIES

Functions of Secretary of State

36 General duty of Secretary of State
(1) The Secretary of State shall exercise his powers under the provisions of this Act referred to in subsection (2) in such manner and to such extent as appears to him to be best calculated to promote the efficiency and effectiveness of the police.
(2) The provisions of this Act mentioned in subsection (1) are—
  (a) Part I;
  (b) this Part;
  (c) Part III (other than sections 61 and 62);
  (d) in Chapter II of Part IV, section 85 and Schedule 6; and
  (e) in Part V, section 95.

37A Setting of strategic priorities for police authorities
(1) The Secretary of State may determine strategic priorities for the policing of the areas of all police authorities to which this section applies.
(2) Before determining any such priorities the Secretary of State shall consult—
  (a) the Association of Police Authorities, and
  (b) the Association of Chief Police Officers.
(3) The Secretary of State shall arrange for any priorities determined under this section to be published in such manner as he considers appropriate.
(4) The police authorities to which this section applies are those established under section 3 and the Metropolitan Police Authority.

38 Setting of performance targets
(1) Where a strategic priority has been determined under section 37A, the Secretary of State may direct police authorities to establish levels of performance ("performance targets") to be aimed at in seeking to give effect to that priority.
(2) A direction under this section may be given to all police authorities to which section 37A applies or to one or more particular authorities.
(3) A direction given under this section may impose conditions with which the performance targets must conform, and different conditions may be imposed for different authorities.
(4) The Secretary of State shall arrange for any direction given under this section to be published in such manner as appears to him to be appropriate.
(5) A police authority that is given a direction under this section shall comply with it.

39 Codes of practice

(1) The Secretary of State may issue codes of practice relating to the discharge by police authorities established under section 3 and the Metropolitan Police Authority of any of their functions.

(2) The Secretary of State may from time to time revise the whole or part of any code of practice issued under this section.

(3) The Secretary of State shall lay before Parliament a copy of any code of practice, and of any revision of a code of practice, issued by him under this section.

39A Codes of practice for chief officers

(1) If the Secretary of State considers it necessary to do so for the purpose of promoting the efficiency and effectiveness generally of the police forces maintained for police areas in England and Wales, he may issue codes of practice relating to the discharge of their functions by the chief officers of police of those forces.

...

40 Power to give directions in relation to police force

(1) Where the Secretary of State is satisfied that the whole or any part of a police force is failing to discharge any of its functions in an effective manner, whether generally or in particular respects, he may direct the police authority responsible for maintaining the force to take specified measures for the purpose of remedying the failure.

(2) Where the Secretary of State is satisfied that the whole or a part of a police force will fail to discharge any of its functions in an effective manner, whether generally or in particular respects, unless remedial measures are taken, he may direct the police authority responsible for maintaining the force to take specified measures in order to prevent such a failure occurring.

...

(4) The Secretary of State shall not give a direction under this section in relation to any police force unless—

(a) the police authority responsible for maintaining the force and the chief officer of police of that force have each been given such information about the Secretary of State's grounds for proposing to give that direction as he considers appropriate for enabling them to make representations or proposals under the following paragraphs of this subsection;

(b) that police authority and chief officer have each been given an opportunity of making representations about those grounds;

(c) that police authority and chief officer have each had an opportunity of making proposals for the taking of remedial measures that would make the giving of the direction unnecessary; and

(d) the Secretary of State has considered any such representations and any such proposals.

...

(7) A police authority that is given a direction under this section shall comply with it.

40A Power to give directions in relation to police authority

(1) Where the Secretary of State is satisfied that a police authority is failing to discharge any of its functions in an effective manner, whether generally or in particular respects, he may direct the police authority to take specified measures for the purpose of remedying the failure.

(2) Where the Secretary of State is satisfied that a police authority will fail to discharge any of its functions in an effective manner, whether generally or in particular respects, unless remedial measures are taken, he may direct the police authority to take specified measures in order to prevent such a failure occurring.

...

(4) The Secretary of State shall not give a direction under this section in relation to a police authority unless—

(a) the police authority has been given such information about the Secretary of State's grounds for proposing to give that direction as he considers appropriate for enabling it to make representations or proposals under the following paragraphs of this subsection;
(b) the police authority has been given an opportunity of making representations about those grounds;
(c) the police authority has had an opportunity of making proposals for the taking of remedial measures that would make the giving of the direction unnecessary; and
(d) the Secretary of State has considered any such representations and any such proposals.

...

(7) A police authority that is given a direction under this section shall comply with it.

...

41 Directions as to minimum budget

(1) The power of the Secretary of State to give directions under section 40 or 40A to a police authority established under section 3 shall include power to direct the authority that the amount of its budget requirement for any financial year (under section 43 of the Local Government Finance Act 1992) shall not be less than an amount specified in the direction.

(2)–(4)...

42 Removal of chief constables, etc

(1) The Secretary of State may—
    (a) require the Metropolitan Police Authority to exercise its power under section 9E to call upon the Commissioner or Deputy Commissioner, in the interests of efficiency or effectiveness, to retire or to resign; or
    (b) require a police authority maintaining a police force under section 2 to exercise its power under section 11 to call upon the chief constable of that force, in the interests of efficiency or effectiveness, to retire or to resign.

(1A) The Secretary of State may also, in any case falling within subsection (1B) in which he considers that it is necessary for the maintenance of public confidence in the force in question—
    (a) require the Metropolitan Police Authority to suspend the Commissioner or Deputy Commissioner from duty; or
    (b) require a police authority maintaining a police force under section 2 to suspend the chief constable of that force from duty.

(1B) The cases falling within this subsection are—
    (a) where the Secretary of State is proposing to exercise his power under subsection (1) in relation to the Metropolitan Police Authority or, as the case may be, the other police authority in question, or is proposing to consider so exercising that power;
    (b) where the Metropolitan Police Authority or the other police authority in question is itself proposing to exercise its power to call upon the Commissioner or Deputy Commissioner or, as the case may be, the chief constable of the force in question to retire or to resign, or is proposing to consider so exercising that power; and
    (c) where the power mentioned in paragraph (a) or (b) has been exercised but the retirement or resignation has not yet taken effect.

(2) Before requiring the exercise by the Metropolitan Police Authority or any other police authority of its power to call upon the Commissioner or Deputy Commissioner or the chief constable of the force in question to retire or to resign, the Secretary of State shall—
    (a) give the officer concerned a notice in writing—
        (i) informing him of the Secretary of State's intention to require the exercise of that power; and
        (ii) explaining the Secretary of State's grounds for requiring the exercise of that power; and
    (b) give that officer an opportunity to make representations to the Secretary of State.

(2A) Where the Secretary of State gives a notice under subsection (2)(a), he shall send a copy of the notice to the Metropolitan Police Authority or other police authority concerned.
(2B) The Secretary of State shall consider any representations made to him under subsection (2).
(3) Where the Secretary of State proposes to require the exercise of a power mentioned in subsection (1), he shall, appoint one or more persons (one at least of whom shall be a person who is not an officer of police or of a Government department) to hold an inquiry and report to him and shall consider any report made under this subsection.
(3A) At an inquiry held under subsection (3)—
  (a) the Commissioner, Deputy Commissioner or, as the case may be, the chief constable in question shall be entitled, in accordance with any regulations under section 42A, to make representations to the inquiry;
  (b) the Metropolitan Police Authority or, as the case may be, the police authority concerned shall be entitled, in accordance with any regulations made under section 42A, to make representations to the inquiry.
(3B) The entitlement of the Commissioner, Deputy Commissioner or, as the case may be, the chief constable in question to make representations shall include the entitlement to make them in person.
(4) The costs incurred by the Commissioner, the Deputy Commissioner or a chief constable in respect of an inquiry under this section, taxed in such manner as the Secretary of State may direct, shall be defrayed out of the police fund.
(4A) If the Secretary of State exercises the power conferred by subsection (1) in relation to the Commissioner or the Deputy Commissioner or a chief constable, the Metropolitan Police Authority or other police authority concerned—
  (a) shall not be required to seek the Secretary of State's approval before calling upon the Commissioner or Deputy Commissioner or chief constable in question, in the interests of efficiency or effectiveness, to retire or to resign; and
  (b) shall not be required to give the Commissioner, the Deputy Commissioner or the chief constable a written explanation of the authority's grounds for calling upon him to retire or to resign, to give him an opportunity to make representations to it or to consider any representations made by him.
(4B) In this section "the Commissioner" means the Commissioner of Police of the Metropolis and "the Deputy Commissioner" means the Deputy Commissioner of Police of the Metropolis.
(4C) In this section a reference to the police authority concerned, in relation to a chief constable, is to the police authority which maintains the police force of which he is chief constable.

43 Reports from police authorities
(1) A police authority shall, whenever so required by the Secretary of State, submit to the Secretary of State a report on such matters connected with the discharge of the authority's functions, or otherwise with the policing of its area, as may be specified in the requirement.
(2) A requirement under subsection (1) may specify the form in which a report is to be given.
(3) The Secretary of State may arrange, or require the police authority to arrange, for a report under this section to be published in such manner as appears to him to be appropriate.

44 Reports from chief constables
(1) The Secretary of State may require a chief constable to submit to him a report on such matters as may be specified in the requirement, being matters connected with the policing of the chief constable's police area.
(2) A requirement under subsection (1) may specify the form in which a report is to be given.
(3) The Secretary of State may arrange, or require the chief constable to arrange, for a report under this section to be published in such manner as appears to the Secretary of State to be appropriate.
(4) Every chief constable shall, as soon as possible after the end of each financial year, submit to the Secretary of State the like report as is required by section 22(1) to be submitted to the police authority.

46 Police grant

(1) Subject to the following provisions of this section, the Secretary of State shall for each financial year make grants for police purposes to—
 (a) police authorities for areas other than the metropolitan police district, and
 (b) the Receiver for the Metropolitan Police District;
 and in those provisions references to police authorities shall be taken as including references to the Receiver.

(2) For each financial year the Secretary of State shall with the approval of the Treasury determine—
 (a) the aggregate amount of grants to be made under this section, and
 (b) the amount of the grant to be made to each authority;
 and any determination may be varied by further determinations under this subsection.

(3) The Secretary of State shall prepare a report setting out any determination under subsection (2), and stating the considerations which he took into account in making the determination.

(4) In determining the allocation among police authorities of the whole or any part of the aggregate amount of grants, the Secretary of State may exercise his discretion by applying such formulae or other rules as he considers appropriate.

(5) The considerations which the Secretary of State takes into account in making a determination under subsection (2), and the formulae and other rules referred to in subsection (4), may be different for different authorities or different classes of authority.

...

50 Regulations for police forces

(1) Subject to the provisions of this section, the Secretary of State may make regulations as to the government, administration and conditions or service of police forces.

(2) Without prejudice to the generality of subsection (1), regulations under this section may make provision with respect to—
 (a) the ranks to be held by members of police forces;
 (b) the qualifications for appointment and promotion of members of police forces;
 (c) periods of service on probation;
 (d) voluntary retirement of members of police forces;
 (e) the conduct, efficiency and effectiveness of members of police forces and the maintenance of discipline;
 (f) the suspension of members of a police force from membership of that force and from their office as constable;
 (g) the maintenance of personal records of members of police forces;
 (h) the duties which are or are not to be performed by members of police forces;
 (i) the treatment as occasions of police duty of attendance at meetings of the Police Federations and of any body recognised by the Secretary of State for the purposes of section 64;
 (j) the hours of duty, leave, pay and allowances of members of police forces; and
 (k) the issue, use and return of police clothing, personal equipment and accoutrements.

(3) Without prejudice to the powers conferred by this section, regulations under this section shall—
 (a) establish, or make provision for the establishment of, procedures for cases in which a member of a police force may be dealt with by dismissal, requirement to resign, reduction in rank, reduction in rate of pay, fine, reprimand or caution, and
 (b) make provision for securing that any case in which a senior officer may be dismissed or dealt with in any of the other ways mentioned in paragraph (a) is decided—
  (i) where he is a member of the metropolitan police force, by the Commissioner of Police of the Metropolis, and
  (ii) where he is a member of any other force, by the police authority which maintains the force or by a committee of that authority.

For the purposes of this subsection "senior officer" means a member of a police force holding a rank above that of chief superintendent.

(4) In relation to any matter as to which provision may be made by regulations under this section, the regulations may, subject to subsection (3)(b),—
  (a) authorise or require provision to be made by, or confer discretionary powers on, the Secretary of State, police authorities, chief officers of police or other persons, or
  (b) authorise or require the delegation by any person of functions conferred on that person by or under the regulations.
(5) Regulations under this section for regulating pay and allowances may be made with retrospective effect to any date specified in the regulations, but nothing in this subsection shall be construed as authorising pay or allowances payable to any person to be reduced retrospectively.
(6) Regulations under this section as to conditions of service shall secure that appointments for fixed terms are not made except where the person appointed holds the rank of superintendent or a higher rank.

...

Inspectors of constabulary

54 Appointment and functions of inspectors of constabulary

(1) Her Majesty may appoint such number of inspectors (to be known as "Her Majesty's Inspectors of Constabulary") as the Secretary of State may with the consent of the Treasury determine, and of the persons so appointed one may be appointed as chief inspector of constabulary.
(2) The inspectors of constabulary shall inspect, and report to the Secretary of State on the efficiency and effectiveness of, every police force maintained for a police area and the Central Police Training and Development Authority.
(2A) The inspectors of constabulary may inspect, and report to the Secretary of State on, a police authority's compliance with the requirements of Part I of the Local Government Act 1999 (best value).
(2B) The Secretary of State may at any time require the inspectors of constabulary to carry out an inspection under this section of a police force maintained for any police area; and a requirement under this subsection may include a requirement for the inspection to be confined to a particular part of the force in question, to particular matters or to particular activities of that force.
(2C) Where the inspectors carry out an inspection under subsection (2B), they shall send a report on that inspection to the Secretary of State.

...

(3) The inspectors of constabulary shall carry out such other duties for the purpose of furthering police efficiency and effectiveness as the Secretary of State may from time to time direct.

...

(4) The chief inspector of constabulary shall in each year submit to the Secretary of State a report in such form as the Secretary of State may direct, and the Secretary of State shall lay a copy of that report before Parliament.
(5) The inspectors of constabulary shall be paid such salary and allowances as the Secretary of State may with the consent of the Treasury determine.
(6) Schedule 4A (which makes further provision about the Inspectors of Constabulary) has effect.

55 Publication of reports

(1) Subject to subsection (2), the Secretary of State shall arrange for any report received by him under section 54(2) or (2A) or (2C) to be published in such manner as appears to him to be appropriate.
(2) The Secretary of State may exclude from publication under subsection (1) any part of a report if, in his opinion, the publication of that part—
  (a) would be against the interests of national security, or
  (b) might jeopardise the safety of any person.
(3) The Secretary of State shall send a copy of the published report—

(a) ... to the police authority maintaining the police force to which the report relates, and
(b) to the chief officer of police of that police force.
(4) The police authority shall invite the chief officer of police to submit comments on the published report to the authority before such date as it may specify.
(5) The police authority shall prepare comments on the published report and shall arrange for—
   (a) its comments,
   (b) any comments submitted by the chief officer of police in accordance with subsection (4), and
   (c) any response which the authority has to the comments submitted by the chief officer of police,
   to be published in such manner as appears to the authority to be appropriate.
(6) The police authority (except where it is the Secretary of State) shall send a copy of any document published under subsection (5) to the Secretary of State.
...

PART III
POLICE REPRESENTATIVE INSTITUTIONS

59 Police Federation
(1) There shall continue to be a Police Federation for England and Wales and a Police Federation of Scotland for the purpose of representing members of the police forces in those countries respectively in all matters affecting their welfare and efficiency, except for—
   (a) questions of promotion affecting individuals, and
   (b) (subject to subsection (2)) questions of discipline affecting individuals.
(2) A Police Federation may represent a member of a police force at any proceedings brought under regulations made in accordance with section 50(3) above or section 26(2A) of the Police (Scotland) Act 1967 or on an appeal from any such proceedings.
(3) Except on an appeal to a police appeals tribunal or as provided by section 84, a member of a police force may only be represented under subsection (2) by another member of a police force.
(4) The Police Federations shall act through local and central representative bodies.
(5) The Police Federations and every branch of a Federation shall be entirely independent of, and subject to subsection (6) unassociated with, any body or person outside the police service, but may employ persons outside the police service in an administrative or advisory capacity.
(6) The Secretary of State—
   (a) may authorise a Police Federation or a branch of a Federation to be associated with a person or body outside the police service in such cases and manner, and subject to such conditions and restrictions, as he may specify, and
   (b) may vary or withdraw an authorisation previously given;
   and anything for the time being so authorised shall not be precluded by subsection (5).
(7) This section applies to police cadets as it applies to members of police forces, and references to the police service shall be construed accordingly.
(7A) For the purposes of subsection (1), a member of staff of the National Policing Improvement Agency who is—
   (a) a constable;
   (b) a employee of the Agency,
   shall be treated as a member of a police force in England and Wales and reference in this section to police service shall be construed accordingly.
...

60 Regulations for Police Federation
(1) The Secretary of State may by regulations—
   (a) prescribe the constitution and proceedings of the Police Federations, or
   (b) authorise the Federations to make rules concerning such matters relating to their constitution and proceedings as may be specified in the regulations.

(2) Without prejudice to the generality of subsection (1), regulations under this section may make provision—
(a) with respect to the membership of the Federations;
(b) with respect to the raising of funds by the Federations by voluntary subscription and the use and management of funds derived from such subscriptions;
(c) with respect to the manner in which representations may be made by committees or bodies of the Federations to police authorities, chief officers of police and the Secretary of State;
(d) for the payment by the Secretary of State of expenses incurred in connection with the Federations and for the use by the Federations of premises provided by police authorities for police purposes; and
(e) for modifying any regulations under the Police Pensions Act 1976, section 50 above or section 26 of the Police (Scotland) Act 1967 in relation to any member of a police force who is the secretary or an officer of a Police Federation and for requiring the appropriate Federation to make contributions in respect of the pay, pension or allowances payable to or in respect of any such person.

. . .

64 Membership of trade unions

(1) Subject to the following provisions of this section, a member of a police force shall not be a member of any trade union, or of any association having for its objects, or one of its objects, to control or influence the pay, pensions or conditions of service of any police force.

(2) Where a person was a member of a trade union before becoming a member of a police force, he may, with the consent of the chief officer of police, continue to be a member of that union during the time of his service in the police force.

(3) . . .

(4) This section applies to police cadets as it applies to members of a police force, and references to a police force or to service in a police force shall be construed accordingly.

. . .

(4C) This section applies to a member of the staff of the National Policing Improvement Agency who is—
(a) a constable, and
(b) an employee of the Agency,
as it applies to a member of a police force, and references to a police force or to service in a police force shall be construed accordingly.

(4D) In its application by virtue of subsection (4C), subsection (2) shall have effect as if the reference to the chief officer of police were a reference to the chief executive of the National Policing Improvement Agency.

. . .

(5) Nothing in this section applies to membership of the Police Federations, or of any body recognised by the Secretary of State for the purposes of this section as representing members of police forces who are not members of those Federations.

PART IV
COMPLAINTS, DISCIPLINARY PROCEEDINGS ETC.

CHAPTER II
DISCIPLINARY AND OTHER PROCEEDINGS

84 Representation at disciplinary and other proceedings

(1) A member of a police force of the rank of chief superintendent or below may not be dismissed, required to resign or reduced in rank by a decision taken in proceedings under regulations made in accordance with section 50(3)(a) unless he has been given an opportunity to elect to be legally represented at any hearing held in the course of those proceedings.

(2) Where a member of a police force makes an election to which subsection (1) refers, he may be represented at the hearing, at his option, either by counsel or by a solicitor.

(3) Except in a case where a member of a police force of the rank of chief superintendent or below has been given an opportunity to elect to be legally represented and has so elected, he may be represented at the hearing only by another member of a police force.

(4) Regulations under section 50 shall specify—
   (a) a procedure for notifying a member of a police force of the effect of subsections (1) to (3) above,
   (b) when he is to be notified of the effect of those subsections, and
   (c) when he is to give notice whether he wishes to be legally represented at the hearing.

(5) If a member of a police force—
   (a) fails without reasonable cause to give notice in accordance with the regulations that he wishes to be legally represented, or
   (b) gives notice in accordance with the regulations that he does not wish to be legally represented,
   he may be dismissed, required to resign or reduced in rank without his being legally represented.

(6) If a member of a police force has given notice in accordance with the regulations that he wishes to be legally represented, the case against him may be presented by counsel or a solicitor whether or not he is actually so represented.

85 Appeals against dismissal etc.

(1) A member of a police force who is dismissed, required to resign or reduced in rank by a decision taken in proceedings under regulations made in accordance with section 50(3) may appeal to a police appeals tribunal against the decision except where he has a right of appeal to some other person; and in that case he may appeal to a police appeals tribunal from any decision of that other person as a result of which he is dismissed, required to resign or reduced in rank.

(2) Where a police appeals tribunal allows an appeal it may, if it considers that it is appropriate to do so, make an order dealing with the appellant in a way—
   (a) which appears to the tribunal to be less severe than the way in which he was dealt with by the decision appealed against, and
   (b) in which he could have been dealt with by the person who made that decision.

(3) The Secretary of State may make rules as to the procedure on appeals to police appeals tribunals under this section.

...

88 Liability for wrongful acts of constables

(1) The chief officer of police for a police area shall be liable in respect of any unlawful conduct of constables under his direction and control in the performance or purported performance of their functions in like manner as a master is liable in respect of any unlawful conduct of his servants in the course of their employment, and accordingly shall in respect of a tort be treated for all purposes as a joint tortfeasor.

(2) There shall be paid out of the police fund—
   (a) any damages or costs awarded against the chief officer of police in any proceedings brought against him by virtue of this section and any costs incurred by him in any such proceedings so far as not recovered by him in the proceedings; and
   (b) any sum required in connection with the settlement of any claim made against the chief officer of police by virtue of this section, if the settlement is approved by the police authority.

(3) Any proceedings in respect of a claim made by virtue of this section shall be brought against the chief officer of police for the time being or, in the case of a vacancy in that office, against the person for the time being performing the functions of the chief officer of police; and references in subsections (1) and (2) to the chief officer of police shall be construed accordingly.

(4) A police authority may, in such cases and to such extent as appear to it to be appropriate, pay out of the police fund—
 (a) any damages or costs awarded against a person to whom this subsection applies in proceedings for a tort committed by that person,
 (b) any costs incurred and not recovered by such a person in such proceedings, and
 (c) any sum required in connection with the settlement of a claim that has or might have given rise to such proceedings.
(5) Subsection (4) applies to a person who is—
 (a) a member of the police force maintained by the police authority,
 (b) a constable for the time being required to serve with that force by virtue of section 24 or 98 of this Act, or
 (c) a special constable appointed for the authority's police area.

. . .

PART V
MISCELLANEOUS AND GENERAL

Offences

89 Assaults on constables

(1) Any person who assaults a constable in the execution of his duty, or a person assisting a constable in the execution of his duty, shall be guilty of an offence and liable on summary conviction to imprisonment for a term not exceeding six months or to a fine not exceeding level 5 on the standard scale, or to both.
(2) Any person who resists or wilfully obstructs a constable in the execution of his duty, or a person assisting a constable in the execution of his duty, shall be guilty of an offence and liable on summary conviction to imprisonment for a term not exceeding one month [*51 weeks*] or to a fine not exceeding level 3 on the standard scale, or to both.
(3) This section also applies to a constable who is a member of a police force maintained in Scotland or Northern Ireland when he is executing a warrant, or otherwise acting in England and Wales, by virtue of any enactment conferring powers on him in England and Wales.

. . .

90 Impersonation, etc.

(1) Any person who with intent to deceive impersonates a member of a police force or special constable, or makes any statement or does any act calculated falsely to suggest that he is such a member or constable, shall be guilty of an offence and liable on summary conviction to imprisonment for a term not exceeding six months or to a fine not exceeding level 5 on the standard scale, or to both.
(2) Any person who, not being a constable, wears any article of police uniform in circumstances where it gives him an appearance so nearly resembling that of a member of a police force as to be calculated to deceive shall be guilty of an offence and liable on summary conviction to a fine not exceeding level 3 on the standard scale.
(3) Any person who, not being a member of a police force or special constable, has in his possession any article of police uniform shall, unless he proves that he obtained possession of that article lawfully and has possession of it for a lawful purpose, be guilty of an offence and liable on summary conviction to a fine not exceeding level 1 on the standard scale.
(4) In this section—
 (a) "article of police uniform" means any article of uniform or any distinctive badge or mark or document of identification usually issued to members of police forces or special constables, or anything having the appearance of such an article, badge, mark or document, and
 (ab) "member of a police force" includes a member of the staff of the National Policing Improvement Agency who is a constable, and
 (b) "special constable" means a special constable appointed for a police area.

91 Causing disaffection
(1) Any person who causes, or attempts to cause, or does any act calculated to cause, disaffection amongst the members of any police force, or induces or attempts to induce, or does any act calculated to induce, any member of a police force to withhold his services, shall be guilty of an offence and liable—
   (a) on summary conviction, to imprisonment for a term not exceeding six months or to a fine not exceeding the statutory maximum, or to both;
   (b) on conviction on indictment, to imprisonment for a term not exceeding two years or to a fine, or to both.
. . .

93 Acceptance of gifts and loans
(1) A police authority may, in connection with the discharge of any of its functions, accept gifts of money, and gifts or loans of other property, on such terms as appear to the authority to be appropriate.
(2) The terms on which gifts or loans are accepted under subsection (1) may include terms providing for the commercial sponsorship of any activity of the police authority or of the police force maintained by it.
. . .

96 Arrangements for obtaining the views of the community on policing
(1) Arrangements shall be made for each police area for obtaining—
   (a) the views of people in that area about matters concerning the policing of the area, and
   (b) their co-operation with the police in preventing crime and anti-social behaviour in that area.
(2) . . .
. . .
(6) The Common Council of the City of London shall issue guidance to the Commissioner of Police for the City of London concerning arrangements for the City of London police area; and the Commissioner shall make arrangements under this section after taking account of that guidance.
. . .

SCHEDULE 2
POLICE AUTHORITIES ESTABLISHED UNDER SECTION 3

Membership of police authorities

1. (1) The Secretary of State shall by regulations make provision in relation to the membership of police authorities established under section 3.
   (2) Regulations under this paragraph shall provide for a police authority to consist of—
      (a) persons who are members of a relevant council, and
      (b) other persons, including at least one lay justice.
   (3) Those regulations shall—
      (a) specify the number of members falling within paragraph (a) and paragraph (b) of sub-paragraph (2), and
      (b) secure that the majority of members of a police authority are persons falling within paragraph (a) of that sub-paragraph.
   (4) Those regulations may make further provision as to qualification for membership, and may provide for a specified number of the members of a police authority to be persons of a specified description.
   (5) Those regulations may include provision as to—
      (a) how a member is to be appointed;
      (b) disqualification for membership;
      (c) the tenure of office of a member (including the circumstances in which a member ceases to hold office or may be removed or suspended from office);

(d) re-appointment as a member;
(e) the validity of acts and proceedings of a person appointed as a member in the event of his disqualification or lack of qualification;
(f) the validity of proceedings of a police authority in the event of a vacancy in membership or of a defect in the appointment of a member or in the composition of the authority;
(g) the payment of remuneration and allowances to a member and the reimbursement of expenses.

Appointment of councillor members

2. Regulations under paragraph 1 shall provide that—
   (a) in the case of a police authority in relation to which there is only one relevant council, the members falling within paragraph 1(2)(a) are to be appointed by that council;
   (b) in any other case, those members are to be appointed by a joint committee consisting of persons appointed by the relevant councils from among their own members.

Appointment of other members

3. (1) Regulations under paragraph 1 shall provide that the members falling within paragraph 1(2)(b) are to be appointed—
   (a) by the existing members of the authority,
   (b) from among persons on a short-list prepared by a selection panel.
   (2) Those regulations may make provision as to qualification for membership of a selection panel, and may provide for a specified number of the members of a panel to be persons of a specified description.
   (3) Those regulations may include provision as to—
   (a) the number of members of a selection panel;
   (b) how and by whom a member of a panel is to be appointed;
   (c) disqualification for membership;
   (d) the tenure of office of a member of a panel (including the circumstances in which a member ceases to hold office or may be removed or suspended from office);
   (e) re-appointment as a member of a panel;
   (f) the conduct of proceedings of a panel, including any procedures that a panel is to follow;
   (g) the validity of acts and proceedings of a person appointed as a member of a panel in the event of his disqualification or lack of qualification;
   (h) the validity of proceedings of a panel in the event of a vacancy in membership or of a defect in the appointment of a member or in the composition of the panel;
   (i) the payment of remuneration and allowances to a member of a panel and the reimbursement of expenses.

...

SCHEDULE 2A
THE METROPOLITAN POLICE AUTHORITY

Membership of Authority

1. (1) The Secretary of State shall by regulations make provision in relation to the membership of the Metropolitan Police Authority.
   (2) Regulations under this paragraph shall provide for the Authority to consist of—
   (a) persons appointed from among the persons specified in sub-paragraph (3), and
   (b) other persons, including at least one lay justice.
   (3) The persons referred to in sub-paragraph (2)(a) are—
   (a) the Mayor of London, and
   (b) members of the London Assembly.
   (4) Regulations under this paragraph shall—
   (a) specify the number of members falling within paragraph (a) and paragraph (b) of sub-paragraph (2), and

(b) secure that the majority of members of the Authority are persons falling within paragraph (a) of that sub-paragraph.

(5) Those regulations may make further provision as to qualification for membership, and may provide for a specified number of the members of the Authority to be persons of a specified description.

(6) Those regulations may include provision as to—
   (a) how a member is to be appointed;
   (b) disqualification for membership;
   (c) the tenure of office of a member (including the circumstances in which a member ceases to hold office or may be removed or suspended from office);
   (d) re-appointment as a member;
   (e) the validity of acts and proceedings of a person appointed as a member in the event of his disqualification or lack of qualification;
   (f) the validity of proceedings of the Authority in the event of a vacancy in membership or of a defect in the appointment of a member or in the composition of the Authority;
   (g) the payment of remuneration and allowances to a member and the reimbursement of expenses.

Appointment of members from London Assembly etc

2. Regulations under paragraph 1 shall provide that the members falling within paragraph 1(2)(a) are to be appointed by the Mayor of London.

Appointment of other members

3. (1) Regulations under paragraph 1 shall provide that—
   (a) one of the members falling within paragraph 1(2)(b) is to be appointed by the Secretary of State, and
   (b) the other members are to be appointed by the existing members of the Metropolitan Police Authority from among persons on a short-list prepared by a selection panel.

(2) Those regulations may make provision as to qualification for membership of a selection panel, and may provide for a specified number of the members of a panel to be persons of a specified description.

(3) Those regulations may include provision as to—
   (a) the number of members of a selection panel;
   (b) how and by whom a member of a panel is to be appointed;
   (c) disqualification for membership;
   (d) the tenure of office of a member of a panel (including the circumstances in which a member ceases to hold office or may be removed or suspended from office);
   (e) re-appointment as a member of a panel;
   (f) the conduct of proceedings of a panel, including any procedures that a panel is to follow;
   (g) the validity of acts and proceedings of a person appointed as a member of a panel in the event of his disqualification or lack of qualification;
   (h) the validity of proceedings of a panel in the event of a vacancy in membership or of a defect in the appointment of a member or in the composition of the panel;
   (i) the payment of remuneration and allowances to a member of a panel and the reimbursement of expenses.

SCHEDULE 4
FORM OF DECLARATION

I,. . . . . of. . . . . do solemnly and sincerely declare and affirm that I will well and truly serve Our Sovereign Lady the Queen in the office of constable, without favour or affection, malice or ill will; and that I will to the best of my power cause the peace to be kept and preserved, and prevent all offences against the persons and properties of Her Majesty's subjects; and that while I continue to hold the said office I will to the best of my skill and knowledge discharge all the duties thereof faithfully according to law.

POLICE ACT 1997
(1997, c. 50)

An Act to make provision for the National Criminal Intelligence Service and the National Crime Squad; to make provision about entry on and interference with property and with wireless telegraphy in the course of the prevention or detection of serious crime; to make provision for the Police Information Technology Organisation; to provide for the issue of certificates about criminal records; to make provision about the administration and organisation of the police; to repeal certain enactments about rehabilitation of offenders; and for connected purposes. [21 March 1997]

PART III
AUTHORISATION OF ACTION IN RESPECT OF PROPERTY

Authorisations

93 Authorisations to interfere with property etc.

(1) Where subsection (2) applies, an authorising officer may authorise—
   (a) the taking of such action, in respect of such property in the relevant area, as he may specify,
   (ab) the taking of such action falling within subsection (1A) in respect of property outside the relevant area, as he may specify, or
   (b) the taking of such action in the relevant area as he may specify, in respect of wireless telegraphy.

(1A) The action falling within this subsection is action for maintaining or retrieving any equipment, apparatus or device the placing or use of which in the relevant area has been authorised under this Part or Part II of the Regulation of Investigatory Powers Act 2000 or under any enactment contained in or made under an Act of the Scottish Parliament which makes provision equivalent to that made by Part II of that Act of 2000.

(1B) Subsection (1) applies where the authorising officer is a member of the staff of the Serious Organised Crime Agency, customs officer or an officer of the Office of Fair Trading with the omission of—
   (a) the words "in the relevant area" in each place where they occur; and
   (b) paragraph (ab).

(2) This subsection applies where the authorising officer believes—
   (a) that it is necessary for the action specified to be taken for the purpose of preventing or detecting serious crime, and
   (b) that the taking of the action is proportionate to what the action seeks to achieve.

(2A) Subsection (2) applies where the authorising officer is the Chief Constable or the Deputy Chief Constable of the Police Service of Northern Ireland as if the reference in subsection (2)(a) to preventing or detecting serious crime included a reference to the interests of national security.

(2AA) Where the authorising officer is the chairman of the Office of Fair Trading, the only purpose falling within subsection (2)(a) is the purpose of preventing or detecting an offence under section 188 of the Enterprise Act 2002.

(2B) The matters to be taken into account in considering whether the requirements of subsection (2) are satisfied in the case of any authorisation shall include whether what it is thought necessary to achieve by the authorised action could reasonably be achieved by other means.

(3) An authorising officer shall not give an authorisation under this section except on an application made—
   (a) if the authorising officer is within subsection (5)(a) to (ea) or (ee), by a member of his police force,
   (aa) if the authorising officer is within subsection (5)(eb) to (ed), by a member, as the case may be, of the Royal Navy Police, the Royal Military Police or the Royal Air Force Police,
   (b) if the authorising officer is within (5)(f), by a member of the staff of the Serious Organised Crime Agency.

   . . .

(d) if the authorising officer is within subsection (5)(h), by an officer of Revenue and Customs, or
(e) if the authorising officer is within subsection (5)(i), by an officer of the Office of Fair Trading.
...
(4) For the purposes of subsection (2), conduct which constitutes one or more offences shall be regarded as serious crime if, and only if,—
(a) it involves the use of violence, results in substantial financial gain or is conduct by a large number of persons in pursuit of a common purpose, or
(b) the offence or one of the offences is an offence for which a person who has attained the age of twenty-one (*eighteen in relation to England and Wales*) and has no previous convictions could reasonably be expected to be sentenced to imprisonment for a term of three years or more,
and, where the authorising officer is within subsection (5)(h), it relates to an assigned matter within the meaning of section 1(1) of the Customs and Excise Management Act 1979.
(5) In this section "authorising officer" means—
(a) the chief constable of a police force maintained under section 2 of the Police Act 1996 (maintenance of police forces for areas in England and Wales except London);
(b) the Commissioner, or an Assistant Commissioner, of Police of the Metropolis;
(c) the Commissioner of Police for the City of London;
(d) the chief constable of a police force maintained under or by virtue of section 1 of the Police (Scotland) Act 1967 (maintenance of police forces for areas in Scotland);
(e) the Chief Constable or a Deputy Chief Constable of the Police Service of Northern Ireland;
(ea) the Chief Constable of the Ministry of Defence Police;
(eb) the Provost Marshal of the Royal Navy Police;
(ec) the Provost Marshal of the Royal Military Police;
(ed) the Provost Marshal of the Royal Air Force Police;
(ee) the Chief Constable of the British Transport Police;
(f) the Director General of the Serious Organised Crime Agency, or any member of staff of that Agency who is designated for the purposes of this paragraph by that Director General;
...
(h) an officer of Revenue and Customs is a senior official within the meaning of the Regulation of Investigatory Powers Act 2000 and who is designated for the purposes of this paragraph by the Commissioners of Her Majesty's Revenue and Customs.
...
(7) The powers conferred by, or by virtue of, this section are additional to any other powers which a person has as a constable either at common law or under or by virtue of any other enactment and are not to be taken to affect any of those other powers.

95 Authorisations: form and duration etc.

(1) An authorisation shall be in writing, except that in an urgent case an authorisation (other than one given by virtue of section 94) may be given orally.
(2) An authorisation shall, unless renewed under subsection (3), cease to have effect—
(a) if given orally or by virtue of section 94, at the end of the period of 72 hours beginning with the time when it took effect;
(b) in any other case, at the end of the period of three months beginning with the day on which it took effect.
(3) If at any time before an authorisation would cease to have effect the authorising officer who gave the authorisation, or in whose absence it was given, considers it necessary for the authorisation to continue to have effect for the purpose for which it was issued, he may, in writing, renew it for a period of three months beginning with the day on which it would cease to have effect.

(4) A person shall cancel an authorisation given by him if satisfied that the authorisation is one in relation to which the requirement of paragraphs (a) to (b) of section 93(2) are no longer satisfied.

...

96 Notification of authorisations etc.
(1) Where a person gives, renews or cancels an authorisation, he shall, as soon as is reasonably practicable and in accordance with arrangements made by the Chief Commissioner, give notice in writing that he has done so to a Commissioner appointed under section 91(1)(b).
(2) Subject to subsection (3), a notice under this section shall specify such matters as the Secretary of State may by order prescribe.
(3) A notice under this section of the giving or renewal of an authorisation shall specify—
   (a) whether section 97 applies to the authorisation or renewal, and
   (b) where that section does not apply by virtue of subsection (3) of that section, the grounds on which the case is believed to be one of urgency.
(4) Where a notice is given to a Commissioner under this section, he shall, as soon as is reasonably practicable, scrutinise the notice.

...

Authorisations requiring approval

97 Authorisations requiring approval
(1) An authorisation to which this section applies shall not take effect until—
   (a) it has been approved in accordance with this section by a Commissioner appointed under section 91(1)(b), and
   (b) the person who gave the authorisation has been notified under subsection (4).
(2) Subject to subsection (3), this section applies to an authorisation if, at the time it is given, the person who gives it believes—
   (a) that any of the property specified in the authorisation—
      (i) is used wholly or mainly as a dwelling or as a bedroom in a hotel, or
      (ii) constitutes office premises, or
   (b) that the action authorised by it is likely to result in any person acquiring knowledge of—
      (i) matters subject to legal privilege,
      (ii) confidential personal information, or
      (iii) confidential journalistic material.
(3) This section does not apply to an authorisation where the person who gives it believes that the case is one of urgency.
(4) Where a Commissioner receives a notice under section 96 which specifies that this section applies to the authorisation, he shall as soon as is reasonably practicable—
   (a) decide whether to approve the authorisation or refuse approval, and
   (b) give written notice of his decision to the person who gave the authorisation.
(5) A Commissioner shall approve an authorisation if, and only if, he is satisfied that there are reasonable grounds for believing the matters specified in section 93(2).

...

98 Matters subject to legal privilege
(1) Subject to subsection (5) below, in section 97 "matters subject to legal privilege" means matters to which subsection (2), (3) or (4) below applies.
(2) This subsection applies to communications between a professional legal adviser and—
   (a) his client, or
   (b) any person representing his client,
   which are made in connection with the giving of legal advice to the client.
(3) This subsection applies to communications—
   (a) between a professional legal adviser and his client or any person representing his client, or

(b) between a professional legal adviser or his client or any such representative and any other person,

which are made in connection with or in contemplation of legal proceedings and for the purposes of such proceedings.

(4) This subsection applies to items enclosed with or referred to in communications of the kind mentioned in subsection (2) or (3) and made—
   (a) in connection with the giving of legal advice, or
   (b) in connection with or in contemplation of legal proceedings and for the purposes of such proceedings.

(5) For the purposes of section 97—
   (a) communications and items are not matters subject to legal privilege when they are in the possession of a person who is not entitled to possession of them, and
   (b) communications and items held, or oral communications made, with the intention of furthering a criminal purpose are not matters subject to legal privilege.

99   Confidential personal information

(1) In section 97 "confidential personal information" means—
   (a) personal information which a person has acquired or created in the course of any trade, business, profession or other occupation or for the purposes of any paid or unpaid office, and which he holds in confidence, and
   (b) communications as a result of which personal information—
      (i) is acquired or created as mentioned in paragraph (a), and
      (ii) is held in confidence.

(2) For the purposes of this section "personal information" means information concerning an individual (whether living or dead) who can be identified from it and relating—
   (a) to his physical or mental health, or
   (b) to spiritual counselling or assistance given or to be given to him.

(3) A person holds information in confidence for the purposes of this section if he holds it subject—
   (a) to an express or implied undertaking to hold it in confidence, or
   (b) to a restriction on disclosure or an obligation of secrecy contained in any enactment (including an enactment contained in an Act passed after this Act).

100   Confidential journalistic material

(1) In section 97 "confidential journalistic material" means—
   (a) material acquired or created for the purposes of journalism which—
      (i) is in the possession of persons who acquired or created it for those purposes,
      (ii) is held subject to an undertaking, restriction or obligation of the kind mentioned in section 99(3), and
      (iii) has been continuously held (by one or more persons) subject to such an undertaking, restriction or obligation since it was first acquired or created for the purposes of journalism, and
   (b) communications as a result of which information is acquired for the purposes of journalism and held as mentioned in paragraph (a)(ii).

(2) For the purposes of subsection (1), a person who receives material, or acquires information, from someone who intends that the recipient shall use it for the purposes of journalism is to be taken to have acquired it for those purposes.

103   Quashing of authorisations etc.

(1) Where, at any time, a Commissioner appointed under section 91(1)(b) is satisfied that, at the time an authorisation was given or renewed, there were no reasonable grounds for believing the matters specified in section 93(2), he may quash the authorisation or, as the case may be, renewal.

(2) Where, in the case of an authorisation or renewal to which section 97 does not apply, a Commissioner appointed under section 91(1)(b) is at any time satisfied that, at the time the authorisation was given or, as the case may be, renewed,—

(a) there were reasonable grounds for believing any of the matters specified in subsection (2) of section 97, and
(b) there were no reasonable grounds for believing the case to be one of urgency for the purposes of subsection (3) of that section,
he may quash the authorisation or, as the case may be, renewal.
(3) Where a Commissioner quashes an authorisation or renewal under subsection (1) or (2), he may order the destruction of any records relating to information obtained by virtue of the authorisation (or, in the case of a renewal, relating wholly or partly to information so obtained after the renewal) other than records required for pending criminal or civil proceedings.
. . .

Appeals

104 Appeals by authorising officers
(1) An authorising officer who gives an authorisation, or in whose absence it is given, may, within the prescribed period, appeal to the Chief Commissioner against—
   (a) any refusal to approve the authorisation or any renewal of it under section 97;
   (b) any decision to quash the authorisation, or any renewal of it, under subsection (1) of section 103;
   (c) any decision to quash the authorisation, or any renewal of it, under subsection (2) of that section;
   (d) any decision to cancel the authorisation under subsection (4) of that section;
   (e) any decision to order the destruction of records under subsection (5) of that section;
   (f) any refusal to make an order under subsection (6) of that section;
   (g) . . .
(2) In subsection (1), "the prescribed period" means the period of seven days beginning with the day on which the refusal, decision or, as the case may be, determination appealed against is reported to the authorising officer.
(3) In determining an appeal within subsection (1)(a), the Chief Commissioner shall, if he is satisfied that there are reasonable grounds for believing the matters specified in section 93(2), allow the appeal and direct the Commissioner to approve the authorisation or renewal under that section.
. . .

General

107 Supplementary provisions relating to Commissioners
(1) The Chief Commissioner shall keep under review the performance of functions under this Part.
(2) The Chief Commissioner shall make an annual report on the matters with which he is concerned to the Prime Minister and to the Scottish Ministers and may at any time report to him or them (as the case may require) on anything relating to any of those matters.
(3) The Prime Minister shall lay before each House of Parliament a copy of each annual report made by the Chief Commissioner under subsection (2) together with a statement as to whether any matter has been excluded from that copy in pursuance of subsection (4) below.
(3A) The Scottish Ministers shall lay before the Scottish Parliament a copy of each annual report made by the Chief Commissioner under subsection (2), together with a statement as to whether any matter has been excluded from that copy in pursuance of subsection (4) below.
(4) The Prime Minister may exclude a matter from the copy of a report as laid before each House of Parliament, if it appears to him, after consultation with the Chief Commissioner and the Scottish Ministers, that the publication of that matter in the report would be prejudicial to any of the purposes for which authorisations may be given or granted under this Part of this Act or Part II of the Regulation of Investigatory Powers Act 2000 or under any enactment contained in or made under an act of the Scottish Parliament which makes provision equivalent to that made by Part II of that Act of 2000 or to the discharge of—
   (a) the functions of any police authority,

(b) the functions of the Serious Organised Crime Agency, or

...

(c) the duties of the Commissioners for Her Majesty's Revenue and Customs,

...

(6) ...

CRIME AND DISORDER ACT 1998
(1998, c. 37)

An Act to make provision for preventing crime and disorder; to create certain racially-aggravated offences; to abolish the rebuttable presumption that a child is doli incapax and to make provision as to the effect of a child's failure to give evidence at his trial; to abolish the death penalty for treason and piracy; to make changes to the criminal justice system; to make further provision for dealing with offenders; to make further provision with respect to remands and committals for trial and the release and recall of prisoners; to amend Chapter I of Part II of the Crime (Sentences) Act 1997 and to repeal Chapter I of Part III of the Crime and Punishment (Scotland) Act 1997; to make amendments designed to facilitate, or otherwise desirable in connection with, the consolidation of certain enactments; and for connected purposes. [31 July 1998]

Crime and disorder: general

1   Anti-social behaviour orders

(1) An application for an order under this section may be made by a relevant authority if it appears to the authority that the following conditions are fulfilled with respect to any person aged 10 or over, namely—

(a) that the person has acted, since the commencement date, in an anti-social manner, that is to say, in a manner that caused or was likely to cause harassment, alarm or distress to one or more persons not of the same household as himself; and

(b) that such an order is necessary to protect relevant persons from further anti-social acts by him.

(1A) In this section and sections 1B and 1E "relevant authority" means—

(a) the council for the local government area;

(aa) in relation to England, a county council;

(b) the chief officer of police of any police force maintained for a police area;

(c) the chief constable of the British Transport Police Force; . . .

(d) any person registered under section 1 of the Housing Act 1996 as a social landlord who provides or manages any houses or hostel in a local government area; or

(e) a housing action trust established by order in pursuance of section 62 of the Housing Act 1988.

(1B) In this section "relevant persons" means—

(a) in relation to a relevant authority falling within paragraph (a) of subsection (1A), persons within the local government area of that council;

(aa) in relation to a relevant authority falling within paragraph (aa) of subsection (1A), persons within the county of the county council;

(b) in relation to a relevant authority falling within paragraph (b) of that subsection, persons within the police area;

(c) in relation to a relevant authority falling within paragraph (c) of that subsection—

(i) persons who are within or likely to be within a place specified in section 31(1)(a) to (f) of the Railways and Transport Safety Act 2003 in a local government area; or

(ii) persons who are within or likely to be within such a place;

(d) in relation to a relevant authority falling within paragraph (d) or (e) of that subsection—

(i) persons who are residing in or who are otherwise on or likely to be on premises provided or managed by that authority; or

(ii) persons who are in the vicinity of or likely to be in the vicinity of such premises.
(2) ...
(3) Such an application shall be made by complaint to a magistrates' court.
(4) If, on such an application, it is proved that the conditions mentioned in subsection (1) above are fulfilled, the magistrates' court may make an order under this section (an "anti-social behaviour order") which prohibits the defendant from doing anything described in the order.
(5) For the purpose of determining whether the condition mentioned in subsection (1)(a) above is fulfilled, the court shall disregard any act of the defendant which he shows was reasonable in the circumstances.
(5A) Nothing in this section affects the operation of section 127 of the Magistrates' Courts Act 1980 (limitation of time in respect of time informations laid or complaints made in magistrates' court).
(6) The prohibitions that may be imposed by an anti-social behaviour order are those necessary for the purpose of protecting persons (whether relevant persons or persons elsewhere in England and Wales) from further anti-social acts by the defendant.
(7) An anti-social behaviour order shall have effect for a period (not less than two years) specified in the order or until further order.
(8) Subject to subsection (9) below, the applicant or the defendant may apply by complaint to the court which made an anti-social behaviour order for it to be varied or discharged by a further order.
(9) Except with the consent of both parties, no anti-social behaviour order shall be discharged before the end of the period of two years beginning with the date of service of the order.
(10) If without reasonable excuse a person does anything which he is prohibited from doing by an anti-social behaviour order, he is guilty of an offence and liable—
   (a) on summary conviction, to imprisonment for a term not exceeding six months or to a fine not exceeding the statutory maximum, or to both; or
   (b) on conviction on indictment, to imprisonment for a term not exceeding five years or to a fine, or to both.
(10A) The following may bring proceedings for an offence under subsection (10)—
   (a) a council which is a relevant authority;
   (b) the council for the local government area in which a person in respect of whom an anti-social behaviour order has been made resides or appears to reside.
(10B) If proceedings for an offence under subsection (10) are brought in a youth court section 47(2) of the Children and Young Persons Act 1933 has effect as if the persons entitled to be present at a sitting for the purposes of those proceedings include one person authorised to be present by a relevant authority.
...

4   Appeals against orders

(1) An appeal shall lie to the Crown Court against the making by a magistrates' court of an anti-social behaviour order, an individual support order or an order under section 1D above.
(2) On such an appeal the Crown Court—
   (a) may make such orders as may be necessary to give effect to its determination of the appeal; and
   (b) may also make such incidental or consequential orders as appear to it to be just.
(3) Any order of the Crown Court made on an appeal under this section (other than one directing that an application be re-heard by a magistrates' court) shall, for the purposes of section 1(8) or 1AB(6) above, be treated as if it were an order of the magistrates' court from which the appeal was brought and not an order of the Crown Court.

11   Child safety orders

(1) Subject to subsection (2) below, if a magistrates' court, on the application of a local authority, is satisfied that one or more of the conditions specified in subsection (3) below are fulfilled with respect to a child under the age of 10, it may make an order (a "child safety order") which—

(a) places the child, for a period (not exceeding the permitted maximum) specified in the order, under the supervision of the responsible officer; and
(b) requires the child to comply with such requirements as are so specified.

(2) A court shall not make a child safety order unless it has been notified by the Secretary of State that arrangements for implementing such orders are available in the area in which it appears that the child resides or will reside and the notice has not been withdrawn.

(3) The conditions are—
(a) that the child has committed an act which, if he had been aged 10 or over, would have constituted an offence;
(b) that a child safety order is necessary for the purpose of preventing the commission by the child of such an act as is mentioned in paragraph (a) above;
(c) that the child has contravened a ban imposed by a curfew notice; and
(d) that the child has acted in a manner that caused or was likely to cause harassment, alarm or distress to one or more persons not of the same household as himself.

(4) The maximum period permitted for the purposes of subsection (1)(a) above is twelve months . . .

(5) The requirements that may be specified under subsection (1)(b) above are those which the court considers desirable in the interests of—
(a) securing that the child receives appropriate care, protection and support and is subject to proper control; or
(b) preventing any repetition of the kind of behaviour which led to the child safety order being made.

(6) Proceedings under this section or section 12 below shall be family proceedings for the purposes of the 1989 Act or section 65 of the Magistrates' Courts Act 1980 ("the 1980 Act"); and the standard of proof applicable to such proceedings shall be that applicable to civil proceedings.

(7) In this section "local authority" has the same meaning as in the 1989 Act.

(8) In this section and section 12 below, "responsible officer", in relation to a child safety order, means one of the following who is specified in the order, namely—
(a) a social worker of a local authority . . .; and
(b) a member of a youth offending team.

13 Appeals against child safety orders

(1) An appeal shall lie to the High Court against the making by a magistrates' court of a child safety order; and on such an appeal the High Court—
(a) may make such orders as may be necessary to give effect to its determination of the appeal; and
(b) may also make such incidental or consequential orders as appear to it to be just.

. . .

14 Local child curfew schemes

(1) A local authority or a chief officer of police may make a scheme (a "local child curfew scheme") for enabling the authority or (as the case may be) the officer—
(a) subject to and in accordance with the provisions of the scheme; and
(b) if, after such consultation as is required by the scheme, the authority or (as the case may be the officer considers it necessary to do so for the purpose of maintaining order,
to give a notice imposing, for a specified period (not exceeding 90 days), a ban to which subsection (2) below applies.

(2) This subsection applies to a ban on children of specified ages (under 16) being in a public place within a specified area—
(a) during specified hours (between 9 am and 6 am); and
(b) otherwise than under the effective control of a parent or a responsible person aged 18 or over.

(3) Before making a local child curfew scheme, a local authority shall consult—
(a) every chief officer of police any part of whose police area lies within its area; and

(b) such other persons or bodies as it considers appropriate.
(3A) Before making a local child curfew scheme, a chief officer of police shall consult—
   (a) every local authority any part of whose area lies within the area to be specified; and
   (b) such other persons as he considers appropriate.
(4) A local child curfew scheme shall, if made by a local authority, be made under the common seal of the authority.
(4A) A local child curfew scheme shall not have effect until it is confirmed by the Secretary of State.
(5) The Secretary of State—
   (a) may confirm, or refuse to confirm, a local curfew scheme submitted under this section for confirmation; and
   (b) may fix the date on which such a scheme is to come into operation;
   and if no date is so fixed, the scheme shall come into operation at the end of the period of one month beginning with the date of its confirmation.
(6) A notice given under a local child curfew scheme (a "curfew notice") may specify different hours in relation to children of different ages.
(7), (8) . . .

15 Contravention of curfew notices
(1) Subsections (2) and (3) below apply where a constable has reasonable cause to believe that a child is in contravention of a ban imposed by a curfew notice.
(2) The constable shall, as soon as practicable, inform the local authority for the area that the child has contravened the ban.
(3) The constable may remove the child to the child's place of residence unless he has reasonable cause to believe that the child would, if removed to that place, be likely to suffer significant harm.

. . .

PART II
CRIMINAL LAW

Racially or religiously aggravated offences: England and Wales

28 Meaning of "racially or religously aggravated"
(1) An offence is racially or religiously aggravated for the purposes of sections 29 to 32 below if—
   (a) at the time of committing the offence, or immediately before or after doing so, the offender demonstrates towards the victim of the offence hostility based on the victim's membership (or presumed membership) of a racial group; or
   (b) the offence is motivated (wholly or partly) by hostility towards members of a racial group based on their membership of that group.
(2) In subsection (1)(a) above—
   "membership", in relation to a racial or religious group, includes association with members of that group;
   "presumed" means presumed by the offender.
(3) It is immaterial for the purposes of paragraph (a) or (b) of subsection (1) above whether or not the offender's hostility is also based, to any extent, on any other factor not mentioned in that paragraph.
(4) In this section "racial group" means a group of persons defined by reference to race, colour, nationality (including citizenship) or ethnic or national origins.
(5) In this section "religious group" means a group of persons defined by reference to religious belief or lack of religious belief.

29 Racially or religiously aggravated assaults
(1) A person is guilty of an offence under this section if he commits—
   (a) an offence under section 20 of the Offences Against the Person Act 1861 (malicious wounding or grievous bodily harm);

(b) an offence under section 47 of that Act (actual bodily harm); or
(c) common assault,
which is racially or religiously aggravated for the purposes of this section.
(2) A person guilty of an offence falling within subsection (1)(a) or (b) above shall be liable—
   (a) on summary conviction, to imprisonment for a term not exceeding six months or to a fine not exceeding the statutory maximum, or to both;
   (b) on conviction on indictment, to imprisonment for a term not exceeding seven years or to a fine, or to both.
(3) A person guilty of an offence falling within subsection (1)(c) above shall be liable—
   (a) on summary conviction, to imprisonment for a term not exceeding six months or to a fine not exceeding the statutory maximum, or to both;
   (b) on conviction on indictment, to imprisonment for a term not exceeding two years or to a fine, or to both.

30 Racially or religiously aggravated criminal damage

(1) A person is guilty of an offence under this section if he commits an offence under section 1(1) of the Criminal Damage Act 1971 (destroying or damaging property belonging to another) which is racially or religiously aggravated for the purposes of this section.
(2) A person guilty of an offence under this section shall be liable—
   (a) on summary conviction, to imprisonment for a term not exceeding six months or to a fine not exceeding the statutory maximum, or to both;
   (b) on conviction on indictment, to imprisonment for a term not exceeding fourteen years or to a fine, or to both.
(3) For the purposes of this section, section 28(1)(a) above shall have effect as if the person to whom the property belongs or is treated as belonging for the purposes of that Act were the victim of the offence.

31 Racially or religiously aggravated public order offences

(1) A person is guilty of an offence under this section if he commits—
   (a) an offence under section 4 of the Public Order Act 1986 (fear or provocation of violence);
   (b) an offence under section 4A of that Act (intentional harassment, alarm or distress); or
   (c) an offence under section 5 of that Act (harassment, alarm or distress), which is racially or religiously aggravated for the purposes of this section.
. . .
(4) A person guilty of an offence falling within subsection (1)(a) or (b) above shall be liable—
   (a) on summary conviction, to imprisonment for a term not exceeding six months or to a fine not exceeding the statutory maximum, or to both;
   (b) on conviction on indictment, to imprisonment for a term not exceeding two years or to a fine, or to both.
(5) A person guilty of an offence falling within subsection (1)(c) above shall be liable on summary conviction to a fine not exceeding level 4 on the standard scale.
. . .

32 Racially or religiously aggravated harassment etc.

(1) A person is guilty of an offence under this section if he commits—
   (a) an offence under section 2 of the Protection from Harassment Act 1997 (offence of harassment); or
   (b) an offence under section 4 of that Act (putting people in fear of violence),
   which is racially or religiously aggravated for the purposes of this section.
. . .
(3) A person guilty of an offence falling within subsection (1)(a) above shall be liable—
   (a) on summary conviction, to imprisonment for a term not exceeding six months or to a fine not exceeding the statutory maximum, or to both;
   (b) on conviction on indictment, to imprisonment for a term not exceeding two years or to a fine, or to both.

(4) A person guilty of an offence falling within subsection (1)(b) above shall be liable—
  (a) on summary conviction, to imprisonment for a term not exceeding six months or to a fine not exceeding the statutory maximum, or to both;
  (b) on conviction on indictment, to imprisonment for a term not exceeding seven years or to a fine, or to both.

...

Miscellaneous

34 Abolition of rebuttable presumption that a child is doli incapax

The rebuttable presumption of criminal law that a child aged 10 or over is incapable of committing an offence is hereby abolished.

36 Abolition of death penalty for treason and piracy

(1) In section I of the Treason Act (Ireland) 1537 (practising any harm etc to, or slandering, the King, Queen or heirs apparent punishable as high treason), for the words "have and suffer such pains of death and" there shall be substituted the words "be liable to imprisonment for life and to such".

(2) In the following enactments, namely—
  (a) section II of the Crown of Ireland Act 1542 (occasioning disturbance etc to the crown of Ireland punishable as high treason);
  (b) section XII of the Act of Supremacy (Ireland) 1560 (penalties for maintaining or defending foreign authority);
  (c) section 3 of the Treason Act 1702 (endeavouring to hinder the succession to the Crown etc punishable as high treason);
  (d) section I of the Treason Act (Ireland) 1703 (which makes corresponding provision),
  for the words "suffer pains of death" there shall be substituted the words "be liable to imprisonment for life".

(3) The following enactments shall cease to have effect, namely—
  (a) the Treason Act 1790;
  (b) the Treason Act 1795.

(4) In section 1 of the Treason Act 1814 (form of sentence in case of high treason), for the words "such person shall be hanged by the neck until such person be dead", there shall be substituted the words "such person shall be liable to imprisonment for life".

(5) In section 2 of the Piracy Act 1837 (punishment of piracy when murder is attempted), for the words "and being convicted thereof shall suffer death" there shall be substituted the words "and being convicted thereof shall be liable to imprisonment for life".

(6) The following enactments shall cease to have effect, namely—
  (a) the Sentence of Death (Expectant Mothers) Act 1931; and
  (b) sections 32 and 33 of the Criminal Justice Act (Northern Ireland) 1945 (which make corresponding provision).

HUMAN RIGHTS ACT 1998
(1998, c 42)

An Act to give further effect to rights and freedoms guaranteed under the European Convention on Human Rights; to make provision with respect to holders of certain judicial offices who become judges of the European Court of Human Rights; and for connected purposes. [9 November 1998]

Introduction

1 The Convention Rights

(1) In this Act "the Convention rights" means the rights and fundamental freedoms set out in—
  (a) Articles 2 to 12 and 14 of the Convention,
  (b) Articles 1 to 3 of the First Protocol, and
  (c) Article 1 of the Thirteenth Protocol,

as read with Articles 16 to 18 of the Convention.
- (2) Those Articles are to have effect for the purposes of this Act subject to any designated derogation or reservation (as to which see sections 14 and 15).
- (3) The Articles are set out in Schedule 1.
- (4) The Secretary of State may by order make such amendments to this Act as he considers appropriate to reflect the effect, in relation to the United Kingdom, of a protocol.
- (5) In subsection (4) "protocol" means a protocol to the Convention—
  - (a) which the United Kingdom has ratified; or
  - (b) which the United Kingdom has signed with a view to ratification.
- (6) No amendment may be made by an order under subsection (4) so as to come into force before the protocol concerned is in force in relation to the United Kingdom.

2 Interpretation of Convention rights

- (1) A court or tribunal determining a question which has arisen in connection with a Convention right must take into account any—
  - (a) judgment, decision, declaration or advisory opinion of the European Court of Human Rights,
  - (b) opinion of the Commission given in a report adopted under Article 31 of the Convention,
  - (c) decision of the Commission in connection with Article 26 or 27(2) of the Convention, or
  - (d) decision of the Committee of Ministers taken under Article 46 of the Convention,

  whenever made or given, so far as, in the opinion of the court or tribunal, it is relevant to the proceedings in which that question has arisen.
- (2) Evidence of any judgment, decision, declaration or opinion of which account may have to be taken under this section is to be given in proceedings before any court or tribunal in such manner as may be provided by rules.
- (3) In this section "rules" means rules of court or, in the case of proceedings before a tribunal, rules made for the purposes of this section—
  - (a) by . . . the Lord Chancellor or the Secretary of State, in relation to any proceedings outside Scotland;
  - (b) by the Secretary of State, in relation to proceedings in Scotland; or
  - (c) by a Northern Ireland department, in relation to proceedings before a tribunal in Northern Ireland—
    - (i) which deals with transferred matters; and
    - (ii) for which no rules made under paragraph (a) are in force.

Legislation

3 Interpretation of legislation

- (1) So far as it is possible to do so, primary legislation and subordinate legislation must be read and given effect in a way which is compatible with the Convention rights.
- (2) This section—
  - (a) applies to primary legislation and subordinate legislation whenever enacted;
  - (b) does not affect the validity, continuing operation or enforcement of any incompatible primary legislation; and
  - (c) does not affect the validity, continuing operation or enforcement of any incompatible subordinate legislation if (disregarding any possibility of revocation) primary legislation prevents removal of the incompatibility.

4 Declaration of incompatibility

- (1) Subsection (2) applies in any proceedings in which a court determines whether a provision of primary legislation is compatible with a Convention right.
- (2) If the court is satisfied that the provision is incompatible with a Convention right, it may make a declaration of that incompatibility.

(3) Subsection (4) applies in any proceedings in which a court determines whether a provision of subordinate legislation, made in the exercise of a power conferred by primary legislation, is compatible with a Convention right.

(4) If the court is satisfied—
   (a) that the provision is incompatible with a Convention right, and
   (b) that (disregarding any possibility of revocation) the primary legislation concerned prevents removal of the incompatibility,
   it may make a declaration of that incompatibility.

(5) In this section "court" means—
   (a) the House of Lords [*the Supreme Court*];
   (b) the Judicial Committee of the Privy Council;
   (c) the Courts-Martial Appeal Court [*Court Martial Appeal Court*];
   (d) in Scotland, the High Court of Justiciary sitting otherwise than as a trial court or the Court of Session;
   (e) in England and Wales or Northern Ireland, the High Court or the Court of Appeal;
   (f) the Court of Protection, in any matter being dealt with by the President of the Family Division, the Vice-Chancellor or a puisne judge of the High Court.

(6) A declaration under this section ("a declaration of incompatibility")—
   (a) does not affect the validity, continuing operation or enforcement of the provision in respect of which it is given; and
   (b) is not binding on the parties to the proceedings in which it is made.

5 Right of Crown to intervene

(1) Where a court is considering whether to make a declaration of incompatibility, the Crown is entitled to notice in accordance with rules of court.

(2) In any case to which subsection (1) applies—
   (a) a Minister of the Crown (or a person nominated by him),
   (b) a member of the Scottish Executive,
   (c) a Northern Ireland Minister,
   (d) a Northern Ireland department,
   is entitled, on giving notice in accordance with rules of court, to be joined as a party to the proceedings.

(3) Notice under subsection (2) may be given at any time during the proceedings.

(4) A person who has been made a party to criminal proceedings (other than in Scotland) as the result of a notice under subsection (2) may, with leave, appeal to the House of Lords [*Supreme Court*] against any declaration of incompatibility made in the proceedings.

(5) In subsection (4)—
   "criminal proceedings" includes all proceedings before the Courts-Martial Appeal Court [*Court Martial Appeal Court*]; and
   "leave" means leave granted by the court making the declaration of incompatibility or by the House of Lords [*Supreme Court*].

Public authorities

6 Acts of public authorities

(1) It is unlawful for a public authority to act in a way which is incompatible with a Convention right.

(2) Subsection (1) does not apply to an act if—
   (a) as the result of one or more provisions of primary legislation, the authority could not have acted differently; or
   (b) in the case of one or more provisions of, or made under, primary legislation which cannot be read or given effect in a way which is compatible with the Convention rights, the authority was acting so as to give effect to or enforce those provisions.

(3) In this section "public authority" includes—
   (a) a court or tribunal, and
   (b) any person certain of whose functions are functions of a public nature,

but does not include either House of Parliament or a person exercising functions in connection with proceedings in Parliament.

(4) *In subsection (3) "Parliament" does not include the House of Lords in its judicial capacity.*

(5) In relation to a particular act, a person is not a public authority by virtue only of subsection (3)(b) if the nature of the act is private.

(6) "An act" includes a failure to act but does not include a failure to—
   (a) introduce in, or lay before, Parliament a proposal for legislation; or
   (b) make any primary legislation or remedial order.

Note: Section 6(4) will be repealed when the Supreme Court is established under the Constitutional Reform Act 2005 and the judicial functions of the House of Lords transferred.

7 Proceedings

(1) A person who claims that a public authority has acted (or proposes to act) in a way which is made unlawful by section 6(1) may—
   (a) bring proceedings against the authority under this Act in the appropriate court or tribunal, or
   (b) rely on the Convention right or rights concerned in any legal proceedings,
but only if he is (or would be) a victim of the unlawful act.

...

(3) If the proceedings are brought on an application for judicial review, the applicant is to be taken to have a sufficient interest in relation to the unlawful act only if he is, or would be, a victim of that act.

(4) If the proceedings are made by way of a petition for judicial review in Scotland, the applicant shall be taken to have title and interest to sue in relation to the unlawful act only if he is, or would be, a victim of that act.

(5) Proceedings under subsection (1)(a) must be brought before the end of—
   (a) the period of one year beginning with the date on which the act complained of took place; or
   (b) such longer period as the court or tribunal considers equitable having regard to all the circumstances,
but that is subject to any rule imposing a stricter time limit in relation to the procedure in question.

(6) In subsection (1)(b) "legal proceedings" includes—
   (a) proceedings brought by or at the instigation of a public authority; and
   (b) an appeal against the decision of a court or tribunal.

(7) For the purposes of this section, a person is a victim of an unlawful act only if he would be a victim for the purposes of Article 34 of the Convention if proceedings were brought in the European Court of Human Rights in respect of that act.

(8) Nothing in this Act creates a criminal offence.

...

8 Judicial remedies

(1) In relation to any act (or proposed act) of a public authority which the court finds is (or would be) unlawful, it may grant such relief or remedy, or make such order, within its powers as it considers just and appropriate.

(2) But damages may be awarded only by a court which has power to award damages, or to order the payment of compensation, in civil proceedings.

(3) No award of damages is to be made unless, taking account of all the circumstances of the case, including—
   (a) any other relief or remedy granted, or order made, in relation to the act in question (by that or any other court), and
   (b) the consequences of any decision (of that or any other court) in respect of that act,
the court is satisfied that the award is necessary to afford just satisfaction to the person in whose favour it is made.

(4) In determining—

(a) whether to award damages, or

(b) the amount of an award,

the court must take into account the principles applied by the European Court of Human Rights in relation to the award of compensation under Article 41 of the Convention.

...

9 Judicial acts

(1) Proceedings under section 7(1)(a) in respect of a judicial act may be brought only—
   (a) by exercising a right of appeal;
   (b) on an application (in Scotland a petition) for judicial review; or
   (c) in such other forum as may be prescribed by rules.

(2) That does not affect any rule of law which prevents a court from being the subject of judicial review.

(3) In proceedings under this Act in respect of a judicial act done in good faith, damages may not be awarded otherwise than to compensate a person to the extent required by Article 5(5) of the Convention.

(4) An award of damages permitted by subsection (3) is to be made against the Crown; but no award may be made unless the appropriate person, if not a party to the proceedings, is joined.

(5) In this section—

"appropriate person" means the Minister responsible for the court concerned, or a person or government department nominated by him;

"court" includes a tribunal;

"judge" includes a member of a tribunal, a justice of the peace (or, in Northern Ireland, a lay magistrate) and a clerk or other officer entitled to exercise the jurisdiction of a court;

"judicial act" means a judicial act of a court and includes an act done on the instructions, or on behalf, of a judge; and

"rules" has the same meaning as in section 7(9).

Remedial action

10 Power to take remedial action

(1) This section applies if—
   (a) a provision of legislation has been declared under section 4 to be incompatible with a Convention right and, if an appeal lies—
      (i) all persons who may appeal have stated in writing that they do not intend to do so;
      (ii) the time for bringing an appeal has expired and no appeal has been brought within that time; or
      (iii) an appeal brought within that time has been determined or abandoned; or
   (b) it appears to a Minister of the Crown or Her Majesty in Council that, having regard to a finding of the European Court of Human Rights made after the coming into force of this section in proceedings against the United Kingdom, a provision of legislation is incompatible with an obligation of the United Kingdom arising from the Convention.

(2) If a Minister of the Crown considers that there are compelling reasons for proceeding under this section, he may by order make such amendments to the legislation as he considers necessary to remove the incompatibility.

(3) If, in the case of subordinate legislation, a Minister of the Crown considers—
   (a) that it is necessary to amend the primary legislation under which the subordinate legislation in question was made, in order to enable the incompatibility to be removed, and
   (b) that there are compelling reasons for proceeding under this section,

he may by order make such amendments to the primary legislation as he considers necessary.

(4) This section also applies where the provision in question is in subordinate legislation and has been quashed, or declared invalid, by reason of incompatibility with a Convention right and the Minister proposes to proceed under paragraph 2(b) of Schedule 2.

...

Other rights and proceedings

11 Safeguard for existing human rights

A person's reliance on a Convention right does not restrict—
(a) any other right or freedom conferred on him by or under any law having effect in any part of the United Kingdom; or
(b) his right to make any claim or bring any proceedings which he could make or bring apart from sections 7 to 9.

12 Freedom of expression

(1) This section applies if a court is considering whether to grant any relief which, if granted, might affect the exercise of the Convention right to freedom of expression.
(2) If the person against whom the application for relief is made ("the respondent") is neither present nor represented, no such relief is to be granted unless the court is satisfied—
　(a) that the applicant has taken all practicable steps to notify the respondent; or
　(b) that there are compelling reasons why the respondent should not be notified.
(3) No such relief is to be granted so as to restrain publication before trial unless the court is satisfied that the applicant is likely to establish that publication should not be allowed.
(4) The court must have particular regard to the importance of the Convention right to freedom of expression and, where the proceedings relate to material which the respondent claims, or which appears to the court, to be journalistic, literary or artistic material (or to conduct connected with such material), to—
　(a) the extent to which—
　　(i) the material has, or is about to, become available to the public; or
　　(ii) it is, or would be, in the public interest for the material to be published;
　(b) any relevant privacy code.
(5) In this section—
"court" includes a tribunal; and
"relief" includes any remedy or order (other than in criminal proceedings).

13 Freedom of thought, conscience and religion

(1) 'If a court's determination of any question arising under this Act might affect the exercise by a religious organisation (itself or its members collectively) of the Convention right to freedom of thought, conscience and religion, it must have particular regard to the importance of that right.
(2) In this section "court" includes a tribunal.

Derogations and reservations

14 Derogations

(1) In this Act "designated derogation" means any derogation by the United Kingdom from an Article of the Convention, or of any protocol to the Convention, which is designated for the purposes of this Act in an order made by the Secretary of State.
(2) ...
(3) If a designated derogation is amended or replaced it ceases to be a designated derogation.
(4) But subsection (3) does not prevent the Secretary of State from exercising his power under subsection (1) to make a fresh designation order in respect of the Article concerned.
(5) ...
(6) A designation order may be made in anticipation of the making by the United Kingdom of a proposed derogation.

15 Reservations

(1) In this Act "designated reservation" means—

    (a) the United Kingdom's reservation to Article 2 of the First Protocol to the Convention; and
    (b) any other reservation by the United Kingdom to an Article of the Convention, or of any protocol to the Convention, which is designated for the purposes of this Act in an order made by the Secretary of State.
(2) The text of the reservation referred to in subsection (1)(a) is set out in Part II of Schedule 3.
(3) If a designated reservation is withdrawn wholly or in part it ceases to be a designated reservation.
(4) But subsection (3) does not prevent the Secretary of State from exercising his power under subsection (1)(b) to make a fresh designation order in respect of the Article concerned.
(5) The Secretary of State must by order make such amendments to this Act as he considers appropriate to reflect—
    (a) any designation order; or
    (b) the effect of subsection (3).

16 Period for which designated derogations have effect

(1) If it has not already been withdrawn by the United Kingdom, a designated derogation ceases to have effect for the purposes of this Act at the end of the period of five years beginning with the date on which designating it was made.
(2) At any time before the period—
    (a) fixed by subsection (1)(a), or
    (b) extended by an order under this subsection,
    comes to an end, the Secretary of State may by order extend it by a further period of five years.
(3) An order under section 14(1) ceases to have effect at the end of the period for consideration, unless a resolution has been passed by each House approving the order.
(4) Subsection (3) does not affect—
    (a) anything done in reliance on the order; or
    (b) the power to make a fresh order under section 14(1).

. . .

Parliamentary procedure

19 Statements of compatibility

(1) A Minister of the Crown in charge of a Bill in either House of Parliament must, before Second Reading of the Bill—
    (a) make a statement to the effect that in his view the provisions of the Bill are compatible with the Convention rights ("a statement of compatibility"); or
    (b) make a statement to the effect that although he is unable to make a statement of compatibility the government nevertheless wishes the House to proceed with the Bill.
(2) The statement must be in writing and be published in such manner as the Minister making it considers appropriate.

Supplemental

20 Orders etc. under this Act

(1) Any power of a Minister of the Crown to make an order under this Act is exercisable by statutory instrument.

SCHEDULE 2
REMEDIAL ORDERS

Orders

1. (1) A remedial order may—
    (a) contain such incidental, supplemental, consequential or transitional provision as the person making it considers appropriate;
    (b) be made so as to have effect from a date earlier than that on which it is made;

(c) make provision for the delegation of specific functions;
(d) make different provision for different cases.

(2) The power conferred by sub-paragraph (1)(a) includes—
  (a) power to amend primary legislation (including primary legislation other than that which contains the incompatible provision); and
  (b) power to amend or revoke subordinate legislation (including subordinate legislation other than that which contains the incompatible provision).

(3) A remedial order may be made so as to have the same extent as the legislation which it affects.

(4) No person is to be guilty of an offence solely as a result of the retrospective effect of a remedial order.

Procedure

2. No remedial order may be made unless—
  (a) a draft of the order has been approved by a resolution of each House of Parliament made after the end of the period of 60 days beginning with the day on which the draft was laid; or
  (b) it is declared in the order that it appears to the person making it that, because of the urgency of the matter, it is necessary to make the order without a draft being so approved.

. . .

Calculating periods

6. In calculating any period for the purposes of this Schedule, no account is to be taken of any time during which—
  (a) Parliament is dissolved or prorogued; or
  (b) both Houses are adjourned for more than four days.

7. (1) This paragraph applies in relation to—
  (a) any remedial order made, and any draft of such an order proposed to be made,—
    (i) by the Scottish Ministers; or
    (ii) within devolved competence (within the meaning of the Scotland Act 1998) by Her Majesty in Council; and
  (b) any document or statement to be laid in connection with such an order (or proposed order).

(2) This Schedule has effect in relation to any such order (or proposed order), document or statement subject to the following modifications.

(3) Any reference to Parliament, each House of Parliament or both Houses of Parliament shall be construed as a reference to the Scottish Parliament.

(4) Paragraph 6 does not apply and instead, in calculating any period for the purposes of this Schedule, no account is to be taken of any time during which the Scottish Parliament is dissolved or is in recess for more than four days.

SCOTLAND ACT 1998
(1998, c. 46)

An Act to provide for the establishment of a Scottish Parliament and Administration and other changes in the government of Scotland; to provide for changes in the constitution and functions of certain public authorities; to provide for the variation of the basic rate of income tax in relation to income of Scottish taxpayers in accordance with a resolution of the Scottish Parliament; to amend the law about parliamentary constituencies in Scotland; and for connected purposes. [19 November 1998]

PART I
THE SCOTTISH PARLIAMENT

The Scottish Parliament

1 The Scottish Parliament
(1) There shall be a Scottish Parliament.

(2) One member of the Parliament shall be returned for each constituency (under the simple majority system) at an election held in the constituency.

(3) Members of the Parliament for each region shall be returned at a general election under the additional member system of proportional representation provided for in this part and vacancies among such members shall be filled in accordance with this Part.

(4) The validity of any proceedings of the Parliament is not affected by any vacancy in its membership.

(5) Schedule 1 (which makes provision for the constituencies and regions for the purposes of this Act and the number of regional members) shall have effect.

General elections

2 Ordinary general elections

(1) The day on which the poll at the first ordinary general election for membership of the Parliament shall be held, and the day, time and place for the meeting of the Parliament following that poll, shall be appointed by order made by the Secretary of State.

(2) The poll at subsequent ordinary general elections shall be held on the first Thursday in May in the fourth calendar year following that in which the previous ordinary general election was held, unless the day of the poll is determined by a proclamation under subsection (5).

(3) If the poll is to be held on the first Thursday in May, the Parliament—
  (a) is dissolved by virtue of this section at the beginning of the minimum period which ends with that day, and
  (b) shall meet within the period of seven days beginning immediately after the day of the poll.

(4) In subsection (3), "the minimum period" means the period determined in accordance with an order under section 12(1).

(5) If the Presiding Officer proposes a day for the holding of the poll which is not more than one month earlier, nor more than one month later, than the first Thursday in May, Her Majesty may by proclamation under the Scottish Seal—
  (a) dissolve the Parliament,
  (b) require the poll at the election to be held on the day proposed, and
  (c) require the Parliament to meet within the period of seven days beginning immediately after the day of the poll.

(6) In this Act "the Scottish Seal" means Her Majesty's Seal appointed by the Treaty of Union to be kept and used in Scotland in place of the Great Seal of Scotland.

5 Candidates

(1) At a general election, the candidates may stand for return as constituency members or regional members.

(2) A person may not be a candidate to be a constituency member for more than one constituency.

(3) The candidates to be regional members shall be those included in a list submitted under subsection (4) or individual candidates.

(4) Any registered political party may submit to the regional returning officer a list of candidates to be regional members for a particular region (referred to in this Act, in relation to the region, as the party's "regional list").

(5) A registered political party's regional list has effect in relation to the general election and any vacancy occurring among the regional members after that election and before the next general election.

(6) Not more than twelve persons may be included in the list (but the list may include only one person).

(7) A registered political party's regional list must not include a person—
  (a) who is included in any other list submitted under subsection (4) for the region or any list submitted under that subsection for another region,
  (b) who is an individual candidate to be a regional member for the region or another region,

(c) who is a candidate to be a constituency member for a constituency not included in the region, or
(d) who is a candidate to be a constituency member for a constituency included in the region but is not a candidate of that party.

(8) A person may not be an individual candidate to be a regional member for a particular region if he is—
(a) included in a list submitted under subsection (4) for the region or another region,
(b) an individual candidate to be a regional member for another region,
(c) a candidate to be a constituency member for a constituency not included in the region, or
(d) a candidate of any registered political party to be a constituency member for a constituency included in the region.

(9) In this Act, "registered political party" means a party registered under Part II of the Political Parties, Elections and Referendums Act 2000.

6 Poll for regional members

(1) This section and sections 7 and 8 are about the return of regional members at a general election.
(2) In each of the constituencies for the Parliament, a poll shall be held at which each person entitled to vote as elector may give a vote (referred to in this Act as a "regional vote") for—
(a) a registered political party which has submitted a regional list, or
(b) an individual candidate to be a regional member for the region.
(3) The right conferred on a person by subsection (2) is in addition to any right the person may have to vote in any poll for the return of a constituency member.

7 Calculation of regional figures

(1) The persons who are to be returned as constituency members for constituencies included in the region must be determined before the persons who are to be returned as the regional members for the region.
(2) For each registered political party which has submitted a regional list, the regional figure for the purposes of section 8 is—
(a) the total number of regional votes given for the party in all the constituencies included in the region,
divided by
(b) the aggregate of one plus the number of candidates of the party returned as constituency members for any of those constituencies.
(3) Each time a seat is allocated to the party under section 8, that figure shall be recalculated by increasing (or further increasing) the aggregate in subsection (2)(b) by one.
(4) For each individual candidate to be a regional member for the region, the regional figure for the purposes of section 8 is the total number of regional votes given for him in all the constituencies included in the region.

8 Allocation of seats to regional members

(1) The first regional member seat shall be allocated to the registered political party or individual candidate with the highest regional figure.
(2) the second and subsequent regional member seats shall be allocated to the registered political party or individual candidate with the highest regional figure, after any recalculation required by section 7(3) has been carried out.
(3) An individual candidate already returned as a constituency or regional member shall be disregarded.
(4) Seats for the region which are allocated to a registered political party shall be filled by the persons in the party's regional list in the order in which they appear in the list.
(5) For the purposes of this section and section 10, a person in a registered political party's regional list who is returned as a member of the Parliament shall be treated as ceasing to be in the list (even if his return is void).

(6) Once a party's regional list has been exhausted (by the return of persons included in it as constituency members or by the previous application of subsection (1) or (2)) the party shall be disregarded.

(7) If (on the application of subsection (1) or any application of subsection (2)) the highest figure is the regional figure of two or more parties or individual candidates—
   (a) the subsection in question shall apply to each of them; or
   (b) if paragraph (a) would result in more than the correct number of seats for the region being allocated, the subsection in question shall apply as if the regional figure for each of those parties or candidates had been adjusted in accordance with subsection (8).

(8) The regional figure for a party or candidate is adjusted in accordance with this subsection by—
   (a) adding one vote to the total number of regional votes given for the party or candidate in all the constituencies included in the region; and
   (b) (in the case of a party) recalculating the regional figure accordingly.

(9) If, on the application of the subsection in question in accordance with subsection (7)(b), seats would be allocated to two or more parties or individual candidates and that would result in more than the correct number of seats for the region being allocated, the regional returning officer shall decide between them by lot.

Franchise and conduct of elections

11 Electors

(1) The persons entitled to vote as electors at an election for membership of the parliament held in any constituency are those who on the day of the poll—
   (a) would be entitled to vote as electors at a local government election in an electoral area falling wholly or partly within the constituency, and
   (b) are registered in the register of local government electors at an address within the constituency.

(2) A person is not entitled to vote as elector in any constituency—
   (a) more than once at a poll for the return of a constituency member, or
   (b) more than once at a poll for the return of regional members,
   or to vote as elector in more than one constituency at a general election.

Duration of membership

13 Term of office of members

The term of office of a member of the Parliament begins on the day on which the member is declared to be returned and ends with the dissolution of the Parliament.

14 Resignation of members

A member of the Parliament may at any time resign his seat by giving notice in writing to the Presiding Officer.

Disqualification

15 Disqualification from membership of the Parliament

(1) A person is disqualified from being a member of the Parliament (subject to section 16) if—
   (a) he is disqualified from being a member of the House of Commons under paragraphs (a) to (e) of section 1(1) of the House of Commons Disqualification Act 1975 (judges, civil servants, members of the armed forces, members of police forces and members of foreign legislatures),
   (b) he is disqualified otherwise than under that Act (either generally or in relation to a particular parliamentary constituency) from being a member of the House of Commons or from sitting and voting in it,
   (c) he is a Lord of Appeal in Ordinary, or
   (d) he is an office-holder of a description specified in an Order in Council made by Her Majesty under this subsection.

(2) An office-holder of a description specified in an Order in Council made by Her Majesty under this subsection is disqualified from being a member of the Parliament for any constituency or region of a description specified in the Order in relation to the office-holder.

(3) In this section "office-holder" includes employee or other post-holder.

16 Exceptions and relief from disqualification

(1) A person is not disqualified from being a member of the Parliament merely because—
   (a) he is a peer (whether of the United Kingdom, Great Britain, England or Scotland), or
   (b) he is a Lord Spiritual.

(2) A citizen of the European Union who is resident in the United Kingdom is not disqualified from being a member of the Parliament merely because of section 3 of the Act of Settlement (disqualification of persons born outside the United Kingdom other than certain Commonwealth citizens and citizens of the Republic of Ireland).

...

Presiding Officer and administration

19 Presiding Officer

(1) The Parliament shall, at its first meeting following a general election, elect from among its members a Presiding Officer and two deputies.

(2) A person elected Presiding Officer or deputy shall hold office until the conclusion of the next election for Presiding Officer under subsection (1) unless he previously resigns, ceases to be a member of the Parliament otherwise than by virtue of a dissolution or is removed from office by resolution of the Parliament.

(3) If the Presiding Officer or a deputy ceases to hold office before the Parliament is dissolved, the Parliament shall elect another from among its members to fill his place.

(4) The Presiding Officer's functions may be exercised by a deputy if the office of Presiding Officer is vacant or the Presiding Officer is for any reason unable to act.

(5) The Presiding Officer may (subject to standing orders) authorise any deputy to exercise functions on his behalf.

(6) Standing orders may include provision as to the participation (including voting) of the Presiding Officer and deputies in the proceedings of the Parliament.

(7) The validity of any act of the Presiding Officer or a deputy is not affected by any defect in his election.

Proceedings etc.

22 Standing orders

(1) The proceedings of the Parliament shall be regulated by standing orders.

...

Legislation

28 Acts of the Scottish Parliament

(1) Subject to section 29, the Parliament may make laws, to be known as Acts of the Scottish Parliament.

(2) Proposed Acts of the Scottish Parliament shall be known as Bills; and a Bill shall become an Act of the Scottish Parliament when it has been passed by the Parliament and has received Royal Assent.

(3) A Bill receives Royal Assent at the beginning of the day on which Letters Patent under the Scottish Seal signed with Her Majesty's own hand signifying Her Assent are recorded in the Register of the Great Seal.

(4) The date of Royal Assent shall be written on the Act of the Scottish Parliament by the Clerk, and shall form part of the Act.

(5) the validity of an Act of the Scottish Parliament is not affected by any invalidity in the proceedings of the Parliament leading to its enactment.

(6) Every Act of the Scottish Parliament shall be judicially noticed.

(7) This section does not affect the power of the Parliament of the United Kingdom to make laws for Scotland.

29 Legislative competence

(1) An Act of the Scottish Parliament is not law so far as any provision of the Act is outside the legislative competence of the Parliament.

(2) A provision is outside the competence so far as any of the following paragraphs apply—
   (a) it would form part of the law of a country or territory other than Scotland, or confer or remove functions exercisable otherwise than in or as regards Scotland,
   (b) it relates to reserved matters,
   (c) it is in breach of the restrictions in Schedule 4.
   (d) it is incompatible with any of the Convention rights or with Community law,
   (e) it would remove the Lord Advocate from his position as head of the systems of criminal prosecution and investigation of deaths in Scotland.

(3) For the purposes of this section, the question whether a provision of an Act of the Scottish Parliament relates to a reserved matter is to be determined, subject to subsection (4), by reference to the purpose of the provision, having regard (among other things) to its effect in all the circumstances.

(4) A provision which—
   (a) would otherwise not relate to reserved matters, but
   (b) makes modifications of Scots private law, or Scots criminal law, as it applies to reserved matters,
   is to be treated as relating to reserved matters unless the purpose of the provision is to make he law in question apply consistently to reserved matters and otherwise.

30 Legislative competence: supplementary

(1) Schedule 5 (which defines reserved matters) shall have effect.

...

31 Scrutiny of Bills before introduction

(1) A member of the Scottish Executive in charge of a Bill shall, on or before introduction of the Bill in the Parliament state that in his view the provisions of the Bill would be within the legislative competence of the Parliament.

(2) The Presiding Officer shall, on or before the introduction of a Bill in the Parliament, decide whether or not in his view the provisions of the Bill would be within the legislative competence of the Parliament and state his decision.

(3) The form of any statement, and the manner in which it is to be made, shall be determined under standing orders, and standing orders may provide for any statement to be published.

32 Submission of Bills for Royal Assent

(1) It is for the Presiding Officer to submit Bills for Royal Assent.

(2) The Presiding Officer shall not submit a Bill for Royal Assent at any time when—
   (a) the Advocate General, the Lord Advocate or the Attorney General is entitled to make a reference in relation to the Bill under section 33,
   (b) any such reference has been made but has not been decided or otherwise disposed of by the Judicial Committee [*Supreme Court*], or
   (c) an order may be made in relation to the Bill under section 35.

(3) The Presiding Officer shall not submit a Bill in its unamended form for Royal Assent if—
   (a) the Judicial Committee [*Supreme Court*] have decided that the Bill or any provision of it would not be within the legislative competence of the Parliament, or
   (b) a reference made in relation to the Bill under section 33 has been withdrawn following a request for withdrawal of the reference under section 34(2)(b).

(4) In this Act—
   "Advocate General" means the Advocate General for Scotland,
   "Judicial Committee" means the Judicial Committee of the Privy Council.

33 Scrutiny of bills by the Judicial Committee [*Supreme Court*]

(1) The Advocate General, the Lord Advocate or the Attorney General may refer the question of whether a Bill or any provision of a Bill would be within the legislative competence of the Parliament to the Judicial Committee [*Supreme Court*] for decision.

(2) Subject to subsection (3), he may make a reference in relation to a Bill at any time during—
 (a) the period of four weeks beginning with the passing of the Bill, and
 (b) any period of four weeks beginning with any subsequent approval of the Bill in accordance with standing orders made by virtue of section 36(5).

(3) He shall not make a reference in relation to a Bill if he has notified the Presiding Officer that he does not intend to make a reference in relation to the Bill, unless the Bill has been approved as mentioned in subsection (2)(b) since the notification.

36 Stages of Bills

(1) Standing orders shall include provision—
 (a) for general debate on a Bill with an opportunity for members to vote on its general principles,
 (b) for the consideration of, and an opportunity for members to vote on, the details of a Bill, and
 (c) for a final stage at which a Bill can be passed or rejected.

(2) Subsection (1) does not prevent standing orders making provision to enable the Parliament to expedite proceedings in relation to a particular Bill.

(3) Standing orders may make provision different from that required by subsection (1) for the procedure applicable to Bills of any of the following kinds—
 (a) Bills which restate the law,
 (b) Bills which repeal spent enactments,
 (c) private Bills.

(4) Standing orders shall provide for an opportunity for the reconsideration of a Bill after its passing if (and only if)—
 (a) the Judicial Committee decide [*Supreme Court decides*] that the Bill or any provision of it would not be within the legislative competence of the Parliament,
 (b) a reference made in relation to the Bill under section 33 is withdrawn following a request for withdrawal of the reference under section 34(2)(b), or
 (c) an order is made in relation to the Bill under section 35.

(5) Standing orders shall, in particular, ensure that any Bill amended on reconsideration is subject to a final stage at which it can be approved or rejected.

(6) References in subsection (4), sections 28(2) and 38(1)(a) and paragraph 7 of Schedule 3 to the passing of a Bill shall, in the case of a Bill which has been amended on reconsideration, be read as references to the approval of the Bill.

Other provisions

37 Acts of Union

The Union with Scotland Act 1706 and the Union with England Act 1707 have effect subject to this Act.

39 Members' interests

(1) Provision shall be made for a register of interests of members of the Parliament and for the register to be published and made available for public inspection.

(2) Provision shall be made—
 (a) requiring members of the Parliament to register in that register financial interests (including benefits in kind), as defined for the purposes of this paragraph,
 (b) requiring that any member of the Parliament who has a financial interest (including benefits in kind), as defined for the purposes of this paragraph, in any matter declares that interest before taking part in any proceedings of the Parliament relating to that matter.

(3) Provision made in pursuance of subsection (2) shall include any provision which the Parliament considers appropriate for preventing or restricting the participation in proceedings of the Parliament of a member with an interest defined for the purposes of subsection (2)(a) or (b) in a matter to which the proceedings relate.

(4) Provision shall be made prohibiting a member of the Parliament from—
 (a) advocating or initiating any cause or matter on behalf of any person, by any means specified in the provision, in consideration of any payment or benefit in kind of a description so specified, or
 (b) urging, in consideration of any such payment or benefit in kind, any other member on behalf of any person by any such means.

(5) Provision made in pursuance of subsections (2) to (4) shall include any provision which the Parliament considers appropriate for excluding from proceedings of the Parliament any member who fails to comply with, or contravenes, any provision made in pursuance of those subsections.

(6) Any member of the Parliament who—
 (a) takes part in any proceedings of the Parliament without having complied with, or in contravention of, any provision made in pursuance of subsection (2) or (3), or
 (b) contravenes any provision made in pursuance of subsection (4),
 is guilty of an offence.

(7) A person guilty of an offence under subsection (6) is liable on summary conviction to a fine not exceeding level 5 on the standard scale.

(8) In this section—
 (a) "provision" means provision made by or under an Act of the Scottish Parliament,
 (b) references to members of the Parliament include references to the Lord Advocate and the Solicitor General for Scotland, whether or not they are such members.

Legal issues

40 Proceedings by or against the Parliament etc.

(1) Proceedings by or against the Parliament shall be instituted by or (as the case may be) against the Parliamentary corporation on behalf of the Parliament.

(2) Proceedings by or against—
 (a) the Presiding Officer or a deputy, or
 (b) any member of the staff of the Parliament,
 shall be instituted by or (as the case may be) against the corporation on his behalf.

(3) In any proceedings against the Parliament, the court shall not make an order for suspension, interdict, reduction or specific performance (or other like order) but may instead make a declarator.

(4) In any proceedings against—
 (a) any member of the Parliament,
 (b) the Presiding Officer or a deputy,
 (c) any member of the staff of the Parliament, or
 (d) the Parliamentary corporation,
 the court shall not make an order for suspension, interdict, reduction or specific performance (or other like order) if the effect of doing so would be to give any relief against the Parliament which could not have been given in proceedings against the Parliament.

(5) References in this section to an order include an interim order.

41 Defamatory statements

(1) For the purposes of the law of defamation—
 (a) any statement made in proceedings of the Parliament, and
 (b) the publication under the authority of the Parliament of any statement,
 shall be absolutely privileged.

(2) In subsection (1), "statement" has the same meaning as in the Defamation Act 1996.

42 Contempt of court

(1) The strict liability rule shall not apply in relation to any publication—
   (a) made in proceedings of the Parliament in relation to a Bill or subordinate legislation, or
   (b) to the extent that it consists of a fair and accurate report of such proceedings made in good faith.
(2) In subsection (1), "the strict liability rule" and "publication" have the same meanings as in the Contempt of Court Act 1981.

43 Corrupt practices

The Parliament shall be a public body for the purposes of the Prevention of Corruption Acts 1889 to 1916.

PART II
THE SCOTTISH ADMINISTRATION

Ministers and their staff

44 The Scottish Executive

(1) There shall be a Scottish Executive, whose members shall be—
   (a) the First Minister,
   (b) such Ministers as the First Minister may appoint under section 47, and
   (c) the Lord Advocate and the Solicitor General for Scotland.
(2) The members of the Scottish Executive are referred to collectively as the Scottish Ministers.
(3) A person who holds a Ministerial office may not be appointed a member of the Scottish Executive; and if a member of the Scottish Executive is appointed to a Ministerial office he shall cease to hold office as a member of the Scottish Executive.
(4) In subsection (3), references to a member of the Scottish Executive include a junior Scottish Minister and "Ministerial office" has the same meaning as in section 2 of the House of Commons Disqualification Act 1975.

45 The First Minister

(1) The First Minister shall be appointed by Her Majesty from among the members of the Parliament and shall hold office at Her Majesty's pleasure.
(2) the First Minister may at any time tender his resignation to Her Majesty and shall do so if the Parliament resolves that the Scottish Executive no longer enjoys the confidence of the Parliament.
(3) The First Minister shall cease to hold office if a person is appointed in his place.
(4) If the office of First Minister is vacant or he is for any reason unable to act, the functions exercisable by him shall be exercisable by a person designated by the Presiding Officer.
(5) A person shall be so designated only if—
   (a) he is a member of the Parliament, or
   (b) if the Parliament has been dissolved, he is a person who ceased to be a member by virtue of the dissolution.
(6) Functions exercisable by a person by virtue of subsection (5)(a) shall continue to be exercisable by him even if the Parliament is dissolved.
(7) The First Minister shall be the Keeper of the Scottish Seal.

46 Choice of the First Minister

(1) If one of the following events occurs, the Parliament shall within the period allowed nominate one of its members for appointment as First Minister.
(2) The events are—
   (a) the holding of a poll at a general election,
   (b) the First Minister tendering his resignation to Her Majesty,
   (c) the office of First Minister becoming vacant (otherwise than in consequence of his so tendering his resignation),

(d) the First Minister ceasing to be a member of the Parliament otherwise than by virtue of a dissolution.
(3) The period allowed is the period of 28 days which begins with the day on which the event in question occurs; but—
　(a) if another of those events occurs within the period allowed, that period shall be extended (subject to paragraph (b)) so that it ends with the period of 28 days beginning with the day on which that other event occurred, and
　(b) the period shall end if the Parliament passes a resolution under section 3(1)(a) or when Her Majesty appoints a person as First Minister.
(4) The Presiding Officer shall recommend to Her Majesty the appointment of any member of the Parliament who is nominated by the Parliament under this section.

47　Ministers
(1) The First Minister may, with the approval of Her Majesty, appoint Ministers from among the members of the Parliament.
. . .

48　The Scottish Law Officers
(1) It is for the First Minister to recommend to Her Majesty the appointment or removal of a person as Lord Advocate or Solicitor General for Scotland; but he shall not do so without the agreement of the Parliament.
. . .

Ministerial functions

53　General transfer of functions
(1) The functions mentioned in subsection (2) shall, so far as they are exercisable within devolved competence, be exercisable by the Scottish Ministers instead of by a Minister of the Crown.
(2) Those functions are—
　(a) those of Her Majesty's prerogative and other executive functions which are exercisable on behalf of Her Majesty by a Minister of the Crown,
　(b) other functions conferred on a Minister of the Crown by a prerogative instrument, and
　(c) functions conferred on a Minister of the Crown by any pre-commencement enactment, but do not include any retained functions of the Lord Advocate.
. . .

54　Devolved competence
(1) References in this Act to the exercise of a function being within or outside devolved competence are to be read in accordance with this section.
(2) It is outside devolved competence—
　(a) to make any provision by subordinate legislation which would be outside the legislative competence of the Parliament if it were included in an Act of the Scottish Parliament, or
　(b) to confirm or approve any subordinate legislation containing such provision.
(3) In the case of any function other than a function of making, confirming or approving subordinate legislation, it is outside devolved competence to exercise the function (or exercise it in any way) so far as a provision of an Act of the Scottish Parliament conferring the function (or, as the case may be, conferring it so as to be exercisable in that way) would be outside the legislative competence of the Parliament.

57　Community law and Convention rights
(1) Despite the transfer to the Scottish Ministers by virtue of section 53 of functions in relation to observing and implementing obligations under Community law, any function of a minister of the Crown in relation to any matter shall continue to be exercisable by him as regards Scotland for the purposes specified in section 2(2) of the European Communities Act 1972.

(2) A member of the Scottish Executive has no power to make any subordinate legislation, or to do any other act, so far as the legislation or act is incompatible with any of the Convention rights or with Community law.

(3) Subsection (2) does not apply to an act of the Lord Advocate—
   (a) in prosecuting any offence, or
   (b) in his capacity as head of the systems of criminal prosecution and investigation of deaths in Scotland,
   which, because of subsection (2) of section 6 of the Human Rights Act 1998, is not unlawful under subsection (1) of that section.

Miscellaneous

91 Maladministration

(1) The Parliament shall make provision for the investigation of relevant complaints made to its members in respect of any action taken by or on behalf of—
   (a) a member of the Scottish Executive in the exercise of functions conferred on the Scottish Ministers, or
   (b) any other office-holder in the Scottish Administration.

(2) For the purposes of subsection (1), a complaint is a relevant complaint if it is a complaint of a kind which could be investigated under the Parliamentary Commissioner Act 1967 if it were made to a member of the House of Commons in respect of a government department or other authority to which that Act applies.

(3) The Parliament may make provision for the investigation of complaints in respect of—
   (a) any action taken by or on behalf of an office-holder in the Scottish Administration,
   (b) any action taken by or on behalf of the Parliamentary corporation,
   (c) any action taken by or on behalf of a Scottish public authority with mixed functions or no reserved functions, or
   (d) any action concerning Scotland and not relating to reserved matters which is taken by or on behalf of a cross-border public authority.

(4) In making provision of the kind required by subsection (1), the Parliament shall have regard (among other things) to the Act of 1967.

. . .

Juridical

98 Devolution issues

Schedule 6 (which makes provision in relation to devolution issues) shall have effect.

99 Rights and liabilities of the Crown in different capacities

(1) Rights and liabilities may arise between the Crown in right of Her Majesty's Government in the United Kingdom and the Crown in right of the Scottish Administration by virtue of a contract, by operation of law or by virtue of an enactment as they may arise between subjects.

(2) Property and liabilities may be transferred between the Crown in one of those capacities and the Crown in the other capacity as they may be transferred between subjects; and they may together create, vary or extinguish any property or liability as subjects may.

(3) Proceedings in respect of—
   (a) any property or liabilities to which the Crown in one of those capacities is entitled or subject under subsection (1) or (2), or
   (b) the exercise of, or failure to exercise, any function exercisable by an office-holder of the Crown in one of those capacities,
   may be instituted by the Crown in either capacity; and the Crown in the other capacity may be a separate party in the proceedings.

(4) This section applies to a unilateral obligation as it applies to a contract.

(5) In this section—
   "office-holder", in relation to the Crown in right of Her Majesty's Government in the United Kingdom, means any minister of the Crown or other office-holder under the Crown in that

capacity and, in relation to the Crown in right of the Scottish Administration, means any office-holder in the Scottish Administration,

"subject" means a person not acting on behalf of the Crown.

100 Human rights

(1) This Act does not enable a person—
   (a) to bring any proceedings in a court or tribunal on the ground that an act is incompatible with the Convention rights, or
   (b) to rely on any of the Convention rights in any such proceedings,
   unless he would be a victim for the purposes of Article 34 of the Convention (within the meaning of the Human Rights Act 1998) if proceedings in respect of the act were brought in the European Court of Human Rights.

(2) Subsection (1) does not apply to the Lord Advocate, the Advocate General, the Attorney General, *the Advocate General for Northern Ireland* or the Attorney General for Northern Ireland.

(3) This Act does not enable a court or tribunal to award any damages in respect of an act which is incompatible with any of the Convention rights which it could not award if section 8(3) and (4) of the Human Rights Act 1998 applied.

(4) In this section "act" means—
   (a) making any legislation,
   (b) any other act or failure to act, if it is the act or failure of a member of the Scottish Executive.

101 Interpretation of Acts of the Scottish Parliament etc.

(1) This section applies to—
   (a) any provision of an Act of the Scottish Parliament, or of a Bill for such an Act, and
   (b) any provision of subordinate legislation made, confirmed or approved, or purporting to be made, confirmed or approved, by a member of the Scottish Executive,
   which could be read in such a way as to be outside competence.

(2) Such a provision is to be read as narrowly as is required for it to be within competence, if such a reading is possible, and is to have effect accordingly.

(3) In this section "competence"—
   (a) in relation to an Act of the Scottish Parliament, or a Bill for such an Act, means the legislative competence of the Parliament, and
   (b) in relation to subordinate legislation, means the powers conferred by virtue of this Act.

102 Powers of courts or tribunals to vary retrospective decisions

(1) This section applies where any court or tribunal decides that—
   (a) an Act of the Scottish Parliament or any provision of such an Act is not within the legislative competence of the Parliament, or
   (b) a member of the Scottish Executive does not have the power to make, confirm or approve a provision of subordinate legislation that he has purported to make, confirm or approve.

(2) The court or tribunal may make an order—
   (a) removing or limiting any retrospective effect of the decision, or
   (b) suspending the effect of the decision for any period and on any conditions to allow the defect to be corrected.

(3) In deciding whether to make an order under this section, the court or tribunal shall (among other things) have regard to the extent to which persons who are not parties to the proceedings would otherwise be adversely affected.

(4) Where a court or tribunal is considering whether to make an order under this section, it shall order intimation of that fact to be given to—
   (a) the Lord Advocate, and
   (b) the appropriate law officer, where the decision mentioned in subsection (1) relates to a devolution issue (within the meaning of Schedule 6),
   unless the person to whom the intimation would be given is a party to the proceedings.

(5) A person to whom intimation is given under subsection (4) may take part as a party in the proceedings so far as they relate to the making of the order.

...

107 Legislative power to remedy ultra vires acts

Subordinate legislation may make such provision as the person making the legislation considers necessary or expedient in consequence of—
(a) an Act of the Scottish Parliament or any provision of an Act of the Scottish Parliament which is not, or may not be, within the legislative competence of the Parliament, or
(b) any purported exercise by a member of the Scottish Executive of his functions which is not, or may not be, an exercise or a proper exercise of those functions.

SCHEDULE 4
ENACTMENTS ETC. PROTECTED FROM MODIFICATION
PART I
THE PROTECTED PROVISIONS

Particular enactments

1. (1) An Act of the Scottish Parliament cannot modify, or confer power by subordinate legislation to modify, any of the following provisions.
   (2) The provisions are—
   (a) Articles 4 and 6 of the Union with Scotland Act 1706 and of the Union with England Act 1707 so far as they relate to freedom of trade,
   (b) the Private Legislation Procedure (Scotland) Act 1936,
   (c) the following provisions of the European Communities Act 1972—
   Section 1 and Schedule 1,
   Section 2, other than subsection (2), the words following "such Community obligation" in subsection (3) and the words "subject to Schedule 2 to this Act" in subsection (4),
   Section 3(1) and (2),
   Section 11(2),
   (d) paragraphs 5(3)(b) and 15(4)(b) of Schedule 32 to the Local Government, Planning and Land Act 1980 (designation of enterprise zones),
   (e) sections 140A to 140G of the Social Security Administration Act 1992 (rent rebate and rent allowance subsidy and council tax benefit),
   (f) the Human Rights Act 1998.

The law on reserved matters

2. (1) An Act of the Scottish Parliament cannot modify, or confer power by subordinate legislation to modify, the law on reserved matters.
   (2) In this paragraph, "the law on reserved matters" means—
   (a) any enactment the subject-matter of which is a reserved matter and which is comprised in an Act of Parliament or subordinate legislation under an Act of Parliament, and
   (b) any rule of law which is not contained in an enactment and the subject-matter of which is a reserved matter,
   and in this sub-paragraph "Act of Parliament" does not include this Act.
   (3) Sub-paragraph (1) applies in relation to a rule of Scots private law or Scots criminal law (whether or not contained in an enactment) only to the extent that the rule in question is special to a reserved matter or the subject-matter of the rule is—
   (a) interest on sums due in respect of taxes or excise duties and refunds of such taxes or duties,
   (b) the obligations, in relation to occupational or personal pension schemes, of the trustees or managers,
   (c) the obligations under an order made by virtue of section 12A(2) or (3) of the Family Law (Scotland) Act 1985 (orders relating to pensions lump sums) of the person

responsible for a pension arrangement other than an occupational or personal pension scheme; or

(d) the obligations under Chapter I of Part IV of the Welfare Reform and Pensions Act 1999 (sharing of rights under pension arrangements) of the person responsible for such a pension arrangement; or

(e) the effect of Chapter II of Part IV of that Act of 1999 (sharing of rights in state pension schemes) as read with Part II of the Social Security Contributions and Benefits Act 1992 (contributory benefits).

(4) In sub-paragraph (3)(c) "pension arrangement" and "person responsible for a pension arrangement" have the same meaning as in section 27(1) of the Family Law (Scotland) Act 1985.

3. (1) Paragraph 2 does not apply to modifications which—
    (a) are incidental to, or consequential on, provision made (whether by virtue of the Act in question or another enactment) which does not relate to reserved matters, and
    (b) do not have a greater effect on reserved matters than is necessary to give effect to the purpose of the provision.

(2) In determining for the purposes of sub-paragraph (1)(b) what is necessary to give effect to the purpose of a provision, any power to make laws other than the power of the Parliament is to be disregarded.

This Act

4. (1) An Act of the Scottish Parliament cannot modify, or confer power by subordinate legislation to modify, this Act.

    . . .

. . .

PART II
GENERAL EXCEPTIONS

Restatement, etc.

7. (1) Part I of this Schedule does not prevent an Act of the Scottish Parliament—
    (a) restating the law (or restating it with such modifications as are not prevented by that Part), or
    (b) repealing any spent enactment,
    or conferring power by subordinate legislation to do so.

(2) For the purposes of paragraph 2, the law on reserved matters includes any restatement in an Act of the Scottish Parliament, or subordinate legislation under such an Act, of the law on reserved matters if the subject-matter of the restatement is a reserved matter.

Effect of Interpretation Act 1978

8. Part I of this Schedule does not prevent the operation of any provision of the Interpretation Act 1978.

Change of title etc.

9. (1) Part I of this Schedule does not prevent an Act of the Scottish Parliament amending, or conferring power by subordinate legislation to amend, any enactment by changing—
    (a) any of the titles referred to in sub-paragraph (2), or
    (b) any reference to a declarator,
    in consequence of any provision made by or under an Act of the Scottish Parliament.

(2) The titles are those of—
    (a) any court or tribunal or any judge, chairman or officer of a court or tribunal,
    (b) any holder of an office in the Scottish Administration which is not a ministerial office or any member of the staff of the Scottish Administration,
    (c) any register.

. . .

SCHEDULE 5
RESERVED MATTERS
PART I
GENERAL RESERVATIONS

The Constitution

1. The following aspects of the constitution are reserved matters, that is—
   (a) the Crown, including succession to the Crown and a regency,
   (b) the Union of the Kingdoms of Scotland and England,
   (c) the Parliament of the United Kingdom,
   (d) the continued existence of the High Court of Justiciary as a criminal court of first instance and of appeal,
   (e) the continued existence of the Court of Session as a civil court of first instance and of appeal.

2. (1) Paragraph 1 does not reserve—
   (a) Her Majesty's prerogative and other executive functions,
   (b) functions exercisable by any person acting on behalf of the Crown, or
   (c) any office in the Scottish Administration.
   (2) Sub-paragraph (1) does not affect the reservation by paragraph 1 of honours and dignities or the functions of the Lord Lyon King of Arms so far as relating to the granting of arms; but this sub-paragraph does not apply to the Lord Lyon King of Arms in his judicial capacity.
   (3) Sub-paragraph (1) does not affect the reservation by paragraph 1 of the management (in accordance with any enactment regulating the use of land) of the Crown Estate.
   (4) Sub-paragraph (1) does not affect the reservation by paragraph 1of the functions of the Security Service, the Secret Intelligence Service and the Government Communications Headquarters.
   (5) Sub-paragraph 1 does not affect the reservation by paragraph 1 of the functions exercisable through the Export Credits Guarantee Department.

3. (1) Paragraph 1 does not reserve property belonging to Her Majesty in right of the Crown or belonging to any person acting on behalf of the Crown or held in trust for Her Majesty for the purposes of any person acting on behalf of the Crown.
   (2) Paragraph 1 does not reserve the ultimate superiority of the Crown or the superiority of the Prince and Steward of Scotland.
   (3) Sub-paragraph (1) does not affect the reservation by paragraph 1 of—
   (a) the hereditary revenues of the Crown, other than revenues from bona vacantia, ultimus haeres and treasure trove,
   (b) the royal arms and standard,
   (c) the compulsory acquisition of property held or used by a Minister of the Crown or government department.

4. (1) Paragraph 1 does not reserve property held by Her Majesty in Her private capacity.
   (2) Sub-paragraph (1) does not affect the reservation by paragraph 1 of the subject-matter of the Crown Private Estates Acts 1800 to 1873.

5. Paragraph 1 does not reserve the use of the Scottish Seal.

Political parties

6. The registration and funding of political parties is a reserved matter but this paragraph does not reserve making payments to any political party for the purpose of assisting members of the Parliament who are connected with the party to perform their Parliamentary duties.

Foreign affairs etc.

7. (1) International relations, including relations with territories outside the United Kingdom, the European Communities (and their institutions) and other international organisations, regulation of international trade, and international development assistance and co-operation are reserved matters.

(2) Sub-paragraph (1) does not reserve—
 (a) observing and implementing international obligations, obligations under the Human Rights Convention and obligations under Community law,
 (b) assisting Ministers of the Crown in relation to any matter to which that sub-paragraph applies.

Public service

8. (1) the Civil Service of the State is a reserved matter.
 (2) Sub-paragraph (1) does not reserve the subject-matter of—
  (a) Part I of the Sheriff Courts and Legal Officers (Scotland) Act 1927 (appointment of sheriff clerks and procurators fiscal etc.),
  (b) Part III of the Administration of Justice (Scotland) Act 1933 (officers of the High Court of Justiciary and of the Court of Session).

Defence

9. (1) The following are reserved matters—
  (a) the defence of the realm,
  (b) the naval, military or air forces of the Crown, including reserve forces,
  (c) visiting forces,
  (d) international headquarters and defence organisations,
  (e) trading with the enemy and enemy property.
 (2) Sub-paragraph (1) does not reserve—
  (a) the exercise of civil defence functions by any person otherwise than as a member of any force or organisation referred to in sub-paragraph (1)(b) to (d) or any other force or organisation reserved by virtue of sub-paragraph (1)(a),
  (b) the conferral of enforcement powers in relation to sea fishing.

Treason

10. Treason (including constructive treason), treason felony and misprison of treason are reserved matters.

PART II

SPECIFIC RESERVATIONS

Preliminary

1. The matters to which any of the Sections in this Part apply are reserved matters for the purposes of this Act.
2. A Section applies to any matter described or referred to in it when read with any illustrations, exceptions or interpretation provisions in that Section.
3. Any illustrations, exceptions or interpretation provisions in a Section relate only to that Section (so that an entry under the heading "exceptions" does not affect any other Section).

Reservations

Head A — Financial and Economic Matters
Head B — Home Affairs
Head C — Trade and Industry
Head D — Energy
Head E — Transport
Head F — Social Security
Head G — Regulation of the Professions
Head H — Employment
Head J — Health and Medicines
Head K — Media and Culture
Head L — Miscellaneous

Note: Only the headings are reproduced here.

SCHEDULE 6
DEVOLUTION ISSUES
PART I
PRELIMINARY

1. In this Schedule "devolution issue" means—
   (a) a question whether an Act of the Scottish Parliament or any provision of an Act of the Scottish Parliament is within the legislative competence of the Parliament,
   (b) a question whether any function (being a function which any person has purported, or is proposing, to exercise) is a function of the Scottish Ministers, the First Minister or the Lord Advocate.
   (c) a question whether the purported or proposed exercise of a function by a member of the Scottish Executive is, or would be, within devolved competence,
   (d) a question whether a purported or proposed exercise of a function by a member of the Scottish Executive is, or would be incompatible with any of the Convention rights or with Community law,
   (e) a question whether a failure to act by a member of the Scottish Executive is incompatible with any of the Convention rights or with Community law,
   (f) any other question about whether a function is exercisable within devolved competence or in or as regards Scotland and any other question arising by virtue of this Act about reserved matters.
2. A devolution issue shall not be taken to arise in any proceedings merely because of any contention of a party to the proceedings which appears to the court or tribunal before which the proceedings take place to be frivolous or vexatious.

...

PART III
PROCEEDINGS IN ENGLAND AND WALES

Application of Part III

14. This Part of this Schedule applies in relation to devolution issues in proceedings in England and Wales.

Institution of proceedings

15. (1) Proceedings for the determination of a devolution issue may be instituted by the Attorney General.
    (2) The Lord Advocate may defend any such proceedings.
    (3) This paragraph is without prejudice to any power to institute or defend proceedings exercisable apart from this paragraph by any person.

Notice of devolution issue

16. A court or tribunal shall order notice of any devolution issue which arises in any proceedings before it to be given to the Attorney General and the Lord Advocate (unless the person to whom the notice would be given is a party to the proceedings).
17. A person to whom notice is given in pursuance of paragraph 16 may take part as a party in the proceedings, so far as they relate to a devolution issue.

Reference of devolution issue to High Court or Court of Appeal

18. A magistrates' court may refer any devolution issue which arises in proceedings (other than criminal proceedings) before it to the High Court.
19. (1) A court may refer any devolution issue which arises in proceedings (other than criminal proceedings) before it to the Courts of Appeal.
    (2) Sub-paragraph (1) does not apply to—
        (a) a magistrates' court, the Court of Appeal or the House of Lords [*Supreme Court*], or
        (b) the High Court if the devolution issue arises in proceedings on a reference under paragraph 18.

20. A tribunal from which there is no appeal shall refer any devolution issue which arises in proceedings before it to the Court of Appeal; and any other tribunal may make such a reference.
21. A court, other than the House of Lords [*Supreme Court*] or the Court of Appeal, may refer any devolution issue which arises in criminal proceedings before it to—
   (a) the High Court (if the proceedings are summary proceedings), or
   (b) the Court of Appeal (if the proceedings are proceedings on indictment).

References from Court of Appeal to Judicial Committee [Supreme Court]

22. The Court of Appeal may refer any devolution issue which arises in proceedings before it (otherwise than on a reference under paragraph 19, 20 or 21) to the Judicial Committee.

Appeals from superior courts to Judicial Committee [Supreme Court]

23. An appeal against a determination of a devolution issue by the High Court or the Court of Appeal on a reference under paragraph 18, 19, 20 or 21 shall lie to the Judicial Committee [*Supreme Court*], but only with leave of the High Court or (as the case may be) the Court of Appeal or, failing such leave, with special leave of the Judicial Committee [*Supreme Court*].

. . .

PART V
GENERAL

Proceedings in the House of Lords [Supreme Court]

32. . . .

Direct references to Judicial Committee [Supreme Court]

33. The Lord Advocate, the Advocate General, the Attorney General or the Attorney General for Northern Ireland *[Advocate General for Northern Ireland]* may require any court or tribunal to refer to the Judicial Committee [*Supreme Court*] any devolution issue which has arisen in proceedings before it to which he is a party.
34. The Lord Advocate, the Attorney General, the Advocate General or the Attorney General for Northern Ireland *[Advocate General for Northern Ireland]* may refer to the Judicial Committee [*Supreme Court*] any devolution issue which is not the subject of proceedings.
35. (1) This paragraph applies where a reference is made under paragraph 34 in relation to a devolution issue which relates to the proposed exercise of a function by a member of the Scottish Executive.
   (2) The person making the reference shall notify a member of the Scottish Executive of that fact.
   (3) No member of the Scottish Executive shall exercise the function in the manner proposed during the period beginning with the receipt of the notification under sub-paragraph (2) and ending with the reference being decided or otherwise disposed of.
   (4) Proceedings relating to any possible failure by a member of the Scottish Executive to comply with sub-paragraph (3) may be instituted by the Advocate General.
   (5) Sub-paragraph (4) is without prejudice to any power to institute proceedings exercisable apart from that sub-paragraph by any person.

Expenses

36. (1) A court or tribunal before which any proceedings take place may take account of any additional expense of the kind mentioned in sub-paragraph (3) in deciding any question as to costs or expenses.
   (2) In deciding any such question, the court or tribunal may award the whole or part of the additional expense as costs or (as the case may be) expenses to the party who incurred it (whatever the decision on the devolution issue).
   (3) The additional expense is any additional expense which the court or tribunal considers that any party to the proceedings has incurred as a result of the participation of any person in pursuance of paragraph 6, 17 or 27.

Procedure of courts and tribunals

37. Any power to make provision for regulating the procedure before any court or tribunal shall include power to make provision for the purposes of this Schedule including, in particular, provision—
    (a) for prescribing the stage in the proceedings at which a devolution issue is to be raised or referred,
    (b) for the sisting or staying of proceedings for the purpose of any proceedings under this Schedule, and
    (c) for determining the manner in which and the time within which any intimation or notice is to be given.

Interpretation

38. Any duty or power conferred by this Schedule to refer a devolution issue to a court shall be construed as a duty or (as the case may be) power to refer the issue to the court for decision.

...

NORTHERN IRELAND ACT 1998
(1998, c. 47)

An Act to make new provision for the government of Northern Ireland for the purpose of implementing the agreement reached at multi-party talks on Northern Ireland set out in Command Paper 3883.

[19 November 1998]

PART I
PRELIMINARY

1 Status of Northern Ireland

(1) It is hereby declared that Northern Ireland in its entirety remains part of the United Kingdom and shall not cease to be so without the consent of a majority of the people of Northern Ireland voting in a poll held for the purposes of this section in accordance with Schedule 1.

(2) But if the wish expressed by a majority in such a poll is that Northern Ireland should cease to be part of the United Kingdom and form part of a united Ireland the Secretary of State shall lay before Parliament such proposals to give effect to that wish as may be agreed between Her Majesty's Government in the United Kingdom and the Government of Ireland.

PART II
LEGISLATIVE POWERS

General

5 Acts of the Northern Ireland Assembly

(1) Subject to sections 6 to 8, the Assembly may make laws, to be known as Acts.

(2) A Bill shall become an Act when it has been passed by the Assembly and has received Royal Assent.

(3) A Bill receives Royal Assent at the beginning of the day on which Letters Patent under the Great Seal of Northern Ireland signed with Her Majesty's own hand signifying Her Assent are notified to the Presiding Officer.

(4) The date of Royal Assent shall be written on the Act by the Presiding Officer, and shall form part of the Act.

(5) The validity of any proceedings leading to the enactment of an Act of the Assembly shall not be called into question in any legal proceedings.

(6) This section does not affect the power of the Parliament of the United Kingdom to make laws for Northern Ireland, but an Act of the Assembly may modify any provision made by or under an Act of Parliament in so far as it is part of the law of Northern Ireland.

6 Legislative competence

(1) A provision of an Act is not law if it is outside the legislative competence of the Assembly.

(2) A provision is outside that competence if any of the following paragraphs apply—
   (a) it would form part of the law of a country or territory other than Northern Ireland, or confer or remove functions exercisable otherwise than in or as regards Northern Ireland;
   (b) it deals with an excepted matter and is not ancillary to other provisions (whether in the Act or previously enacted) dealing with reserved or transferred matters;
   (c) it is incompatible with any of the Convention rights;
   (d) it is incompatible with Community law;
   (e) it discriminates against any person or class of person on the ground of religious belief or political opinion;
   (f) it modifies an enactment in breach of section 7.

(3) For the purposes of this Act, a provision is ancillary to other provisions if it is a provision—
   (a) which provides for the enforcement of those other provisions or is otherwise necessary or expedient for making those other provisions effective; or
   (b) which is otherwise incidental to, or consequential on, those provisions;

and references in this Act to provisions previously enacted are references to provisions contained in, or in any instrument made under, other Northern Ireland legislation or an Act of Parliament

(4) Her Majesty may by Order in Council specify functions which are to be treated, for such purposes of this Act as may be specified, as being, or as not being, functions which are exercisable in or as regards Northern Ireland.

(5) No recommendation shall be made to Her Majesty to make an Order in Council under subsection (4) unless a draft of the Order has been laid before and approved by resolution of each House of Parliament.

7 Entrenched enactments

(1) Subject to subsection (2), the following enactments shall not be modified by an Act of the Assembly or subordinate legislation made, confirmed or approved by a Minister or Northern Ireland department—
   (a) the European Communities Act 1972;
   (b) the Human Rights Act 1998;
   (c) section 43(1) to (6) and (8), section 67, sections 84 to 86, section 95(3) and (4) and section 98; and
   (d) section 1 and section 84 of the Justice (Northern Ireland) Act 2002.

(2) Subsection (1) does not prevent an Act of the Assembly or subordinate legislation modifying section 3(3) or (4) or 11(1) of the European Communities Act 1972.

(3) In this Act "Minister", unless the context otherwise requires, means the First Minister, the deputy First Minister or a Northern Ireland Minister.

Scrutiny and stages of Bills

9 Scrutiny by Ministers

(1) A Minister in charge of a Bill shall, on or before introduction of it in the Assembly, make a statement to the effect that in his view the Bill would be within the legislative competence of the Assembly.

(2) The statement shall be in writing and shall be published in such manner as the Minister making the statement considers appropriate.

10 Scrutiny by Presiding Officer

(1) Standing orders shall ensure that a Bill is not introduced in the Assembly if the Presiding Officer decides that any provision of it would not be within the legislative competence of the Assembly.

(2) Subject to subsection (3)—

(a) the Presiding Officer shall consider a Bill both on its introduction and before the Assembly enters on its final stage; and
(b) if he considers that the Bill contains—
  (i) any provision which deals with an excepted matter and is ancillary to other provisions (whether in the Bill or previously enacted) dealing with reserved or transferred matters; or
  (ii) any provision which deals with a reserved matter,
he shall refer it to the Secretary of State; and
(c) the Assembly shall not proceed with the Bill or, as the case may be, enter on its final stage unless—
  (i) the Secretary of State's consent to the consideration of the Bill by the Assembly is signified; or
  (ii) the Assembly is informed that in his opinion the Bill does not contain any such provision as is mentioned in paragraph (b)(i) and (ii).
(3) Subsection (2)(b) and (c) shall not apply—
(a) where, in the opinion of the Presiding Officer, each provision of the Bill which deals with an excepted or reserved matter is ancillary to other provisions (whether in the Bill or previously enacted) dealing with transferred matters only; or
(b) on the introduction of a Bill, where the Bill has been endorsed with a statement that the Secretary of State has consented to the Assembly considering the Bill.
(4) In this section and section 14 "final stage", in relation to a Bill, means the stage in the Assembly's proceedings at which the Bill falls finally to be passed or rejected.

11 Scrutiny by the Judicial Committee [*Supreme Court*]
(1) The Attorney General for Northern Ireland may refer the question of whether a provision of a Bill would be within the legislative competence of the Assembly to the Judicial Committee [*Supreme Court*] for decision.
(2) Subject to subsection (3), he may make a reference in relation to a provision of a Bill at any time during—
(a) the period of four weeks beginning with the passing of the Bill, and
(b) the period of four weeks beginning with any subsequent approval of the Bill in accordance with standing orders made by virtue of section 13(6).
(3) If he notifies the Presiding Officer that he does not intend to make a reference in relation to a provision of a Bill, he shall not make such a reference unless, after the notification, the Bill is approved as mentioned in subsection (2)(b).
(4) If the Judicial Committee [*Supreme Court*] decide that any provision of a Bill would be within the legislative competence of the Assembly, their decision shall be taken as applying also to that provision if contained in the Act when enacted.

13 Stages of Bills
(1) Standing orders shall include provision—
(a) for general debate on a Bill with an opportunity for members to vote on its general principles;
(b) for the consideration of, and an opportunity for members to vote on, the details of a Bill; and
(c) for a final stage at which a Bill can be passed or rejected but not amended.
(2) Standing orders may, in relation to different types of Bill, modify provisions made in pursuance of subsection (1)(a) or (b).
(3) Standing orders—
(a) shall include provision for establishing such a committee as is mentioned in paragraph 11 of Strand One of the Belfast Agreement;
(b) may include provision for the details of a Bill to be considered by the committee in such circumstances as may be specified in the orders.
(4) Standing orders shall include provision—

(a) requiring the Presiding Officer to send a copy of each Bill, as soon as reasonably practicable after introduction, to the Northern Ireland Human Rights Commission; and
(b) enabling the Assembly to ask the Commission, where the Assembly thinks fit, to advise whether a Bill is compatible with human rights (including the Convention rights).

(5) Standing orders shall provide for an opportunity for the reconsideration of a Bill after its passing if (and only if)—
(a) the Judicial Committee [*Supreme Court*] decide that any provision of the Bill would not be within the legislative competence of the Assembly;
(b) a reference made in relation to a provision of the Bill under section 11 has been withdrawn following a request for withdrawal under section 12;
(c) a decision is made in relation to the Bill under section 14(4) or (5); or
(d) a motion under section 15(1) is passed by either House of Parliament.

(6) Standing orders shall, in particular, ensure that any Bill amended on reconsideration is subject to a final stage at which it can be approved or rejected but not amended.

(7) References in subsection (5) and other provisions of this Act to the passing of a Bill shall, in the case of a Bill which has been amended on reconsideration, be read as references to the approval of the Bill.

Royal Assent

14 Submission by Secretary of State
(1) It shall be the Secretary of State who submits Bills for Royal Assent.
. . .

PART III
EXECUTIVE AUTHORITIES

Authorities

16A Appointment of First Minister, deputy First Minister and Northern Ireland Ministers following Assembly election

(1) This section applies where an Assembly is elected under section 31 or 32.
(2) All Northern Ireland Ministers shall cease to hold office.
(3) Within a period of seven days beginning with the first meeting of the Assembly—
(a) the offices of First Minister and deputy First Minister shall be filled by applying subsections (4) to (7); and
(b) the Ministerial offices to be held by Northern Ireland Ministers shall be filled by applying section 18(2) to (6).
(4) The nominating officer of the largest political party of the largest political designation shall nominate a member of the Assembly to be the First Minister.
(5) The nominating officer of the largest political party of the second largest political designation shall nominate a member of the Assembly to be the deputy First Minister.
(6) If the persons nominated do not take up office within a period specified in standing orders, further nominations shall be made under subsections (4) and (5).
(7) Subsections (4) to (6) shall be applied as many times as may be necessary to secure that the offices of First Minister and deputy First Minister are filled.
(8) But no person may take up office as First Minister, deputy First Minister or Northern Ireland Minister by virtue of this section after the end of the period mentioned in subsection (3) (see further section 32(3)).
(9) The persons nominated under subsections (4) and (5) shall not take up office until each of them has affirmed the terms of the pledge of office.
(10) Subject to the provisions of this Part, the First Minister and the deputy First Minister shall hold office until immediately before those offices are next filled by virtue of this section.
(11) The holder of the office of First Minister or deputy First Minister may by notice in writing to the Presiding Officer designate a Northern Ireland Minister to exercise the functions of that office—

(a) during any absence or incapacity of the holder; or
(b) during any vacancy in that office arising otherwise than under section 16B(2),
but a person shall not have power to act by virtue of paragraph (a) for a continuous period exceeding six weeks.

(12) This section shall be construed in accordance with, and is subject to, section 16C

16B Vacancies in the office of First Minister or deputy First Minister
(1) The First Minister or the deputy First Minister—
   (a) may at any time resign by notice in writing to the Presiding Officer; and
   (b) shall cease to hold office if he ceases to be a member of the Assembly otherwise than by virtue of a dissolution.
(2) If either the First Minister or the deputy First Minister ceases to hold office at any time, whether by resignation or otherwise, the other—
   (a) shall also cease to hold office at that time; but
   (b) may continue to exercise the functions of his office until immediately before those offices are filled in accordance with this section.
(3) Where the offices of the First Minister and the deputy First Minister become vacant at any time, they shall be filled by applying subsections (4) to (7) within a period of seven days beginning with that time.
(4) The nominating officer of the largest political party of the largest political designation shall nominate a member of the Assembly to be the First Minister.
(5) The nominating officer of the largest political party of the second largest political designation shall nominate a member of the Assembly to be the deputy First Minister.
(6) If the persons nominated do not take up office within a period specified in standing orders, further nominations shall be made under subsections (4) and (5).
(7) Subsections (4) to (6) shall be applied as many times as may be necessary to secure that the offices of First Minister and deputy First Minister are filled.
(8) But no person may take up office as First Minister or deputy First Minister under this section after the end of the period mentioned in subsection (3) (see further section 32(3)).
(9) The persons nominated under subsections (4) and (5) shall not take up office until each of them has affirmed the terms of the pledge of office.
(10) This section shall be construed in accordance with, and is subject to, section 16C

16C Sections 16A and 16B: supplementary
(1) In sections 16A and 16B and this section "nominating officer", in relation to a party, means—
   (a) the person registered under Part 2 of the Political Parties, Elections and Referendums Act 2000 as the party's nominating officer; or
   (b) a member of the Assembly nominated by him for the purposes of this section.
(2) For the purposes of sections 16A and 16B and this section—
   (a) the size of a political party is to be determined by reference to the number of seats in the Assembly which were held by members of the party on the day on which the Assembly first met following its election; but
   (b) if two or more parties are taken by virtue of paragraph (a) to be of the same size, the respective sizes of those parties is to be determined by reference to the number of first preference votes cast for the parties at the last general election of members of the Assembly;
(this is subject to subsections (7) and (8)).
(3) For the purposes of sections 16A and 16B and this section, a political party to which one or more members of the Assembly belong is to be taken—
   (a) to be of the political designation "Nationalist" if, at the relevant time (see subsection (11)), more than half of the members of the Assembly who belonged to the party were designated Nationalists;
   (b) to be of the political designation "Unionist" if, at the relevant time, more than half of the members of the Assembly who belonged to the party were designated Unionists;
   (c) otherwise, to be of the political designation "Other".

(4) For the purposes of sections 16A and 16B and this section—
  (a) the size of the political designation "Nationalist" is to be taken to be equal to the number of members of the Assembly who, at the relevant time, were designated Nationalists;
  (b) the size of the political designation "Unionist" is to be taken to be equal to the number of members of the Assembly who, at the relevant time, were designated Unionists;
  (c) the size of the political designation "Other" is to be taken to be equal to the number of members of the Assembly who, at the relevant time, were neither designated Nationalists nor designated Unionists.
(5) But if two or more political designations are taken by virtue of subsection (4) to be of the same size, the respective sizes of those designations is to be determined by reference to the aggregate number of first preference votes cast, at the last general election of members of the Assembly, for members of the Assembly who, at the relevant time, were—
  (a) designated Nationalists (in the case of the political designation "Nationalist");
  (b) designated Unionists (in the case of the political designation "Unionist"); or
  (c) neither designated Nationalists nor designated Unionists (in the case of the political designation "Other").
(6) If at any time the party which is the largest political party of the largest political designation is not the largest political party—
  (a) any nomination to be made at that time under section 16A(4) or 16B(4) shall instead be made by the nominating officer of the largest political party; and
  (b) any nomination to be made at that time under section 16A(5) or 16B(5) shall instead be made by the nominating officer of the largest political party of the largest political designation.
(7) Where—
  (a) the Assembly has resolved under section 30(2) that a political party does not enjoy its confidence; and
  (b) the party's period of exclusion (see subsection (12)) under that provision has not come to an end,
  subsection (2)(a) above shall have effect as if the number of seats in the Assembly which were held by members of the party on the day on which the Assembly first met following its election was nil.
(8) Where—
  (a) the Secretary of State has given a direction under section 30A(5) in respect of a political party; and
  (b) the party's period of exclusion under that provision has not come to an end,
  subsection (2)(a) above shall have effect as if the number of seats in the Assembly which were held by members of the party on the day on which the Assembly first met following its election was nil.
(9) Where—
  (a) a person nominated by the nominating officer of a political party ceased to hold office as First Minister or deputy First Minister as a result of a resolution of the Assembly under section 30(2) or a direction of the Secretary of State under section 30A(5); and
  (b) the party's period of exclusion under section 30(2) or 30A(5) subsequently comes to an end otherwise than by virtue of the dissolution of the Assembly,
  the First Minister and the deputy First Minister shall cease to hold office when the party's period of exclusion under that provision comes to an end (unless any period of exclusion of the party under the other provision has not come to an end).
(10) But where a direction under section 30A(5) ceases to have effect under section 95A(6) or (7), its so ceasing to have effect shall for the purposes of subsection (9) be taken not to involve the coming to an end of a period of exclusion under section 30A(5).
(11) In this section "the relevant time" means the end of the day on which the Assembly first met following its election.

(12) In this section, a reference to a period of exclusion under any provision is, in the case of a period of exclusion under that provision which has been extended, a reference to that period as extended.

(13) Standing orders may make further provision in connection with the making of nominations under sections 16A and 16B.

(14) In this Act "the pledge of office" means the pledge of office which, together with the code of conduct to which it refers, is set out in Schedule 4

17 Ministerial offices

(1) The First Minister and the deputy First Minister acting jointly may at any time, and shall where subsection (2) applies, determine—
   (a) the number of Ministerial offices to be held by Northern Ireland Ministers; and
   (b) the functions to be exercisable by the holder of each such office.

(2) This subsection applies where provision is made by an Act of the Assembly for establishing a new Northern Ireland department or dissolving an existing one.

(3) In making a determination under subsection (1), the First Minister and the deputy First Minister shall ensure that the functions exercisable by those in charge of the different Northern Ireland departments existing at the date of the determination are exercisable by the holders of different Ministerial offices.

(4) The number of Ministerial offices shall not exceed 10 or such greater number as the Secretary of State may by order provide.

(5) A determination under subsection (1) shall not have effect unless it is approved by a resolution of the Assembly passed with cross-community support.

18 Northern Ireland Ministers

(1) Where—
   (a) ...
   (b) a determination under section 17(1) takes effect;
   (c) a resolution which causes one or more Ministerial offices to become vacant is passed under section 30(2);
   ...
   (da) the period of exclusion imposed by a resolution under section 30(2) or 30A(5) comes to an end; or
   (e) such other circumstances obtain as may be specified in standing orders,
   all Northern Ireland Ministers shall cease to hold office and the Ministerial offices shall be filled by applying subsections (2) to (6) within a period so specified.

...

20 The Executive Committee

(1) There shall be an Executive Committee of each Assembly consisting of the First Minister, the deputy First Minister and the Northern Ireland Ministers.

(2) The First Minister and the deputy First Minister shall be chairmen of the Committee.

(3) The Committee shall have the functions set out in paragraphs 19 and 20 of Strand One of the Belfast Agreement.

(4) The Committee shall also have the function of discussing and agreeing upon—
   (a) significant or controversial matters that are clearly outside the scope of the agreed programme referred to in paragraph 20 of Strand One of that Agreement;
   (b) significant or controversial matters that the First Minister and deputy First Minister acting jointly have determined to be matters that should be considered by the Executive Committee.

22 Statutory functions

(1) An Act of the Assembly or other enactment may confer functions on a Minister (but not a junior Minister) or a Northern Ireland department by name.

(2) Functions conferred on a Northern Ireland department by an enactment passed or made before the appointed day shall, except as provided by an Act of the Assembly or other subsequent enactment, continue to be exercisable by that department.

23 **Prerogative and executive powers**
(1) The executive power in Northern Ireland shall continue to be vested in Her Majesty.
. . .

24 **Community law, Convention rights etc.**
(1) A Minister or Northern Ireland department has no power to make, confirm or approve any subordinate legislation, or to do any act, so far as the legislation or act—
   (a) is incompatible with any of the Convention rights;
   (b) is incompatible with Community law;
   (c) discriminates against a person or class of person on the ground of religious belief or political opinion;
   (d) in the case of an act, aids or incites another person to discriminate against a person or class of person on that ground; or
   (e) in the case of legislation, modifies an enactment in breach of section 7.
. . .

25 **Excepted and reserved matters**
(1) If any subordinate legislation made, confirmed or approved by, a Minister or Northern Ireland department contains a provision dealing with an excepted or reserved matter, the Secretary of State may by order revoke the legislation.
(2) An order made under subsection (1) shall recite the reasons for revoking the legislation and may make provision having retrospective effect.

26 **International obligations**
(1) If the Secretary of State considers that any action proposed to be taken by a Minister or Northern Ireland department would be incompatible with any international obligations, with the interests of defence or national security or with the protection of public safety or public order, he may by order direct that the proposed action shall not be taken.
. . .

PART IV
THE NORTHERN IRELAND ASSEMBLY

Presiding Officer and Commission

39 **Presiding Officer**
(1) Each Assembly shall as its first business elect from among its members a Presiding Officer and deputies.
. . .

40 **Commission**
(1) There shall be a body corporate, to be known as the Northern Ireland Assembly Commission ("the Commission"), to perform—
   (a) the functions conferred on the Commission by virtue of any enactment; and
   (b) any functions conferred on the Commission by resolution of the Assembly.
. . .

Proceedings etc.

41 **Standing orders**
(1) The proceedings of the Assembly shall be regulated by standing orders.
. . .

42 **Petitions of concern**
(1) If 30 members petition the Assembly expressing their concern about a matter which is to be voted on by the Assembly, the vote on that matter shall require cross-community support.

(2) Standing orders shall make provision with respect to the procedure to be followed in petitioning the Assembly under this section, including provision with respect to the period of notice required.

(3) Standing orders shall provide that the matter to which a petition under this section relates may be referred, in accordance with paragraphs 11 and 13 of Strand One of the Belfast Agreement, to the committee established under section 13(3)(a).

43 Members' interests

(1) Standing orders shall include provision for a register of interests of members of the Assembly, and for—
  (a) registrable interests (as defined in standing orders) to be registered in it; and
  (b) the register to be published and made available for public inspection.

...

PART VII
HUMAN RIGHTS AND EQUAL OPPORTUNITIES

Human rights

68 The Northern Ireland Human Rights Commission

(1) There shall be a body corporate to be known as the Northern Ireland Human Rights Commission.

(2) The Commission shall consist of a Chief Commissioner and other Commissioners appointed by the Secretary of State.

(3) In making appointments under this section, the Secretary of State shall as far as practicable secure that the Commissioners, as a group, are representative of the community in Northern Ireland.

(4) Schedule 7 (which makes supplementary provision about the Commission) shall have effect.

69 The Commission's functions

(1) The Commission shall keep under review the adequacy and effectiveness in Northern Ireland of law and practice relating to the protection of human rights.

(2) The Commission shall, before the end of the period of two years beginning with the commencement of this section, make to the Secretary of State such recommendations as it thinks fit for improving—
  (a) its effectiveness;
  (b) the adequacy and effectiveness of the functions conferred on it by this Part; and
  (c) the adequacy and effectiveness of the provisions of this Part relating to it.

(3) The Commission shall advise the Secretary of State and the Executive Committee of the Assembly of legislative and other measures which ought to be taken to protect human rights—
  (a) as soon as reasonably practicable after receipt of a general or specific request for advice; and
  (b) on such other occasions as the Commission thinks appropriate.

(4) The Commission shall advise the Assembly whether a Bill is compatible with human rights—
  (a) as soon as reasonably practicable after receipt of a request for advice; and
  (b) on such other occasions as the Commission thinks appropriate.

(5) The Commission may—
  (a) give assistance to individuals in accordance with section 70; and
  (b) bring proceedings involving law or practice relating to the protection of human rights.

(6) The Commission shall promote understanding and awareness of the importance of human rights in Northern Ireland; and for this purpose it may undertake, commission or provide financial or other assistance for—
  (a) research; and
  (b) educational activities.

(7) The Secretary of State shall request the Commission to provide advice of the kind referred to in paragraph 4 of the Human Rights section of the Belfast Agreement.
(8) For the purpose of exercising its functions under this section the Commission may conduct such investigations as it considers necessary or expedient.
(8A) The Commission shall publish a report of its finding on an investigation.
(9) The Commission may decide to publish its advice and the outcome of its research . . .
(10) The Commission shall do all that it can to ensure the establishment of the committee referred to in paragraph 10 of that section of that Agreement.
(11) In this section—
    (a) a reference to the Assembly includes a reference to a committee of the Assembly;
    (b) "human rights" includes the Convention rights.

70 Assistance by Commission
(1) This section applies to—
    (a) proceedings involving law or practice relating to the protection of human rights which a person in Northern Ireland has commenced, or wishes to commence; or
    (b) proceedings in the course of which such a person relies, or wishes to rely, on such law or practice.
(2) Where the person applies to the Northern Ireland Human Rights Commission for assistance in relation to proceedings to which this section applies, the Commission may grant the application on any of the following grounds—
    (a) that the case raises a question of principle;
    (b) that it would be unreasonable to expect the person to deal with the case without assistance because of its complexity, or because of the person's position in relation to another person involved, or for some other reason;
    (c) that there are other special circumstances which make it appropriate for the Commission to provide assistance.
(3) Where the Commission grants an application under subsection (2) it may—
    (a) provide, or arrange for the provision of, legal advice;
    (b) arrange for the provision of legal representation;
    (c) provide any other assistance which it thinks appropriate.
(4) Arrangements made by the Commission for the provision of assistance to a person may include provision for recovery of expenses from the person in certain circumstances.

71 Restrictions on application of rights
(1) Nothing in section 6(2)(c), 24(1)(a) or 69(5)(b) shall enable a person—
    (a) to bring any proceedings in a court or tribunal on the aground that any legislation or act is incompatible with the Convention rights; or
    (b) to rely on any of the Convention rights in any such proceedings,
    unless he would be a victim for the purposes of article 34 of the Convention if proceedings in respect of the legislation or act were brought in the European Court of Human Rights.
(2) Subsection (1) does not apply to the Attorney General, the Attorney General for Northern Ireland, the Advocate General for Scotland or the Lord Advocate.
. . .
(3) Section 6(2)(c)—
    (a) does not apply to a provision of an Act of the Assembly if the passing of the Act is, by virtue of subsection (2) of section 6 of the Human Rights Act 1998, not unlawful under subsection (1) of that section; and
    (b) does not enable a court or tribunal to award in respect of the passing of an Act of the Assembly any damages which it could not award on finding the passing of the Act unlawful under that subsection.
(4) Section 24(1)(a)—
    (a) does not apply to an act which, by virtue of subsection (2) of section 6 of the Human Rights Act 1998, is not unlawful under subsection (1) of that section; and

(b) does not enable a court or tribunal to award in respect of an act any damages which it could not award on finding the act unlawful under that subsection.

(5) In this section "the Convention" has the same meaning as in the Human Rights Act 1998.

PART VIII
MISCELLANEOUS

80 Legislative power to remedy ultra vires acts

(1) The Secretary of State may by order make such provision as he considers necessary or expedient in consequence of—
   (a) any provision of an Act of the Assembly which is not, or may not be, within the legislative competence of the Assembly; or
   (b) any purported exercise by a Minister or Northern Ireland department of his or its functions which is not, or may not be, a valid exercise of those functions.

(2) An order under this section may—
   (a) make provision having retrospective effect;
   (b) make consequential or supplementary provision, including provision amending or repealing any Northern Ireland legislation, or any instrument made under such legislation;
   (c) make transitional or saving provision.

83 Interpretation of Acts of the Assembly etc.

(1) This section applies where—
   (a) any provision of an Act of the Assembly, or of a Bill for such an Act, could be read either—
      (i) in such a way as to be within the legislative competence of the Assembly; or
      (ii) in such a way as to be outside that competence; or
   (b) any provision of subordinate legislation made, confirmed or approved, or purporting to be made, confirmed or approved, by a Northern Ireland authority could be read either—
      (i) in such a way as not to be invalid by reason of section 24 or, as the case may be, section 76; or
      (ii) in such a way as to be invalid by reason of that section.

(2) The provision shall be read in the way which makes it within that competence or, as the case may be, does not make it invalid by reason of that section, and shall have effect accordingly.

(3) In this section "Northern Ireland authority" means a Minister, a Northern Ireland department or a public authority (within the meaning of section 76) carrying out functions relating to Northern Ireland.

. . .

HOUSE OF LORDS ACT 1999
(1999, c. 34)

An Act to restrict membership of the House of Lords by virtue of a hereditary peerage; to make related provision about disqualifications for voting at elections to and for membership of the House of Commons; and for connected purposes. [11 November 1999]

1 Exclusion of hereditary peers

No-one shall be a member of the House of Lords by virtue of a hereditary peerage.

2 Exception from section 1

(1) Section 1 shall not apply in relation to anyone excepted from it by or in accordance with Standing Orders of the House.

(2) At any time 90 people shall be excepted from section 1; but anyone excepted as holder of the office of Earl Marshal, or as performing the office of Lord Great Chamberlain, shall not count towards that limit.

(3) Once excepted from section 1, a person shall continue to be so throughout his life (until an Act of Parliament provides to the contrary).

(4) Standing Orders shall make provision for filling vacancies among the people excepted from section 1; and in any case where—
  (a) the vacancy arises on a death occurring after the end of the first Session of the next Parliament after that in which this Act is passed, and
  (b) the deceased person was excepted in consequence of an election,
  that provision shall require the holding of a by-election.

(5) A person may be excepted from section 1 by or in accordance with Standing Orders made in anticipation of the enactment or commencement of this section.

(6) Any question whether a person is excepted from section 1 shall be decided by the Clerk of the Parliaments, whose certificate shall be conclusive.

3 Removal of disqualifications in relation to the House of Commons

(1) The holder of a hereditary peerage shall not be disqualified by virtue of that peerage for—
  (a) voting at elections to the House of Commons, or
  (b) being, or being elected as, a member of that House.

(2) Subsection (1) shall not apply in relation to anyone excepted from section 1 by virtue of section 2.

6 Interpretation and short title

(1) In this Act "hereditary peerage" includes the principality of Wales and the earldom of Chester.

. . .

FREEDOM OF INFORMATION ACT 2000
(2000, c. 36)

An Act to make provision for the disclosure of information held by public authorities or by persons providing services for them and to amend the Data Protection Act 1998 and the Public Records Act 1958; and for connected purposes. [30 November 2000]

PART I
ACCESS TO INFORMATION HELD BY PUBLIC AUTHORITIES

Right to information

1 General right of access to information held by public authorities

(1) Any person making a request for information to a public authority is entitled—
  (a) to be informed in writing by the public authority whether it holds information of the description specified in the request, and
  (b) if that is the case, to have that information communicated to him.

(2) Subsection (1) has effect subject to the following provisions of this section and to the provisions of sections 2, 9, 12 and 14.

(3) Where a public authority—
  (a) reasonably requires further information in order to identify and locate the information requested, and
  (b) has informed the applicant of that requirement,
  the authority is not obliged to comply with subsection (1) unless it is supplied with that further information.

(4) The information—
  (a) in respect of which the applicant is to be informed under subsection (1)(a), or
  (b) which is to be communicated under subsection (1)(b),
  is the information in question held at the time when the request is received, except that account may be taken of any amendment or deletion made between that time and the time when the information is to be communicated under subsection (1)(b), being an amendment or deletion that would have been made regardless of the receipt of the request.

(5) A public authority is to be taken to have complied with subsection (1)(a) in relation to any information if it has communicated the information to the applicant in accordance with subsection (1)(b).

(6) In this Act, the duty of a public authority to comply with subsection (1)(a) is referred to as "the duty to confirm or deny".

2 Effect of the exemptions in Part II

(1) Where any provision of Part II states that the duty to confirm or deny does not arise in relation to any information, the effect of the provision is that where either—
  (a) the provision confers absolute exemption, or
  (b) in all the circumstances of the case, the public interest in maintaining the exclusion of the duty to confirm or deny outweighs the public interest in disclosing whether the public authority holds the information,
section 1(1)(a) does not apply.

(2) In respect of any information which is exempt information by virtue of any provision of Part II, section 1(1)(b) does not apply if or to the extent that—
  (a) the information is exempt information by virtue of a provision conferring absolute exemption, or
  (b) in all the circumstances of the case, the public interest in maintaining the exemption outweighs the public interest in disclosing the information.

(3) For the purposes of this section, the following provisions of Part II (and no others) are to be regarded as conferring absolute exemption—
  (a) section 21,
  (b) section 23,
  (c) section 32,
  (d) section 34,
  (e) section 36 so far as relating to information held by the House of Commons or the House of Lords,
  (f) in section 40—
    (i) subsection (1), and
    (ii) subsection (2) so far as relating to cases where the first condition referred to in that subsection is satisfied by virtue of subsection (3)(a)(i) or (b) of that section,
  (g) section 41, and
  (h) section 44.

3 Public authorities

(1) In this Act "public authority" means—
  (a) subject to section 4(4), any body which, any other person who, or the holder of any office which—
    (i) is listed in Schedule 1, or
    (ii) is designated by order under section 5, or
  (b) a publicly-owned company as defined by section 6.

(2) For the purposes of this Act, information is held by a public authority if—
  (a) it is held by the authority, otherwise than on behalf of another person, or
  (b) it is held by another person on behalf of the authority.

6 Publicly-owned companies

(1) A company is a "publicly-owned company" for the purposes of section 3(1)(b) if—
  (a) it is wholly owned by the Crown, or
  (b) it is wholly owned by any public authority listed in Schedule 1 other than—
    (i) a government department, or
    (ii) any authority which is listed only in relation to particular information.

. . .

8 Request for information

(1) In this Act any reference to a "request for information" is a reference to such a request which—

(a) is in writing,
(b) states the name of the applicant and an address for correspondence, and
(c) describes the information requested.
(2) For the purposes of subsection (1)(a), a request is to be treated as made in writing where the text of the request—
(a) is transmitted by electronic means,
(b) is received in legible form, and
(c) is capable of being used for subsequent reference.

9   Fees

(1) A public authority to whom a request for information is made may, within the period for complying with section 1(1), give the applicant a notice in writing (in this Act referred to as a "fees notice") stating that a fee of an amount specified in the notice is to be charged by the authority for complying with section 1(1).
(2) Where a fees notice has been given to the applicant, the public authority is not obliged to comply with section 1(1) unless the fee is paid within the period of three months beginning with the day on which the fees notice is given to the applicant.
(3) Subject to subsection (5), any fee under this section must be determined by the public authority in accordance with regulations made by the Secretary of State.
. . .

10   Time for compliance with request

(1) Subject to subsections (2) and (3), a public authority must comply with section 1(1) promptly and in any event not later than the twentieth working day following the date of receipt.
(2) Where the authority has given a fees notice to the applicant and the fee is paid in accordance with section 9(2), the working days in the period beginning with the day on which the fees notice is given to the applicant and ending with the day on which the fee is received by the authority are to be disregarded in calculating for the purposes of subsection (1) the twentieth working day following the date of receipt.
. . .

11   Means by which communication to be made

(1) Where, on making his request for information, the applicant expresses a preference for communication by any one or more of the following means, namely—
(a) the provision to the applicant of a copy of the information in permanent form or in another form acceptable to the applicant,
(b) the provision to the applicant of a reasonable opportunity to inspect a record containing the information, and
(c) the provision to the applicant of a digest or summary of the information in permanent form or in another form acceptable to the applicant,
the public authority shall so far as reasonably practicable give effect to that preference.
(2) In determining for the purposes of this section whether it is reasonably practicable to communicate information by particular means, the public authority may have regard to all the circumstances, including the cost of doing so.
(3) Where the public authority determines that it is not reasonably practicable to comply with any preference expressed by the applicant in making his request, the authority shall notify the applicant of the reasons for its determination.
(4) Subject to subsection (1), a public authority may comply with a request by communicating information by any means which are reasonable in the circumstances.

12   Exemption where cost of compliance exceeds appropriate limit

(1) Section 1(1) does not oblige a public authority to comply with a request for information if the authority estimates that the cost of complying with the request would exceed the appropriate limit.

(2) Subsection (1) does not exempt the public authority from its obligation to comply with paragraph (a) of section 1(1) unless the estimated cost of complying with that paragraph alone would exceed the appropriate limit.

(3) In subsections (1) and (2) "the appropriate limit" means such amount as may be prescribed, and different amounts may be prescribed in relation to different cases.

(4) The Secretary of State may by regulations provide that, in such circumstances as may be prescribed, where two or more requests for information are made to a public authority—
  (a) by one person, or
  (b) by different persons who appear to the public authority to be acting in concert or in pursuance of a campaign,
  the estimated cost of complying with any of the requests is to be taken to be the estimated total cost of complying with all of them.

(5) The Secretary of State may by regulations make provision for the purposes of this section as to the costs to be estimated and as to the manner in which they are to be estimated.

14 Vexatious or repeated requests

(1) Section 1(1) does not oblige a public authority to comply with a request for information if the request is vexatious.

(2) Where a public authority has previously complied with a request for information which was made by any person, it is not obliged to comply with a subsequent identical or substantially similar request from that person unless a reasonable interval has elapsed between compliance with the previous request and the making of the current request.

16 Duty to provide advice and assistance

(1) It shall be the duty of a public authority to provide advice and assistance, so far as it would be reasonable to expect the authority to do so, to persons who propose to make, or have made, requests for information to it.

(2) Any public authority which, in relation to the provision of advice or assistance in any case, conforms with the code of practice under section 45 is to be taken to comply with the duty imposed by subsection (1) in relation to that case.

Refusal of request

17 Refusal of request

(1) A public authority which, in relation to any request for information, is to any extent relying on a claim that any provision of Part II relating to the duty to confirm or deny is relevant to the request or on a claim that information is exempt information must, within the time for complying with section 1(1), give the applicant a notice which—
  (a) states that fact,
  (b) specifies the exemption in question, and
  (c) states (if that would not otherwise be apparent) why the exemption applies.

...

(3) A public authority which, in relation to any request for information, is to any extent relying on a claim that subsection (1)(b) or (2)(b) of section 2 applies must, either in the notice under subsection (1) or in a separate notice given within such time as is reasonable in the circumstances, state the reasons for claiming—
  (a) that, in all the circumstances of the case, the public interest in maintaining the exclusion of the duty to confirm or deny outweighs the public interest in disclosing whether the authority holds the information, or
  (b) that, in all the circumstances of the case, the public interest in maintaining the exemption outweighs the public interest in disclosing the information.

(4) A public authority is not obliged to make a statement under subsection (1)(c) or (3) if, or to the extent that, the statement would involve the disclosure of information which would itself be exempt information.

(5) A public authority which, in relation to any request for information, is relying on a claim that section 12 or 14 applies must, within the time for complying with section 1(1), give the applicant a notice stating that fact.

. . .

The Information Commissioner and the Information Tribunal

18 The Information Commissioner and the Information Tribunal

(1) The Data Protection Commissioner shall be known instead as the Information Commissioner.
(2) The Data Protection Tribunal shall be known instead as the Information Tribunal.
(3) In this Act—
  (a) the Information Commissioner is referred to as "the Commissioner", and
  (b) the Information Tribunal is referred to as "the Tribunal".

. . .

Publication schemes

19 Publication schemes

(1) It shall be the duty of every public authority—
  (a) to adopt and maintain a scheme which relates to the publication of information by the authority and is approved by the Commissioner (in this Act referred to as a "publication scheme"),
  (b) to publish information in accordance with its publication scheme, and
  (c) from time to time to review its publication scheme.
(2) A publication scheme must—
  (a) specify classes of information which the public authority publishes or intends to publish,
  (b) specify the manner in which information of each class is, or is intended to be, published, and
  (c) specify whether the material is, or is intended to be, available to the public free of charge or on payment.
(3) in adopting or reviewing a publication scheme, a public authority shall have regard to the public interest—
  (a) in allowing public access to information held by the authority, and
  (b) in the publication of reasons for decisions made by the authority.
(4) A public authority shall publish its publication scheme in such manner as it thinks fit.
(5) The Commissioner may, when approving a scheme, provide that his approval is to expire at the end of a specified period.
(6) Where the Commissioner has approved the publication scheme of any public authority, he may at any time give notice to the public authority revoking his approval of the scheme as from the end of the period of six months beginning with the day on which the notice is given.
(7) Where the Commissioner—
  (a) refuses to approve a proposed publication scheme, or
  (b) revokes his approval of a publication scheme,
  he must give the public authority a statement of his reasons for doing so.

20 Model publication schemes

(1) The Commissioner may from time to time approve, in relation to public authorities falling within particular classes, model publication schemes prepared by him or by other persons.
(2) Where a public authority falling within the class to which an approved model scheme relates adopts such a scheme without modification, no further approval of the Commissioner is required so long as the model scheme remains approved; and where such an authority adopts such a scheme with modifications, the approval of the Commissioner is required only in relation to the modifications.

. . .

PART II
EXEMPT INFORMATION

21 Information accessible to applicant by other means

(1) Information which is reasonably accessible to the applicant otherwise than under section 1 is exempt information.

(2) For the purposes of subsection (1)—
   (a) information may be reasonably accessible to the applicant even though it is accessible only on payment, and
   (b) information is to be taken to be reasonably accessible to the applicant if it is information which the public authority or any other person is obliged by or under any enactment to communicate (otherwise than by making the information available for inspection) to members of the public on request, whether free of charge or on payment.

(3) For the purposes of subsection (1), information which is held by a public authority and does not fall within subsection (2)(b) is not to be regarded as reasonably accessible to the applicant merely because the information is available from the public authority itself on request, unless the information is made available in accordance with the authority's publication scheme and any payment required is specified in, or determined in accordance with, the scheme.

22 Information intended for future publication

(1) Information is exempt information if—
   (a) the information is held by the public authority with a view to its publication, by the authority or any other person, at some future date (whether determined or not),
   (b) the information was already held with a view to such publication at the time when the request for information was made, and
   (c) it is reasonable in all the circumstances that the information should be withheld from disclosure until the date referred to in paragraph (a).

(2) The duty to confirm or deny does not arise if, or to the extent that, compliance with section 1(1)(a) would involve the disclosure of any information (whether or, not already recorded) which falls within subsection (1).

23 Information supplied by, or relating to, bodies dealing with security matters

(1) Information held by a public authority is exempt information if it was directly or indirectly supplied to the public authority by, or relates to, any of the bodies specified in subsection (3).

(2) A certificate signed by a Minister of the Crown certifying that the information to which it applies was directly or indirectly supplied by, or relates to, any of the bodies specified in subsection (3) shall, subject to section 60, be conclusive evidence of that fact.

(3) The bodies referred to in subsections (1) and (2) are—
   (a) the Security Service,
   (b) the Secret Intelligence Service,
   (c) the Government Communications Headquarters,
   (d) the special forces,
   (e) the Tribunal established under section 65 of the Regulation of Investigatory Powers Act 2000,
   (f) the Tribunal established under section 7 of the Interception of Communications Act 1985,
   (g) the Tribunal established under section 5 of the Security Service Act 1989,
   (h) the Tribunal established under section 9 of the Intelligence Services Act 1994,
   (i) the Security Vetting Appeals Panel,
   (j) the Security Commission,
   (k) the National Criminal Intelligence Service,
   (l) the Service Authority for the National Criminal Intelligence Service,
   (m) the Serious Organised Crime Agency.

...

24 **National security**
(1) Information which does not fall within section 23(1) is exempt information if exemption from section 1(1)(b) is required for the purpose of safeguarding national security.
(2) The duty to confirm or deny does not arise if, or to the extent that, exemption from section 1(1)(a) is required for the purpose of safeguarding national security.
(3) A certificate signed by a Minister of the Crown certifying that exemption from section 1(1)(b), or from section 1(1)(a) and (b), is, or at any time was, required for the purpose of safeguarding national security shall, subject to section 60, be conclusive evidence of that fact.
(4) A certificate under subsection (3) may identify the information to which it applies by means of a general description and may be expressed to have prospective effect.

26 **Defence**
(1) Information is exempt information if its disclosure under this Act would, or would be likely to, prejudice—
 (a) the defence of the British Islands or of any colony, or
 (b) the capability, effectiveness or security of any relevant forces.
(2) In subsection (1)(b) "relevant forces" means—
 (a) the armed forces of the Crown, and
 (b) any forces co-operating with those forces,
 or any part of any of those forces.
(3) The duty to confirm or deny does not arise if, or to the extent that, compliance with section 1(1)(a) would, or would be likely to, prejudice any of the matters mentioned in subsection (1).

27 **International relations**
(1) Information is exempt information if its disclosure under this Act would, or would be likely to, prejudice—
 (a) relations between the United Kingdom and any other State,
 (b) relations between the United Kingdom and any international organisation or international court,
 (c) the interests of the United Kingdom abroad, or
 (d) the promotion or protection by the United Kingdom of its interests abroad.
(2) Information is also exempt information if it is confidential information obtained from a State other than the United Kingdom or from an international organisation or international court.
(3) For the purposes of this section, any information obtained from a State, organisation or court is confidential at any time while the terms on which it was obtained require it to be held in confidence or while the circumstances in which it was obtained make it reasonable for the State, organisation or court to expect that it will be so held.
(4) The duty to confirm or deny does not arise if, or to the extent that, compliance with section 1(1)(a)—
 (a) would, or would be likely to, prejudice any of the matters mentioned in subsection (1), or
 (b) would involve the disclosure of any information (whether or not already recorded) which is confidential information obtained from a State other than the United Kingdom or from an international organisation or international court.

...

28 **Relations within the United Kingdom**
(1) Information is exempt information if its disclosure under this Act would, or would be likely to, prejudice relations between any administration in the United Kingdom and any other such administration.
(2) In subsection (1) "administration in the United Kingdom" means—

(a) the government of the United Kingdom,
(b) the Scottish Administration,
(c) the Executive Committee of the Northern Ireland Assembly, or
(d) the Welsh Assembly Government.
(3) The duty to confirm or deny does not arise if, or to the extent that, compliance with section 1(1)(a) would, or would be likely to, prejudice any of the matters mentioned in subsection (1).

29 The economy
(1) Information is exempt information if its disclosure under this Act would, or would be likely to, prejudice—
 (a) the economic interests of the United Kingdom or of any part of the United Kingdom, or
 (b) the financial interests of any administration in the United Kingdom, as defined by section 28(2).
(2) The duty to confirm or deny does not arise if, or to the extent that, compliance with section 1(1)(a) would, or would be likely to, prejudice any of the matters mentioned in subsection (1).

30 Investigations and proceedings conducted by public authorities
(1) Information held by a public authority is exempt information if it has at any time been held by the authority for the purposes of—
 (a) any investigation which the public authority has a duty to conduct with a view to it being ascertained—
  (i) whether a person should be charged with an offence, or
  (ii) whether a person charged with an offence is guilty of it,
 (b) any investigation which is conducted by the authority and in the circum-stances may lead to a decision by the authority to institute criminal proceedings which the authority has power to conduct, or
 (c) any criminal proceedings which the authority has power to conduct.
(2) Information held by a public authority is exempt information if—
 (a) it was obtained or recorded by the authority for the purposes of its functions relating to—
  (i) investigations falling within subsection (1)(a) or (b),
  (ii) criminal proceedings which the authority has power to conduct,
  (iii) investigations (other than investigations falling within subsection (1)(a) or (b)) which are conducted by the authority for any of the purposes specified in section 31(2) and either by virtue of Her Majesty's prerogative or by virtue of powers conferred by or under any enactment, or
  (iv) civil proceedings which are brought by or on behalf of the authority and arise out of such investigations, and
 (b) it relates to the obtaining of information from confidential sources.
(3) The duty to confirm or deny does not arise in relation to information which is (or if it were held by the public authority would be) exempt information by virtue of subsection (1) or (2).
...

31 Law enforcement
(1) Information which is not exempt information by virtue of section 30 is exempt information if its disclosure under this Act would, or would be likely to, prejudice—
 (a) the prevention or detection of crime,
 (b) the apprehension or prosecution of offenders,
 (c) the administration of justice,
 (d) the assessment or collection of any tax or duty or of any imposition of a similar nature,
 (e) the operation of the immigration controls,
 (f) the maintenance of security and good order in prisons or in other institutions where persons are lawfully detained,

(g) the exercise by any public authority of its functions for any of the purposes specified in subsection (2),
(h) any civil proceedings which are brought by or on behalf of a public authority and arise out of an investigation conducted, for any of the purposes specified in subsection (2), by or on behalf of the authority by virtue of Her Majesty's prerogative or by virtue of powers conferred by or under an enactment, or
(i) any inquiry held under the Fatal Accidents and Sudden Deaths Inquiries (Scotland) Act 1976 to the extent that the inquiry arises out of an investigation conducted, for any of the purposes specified in subsection (2), by or on behalf of the authority by virtue of Her Majesty's prerogative or by virtue of powers conferred by or under an enactment.

(2) The purposes referred to in subsection (1)(g) to (i) are—
(a) the purpose of ascertaining whether any person has failed to comply with the law,
(b) the purpose of ascertaining whether any person is responsible for any conduct which is improper,
(c) the purpose of ascertaining whether circumstances which would justify regulatory action in pursuance of any enactment exist or may arise,
(d) the purpose of ascertaining a person's fitness or competence in relation to the management of bodies corporate or in relation to any profession or other activity which he is, or seeks to become, authorised to carry on,
(e) the purpose of ascertaining the cause of an accident,
(f) the purpose of protecting charities against misconduct or mismanagement (whether by trustees or other persons) in their administration,
(g) the purpose of protecting the property of charities from loss or misapplication,
(h) the purpose of recovering the property of charities,
(i) the purpose of securing the health, safety and welfare of persons at work, and
(j) the purpose of protecting persons other than persons at work against risk to health or safety arising out of or in connection with the actions of persons at work.

(3) The duty to confirm or deny does not arise if, or to the extent that, compliance with section 1(1)(a) would, or would be likely to, prejudice any of the matters mentioned in subsection (1).

32 Court records, etc.

(1) Information held by a public authority is exempt information if it is held only by virtue of being contained in—
(a) any document filed with, or otherwise placed in the custody of, a court for the purposes of proceedings in a particular cause or matter,
(b) any document served upon, or by, a public authority for the purposes of proceedings in a particular cause or matter, or
(c) any document created by—
(i) a court, or
(ii) a member of the administrative staff of a court,
for the purposes of proceedings in a particular cause or matter.

. . .

33 Audit functions

(1) This section applies to any public authority which has functions in relation to—
(a) the audit of the accounts of other public authorities, or
(b) the examination of the economy, efficiency and effectiveness with which other public authorities use their resources in discharging their functions.

(2) Information held by a public authority to which this section applies is exempt information if its disclosure would, or would be likely to, prejudice the exercise of any of the authority's functions in relation to any of the matters referred to in subsection (1).

(3) The duty to confirm or deny does not arise in relation to a public authority to which this section applies if, or to the extent that, compliance with section 1(1)(a) would, or would be likely to, prejudice the exercise of any of the authority's functions in relation to any of the matters referred to in subsection (1).

34 Parliamentary privilege

(1) Information is exempt information if exemption from section 1(1)(b) is required for the purpose of avoiding an infringement of the privileges of either House of Parliament.

(2) The duty to confirm or deny does not apply if, or to the extent that, exemption from section 1(1)(a) is required for the purpose of avoiding an infringement of the privileges of either House of Parliament.

(3) A certificate signed by the appropriate authority certifying that exemption from section 1(1)(b), or from section 1(1)(a) and (b), is, or at any time was, required for the purpose of avoiding an infringement of the privileges of either House of Parliament shall be conclusive evidence of that fact.

(4) In subsection (3) "the appropriate authority" means—
 (a) in relation to the House of Commons, the Speaker of that House, and
 (b) in relation to the House of Lords, the Clerk of the Parliaments.

35 Formulation of government policy, etc.

(1) Information held by a government department or by the Welsh Assembly Government is exempt information if it relates to—
 (a) the formulation or development of government policy,
 (b) Ministerial communications,
 (c) the provision of advice by any of the Law Officers or any request for the provision of such advice, or
 (d) the operation of any Ministerial private office.

(2) Once a decision as to government policy has been taken, any statistical information used to provide an informed background to the taking of the decision is not to be regarded—
 (a) for the purposes of subsection (1)(a), as relating to the formulation or development of government policy, or
 (b) for the purposes of subsection (1)(b), as relating to Ministerial communications.

(3) The duty to confirm or deny does not arise in relation to information which is (or if it were held by the public authority would be) exempt information by virtue of subsection (1).

(4) In making any determination required by section 2(1)(b) or (2)(b) in relation to information which is exempt information by virtue of subsection (1)(a), regard shall be had to the particular public interest in the disclosure of factual information which has been used, or is intended to be used, to provide informed background to decision-taking.

...

36 Prejudice to effective conduct of public affairs

(1) This section applies to—
 (a) information which is held by a government department or by the Welsh Assembly Government and is not exempt information by virtue of section 35, and
 (b) information which is held by any other public authority.

(2) Information to which this section applies is exempt information if, in the reasonable opinion of a qualified person, disclosure of the information under this Act—
 (a) would, or would be likely to, prejudice—
  (i) the maintenance of the convention of the collective responsibility of Ministers of the Crown, or
  (ii) the work of the Cabinet of the Welsh Assembly Government, or
  (iii) the work of the executive committee of the National Assembly for Wales,
 (b) would, or would be likely to, inhibit—
  (i) the free and frank provision of advice, or
  (ii) the free and frank exchange of views for the purposes of deliberation, or
 (c) would otherwise prejudice, or would be likely otherwise to prejudice, the effective conduct of public affairs.

(3) The duty to confirm or deny does not arise in relation to information to which this section applies (or would apply if held by the public authority) if, or to the extent that, in the reasonable opinion of a qualified person, compliance with section 1(1)(a) would, or would be likely to, have any of the effects mentioned in subsection (2).

(4) In relation to statistical information, subsections (2) and (3) shall have effect with the omission of the words "in the reasonable opinion of a qualified person".

(5) In subsections (2) and (3) "qualified person" —
   (a) in relation to information held by a government department in the charge of a Minister of the Crown, means any Minister of the Crown,
   (b) in relation to information held by a Northern Ireland department, means the Northern Ireland Minister in charge of the department,
   (c) in relation to information held by any other government department, means the commissioners or other person in charge of that department,
   (d) in relation to information held by the House of Commons, means the Speaker of that House,
   (e) in relation to information held by the House of Lords, means the Clerk of the Parliaments,
   (f) in relation to information held by the Northern Ireland Assembly, means the Presiding Officer,
   (g) in relation to information held by the Welsh Assembly Government, means the Welsh Ministers or the Counsel General to the Welsh Assembly Government,
   . . .
. . .

37 Communications with Her Majesty, etc. and honours

(1) Information is exempt information if it relates to—
   (a) communications with Her Majesty, with other members of the Royal Family or with the Royal Household, or
   (b) the conferring by the Crown of any honour or dignity.

(2) The duty to confirm or deny does not arise in relation to information which is (or if it were held by the public authority would be) exempt information by virtue of subsection (1).

38 Health and safety

(1) Information is exempt information if its disclosure under this Act would, or would be likely to—
   (a) endanger the physical or mental health of any individual, or
   (b) endanger the safety of any individual.

(2) The duty to confirm or deny does not arise if, or to the extent that, compliance with section 1(1)(a) would, or would be likely to, have either of the effects mentioned in subsection (1).

39 Environmental information

(1) Information is exempt information if the public authority holding it—
   (a) is obliged by environmental information regulations to make the information available to the public in accordance with the regulations, or
   (b) would be so obliged but for any exemption contained in the regulations.

(1A) In subsection (1) "environmental information regulations" means—
   (a) regulations made under section 74, or
   (b) regulations made under section 2(2) of the European Communities Act 1972 for the purpose of implementing any Community obligation relating to public access to, and the dissemination of, information on the environment.

(2) The duty to confirm or deny does not arise in relation to information which is (or if it were held by the public authority would be) exempt information by virtue of subsection (1).

(3) Subsection (1)(a) does not limit the generality of section 21(1).

40 Personal information

(1) Any information to which a request for information relates is exempt information if it constitutes personal data of which the applicant is the data subject.

(2) Any information to which a request for information relates is also exempt information if—
   (a) it constitutes personal data which do not fall within subsection (1), and
   (b) either the first or the second condition below is satisfied.

(3) The first condition is—
   (a) in a case where the information falls within any of paragraphs (a) to (d) of the definition of "data" in section 1(1) of the Data Protection Act 1998, that the disclosure of the information to a member of the public otherwise than under this Act would contravene—
      (i) any of the data protection principles, or
      (ii) section 10 of that Act (right to prevent processing likely to cause damage or distress), and
   (b) in any other case, that the disclosure of the information to a member of the public otherwise than under this Act would contravene any of the data protection principles if the exemptions in section 33A(1) of the Data Protection Act 1998 (which relate to manual data held by public authorities) were disregarded.
(4) The second condition is that by virtue of any provision of Part IV of the Data Protection Act 1998 the information is exempt from section 7(1)(c) of that Act (data subject's right of access to personal data).
(5) The duty to confirm or deny—
   (a) does not arise in relation to information which is (or if it were held by the public authority would be) exempt information by virtue of subsection (1), and
   (b) does not arise in relation to other information if or to the extent that either—
      (i) the giving to a member of the public of the confirmation or denial that would have to be given to comply with section 1(1)(a) would (apart from this Act) contravene any of the data protection principles or section 10 of the Data Protection Act 1998 or would do so if the exemptions in section 33A(1) of that Act were disregarded, or
      (ii) by virtue of any provision of Part IV of the Data Protection Act 1998 the information is exempt from section 7(1)(a) of that Act (data subject's right to be informed whether personal data being processed).
(6) In determining for the purposes of this section whether anything done before 24th October 2007 would contravene any of the data protection principles, the exemptions in Part III of Schedule 8 to the Data Protection Act 1998 shall be disregarded.
(7) In this section—
"the data protection principles" means the principles set out in Part I of Schedule 1 to the Data Protection Act 1998, as read subject to Part II of that Schedule and section 27(1) of that Act;
"data subject" has the same meaning as in section 1(1) of that Act;
"personal data" has the same meaning as in section 1(1) of that Act.

41 Information provided in confidence

(1) Information is exempt information if—
   (a) it was obtained by the public authority from any other person (including another public authority), and
   (b) the disclosure of the information to the public (otherwise than under this Act) by the public authority holding it would constitute a breach of confidence actionable by that or any other person.
(2) The duty to confirm or deny does not arise if, or to the extent that, the confirmation or denial that would have to be given to comply with section 1(1)(a) would (apart from this Act) constitute an actionable breach of confidence.

42 Legal professional privilege

(1) Information in respect of which a claim to legal professional privilege or, in Scotland, to confidentiality of communications could be maintained in legal proceedings is exempt information.
(2) The duty to confirm or deny does not arise if, or to the extent that, compliance with section 1(1)(a) would involve the disclosure of any information (whether or not already recorded) in respect of which such a claim could be maintained in legal proceedings.

43 Commercial interests
  (1) Information is exempt information if it constitutes a trade secret.
  (2) Information is exempt information if its disclosure under this Act would, or would be likely to, prejudice the commercial interests of any person (including the public authority holding it).
  (3) The duty to confirm or deny does not arise if, or to the extent that, compliance with section 1(1)(a) would, or would be likely to, prejudice the interests mentioned in subsection (2).

44 Prohibitions on disclosure
  (1) Information is exempt information if its disclosure (otherwise than under this Act) by the public authority holding it—
    (a) is prohibited by or under any enactment,
    (b) is incompatible with any Community obligation, or
    (c) would constitute or be punishable as a contempt of court.
  (2) The duty to confirm or deny does not arise if the confirmation or denial that would have to be given to comply with section 1(1)(a) would (apart from this Act) fall within any of paragraphs (a) to (c) of subsection (1).

PART III
GENERAL FUNCTIONS OF SECRETARY OF STATE AND INFORMATION COMMISSIONER

45 Issue of code of practice ...
  (1) The Secretary of State shall issue, and may from time to time revise, a code of practice providing guidance to public authorities as to the practice which it would, in his opinion, be desirable for them to follow in connection with the discharge of the authorities' functions under Part I.
  (2) The code of practice must, in particular, include provision relating to—
    (a) the provision of advice and assistance by public authorities to persons who propose to make, or have made, requests for information to them,
    (b) the transfer of requests by one public authority to another public authority by which the information requested is or may be held,
    (c) consultation with persons to whom the information requested relates or persons whose interests are likely to be affected by the disclosure of information,
    (d) the inclusion in contracts entered into by public authorities of terms relating to the disclosure of information, and
    (e) the provision by public authorities of procedures for dealing with complaints about the handling by them of requests for information.
  (3) The code may make different provision for different public authorities.
  (4) Before issuing or revising any code under this section, the Secretary of State shall consult the Commissioner.
  (5) The Secretary of State shall lay before each House of Parliament any code or revised code made under this section.

47 General functions of Commissioner
  (1) It shall be the duty of the Commissioner to promote the following of good practice by public authorities and, in particular, so to perform his functions under this Act as to promote the observance by public authorities of—
    (a) the requirements of this Act, and
    (b) the provisions of the codes of practice under sections 45 and 46.
  (2) The Commissioner shall arrange for the dissemination in such form and manner as he considers appropriate of such information as it may appear to him expedient to give to the public—
    (a) about the operation of this Act,
    (b) about good practice, and
    (c) about other matters within the scope of his functions under this Act, and may give advice to any person as to any of those matters.

(3) The Commissioner may, with the consent of any public authority, assess whether that authority is following good practice.

...

49 Reports to be laid before Parliament
(1) The Commissioner shall lay annually before each House of Parliament a general report on the exercise of his functions under this Act.
(2) The Commissioner may from time to time lay before each House of Parliament such other reports with respect to those functions as he thinks fit.

PART IV
ENFORCEMENT

50 Application for decision by Commissioner
(1) Any person (in this section referred to as "the complainant") may apply to the Commissioner for a decision whether, in any specified respect, a request for information made by the complainant to a public authority has been dealt with in accordance with the requirements of Part I.
(2) On receiving an application under this section, the Commissioner shall make a decision unless it appears to him—
   (a) that the complainant has not exhausted any complaints procedure which is provided by the public authority in conformity with the code of practice under section 45,
   (b) that there has been undue delay in making the application,
   (c) that the application is frivolous or vexatious, or
   (d) that the application has been withdrawn or abandoned.
(3) Where the Commissioner has received an application under this section, he shall either—
   (a) notify the complainant that he has not made any decision under this section as a result of the application and of his grounds for not doing so, or
   (b) serve notice of his decision (in this Act referred to as a "decision notice") on the complainant and the public authority.
(4) Where the Commissioner decides that a public authority—
   (a) has failed to communicate information, or to provide confirmation or denial, in a case where it is required to do so by section 1(1), or
   (b) has failed to comply with any of the requirements of sections 11 and 17, the decision notice must specify the steps which must be taken by the authority for complying with that requirement and the period within which they must be taken.
(5) A decision notice must contain particulars of the right of appeal conferred by section 57.

...

TERRORISM ACT 2000
(2000, c. 11)

An Act to make provision about terrorism; and to make temporary provision for Northern Ireland about the prosecution and punishment of certain offences, the preservation of peace and the maintenance of order. [20 July 2000]

PART I
INTRODUCTORY

1 Terrorism: interpretation
(1) In this Act "terrorism" means the use or threat of action where—
   (a) the action falls within subsection (2),
   (b) the use or threat is designed to influence the government or an international governmental organisation or to intimidate the public or a section of the public, and
   (c) the use or threat is made for the purpose of advancing a political, religious or ideological cause.

(2) Action falls within this subsection if it—
   (a) involves serious violence against a person,
   (b) involves serious damage to property,
   (c) endangers a person's life, other than that of the person committing the action,
   (d) creates a serious risk to the health or safety of the public or a section of the public, or
   (e) is designed seriously to interfere with or seriously to disrupt an electronic system.
(3) The use or threat of action falling within subsection (2) which involves the use of firearms or explosives is terrorism whether or not subsection (1)(b) is satisfied.
(4) In this section—
   (a) "action" includes action outside the United Kingdom,
   (b) a reference to any person or to property is a reference to any person, or to property, wherever situated,
   (c) a reference to the public includes a reference to the public of a country other than the United Kingdom, and
   (d) "the government" means the government of the United Kingdom, of a Part of the United Kingdom or of a country other than the United Kingdom.
(5) In this Act a reference to action taken for the purposes of terrorism includes a reference to action taken for the benefit of a proscribed organisation.

PART II
PROSCRIBED ORGANISATIONS

Procedure

3 Proscription

(1) For the purposes of this Act an organisation is proscribed if—
   (a) it is listed in Schedule 2, or
   (b) it operates under the same name as an organisation listed in that Schedule.
(2) Subsection (1)(b) shall not apply in relation to an organisation listed in Schedule 2 if its entry is the subject of a note in that Schedule.
(3) The Secretary of State may by order—
   (a) add an organisation to Schedule 2;
   (b) remove an organisation from that Schedule,
   (c) amend that Schedule in some other way.
(4) The Secretary of State may exercise his power under subsection (3)(a) in respect of an organisation only if he believes that it is concerned in terrorism.
(5) For the purposes of subsection (4) an organisation is concerned in terrorism if it—
   (a) commits or participates in acts of terrorism,
   (b) prepares for terrorism,
   (c) promotes or encourages terrorism, or
   (d) is otherwise concerned in terrorism.
(5A) The cases in which an organisation promotes or encourages terrorism for the purposes of subsection (5)(c) include any case in which activities of the organisation—
   (a) include the unlawful glorification of the commission or preparation (whether in the past, in the future or generally) of acts of terrorism; or
   (b) are carried out in a manner that ensures that the organisation is associated with statements containing any such glorification.
(5B) The glorification of any conduct is unlawful for the purposes of subsection (5A) if there are persons who may become aware of it who could reasonably be expected to infer that what is being glorified, is being glorified as—
   (a) conduct that should be emulated in existing circumstances, or
   (b) conduct that is illustrative of a type of conduct that should be so emulated.
(5C) In this section—
   'glorification' includes any form of praise or celebration, and cognate expressions are to be construed accordingly;

'statement' includes a communication without words consisting of sounds or images or both.

(6) Where the Secretary of State believes—
   (a) that an organisation listed in Schedule 2 is operating wholly or partly under a name that is not specified in that Schedule (whether as well as or instead of under the specified name), or
   (b) that an organisation that is operating under a name that is not so specified is otherwise for all practical purposes the same as an organisation so listed,
   he may, by order, provide that the name that is not specified in that Schedule is to be treated as another name for the listed organisation.

(7) Where an order under subsection (6) provides for a name to be treated as another name for an organisation, this Act shall have effect in relation to acts occurring while—
   (a) the order is in force, and
   (b) the organisation continues to be listed in Schedule 2,
   as if the organisation were listed in that Schedule under the other name, as well as under the name specified in the Schedule.

(8) The Secretary of State may at any time by order revoke an order under subsection (6) or otherwise provide for a name specified in such an order to cease to be treated as a name for a particular organisation.

(9) Nothing in subsections (6) to (8) prevents any liability from being established in any proceedings by proof that an organisation is the same as an organisation listed in Schedule 2, even though it is or was operating under a name specified neither in Schedule 2 nor in an order under subsection (6).

4 Deproscription: application

(1) An application may be made to the Secretary of State for an order under section 3(3) or (8)—
   (a) removing an organisation from Schedule 2, or
   (b) providing for a name to cease to be treated as a name for an organisation listed in that Schedule.

(2) An application may be made by—
   (a) the organisation, or
   (b) any person affected by the organisation's proscription or by the treatment of the name as a name for the organisation.

(3) The Secretary of State shall make regulations prescribing the procedure for applications under this section.

(4) The regulations shall, in particular—
   (a) require the Secretary of State to determine an application within a specified period of time, and
   (b) require an application to state the grounds on which it is made.

5 Deproscription: appeal

(1) There shall be a commission, to be known as the Proscribed Organisations Appeal Commission.

(2) Where an application under section 4 has been refused, the applicant may appeal to the Commission.

(3) The Commission shall allow an appeal against a refusal to deproscribe an organisation or to provide for a name to cease to be treated as a name for an organisation if it considers that the decision to refuse was flawed when considered in the light of the principles applicable on an application for judicial review.

(4) Where the Commission allows an appeal under this section . . ., it may make an order under this subsection.

(5) Where an order is made under subsection (4) in respect of an appeal against a refusal to deproscribe an organisation the Secretary of State shall as soon as is reasonably practicable—

(a) lay before Parliament, in accordance with section 123(4), the draft of an order under section 3(3)(b) removing the organisation from the list in Schedule 2, or
(b) make an order removing the organisation from the list in Schedule 2 in pursuance of section 123(5).
(5A) Where an order is made under subsection (4) in respect of an appeal against a refusal to provide for a name to cease to be treated as a name for an organisation, the Secretary of State shall, as soon as is reasonably practicable, make an order under section 3(8) providing that the name in question is to cease to be so treated in relation to that organisation.
(6) Schedule 3 (constitution of the Commission and procedure) shall have effect.

6 Further appeal

(1) A party to an appeal under section 5 which the, Proscribed Organisations Appeal Commission has determined may bring a further appeal on a question of law to—
 (a) the Court of Appeal, if the first appeal was heard in England and Wales,
 (b) the Court of Session, if the first appeal was heard in Scotland, or
 (c) the Court of Appeal in Northern Ireland, if the first appeal was heard in Northern Ireland.
(2) An appeal under subsection (1) may be brought only with the permission—
 (a) of the Commission, or
 (b) where the Commission refuses permission, of the court to which the appeal would be brought.
(3) An order under section 5(4) shall not require the Secretary of State to take any action until the final determination or disposal of an appeal under this section (including any appeal to the House of Lords [*Supreme Court*]).

Offences

11 Membership

(1) A person commits an offence if he belongs or professes to belong to a proscribed organisation.
(2) It is a defence for a person charged with an offence under subsection (1) to prove—
 (a) that the organisation was not proscribed on the last (or only) occasion on which he became a member or began to profess to be a member, and
 (b) that he has not taken part in the activities of the organisation at any time while it was proscribed.
(3) A person guilty of an offence under this section shall be liable—
 (a) on conviction on indictment, to imprisonment for a term not exceeding ten years, to a fine or to both, or
 (b) on summary conviction, to imprisonment for a term not exceeding six months, to a fine not exceeding the statutory maximum or to both.

. . .

12 Support

(1) A person commits an offence if—
 (a) he invites support for a proscribed organisation, and
 (b) the support is not, or is not restricted to, the provision of money or other property (within the meaning of section 15).
(2) A person commits an offence if he arranges, manages or assists in arranging or managing a meeting which he knows is—
 (a) to support a proscribed organisation,
 (b) to further the activities of a proscribed organisation, or
 (c) to be addressed by a person who belongs or professes to belong to a proscribed organisation.
(3) A person commits an offence if he addresses a meeting and the purpose of his address is to encourage support for a proscribed organisation or to further its activities.

(4) Where a person is charged with an offence under subsection (2)(c) in respect of a private meeting it is a defence for him to prove that he had no reasonable cause to believe that the address mentioned in subsection (2)(c) would support a proscribed organisation or further its activities.

(5) In subsections (2) to (4)—
    (a) "meeting" means a meeting of three or more persons, whether or not the public are admitted, and
    (b) a meeting is private if the public are not admitted.

(6) A person guilty of an offence under this section shall be liable—
    (a) on conviction on indictment, to imprisonment for a term not exceeding ten years, to a fine or to both, or
    (b) on summary conviction, to imprisonment for a term not exceeding six months, to a fine not exceeding the statutory maximum or to both.

13 Uniform

(1) A person in a public place commits an offence if he—
    (a) wears an item of clothing, or
    (b) wears, carries or displays an article,
in such a way or in such circumstances as to arouse reasonable suspicion that he is a member or supporter of a proscribed organisation.

(2) A constable in Scotland may arrest a person without a warrant if he has reasonable grounds to suspect that the person is guilty of an offence under this section.

(3) A person guilty of an offence under this section shall be liable on summary conviction to—
    (a) imprisonment for a term not exceeding six months,
    (b) a fine not exceeding level 5 on the standard scale, or
    (c) both.

Offences

15 Fund-raising

(1) A person commits an offence if he—
    (a) invites another to provide money or other property, and
    (b) intends that it should be used, or has reasonable cause to suspect that it may be used, for the purposes of terrorism.

(2) A person commits an offence if he—
    (a) receives money or other property, and
    (b) intends that it should be used, or has reasonable cause to suspect that it may be used, for the purposes of terrorism.

(3) A person commits an offence if he—
    (a) provides money or other property, and
    (b) knows or has reasonable cause to suspect that it will or may be used for the purposes of terrorism.

(4) In this section a reference to the provision of money or other property is a reference to its being given, lent or otherwise made available, whether or not for consideration.

19 Disclosure of information: duty

(1) This section applies where a person—
    (a) believes or suspects that another person has committed an offence under any of sections 15 to 18, and
    (b) bases his belief or suspicion on information which comes to his attention in the course of a trade, profession, business or employment.

(1A) But this section does not apply if the information came to the person in the course of a business in the regulated sector.

(2) The person commits an offence if he does not disclose to a constable as soon as is reasonably practicable—
    (a) his belief or suspicion, and

(b) the information on which it is based.
(3) It is a defence for a person charged with an offence under subsection (2) to prove that he had a reasonable excuse for not making the disclosure.
(4) Where—
  (a) a person is in employment,
  (b) his employer has established a procedure for the making of disclosures of the matters specified in subsection (2), and
  (c) he is charged with an offence under that subsection,
  it is a defence for him to prove that he disclosed the matters specified in that subsection in accordance with the procedure.
(5) Subsection (2) does not require disclosure by a professional legal adviser of—
  (a) information which he obtains in privileged circumstances, or
  (b) a belief or suspicion based on information which he obtains in privileged circumstances.
(6) For the purpose of subsection (5) information is obtained by an adviser in privileged circumstances if it comes to him, otherwise than with a view to furthering a criminal purpose—
  (a) from a client or a client's representative, in connection with the provision of legal advice by the adviser to the client,
  (b) from a person seeking legal advice from the adviser, or from the person's representative, or
  (c) from any person, for the purpose of actual or contemplated legal proceedings.
...

22 Penalties

A person guilty of an offence under any of sections 15 to 18 shall be liable—
(a) on conviction on indictment, to imprisonment for a term not exceeding 14 years, to a fine or to both, or
(b) on summary conviction, to imprisonment for a term not exceeding six months, to a fine not exceeding the statutory maximum or to both.

23 Forfeiture

(1) The court by or before which a person is convicted of an offence under any of sections 15 to 18 may make a forfeiture order in accordance with the provisions of this section.
...

PART V
COUNTER-TERRORIST POWERS

Suspected terrorists

40 Terrorist: interpretation

(1) In this Part "terrorist" means a person who—
  (a) has committed an offence under any of sections 11, 12, 15 to 18, 54 and 56 to 63, or
  (b) is or has been concerned in the commission, preparation or instigation of acts of terrorism.
(2) The reference in subsection (1)(b) to a person who has been concerned in the commission, preparation or instigation of acts of terrorism includes a reference to a person who has been, whether before or after the passing of this Act, concerned in the commission, preparation or instigation of acts of terrorism within the meaning given by section 1.

41 Arrest without warrant

(1) A constable may arrest without a warrant a person whom he reasonably suspects to be a terrorist.
(2) Where a person is arrested under this section the provisions of Schedule 8 (detention: treatment, review and extension) shall apply.

(3) Subject to subsections (4) to (7), a person detained under this section shall (unless detained under any other power) be released not later than the end of the period of 48 hours beginning—
   (a) with the time of his arrest under this section, or
   (b) if he was being detained under Schedule 7 when he was arrested under this section, with the time when his examination under that Schedule began.
(4) If on a review of a person's detention under Part II of Schedule 8 the review officer does not authorise continued detention, the person shall (unless detained in accordance with subsection (5) or (6) or under any other power) be released.
(5) Where a police officer intends to make an application for a warrant under paragraph 29 of Schedule 8 extending a person's detention, the person may be detained pending the making of the application.
(6) Where an application has been made under paragraph 29 or 36 of Schedule 8 in respect of a person's detention, he may be detained pending the conclusion of proceedings on the application.
(7) Where an application under paragraph 29 or 36 of Schedule 8 is granted in respect of a person's detention, he may be detained, subject to paragraph 37 of that Schedule, during the period specified in the warrant.
(8) The refusal of an application in respect of a person's detention under paragraph 29 or 36 of Schedule 8 shall not prevent his continued detention in accordance with this section.
(9) A person who has the powers of a constable in one Part of the United Kingdom may exercise the power under subsection (1) in any Part of the United Kingdom.

42 Search of premises

(1) A justice of the peace may on the application of a constable issue a warrant in relation to specified premises if he is satisfied that there are reasonable grounds for suspecting that a person whom the constable reasonably suspects to be a person falling within section 40(1)(b) is to be found there.
(2) A warrant under this section shall authorise any constable to enter and search the specified premises for the purpose of arresting the person referred to in subsection (1) under section 41.
(3) In the application of subsection (1) to Scotland—
   (a) "justice of the peace" includes the sheriff, and
   (b) the justice of the peace or sheriff can be satisfied as mentioned in that subsection only by having heard evidence on oath.

43 Search of persons

(1) A constable may stop and search a person whom he reasonably suspects to be a terrorist to discover whether he has in his possession anything which may constitute evidence that he is a terrorist.
(2) A constable may search a person arrested under section 41 to discover whether he has in his possession anything which may constitute evidence that he is a terrorist.
(3) A search of a person under this section must be carried out by someone of the same sex.
(4) A constable may seize and retain anything which he discovers in the course of a search of a person under subsection (1) or (2) and which he reasonably suspects may constitute evidence that the person is a terrorist.
(5) A person who has the powers of a constable in one Part of the United Kingdom may exercise a power under this section in any Part of the United Kingdom.

Inciting terrorism overseas

59 England and Wales

(1) A person commits an offence if—
   (a) he incites another person to commit an act of terrorism wholly or partly outside the United Kingdom, and

(b) the act would, if committed in England and Wales, constitute one of the offences listed in subsection (2).
(2) Those offences are—
 (a) murder,
 (b) an offence under section 18 of the Offences against the Person Act 1861 (wounding with intent),
 (c) an offence under section 23 or 24 of that Act (poison),
 (d) an offence under section 28 or 29 of that Act (explosions), and
 (e) an offence under section 1(2) of the Criminal Damage Act 1971 (endangering life by damaging property).
(3) A person guilty of an offence under this section shall be liable to any penalty to which he would be liable on conviction of the offence listed in subsection (2) which corresponds to the act which he incites.
(4) For the purposes of subsection (1) it is immaterial whether or not the person incited is in the United Kingdom at the time of the incitement.
(5) Nothing in this section imposes criminal liability on any person acting on behalf of, or holding office under, the Crown.

Terrorist bombing and finance offences

62 Terrorist bombing: jurisdiction
(1) If—
 (a) a person does anything outside the United Kingdom as an act of terrorism or for the purposes of terrorism, and
 (b) his action would have constituted the commission of one of the offences listed in subsection (2) if it had been done in the United Kingdom,
he shall be guilty of the offence.
(2) The offences referred to in subsection (1)(b) are—
 (a) an offence under section 2, 3 or 5 of the Explosive Substances Act 1883 (causing explosions, &c.),
 (b) an offence under section 1 of the Biological Weapons Act 1974 (biological weapons), and
 (c) an offence under section 2 of the Chemical Weapons Act 1996 (chemical weapons).

PART VIII
GENERAL

114 Police powers
(1) A power conferred by virtue of this Act on a constable—
 (a) is additional to powers which he has at common law or by virtue of any other enactment, and
 (b) shall not be taken to affect those powers.
(2) A constable may if necessary use reasonable force for the purpose of exercising a power conferred on him by virtue of this Act (apart from paragraphs 2 and 3 of Schedule 7).
(3) Where anything is seized by a constable under a power conferred by virtue of this Act, it may (unless the contrary intention appears) be retained for so long as is necessary in all the circumstances.

116 Powers to stop and search
(1) A power to search premises conferred by virtue of this Act shall be taken to include power to search a container.
(2) A power conferred by virtue of this Act to stop a person includes power to stop a vehicle (other than an aircraft which is airborne).
(3) A person commits an offence if he fails to stop a vehicle when required to do so by virtue of this section.
(4) A person guilty of an offence under subsection (3) shall be liable on summary conviction to—

(a) imprisonment for a term not exceeding six months,
(b) a fine not exceeding level 5 on the standard scale, or
(c) both.

SCHEDULE 2
PROSCRIBED ORGANISATIONS

The Irish Republican Army.
Cumann na mBan.
Fianna na hEireann.
The Red Hand Commando.
Saor Eire.
The Ulster Freedom Fighters.
The Ulster Volunteer Force.
The Irish National Liberation Army.
The Irish People's Liberation Organisation.
The Ulster Defence Association.
The Loyalist Volunteer Force.
The Continuity Army Council.
The Orange Volunteers.
The Red Hand Defenders.
Al-Qa'ida
Egyptian Islamic Jihad
Al-Gama'at al-Islamiya
Armed Islamic Group (Groupe Islamique Armée) (GIA)
Salafist Group for Call and Combat (Groupe Salafiste pour la Prédication et le Combat) (GSPC)
Babbar Khalsa
International Sikh Youth Federation
Harakat Mujahideen
Jaish e Mohammed
Lashkar e Tayyaba
Liberation Tigers of Tamil Eelam (LTTE)
Hizballah External Security Organisation
Hamas-Izz al-Din al-Qassem Brigades
Palestinian Islamic Jihad—Shaqaqi
Abu Nidal Organisation
Islamic Army of Aden
Mujaheddin e Khalq
Kurdistan Workers' Party (Partiya Karkeren Kurdistan) (PKK)
Revolutionary Peoples' Liberation Party—Front (Devrimci Halk Kurtulus Partisi-Cephesi) (DHKP-C)
Basque Homeland and Liberty (Euskadi ta Askatasuna) (ETA)
17 November Revolutionary Organisation (N17)
Abu Sayyaf Group
Asbat Al-Ansar
Islamic Movement of Uzbekistan
Jemaah Islamiyah
Al Ittihad Al Islamia
Ansar al Islam
Ansar al Sunna
Groupe Islamique Combattant Marocain
Harakat-ul-Jihad-ul-Islami
Harakat-ul-Jihad-ul-Islami (Bangladesh)
Harakat-ul-Mujahideen/Alami
Hezb-e Islami Gulbuddin
Islamic Jihad Union

Jamaat ul-Furquan
Jundallah
Khuddam ul-Islam
Lashkar-e Jhangvi
Libyan Islamic Fighting Group
Sipah-e Sahaba Pakistan
Al-Ghurabaa
The Saved Sect
Baluchistan Liberation Army
Teyrebaz Azadiye Kurdistan
Jammat-ul Mujahadeen Bangladesh
Tehrik Nefaz-e-Shariat Muhammadi

SCHEDULE 3
THE PROSCRIBED ORGANISATIONS APPEAL COMMISSION

Constitution and administration

1. (1) The Commission shall consist of members appointed by the Lord Chancellor.
   (2) The Lord Chancellor shall appoint one of the members as chairman.
   (3) A member shall hold and vacate office in accordance with terms of his appointment.
   (4) A member may resign at any time by notice in writing to the Lord Chancellor.

. . .

Procedure

4. (1) The Commission shall sit at such times and in such places as the Lord Chancellor may direct after consulting the following—
   (a) the Lord Chief Justice of England and Wales;
   (b) the Lord President of the Court of Session;
   (c) the Lord Chief Justice of Northern Ireland.
   (2) The Commission may sit in two or more divisions.
   (3) At each sitting of the Commission—
   (a) three members shall attend,
   (b) one of the members shall be a person who holds or has held high judicial office (within the meaning of the Appellate Jurisdiction Act 1876), and
   (c) the chairman or another member nominated by him shall preside and report the Commission's decision.

5. (1) The Lord Chancellor may make rules—
   (a) regulating the exercise of the right of appeal to the Commission;
   (b) prescribing practice and procedure to be followed in relation to proceedings before the Commission;
   (c) providing for proceedings before the Commission to be determined without an oral hearing in specified circumstances;
   (d) making provision about evidence in proceedings before the Commission (including provision about the burden of proof and admissibility of evidence);
   (e) making provision about proof of the Commission's decisions.
   (2) In making the rules the Lord Chancellor shall, in particular, have regard to the need to secure—
   (a) that decisions which are the subject of appeals are properly reviewed, and
   (b) that information is not disclosed contrary to the public interest.

. . .

SCHEDULE 6
FINANCIAL INFORMATION

Orders

1. (1) Where an order has been made under this paragraph in relation to a terrorist investigation, a constable named in the order may require a financial institution to which the order applies to provide customer information for the purposes of the investigation.

    ...

   (2) The information shall be provided—
      (a) in such manner and within such time as the constable may specify, and
      (b) notwithstanding any restriction on the disclosure of information imposed by statute or otherwise.
   (3) An institution which fails to comply with a requirement under this paragraph shall be guilty of an offence.
   (4) It is a defence for an institution charged with an offence under sub-paragraph (3) to prove—
      (a) that the information required was not in the institution's possession, or
      (b) that it was not reasonably practicable for the institution to comply with the requirement.
   (5) An institution guilty of an offence under sub-paragraph (3) shall be liable on summary conviction to a fine not exceeding level 5 on the standard scale.

Procedure

2. An order under paragraph 1 may be made only on the application of—
   (a) in England and Wales or Northern Ireland, a police officer of at least the rank of superintendent, or
   (b) in Scotland, the procurator fiscal.
3. An order under paragraph 1 may be made only by—
   (a) in England and Wales, a Circuit judge, or a District Judge (Magistrates' Courts),
   (b) in Scotland, the sheriff, or
   (c) in Northern Ireland, a Crown Court judge.
4. (1) Criminal Procedure Rules may make provision about the procedure for an application under paragraph 1.
   (2) The High Court of Justiciary may, by Act of Adjournal, make provision about the procedure for an application under paragraph 1.
   (3) Crown Court rules may make provision about the procedure for an application under paragraph 1.

Criteria for making order

5. An order under paragraph 1 may be made only if the person making it is satisfied that—
   (a) the order is sought for the purposes of a terrorist investigation,
   (b) the tracing of terrorist property is desirable for the purposes of the investigation, and
   (c) the order will enhance the effectiveness of the investigation.

HOUSE OF COMMONS (REMOVAL OF CLERGY DISQUALIFICATION) ACT 2001
(2001, c. 13)

An Act to remove any disqualification from membership of the House of Commons that arises by reason of a person having been ordained or being a minister of a religious denomination and to continue the disqualification of Lords Spiritual from such membership. [11 May 2001]

1 Removal of disqualification of clergy

(1) A person is not disqualified from being or being elected as a member of the House of Commons merely because he has been ordained or is a minister of any religious denomination.

(2) But a person is disqualified from being or being elected as a member of that House if he is a Lord Spiritual.
(3) Accordingly—
    (a) Schedule 1 (which makes amendments consequential on this section) has effect, and
    (b) the enactments mentioned in Schedule 2 (which relate to the disqualification of clergy from membership of the House of Commons) are repealed to the extent specified in that Schedule.

CRIMINAL JUSTICE AND POLICE ACT 2001
(2001, c. 16)

An Act to make provision for combatting crime and disorder; to make provision about the disclosure of information relating to criminal matters and about powers of search and seizure; to amend the Police and Criminal Evidence Act 1984, the Police and Criminal Evidence (Northern Ireland) Order 1989 and the Terrorism Act 2000; to make provision about the police, the National Criminal Intelligence Service and the National Crime Squad; to make provision about the powers of the courts in relation to criminal matters; and for connected purposes. [11 May 2001]

PART 2
POWERS OF SEIZURE

Additional powers of seizure

50 Additional powers of seizure from premises
(1) Where—
    (a) a person who is lawfully on any premises finds anything on those premises that he has reasonable grounds for believing may be or may contain something for which he is authorised to search on those premises,
    (b) a power of seizure to which this section applies or the power conferred by subsection (2) would entitle him, if he found it, to seize whatever it is that he has grounds for believing that thing to be or to contain, and
    (c) in all the circumstances, it is not reasonably practicable for it to be determined, on those premises—
        (i) whether what he has found is something that he is entitled to seize, or
        (ii) the extent to which what he has found contains something that he is entitled to seize,
    that person's powers of seizure shall include power under this section to seize so much of what he has found as it is necessary to remove from the premises to enable that to be determined.
(2) Where—
    (a) a person who is lawfully on any premises finds anything on those premises ("the seizable property") which he would be entitled to seize but for its being comprised in something else that he has (apart from this subsection) no power to seize,
    (b) the power under which that person would have power to seize the seizable property is a power to which this section applies, and
    (c) in all the circumstances it is not reasonably practicable for the seizable property to be separated, on those premises, from that in which it is comprised,
    that person's powers of seizure shall include power under this section to seize both the seizable property and that from which it is not reasonably practicable to separate it.
(3) The factors to be taken into account in considering, for the purposes of this section, whether or not it is reasonably practicable on particular premises for something to be determined, or for something to be separated from something else, shall be confined to the following—
    (a) how long it would take to carry out the determination or separation on those premises;
    (b) the number of persons that would be required to carry out that determination or separation on those premises within a reasonable period;

(c) whether the determination or separation would (or would if carried out on those premises) involve damage to property;
(d) the apparatus or equipment that it would be necessary or appropriate to use for the carrying out of the determination or separation; and
(e) in the case of separation, whether the separation—
  (i) would be likely, or
  (ii) if carried out by the only means that are reasonably practicable on those premises, would be likely,
to prejudice the use of some or all of the separated seizable property for a purpose for which something seized under the power in question is capable of being used.

...

(5) This section applies to each of the powers of seizure specified in Part 1 of Schedule 1.

...

51 Additional powers of seizure from the person

(1) Where—
  (a) a person carrying out a lawful search of any person finds something that he has reasonable grounds for believing may be or may contain something for which he is authorised to search,
  (b) a power of seizure to which this section applies or the power conferred by subsection (2) would entitle him, if he found it, to seize whatever it is that he has grounds for believing that thing to be or to contain, and
  (c) in all the circumstances it is not reasonably practicable for it to be determined, at the time and place of the search—
    (i) whether what he has found is something that he is entitled to seize, or
    (ii) the extent to which what he has found contains something that he is entitled to seize,
that person's powers of seizure shall include power under this section to seize so much of what he has found as it is necessary to remove from that place to enable that to be determined.

(2) Where—
  (a) a person carrying out a lawful search of any person finds something ("the seizable property") which he would be entitled to seize but for its being comprised in something else that he has (apart from this subsection) no power to seize,
  (b) the power under which that person would have power to seize the seizable property is a power to which this section applies, and
  (c) in all the circumstances it is not reasonably practicable for the seizable property to be separated, at the time and place of the search, from that in which it is comprised,
that person's powers of seizure shall include power under this section to seize both the seizable property and that from which it is not reasonably practicable to separate it.

(3) The factors to be taken into account in considering, for the purposes of this section, whether or not it is reasonably practicable, at the time and place of a search, for something to be determined, or for something to be separated from something else, shall be confined to the following—
  (a) how long it would take to carry out the determination or separation at that time and place;
  (b) the number of persons that would be required to carry out that determination or separation at that time and place within a reasonable period;
  (c) whether the determination or separation would (or would if carried out at that time and place) involve damage to property;
  (d) the apparatus or equipment that it would be necessary or appropriate to use for the carrying out of the determination or separation; and
  (e) in the case of separation, whether the separation—
    (i) would be likely, or
    (ii) if carried out by the only means that are reasonably practicable at that time and place, would be likely,

to prejudice the use of some or all of the separated seizable property for a purpose for which something seized under the power in question is capable of being used.

(4) Section 19(6) of the 1984 Act and Article 21(6) of the Police and Criminal Evidence (Northern Ireland) Order 1989 (powers of seizure not to include power to seize anything a person has reasonable grounds for believing is legally privileged) shall not apply to the power of seizure conferred by subsection (2).

(5) This section applies to each of the powers of seizure specified in Part 2 of Schedule 1.

52 Notice of exercise of power under s. 50 or 51

(1) Where a person exercises a power of seizure conferred by section 50, it shall (subject to subsections (2) and (3)) be his duty, on doing so, to give to the occupier of the premises a written notice—
 (a) specifying what has been seized in reliance on the powers conferred by that section;
 (b) specifying the grounds on which those powers have been exercised;
 (c) setting out the effect of sections 59 to 61;
 (d) specifying the name and address of the person to whom notice of an application under section 59(2) to the appropriate judicial authority in respect of any of the seized property must be given; and
 (e) specifying the name and address of the person to whom an application may be made to be allowed to attend the initial examination required by any arrangements made for the purposes of section 53(2).

(2) Where it appears to the person exercising on any premises a power of seizure conferred by section 50—
 (a) that the occupier of the premises is not present on the premises at the time of the exercise of the power, but
 (b) that there is some other person present on the premises who is in charge of the premises,
subsection (1) of this section shall have effect as if it required the notice under that subsection to be given to that other person.

(3) Where it appears to the person exercising a power of seizure conferred by section 50 that there is no one present on the premises to whom he may give a notice for the purposes of complying with subsection (1) of this section, he shall, before leaving the premises, instead of complying with that subsection, attach a notice such as is mentioned in that subsection in a prominent place to the premises.

(4) Where a person exercises a power of seizure conferred by section 51 it shall be his duty, on doing so, to give a written notice to the person from whom the seizure is made—
 (a) specifying what has been seized in reliance on the powers conferred by that section;
 (b) specifying the grounds on which those powers have been exercised;
 (c) setting out the effect of sections 59 to 61;
 (d) specifying the name and address of the person to whom notice of any application under section 59(2) to the appropriate judicial authority in respect of any of the seized property must be given; and
 (e) specifying the name and address of the person to whom an application may be made to be allowed to attend the initial examination required by any arrangements made for the purposes of section 53(2).

. . .

Return or retention of seized property

53 Examination and return of property seized under s. 50 or 51

(1) This section applies where anything has been seized under a power conferred by section 50 or 51.

(2) It shall be the duty of the person for the time being in possession of the seized property in consequence of the exercise of that power to secure that there are arrangements in force which (subject to section 61) ensure—
 (a) that an initial examination of the property is carried out as soon as reasonably practicable after the seizure;

(b) that that examination is confined to whatever is necessary for determining how much of the property falls within subsection (3);
(c) that anything which is found, on that examination, not to fall within subsection (3) is separated from the rest of the seized property and is returned as soon as reasonably practicable after the examination of all the seized property has been completed; and
(d) that, until the initial examination of all the seized property has been completed and anything which does not fall within subsection (3) has been returned, the seized property is kept separate from anything seized under any other power.

(3) The seized property falls within this subsection to the extent only—
(a) that it is property for which the person seizing it had power to search when he made the seizure but is not property the return of which is required by section 54;
(b) that it is property the retention of which is authorised by section 56; or
(c) that it is something which, in all the circumstances, it will not be reasonably practicable, following the examination, to separate from property falling within paragraph (a) or (b).

(4) In determining for the purposes of this section the earliest practicable time for the carrying out of an initial examination of the seized property, due regard shall be had to the desirability of allowing the person from whom it was seized, or a person with an interest in that property, an opportunity of being present or (if he chooses) of being represented at the examination.

(5) In this section, references to whether or not it is reasonably practicable to separate part of the seized property from the rest of it are references to whether or not it is reasonably practicable to do so without prejudicing the use of the rest of that property, or a part of it, for purposes for which (disregarding the part to be separated) the use of the whole or of a part of the rest of the property, if retained, would be lawful.

54 Obligation to return items subject to legal privilege

(1) If, at any time after a seizure of anything has been made in exercise of a power of seizure to which this section applies—
(a) it appears to the person for the time being having possession of the seized property in consequence of the seizure that the property—
(i) is an item subject to legal privilege, or
(ii) has such an item comprised in it,
and
(b) in a case where the item is comprised in something else which has been lawfully seized, it is not comprised in property falling within subsection (2),
it shall be the duty of that person to secure that the item is returned as soon as reasonably practicable after the seizure.

(2) Property in which an item subject to legal privilege is comprised falls within this subsection if—
(a) the whole or a part of the rest of the property is property falling within subsection (3) or property the retention of which is authorised by section 56; and
(b) in all the circumstances, it is not reasonably practicable for that item to be separated from the rest of that property (or, as the case may be, from that part of it) without prejudicing the use of the rest of that property, or that part of it, for purposes for which (disregarding that item) its use, if retained, would be lawful.

(3) Property falls within this subsection to the extent that it is property for which the person seizing it had power to search when he made the seizure, but is not property which is required to be returned under this section or section 55.

(4) This section applies—
(a) to the powers of seizure conferred by sections 50 and 51;
(b) to each of the powers of seizure specified in Parts 1 and 2 of Schedule 1; and
(c) to any power of seizure (not falling within paragraph (a) or (b)) conferred on a constable by or under any enactment, including an enactment passed after this Act.

55 Obligation to return excluded and special procedure material
(1) If, at any time after a seizure of anything has been made in exercise of a power to which this section applies—
   (a) it appears to the person for the time being having possession of the seized property in consequence of the seizure that the property—
      (i) is excluded material or special procedure material, or
      (ii) has any excluded material or any special procedure material comprised in it,
   (b) its retention is not authorised by section 56, and
   (c) in a case where the material is comprised in something else which has been lawfully seized, it is not comprised in property falling within subsection (2) or (3),
   it shall be the duty of that person to secure that the item is returned as soon as reasonably practicable after the seizure.
(2) Property in which any excluded material or special procedure material is comprised falls within this subsection if—
   (a) the whole or a part of the rest of the property is property for which the person seizing it had power to search when he made the seizure but is not property the return of which is required by this section or section 54; and
   (b) in all the circumstances, it is not reasonably practicable for that material to be separated from the rest of that property (or, as the case may be, from that part of it) without prejudicing the use of the rest of that property, or that part of it, for purposes for which (disregarding that material) its use, if retained, would be lawful.
(3) Property in which any excluded material or special procedure material is comprised falls within this subsection if—
   (a) the whole or a part of the rest of the property is property the retention of which is authorised by section 56; and
   (b) in all the circumstances, it is not reasonably practicable for that material to be separated from the rest of that property (or, as the case may be, from that part of it) without prejudicing the use of the rest of that property, or that part of it, for purposes for which (disregarding that material) its use, if retained, would be lawful.
(4) This section applies (subject to subsection (5)) to each of the powers of seizure specified in Part 3 of Schedule 1.
. . .

56 Property seized by constables etc.
(1) The retention of—
   (a) property seized on any premises by a constable who was lawfully on the premises,
   (b) property seized on any premises by a relevant person who was on the premises accompanied by a constable, and
   (c) property seized by a constable carrying out a lawful search of any person,
   is authorised by this section if the property falls within subsection (2) or (3).
(2) Property falls within this subsection to the extent that there are reasonable grounds for believing—
   (a) that it is property obtained in consequence of the commission of an offence; and
   (b) that it is necessary for it to be retained in order to prevent its being concealed, lost, damaged, altered or destroyed.
(3) Property falls within this subsection to the extent that there are reasonable grounds for believing—
   (a) that it is evidence in relation to any offence; and
   (b) that it is necessary for it to be retained in order to prevent its being concealed, lost, altered or destroyed.
(4) Nothing in this section authorises the retention (except in pursuance of section 54(2)) of anything at any time when its return is required by section 54.
(4A) Subsection (1)(a) includes property seized on any premises—
   (a) by a person authorised under section 16(2) of the 1984 Act to accompany a constable executing a warrant, or

(b) by a person accompanying a constable under section 2(6) of the Criminal Justice Act 1987 in the execution of a warrant under section 2(4) of that Act.

...

58 Person to whom seized property is to be returned

(1) Where—
   (a) anything has been seized in exercise of any power of seizure, and
   (b) there is an obligation under this Part for the whole or any part of the seized property to be returned,
   the obligation to return it shall (subject to the following provisions of this section) be an obligation to return it to the person from whom it was seized.
(2) Where—
   (a) any person is obliged under this Part to return anything that has been seized to the person from whom it was seized, and
   (b) the person under that obligation is satisfied that some other person has a better right to that thing than the person from whom it was seized,
   his duty to return it shall, instead, be a duty to return it to that other person or, as the case may be, to the person appearing to him to have the best right to the thing in question.
(3) Where different persons claim to be entitled to the return of anything that is required to be returned under this Part, that thing may be retained for as long as is reasonably necessary for the determination in accordance with subsection (2) of the person to whom it must be returned.
(4) References in this Part to the person from whom something has been seized, in relation to a case in which the power of seizure was exercisable by reason of that thing's having been found on any premises, are references to the occupier of the premises at the time of the seizure.

...

Remedies and safeguards

59 Application to the appropriate judicial authority

(1) This section applies where anything has been seized in exercise, or purported exercise, of a relevant power of seizure.
(2) Any person with a relevant interest in the seized property may apply to the appropriate judicial authority, on one or more of the grounds mentioned in subsection (3), for the return of the whole or a part of the seized property.
(3) Those grounds are—
   (a) that there was no power to make the seizure;
   (b) that the seized property is or contains an item subject to legal privilege that is not comprised in property falling within section 54(2);
   (c) that the seized property is or contains any excluded material or special procedure material which—
      (i) has been seized under a power to which section 55 applies;
      (ii) is not comprised in property falling within section 55(2) or (3); and
      (iii) is not property the retention of which is authorised by section 56;
   (d) that the seized property is or contains something seized under section 50 or 51 which does not fall within section 53(3);
   and subsections (5) and (6) of section 55 shall apply for the purposes of paragraph (c) as they apply for the purposes of that section.
(4) Subject to subsection (6), the appropriate judicial authority, on an application under subsection (2), shall—
   (a) if satisfied as to any of the matters mentioned in subsection (3), order the return of so much of the seized property as is property in relation to which the authority is so satisfied; and
   (b) to the extent that that authority is not so satisfied, dismiss the application.
(5) The appropriate judicial authority—

(a) on an application under subsection (2),
(b) on an application made by the person for the time being having possession of anything in consequence of its seizure under a relevant power of seizure, or
(c) on an application made—
   (i) by a person with a relevant interest in anything seized under section 50 or 51, and
   (ii) on the grounds that the requirements of section 53(2) have not been or are not being complied with,
may give such directions as the authority thinks fit as to the examination, retention, separation or return of the whole or any part of the seized property.

(6) On any application under this section, the appropriate judicial authority may authorise the retention of any property which—
(a) has been seized in exercise, or purported exercise, of a relevant power of seizure, and
(b) would otherwise fall to be returned,
if that authority is satisfied that the retention of the property is justified on grounds falling within subsection (7).

(7) Those grounds are that (if the property were returned) it would immediately become appropriate—
(a) to issue, on the application of the person who is in possession of the property at the time of the application under this section, a warrant in pursuance of which, or of the exercise of which, it would be lawful to seize the property; or
(b) to make an order under—
   (i) paragraph 4 of Schedule 1 to the 1984 Act,
   (ii) paragraph 4 of Schedule 1 to the Police and Criminal Evidence (Northern Ireland) Order 1989,
   (iii) section 20BA of the Taxes Management Act 1970, or
   (iv) paragraph 5 of Schedule 5 to the Terrorism Act 2000,
under which the property would fall to be delivered up or produced to the person mentioned in paragraph (a).

(8) Where any property which has been seized in exercise, or purported exercise, of a relevant power of seizure has parts ("part A" and "part B") comprised in it such that—
(a) it would be inappropriate, if the property were returned, to take any action such as is mentioned in subsection (7) in relation to part A,
(b) it would (or would but for the facts mentioned in paragraph (a)) be appropriate, if the property were returned, to take such action in relation to part B, and
(c) in all the circumstances, it is not reasonably practicable to separate part A from part B without prejudicing the use of part B for purposes for which it is lawful to use property seized under the power in question,
the facts mentioned in paragraph (a) shall not be taken into account by the appropriate judicial authority in deciding whether the retention of the property is justified on grounds falling within subsection (7).

. . .

61   The duty to secure

(1) The duty to secure that arises under this section is a duty of the person for the time being having possession, in consequence of the seizure, of the seized property to secure that arrangements are in force that ensure that the seized property (without being returned) is not, at any time after the giving of the notice of the application under section 60(1), either—
(a) examined or copied, or
(b) put to any use to which its seizure would, apart from this subsection, entitle it to be put,
except with the consent of the applicant or in accordance with the directions of the appropriate judicial authority.

(2) Subsection (1) shall not have effect in relation to any time after the withdrawal of the application to which the notice relates.

. . .

Construction of Part 2

63 **Copies**
(1) Subject to subsection (3)—
    (a) in this Part, "seize" includes "take a copy of", and cognate expressions shall be construed accordingly;
    (b) this Part shall apply as if any copy taken under any power to which any provision of this Part applies were the original of that of which it is a copy; and
    (c) for the purposes of this Part, except sections 50 and 51, the powers mentioned in subsection (2) (which are powers to obtain hard copies etc. of information which is stored in electronic form) shall be treated as powers of seizure, and references to seizure and to seized property shall be construed accordingly.

. . .

ANTI-TERRORISM, CRIME AND SECURITY ACT 2001
(2001, c. 24)

An Act to amend the Terrorism Act 2000; to make further provision about terrorism and security; to provide for the freezing of assets; to make provision about immigration and asylum; to amend or extend the criminal law and powers for preventing crime and enforcing that law; to make provision about the control of pathogens and toxins; to provide for the retention of communications data; to provide for implementation of Title VI of the Treaty on European Union; and for connected purposes.

[14 December 2001]

PART 1
TERRORIST PROPERTY

1 **Forfeiture of terrorist cash**
(1) Schedule 1 (which makes provision for enabling cash which—
    (a) is intended to be used for the purposes of terrorism,
    (b) consists of resources of an organisation which is a proscribed organisation, or
    (c) is, or represents, property obtained through terrorism,
    to be forfeited in civil proceedings before a magistrates' court or (in Scotland) the sheriff) is to have effect.
(2) The powers conferred by Schedule 1 are exercisable in relation to any cash whether or not any proceedings have been brought for an offence in connection with the cash.

. . .

PART 2
FREEZING ORDERS

Orders

4 **Power to make order**
(1) The Treasury may make a freezing order if the following two conditions are satisfied.
(2) The first condition is that the Treasury reasonably believe that—
    (a) action to the detriment of the United Kingdom's economy (or part of it) has been or is likely to be taken by a person or persons, or
    (b) action constituting a threat to the life or property of one or more nationals of the United Kingdom or residents of the United Kingdom has been or is likely to be taken by a person or persons.
(3) If one person is believed to have taken or to be likely to take the action the second condition is that the person is—
    (a) the government of a country or territory outside the United Kingdom, or
    (b) a resident of a country or territory outside the United Kingdom.

        (4) If two or more persons are believed to have taken or to be likely to take the action the second condition is that each of them falls within paragraph (a) or (b) of subsection (3); and different persons may fall within different paragraphs.

5   Contents of order
   (1) A freezing order is an order which prohibits persons from making funds available to or for the benefit of a person or persons specified in the order.
   (2) The order must provide that these are the persons who are prohibited—
      (a) all persons in the United Kingdom, and
      (b) all persons elsewhere who are nationals of the United Kingdom or are bodies incorporated under the law of any part of the United Kingdom or are Scottish partnerships.
   (3) The order may specify the following (and only the following) as the person or persons to whom or for whose benefit funds are not to be made available—
      (a) the person or persons reasonably believed by the Treasury to have taken or to be likely to take the action referred to in section 4;
      (b) any person the Treasury reasonably believe has provided or is likely to provide assistance (directly or indirectly) to that person or any of those persons.
   (4) A person may be specified under subsection (3) by—
      (a) being named in the order, or
      (b) falling within a description of persons set out in the order.
   (5) The description must be such that a reasonable person would know whether he fell within it.
   (6) Funds are financial assets and economic benefits of any kind.

Orders: procedure etc.

10   Procedure for making freezing orders
   (1) A power to make a freezing order is exercisable by statutory instrument.
   (2) A freezing order—
      (a) must be laid before Parliament after being made;
      (b) ceases to have effect at the end of the relevant period unless before the end of that period the order is approved by a resolution of each House of Parliament (but without that affecting anything done under the order or the power to make a new order).
   (3) The relevant period is a period of 28 days starting with the day on which the order is made.
   (4) In calculating the relevant period no account is to be taken of any time during which Parliament is dissolved or prorogued or during which both Houses are adjourned for more than 4 days.
   (5) If the Treasury propose to make a freezing order in the belief that the condition in section 4(2)(b) is satisfied, they must not make the order unless they consult the Secretary of State.

POLICE REFORM ACT 2002
(2002, c. 30)

An Act to make new provision about the supervision, administration, functions and conduct of police forces, police officers and other persons serving with, or carrying out functions in relation to, the police; to amend police powers and to provide for the exercise of police powers by persons who are not police officers; to amend the law relating to anti-social behaviour orders; to amend the law relating to sex offender orders; and for connected purposes. [24 July 2002]

PART 2
COMPLAINTS AND MISCONDUCT

The Independent Police Complaints Commission

9   The Independent Police Complaints Commission
   (1) There shall be a body corporate to be known as the Independent Police Complaints Commission (in this Part referred to as "the Commission").

(2) The Commission shall consist of—
    (a) a chairman appointed by Her Majesty; and
    (b) not less than ten other members appointed by the Secretary of State.
(3) A person shall not be appointed as the chairman of the Commission, or as another member of the Commission, if—
    (a) he holds or has held office as a constable in any part of the United Kingdom;
    (b) he is or has been under the direction and control of a chief officer or of any person holding an equivalent office in Scotland or Northern Ireland;
    (c) he is a person in relation to whom a designation under section 39 is or has been in force;
    (d) he is a person in relation to whom an accreditation under section 41 or 41A is or has been in force;
    (da) he is or has been the chairman or a member of, or a member of the staff of, the Serious Organised Crime Agency;
    (db) he is or has been—
        (i) the chairman or chief executive of, or
        (ii) another member of, or
        (iii) another member of the staff of,
        the National Policing Improvement Agency.
    (e) he . . . has been a member of the National Criminal Intelligence Service or the National Crime Squad; or
    (f) he is or has at any time been a member of a body of constables which at the time of his membership is or was a body of constables in relation to which any procedures are or were in force by virtue of an agreement or order under—
        (i) section 26 of this Act; or
        (ii) section 78 of the 1996 Act or section 96 of the 1984 Act (which made provision corresponding to that made by section 26 of this Act).
(4) An appointment made in contravention of subsection (3) shall have no effect.
(5) The Commission shall not—
    (a) be regarded as the servant or agent of the Crown; or
    (b) enjoy any status, privilege or immunity of the Crown;
    and the Commission's property shall not be regarded as property of, or property held on behalf of, the Crown.
(6) Schedule 2 (which makes further provision in relation to the Commission) shall have effect.
(7) The Police Complaints Authority shall cease to exist on such day as the Secretary of State may by order appoint.

10   General functions of the Commission
(1) The functions of the Commission shall be—
    (a) to secure the maintenance by the Commission itself, and by police authorities and chief officers, of suitable arrangements with respect to the matters mentioned in subsection (2);
    (b) to keep under review all arrangements maintained with respect to those matters;
    (c) to secure that arrangements maintained with respect to those matters comply with the requirements of the following provisions of this Part, are efficient and effective and contain and manifest an appropriate degree of independence;
    (d) to secure that public confidence is established and maintained in the existence of suitable arrangements with respect to those matters and with the operation of the arrangements that are in fact maintained with respect to those matters;
    (e) to make such recommendations, and to give such advice, for the modification of the arrangements maintained with respect to those matters, and also of police practice in relation to other matters, as appear, from the carrying out by the Commission of its other functions, to be necessary or desirable;
    (f) to such extent as it may be required to do so by regulations made by the Secretary of State, to carry out functions in relation to bodies of constables maintained otherwise

than by police authorities which broadly correspond to those conferred on the Commission in relation to police forces by the preceding paragraphs of this subsection;
  (g) to carry out functions in relation to the Serious Organised Crime Agency which correspond to those conferred on the Commission in relation to police forces by paragraph (e) of this subsection; and
  (h) to carry out functions in relation to the National Policing Improvement Agency.
(2) Those matters are—
  (a) the handling of complaints made about the conduct of persons serving with the police;
  (b) the recording of matters from which it appears that there may have been conduct by such persons which constitutes or involves the commission of a criminal offence or behaviour justifying disciplinary proceedings;
  (ba) the recording of matters from which it appears that a person has died or suffered serious injury during, or following, contact with a person serving with the police;
  (c) the manner in which any such complaints or any such matters as are mentioned in paragraph (b) or (ba) are investigated or otherwise handled and dealt with.
(3) The Commission shall also have the functions which are conferred on it by—
  (a) . . .
  (b) any agreement or order under section 26 of this Act (other bodies of constables);
  (ba) any agreement under section 26A of this Act (Serious Organised Crime Agency);
  (bb) any agreement under section 26B of this Act (National Policing Improvement Agency);
  (c) any regulations under section 39 of this Act (police powers for contracted-out staff); or
  (d) any regulations or arrangements relating to disciplinary or similar proceedings against persons serving with the police, or against members of . . . any body of constables maintained otherwise than by a police authority.
(4) It shall be the duty of the Commission—
  (a) to exercise the powers and perform the duties conferred on it by the following provisions of this Part in the manner that it considers best calculated for the purpose of securing the proper carrying out of its functions under subsections (1) and (3); and
  (b) to secure that arrangements exist which are conducive to, and facilitate, the reporting of misconduct by persons in relation to whose conduct the Commission has functions.
(5) It shall also be the duty of the Commission—
  (a) to enter into arrangements with the chief inspector of constabulary for the purpose of securing co-operation, in the carrying out of their respective functions, between the Commission and the inspectors of constabulary; and
  (b) to provide those inspectors with all such assistance and co-operation as may be required by those arrangements, or as otherwise appears to the Commission to be appropriate, for facilitating the carrying out by those inspectors of their functions.
(6) Subject to the other provisions of this Part, the Commission may do anything which appears to it to be calculated to facilitate, or is incidental or conducive to, the carrying out of its functions.
(7) The Commission may, in connection with the making of any recommendation or the giving of any advice to any person for the purpose of carrying out—
  (a) its function under subsection (1)(e),
  (b) any corresponding function conferred on it by virtue of subsection (1)(f), or
  (c) its function under subsection (1)(g) or (h),
  impose any such charge on that person for anything done by the Commission for the purposes of, or in connection with, the carrying out of that function as it thinks fit.
(8) Nothing in this Part shall confer any function on the Commission in relation to so much of any complaint or conduct matter as relates to the direction and control of a police force by—
  (a) the chief officer of police of that force; or
  (b) a person for the time being carrying out the functions of the chief officer of police of that force.

11 Reports to the Secretary of State

(1) As soon as practicable after the end of each of its financial years, the Commission shall make a report to the Secretary of State on the carrying out of its functions during that year.

(2) The Commission shall also make such reports to the Secretary of State about matters relating generally to the carrying out of its functions as he may, from time to time, require.

(3) The Commission may, from time to time, make such other reports to the Secretary of State as it considers appropriate for drawing his attention to matters which—
   (a) have come to the Commission's notice; and
   (b) are matters that it considers should be drawn to his attention by reason of their gravity or of other exceptional circumstances.

(4) The Commission shall prepare such reports containing advice and recommendations as it thinks appropriate for the purpose of carrying out—
   (a) its function under subsection (1)(e) of section 10; or
   (b) any corresponding function conferred on it by virtue of subsection (1)(f) of that section.

(5) Where the Secretary of State receives any report under this section, he shall—
   (a) in the case of every annual report under subsection (1), and
   (b) in the case of any other report, if and to the extent that he considers it appropriate to do so,
   lay a copy of the report before Parliament and cause the report to be published.

(6) The Commission shall send a copy of every annual report under subsection (1)—
   (a) to every police authority;
   (b) to the Service Authority for the National Criminal Intelligence Service;
   (c) ...
   (d) to every authority that is maintaining a body of constables in relation to which any procedures are for the time being in force by virtue of any agreement or order under section 26 or by virtue of subsection (9) of that section, and
   (e) to the National Policing Improvement Agency.

(7) The Commission shall send a copy of every report under subsection (3)—
   (a) to any police authority that appears to the Commission to be concerned; and
   (b) to the chief officer of police of any police force that appears to it to be concerned.

(8) Where a report under subsection (3) relates to the Serious Organised Crime Agency, the Commission shall send a copy of that report to the Agency . . .

(9) Where a report under subsection (3) relates to a body of constables maintained by an authority other than a police authority, the Commission shall send a copy of that report—
   (a) to that authority; and
   (b) to the person having the direction and control of that body of constables.

(9A) Where a report under subsection (3) relates to the National Policing Improvement Agency, the Commission shall send a copy of that report to the Agency.

(10) The Commission shall send a copy of every report under subsection (4) to—
   (a) the Secretary of State;
   (b) every police authority;
   (c) every chief officer;
   (d) the Serious Organised Crime Agency;
   (e) ...
   (f) every authority that is maintaining a body of constables in relation to which any procedures are for the time being in force by virtue of any agreement or order under section 26 or by virtue of subsection (9) of that section;
   (g) every person who has the direction and control of such a body of constables; and
   (h) the National Policing Improvement Agency.

(11) The Commission shall send a copy of every report made or prepared by it under subsection (3) or (4) to such of the persons (in addition to those specified in the preceding subsections) who—
   (a) are referred to in the report, or

Application of Part 2

12 Complaints, matters and persons to which Part 2 applies

(1) In this Part references to a complaint are references (subject to the following provisions of this section) to any complaint about the conduct of a person serving with the police which is made (whether in writing or otherwise) by—
 (a) a member of the public who claims to be the person in relation to whom the conduct took place;
 (b) a member of the public not falling within paragraph (a) who claims to have been adversely affected by the conduct;
 (c) a member of the public who claims to have witnessed the conduct;
 (d) a person acting on behalf of a person falling within any of paragraphs (a) to (c).

(2) In this Part "conduct matter" means (subject to the following provisions of this section, paragraph 2(4) of Schedule 3 and any regulations made by virtue of section 23(2)(d)) any matter which is not and has not been the subject of a complaint but in the case of which there is an indication (whether from the circumstances or otherwise) that a person serving with the police may have—
 (a) committed a criminal offence; or
 (b) behaved in a manner which would justify the bringing of disciplinary proceedings.

. . .

(3) The complaints that are complaints for the purposes of this Part by virtue of subsection (1)(b) do not, except in a case falling within subsection (4), include any made by or on behalf of a person who claims to have been adversely affected as a consequence only of having seen or heard the conduct, or any of the alleged effects of the conduct.

(4) A case falls within this subsection if—
 (a) it was only because the person in question was physically present, or sufficiently nearby, when the conduct took place or the effects occurred that he was able to see or hear the conduct or its effects; or
 (b) the adverse effect is attributable to, or was aggravated by, the fact that the person in relation to whom the conduct took place was already known to the person claiming to have suffered the adverse effect.

(5) For the purposes of this section a person shall be taken to have witnessed conduct if, and only if—
 (a) he acquired his knowledge of that conduct in a manner which would make him a competent witness capable of giving admissible evidence of that conduct in criminal proceedings; or
 (b) he has in his possession or under his control anything which would in any such proceedings constitute admissible evidence of that conduct.

(6) For the purposes of this Part a person falling within subsection 1(a) to (c) to shall not be taken to have authorised another person to act on his behalf unless—
 (a) that other person is for the time being designated for the purposes of this Part by the Commission as a person through whom complaints may be made, or he is of a description of persons so designated; or
 (b) the other person has been given, and is able to produce, the written consent to his so acting of the person on whose behalf he acts.

(7) For the purposes of this Part, a person is serving with the police if—
 (a) he is a member of a police force;
 (b) he is an employee of a police authority who is under the direction and control of a chief officer; or
 (c) he is a special constable who is under the direction and control of a chief officer.

Handling of complaints, conduct matters and DSI matters etc.

13 Handling of complaints, conduct matters and DSI matters etc.

Schedule 3 (which makes provision for the handling of complaints, conduct matters and DSI matters and for the carrying out of investigations) shall have effect subject to section 14(1).

14 Direction and control matters

(1) Nothing in Schedule 3 shall have effect with respect to so much of any complaint as relates to the direction and control of a police force by—
   (a) the chief officer of police of that force; or
   (b) a person for the time being carrying out the functions of the chief officer of police of that force.

(2) The Secretary of State may issue guidance to chief officers and to police authorities about the handling of so much of any complaint as relates to the direction and control of a police force by such a person as is mentioned in subsection (1).

(3) It shall be the duty of a chief officer and of a police authority when handling any complaint relating to such a matter to have regard to any guidance issued under subsection (2).

Co-operation, assistance and information

15 General duties of police authorities, chief officers and inspectors

(1) It shall be the duty of—
   (a) every police authority maintaining a police force,
   (b) the chief officer of police of every police force, and
   (c) every inspector of constabulary carrying out any of his functions in relation to a police force,
   to ensure that it or he is kept informed, in relation to that force, about all matters falling within subsection (2).

(1A) It shall be the duty of the Serious Organised Crime Agency to ensure that it is kept informed, in relation to the Agency, about all matters falling within subsection (2).

(1B) It shall be the duty of the National Policing Improvement Agency to ensure that it is kept informed, in relation to that Agency, about all matters falling within subsection (2).

(2) Those matters are—
   (a) matters with respect to which any provision of this Part has effect;
   (b) anything which is done under or for the purposes of any such provision; and
   (c) any obligations to act or refrain from acting that have arisen by or under this Part but have not yet been complied with, or have been contravened.

(3) Where—
   (a) a police authority maintaining any police force requires the chief officer of that force or of any other force to provide a member of his force for appointment under paragraph 16, 17 or 18 of Schedule 3,
   (b) the chief officer of police of any police force requires the chief officer of police of any other police force to provide a member of that other force for appointment under any of those paragraphs, or
   (c) a police authority or chief officer requires the Director General of the Serious Organised Crime Agency to provide a member of the staff of that Agency for appointment under any of those paragraphs,
   it shall be the duty of the chief officer or Director General to whom the requirement is addressed to comply with it.

(4) It shall be the duty of—
   (a) every police authority maintaining a police force,
   (b) the chief officer of police of every police force, and
   (c) the Serious Organised Crime Agency
   (d) ...
   to provide the Commission and every member of the Commission's staff with all such assistance as the Commission or that member of staff may reasonably require for the

purposes of, or in connection with, the carrying out of any investigation by the Commission under this Part.

(5) It shall be the duty of—
   (a) every police authority maintaining a police force,
   (b) the chief officer of every police force, and
   (c) the Serious Organised Crime Agency
   (d) ...
   to ensure that a person appointed under paragraph 16, 17 or 18 of Schedule 3 to carry out an investigation is given all such assistance and co-operation in the carrying out of that investigation as that person may reasonably require

(6) The duties imposed by subsections (4) and (5) on a police authority maintaining a police force and on the chief officer of such a force and on the Serious Organised Crime Agency have effect—
   (a) irrespective of whether the investigation relates to the conduct of a person who is or has been a member of that force or a member of staff of the Agency; and
   (b) irrespective of who has the person appointed to carry out the investigation under his direction and control;
   but a chief officer of a third force may be required to give assistance and co-operation under subsection (5) only with the approval of the chief officer of the force to which the person who requires it belongs . . .

(7) In subsection (6) "third force", in relation to an investigation, means a police force other than—
   (a) the force to which the person carrying out the investigation belongs; or
   (b) the force to which the person whose conduct is under investigation belonged at the time of the conduct;
   . . .

17 Provision of information to the Commission

(1) It shall be the duty of—
   (a) every police authority, and
   (b) every chief officer,
   at such times, in such circumstances and in accordance with such other requirements as may be set out in regulations made by the Secretary of State, to provide the Commission with all such information and documents as may be specified or described in regulations so made.

(2) It shall also be the duty of every police authority and of every chief officer—
   (a) to provide the Commission with all such other information and documents specified or described in a notification given by the Commission to that authority or chief officer, and
   (b) to produce or deliver up to the Commission all such evidence and other things so specified or described,
   as appear to the Commission to be required by it for the purposes of the carrying out of any of its functions.

(3) Anything falling to be provided, produced or delivered up by any person in pursuance of a requirement imposed under subsection (2) must be provided, produced or delivered up in such form, in such manner and within such period as may be specified in—
   (a) the notification imposing the requirement; or
   (b) in any subsequent notification given by the Commission to that person for the purposes of this subsection.

(4) Nothing in this section shall require a police authority or chief officer—
   (a) to provide the Commission with any information or document, or to produce or deliver up any other thing, before the earliest time at which it is practicable for that authority or chief officer to do so; or
   (b) to provide, produce or deliver up anything at all in a case in which it never becomes practicable for that authority or chief officer to do so.

(5) A requirement imposed by any regulations or notification under this section may authorise or require information or documents to which it relates to be provided to the Commission electronically.

(6) In this section—
"chief officer" includes the chief executive of the National Policing Improvement Agency;
"police authority" includes the National Policing Improvement Agency.

18 Inspections of police premises on behalf of the Commission

(1) Where—
   (a) the Commission requires—
      (i) a police authority maintaining any police force, or
      (ii) the chief officer of police of any such force,
   to allow a person nominated for the purpose by the Commission to have access to any premises occupied for the purposes of that force and to documents and other things on those premises, and
   (b) the requirement is imposed for any of the purposes mentioned in subsection (2),
   it shall be the duty of the authority or, as the case may be, of the chief officer to secure that the required access is allowed to the nominated person.

(2) Those purposes are—
   (a) the purposes of any examination by the Commission of the efficiency and effectiveness of the arrangements made by the force in question for handling complaints or dealing with recordable conduct matters or DSI matters;
   (b) the purposes of any investigation by the Commission under this Part or of any investigation carried out under its supervision or management.

(3) A requirement imposed under this section for the purposes mentioned in subsection (2)(a) must be notified to the authority or chief officer at least 48 hours before the time at which access is required.

(4) Where—
   (a) a requirement imposed under this section for the purposes mentioned in subsection (2)(a) requires access to any premises, document or thing to be allowed to any person, but
   (b) there are reasonable grounds for not allowing that person to have the required access at the time at which he seeks to have it,
   the obligation to secure that the required access is allowed shall have effect as an obligation to secure that the access is allowed to that person at the earliest practicable time after there cease to be any such grounds as that person may specify.

(5) The provisions of this section are in addition to, and without prejudice to—
   (a) the rights of entry, search and seizure that are or may be conferred on—
      (i) a person designated for the purposes of paragraph 19 of Schedule 3, or
      (ii) any person who otherwise acts on behalf of the Commission,
   in his capacity as a constable or as a person with the powers and privileges of a constable; or
   (b) the obligations of police authorities and chief officers under sections 15 and 17.

19 Use of investigatory powers by or on behalf of the Commission

(1) The Secretary of State may by order make such provision as he thinks appropriate for the purpose of authorising—
   (a) the use of directed and intrusive surveillance, and
   (b) the conduct and use of covert human intelligence sources,
   for the purposes of, or for purposes connected with, the carrying out of the Commission's functions.

(2) An order under this section may, for the purposes of or in connection with any such provision as is mentioned in subsection (1), provide for—
   (a) Parts 2 and 4 the Regulation of Investigatory Powers Act 2000 (surveillance and covert human intelligence sources and scrutiny of investigatory powers), and
   (b) Part 3 of the 1997 Act (authorisations in respect of property),

to have effect with such modifications as may be specified in the order.
(3) The Secretary of State shall not make an order containing (with or without any other provision) any provision authorised by this section unless a draft of that order has been laid before Parliament and approved by a resolution of each House.
(4) Expressions used in this section and in Part 2 of the Regulation of Investigatory Powers Act 2000 have the same meanings in this section as in that Part.

20 Duty to keep the complainant informed

(1) In any case in which there is an investigation of a complaint in accordance with the provisions of Schedule 3—
 (a) by the Commission, or
 (b) under its management,
it shall be the duty of the Commission to provide the complainant with all such information as will keep him properly informed, while the investigation is being carried out and subsequently, of all the matters mentioned in subsection (4).
(2) In any case in which there is an investigation of a complaint in accordance with the provisions of Schedule 3—
 (a) by the appropriate authority on its own behalf, or
 (b) under the supervision of the Commission,
it shall be the duty of the appropriate authority to provide the complainant with all such information as will keep him properly informed, while the investigation is being carried out and subsequently, of all the matters mentioned in subsection (4).
(3) Where subsection (2) applies, it shall be the duty of the Commission to give the appropriate authority all such directions as it considers appropriate for securing that that authority complies with its duty under that subsection; and it shall be the duty of the appropriate authority to comply with any direction given to it under this subsection.
(4) The matters of which the complainant must be kept properly informed are—
 (a) the progress of the investigation;
 (b) any provisional findings of the person carrying out the investigation;
 (c) whether any report has been submitted under paragraph 22 of Schedule 3;
 (d) the action (if any) that is taken in respect of the matters dealt with in any such report; and
 (e) the outcome of any such action.
(5) The duties imposed by this section on the Commission and the appropriate authority in relation to any complaint shall be performed in such manner, and shall have effect subject to such exceptions, as may be provided for by regulations made by the Secretary of State.
(6) The Secretary of State shall not by regulations provide for any exceptions from the duties imposed by this section except so far as he considers it necessary to do so for the purpose of—
 (a) preventing the premature or inappropriate disclosure of information that is relevant to, or may be used in, any actual or prospective criminal proceedings;
 (b) preventing the disclosure of information in any circumstances in which it has been determined in accordance with the regulations that its non-disclosure—
  (i) is in the interests of national security;
  (ii) is for the purposes of the prevention or detection of crime, or the apprehension or prosecution of offenders;
  (iii) is required on proportionality grounds; or
  (iv) is otherwise necessary in the public interest.
(7) The non-disclosure of information is required on proportionality grounds if its disclosure would cause, directly or indirectly, an adverse effect which would be disproportionate to the benefits arising from its disclosure.
(8) Regulations under this section may include provision framed by reference to the opinion of, or a determination by, the Commission or any police authority or chief officer.
(9) It shall be the duty of a person appointed to carry out an investigation under this Part to provide the Commission or, as the case may be, the appropriate authority with all such

information as the Commission or that authority may reasonably require for the purpose of performing its duty under this section.

21 Duty to provide information for other persons

(1) A person has an interest in being kept properly informed about the handling of a complaint or recordable conduct matter or DSI matter if—
  (a) it appears to the Commission or to an appropriate authority that he is a person falling within subsection (2) or (2A); and
  (b) that person has indicated that he consents to the provision of information to him in accordance with this section and that consent has not been withdrawn.

(2) A person falls within this subsection if (in the case of a complaint or recordable conduct matter)—
  (a) he is a relative of a person whose death is the alleged result from the conduct complained of or to which the recordable conduct matter relates;
  (b) he is a relative of a person whose serious injury is the alleged result from that conduct and that person is incapable of making a complaint;
  (c) he himself has suffered serious injury as the alleged result of that conduct.

(2A) A person falls within this subsection if (in the case of a DSI matter)—
  (a) he is a relative of the person who has died;
  (b) he is a relative of the person who has suffered serious injury and that person is incapable of making a complaint;
  (c) he himself is the person who has suffered serious injury.

(3) A person who does not fall within subsection (2) or (2A) has an interest in being kept properly informed about the handling of a complaint or recordable conduct matter or DSI matter if—
  (a) the Commission or an appropriate authority considers that he has an interest in the handling of the complaint or recordable conduct matter or DSI matter which is sufficient to make it appropriate for information to be provided to him in accordance with this section; and
  (b) he has indicated that he consents to the provision of information to him in accordance with this section.

(4) In relation to a complaint, this section confers no rights on the complainant.

(5) A person who has an interest in being kept properly informed about the handling of a complaint or conduct matter or DSI matter is referred to in this section as an "interested person".

(6) In any case in which there is an investigation of the complaint or recordable conduct matter or DSI matter in accordance with the provisions of Schedule 3—
  (a) by the Commission, or
  (b) under its management,
it shall be the duty of the Commission to provide the interested person with all such information as will keep him properly informed, while the investigation is being carried out and subsequently, of all the matters mentioned in subsection (9).

(7) In any case in which there is an investigation of the complaint or recordable conduct matter or DSI matter in accordance with the provisions of Schedule 3—
  (a) by the appropriate authority on its own behalf, or
  (b) under the supervision of the Commission,
it shall be the duty of the appropriate authority to provide the interested person with all such information as will keep him properly informed, while the investigation is being carried out and subsequently, of all the matters mentioned in subsection (9).

(8) Where subsection (7) applies, it shall be the duty of the Commission to give the appropriate authority all such directions as it considers appropriate for securing that that authority complies with its duty under that subsection; and it shall be the duty of the appropriate authority to comply with any direction given to it under this subsection.

(9) The matters of which the interested person must be kept properly informed are—
  (a) the progress of the investigation;

(b) any provisional findings of the person carrying out the investigation;
(ba) whether the Commission or the appropriate authority has made a determination under paragraph 21A of Schedule 3;
(c) whether any report has been submitted under paragraph 22 *or 24A* of Schedule 3;
(d) the action (if any) that is taken in respect of the matters dealt with in any such report; and
(e) the outcome of any such action.

(10) The duties imposed by this section on the Commission and the appropriate authority in relation to any complaint or recordable conduct matter or DSI matter shall be performed in such manner, and shall have effect subject to such exceptions, as may be provided for by regulations made by the Secretary of State.

(11) Subsections (6) to (9) of section 20 apply for the purposes of this section as they apply for the purposes of that section.

(12) In this section "relative" means a person of a description prescribed in regulations made by the Secretary of State.

Guidance and regulations

22 Power of the Commission to issue guidance

(1) The Commission may issue guidance—
 (a) to police authorities,
 (b) to chief officers, and
 (c) to persons who are serving with the police otherwise than as chief officers,
concerning the exercise or performance, by the persons to whom the guidance is issued, of any of the powers or duties specified in subsection (2).

(2) Those powers and duties are—
 (a) those that are conferred or imposed by or under this Part; and
 (b) those that are otherwise conferred or imposed but relate to—
  (i) the handling of complaints;
  (ii) the means by which recordable conduct matters or DSI matters are dealt with; or
  (iii) the detection or deterrence of misconduct by persons serving with the police.

(3) Before issuing any guidance under this section, the Commission shall consult with—
 (a) the Association of Police Authorities;
 (b) the Association of Chief Police Officers; and
 (c) such other persons as it thinks fit.

(4) The approval of the Secretary of State shall be required for the issue by the Commission of any guidance under this section.

(5) Without prejudice to the generality of the preceding provisions of this section, the guidance that may be issued under this section includes—
 (a) guidance about the handling of complaints which have not yet been recorded and about dealing with recordable conduct matters or DSI matters that have not been recorded;
 (b) guidance about the procedure to be followed by the appropriate authority when recording a complaint or any recordable conduct matter;
 (c) guidance about—
  (i) how to decide whether a complaint is suitable for being subjected to local resolution; and
  (ii) about the information to be provided to a person before his consent to such resolution is given;
 (d) guidance about how to protect the scene of an incident or alleged incident which—
  (i) is or may become the subject-matter of a complaint; or
  (ii) is or may involve a recordable conduct matter or DSI matter;
 (e) guidance about the circumstances in which it is appropriate (where it is lawful to do so)—

(i) to disclose to any person, or to publish, any information about an investigation of a complaint or conduct matter or DSI matter; or
(ii) to provide any person with, or to publish, any report or other document relating to such an investigation;
(f) guidance about the matters to be included in a memorandum under paragraph 23 or 25 of Schedule 3 and about the manner in which, and the place at which, such a memorandum is to be delivered to the Commission.
(6) Nothing in this section shall authorise the issuing of any guidance about a particular case.
(7) It shall be the duty of every person to whom any guidance under this section is issued to have regard to that guidance in exercising or performing the powers and duties to which the guidance relates.
(8) A failure by a person to whom guidance under this section is issued to have regard to the guidance shall be admissible in evidence in any disciplinary proceedings or on any appeal from a decision taken in any such proceedings.

Interpretation of Part 2

29 Interpretation of Part 2

(1) In this Part—
"the appropriate authority"—
(a) in relation to a person serving with the police or in relation to any complaint, conduct matter or investigation relating to the conduct of such a person, means—
(i) if that person is a senior officer, the police authority for the area of the police force of which he is a member; and
(ii) if he is not a senior officer, the chief officer under whose direction and control he is; and
(b) in relation to a death or serious injury matter, means—
(i) if the relevant officer is a senior officer, the police authority for the area of the police force of which he is a member; and
(ii) if he is not a senior officer, the chief officer under whose direction and control he is.
"chief officer" means the chief officer of police of any police force;
"the Commission" has the meaning given by section 9(1);
"complainant" shall be construed in accordance with subsection (2);
"complaint" has the meaning given by section 12;
"conduct" includes acts, omissions and statements (whether actual, alleged or inferred);
"conduct matter" has the meaning given by section 12;
"death or serious injury matter" and "DSI matter" have the meaning given in section 12;
"disciplinary proceedings" means—
(a) in relation to a member of a police force or a special constable, proceedings under any regulations made by virtue of section 50 or 51 of the 1996 Act and identified as disciplinary proceedings by those regulations; and
(b) in relation to a person serving with the police who is not a member of a police force or a special constable, proceedings identified as such by regulations made by the Secretary of State for the purposes of this Part;
"document" means anything in which information of any description is recorded;
"information" includes estimates and projections, and statistical analyses;
"local resolution", in relation to a complaint, means the handling of that complaint in accordance with a procedure which—
(a) does not involve a formal investigation; and
(b) is laid down by regulations under paragraph 8 of Schedule 3 for complaints which it has been decided, in accordance with paragraph 6 of that Schedule, to subject to local resolution;
"person complained against", in relation to a complaint, means the person whose conduct is the subject-matter of the complaint;

"recordable conduct matter" means (subject to any regulations under section 23(2)(d))—
(a) a conduct matter that is required to be recorded by the appropriate authority under paragraph 10 or 11 of Schedule 3 or has been so recorded; or
(b) except in sub-paragraph (4) of paragraph 2 of Schedule 3, any matter brought to the attention of the appropriate authority under that sub-paragraph;
"relevant force", in relation to the appropriate authority, means—
(a) if that authority is a police authority, the police force maintained by it; and
(b) if that authority is the chief officer of police of a police force, his force;
"senior officer" means a member of a police force holding a rank above that of chief superintendent;
"serious injury" means a fracture, a deep cut, a deep laceration or an injury causing damage to an internal organ or the impairment of any bodily function;
"serving with the police", in relation to any person, shall be construed in accordance with section 12(7).
. . .

(2) References in this Part, in relation to anything which is or purports to be a complaint, to the complainant are references—
(a) except in the case of anything which is or purports to be a complaint falling within section 12(1)(d), to the person by whom the complaint or purported complaint was made; and
(b) in that case, to the person on whose behalf the complaint or purported complaint was made;
but where any person is acting on another's behalf for the purposes of any complaint or purported complaint, anything that is to be or may be done under this Part by or in relation to the complainant may be done, instead, by or in relation to the person acting on the complainant's behalf.

(3) Subject to subsection (4), references in this Part, in relation to any conduct or anything purporting to be a complaint about any conduct, to a member of the public include references to any person falling within any of the following paragraphs (whether at the time of the conduct or at any subsequent time)—
(a) a person serving with the police;
(b) a member of the Serious Organised Crime Agency;
(c) a member of the staff of the National Policing Improvment Agency; or
(d) a person engaged on relevant service, within the meaning of section 97(1)(a) . . . or (d) of the 1996 Act (temporary service of various kinds).

(4) In this Part references, in relation to any conduct or to anything purporting to be a complaint about any conduct, to a member of the public do not include references to—
(a) a person who, at the time when the conduct is supposed to have taken place, was under the direction and control of the same chief officer as the person whose conduct it was; or
(b) a person who—
(i) at the time when the conduct is supposed to have taken place, in relation to him, or
(ii) at the time when he is supposed to have been adversely affected by it, or to have witnessed it,
was on duty in his capacity as a person falling within subsection (3)(a) to (d).

(5) For the purposes of this Part a person is adversely affected if he suffers any form of loss or damage, distress or inconvenience, if he is put in danger or if he is otherwise unduly put at risk of being adversely affected.

(6) References in this Part to the investigation of any complaint or matter by the appropriate authority on its own behalf, under the supervision of the Commission, under the management of the Commission or by the Commission itself shall be construed as references to its investigation in accordance with paragraph 16, 17, 18 or, as the case may be, 19 of Schedule 3.

(7) The Commissioner of Police for the City of London shall be treated for the purposes of this Part as if he were a member of the City of London police force.

PART 4
POLICE POWERS ETC.

CHAPTER 1
EXERCISE OF POLICE POWERS ETC. BY CIVILIANS

38 Police powers for police authority employees

(1) The chief officer of police of any police force may designate any person who—
  (a) is employed by the police authority maintaining that force, and
  (b) is under the direction and control of that chief officer,
  as an officer of one or more of the descriptions specified in subsection (2).
(2) The description of officers are as follows—
  (a) community support officer;
  (b) investigating officer;
  (c) detention officer;
  (d) escort officer;
  (e) staff custody officer.
(3) ...
(4) A chief officer of police . . . shall not designate a person under this section unless he is satisfied that that person—
  (a) is a suitable person to carry out the functions for the purposes of which he is designated;
  (b) is capable of effectively carrying out those functions; and
  (c) has received adequate training in the carrying out of those functions and in the exercise and performance of the powers and duties to be conferred or enforced on him by virtue of the designation.
(5) A person designated under this section shall have the powers and duties conferred or imposed on him by the designation.
(5A) A person designated under this section as a community support officer shall also have the standard powers and duties of a community support officer (see section 38A(2)).
(6) Powers and duties may be conferred or imposed on a designated person by means only of the application to him by his designation of provisions of the applicable Part of Schedule 4 that are to apply to the designated person; and for this purpose the applicable Part of that Schedule is—
  (a) in the case of a person designated as a community support officer, Part 1;
  (b) in the case of a person designated as an investigating officer, Part 2;
  (c) in the case of a person designated as a detention officer, Part 3; and
  (d) in the case of a person designated as an escort officer, Part 4.
  (e) in the case of a person designated as a staff custody officer, Part 4.
(6A) Subsection (6) has effect subject to subsection (5A) and (8).
(7) An employee of a police authority . . . authorised or required to do anything by virtue of a designation under this section—
  (a) shall not be authorised or required by virtue of that designation to engage in any conduct otherwise than in the course of that employment; and
  (b) shall be so authorised or required subject to such restrictions and conditions (if any) as may be specified in his designation.
(8) Where any power exercisable by any person in reliance on his designation under this section is a power which, in the case of its exercise by a constable, includes or is supplemented by a power to use reasonable force, any person exercising that power in reliance on that designation shall have the same entitlement as a constable to use reasonable force.

(9) Where any power exercisable by any person in reliance on his designation under this section includes power to use force to enter any premises, that power shall not be exercisable by that person except—
   (a) in the company, and under the supervision, of a constable; or
   (b) for the purpose of saving life or limb or preventing serious damage to property.

...

39 Police powers for contracted-out staff

(1) This section applies if a police authority has entered into a contract with a person ("the contractor") for the provision of services relating to the detention or escort of persons who have been arrested or are otherwise in custody.

(2) The chief officer of police of the police force maintained by that police authority may designate any person who is an employee of the contractor as either or both of the following—
   (a) a detention officer; or
   (b) an escort officer.

(3) A person designated under this section shall have the powers and duties conferred or imposed on him by the designation.

(4) A chief officer of police shall not designate a person under this section unless he is satisfied that that person—
   (a) is a suitable person to carry out the functions for the purposes of which he is designated;
   (b) is capable of effectively carrying out those functions; and
   (c) has received adequate training in the carrying out of those functions and in the exercise and performance of the powers and duties to be conferred on him by virtue of the designation.

(5) A chief officer of police shall not designate a person under this section unless he is satisfied that the contractor is a fit and proper person to supervise the carrying out of the functions for the purposes of which that person is designated.

(6) Powers and duties may be conferred or imposed on a designated person by means only of the application to him by his designation of provisions of the applicable Part of Schedule 4 that are to apply to the designated person; and for this purpose the applicable Part of that Schedule is—
   (a) in the case of a person designated as a detention officer, Part 3; and
   (b) in the case of a person designated as an escort officer, Part 4.

(7) An employee of the contractor authorised or required to do anything by virtue of a designation under this section—
   (a) shall not be authorised or required by virtue of that designation to engage in any conduct otherwise than in the course of that employment; and
   (b) shall be so authorised or required subject to such restrictions and conditions (if any) as may be specified in his designation.

(8) Where any power exercisable by any person in reliance on his designation under this section is a power which, in the case of its exercise by a constable, includes or is supplemented by a power to use reasonable force, any person exercising that power in reliance on that designation shall have the same entitlement as a constable to use reasonable force.

(9) The Secretary of State may by regulations make provision for the handling of complaints relating to, or other instances of misconduct involving, the carrying out by any person designated under this section of the functions for the purposes of which any power or duty is conferred or imposed by his designation.

(10) Regulations under subsection (9) may, in particular, provide that any provision made by Part 2 of this Act with respect to complaints against persons serving with the police is to apply, with such modifications as may be prescribed by them, with respect to complaints against persons designated under this section.

(11) Before making regulations under this section, the Secretary of State shall consult with—
   (a) the Association of Police Authorities;

(b) the Association of Chief Police Officers;
(c) the Independent Police Complaints Commission; and
(d) such other persons as he thinks fit.

(12) A designation under this section, unless it is previously withdrawn or ceases to have effect in accordance with subsection (13), shall remain in force for such period as may be specified in the designation; but it may be renewed at any time with effect from the time when it would otherwise expire.

(13) A designation under this section shall cease to have effect—
(a) if the designated person ceases to be an employee of the contractor; or
(b) if the contract between the police authority and the contractor is terminated or expires.

40 Community safety accreditation schemes

(1) The chief officer of police of any police force may, if he considers that it is appropriate to do so for the purposes specified in subsection (3), establish and maintain a scheme ("a community safety accreditation scheme").

(2) A community safety accreditation scheme is a scheme for the exercise in the chief officer's police area by persons accredited by him under section 41 of the powers conferred by their accreditations under that section.

(3) Those purposes are—
(a) contributing to community safety and security; and
(b) in co-operation with the police force for the area, combatting crime and disorder, public nuisance and other forms of anti-social behaviour.

(4) Before establishing a community safety accreditation scheme for his police area, a chief officer of any police force (other than the Commissioner of Police of the Metropolis) must consult with—
(a) the police authority maintaining that force, and
(b) every local authority any part of whose area lies within the police area.

(5) Before establishing a community safety accreditation scheme for the metropolitan police district, the Commissioner of Police of the Metropolis must consult with—
(a) the Metropolitan Police Authority;
(b) the Mayor of London; and
(c) every local authority any part of whose area lies within the metropolitan police district.

(6) In subsections (4)(b) and (5)(c) "local authority" means—
(a) in relation to England, a district council, a London borough council, the Common Council of the City of London or the Council of the Isles of Scilly; and
(b) in relation to Wales, a county council or a county borough council.

(7) Every police plan under section 8 of the 1996 Act which is issued after the commencement of this section, and every draft of such a plan which is submitted by a chief officer of police to a police authority after the commencement of this section, must set out—
(a) whether a community safety accreditation scheme is maintained for the police area in question;
(b) if not, whether there is any proposal to establish such a scheme for that area during the period to which the plan relates;
(c) particulars of any such proposal or of any proposal to modify during that period any community safety accreditation scheme that is already maintained for that area;
(d) the extent (if any) of any arrangements for provisions specified in Schedule 4 to be applied to designated persons employed by the police authority; and
(e) the respects in which any community safety accreditation scheme that is maintained or proposed will be supplementing those arrangements during the period to which the plan relates.

(8) A community safety accreditation scheme must contain provision for the making of arrangements with employers who—
(a) are carrying on business in the police area in question, or
(b) are carrying on business in relation to the whole or any part of that area or in relation to places situated within it,

for those employers to supervise the carrying out by their employees of the community safety functions for the purposes of which powers are conferred on those employees by means of accreditations under section 41.

(9) It shall be the duty of a chief officer of police who establishes and maintains a community safety accreditation scheme to ensure that the employers of the persons on whom powers are conferred by the grant of accreditations under section 41 have established and maintain satisfactory arrangements for handling complaints relating to the carrying out by those persons of the functions for the purposes of which the powers are conferred.

Note: Section 40(7) will be repealed when s 52 of the Police and Justice Act 2006 comes into force.

41A   Accreditation of weights and measures inspectors

(1) The chief officer of police of any police force may, on the making of an application for the purpose by such person and in such manner as he may require, grant accreditation under this section to a weights and measures inspector.

(2) A weights and measures inspector to whom an accreditation under this section granted by a chief officer of police may exercise the powers conferred by the accreditation in the chief officer's police area.

(3) Schedule 5A (which sets out the powers that may be conferred on inspectors accredited under this section) shall have effect.

...

42   Supplementary provisions relating to designations and accreditations

(1) A person who exercises or performs any power or duty in relation to any person in reliance on his designation under section 38 or 39 or his accreditation under section 41 or 41A, or who purports to do so, shall produce that designation or accreditation to that person, if requested to do so.

(2) A power exercisable by any person in reliance on his designation by a chief officer of police under section 38 or 39 or his accreditation under section 41 shall be exercisable only by a person wearing such uniform as may be—

(a) determined or approved for the purposes of this Chapter by the chief officer of police who granted the designation or accreditation; and

(b) identified or described in the designation or accreditation;

and, in the case of an accredited person, such a power shall be exercisable only if he is also wearing such badge as may be specified for the purposes of this subsection by the Secretary of State, and is wearing it in such manner, or in such place, as may be so specified.

(3) A chief officer of police who has granted a designation or accreditation to any person under section 38, 39 or 41 or an accreditation to any weights and measures inspector under section 41A may at any time, by notice to the designated or accredited person or accredited inspector, modify or withdraw that designation or accreditation.

(4) ...

(5) Where any person's designation under section 39 is modified or withdrawn, the chief officer giving notice of the modification or withdrawal shall send a copy of the notice to the contractor responsible for supervising that person in the carrying out of the functions for the purposes of which the designation was granted.

(6) Where any person's accreditation under section 41 is modified or withdrawn, the chief officer giving notice of the modification or withdrawal shall send a copy of the notice to the employer responsible for supervising that person in the carrying out of the functions for the purposes of which the accreditation was granted.

(7) For the purposes of determining liability for the unlawful conduct of employees of a police authority, conduct by such an employee in reliance or purported reliance on a designation under section 38 shall be taken to be conduct in the course of his employment by the police authority; and, in the case of a tort, that authority shall fall to be treated as a joint tortfeasor accordingly.

(8) ...

(9) For the purposes of determining liability for the unlawful conduct of employees of a contractor (within the meaning of section 39), conduct by such an employee in reliance or purported reliance on a designation under that section shall be taken to be conduct in the course of his employment by that contractor; and, in the case of a tort, that contractor shall fall to be treated as a joint tortfeasor accordingly.

(10) For the purposes of determining liability for the unlawful conduct of employees of a person with whom a chief officer of police has entered into any arrangements for the purposes of a community safety accreditation scheme, conduct by such an employee in reliance or purported reliance on an accreditation under section 41 shall be taken to be conduct in the course of his employment by that employer; and, in the case of a tort, that employer shall fall to be treated as a joint tortfeasor accordingly.

...

46 Offences against designated and accredited persons etc.

...

(2) Any person who resists or wilfully obstructs—
   (a) a designated person in the execution of his duty,
   (b) an accredited person in the execution of his duty,
   (ba) an accredited inspector in the exercise of his duty, or
   (c) a person assisting a designated or accredited person or accredited inspector in the execution of his duty,
is guilty of an offence and shall be liable, on summary conviction, to imprisonment for a term not exceeding one month [*51 weeks*] or to a fine not exceeding level 3 on the standard scale, or to both.

...

(4) In this section references to the execution by a designated person, accredited person or an accredited inspector of his duty are references to his exercising any power or performing any duty which is his by virtue of his designation or accreditation.

47 Interpretation of Chapter 1

(1) In this Chapter—
"accredited inspector" means a weights and measures inspector in relation to whom an accreditation under section 41A is for the time being in force;
"accredited person" means a person in relation to whom an accreditation under section 41 is for the time being in force;
"community safety functions" means any functions the carrying out of which would be facilitated by the ability to exercise one or more of the powers mentioned in Schedule 5;
"conduct" includes omissions and statements;
"designated person" means a person in relation to whom a designation under section 38 or 39 is for the time being in force;

...

(2) In this Chapter—
   (a) references to carrying on business include references to carrying out functions under any enactment; and
   (b) references to the employees of a person carrying on business include references to persons holding office under a person, and references to employers shall be construed accordingly.

CHAPTER 2
PROVISIONS MODIFYING AND SUPPLEMENTING POLICE POWERS

Power to require name and address

50 Persons acting in an anti-social manner

(1) If a constable in uniform has reason to believe that a person has been acting, or is acting, in an anti-social manner (within the meaning of section 1 of the Crime and Disorder Act 1998

(anti-social behaviour orders)), he may require that person to give his name and address to the constable.

(2) Any person who—
  (a) fails to give his name and address when required to do so under subsection (1), or
  (b) gives a false or inaccurate name or address in response to a requirement under that subsection, is guilty of an offence and shall be liable, on summary conviction, to a fine not exceeding level 3 on the standard scale.

Persons in police detention

51 Independent custody visitors for places of detention

(1) Every police authority shall—
  (a) make arrangements for detainees to be visited by persons appointed under the arrangements ("independent custody visitors"); and
  (b) keep those arrangements under review and from time to time revise them as they think fit.

(2) The arrangements must secure that the persons appointed under the arrangements are independent of both—
  (a) the police authority; and
  (b) the chief officer of police of the police force maintained by that authority.

(3) The arrangements may confer on independent custody visitors such powers as the police authority considers necessary to enable them to carry out their functions under the arrangements and may, in particular, confer on them powers—
  (a) to require access to be given to each police station;
  (b) to examine records relating to the detention of persons there;
  (c) to meet detainees there for the purposes of a discussion about their treatment and conditions while detained; and
  (d) to inspect the facilities there including in particular, cell accommodation, washing and toilet facilities and the facilities for the provision of food.

(4) The arrangements may include provision for access to a detainee to be denied to independent custody visitors if—
  (a) it appears to an officer of or above the rank of inspector that there are grounds for denying access at the time it is requested;
  (b) the grounds are grounds specified for the purposes of paragraph (a) in the arrangements; and
  (c) the procedural requirements imposed by the arrangements in relation to a denial of access are complied with.

(5) Grounds shall not be specified in any arrangements for the purposes of subsection (4)(a) unless they are grounds for the time being set out for the purposes of this subsection in the code of practice issued by the Secretary of State under subsection (6).

(6) The Secretary of State shall issue, and may from time to time revise, a code of practice as to the carrying out by police authorities and independent custody visitors of their functions under the arrangements.

(7) Before issuing or revising a code of practice under this section, the Secretary of State shall consult with—
  (a) the Association of Police Authorities;
  (b) the Association of Chief Police Officers; and
  (c) such other persons as he thinks fit.

(8) The Secretary of State shall lay any code of practice issued by him under this section, and any revisions of any such code, before Parliament.

(9) Police authorities and independent custody visitors shall have regard to the code of practice for the time being in force under subsection (6) in the carrying out of their functions under the preceding provisions of this section.

(10) In this section "detainee", in relation to arrangements made under this section, means a person detained in a police station in the police area of the police authority.

Seizure of motor vehicles

59 Vehicles used in manner causing alarm, distress or annoyance

(1) Where a constable in uniform has reasonable grounds for believing that a motor vehicle is being used on any occasion in a manner which—
  (a) contravenes section 3 or 34 of the Road Traffic Act 1988 (careless and inconsiderate driving and prohibition of off-road driving), and
  (b) is causing, or is likely to cause, alarm, distress or annoyance to members of the public, he shall have the powers set out in subsection (3).

(2) A constable in uniform shall also have the powers set out in subsection (3) where he has reasonable grounds for believing that a motor vehicle has been used on any occasion in a manner falling within subsection (1).

(3) Those powers are—
  (a) power, if the motor vehicle is moving, to order the person driving it to stop the vehicle;
  (b) power to seize and remove the motor vehicle;
  (c) power, for the purposes of exercising a power falling within paragraph (a) or (b), to enter any premises on which he has reasonable grounds for believing the motor vehicle to be;
  (d) power to use reasonable force, if necessary, in the exercise of any power conferred by any of paragraphs to (a) to (c).

(4) A constable shall not seize a motor vehicle in the exercise of the powers conferred on him by this section unless—
  (a) he has warned the person appearing to him to be the person whose use falls within subsection (1) that he will seize it, if that use continues or is repeated; and
  (b) it appears to him that the use has continued or been repeated after the warning.

(5) Subsection (4) does not require a warning to be given by a constable on any occasion on which he would otherwise have the power to seize a motor vehicle under this section if—
  (a) the circumstances make it impracticable for him to give the warning;
  (b) the constable has already on that occasion given a warning under that subsection in respect of any use of that motor vehicle or of another motor vehicle by that person or any other person;
  (c) the constable has reasonable grounds for believing that such a warning has been given on that occasion otherwise than by him; or
  (d) the constable has reasonable grounds for believing that the person whose use of that motor vehicle on that occasion would justify the seizure is a person to whom a warning under that subsection has been given (whether or not by that constable or in respect the same vehicle or the same or a similar use) on a previous occasion in the previous twelve months.

(6) A person who fails to comply with an order under subsection (3)(a) is guilty of an offence and shall be liable, on summary conviction, to a fine not exceeding level 3 on the standard scale.

(7) Subsection (3)(c) does not authorise entry into a private dwelling house.

(8) The powers conferred on a constable by this section shall be exercisable only at a time when regulations under section 60 are in force.

(9) In this section—
"driving" has the same meaning as in the Road Traffic Act 1988;
"motor vehicle" means any mechanically propelled vehicle, whether or not it is intended or adapted for use on roads; and
"private dwelling house" does not include any garage or other structure occupied with the dwelling house, or any land appurtenant to the dwelling house.

60 Retention etc. of vehicles seized under section 59

(1) The Secretary of State may by regulations make provision as to—
  (a) the removal and retention of motor vehicles seized under section 59; and
  (b) the release or disposal of such motor vehicles.

(2) Regulations under subsection (1) may, in particular, make provision—
   (a) for the giving of notice of the seizure of a motor vehicle under section 59 to a person who is the owner of that vehicle or who, in accordance with the regulations, appears to be its owner;
   (b) for the procedure by which a person who claims to be the owner of a motor vehicle seized under section 59 may seek to have it released;
   (c) for requiring the payment of fees, charges or costs in relation to the removal and retention of such a motor vehicle and to any application for its release;
   (d) as to the circumstances in which a motor vehicle seized under section 59 may be disposed of:
   (e) as to the destination—
      (i) of any fees or charges payable in accordance with the regulations; and
      (ii) of the proceeds (if any) arising from the disposal of a motor vehicle seized under section 59;
   (f) for the delivery to a local authority, in circumstances prescribed by or determined in accordance with the regulations, of any motor vehicle seized under section 59.
(3) Regulations under subsection (1) must provide that a person who would otherwise be liable to pay any fee or charge under the regulations shall not be liable to pay it if—
   (a) the use by reference to which the motor vehicle in question was seized was not a use by him; and
   (b) he did not know of the use of the vehicle in the manner which led to its seizure, had not consented to its use in that manner and could not, by the taking of reasonable steps, have prevented its use in that manner.
(4) In this section—
"local authority"—
   (a) in relation to England, means the council of a county, metropolitan district or London borough, the Common Council of the City of London or Transport for London; and
   (b) in relation to Wales, means the council of a county or county borough; "motor vehicle" has the same meaning as in section 59.

ANTI-SOCIAL BEHAVIOUR ACT 2003
(2003, c. 38)

An Act to make provision in connection with anti-social behaviour. [20 November 2003]

PART 4
DISPERSAL OF GROUPS ETC.

30 Dispersal of groups and removal of persons under 16 to their place of residence

(1) This section applies where a relevant officer has reasonable grounds for believing—
   (a) that any members of the public have been intimidated, harassed, alarmed or distressed as a result of the presence or behaviour of groups of two or more persons in public places in any locality in his police area (the "relevant locality"), and
   (b) that anti-social behaviour is a significant and persistent problem in the relevant locality.
(2) The relevant officer may give an authorisation that the powers conferred on a constable in uniform by subsections (3) to (6) are to be exercisable for a period specified in the authorisation which does not exceed 6 months.
(3) Subsection (4) applies if a constable in uniform has reasonable grounds for believing that the presence or behaviour of a group of two or more persons in any public place in the relevant locality has resulted, or is likely to result, in any members of the public being intimidated, harassed, alarmed or distressed.
(4) The constable may give one or more of the following directions, namely—
   (a) a direction requiring the persons in the group to disperse (either immediately or by such time as he may specify and in such way as he may specify),

(b) a direction requiring any of those persons whose place of residence is not within the relevant locality to leave the relevant locality or any part of the relevant locality (either immediately or by such time as he may specify and in such way as he may specify), and

(c) a direction prohibiting any of those persons whose place of residence is not within the relevant locality from returning to the relevant locality or any part of the relevant locality for such period (not exceeding 24 hours) from the giving of the direction as he may specify;

but this subsection is subject to subsection (5).

(5) A direction under subsection (4) may not be given in respect of a group of persons—

    (a) who are engaged in conduct which is lawful under section 220 of the Trade Union and Labour Relations (Consolidation) Act 1992, or

    (b) who are taking part in a public procession of the kind mentioned in section 11(1) of the Public Order Act 1986 in respect of which—

        (i) written notice has been given in accordance with section 11 of that Act, or

        (ii) such notice is not required to be given as provided by subsections (1) and (2) of that section.

(6) If, between the hours of 9pm and 6am, a constable in uniform finds a person in any public place in the relevant locality who he has reasonable grounds for believing—

    (a) is under the age of 16, and

    (b) is not under the effective control of a parent or a responsible person aged 18 or over,

he may remove the person to the person's place of residence unless he has reasonable grounds for believing that the person would, if removed to that place, be likely to suffer significant harm.

(7) In this section any reference to the presence or behaviour of a group of persons is to be read as including a reference to the presence or behaviour of any one or more of the persons in the group.

31 Authorisations: supplemental

(1) An authorisation—

    (a) must be in writing,

    (b) must be signed by the relevant officer giving it, and

    (c) must specify—

        (i) the relevant locality,

        (ii) the grounds on which the authorisation is given, and

        (iii) the period during which the powers conferred by section 30(3) to (6) are exercisable.

(2) An authorisation may not be given without the consent of the local authority or each local authority whose area includes the whole or part of the relevant locality.

(3) Publicity must be given to an authorisation by either or both of the following methods—

    (a) publishing an authorisation notice in a newspaper circulating in the relevant locality,

    (b) posting an authorisation notice in some conspicuous place or places within the relevant locality.

(4) An "authorisation notice" is a notice which—

    (a) states the authorisation has been given,

    (b) specifies the relevant locality, and

    (c) specifies the period during which the powers conferred by section 30(3) to (6) are exercisable.

(5) Subsection (3) must be complied with before the beginning of the period mentioned in subsection (4)(c).

(6) An authorisation may be withdrawn by—

    (a) the relevant officer who gave it, or

    (b) any other relevant officer whose police area includes the relevant locality and whose rank is the same as or higher than that of the relevant officer mentioned in paragraph (a).

(7) Before the withdrawal of an authorisation, consultation must take place with any local authority whose area includes the whole or part of the relevant locality.

(8) The withdrawal of an authorisation does not affect the exercise of any power pursuant to that authorisation which occurred prior to its withdrawal.

(9) The giving or withdrawal of an authorisation does not prevent the giving of a further authorisation in respect of a locality which includes the whole or any part of the relevant locality to which the earlier authorisation relates.

(10) In this section "authorisation" means an authorisation under section 30.

32 Powers under section 30: supplemental

(1) A direction under section 30(4)—
   (a) may be given orally,
   (b) may be given to any person individually or to two or more persons together, and
   (c) may be withdrawn or varied by the person who gave it.

(2) A person who knowingly contravenes a direction given to him under section 30(4) commits an offence and is liable on summary conviction to—
   (a) a fine not exceeding level 4 on the standard scale, or
   (b) imprisonment for a term not exceeding 3 months,
   or to both.

(3) ...

(4) Where the power under section 30(6) is exercised, any local authority whose area includes the whole or part of the relevant locality must be notified of that fact.

36 Interpretation

In this Part—

"anti-social behaviour" means behaviour by a person which causes or is likely to cause harassment, alarm or distress to one or more other persons not of the same household as the person,

"local authority" means—
(a) in relation to England, a district council, a county council that is the council for a county in which there are no district councils, a London borough council, the Common Council of the City of London or the Council of the Isles of Scilly,
(b) in relation to Wales, a county council or a county borough council,

"public place" means—
   (a) any highway, and
   (b) any place to which at the material time the public or any section of the public has access, on payment or otherwise, as of right or by virtue of express or implied permission,

"relevant locality" has the same meaning as in section 30,

"relevant officer" means a police officer of or above the rank of superintendent.

CRIMINAL JUSTICE ACT 2003
(2003, c. 44)

An Act to make provision about criminal justice (including the powers and duties of the police) and about dealing with offenders; to amend the law relating to jury service; to amend Chapter 1 of Part 1 of the Crime and Disorder Act 1998 and Part 5 of the Police Act 1997; to make provision about civil proceedings brought by offenders; and for connected purposes. [20 November 2003]

PART 4
CHARGING ETC

29 New method of instituting proceedings

(1) A public prosecutor may institute criminal proceedings against a person by issuing a document (a "written charge") which charges the person with an offence.

(2) Where a public prosecutor issues a written charge, it must at the same time issue a document (a "requisition") which requires the person to appear before a magistrates' court to answer the written charge.
(3) The written charge and requisition must be served on the person concerned, and a copy of both must be served on the court named in the requisition.
(4) *In consequence of subsections (1) to (3), a public prosecutor is not to have the power to lay an information for the purpose of obtaining the issue of a summons under section 1 of the Magistrates' Courts Act 1980.*
(5) In this section "public prosecutor" means—
   (a) a police force or a person authorised by a police force to institute criminal proceedings,
   (b) the Director of the Serious Fraud Office or a person authorised by him to institute criminal proceedings,
   (c) the Director of Public Prosecutions or a person authorised by him to institute criminal proceedings,
   (ca) the Director of Revenue and Customs Prosecutions or a person authorised by him to institute criminal proceedings,
   (cb) the Director of the Serious Organised Crime Agency or a person authorised by him to institute criminal proceedings,
   (d) the Attorney General or a person authorised by him to institute criminal proceedings,
   (e) a Secretary of State or a person authorised by a Secretary of State to institute criminal proceedings,
   (f) the Commissioners of Inland Revenue or a person authorised by them to institute criminal proceedings,
   (g) the Commissioners of Customs and Excise or a person authorised by them to institute criminal proceedings, or
   (h) a person specified in an order made by the Secretary of State for the purposes of this section or a person authorised by such a person to institute criminal proceedings.
(6) In subsection (5) "police force" has the meaning given by section 3(3) of the Prosecution of Offences Act 1985.

30 Further provision about new method

(1) Criminal Procedure Rules may make—
   (a) provision as to the form, content, recording, authentication and service of written charges or requisitions, and
   (b) such other provision in relation to written charges or requisitions as appears to the Criminal Procedure Rule Committee to be necessary or expedient.
(2) Without limiting subsection (1), the provision which may be made by virtue of that subsection includes provision—
   (a) which applies (with or without modifications), or which disapplies, the provision of any enactment relating to the service of documents,
   (b) for or in connection with the issue of further requisitions.
(3) Nothing in subsection (1) or (2) is to be taken as affecting the generality of section 144(1) of that Act.
(4) Nothing in section 29 affects—
   (a) the power of a public prosecutor to lay an information for the purpose of obtaining the issue of a warrant under section 1 of the Magistrates' Courts Act 1980,
   (b) the power of a person who is not a public prosecutor to lay an information for the purpose of obtaining the issue of a summons or warrant under section 1 of that Act, or
   (c) any power to charge a person with an offence whilst he is in custody.
(5) Except where the context otherwise requires, in any enactment contained in an Act passed before this Act—
   (a) any reference (however expressed) which is or includes a reference to an information within the meaning of section 1 of the Magistrates' Courts Act 1980 (or to the laying

of such an information) is to be read as including a reference to a written charge (or to the issue of a written charge),
    (b) any reference (however expressed) which is or includes a reference to a summons under section 1 of the Magistrates' Courts Act 1980 (or to a justice of the peace issuing such a summons) is to be read as including a reference to a requisition (or to a public prosecutor issuing a requisition).
(6) Subsection (5) does not apply to section 1 of the Magistrates' Courts Act 1980.
(7) The reference in subsection (5) to an enactment contained in an Act passed before this Act includes a reference to an enactment contained in that Act as a result of an amendment to that Act made by this Act or by any other Act passed in the same Session as this Act.
(8) In this section "public prosecutor", "requisition" and "written charge" have the same meaning as in section 29.

PREVENTION OF TERRORISM ACT 2005
(2005, c 2)

An Act to provide for the making against individuals involved in terrorism-related activity of orders imposing obligations on them for purposes connected with preventing or restricting their further involvement in such activity; to make provision about appeals and other proceedings relating to such orders; and for connected purposes. [11 March 2005]

Control orders

1   Power to make control orders
(1) In this Act "control order" means an order against an individual that imposes obligations on him for purposes connected with protecting members of the public from a risk of terrorism.
(2) The power to make a control order against an individual shall be exercisable—
    (a) except in the case of an order imposing obligations that are incompatible with the individual's right to liberty under Article 5 of the Human Rights Convention, by the Secretary of State; and
    (b) in the case of an order imposing obligations that are or include derogating obligations, by the court on an application by the Secretary of State.
(3) The obligations that may be imposed by a control order made against an individual are any obligations that the Secretary of State or (as the case may be) the court considers necessary for purposes connected with preventing or restricting involvement by that individual in terrorism-related activity.
(4) Those obligations may include, in particular—
    (a) a prohibition or restriction on his possession or use of specified articles or substances;
    (b) a prohibition or restriction on his use of specified services or specified facilities, or on his carrying on specified activities;
    (c) a restriction in respect of his work or other occupation, or in respect of his business;
    (d) a restriction on his association or communications with specified persons or with other persons generally;
    (e) a restriction in respect of his place of residence or on the persons to whom he gives access to his place of residence;
    (f) a prohibition on his being at specified places or within a specified area at specified times or on specified days;
    (g) a prohibition or restriction on his movements to, from or within the United Kingdom, a specified part of the United Kingdom or a specified place or area within the United Kingdom;
    (h) a requirement on him to comply with such other prohibitions or restrictions on his movements as may be imposed, for a period not exceeding 24 hours, by directions given to him in the specified manner, by a specified person and for the purpose of securing compliance with other obligations imposed by or under the order;

(i) a requirement on him to surrender his passport, or anything in his possession to which a prohibition or restriction imposed by the order relates, to a specified person for a period not exceeding the period for which the order remains in force;

(j) a requirement on him to give access to specified persons to his place of residence or to other premises to which he has power to grant access;

(k) a requirement on him to allow specified persons to search that place or any such premises for the purpose of ascertaining whether obligations imposed by or under the order have been, are being or are about to be contravened;

(l) a requirement on him to allow specified persons, either for that purpose or for the purpose of securing that the order is complied with, to remove anything found in that place or on any such premises and to subject it to tests or to retain it for a period not exceeding the period for which the order remains in force;

(m) a requirement on him to allow himself to be photographed;

(n) a requirement on him to co-operate with specified arrangements for enabling his movements, communications or other activities to be monitored by electronic or other means;

(o) a requirement on him to comply with a demand made in the specified manner to provide information to a specified person in accordance with the demand;

(p) a requirement on him to report to a specified person at specified times and places.

(5) Power by or under a control order to prohibit or restrict the controlled person's movements includes, in particular, power to impose a requirement on him to remain at or within a particular place or area (whether for a particular period or at particular times or generally).

(6) The reference in subsection (4)(n) to co-operating with specified arrangements for monitoring includes a reference to each of the following—
(a) submitting to procedures required by the arrangements;
(b) wearing or otherwise using apparatus approved by or in accordance with the arrangements;
(c) maintaining such apparatus in the specified manner;
(d) complying with directions given by persons carrying out functions for the purposes of those arrangements.

(7) The information that the controlled person may be required to provide under a control order includes, in particular, advance information about his proposed movements or other activities.

(8) A control order may provide for a prohibition, restriction or requirement imposed by or under the order to apply only where a specified person has not given his consent or approval to what would otherwise contravene the prohibition, restriction or requirement.

(9) For the purposes of this Act involvement in terrorism-related activity is any one or more of the following—
(a) the commission, preparation or instigation of acts of terrorism;
(b) conduct which facilitates the commission, preparation or instigation of such acts, or which is intended to do so;
(c) conduct which gives encouragement to the commission, preparation or instigation of such acts, or which is intended to do so;
(d) conduct which gives support or assistance to individuals who are known or believed to be involved in terrorism-related activity;
and for the purposes of this subsection it is immaterial whether the acts of terrorism in question are specific acts of terrorism or acts of terrorism generally.

(10) In this Act—
"derogating obligation" means an obligation on an individual which—
(a) is incompatible with his right to liberty under Article 5 of the Human Rights Convention; but
(b) is of a description of obligations which, for the purposes of the designation of a designated derogation, is set out in the designation order;

"designated derogation" has the same meaning as in the Human Rights Act 1998 (see section 14(1) of that Act);

"designation order", in relation to a designated derogation, means the order under section 14(1) of the Human Rights Act 1998 by which the derogation is designated.

2 Making of non-derogating control orders

(1) The Secretary of State may make a control order against an individual if he—
   (a) has reasonable grounds for suspecting that the individual is or has been involved in terrorism-related activity; and
   (b) considers that it is necessary, for purposes connected with protecting members of the public from a risk of terrorism, to make a control order imposing obligations on that individual.

(2) The Secretary of State may make a control order against an individual who is for the time being bound by a control order made by the court only if he does so—
   (a) after the court has determined that its order should be revoked; but
   (b) while the effect of the revocation has been postponed for the purpose of giving the Secretary of State an opportunity to decide whether to exercise his own powers to make a control order against the individual.

(3) A control order made by the Secretary of State is called a non-derogating control order.

(4) A non-derogating control order—
   (a) has effect for a period of 12 months beginning with the day on which it is made; but
   (b) may be renewed on one or more occasions in accordance with this section.

(5) A non-derogating control order must specify when the period for which it is to have effect will end.

(6) The Secretary of State may renew a non-derogating control order (with or without modifications) for a period of 12 months if he—
   (a) considers that it is necessary, for purposes connected with protecting members of the public from a risk of terrorism, for an order imposing obligations on the controlled person to continue in force; and
   (b) considers that the obligations to be imposed by the renewed order are necessary for purposes connected with preventing or restricting involvement by that person in terrorism-related activity.

. . .

3 Supervision by court of making of non-derogating control orders

(1) The Secretary of State must not make a non-derogating control order against an individual except where—
   (a) having decided that there are grounds to make such an order against that individual, he has applied to the court for permission to make the order and has been granted that permission;
   (b) the order contains a statement by the Secretary of State that, in his opinion, the urgency of the case requires the order to be made without such permission; or
   (c) the order is made before 14th March 2005 against an individual who, at the time it is made, is an individual in respect of whom a certificate under section 21(1) of the Anti-terrorism, Crime and Security Act 2001 is in force.

(2) Where the Secretary of State makes an application for permission to make a non-derogating control order against an individual, the application must set out the order for which he seeks permission and—
   (a) the function of the court is to consider whether the Secretary of State's decision that there are grounds to make that order is obviously flawed;
   (b) the court may give that permission unless it determines that the decision is obviously flawed; and
   (c) if it gives permission, the court must give directions for a hearing in relation to the order as soon as reasonably practicable after it is made.

(3) Where the Secretary of State makes a non-derogating control order against an individual without the permission of the court—
    (a) he must immediately refer the order to the court; and
    (b) the function of the court on the reference is to consider whether the decision of the Secretary of State to make the order he did was obviously flawed.
(4) The court's consideration on a reference under subsection (3)(a) must begin no more than 7 days after the day on which the control order in question was made.
(5) The court may consider an application for permission under subsection (1)(a) or a reference under subsection (3)(a)—
    (a) in the absence of the individual in question;
    (b) without his having been notified of the application or reference; and
    (c) without his having been given an opportunity (if he was aware of the application or reference) of making any representations to the court;
    but this subsection is not to be construed as limiting the matters about which rules of court may be made in relation to the consideration of such an application or reference.
(6) On a reference under subsection (3)(a), the court—
    (a) if it determines that the decision of the Secretary of State to make a non-derogating control order against the controlled person was obviously flawed, must quash the order;
    (b) if it determines that that decision was not obviously flawed but that a decision of the Secretary of State to impose a particular obligation by that order was obviously flawed, must quash that obligation and (subject to that) confirm the order and give directions for a hearing in relation to the confirmed order; and
    (c) in any other case, must confirm the order and give directions for a hearing in relation to the confirmed order.
(7) The directions given under subsection (2)(c) or (6)(b) or (c) must include arrangements for the individual in question to be given an opportunity within 7 days of the court's giving permission or (as the case may be) making its determination on the reference to make representations about—
    (a) the directions already given; and
    (b) the making of further directions.
(8) On a reference under subsection (3)(a), the court may quash a certificate contained in the order for the purposes of subsection (1)(b) if it determines that the Secretary of State's decision that the certificate should be contained in the order was flawed.
(9) The court must ensure that the controlled person is notified of its decision on a reference under subsection (3)(a).
(10) On a hearing in pursuance of directions under subsection (2)(c) or (6)(b) or (c), the function of the court is to determine whether any of the following decisions of the Secretary of State was flawed—
    (a) his decision that the requirements of section 2(1)(a) and (b) were satisfied for the making of the order; and
    (b) his decisions on the imposition of each of the obligations imposed by the order.
(11) In determining—
    (a) what constitutes a flawed decision for the purposes of subsection (2), (6) or (8), or
    (b) the matters mentioned in subsection (10),
    the court must apply the principles applicable on an application for judicial review.
(12) If the court determines, on a hearing in pursuance of directions under subsection (2)(c) or (6)(b) or (c), that a decision of the Secretary of State was flawed, its only powers are—
    (a) power to quash the order;
    (b) power to quash one or more obligations imposed by the order; and
    (c) power to give directions to the Secretary of State for the revocation of the order or for the modification of the obligations it imposes.
(13) In every other case the court must decide that the control order is to continue in force.

(14) If requested to do so by the controlled person, the court must discontinue any hearing in pursuance of directions under subsection (2)(c) or (6)(b) or (c).

4 Power of court to make derogating control orders

(1) On an application to the court by the Secretary of State for the making of a control order against an individual, it shall be the duty of the court—
   (a) to hold an immediate preliminary hearing to determine whether to make a control order imposing obligations that are or include derogating obligations (called a "derogating control order") against that individual; and
   (b) if it does make such an order against that individual, to give directions for the holding of a full hearing to determine whether to confirm the order (with or without modifications).

(2) The preliminary hearing under subsection (1)(a) may be held—
   (a) in the absence of the individual in question;
   (b) without his having had notice of the application for the order; and
   (c) without his having been given an opportunity (if he was aware of the application) of making any representations to the court;
   but this subsection is not to be construed as limiting the matters about which rules of court may be made in relation to that hearing.

(3) At the preliminary hearing, the court may make a control order against the individual in question if it appears to the court—
   (a) that there is material which (if not disproved) is capable of being relied on by the court as establishing that the individual is or has been involved in terrorism-related activity;
   (b) that there are reasonable grounds for believing that the imposition of obligations on that individual is necessary for purposes connected with protecting members of the public from a risk of terrorism;
   (c) that the risk arises out of, or is associated with, a public emergency in respect of which there is a designated derogation from the whole or a part of Article 5 of the Human Rights Convention; and
   (d) that the obligations that there are reasonable grounds for believing should be imposed on the individual are or include derogating obligations of a description set out for the purposes of the designated derogation in the designation order.

(4) The obligations that may be imposed by a derogating control order in the period between—
   (a) the time when the order is made, and
   (b) the time when a final determination is made by the court whether to confirm it,
   include any obligations which the court has reasonable grounds for considering are necessary as mentioned in section 1(3).

(5) At the full hearing under subsection (1)(b), the court may—
   (a) confirm the control order made by the court; or
   (b) revoke the order;
   and where the court revokes the order, it may (if it thinks fit) direct that this Act is to have effect as if the order had been quashed.

(6) In confirming a control order, the court—
   (a) may modify the obligations imposed by the order; and
   (b) where a modification made by the court removes an obligation, may (if it thinks fit) direct that this Act is to have effect as if the removed obligation had been quashed.

(7) At the full hearing, the court may confirm the control order (with or without modifications) only if—
   (a) it is satisfied, on the balance of probabilities, that the controlled person is an individual who is or has been involved in terrorism-related activity;
   (b) it considers that the imposition of obligations on the controlled person is necessary for purposes connected with protecting members of the public from a risk of terrorism;
   (c) it appears to the court that the risk is one arising out of, or is associated with, a public emergency in respect of which there is a designated derogation from the whole or a part of Article 5 of the Human Rights Convention; and

(d) the obligations to be imposed by the order or (as the case may be) by the order as modified are or include derogating obligations of a description set out for the purposes of the designated derogation in the designation order.

...

(10) The power of the court to renew a derogating control order is exercisable on as many occasions as the court thinks fit; but, on each occasion, it is exercisable only if—
  (a) the court considers that it is necessary, for purposes connected with protecting members of the public from a risk of terrorism, for a derogating control order to continue in force against the controlled person;
  (b) it appears to the court that the risk is one arising out of, or is associated with, a public emergency in respect of which there is a designated derogation from the whole or a part of Article 5 of the Human Rights Convention;
  (c) the derogating obligations that the court considers should continue in force are of a description that continues to be set out for the purposes of the designated derogation in the designation order; and
  (d) the court considers that the obligations to be imposed by the renewed order are necessary for purposes connected with preventing or restricting involvement by that person in terrorism-related activity.

...

(13) It shall be immaterial, for the purposes of determining what obligations may be imposed by a control order made by the court, whether the involvement in terrorism-related activity to be prevented or restricted by the obligations is connected with matters in relation to which the requirements of subsection (3)(a) or (7)(a) were satisfied.

5 Arrest and detention pending derogating control order

(1) A constable may arrest and detain an individual if—
  (a) the Secretary of State has made an application to the court for a derogating control order to be made against that individual; and
  (b) the constable considers that the individual's arrest and detention is necessary to ensure that he is available to be given notice of the order if it is made.
(2) A constable who has arrested an individual under this section must take him to the designated place that the constable considers most appropriate as soon as practicable after the arrest.
(3) An individual taken to a designated place under this section may be detained there until the end of 48 hours from the time of his arrest.
(4) If the court considers that it is necessary to do so to ensure that the individual in question is available to be given notice of any derogating control order that is made against him, it may, during the 48 hours following his arrest, extend the period for which the individual may be detained under this section by a period of no more than 48 hours.
(5) An individual may not be detained under this section at any time after—
  (a) he has become bound by a derogating control order made against him on the Secretary of State's application; or
  (b) the court has dismissed the application.
(6) A person who has the powers of a constable in one part of the United Kingdom may exercise the power of arrest under this section in that part of the United Kingdom or in any other part of the United Kingdom.

...

(9) The power to detain an individual under this section includes power to detain him in a manner that is incompatible with his right to liberty under Article 5 of the Human Rights Convention if, and only if—
  (a) there is a designated derogation in respect of the detention of individuals under this section in connection with the making of applications for derogating control orders; and
  (b) that derogation and the designated derogation relating to the power to make the orders applied for are designated in respect of the same public emergency.

...

7 Modification, notification and proof of orders etc.
(1) If while a non-derogating control order is in force the controlled person considers that there has been a change of circumstances affecting the order, he may make an application to the Secretary of State for—
    (a) the revocation of the order; or
    (b) the modification of an obligation imposed by the order;
    and it shall be the duty of the Secretary of State to consider the application.
(2) The Secretary of State may, at any time (whether or not in response to an application by the controlled person)—
    (a) revoke a non-derogating control order;
    (b) relax or remove an obligation imposed by such an order;
    (c) with the consent of the controlled person, modify the obligations imposed by such an order; or
    (d) make to the obligations imposed by such an order any modifications which he considers necessary for purposes connected with preventing or restricting involvement by the controlled person in terrorism-related activity.
(3) The Secretary of State may not make to the obligations imposed by a control order any modification the effect of which is that a non-derogating control order becomes an order imposing a derogating obligation.
(4) An application may be made at any time to the court—
    (a) by the Secretary of State, or
    (b) by the controlled person,
    for the revocation of a derogating control order or for the modification of obligations imposed by such an order.

...

(7) If the court at any time determines that a derogating control order needs to be modified so that it no longer imposes derogating obligations, it must revoke the order.
(8) The controlled person is bound by—
    (a) a control order,
    (b) the renewal of a control order, or
    (c) a modification by virtue of subsection (2)(d) or (5)(c),
    only if a notice setting out the terms of the order, renewal or modification has been delivered to him in person.

...

8 Criminal investigations after making of control order
(1) This section applies where it appears to the Secretary of State—
    (a) that the involvement in terrorism-related activity of which an individual is suspected may have involved the commission of an offence relating to terrorism; and
    (b) that the commission of that offence is being or would fall to be investigated by a police force.
(2) Before making, or applying for the making of, a control order against the individual, the Secretary of State must consult the chief officer of the police force about whether there is evidence available that could realistically be used for the purposes of a prosecution of the individual for an offence relating to terrorism.
(3) If a control order is made against the individual the Secretary of State must inform the chief officer of the police force that the control order has been made and that subsection (4) applies.
(4) It shall then be the duty of the chief officer to secure that the investigation of the individual's conduct with a view to his prosecution for an offence relating to terrorism is kept under review throughout the period during which the control order has effect.

(5) In carrying out his functions by virtue of this section the chief officer must consult the relevant prosecuting authority, but only, in the case of the performance of his duty under subsection (4), to the extent that he considers it appropriate to do so.

(6) The requirements of subsection (5) may be satisfied by consultation that took place wholly or partly before the passing of this Act.

...

9 Offences

(1) A person who, without reasonable excuse, contravenes an obligation imposed on him by a control order is guilty of an offence.

(2) A person is guilty of an offence if—
 (a) a control order by which he is bound at a time when he leaves the United Kingdom requires him, whenever he enters the United Kingdom, to report to a specified person that he is or has been the subject of such an order;
 (b) he re-enters the United Kingdom after the order has ceased to have effect;
 (c) the occasion on which he re-enters the United Kingdom is the first occasion on which he does so after leaving while the order was in force; and
 (d) on that occasion he fails, without reasonable excuse, to report to the specified person in the manner that was required by the order.

(3) A person is guilty of an offence if he intentionally obstructs the exercise by any person of a power conferred by section 7(9).

(4) A person guilty of an offence under subsection (1) or (2) shall be liable—
 (a) on conviction on indictment, to imprisonment for a term not exceeding 5 years or to a fine, or to both;
 (b) on summary conviction in England and Wales, to imprisonment for a term not exceeding 12 months or to a fine not exceeding the statutory maximum, or to both;
 (c) on summary conviction in Scotland or Northern Ireland, to imprisonment for a term not exceeding 6 months or to a fine not exceeding the statutory maximum, or to both.

(5) In relation to an offence committed before the commencement of section 154(1) of the Criminal Justice Act 2003 (c. 44), the reference in subsection (4)(b) to 12 months is to be read as a reference to 6 months.

...

Note: Sections 1–9 continue in force by order (SI 2008/559, art 2) for a period of one year from 11 March 2008.

Appeals and other proceedings

10 Appeals relating to non-derogating control orders

(1) Where—
 (a) a non-derogating control order has been renewed, or
 (b) an obligation imposed by such an order has been modified without the consent of the controlled person,
the controlled person may appeal to the court against the renewal or modification.

(2) In the case of an appeal against a renewal with modifications, the appeal may include an appeal against some or all of the modifications.

(3) Where an application is made by the controlled person to the Secretary of State for—
 (a) the revocation of a non-derogating control order, or
 (b) the modification of an obligation imposed by such an order,
that person may appeal to the court against any decision by the Secretary of State on the application.

(4) The function of the court on an appeal against the renewal of a non-derogating control order, or on an appeal against a decision not to revoke such an order, is to determine whether either or both of the following decisions of the Secretary of State was flawed—
 (a) his decision that it is necessary, for purposes connected with protecting members of the public from a risk of terrorism, for an order imposing obligations on the controlled person to continue in force;

(b) his decision that the obligations to be imposed by the renewed order, or (as the case may be) the obligations imposed by the order to which the application for revocation relates, are necessary for purposes connected with preventing or restricting involvement by that person in terrorism-related activity.

(5) The function of the court on an appeal against a modification of an obligation imposed by a non-derogating control order (whether on a renewal or otherwise), or on an appeal against a decision not to modify such an obligation, is to determine whether the following decision of the Secretary of State was flawed—
(a) in the case of an appeal against a modification, his decision that the modification is necessary for purposes connected with preventing or restricting involvement by the controlled person in terrorism-related activity; and
(b) in the case of an appeal against a decision on an application for the modification of an obligation, his decision that the obligation continues to be necessary for that purpose.

(6) In determining the matters mentioned in subsections (4) and (5) the court must apply the principles applicable on an application for judicial review.

(7) If the court determines on an appeal under this section that a decision of the Secretary of State was flawed, its only powers are—
(a) power to quash the renewal of the order;
(b) power to quash one or more obligations imposed by the order; and
(c) power to give directions to the Secretary of State for the revocation of the order or for the modification of the obligations it imposes.

(8) In every other case, the court must dismiss the appeal.

11 Jurisdiction and appeals in relation to control order decisions etc.

(1) Control order decisions and derogation matters are not to be questioned in any legal proceedings other than—
(a) proceedings in the court; or
(b) proceedings on appeal from such proceedings.

(2) The court is the appropriate tribunal for the purposes of section 7 of the Human Rights Act 1998 (c. 42) in relation to proceedings all or any part of which call a control order decision or derogation matter into question.

(3) No appeal shall lie from any determination of the court in control order proceedings, except on a question of law.

(4) No appeal by any person other than the Secretary of State shall lie from any determination—
(a) on an application for permission under section 3(1)(a); or
(b) on a reference under section 3(3)(a).

. . .

Supplemental

13 Duration of sections 1 to 9

(1) Except so far as otherwise provided under this section, sections 1 to 9 expire at the end of the period of 12 months beginning with the day on which this Act is passed.

(2) The Secretary of State may, by order made by statutory instrument—
(a) repeal sections 1 to 9;
(b) at any time revive those sections for a period not exceeding one year; or
(c) provide that those sections—
(i) are not to expire at the time when they would otherwise expire under subsection (1) or in accordance with an order under this subsection; but
(ii) are to continue in force after that time for a period not exceeding one year.

(3) Before making an order under this section the Secretary of State must consult—
(a) the person appointed for the purposes of section 14(2);
(b) the Intelligence Services Commissioner; and
(c) the Director-General of the Security Service.

(4) No order may be made by the Secretary of State under this section unless a draft of it has been laid before Parliament and approved by a resolution of each House.

(5) Subsection (4) does not apply to an order that contains a declaration by the Secretary of State that the order needs, by reason of urgency, to be made without the approval required by that subsection.

(6) An order under this section that contains such a declaration—
   (a) must be laid before Parliament after being made; and
   (b) if not approved by a resolution of each House before the end of 40 days beginning with the day on which the order was made, ceases to have effect at the end of that period.

(7) Where an order ceases to have effect in accordance with subsection (6), that does not—
   (a) affect anything previously done in reliance on the order; or
   (b) prevent the making of a new order to the same or similar effect.

...

(9) Nothing in this Act about the period for which a control order is to have effect or is renewed enables such an order to continue in force after the provision under which it was made or last renewed has expired or been repealed by virtue of this section.

...

14 Reporting and review

(1) As soon as reasonably practicable after the end of every relevant 3 month period, the Secretary of State must—
   (a) prepare a report about his exercise of the control order powers during that period; and
   (b) lay a copy of that report before Parliament.

(2) The Secretary of State must also appoint a person to review the operation of this Act.

(3) As soon as reasonably practicable after the end of—
   (a) the period of 9 months beginning with the day on which this Act is passed, and
   (b) every 12 month period which ends with the first or a subsequent anniversary of the end of the period mentioned in the preceding paragraph and is a period during the whole or a part of which sections 1 to 9 of this Act were in force,
the person so appointed must carry out a review of the operation of this Act during that period.

(4) The person who conducts a review under this section must send the Secretary of State a report on its outcome as soon as reasonably practicable after completing the review.

(5) That report must also contain the opinion of the person making it on—
   (a) the implications for the operation of this Act of any proposal made by the Secretary of State for the amendment of the law relating to terrorism; and
   (b) the extent (if any) to which the Secretary of State has made use of his power by virtue of section 3(1)(b) to make non-derogating control orders in urgent cases without the permission of the court.

(6) On receiving a report under subsection (4), the Secretary of State must lay a copy of it before Parliament.

(7) The Secretary of State may pay the expenses of a person appointed to carry out a review and may also pay him such allowances as the Secretary of State determines.

...

CONSTITUTIONAL REFORM ACT 2005
(2005, c. 4)

An Act to make provision for modifying the office of Lord Chancellor, and to make provision relating to the functions of that office; to establish a Supreme Court of the United Kingdom, and to abolish the appellate jurisdiction of the House of Lords; to make provision about the jurisdiction of the Judicial Committee of the Privy Council and the judicial functions of the President of the Council; to make other provision about the judiciary, their appointment and discipline; and for connected purposes.

[24 March 2005]

PART 1
THE RULE OF LAW

1 The rule of law

This Act does not adversely affect—
   (a) the existing constitutional principle of the rule of law, or
   (b) the Lord Chancellor's existing constitutional role in relation to that principle.

PART 2
ARRANGEMENTS TO MODIFY THE OFFICE OF LORD CHANCELLOR

Qualifications for office of Lord Chancellor

2 Lord Chancellor to be qualified by experience

   (1) A person may not be recommended for appointment as Lord Chancellor unless he appears to the Prime Minister to be qualified by experience.
   (2) The Prime Minister may take into account any of these—
      (a) experience as a Minister of the Crown;
      (b) experience as a member of either House of Parliament;
      (c) experience as a qualifying practitioner;
      (d) experience as a teacher of law in a university;
      (e) other experience that the Prime Minister considers relevant.
   (3) In this section "qualifying practitioner" means any of these—
      (a) a person who has a Senior Courts qualification, within the meaning of section 71 of the Courts and Legal Services Act 1990;
      (b) an advocate in Scotland or a solicitor entitled to appear in the Court of Session and the High Court of Justiciary;
      (c) a member of the Bar of Northern Ireland or a solicitor of the Court of Judicature of Northern Ireland.

Continued judicial independence

3 Guarantee of continued judicial independence

   (1) The Lord Chancellor, other Ministers of the Crown and all with responsibility for matters relating to the judiciary or otherwise to the administration of justice must uphold the continued independence of the judiciary.
   (2) Subsection (1) does not impose any duty which it would be within the legislative competence of the Scottish Parliament to impose.
   (3) A person is not subject to the duty imposed by subsection (1) if he is subject to the duty imposed by section 1(1) of the Justice (Northern Ireland) Act 2002.
   (4) The following particular duties are imposed for the purpose of upholding that independence.
   (5) The Lord Chancellor and other Ministers of the Crown must not seek to influence particular judicial decisions through any special access to the judiciary.
   (6) The Lord Chancellor must have regard to—
      (a) the need to defend that independence;
      (b) the need for the judiciary to have the support necessary to enable them to exercise their functions;

(c) the need for the public interest in regard to matters relating to the judiciary or otherwise to the administration of justice to be properly represented in decisions affecting those matters.
(7) In this section "the judiciary" includes the judiciary of any of the following—
   (a) the Supreme Court;
   (b) any other court established under the law of any part of the United Kingdom;
   (c) any international court.

...

Representations by senior judges

5   Representations to Parliament

(1) The chief justice of any part of the United Kingdom may lay before Parliament written representations on matters that appear to him to be matters of importance relating to the judiciary, or otherwise to the administration of justice, in that part of the United Kingdom.
(2) In relation to Scotland those matters do not include matters within the legislative competence of the Scottish Parliament, unless they are matters to which a Bill for an Act of Parliament relates.
(3) In relation to Northern Ireland those matters do not include transferred matters within the legislative competence of the Northern Ireland Assembly, unless they are matters to which a Bill for an Act of Parliament relates.

...

Judiciary and courts in England and Wales

7   President of the Courts of England and Wales

(1) The Lord Chief Justice holds the office of President of the Courts of England and Wales and is Head of the Judiciary of England and Wales.
(2) As President of the Courts of England and Wales he is responsible—
   (a) for representing the views of the judiciary of England and Wales to Parliament, to the Lord Chancellor and to Ministers of the Crown generally;
   (b) for the maintenance of appropriate arrangements for the welfare, training and guidance of the judiciary of England and Wales within the resources made available by the Lord Chancellor;
   (c) for the maintenance of appropriate arrangements for the deployment of the judiciary of England and Wales and the allocation of work within courts.
(3) The President of the Courts of England and Wales is president of the courts listed in subsection (4) and is entitled to sit in any of those courts.
(4) The courts are—
   the Court of Appeal
   the High Court
   the Crown Court
   the county courts
   the magistrates' courts.

...

8   *Head and Deputy Head of Criminal Justice*

(1) There is to be a Head of Criminal Justice.
(2) The Head of Criminal Justice is—
   (a) the Lord Chief Justice, or
   (b) if the Lord Chief Justice appoints another person, that person.
(3) The Lord Chief Justice may appoint a person to be Deputy Head of Criminal Justice.
(4) The Lord Chief Justice must not appoint a person under subsection (2)(b) or (3) unless these conditions are met—
   (a) the Lord Chief Justice has consulted the Lord Chancellor;
   (b) the person to be appointed is a judge of the Court of Appeal.

(5) A person appointed under subsection (2)(b) or (3) holds the office to which he is appointed in accordance with the terms of his appointment.

14 Transfer of appointment functions to Her Majesty
Schedule 3 provides for—
- (a) Her Majesty instead of the Lord Chancellor to make appointments to certain offices, and
- (b) the modification of enactments relating to those offices.

15 Other functions of the Lord Chancellor and organisation of the courts
(1) Schedule 4 provides for—
- (a) the transfer of functions to or from the Lord Chancellor,
- (b) the modification of other functions of the Lord Chancellor,
- (c) the modification of enactments relating to those functions, and
- (d) the modification of enactments relating to the organisation of the courts.

...

Speakership of the House of Lords

18 Speakership of the House of Lords
Schedule 6 contains amendments relating to the Speakership of the House of Lords.

PART 3
THE SUPREME COURT

The Supreme Court

23 The Supreme Court
(1) There is to be a Supreme Court of the United Kingdom.
(2) The Court consists of 12 judges appointed by Her Majesty by letters patent.
(3) Her Majesty may from time to time by Order in Council amend subsection (2) so as to increase or further increase the number of judges of the Court.
(4) No recommendation may be made to Her Majesty in Council to make an Order under subsection (3) unless a draft of the Order has been laid before and approved by resolution of each House of Parliament.
(5) Her Majesty may by letters patent appoint one of the judges to be President and one to be Deputy President of the Court.
(6) The judges other than the President and Deputy President are to be styled "Justices of the Supreme Court".
(7) The Court is to be taken to be duly constituted despite any vacancy among the judges of the Court or in the office of President or Deputy President.

Note: An order by which s. 23 comes into force may not be made unless the Lord Chancellor is satisfied that the Supreme Court will be provided with accommodation in accordance with written plans that he has approved, and he may only approve these, having consulted the Lords of Appeal in Ordinary holding office at the time, if he is satisfied that the accommodation will be appropriate for the purposes of the court.

24 First members of the Court
On the commencement of section 23—
- (a) the persons who immediately before that commencement are Lords of Appeal in Ordinary become judges of the Supreme Court,
- (b) the person who immediately before that commencement is the senior Lord of Appeal in Ordinary becomes the President of the Court, and
- (c) the person who immediately before that commencement is the second senior Lord of Appeal in Ordinary becomes the Deputy President of the Court.

Appointment of judges

25 Qualification for appointment
(1) A person is not qualified to be appointed a judge of the Supreme Court unless he has (at any time)—
- (a) held high judicial office for a period of at least 2 years, or

(b) satisfied the judicial-appointment eligibility on a 15-year basis, or
(c) been a qualifying practitioner for a period of at least 15 years.

...

26 Selection of members of the Court

(1) This section applies to a recommendation for an appointment to one of the following offices—
  (a) judge of the Supreme Court;
  (b) President of the Court;
  (c) Deputy President of the Court.
(2) A recommendation may be made only by the Prime Minister.
(3) The Prime Minister—
  (a) must recommend any person whose name is notified to him under section 29;
  (b) may not recommend any other person.
(4) A person who is not a judge of the Court must be recommended for appointment as a judge if his name is notified to the Prime Minister for an appointment as President or Deputy President.
(5) If there is a vacancy in one of the offices mentioned in subsection (1), or it appears to him that there will soon be such a vacancy, the Lord Chancellor must convene a selection commission for the selection of a person to be recommended.

27 Selection process

(1) The commission must—
  (a) determine the selection process to be applied,
  (b) apply the selection process, and
  (c) make a selection accordingly.
(2) As part of the selection process the commission must consult each of the following—
  (a) such of the senior judges as are not members of the commission and are not willing to be considered for selection;
  (b) the Lord Chancellor;
  (c) the First Minister in Scotland;
  (d) the First Minister for Wales;
  (e) the Secretary of State for Northern Ireland.
(3) If for any part of the United Kingdom no judge of the courts of that part is to be consulted under subsection (2)(a), the commission must consult as part of the selection process the most senior judge of the courts of that part who is not a member of the commission and is not willing to be considered for selection.
(4) Subsections (5) to (10) apply to any selection under this section or section 31.
(5) Selection must be on merit.
(6) A person may be selected only if he meets the requirements of section 25.
(7) A person may not be selected if he is a member of the commission.
(8) In making selections for the appointment of judges of the Court the commission must ensure that between them the judges will have knowledge of, and experience of practice in, the law of each part of the United Kingdom.
(9) The commission must have regard to any guidance given by the Lord Chancellor as to matters to be taken into account (subject to any other provision of this Act) in making a selection.
(10) Any selection must be of one person only.

28 Report

(1) After complying with section 27 the commission must submit a report to the Lord Chancellor.
(2) The report must—
  (a) state who has been selected;
  (b) state the senior judges consulted under section 27(2)(a) and any judge consulted under section 27(3);

(c) contain any other information required by the Lord Chancellor.
(3) The report must be in a form approved by the Lord Chancellor.
(4) After submitting the report the commission must provide any further information the Lord Chancellor may require.
(5) When he receives the report the Lord Chancellor must consult each of the following—
    (a) the senior judges consulted under section 27(2)(a);
    (b) any judge consulted under section 27(3);
    (c) the First Minister in Scotland;
    (d) the First Minister for Wales;
    (e) the Secretary of State for Northern Ireland.

29 The Lord Chancellor's options
(1) This section refers to the following stages—
    Stage 1: where a person has been selected under section 27
    Stage 2: where a person has been selected following a rejection or reconsideration at stage 1
    Stage 3: where a person has been selected following a rejection or reconsideration at stage 2.
(2) At stage 1 the Lord Chancellor must do one of the following—
    (a) notify the selection;
    (b) reject the selection;
    (c) require the commission to reconsider the selection.
(3) At stage 2 the Lord Chancellor must do one of the following—
    (a) notify the selection;
    (b) reject the selection, but only if it was made following a reconsideration at stage 1;
    (c) require the commission to reconsider the selection, but only if it was made following a rejection at stage 1.
(4) At stage 3 the Lord Chancellor must notify the selection, unless subsection (5) applies and he makes a notification under it.
(5) If a person whose selection the Lord Chancellor required to be reconsidered at stage 1 or 2 was not selected again at the next stage, the Lord Chancellor may at stage 3 notify that person's name to the Prime Minister.
(6) In this Part references to the Lord Chancellor notifying a selection are references to his notifying to the Prime Minister the name of the person selected.

30 Exercise of powers to reject or require reconsideration
(1) The power of the Lord Chancellor under section 29 to reject a selection at stage 1 or 2 is exercisable only on the grounds that, in the Lord Chancellor's opinion, the person selected is not suitable for the office concerned.
(2) The power of the Lord Chancellor under section 29 to require the commission to reconsider a selection at stage 1 or 2 is exercisable only on the grounds that, in the Lord Chancellor's opinion—
    (a) there is not enough evidence that the person is suitable for the office concerned,
    (b) there is evidence that the person is not the best candidate on merit, or
    (c) there is not enough evidence that if the person were appointed the judges of the Court would between them have knowledge of, and experience of practice in, the law of each part of the United Kingdom.
(3) The Lord Chancellor must give the commission reasons in writing for rejecting or requiring reconsideration of a selection.

31 Selection following rejection or requirement to reconsider
(1) If under section 29 the Lord Chancellor rejects or requires reconsideration of a selection at stage 1 or 2, the commission must select a person in accordance with this section.
(2) If the Lord Chancellor rejects a selection, the commission—
    (a) may not select the person rejected, and

(b) where the rejection is following reconsideration of a selection, may not select the person (if different) whose selection it reconsidered.
(3) If the Lord Chancellor requires a selection to be reconsidered, the commission—
   (a) may select the same person or a different person, but
   (b) where the requirement is following a rejection, may not select the person rejected.
(4) The commission must inform the Lord Chancellor of the person selected following a rejection or requirement to reconsider.

33 Tenure

A judge of the Supreme Court holds that office during good behaviour, but may be removed from it on the address of both Houses of Parliament.

34 Salaries and allowances

(1) A judge of the Supreme Court is entitled to a salary.
. . .
(5) Salaries payable under this section are to be charged on and paid out of the Consolidated Fund of the United Kingdom.
. . .

41 Relation to other courts etc

(1) Nothing in this Part is to affect the distinctions between the separate legal systems of the parts of the United Kingdom.
(2) A decision of the Supreme Court on appeal from a court of any part of the United Kingdom, other than a decision on a devolution matter, is to be regarded as the decision of a court of that part of the United Kingdom.
(3) A decision of the Supreme Court on a devolution matter—
   (a) is not binding on that Court when making such a decision;
   (b) otherwise, is binding in all legal proceedings.
. . .

PART 4
JUDICIAL APPOINTMENTS AND DISCIPLINE

CHAPTER 1
COMMISSION AND OMBUDSMAN

61 The Judicial Appointments Commission

(1) There is to be a body corporate called the Judicial Appointments Commission.
. . .

62 Judicial Appointments and Conduct Ombudsman

(1) There is to be a Judicial Appointments and Conduct Ombudsman.
. . .

CHAPTER 2
APPOINTMENTS

General provisions

63 Merit and good character

(1) Subsections (2) and (3) apply to any selection under this Part by the Commission or a selection panel ("the selecting body").
(2) Selection must be solely on merit.
(3) A person must not be selected unless the selecting body is satisfied that he is of good character.

64 Encouragement of diversity

(1) The Commission, in performing its functions under this Part, must have regard to the need to encourage diversity in the range of persons available for selection for appointments.

(2) This section is subject to section 63.

65 Guidance about procedures

(1) The Lord Chancellor may issue guidance about procedures for the performance by the Commission or a selection panel of its functions of—
  (a) identifying persons willing to be considered for selection under this Part, and
  (b) assessing such persons for the purposes of selection.
(2) The guidance may, among other things, relate to consultation or other steps in determining such procedures.
(3) The purposes for which guidance may be issued under this section include the encouragement of diversity in the range of persons available for selection.

. . .

Lord Chief Justice and Heads of Division

67 Selection of Lord Chief Justice and Heads of Division

(1) Sections 68 to 75 apply to a recommendation for an appointment to one of the following offices—
  (a) Lord Chief Justice;
  (b) Master of the Rolls;
  (c) President of the Queen's Bench Division;
  (d) President of the Family Division;
  (e) Chancellor of the High Court.
(2) Any such recommendation must be made in accordance with those sections and section 96.

70 Selection process

(1) On receiving a request the Commission must appoint a selection panel.
(2) The panel must—
  (a) determine the selection process to be applied,
  (b) apply the selection process, and
  (c) make a selection accordingly.
(3) One person only must be selected for each recommendation to which a request relates.
(4) Subsection (3) applies to selection under this section and to selection under section 75.
(5) If practicable the panel must consult, about the exercise of its functions under this section, the current holder of the office for which a selection is to be made.
(6) A selection panel is a committee of the Commission.

71 Selection panel

(1) The selection panel must consist of four members.
(2) The first member is the most senior England and Wales Supreme Court judge who is not disqualified, or his nominee.
(3) Unless subsection (7) applies, the second member is the Lord Chief Justice or his nominee.
(4) Unless subsection (9) applies, the third member is the chairman of the Commission or his nominee.
(5) The fourth member is a lay member of the Commission designated by the third member.

. . .

SCHEDULE 12   Section 61
THE JUDICIAL APPOINTMENTS COMMISSION
PART 1
THE COMMISSIONERS

The Commissioners

1. The Commission consists of—
  (a) a chairman, and
  (b) 14 other Commissioners,
appointed by Her Majesty on the recommendation of the Lord Chancellor.

2. (1) The chairman must be a lay member.
   (2) Of the other Commissioners—
       (a) 5 must be judicial members,
       (b) 2 must be professional members,
       (c) 5 must be lay members,
       (d) 1 other must be the holder of an office listed in Part 3 of Schedule 14, and
       (e) 1 other must be a lay justice member.
   . . .
   (3) Of the Commissioners appointed as judicial members—
       (a) 1 must be a Lord Justice of Appeal;
       (b) 1 must be a puisne judge of the High Court;
       (c) 1 other must be either a Lord Justice of Appeal or a puisne judge of the High Court;
       (d) 1 must be a circuit judge;
       (e) 1 must be a district judge of a county court, a District Judge (Magistrates' Courts) or a person appointed to an office under section 89 of the Supreme Court Act 1981 (c. 54).
   (4) Of the Commissioners appointed as professional members—
       (a) 1 must be a practising barrister in England and Wales;
       (b) 1 must be a practising solicitor of the Senior Courts of England and Wales.
   . . .
3. A person must not be appointed as a Commissioner if he is employed in the civil service of the State.
. . .

SERIOUS ORGANISED CRIME AND POLICE ACT 2005
(2005, c. 15)

An Act to provide for the establishment and functions of the Serious Organised Crime Agency; to make provision about investigations, prosecutions, offenders and witnesses in criminal proceedings and the protection of persons involved in investigations or proceedings; to make further provision for combatting crime and disorder, including new provision about powers of arrest and search warrants and about parental compensation orders; to make further provision about the police and policing and persons supporting the police; to make provision for protecting certain organisations from interference with their activities; to make provision about criminal records. [7 April 2005]

PART 1
THE SERIOUS ORGANISED CRIME AGENCY

CHAPTER 1
SOCA: ESTABLISHMENT AND ACTIVITIES

Establishment of SOCA

1 **Establishment of Serious Organised Crime Agency**
   (1) There shall be a body corporate to be known as the Serious Organised Crime Agency ("SOCA").
   (2) Schedule 1 makes provision about the constitution, members and staff of SOCA and other matters relating to it.
   (3) Each of the following bodies shall cease to exist on such date as the Secretary of State appoints by order—
       (a) the National Criminal Intelligence Service and its Service Authority, and
       (b) the National Crime Squad and its Service Authority.

Functions

2 **Functions of SOCA as to serious organised crime**
   (1) SOCA has the functions of—
       (a) preventing and detecting serious organised crime, and

        (b) contributing to the reduction of such crime in other ways and to the mitigation of its consequences.
    (2) SOCA's functions under subsection (1) are exercisable subject to subsections (3) to (5) (but subsection (3) does not apply to Scotland).
    (3) If, in exercising its function under subsection (1)(a), SOCA becomes aware of conduct appearing to SOCA to involve serious or complex fraud, SOCA may thereafter exercise that function in relation to the fraud in question only—
        (a) with the agreement of the Director, or an authorised officer, of the Serious Fraud Office, or
        (b) if the Serious Fraud Office declines to act in relation to it.
    (4) If, in exercising its function under subsection (1)(a), SOCA becomes aware of conduct appearing to SOCA to involve revenue fraud, SOCA may thereafter exercise that function in relation to the fraud in question only with the agreement of the Commissioners.
    (5) Before exercising its function under subsection (1)(b) in any way in relation to revenue fraud, SOCA must consult the Commissioners.
    (6) The issue of whether SOCA's function under subsection (1)(a) continued to be exercisable in any circumstances within subsection (3) or (4) may not be raised in any criminal proceedings.
    (7) In this section "revenue fraud" includes fraud relating to taxes, duties and national insurance contributions.
    (8) In this Chapter "the Commissioners" means the Commissioners for Her Majesty's Revenue and Customs.

2A **Functions of SOCA relating to the recovery of assets**
SOCA has the functions conferred on it (whether directly or through its staff by the Proceeds of Crime Act 2002) (functions relating to the recovery of assets).

3 **Functions of SOCA as to information relating to crime**
    (1) SOCA has the function of gathering, storing, analysing and disseminating information relevant to—
        (a) the prevention, detection, investigation or prosecution of offences, or
        (b) the reduction of crime in other ways or the mitigation of its consequences.
    (2) SOCA may disseminate such information to—
        (a) police forces within subsection (3),
        (b) special police forces,
        (c) law enforcement agencies, or
        (d) such other persons as it considers appropriate in connection with any of the matters mentioned in subsection (1)(a) or (b).
    (3) The police forces within this subsection are—
        (a) police forces in the United Kingdom, and
        (b) the States of Jersey Police Force, the salaried police force of the Island of Guernsey and the Isle of Man Constabulary.
    (4) In this section "law enforcement agency" means—
        (a) the Commissioners or any other government department,
        (b) the Scottish Administration,
        (c) any other person who is charged with the duty of investigating offences or charging offenders, or
        (d) any other person who is engaged outside the United Kingdom in the carrying on of activities similar to any carried on by SOCA or a police force.
    (5) In this Chapter "special police force" means—
        (a) the Ministry of Defence Police,
        (b) the British Transport Police Force,
        (c) the Civil Nuclear Constabulary, or
        (d) the Scottish Crime and Drug Enforcement Agency.

General powers

5   SOCA's general powers

(1)   SOCA has the general powers conferred by this section.

(2)   SOCA may—
 (a)   institute criminal proceedings in England and Wales or Northern Ireland;
 (b)   at the request of the chief officer of a police force within section 3(3) or of a special police force, act in support of any activities of that force;
 (c)   at the request of any law enforcement agency, act in support of any activities of that agency;
 (d)   enter into other arrangements for co-operating with bodies or persons (in the United Kingdom or elsewhere) which it considers appropriate in connection with the exercise of any of SOCA's functions under section 2 or 3 or any activities within subsection (3).

(3)   Despite the references to serious organised crime in section 2(1), SOCA may carry on activities in relation to other crime if they are carried on for the purposes of any of the functions conferred on SOCA by section 2 or 3.

(4)   Subsection (3) does not affect the generality of section 3(1).

(5)   SOCA may furnish such assistance as it considers appropriate in response to requests made by any government or other body exercising functions of a public nature in any country or territory outside the United Kingdom.

(6)   Subsection (5) does not apply to any request for assistance which—
 (a)   could be made under section 13 of the Crime (International Co-operation) Act 2003 (c. 32) (requests by overseas authorities to obtain evidence), and
 (b)   is not a request in relation to which SOCA has functions under that section by virtue of an order under section 27(2) of that Act.

(7)   In this section "law enforcement agency" has the meaning given by section 3(4).

Annual plans and reports

7   Annual reports

(1)   As soon as possible after the end of each financial year SOCA must issue a report on the exercise of its functions during that year (an "annual report").

(2)   The annual report must include an assessment of the extent to which the annual plan for that year under section 6 has been carried out.

(3)   SOCA must arrange for the annual report to be published in such manner as it considers appropriate.

(4)   SOCA must send a copy of the annual report to—
 (a)   the Secretary of State,
 (b)   the Scottish Ministers,
 (c)   the Commissioners,
 (d)   each police authority for an area in Great Britain, each joint police board and the Northern Ireland Policing Board,
 (e)   the chief officer of each police force in the United Kingdom, and
 (f)   such other persons as SOCA considers appropriate.

(5)   In subsection (4)(d) the reference to a police authority for an area in Great Britain does not include a constituent authority in an amalgamation scheme approved under section 19(1) of the Police (Scotland) Act 1967.

(6)   The Secretary of State must lay a copy of the annual report before Parliament.

(7)   The Scottish Ministers must lay a copy of the annual report before the Scottish Parliament.

Central supervision and direction

8   General duty of Secretary of State and Scottish Ministers

The Secretary of State and the Scottish Ministers must exercise the powers respectively conferred on him and them under this Chapter in such manner and to such extent as appear to him and them to be best calculated to promote the efficiency and effectiveness of SOCA.

9 Strategic priorities

(1) The Secretary of State may determine strategic priorities for SOCA.
(2) Before determining any such priorities the Secretary of State must consult—
  (a) SOCA,
  (b) the Scottish Ministers, and
  (c) such other persons as he considers appropriate.
(3) The Secretary of State must arrange for any priorities determined under this section to be published in such manner as he considers appropriate.

11 Reports to Secretary of State

(1) The Secretary of State may require SOCA to submit a report to him on such matters—
  (a) connected with the exercise of SOCA's functions, or
  (b) otherwise connected with any of SOCA's activities,
  as may be specified in the requirement.
(2) A report submitted under subsection (1) must be in such form as may be so specified.
(3) The Secretary of State must consult the Scottish Ministers before imposing any requirement under that subsection relating to any functions or activities of SOCA—
  (a) exercised or carried out in Scotland, or
  (b) exercised or carried out outside, but in relation to, Scotland.
(4) The Secretary of State may—
  (a) arrange, or
  (b) require SOCA to arrange,
  for a report under this section to be published in such manner as he considers appropriate.
(5) But the Secretary of State may exclude any part of a report from publication under subsection (4) if, in his opinion, publication of that part—
  (a) would be against the interests of national security, or
  (b) could prejudice the prevention or detection of crime or the apprehension or prosecution of offenders, or
  (c) could jeopardise the safety of any person.

Operational matters

21 Operational responsibility of Director General

(1) The Director General of SOCA has the function of exercising general operational control in relation to the activities carried out in the exercise of SOCA's functions.
(2) This function includes deciding—
  (a) which particular operations are to be mounted in the exercise of any of those functions, and
  (b) how such operations are to be conducted.

Use and disclosure of information

32 Use of information by SOCA

Information obtained by SOCA in connection with the exercise of any of its functions may be used by SOCA in connection with the exercise of any of its other functions.

33 Disclosure of information by SOCA

(1) Information obtained by SOCA in connection with the exercise of any of its functions may be disclosed by SOCA if the disclosure is for any permitted purposes.
(2) "Permitted purposes" means the purposes of any of the following—
  (a) the prevention, detection, investigation or prosecution of criminal offences, whether in the United Kingdom or elsewhere;
  (b) the prevention, detection or investigation of conduct for which penalties other than criminal penalties are provided under the law of any part of the United Kingdom or of any country or territory outside the United Kingdom;
  (c) the exercise of any function conferred on SOCA by section 2, 3 or 5 (so far as not falling within paragraph (a) or (b));

(d) the exercise of any functions of any intelligence service within the meaning of the Regulation of Investigatory Powers Act 2000;
(e) the exercise of any functions under Part 2 of the Football Spectators Act 1989;
(f) the exercise of any function which appears to the Secretary of State to be a function of a public nature and which he designates by order.

(3) A disclosure under this section does not breach—
(a) any obligation of confidence owed by the person making the disclosure, or
(b) any other restriction on the disclosure of information (however imposed).

(4) But nothing in this section authorises—
(a) a disclosure, in contravention of any provisions of the Data Protection Act 1998, of personal data which are not exempt from those provisions,
(b) a disclosure which is prohibited by Part 1 of the Regulation of Investigatory Powers Act 2000, or
(c) a disclosure in contravention of section 35(2).

34 Disclosure of information to SOCA

(1) Any person may disclose information to SOCA if the disclosure is made for the purposes of the exercise by SOCA of any of its functions.

(2) A disclosure under this section does not breach—
(a) any obligation of confidence owed by the person making the disclosure, or
(b) any other restriction on the disclosure of information (however imposed).

(3) But nothing in this section authorises—
(a) a disclosure, in contravention of any provisions of the Data Protection Act 1998, of personal data which are not exempt from those provisions, or
(b) a disclosure which is prohibited by Part 1 of the Regulation of Investigatory Powers Act 2000.

(4) Information may not be disclosed under subsection (1) on behalf of the Commissioners unless the disclosure is authorised by the Commissioners or by an authorised officer of theirs.

35 Restrictions on further disclosure

(1) Information disclosed by SOCA under section 33 to any person or body must not be further disclosed except—
(a) for a purpose connected with any function of that person or body for the purposes of which the information was disclosed by SOCA, or otherwise for any permitted purposes, and
(b) with the consent of SOCA.

(2) Information disclosed to SOCA under any enactment by the Commissioners or a person acting on their behalf must not be further disclosed except—
(a) for any permitted purposes, and
(b) with the consent of the Commissioners or an authorised officer of Revenue and Customs.

(3) Consent under subsection (1) or (2) may be given—
(a) in relation to a particular disclosure, or
(b) in relation to disclosures made in circumstances specified or described in the consent.

(4) In this section "permitted purposes" has the meaning given by section 33(2).

General duties of police etc.

36 General duty of police to pass information to SOCA

(1) The chief officer of a police force in Great Britain must keep SOCA informed of any information relating to crime in his police area that appears to him to be likely to be relevant to the exercise by SOCA of any of its functions.

(2) The Chief Constable of the Police Service of Northern Ireland has a corresponding duty in relation to crime in Northern Ireland.

(3) The chief officer of a special police force must keep SOCA informed of any information relating to crime that he has become aware of in his capacity as chief officer and appears to him to be likely to be relevant to the exercise by SOCA of any of its functions.

37 General duty of police etc. to assist SOCA

(1) It is the duty of every person to whom this section applies to assist SOCA in the exercise of its functions in relation to serious organised crime.

(2) This section applies to—
   (a) any constable,
   (b) any officer of Revenue and Customs, and
   (c) any member of Her Majesty's armed forces or Her Majesty's coastguard.

Miscellaneous and supplementary

41 Directions

Any person to whom a direction is given by the Secretary of State or the Scottish Ministers under this Chapter must comply with the direction.

PART 2
INVESTIGATIONS, PROSECUTIONS, PROCEEDINGS AND PROCEEDS OF CRIME

CHAPTER 1
INVESTIGATORY POWERS OF DPP, ETC.

Introductory

60 Investigatory powers of DPP etc.

(1) This Chapter confers powers on—
   (a) the Director of Public Prosecutions,
   (b) the Director of Revenue and Customs Prosecutions,
   (c) the Lord Advocate, and
   (d) the Director of Public Prosecutions for Northern Ireland,
   in relation to the giving of disclosure notices in connection with the investigation of offences to which this Chapter applies or in connection with a terrorist investigation.

(2) The Director of Public Prosecutions may, to such extent as he may determine, delegate the exercise of his powers under this Chapter to a Crown prosecutor.

(3) The Director of Revenue and Customs Prosecutions may, to such extent as he may determine, delegate the exercise of his powers under this Chapter to a Revenue and Customs Prosecutor.

(4) The Lord Advocate may, to such extent as he may determine, delegate the exercise of his powers under this Chapter to a procurator fiscal.

(4A) The Director of Public Prosecutions for Northern Ireland may, to such extent as he may determine, delegate the exercise of his powers under this Chapter to a Public Prosecutor.

(5) In this Chapter "the Investigating Authority" means—
   (a) the Director of Public Prosecutions,
   (b) the Director of Revenue and Customs Prosecutions,
   (c) the Lord Advocate, or
   (d) the Director of Public Prosecutions for Northern Ireland.

(6) But, in circumstances where the powers of any of those persons are exercisable by any other person by virtue of subsection (2), (3), (4) or (4A), references to "the Investigating Authority" accordingly include any such other person.

(7) In this Chapter "terrorist investigation" means an investigation of—
   (a) the commission, preparation or instigation of acts of terrorism,
   (b) any act or omission which appears to have been for the purposes of terrorism and which consists in or involves the commission, preparation or instigation of an offence, or

(c) the commission, preparation or instigation of an offence under the Terrorism Act 2000 or under Part 1 of the Terrorism Act 2006 other than an offence under section 1 or 2 of that Act.

61 Offences to which this Chapter applies

(1) This Chapter applies to the following offences—
  (a) any offence listed in Schedule 2 to the Proceeds of Crime Act 2002 (lifestyle offences: England and Wales);
  (b) any offence listed in Schedule 4 to that Act (lifestyle offences: Scotland);
  (ba) any offence listed in Schedule 5 to that Act (lifestyle offences: Northern Ireland);
  (c) any offence under sections 15 to 18 of the Terrorism Act 2000 (offences relating to fund-raising, money laundering etc.);
  (d) any offence under section 170 of the Customs and Excise Management Act 1979 (fraudulent evasion of duty) or section 72 of the Value Added Tax Act 1994 (offences relating to VAT) which is a qualifying offence;
  (e) any offence under section 17 of the Theft Act 1968 or section 17 of the Theft Act (Northern Ireland) 1969 (false accounting), or any offence at common law of cheating in relation to the public revenue, which is a qualifying offence;
  (f) any offence under section 1 of the Criminal Attempts Act 1981 or Article 3 of the Criminal Attempts and Conspiracy (Northern Ireland) Order 1983, or in Scotland at common law, of attempting to commit any offence in paragraph (c) or any offence in paragraph (d) or (e) which is a qualifying offence;
  (g) any offence under section 1 of the Criminal Law Act 1977 or Article 9 of the Criminal Attempts and Conspiracy (Northern Ireland) Order 1983, or in Scotland at common law, of conspiracy to commit any offence in paragraph (c) or any offence in paragraph (d) or (e) which is a qualifying offence.
  (h) in England and Wales—
    (i) any common law offence of bribery;
    (ii) any offence under section 1 of the Public Bodies Corrupt Practices Act 1889 (corruption in office);
    (iii) the first two offences under section 1 of the Prevention of Corruption Act 1906 (bribes obtained by or given to agents).

(2) For the purposes of subsection (1) an offence in paragraph (d) or (e) of that subsection is a qualifying offence if the Investigating Authority certifies that in his opinion—
  (a) in the case of an offence in paragraph (d) or an offence of cheating the public revenue, the offence involved or would have involved a loss, or potential loss, to the public revenue of an amount not less than £5,000;
  (b) in the case of an offence under section 17 of the Theft Act 1968, the offence involved or would have involved a loss or gain, or potential loss or gain, of an amount not less than £5,000.

(3) A document purporting to be a certificate under subsection (2) is to be received in evidence and treated as such a certificate unless the contrary is proved.

Disclosure notices

62 Disclosure notices

(1) If it appears to the Investigating Authority—
  (a) that there are reasonable grounds for suspecting that an offence to which this Chapter applies has been committed,
  (b) that any person has information (whether or not contained in a document) which relates to a matter relevant to the investigation of that offence, and
  (c) that there are reasonable grounds for believing that information which may be provided by that person in compliance with a disclosure notice is likely to be of substantial value (whether or not by itself) to that investigation,

he may give, or authorise an appropriate person to give, a disclosure notice to that person.

(1A) If it appears to the Investigating Authority—

(a) that any person has information (whether or not contained in a document) which relates to a matter relevant to a terrorist investigation, and
(b) that there are reasonable grounds for believing that information which may be provided by that person in compliance with a disclosure notice is likely to be of substantial value (whether or not by itself) to that investigation,

he may give, or authorise an appropriate person to give, a disclosure notice to that person.

(2) In this Chapter "appropriate person" means—
(a) a constable,
(b) a member of the staff of SOCA who is for the time being designated under section 43, or
(c) an officer of Revenue and Customs.

But in the application of this Chapter to Northern Ireland, this subsection has effect as if paragraph (b) were omitted.

(3) In this Chapter "disclosure notice" means a notice in writing requiring the person to whom it is given to do all or any of the following things in accordance with the specified requirements, namely—
(a) answer questions with respect to any matter relevant to the investigation;
(b) provide information with respect to any such matter as is specified in the notice;
(c) produce such documents, or documents of such descriptions, relevant to the investigation as are specified in the notice.

(4) In subsection (3) "the specified requirements" means such requirements specified in the disclosure notice as relate to—
(a) the time at or by which,
(b) the place at which, or
(c) the manner in which,

the person to whom the notice is given is to do any of the things mentioned in paragraphs (a) to (c) of that subsection; and those requirements may include a requirement to do any of those things at once.

(5) A disclosure notice must be signed or counter-signed by the Investigating Authority.
(6) This section has effect subject to section 64 (restrictions on requiring information etc.).

63 Production of documents

(1) This section applies where a disclosure notice has been given under section 62.
(2) An authorised person may—
(a) take copies of or extracts from any documents produced in compliance with the notice, and
(b) require the person producing them to provide an explanation of any of them.

(3) Documents so produced may be retained for so long as the Investigating Authority considers that it is necessary to retain them (rather than copies of them) in connection with the investigation for the purposes of which the disclosure notice was given.

(4) If the Investigating Authority has reasonable grounds for believing—
(a) that any such documents may have to be produced for the purposes of any legal proceedings, and
(b) that they might otherwise be unavailable for those purposes,

they may be retained until the proceedings are concluded.

(5) If a person who is required by a disclosure notice to produce any documents does not produce the documents in compliance with the notice, an authorised person may require that person to state, to the best of his knowledge and belief, where they are.

(6) In this section "authorised person" means any appropriate person who either—
(a) is the person by whom the notice was given, or
(b) is authorised by the Investigating Authority for the purposes of this section.

(7) This section has effect subject to section 64 (restrictions on requiring information etc.).

64 Restrictions on requiring information etc.

(1) A person may not be required under section 62 or 63—

(a) to answer any privileged question,
(b) to provide any privileged information, or
(c) to produce any privileged document,
except that a lawyer may be required to provide the name and address of a client of his.

...

(8) A person may not be required under section 62 or 63 to disclose any information or produce any document in respect of which he owes an obligation of confidence by virtue of carrying on any banking business, unless—
(a) the person to whom the obligation of confidence is owed consents to the disclosure or production, or
(b) the requirement is made by, or in accordance with a specific authorisation given by, the Investigating Authority.

...

65 Restrictions on use of statements

(1) A statement made by a person in response to a requirement imposed under section 62 or 63 ("the relevant statement") may not be used in evidence against him in any criminal proceedings unless subsection (2) or (3) applies.
(2) This subsection applies where the person is being prosecuted—
(a) for an offence under section 67 of this Act, or
(b) for an offence under section 5 of the Perjury Act 1911 (c. 6) (false statements made on oath otherwise than in judicial proceedings or made otherwise than on oath), or
(c) for an offence under section 2 of the False Oaths (Scotland) Act 1933 (c. 20) (false statutory declarations and other false statements without oath) or at common law for an offence of attempting to pervert the course, or defeat the ends, of justice, or
(d) for an offence under Article 10 of the Perjury (Northern Ireland) Order 1979.
(3) This subsection applies where the person is being prosecuted for some other offence and—
(a) the person, when giving evidence in the proceedings, makes a statement inconsistent with the relevant statement, and
(b) in the proceedings evidence relating to the relevant statement is adduced, or a question about it is asked, by or on behalf of the person.

Enforcement

66 Power to enter and seize documents

(1) A justice of the peace may issue a warrant under this section if, on an information on oath laid by the Investigating Authority, he is satisfied—
(a) that any of the conditions mentioned in subsection (2) is met in relation to any documents of a description specified in the information, and
(b) that the documents are on premises so specified.
(2) The conditions are—
(a) that a person has been required by a disclosure notice to produce the documents but has not done so;
(b) that it is not practicable to give a disclosure notice requiring their production;
(c) that giving such a notice might seriously prejudice the investigation of an offence to which this Chapter applies.
(3) A warrant under this section is a warrant authorising an appropriate person named in it—
(a) to enter and search the premises, using such force as is reasonably necessary;
(b) to take possession of any documents appearing to be documents of a description specified in the information, or to take any other steps which appear to be necessary for preserving, or preventing interference with, any such documents;
(c) in the case of any such documents consisting of information recorded otherwise than in legible form, to take possession of any computer disk or other electronic storage device which appears to contain the information in question, or to take any other steps which appear to be necessary for preserving, or preventing interference with, that information;

(d) to take copies of or extracts from any documents or information falling within paragraph (b) or (c);
(e) to require any person on the premises to provide an explanation of any such documents or information or to state where any such documents or information may be found;
(f) to require any such person to give the appropriate person such assistance as he may reasonably require for the taking of copies or extracts as mentioned in paragraph (d).

(4) A person executing a warrant under this section may take other persons with him, if it appears to him to be necessary to do so.

(5) A warrant under this section must, if so required, be produced for inspection by the owner or occupier of the premises or anyone acting on his behalf.

(6) If the premises are unoccupied or the occupier is temporarily absent, a person entering the premises under the authority of a warrant under this section must leave the premises as effectively secured against trespassers as he found them.

(7) Where possession of any document or device is taken under this section—
  (a) the document may be retained for so long as the Investigating Authority considers that it is necessary to retain it (rather than a copy of it) in connection with the investigation for the purposes of which the warrant was sought, or
  (b) the device may be retained for so long as he considers that it is necessary to retain it in connection with that investigation,
  as the case may be.

(8) If the Investigating Authority has reasonable grounds for believing—
  (a) that any such document or device may have to be produced for the purposes of any legal proceedings, and
  (b) that it might otherwise be unavailable for those purposes,
  it may be retained until the proceedings are concluded.

(9) Nothing in this section authorises a person to take possession of, or make copies of or take extracts from, any document or information which, by virtue of section 64, could not be required to be produced or disclosed under section 62 or 63.

(10) In the application of this section to Scotland—
  (a) subsection (1) has effect as if, for the words from the beginning to "satisfied—", there were substituted "A sheriff may issue a warrant under this section, on the application of a procurator fiscal, if he is satisfied—";
  (b) subsections (1)(a) and (3)(b) have effect as if, for "in the information", there were substituted "in the application"; and
  (c) subsections (4) to (6) do not have effect.

(11) In the application of this section to Northern Ireland—
  (a) subsection (1) has effect as if, for the words from the beginning to "laid", there were substituted "A lay magistrate may issue a warrant under this section if, on complaint on oath made"; and
  (b) subsections (1)(a) and (3)(b) have effect as if, for "in the information", there were substituted "in the complaint".

67 Offences in connection with disclosure notices or search warrants

(1) A person commits an offence if, without reasonable excuse, he fails to comply with any requirement imposed on him under section 62 or 63.

(2) A person commits an offence if, in purported compliance with any requirement imposed on him under section 62 or 63—
  (a) he makes a statement which is false or misleading, and
  (b) he either knows that it is false or misleading or is reckless as to whether it is false or misleading.
  "False or misleading" means false or misleading in a material particular.

(3) A person commits an offence if he wilfully obstructs any person in the exercise of any rights conferred by a warrant under section 66.

(4) A person guilty of an offence under subsection (1) or (3) is liable on summary conviction—
  (a) to imprisonment for a term not exceeding 51 weeks, or

(b) to a fine not exceeding level 5 on the standard scale,

or to both.

(5) A person guilty of an offence under subsection (2) is liable—
 (a) on conviction on indictment, to imprisonment for a term not exceeding two years or to a fine, or to both;
 (b) on summary conviction, to imprisonment for a term not exceeding 12 months or to a fine not exceeding the statutory maximum, or to both.

(6) In the application of this section to Scotland, the reference to 51 weeks in subsection (4)(a) is to be read as a reference to 12 months.

(7) In the application of this section to Northern Ireland—
 (a) the reference to 51 weeks in subsection (4)(a) is to be read as a reference to 6 months; and
 (b) the reference to 12 months in subsection (5)(b) is to be read as a reference to 6 months.

Supplementary

69 Manner in which disclosure notice may be given

(1) This section provides for the manner in which a disclosure notice may be given under section 62.

(2) The notice may be given to a person by—
 (a) delivering it to him,
 (b) leaving it at his proper address,
 (c) sending it by post to him at that address.

(3) The notice may be given—
 (a) in the case of a body corporate, to the secretary or clerk of that body;
 (b) in the case of a partnership, to a partner or a person having the control or management of the partnership business;
 (c) in the case of an unincorporated association (other than a partnership), to an officer of the association.

(4) For the purposes of this section and section 7 of the Interpretation Act 1978 (service of documents by post) in its application to this section, the proper address of a person is his usual or last-known address (whether residential or otherwise), except that—
 (a) in the case of a body corporate or its secretary or clerk, it is the address of the registered office of that body or its principal office in the United Kingdom,
 (b) in the case of a partnership, a partner or a person having the control or management of the partnership business, it is that of the principal office of the partnership in the United Kingdom, and
 (c) in the case of an unincorporated association (other than a partnership) or an officer of the association, it is that of the principal office of the association in the United Kingdom.

(5) This section does not apply to Scotland.

PART 3

POLICE POWERS ETC.

Exclusion zones

112 Power to direct a person to leave a place

(1) A constable may direct a person to leave a place if he believes, on reasonable grounds, that the person is in the place at a time when he would be prohibited from entering it by virtue of—
 (a) an order to which subsection (2) applies, or
 (b) a condition to which subsection (3) applies.

(2) This subsection applies to an order which—
 (a) was made, by virtue of any enactment, following the person's conviction of an offence, and

            (b) prohibits the person from entering the place or from doing so during a period specified in the order.
    (3) This subsection applies to a condition which—
            (a) was imposed, by virtue of any enactment, as a condition of the person's release from a prison in which he was serving a sentence of imprisonment following his conviction of an offence, and
            (b) prohibits the person from entering the place or from doing so during a period specified in the condition.
    (4) A direction under this section may be given orally.
    (5) Any person who knowingly contravenes a direction given to him under this section is guilty of an offence and liable on summary conviction to imprisonment for a term not exceeding 51 weeks or to a fine not exceeding level 4 on the standard scale, or to both.

. . .

PART 4
PUBLIC ORDER AND CONDUCT IN PUBLIC PLACES ETC.

Trespass on designated site

128 Offence of trespassing on designated site

    (1) A person commits an offence if he enters, or is on, any protected site in England and Wales or Northern Ireland as a trespasser.
    (1A) In this section "protected site" means—
            (a) a nuclear site; or
            (b) a designated site.
    (1B) In this section "nuclear site" means—
            (a) so much of any premises in respect of which a nuclear site licence (within the meaning of the Nuclear Installations Act 1965) is for the time being in force as lies within the outer perimeter of the protection provided for those premises; and
            (b) so much of any other premises of which premises falling within paragraph (a) form a part as lies within that outer perimeter.
    (1C) For this purpose—
            (a) the outer perimeter of the protection provided for any premises is the line of the outermost fences, walls or other obstacles provided or relied on for protecting those premises from intruders; and
            (b) that line shall be determined on the assumption that every gate, door or other barrier across a way through a fence, wall or other obstacle is closed.
    (2) A "designated site" means a site—
            (a) specified or described (in any way) in an order made by the Secretary of State, and
            (b) designated for the purposes of this section by the order.
    (3) The Secretary of State may only designate a site for the purposes of this section if—
            (a) it is comprised in Crown land; or
            (b) it is comprised in land belonging to Her Majesty in Her private capacity or to the immediate heir to the Throne in his private capacity; or
            (c) it appears to the Secretary of State that it is appropriate to designate the site in the interests of national security.
    (4) It is a defence for a person charged with an offence under this section to prove that he did not know, and had no reasonable cause to suspect, that the site in relation to which the offence is alleged to have been committed was a designated site.
    (5) A person guilty of an offence under this section is liable on summary conviction—
            (a) to imprisonment for a term not exceeding 51 weeks, or
            (b) to a fine not exceeding level 5 on the standard scale,
        or to both.
    (6) No proceedings for an offence under this section may be instituted against any person—
            (a) in England and Wales, except by or with the consent of the Attorney General, or

(b) in Northern Ireland, except by or with the consent of the Attorney General for Northern Ireland.

(7) For the purposes of this section a person who is on any protected site as a trespasser does not cease to be a trespasser by virtue of being allowed time to leave the site.

(8) In this section—
  (a) "site" means the whole or part of any building or buildings, or any land, or both;
  (b) "Crown land" means land in which there is a Crown interest or a Duchy interest.

(9) For this purpose—
"Crown interest" means an interest belonging to Her Majesty in right of the Crown, and
"Duchy interest" means an interest belonging to Her Majesty in right of the Duchy of Lancaster or belonging to the Duchy of Cornwall.

(10) In the application of this section to Northern Ireland, the reference to 51 weeks in subsection (5)(a) is to be read as a reference to 6 months.

131 Designated sites: access

(1) The following provisions do not apply to land in respect of which a designation order is in force—
  (a) section 2(1) of the Countryside and Rights of Way Act 2000 (rights of public in relation to access land),
  . . .

(2) The Secretary of State may take such steps as he considers appropriate to inform the public of the effect of any designation order, including, in particular, displaying notices on or near the site to which the order relates.

(3) But the Secretary of State may only—
  (a) display any such notice, or
  (b) take any other steps under subsection (2),
  in or on any building or land, if the appropriate person consents.

(4) The "appropriate person" is—
  (a) a person appearing to the Secretary of State to have a sufficient interest in the building or land to consent to the notice being displayed or the steps being taken, or
  (b) a person acting on behalf of such a person.

(5) In this section a "designation order" means—
  (a) in relation to England and Wales or Northern Ireland, an order under section 128, or
  . . .

Demonstrations in vicinity of Parliament

132 Demonstrating without authorisation in designated area

(1) Any person who—
  (a) organises a demonstration in a public place in the designated area, or
  (b) takes part in a demonstration in a public place in the designated area, or
  (c) carries on a demonstration by himself in a public place in the designated area,
  is guilty of an offence if, when the demonstration starts, authorisation for the demonstration has not been given under section 134(2).

(2) It is a defence for a person accused of an offence under subsection (1) to show that he reasonably believed that authorisation had been given.

(3) Subsection (1) does not apply if the demonstration is—
  (a) a public procession of which notice is required to be given under subsection (1) of section 11 of the Public Order Act 1986, or of which (by virtue of subsection (2) of that section) notice is not required to be given, or
  (b) a public procession for the purposes of section 12 or 13 of that Act.

(4) Subsection (1) also does not apply in relation to any conduct which is lawful under section 220 of the Trade Union and Labour Relations (Consolidation) Act 1992.

(5) If subsection (1) does not apply by virtue of subsection (3) or (4), nothing in sections 133 to 136 applies either.

(6) Section 14 of the Public Order Act 1986 (imposition of conditions on public assemblies) does not apply in relation to a public assembly which is also a demonstration in a public place in the designated area.
(7) In this section and in sections 133 to 136—
    (a) "the designated area" means the area specified in an order under section 138,
    (b) "public place" means any highway or any place to which at the material time the public or any section of the public has access, on payment or otherwise, as of right or by virtue of express or implied permission,
    (c) references to any person organising a demonstration include a person participating in its organisation,
    (d) references to any person organising a demonstration do not include a person carrying on a demonstration by himself,
    (e) references to any person or persons taking part in a demonstration (except in subsection (1) of this section) include a person carrying on a demonstration by himself.

133 Notice of demonstrations in designated area
(1) A person seeking authorisation for a demonstration in the designated area must give written notice to that effect to the Commissioner of Police of the Metropolis (referred to in this section and section 134 as "the Commissioner").
(2) The notice must be given—
    (a) if reasonably practicable, not less than 6 clear days before the day on which the demonstration is to start, or
    (b) if that is not reasonably practicable, then as soon as it is, and in any event not less than 24 hours before the time the demonstration is to start.
(3) The notice must be given—
    (a) if the demonstration is to be carried on by more than one person, by any of the persons organising it,
    (b) if it is to be carried on by a person by himself, by that person.
(4) The notice must state—
    (a) the date and time when the demonstration is to start,
    (b) the place where it is to be carried on,
    (c) how long it is to last,
    (d) whether it is to be carried on by a person by himself or not,
    (e) the name and address of the person giving the notice.
(5) A notice under this section must be given by—
    (a) delivering it to a police station in the metropolitan police district, or
    (b) sending it by post by recorded delivery to such a police station.
(6) Section 7 of the Interpretation Act 1978 (under which service of a document is deemed to have been effected at the time it would be delivered in the ordinary course of post) does not apply to a notice under this section.

134 Authorisation of demonstrations in designated area
(1) This section applies if a notice complying with the requirements of section 133 is received at a police station in the metropolitan police district by the time specified in section 133(2).
(2) The Commissioner must give authorisation for the demonstration to which the notice relates.
(3) In giving authorisation, the Commissioner may impose on the persons organising or taking part in the demonstration such conditions specified in the authorisation and relating to the demonstration as in the Commissioner's reasonable opinion are necessary for the purpose of preventing any of the following—
    (a) hindrance to any person wishing to enter or leave the Palace of Westminster,
    (b) hindrance to the proper operation of Parliament,
    (c) serious public disorder,
    (d) serious damage to property,

(e) disruption to the life of the community,
(f) a security risk in any part of the designated area,
(g) risk to the safety of members of the public (including any taking part in the demonstration).

(4) The conditions may, in particular, impose requirements as to—
 (a) the place where the demonstration may, or may not, be carried on,
 (b) the times at which it may be carried on,
 (c) the period during which it may be carried on,
 (d) the number of persons who may take part in it,
 (e) the number and size of banners or placards used,
 (f) maximum permissible noise levels.

(5) The authorisation must specify the particulars of the demonstration given in the notice under section 133 pursuant to subsection (4) of that section, with any modifications made necessary by any condition imposed under subsection (3) of this section.

(6) The Commissioner must give notice in writing of—
 (a) the authorisation,
 (b) any conditions imposed under subsection (3), and
 (c) the particulars mentioned in subsection (5),
 to the person who gave the notice under section 133.

(7) Each person who takes part in or organises a demonstration in the designated area is guilty of an offence if —
 (a) he knowingly fails to comply with a condition imposed under subsection (3) which is applicable to him (except where it is varied under section 135), or
 (b) he knows or should have known that the demonstration is carried on otherwise than in accordance with the particulars set out in the authorisation by virtue of subsection (5).

(8) It is a defence for a person accused of an offence under subsection (7) to show—
 (a) (in a paragraph (a) case) that the failure to comply, or
 (b) (in a paragraph (b) case) that the divergence from the particulars,
 arose from circumstances beyond his control, or from something done with the agreement, or by the direction, of a police officer.

(9) The notice required by subsection (6) may be sent by post to the person who gave the notice under section 133 at the address stated in that notice pursuant to subsection (4)(e) of that section.

(10) If the person to whom the notice required by subsection (6) is to be given has agreed, it may be sent to him by email or by facsimile transmission at the address or number notified by him for the purpose to the Commissioner (and a notice so sent is "in writing" for the purposes of that subsection).

135 Supplementary directions

(1) This section applies if the senior police officer reasonably believes that it is necessary, in order to prevent any of the things mentioned in paragraphs (a) to (g) of subsection (3) of section 134—
 (a) to impose additional conditions on those taking part in or organising a demonstration authorised under that section, or
 (b) to vary any condition imposed under that subsection or under paragraph (a) (including such a condition as varied under subsection (2)).

(2) The senior police office may give directions to those taking part in or organising the demonstration imposing such additional conditions or varying any such condition already imposed.

(3) A person taking part in or organising the demonstration who knowingly fails to comply with a condition which is applicable to him and which is imposed or varied by a direction under this section is guilty of an offence.

(4) It is a defence for him to show that the failure to comply arose from circumstances beyond his control.

(5) In this section, "the senior police officer" means the most senior in rank of the police officers present at the scene (or any one of them if there are more than one of the same rank).

136 Offences under sections 132 to 135: penalties

(1) A person guilty of an offence under section 132(1)(a) is liable on summary conviction to imprisonment for a term not exceeding 51 weeks, to a fine not exceeding level 4 on the standard scale, or to both.

(2) A person guilty of an offence under section 132(1)(b) or (c) is liable on summary conviction to a fine not exceeding level 3 on the standard scale.

(3) A person guilty of an offence under section 134(7) or 135(3) is liable on summary conviction—
   (a) if the offence was in relation to his capacity as organiser of the demonstration, to imprisonment for a term not exceeding 51 weeks, to a fine not exceeding level 4 on the standard scale, or to both,
   (b) otherwise, to a fine not exceeding level 3 on the standard scale.

(4) A person who is guilty of the offence of inciting another to—
   (a) do anything which would constitute an offence mentioned in subsection (1), (2) or (3), or
   (b) fail to do anything where the failure would constitute such an offence,
is liable on summary conviction to imprisonment for a term not exceeding 51 weeks, to a fine not exceeding level 4 on the standard scale, or to both, notwithstanding section 45(3) of the Magistrates' Courts Act 1980.

(5) ...

137 Loudspeakers in designated area

(1) Subject to subsection (2), a loudspeaker shall not be operated, at any time or for any purpose, in a street in the designated area.

(2) Subsection (1) does not apply to the operation of a loudspeaker—
   (a) in case of emergency,
   (b) for police, fire and rescue authority or ambulance purposes,
   (c) by the Environment Agency, a water undertaker or a sewerage undertaker in the exercise of any of its functions,
   (d) by a local authority within its area,
   (e) for communicating with persons on a vessel for the purpose of directing the movement of that or any other vessel,
   (f) if the loudspeaker forms part of a public telephone system,
   (g) if the loudspeaker is in or fixed to a vehicle and subsection (3) applies,
   (h) otherwise than on a highway, by persons employed in connection with a transport undertaking used by the public, but only if the loudspeaker is operated solely for making announcements to passengers or prospective passengers or to other persons so employed,
   (i) in accordance with a consent granted by a local authority under Schedule 2 to the Noise and Statutory Nuisance Act 1993.

(3) This subsection applies if the loudspeaker referred to in subsection (2)(g)—
   (a) is operated solely for the entertainment of or for communicating with the driver or a passenger of the vehicle (or, if the loudspeaker is or forms part of the horn or similar warning instrument of the vehicle, solely for giving warning to other traffic), and
   (b) is so operated as not to give reasonable cause for annoyance to persons in the vicinity.

(4) A person who operates or permits the operation of a loudspeaker in contravention of subsection (1) is guilty of an offence and is liable on summary conviction to—
   (a) a fine not exceeding level 5 on the standard scale, together with
   (b) a further fine not exceeding £50 for each day on which the offence continues after the conviction.

(5) In this section—

"local authority" means a London borough council (and, in subsection (2)(d), the Greater London Authority),

"street" means a street within the meaning of section 48(1) of the New Roads and Street Works Act 1991 which is for the time being open to the public,

"the designated area" means the area specified in an order under section 138,

"vessel" includes a hovercraft within the meaning of the Hovercraft Act 1968.

(6) In Schedule 2 to the Noise and Statutory Nuisance Act 1993 (consent to the operation of loudspeakers in streets or roads), in paragraph 1(1), at the end add "or of section 137(1) of the Serious Organised Crime and Police Act 2005".

138 The designated area

(1) The Secretary of State may by order specify an area as the designated area for the purposes of sections 132 to 137.

(2) The area may be specified by description, by reference to a map or in any other way.

(3) No point in the area so specified may be more than one kilometre in a straight line from the point nearest to it in Parliament Square.

EQUALITY ACT 2006
(2006, c. 3)

An Act to make provision for the establishment of the Commission for Equality and Human Rights; to dissolve the Equal Opportunities Commission, the Commission for Racial Equality and the Disability Rights Commission; to make provision about discrimination on grounds of religion or belief; to enable provision to be made about discrimination on grounds of sexual orientation; to impose duties relating to sex discrimination on persons performing public functions; to amend the Disability Discrimination Act 1995; and for connected purposes. [16 February 2006]

PART 1
THE COMMISSION FOR EQUALITY AND HUMAN RIGHTS

The Commission

1 Establishment

There shall be a body corporate known as the Commission for Equality and Human Rights.

3 General duty

The Commission shall exercise its functions under this Part with a view to encouraging and supporting the development of a society in which—

(a) people's ability to achieve their potential is not limited by prejudice or discrimination,
(b) there is respect for and protection of each individual's human rights,
(c) there is respect for the dignity and worth of each individual,
(d) each individual has an equal opportunity to participate in society, and
(e) there is mutual respect between groups based on understanding and valuing of diversity and on shared respect for equality and human rights.

4 Strategic plan

(1) The Commission shall prepare a plan showing—
   (a) activities or classes of activity to be undertaken by the Commission in pursuance of its functions under this Act,
   (b) an expected timetable for each activity or class, and
   (c) priorities for different activities or classes, or principles to be applied in determining priorities.

(2) The Commission shall review the plan—
   (a) at least once during the period of three years beginning with its completion,
   (b) at least once during each period of three years beginning with the completion of a review, and
   (c) at such other times as the Commission thinks appropriate.

    (3)   If the Commission thinks it appropriate as a result of a review, the Commission shall revise the plan.

    (4)   The Commission shall send the plan and each revision to the Minister, who shall lay a copy before Parliament.

    (5)   The Commission shall publish the plan and each revision.

Duties

8 Equality and diversity

(1) The Commission shall, by exercising the powers conferred by this Part—
    (a)   promote understanding of the importance of equality and diversity,
    (b)   encourage good practice in relation to equality and diversity,
    (c)   promote equality of opportunity,
    (d)   promote awareness and understanding of rights under the equality enactments,
    (e)   enforce the equality enactments,
    (f)   work towards the elimination of unlawful discrimination, and
    (g)   work towards the elimination of unlawful harassment.

(2) In subsection (1)—
"diversity" means the fact that individuals are different,
"equality" means equality between individuals, and
"unlawful" is to be construed in accordance with section 34.

(3) In promoting equality of opportunity between disabled persons and others, the Commission may, in particular, promote the favourable treatment of disabled persons.

(4) In this Part "disabled person" means a person who—
    (a)   is a disabled person within the meaning of the Disability Discrimination Act 1995, or
    (b)   has been a disabled person within that meaning (whether or not at a time when that Act had effect).

9 Human rights

(1) The Commission shall, by exercising the powers conferred by this Part—
    (a)   promote understanding of the importance of human rights,
    (b)   encourage good practice in relation to human rights,
    (c)   promote awareness, understanding and protection of human rights, and
    (d)   encourage public authorities to comply with section 6 of the Human Rights Act 1998 (compliance with Convention rights).

(2) In this Part "human rights" means—
    (a)   the Convention rights within the meaning given by section 1 of the Human Rights Act 1998, and
    (b)   other human rights.

(3) In determining what action to take in pursuance of this section the Commission shall have particular regard to the importance of exercising the powers conferred by this Part in relation to the Convention rights.

(4) In fulfilling a duty under section 8 or 10 the Commission shall take account of any relevant human rights.

(5) A reference in this Part (including this section) to human rights does not exclude any matter by reason only of its being a matter to which section 8 or 10 relates.

10 Groups

(1) The Commission shall, by exercising the powers conferred by this Part—
    (a) promote understanding of the importance of good relations—
        (i)   between members of different groups, and
        (ii)   between members of groups and others,
    (b)   encourage good practice in relation to relations—
        (i)   between members of different groups, and
        (ii)   between members of groups and others,

(c) work towards the elimination of prejudice against, hatred of and hostility towards members of groups, and
(d) work towards enabling members of groups to participate in society.
(2) In this Part "group" means a group or class of persons who share a common attribute in respect of any of the following matters—
   (a) age,
   (b) disability,
   (c) gender,
   (d) proposed, commenced or completed reassignment of gender (within the meaning given by section 82(1) of the Sex Discrimination Act 1975),
   (e) race,
   (f) religion or belief, and
   (g) sexual orientation.
(3) For the purposes of this Part a reference to a group (as defined in subsection (2)) includes a reference to a smaller group or smaller class, within a group, of persons who share a common attribute (in addition to the attribute by reference to which the group is defined) in respect of any of the matters specified in subsection (2)(a) to (g).
(4) In determining what action to take in pursuance of this section the Commission shall have particular regard to the importance of exercising the powers conferred by this Part in relation to groups defined by reference to race, religion or belief.
(5) The Commission may, in taking action in pursuance of subsection (1) in respect of groups defined by reference to disability and others, promote or encourage the favourable treatment of disabled persons.
(6) The Minister may by order amend the list in subsection (2) so as to—
   (a) add an entry, or
   (b) vary an entry.
(7) This section is without prejudice to the generality of section 8.

11 Monitoring the law
(1) The Commission shall monitor the effectiveness of the equality and human rights enactments.
(2) The Commission may—
   (a) advise central government about the effectiveness of any of the equality and human rights enactments;
   (b) recommend to central government the amendment, repeal, consolidation (with or without amendments) or replication (with or without amendments) of any of the equality and human rights enactments;
   (c) advise central or devolved government about the effect of an enactment (including an enactment in or under an Act of the Scottish Parliament);
   (d) advise central or devolved government about the likely effect of a proposed change of law.
(3) In this section—
   (a) "central government" means Her Majesty's Government,
   (b) "devolved government" means—
      (i) the Scottish Ministers, and
      (ii) the Welsh Assembly Government, and
   (c) a reference to the equality enactments shall be treated as including a reference to any provision of this Act.

General powers

13 Information, advice, &c.
(1) In pursuance of its duties under sections 8 to 10 the Commission may—
   (a) publish or otherwise disseminate ideas or information;
   (b) undertake research;
   (c) provide education or training;

(d) give advice or guidance (whether about the effect or operation of an enactment or otherwise);
(e) arrange for a person to do anything within paragraphs (a) to (d);
(f) act jointly with, co-operate with or assist a person doing anything within paragraphs (a) to (d).
(2) The reference to giving advice in subsection (1)(d) does not include a reference to preparing, or assisting in the preparation of, a document to be used for the purpose of legal proceedings.

Enforcement powers

20 Investigations

(1) The Commission may investigate whether or not a person—
    (a) has committed an unlawful act,
    (b) has complied with a requirement imposed by an unlawful act notice under section 21, or
    (c) has complied with an undertaking given under section 23.
(2) The Commission may conduct an investigation under subsection (1)(a) only if it suspects that the person concerned may have committed an unlawful act.
(3) A suspicion for the purposes of subsection (2) may (but need not) be based on the results of, or a matter arising during the course of, an inquiry under section 16.
(4) Before settling a report of an investigation recording a finding that a person has committed an unlawful act or has failed to comply with a requirement or undertaking the Commission shall—
    (a) send a draft of the report to the person,
    (b) specify a period of at least 28 days during which he may make written representations about the draft, and
    (c) consider any representations made.
(5) Schedule 2 makes supplemental provision about investigations.

TERRORISM ACT 2006
(2006, c. 11)

An Act to make provision for and about offences relating to conduct carried out or capable of being carried out, for purposes connected with terrorism; to amend enactments relating to terrorism; and for connected purposes. [30 March 2006]

PART 1
OFFENCES

Encouragement etc. of terrorism

1 Encouragement of terrorism

(1) This section applies to a statement that is likely to be understood by some or all of the members of the public to whom it is published as a direct or indirect encouragement or other inducement to them to the commission, preparation or instigation of acts of terrorism or Convention offences.
(2) A person commits an offence if—
    (a) he publishes a statement to which this section applies or causes another to publish such a statement; and
    (b) at the time he publishes it or causes it to be published, he—
        (i) intends members of the public to be directly or indirectly encouraged or otherwise induced by the statement to commit, prepare or instigate acts of terrorism or Convention offences; or
        (ii) is reckless as to whether members of the public will be directly or indirectly encouraged or otherwise induced by the statement to commit, prepare or insti-

gate such acts or offences.
(3) For the purposes of this section, the statements that are likely to be understood by members of the public as indirectly encouraging the commission or preparation of acts of terrorism or Convention offences include every statement which—
    (a) glorifies the commission or preparation (whether in the past, in the future or generally) of such acts or offences; and
    (b) is a statement from which those members of the public could reasonably be expected to infer that what is being glorified is being glorified as conduct that should be emulated by them in existing circumstances.
(4) For the purposes of this section the questions how a statement is likely to be understood and what members of the public could reasonably be expected to infer from it must be determined having regard both—
    (a) to the contents of the statement as a whole; and
    (b) to the circumstances and manner of its publication.
(5) It is irrelevant for the purposes of subsections (1) to (3)—
    (a) whether anything mentioned in those subsections relates to the commission, preparation or instigation of one or more particular acts of terrorism or Convention offences, of acts of terrorism or Convention offences of a particular description or of acts of terrorism or Convention offences generally; and,
    (b) whether any person is in fact encouraged or induced by the statement to commit, prepare or instigate any such act or offence.
(6) In proceedings for an offence under this section against a person in whose case it is not proved that he intended the statement directly or indirectly to encourage or otherwise induce the commission, preparation or instigation of acts of terrorism or Convention offences, it is a defence for him to show—
    (a) that the statement neither expressed his views nor had his endorsement (whether by virtue of section 3 or otherwise); and
    (b) that it was clear, in all the circumstances of the statement's publication, that it did not express his views and (apart from the possibility of his having been given and failed to comply with a notice under subsection (3) of that section) did not have his endorsement.
(7) A person guilty of an offence under this section shall be liable—
    (a) on conviction on indictment, to imprisonment for a term not exceeding 7 years or to a fine, or to both;
    (b) on summary conviction in England and Wales, to imprisonment for a term not exceeding 12 months or to a fine not exceeding the statutory maximum, or to both;
    (c) on summary conviction in Scotland or Northern Ireland, to imprisonment for a term not exceeding 6 months or to a fine not exceeding the statutory maximum, or to both.
(8) In relation to an offence committed before the commencement of section 154(1) of the Criminal Justice Act 2003, the reference in subsection (7)(b) to 12 months is to be read as a reference to 6 months.

2 Dissemination of terrorist publications
(1) A person commits an offence if he engages in conduct falling within subsection (2) and, at the time he does so—
    (a) he intends an effect of his conduct to be a direct or indirect encouragement or other inducement to the commission, preparation or instigation of acts of terrorism;
    (b) he intends an effect of his conduct to be the provision of assistance in the commission or preparation of such acts; or
    (c) he is reckless as to whether his conduct has an effect mentioned in paragraph (a) or (b).
(2) For the purposes of this section a person engages in conduct falling within this subsection if he—
    (a) distributes or circulates a terrorist publication;
    (b) gives, sells or lends such a publication;
    (c) offers such a publication for sale or loan;

(d) provides a service to others that enables them to obtain, read, listen to or look at such a publication, or to acquire it by means of a gift, sale or loan;
(e) transmits the contents of such a publication electronically; or
(f) has such a publication in his possession with a view to its becoming the subject of conduct falling within any of paragraphs (a) to (e).

(3) For the purposes of this section a publication is a terrorist publication, in relation to conduct falling within subsection (2), if matter contained in it is likely—
(a) to be understood, by some or all of the persons to whom it is or may become available as a consequence of that conduct, as a direct or indirect encouragement or other inducement to them to the commission, preparation or instigation of acts of terrorism; or
(b) to be useful in the commission or preparation of such acts and to be understood, by some or all of those persons, as contained in the publication, or made available to them, wholly or mainly for the purpose of being so useful to them.

(4) For the purposes of this section matter that is likely to be understood by a person as indirectly encouraging the commission or preparation of acts of terrorism includes any matter which—
(a) glorifies the commission or preparation (whether in the past, in the future or generally) of such acts; and
(b) is matter from which that person could reasonably be expected to infer that what is being glorified is being glorified as conduct that should be emulated by him in existing circumstances.

(5) For the purposes of this section the question whether a publication is a terrorist publication in relation to particular conduct must be determined—
(a) as at the time of that conduct; and
(b) having regard both to the contents of the publication as a whole and to the circumstances in which that conduct occurs.

(6) In subsection (1) references to the effect of a person's conduct in relation to a terrorist publication include references to an effect of the publication on one or more persons to whom it is or may become available as a consequence of that conduct.

(7) It is irrelevant for the purposes of this section whether anything mentioned in subsections (1) to (4) is in relation to the commission, preparation or instigation of one or more particular acts of terrorism, of acts of terrorism of a particular description or of acts of terrorism generally.

(8) For the purposes of this section it is also irrelevant, in relation to matter contained in any article whether any person—
(a) is in fact encouraged or induced by that matter to commit, prepare or instigate acts of terrorism; or
(b) in fact makes use of it in the commission or preparation of such acts.

(9) In proceedings for an offence under this section against a person in respect of conduct to which subsection (10) applies, it is a defence for him to show—
(a) that the matter by reference to which the publication in question was a terrorist publication neither expressed his views nor had his endorsement (whether by virtue of section 3 or otherwise); and
(b) that it was clear, in all the circumstances of the conduct, that that matter did not express his views and (apart from the possibility of his having been given and failed to comply with a notice under subsection (3) of that section) did not have his endorsement.

(10) This subsection applies to the conduct of a person to the extent that—
(a) the publication to which his conduct related contained matter by reference to which it was a terrorist publication by virtue of subsection (3)(a); and
(b) that person is not proved to have engaged in that conduct with the intention specified in subsection (1)(a).

(11) A person guilty of an offence under this section shall be liable—

(a) on conviction on indictment, to imprisonment for a term not exceeding 7 years or to a fine, or to both;
(b) on summary conviction in England and Wales, to imprisonment for a term not exceeding 12 months or to a fine not exceeding the statutory maximum, or to both;
(c) on summary conviction in Scotland or Northern Ireland, to imprisonment for a term not exceeding 6 months or to a fine not exceeding the statutory maximum, or to both.

(12) In relation to an offence committed before the commencement of section 154(1) of the Criminal Justice Act 2003, the reference in subsection (11)(b) to 12 months is to be read as a reference to 6 months.

(13) In this section—
"lend" includes let on hire, and "loan" is to be construed accordingly;
"publication" means an article or record of any description that contains any of the following, or any combination of them—
(a) matter to be read;
(b) matter to be listened to;
(c) matter to be looked at or watched.

3 Application of ss. 1 and 2 to internet activity etc.

(1) This section applies for the purposes of sections 1 and 2 in relation to cases where—
(a) a statement is published or caused to be published in the course of, or in connection with, the provision or use of a service provided electronically; or
(b) conduct falling within section 2(2) was in the course of, or in connection with, the provision or use of such a service.

(2) The cases in which the statement, or the article or record to which the conduct relates, is to be regarded as having the endorsement of a person ("the relevant person") at any time include a case in which—
(a) a constable has given him a notice under subsection (3);
(b) that time falls more than 2 working days after the day on which the notice was given; and
(c) the relevant person has failed, without reasonable excuse, to comply with the notice.

(3) A notice under this subsection is a notice which—
(a) declares that, in the opinion of the constable giving it, the statement or the article or record is unlawfully terrorism-related;
(b) requires the relevant person to secure that the statement or the article or record, so far as it is so related, is not available to the public or is modified so as no longer to be so related;
(c) warns the relevant person that a failure to comply with the notice within 2 working days will result in the statement, or the article or record, being regarded as having his endorsement; and
(d) explains how, under subsection (4), he may become liable by virtue of the notice if the statement, or the article or record, becomes available to the public after he has complied with the notice.

(4) Where—
(a) a notice under subsection (3) has been given to the relevant person in respect of a statement, or an article or record, and he has complied with it, but
(b) he subsequently publishes or causes to be published a statement which is, or is for all practical purposes, the same or to the same effect as the statement to which the notice related, or to matter contained in the article or record to which it related, (a "repeat statement");
the requirements of subsection (2)(a) to (c) shall be regarded as satisfied in the case of the repeat statement in relation to the times of its subsequent publication by the relevant person.

(5) In proceedings against a person for an offence under section 1 or 2 the requirements of subsection (2)(a) to (c) are not, in his case, to be regarded as satisfied in relation to any time by virtue of subsection (4) if he shows that he—

(a) has, before that time, taken every step he reasonably could to prevent a repeat statement from becoming available to the public and to ascertain whether it does; and
(b) was, at that time, a person to whom subsection (6) applied.
(6) This subsection applies to a person at any time when he—
(a) is not aware of the publication of the repeat statement; or
(b) having become aware of its publication, has taken every step that he reasonably could to secure that it either ceased to be available to the public or was modified as mentioned in subsection (3)(b).
(7) For the purposes of this section a statement or an article or record is unlawfully terrorism-related if it constitutes, or if matter contained in the article or record constitutes—
(a) something that is likely to be understood, by any one or more of the persons to whom it has or may become available, as a direct or indirect encouragement or other inducement to the commission, preparation or instigation of acts of terrorism or Convention offences; or
(b) information which—
(i) is likely to be useful to any one or more of those persons in the commission or preparation of such acts; and
(ii) is in a form or context in which it is likely to be understood by any one or more of those persons as being wholly or mainly for the purpose of being so useful.
(8) The reference in subsection (7) to something that is likely to be understood as an indirect encouragement to the commission or preparation of acts of terrorism or Convention offences includes anything which is likely to be understood as—
(a) the glorification of the commission or preparation (whether in the past, in the future or generally) of such acts or such offences; and
(b) a suggestion that what is being glorified is being glorified as conduct that should be emulated in existing circumstances.
(9) In this section "working day" means any day other than—
(a) a Saturday or a Sunday;
(b) Christmas Day or Good Friday; or
(c) a day which is a bank holiday under the Banking and Financial Dealings Act 1971 in any part of the United Kingdom.

4 **Giving of notices under s. 3**
(1) Except in a case to which any of subsections (2) to (4) applies, a notice under section 3(3) may be given to a person only—
(a) by delivering it to him in person; or
(b) by sending it to him, by means of a postal service providing for delivery to be recorded, at his last known address.
(2) Such a notice may be given to a body corporate only—
(a) by delivering it to the secretary of that body in person; or
(b) by sending it to the appropriate person, by means of a postal service providing for delivery to be recorded, at the address of the registered or principal office of the body.
(3) Such a notice may be given to a firm only—
(a) by delivering it to a partner of the firm in person;
(b) by so delivering it to a person having the control or management of the partnership business; or
(c) by sending it to the appropriate person, by means of a postal service providing for delivery to be recorded, at the address of the principal office of the partnership.
(4) Such a notice may be given to an unincorporated body or association only—
(a) by delivering it to a member of its governing body in person; or
(b) by sending it to the appropriate person, by means of a postal service providing for delivery to be recorded, at the address of the principal office of the body or association.
(5) In the case of—
(a) a company registered outside the United Kingdom,

(b) a firm carrying on business outside the United Kingdom, or
(c) an unincorporated body or association with offices outside the United Kingdom,
the references in this section to its principal office include references to its principal office within the United Kingdom (if any).

(6) In this section "the appropriate person" means—
   (a) in the case of a body corporate, the body itself or its secretary;
   (b) in the case of a firm, the firm itself or a partner of the firm or a person having the control or management of the partnership business; and
   (c) in the case of an unincorporated body or association, the body or association itself or a member of its governing body.

(7) For the purposes of section 3 the time at which a notice under subsection (3) of that section is to be regarded as given is—
   (a) where it is delivered to a person, the time at which it is so delivered; and
   (b) where it is sent by a postal service providing for delivery to be recorded, the time recorded as the time of its delivery.

(8) In this section "secretary", in relation to a body corporate, means the secretary or other equivalent officer of the body.

Preparation of terrorist acts and terrorist training

5 Preparation of terrorist acts

(1) A person commits an offence if, with the intention of—
   (a) committing acts of terrorism, or
   (b) assisting another to commit such acts,
   he engages in any conduct in preparation for giving effect to his intention.

(2) It is irrelevant for the purposes of subsection (1) whether the intention and preparations relate to one or more particular acts of terrorism, acts of terrorism of a particular description or acts of terrorism generally.

(3) A person guilty of an offence under this section shall be liable, on conviction on indictment, to imprisonment for life.

6 Training for terrorism

(1) A person commits an offence if—
   (a) he provides instruction or training in any of the skills mentioned in subsection (3); and
   (b) at the time he provides the instruction or training, he knows that a person receiving it intends to use the skills in which he is being instructed or trained—
      (i) for or in connection with the commission or preparation of acts of terrorism or Convention offences; or
      (ii) for assisting the commission or preparation by others of such acts or offences.

(2) A person commits an offence if—
   (a) he receives instruction or training in any of the skills mentioned in subsection (3); and
   (b) at the time of the instruction or training, he intends to use the skills in which he is being instructed or trained—
      (i) for or in connection with the commission or preparation of acts of terrorism or Convention offences; or
      (ii) for assisting the commission or preparation by others of such acts or offences.

(3) The skills are—
   (a) the making, handling or use of a noxious substance, or of substances of a description of such substances;
   (b) the use of any method or technique for doing anything else that is capable of being done for the purposes of terrorism, in connection with the commission or preparation of an act of terrorism or Convention offence or in connection with assisting the commission or preparation by another of such an act or offence; and
   (c) the design or adaptation for the purposes of terrorism, or in connection with the commission or preparation of an act of terrorism or Convention offence, of any method or technique for doing anything.

(4) It is irrelevant for the purposes of subsections (1) and (2)—
  (a) whether any instruction or training that is provided is provided to one or more particular persons or generally;
  (b) whether the acts or offences in relation to which a person intends to use skills in which he is instructed or trained consist of one or more particular acts of terrorism or Convention offences, acts of terrorism or Convention offences of a particular description or acts of terrorism or Convention offences generally; and
  (c) whether assistance that a person intends to provide to others is intended to be provided to one or more particular persons or to one or more persons whose identities are not yet known.
(5) A person guilty of an offence under this section shall be liable-
  (a) on conviction on indictment, to imprisonment for a term not exceeding 10 years or to a fine, or to both;
  (b) on summary conviction in England and Wales, to imprisonment for a term not exceeding 12 months or to a fine not exceeding the statutory maximum, or to both;
  (c) on summary conviction in Scotland or Northern Ireland, to imprisonment for a term not exceeding 6 months or to a fine not exceeding the statutory maximum, or to both.
(6) In relation to an offence committed before the commencement of section 154(1) of the Criminal Justice Act 2003, the reference in subsection (5)(b) to 12 months is to be read as a reference to 6 months.
(7) In this section—
  "noxious substance" means—
  (a) a dangerous substance within the meaning of Part 7 of the Anti-terrorism, Crime and Security Act 2001; or
  (b) any other substance which is hazardous or noxious or which may be or become hazardous or noxious only in certain circumstances;
  "substance" includes any natural or artificial substance (whatever its origin or method of production and whether in solid or liquid form or in the form of a gas or vapour) and any mixture of substances.

7 Powers of forfeiture in respect of offences under s. 6

(1) A court before which a person is convicted of an offence under section 6 may order the forfeiture of anything the court considers to have been in the person's possession for purposes connected with the offence.
(2) Before making an order under subsection (1) in relation to anything the court must give an opportunity of being heard to any person (in addition to the convicted person) who claims to be the owner of that thing or otherwise to have an interest in it.
(3) An order under subsection (1) may not be made so as to come into force at any time before there is no further possibility (disregarding any power to grant permission for the bringing of an appeal out of time) of the order's being varied or set aside on appeal.
(4) Where a court makes an order under subsection (1), it may also make such other provision as appears to it to be necessary for giving effect to the forfeiture.
(5) That provision may include, in particular, provision relating to the retention, handling, destruction or other disposal of what is forfeited.
(6) Provision made by virtue of this section may be varied at any time by the court that made it.

8 Attendance at a place used for terrorist training

(1) A person commits an offence if—
  (a) he attends at any place, whether in the United Kingdom or elsewhere;
  (b) while he is at that place, instruction or training of the type mentioned in section 6(1) of this Act or section 54(1) of the Terrorism Act 2000 (weapons training) is provided there;
  (c) that instruction or training is provided there wholly or partly for purposes connected with the commission or preparation of acts of terrorism or Convention offences; and
  (d) the requirements of subsection (2) are satisfied in relation to that person.

(2) The requirements of this subsection are satisfied in relation to a person if—
   (a) he knows or believes that instruction or training is being provided there wholly or partly for purposes connected with the commission or preparation of acts of terrorism or Convention offences; or
   (b) a person attending at that place throughout the period of that person's attendance could not reasonably have failed to understand that instruction or training was being provided there wholly or partly for such purposes.
(3) It is immaterial for the purposes of this section—
   (a) whether the person concerned receives the instruction or training himself; and
   (b) whether the instruction or training is provided for purposes connected with one or more particular acts of terrorism or Convention offences, acts of terrorism or Convention offences of a particular description or acts of terrorism or Convention offences generally.
(4) A person guilty of an offence under this section shall be liable-
   (a) on conviction on indictment, to imprisonment for a term not exceeding 10 years or to a fine, or to both;
   (b) on summary conviction in England and Wales, to imprisonment for a term not exceeding 12 months or to a fine not exceeding the statutory maximum, or to both;
   (c) on summary conviction in Scotland or Northern Ireland, to imprisonment for a term not exceeding 6 months or to a fine not exceeding the statutory maximum, or to both..
(5) In relation to an offence committed before the commencement of section 154(1) of the Criminal Justice Act 2003, the reference in subsection (4)(b) to 12 months is to be read as a reference to 6 months.
(6) References in this section to instruction or training being provided include references to its being made available.

Offences involving radioactive devices and materials and nuclear facilities and sites

9 Making and possession of devices or materials

(1) A person commits an offence if—
   (a) he makes or has in his possession a radioactive device, or
   (b) he has in his possession radioactive material,
   with the intention of using the device or material in the course of or in connection with the commission or preparation of an act of terrorism or for the purposes of terrorism, or of making it available to be so used.
(2) It is irrelevant for the purposes of subsection (1) whether the act of terrorism to which an intention relates is a particular act of terrorism, an act of terrorism of a particular description or an act of terrorism generally.
(3) A person guilty of an offence under this section shall be liable, on conviction on indictment, to imprisonment for life.
(4) In this section—
   "radioactive device" means—
   (a) a nuclear weapon or other nuclear explosive device;
   (b) a radioactive material dispersal device;
   (c) a radiation-emitting device;
   "radioactive material" means nuclear material or any other radioactive substance which—
   (a) contains nuclides that undergo spontaneous disintegration in a process accompanied by the emission of one or more types of ionising radiation, such as alpha radiation, beta radiation, neutron particles or gamma rays; and
   (b) is capable, owing to its radiological or fissile properties, of—
      (i) causing serious bodily injury to a person;
      (ii) causing serious damage to property;
      (iii) endangering a person's life; or
      (iv) creating a serious risk to the health or safety of the public.
(5) In subsection (4)—

"device" includes any of the following, whether or not fixed to land, namely, machinery, equipment, appliances, tanks, containers, pipes and conduits;
"nuclear material" has the same meaning as in the Nuclear Material (Offences) Act 1983 (see section 6 of that Act).

10 Misuse of devices or material and misuse and damage of facilities

(1) A person commits an offence if he uses—
  (a) a radioactive device, or
  (b) radioactive material,
in the course of or in connection with the commission of an act of terrorism or for the purposes of terrorism.

(2) A person commits an offence if, in the course of or in connection with the commission of an act of terrorism or for the purposes of terrorism, he uses or damages a nuclear facility in a manner which—
  (a) causes a release of radioactive material; or
  (b) creates or increases a risk that such material will be released.

(3) A person guilty of an offence under this section shall be liable, on conviction on indictment, to imprisonment for life.

(4) In this section—
"nuclear facility" means—
  (a) a nuclear reactor, including a reactor installed in or on any transportation device for use as an energy source in order to propel it or for any other purpose; or
  (b) a plant or conveyance being used for the production, storage, processing or transport of radioactive material;
"radioactive device" and "radioactive material" have the same meanings as in section 9.

(5) In subsection (4)—
"nuclear reactor" has the same meaning as in the Nuclear Installations Act 1965 (see section 26 of that Act);
"transportation device" means any vehicle or any space object (within the meaning of the Outer Space Act 1986).

11 Terrorist threats relating to devices, materials or facilities

(1) A person commits an offence if, in the course of or in connection with the commission of an act of terrorism or for the purposes of terrorism—
  (a) he makes a demand—
    (i) for the supply to himself or to another of a radioactive device or of radioactive material;
    (ii) for a nuclear facility to be made available to himself or to another; or
    (iii) for access to such a facility to be given to himself or to another;
  (b) he supports the demand with a threat that he or another will take action if the demand is not met; and
  (c) the circumstances and manner of the threat are such that it is reasonable for the person to whom it is made to assume that there is real risk that the threat will be carried out if the demand is not met.

(2) A person also commits an offence if—
  (a) he makes a threat falling within subsection (3) in the course of or in connection with the commission of an act of terrorism or for the purposes of terrorism; and
  (b) the circumstances and manner of the threat are such that it is reasonable for the person to whom it is made to assume that there is real risk that the threat will be carried out, or would be carried out if demands made in association with the threat are not met.

(3) A threat falls within this subsection if it is—
  (a) a threat to use radioactive material;
  (b) a threat to use a radioactive device; or
  (c) a threat to use or damage a nuclear facility in a manner that releases radioactive material or creates or increases a risk that such material will be released.

(4) A person guilty of an offence under this section shall be liable, on conviction on indictment, to imprisonment for life.
(5) In this section—
"nuclear facility" has the same meaning as in section 10;
"radioactive device" and "radioactive material" have the same meanings as in section 9.

17 Commission of offences abroad
(1) If—
- (a) a person does anything outside the United Kingdom, and
- (b) his action, if done in a part of the United Kingdom, would constitute an offence falling within subsection (2),

he shall be guilty in that part of the United Kingdom of the offence.

(2) The offences falling within this subsection are—
- (a) an offence under section 1 or 6 of this Act so far as it is committed in relation to any statement, instruction or training in relation to which that section has effect by reason of its relevance to the commission, preparation or instigation of one or more Convention offences;
- (b) an offence under any of sections 8 to 11 of this Act;
- (c) an offence under section 11(1) of the Terrorism Act 2000 (membership of proscribed organisations);
- (d) an offence under section 54 of that Act (weapons training);
- (e) conspiracy to commit an offence falling within this subsection;
- (f) inciting a person to commit such an offence;
- (g) attempting to commit such an offence;
- (h) aiding, abetting, counselling or procuring the commission of such an offence.

(3) Subsection (1) applies irrespective of whether the person is a British citizen or, in the case of a company, a company incorporated in a part of the United Kingdom.

(4) In the case of an offence falling within subsection (2) which is committed wholly or partly outside the United Kingdom—
- (a) proceedings for the offence may be taken at any place in the United Kingdom; and
- (b) the offence may for all incidental purposes be treated as having been committed at any such place.

...

18 Liability of company directors etc.
(1) Where an offence under this Part is committed by a body corporate and is proved to have been committed with the consent or connivance of—
- (a) a director, manager, secretary or other similar officer of the body corporate, or
- (b) a person who was purporting to act in any such capacity,

he (as well as the body corporate) is guilty of that offence and shall be liable to be proceeded against and punished accordingly.

(2) Where an offence under this Part—
- (a) is committed by a Scottish firm, and
- (b) is proved to have been committed with the consent or connivance of a partner of the firm,

he (as well as the firm) is guilty of that offence and shall be liable to be proceeded against and punished accordingly.

(3) In this section "director", in relation to a body corporate whose affairs are managed by its members, means a member of the body corporate.

19 Consents to prosecutions
(1) Proceedings for an offence under this Part—
- (a) may be instituted in England and Wales only with the consent of the Director of Public Prosecutions; and

...

(2) But if it appears to the Director of Public Prosecutions or the Director of Public Prosecutions for Northern Ireland that an offence under this Part has been committed for a purpose wholly or partly connected with the affairs of a country other than the United Kingdom, his consent for the purposes of this section may be given only with the permission—
(a) in the case of the Director of Public Prosecutions, of the Attorney General; and
. . .

. . .

Interpretation of Part 1

20 Interpretation of Part 1
(1) Expressions used in this Part and in the Terrorism Act 2000 have the same meanings in this Part as in that Act.
. . .

IDENTITY CARDS ACT 2006
(2006, c. 15)

An Act to make provision for a national scheme of registration of individuals and for the issue of cards capable of being used for identifying registered individuals; to make it an offence for a person to be in possession or control of an identity document to which he is not entitled, or of apparatus, articles or materials for making false identity documents; to amend the Consular Fees Act 1980; to make provision facilitating the verification of information provided with an application for a passport; and for connected purposes. [30 March 2006]

Note: These provisions are not yet in force.

Registration

1 The National Identity Register
(1) It shall be the duty of the Secretary of State to establish and maintain a register of individuals (to be known as "the National Identity Register").
(2) The purposes for which the Register is to be established and maintained are confined to the statutory purposes.
(3) The statutory purposes are to facilitate, by the maintenance of a secure and reliable record of registrable facts about individuals in the United Kingdom—
(a) the provision of a convenient method for such individuals to prove registrable facts about themselves to others who reasonably require proof; and
(b) the provision of a secure and reliable method for registrable facts about such individuals to be ascertained or verified wherever that is necessary in the public interest.
(4) For the purposes of this Act something is necessary in the public interest if, and only if, it is—
(a) in the interests of national security;
(b) for the purposes of the prevention or detection of crime;
(c) for the purposes of the enforcement of immigration controls;
(d) for the purposes of the enforcement of prohibitions on unauthorised working or employment; or
(e) for the purpose of securing the efficient and effective provision of public services.
(5) In this Act "registrable fact", in relation to an individual, means—
(a) his identity;
(b) the address of his principal place of residence in the United Kingdom;
(c) the address of every other place in the United Kingdom or elsewhere where he has a place of residence;
(d) where in the United Kingdom and elsewhere he has previously been resident;

(e) the times at which he was resident at different places in the United Kingdom or elsewhere;
(f) his current residential status;
(g) residential statuses previously held by him;
(h) information about numbers allocated to him for identification purposes and about the documents to which they relate;
(i) information about occasions on which information recorded about him in the Register has been provided to any person; and
(j) information recorded in the Register at his request.
(6) But the registrable facts falling within subsection (5)(h) do not include any sensitive personal data (within the meaning of the Data Protection Act 1998) or anything the disclosure of which would tend to reveal such data.
(7) In this section references to an individual's identity are references to—
(a) his full name;
(b) other names by which he is or has previously been known;
(c) his gender;
(d) his date and place of birth and, if he has died, the date of his death; and
(e) external characteristics of his that are capable of being used for identifying him.
(8) In this section "residential status", in relation to an individual, means—
(a) his nationality;
(b) his entitlement to remain in the United Kingdom; and
(c) where that entitlement derives from a grant of leave to enter or remain in the United Kingdom, the terms and conditions of that leave.

2 Individuals entered in Register

(1) An entry must be made in the Register for every individual who—
(a) is entitled to be entered in it; and
(b) applies to be entered in it.
(2) The individuals entitled to be entered in the Register are—
(a) every individual who has attained the age of 16 and, without being excluded under subsection (3) from an entitlement to be registered, is residing at a place in the United Kingdom; and
(b) every individual of a prescribed description who has resided in the United Kingdom or who is proposing to enter the United Kingdom.
(3) Regulations made by the Secretary of State may provide that an individual residing in the United Kingdom is excluded from an entitlement to be registered if—
(a) he is residing in the United Kingdom in exercise of an entitlement to remain there that will end less than the prescribed period after it was acquired;
(b) he is an individual of a prescribed description who has not yet been resident in the United Kingdom for the prescribed period; or
(c) he is residing in the United Kingdom despite having no entitlement to remain there.
(4) An entry for an individual may be made in the Register (whether or not he has applied to be, or is entitled to be, entered in it) if—
(a) information capable of being recorded in an entry for him is otherwise available to be recorded; and
(b) the Secretary of State considers that the addition of the entry to the Register would be consistent with the statutory purposes.
(5) An entry in the Register consisting of all the information recorded about an individual must be given a unique number, to be known as his National Identity Registration Number; and that number must comply with the prescribed requirements.
(6) The Secretary of State may by order modify the age for the time being specified in subsection (2)(a).
(7) The Secretary of State must not make an order containing (with or without other provision) any provision that he is authorised to make by subsection (6) unless a draft of the order has been laid before Parliament and approved by a resolution of each House.

3 Information recorded in Register

(1) Information—
   (a) may be entered in the Register, and
   (b) once entered, may continue to be recorded there,
   only if and for so long as it is consistent with the statutory purposes for it to be recorded in the Register.

(2) Information may not be recorded in the Register unless it is—
   (a) information the inclusion of which in an individual's entry is authorised by Schedule 1;
   (b) information of a technical nature for use in connection with the administration of the Register;
   (c) information of a technical nature for use in connection with the administration of arrangements made for purposes connected with the issue or cancellation of ID cards; or
   (d) information that must be recorded in the Register in accordance with subsection (3).

(3) Information about an individual must be recorded in his entry in the Register (whether or not it is authorised by Schedule 1) if—
   (a) he has made an application to the Secretary of State requesting the recording of the information as part of his entry;
   (b) the information is of a description identified in regulations made by the Secretary of State as a description of information that may be made the subject of such a request; and
   (c) the Secretary of State considers that it is both practicable and appropriate for it to be recorded in accordance with the applicant's request.

(4) An individual's entry in the Register must include any information falling within paragraph 9 of Schedule 1 that relates to an occasion on which information contained in his entry has been provided to a person without the individual's consent.

(5) Where—
   (a) the Secretary of State and an individual have agreed on what is to be recorded about a matter in that individual's entry in the Register, and
   (b) the Secretary of State has given, and not withdrawn, a direction that what is to be recorded in that individual's case about that matter is to be determined by the agreement,
   there is to be a conclusive presumption for the purposes of this Act that the information to which the direction relates is accurate and complete information about that matter.

(6) The Secretary of State may by order modify the information for the time being set out in Schedule 1.

(7) The Secretary of State must not make an order containing (with or without other provision) any provision for adding information to the information that may be recorded in the Register unless a draft of the order has been laid before Parliament and approved by a resolution of each House.

(8) A statutory instrument containing an order which—
   (a) contains provisions that the Secretary of State is authorised to make by this section, and
   (b) is not an order a draft of which is required to have been laid before Parliament and approved by a resolution of each House,
   shall be subject to annulment in pursuance of a resolution of either House of Parliament.

5 Applications relating to entries in Register

(1) An application by an individual to be entered in the Register may be made either—
   (a) by being included in the prescribed manner in an application for a designated document; or
   (b) by being submitted in the prescribed manner directly to the Secretary of State.

(2) Where an application to be issued with a designated document is made by an individual, the application must do one of the following—

(a) include an application by that individual to be entered in the Register;
(b) state that the individual is already entered in the Register and confirm the contents of his entry;
(c) state that the individual is entered in the Register and confirm the contents of his entry subject to the changes notified in the application.

(3) Where an individual makes—
(a) an application to be entered in the Register, or
(b) an application which for the purposes of this Act confirms (with or without changes) the contents of his entry in the Register,
the application must be accompanied by the prescribed information.

(4) Where an individual has made an application falling within subsection (3)(a) or (b), the Secretary of State may require him to do such one or more of the things specified in subsection (5) as the Secretary of State thinks fit for the purpose of—
(a) verifying information that may be entered in the Register about that individual in consequence of that application; or
(b) otherwise ensuring that there is a complete, up-to-date and accurate entry about that individual in the Register.

(5) The things that an individual may be required to do under subsection (4) are—
(a) to attend at an agreed place and time or (in the absence of agreement) at a specified place and time;
(b) to allow his fingerprints, and other biometric information about himself, to be taken and recorded;
(c) to allow himself to be photographed;
(d) otherwise to provide such information as may be required by the Secretary of State.

(6) Regulations under this section must not require an individual to provide information to another person unless it is information required by the Secretary of State for the statutory purposes.

(7) The power of the Secretary of State to make regulations containing (with or without other provision) any provision that he is authorised to make by this section is exercisable, on the first occasion on which regulations are made under this section, only if a draft of the regulations has been laid before Parliament and approved by a resolution of each House.

ID cards

6 Issue etc. of ID cards

(1) For the purposes of this Act an ID card is a card which—
(a) is issued to an individual by the Secretary of State, or as part of or together with a designated document; and
(b) does, as respects that individual, both of the things specified in subsection (2).

(2) Those things are—
(a) recording registrable facts about the individual that are already recorded as part of his entry in the Register;
(b) carrying data enabling the card to be used for facilitating the making of applications for information recorded in a prescribed part of the individual's entry in the Register, or for otherwise facilitating the provision of that information to a person entitled to be provided with it.

(3) An ID card issued to an individual—
(a) must record only the prescribed information;
(b) must record prescribed parts of it in an encrypted form;
(c) is valid only for the prescribed period; and
(d) remains the property of the person issuing it.

(4) Except in prescribed cases, an ID card must be issued to an individual if he—
(a) is entitled to be entered in the Register or is subject to compulsory registration; and
(b) is an individual about whom the prescribed registrable facts are recorded in the Register;

but this subsection does not require an ID card to be issued as part of or together with a designated document issued on an application made in a case falling within subsection (7)(a) to (c).

(5) In prescribed cases an ID card may be issued to an individual who—
   (a) is not required to be issued with one; but
   (b) is an individual about whom the prescribed registrable facts are recorded in the Register.

(6) An ID card relating to an individual is not to be issued except on an application made by him which either—
   (a) accompanies an application made by him to be entered in the Register; or
   (b) in the prescribed manner confirms (with or without changes) the contents of an entry already made in the Register for that individual.

(7) Where an individual who is not already the holder of an ID card makes an application to be issued with a designated document, his application must, in the prescribed manner, include an application by him to be issued with such a card unless—
   (a) it is being made before 1st January 2010;
   (b) the designated document applied for is a United Kingdom passport (within the meaning of the Immigration Act 1971); and
   (c) the application for that document contains a declaration by that individual that he does not wish to be issued with such a card.

(8) Other applications for the issue of an ID card—
   (a) may be made only in the prescribed manner;
   (b) may be made to the Secretary of State or, in prescribed cases, to a designated documents authority; and
   (c) must be accompanied by the prescribed information;
   and regulations for the purposes of paragraph (b) may authorise an application to be made to a designated documents authority irrespective of whether an application is made to that authority for the issue of a designated document.

(9) The Secretary of State must not make regulations containing (with or without other provision) any provision for prescribing—
   (a) the information to be recorded in or on an ID card,
   (b) the form in which information is to be recorded in or on such a card, or
   (c) the registrable facts which are to be relevant for the purposes of subsection (4)(b),
   unless a draft of the regulations has been laid before Parliament and approved by a resolution of each House.

7 ID cards for those compulsorily registered

(1) This section applies where an individual—
   (a) is subject to compulsory registration; and
   (b) is entered in the Register.

(2) If the individual—
   (a) holds a valid ID card that is due to expire within the prescribed period, or
   (b) does not hold a valid ID card,
   he must apply for one within the prescribed period.

(3) Where an individual applies for an ID card in pursuance of this section, the Secretary of State may require him to do such one or more of the things specified in subsection (4) as the Secretary of State thinks fit for the purpose of—
   (a) verifying information provided for the purposes of the application; or
   (b) otherwise ensuring that there is a complete, up-to-date and accurate entry about that individual in the Register.

(4) The things that an individual may be required to do under subsection (3) are—
   (a) to attend at an agreed place and time or (in the absence of agreement) at a specified place and time;
   (b) to allow his fingerprints, and other biometric information about himself, to be taken and recorded;

            (c) to allow himself to be photographed;
            (d) otherwise to provide such information as may be required by the Secretary of State.
    (5) An individual who contravenes—
            (a) a requirement imposed by subsection (2), or
            (b) a requirement imposed under subsection (3),
        shall be liable to a civil penalty not exceeding £1,000.

8 Functions of persons issuing designated documents

   (1) A designated documents authority may issue a designated document to an individual only if—
            (a) it is satisfied that the requirements imposed by or under this Act in relation to the application for the issue of that document to that individual have been complied with;
            (b) it is satisfied that the Secretary of State has considered and disposed of so much of that application as relates to the making of an entry in the Register or the confirmation (with or without changes) of the contents of such an entry; and
            (c) it has ascertained whether the individual already holds a valid ID card.
   (2) A designated documents authority which issues a designated document to an individual in a case in which—
            (a) the individual does not already hold a valid ID card, and
            (b) the designated document is being issued otherwise than on an application made in a case falling within section 6(7)(a) to (c),
        must ensure that the document is issued together with an ID card satisfying the prescribed requirements.
   (3) Regulations made by the Secretary of State may impose requirements regulating how designated documents authorities handle—
            (a) applications to be entered in the Register that are made to them;
            (b) applications to be issued with ID cards that are made to them (whether or not as part of an application for a designated document); and
            (c) applications made to them that confirm (with or without changes) the contents of an individual's entry in the Register.
   (4) Regulations made by the Secretary of State may also require designated documents authorities to notify the Secretary of State where a designated document that was issued together with an ID card—
            (a) is modified, suspended or revoked; or
            (b) is required to be surrendered.
   (5) The Secretary of State must not make regulations containing (with or without other provision) any provision prescribing requirements for the purposes of subsection (2) unless a draft of the regulations has been laid before Parliament and approved by a resolution of each House.

Maintaining accuracy of Register etc.

9 Power to require information for validating Register

   (1) Where it appears to the Secretary of State that a person on whom a requirement may be imposed under this section may have information in his possession which could be used for verifying—
            (a) something recorded in the Register about an individual,
            (b) something provided to the Secretary of State or a designated documents authority for the purpose of being recorded in an individual's entry in the Register, or
            (c) something otherwise available to the Secretary of State to be recorded about an individual in the Register,
        the Secretary of State may require that person to provide him with the information.
   (2) Where it appears to a designated documents authority that a person on whom a requirement may be imposed under this section may have information in his possession which could be used for verifying—

(a) something that is recorded in the Register about an individual who has applied to the authority for the issue or modification of a designated document or of an ID card, or

(b) something that has been provided to that authority for the purpose of being recorded in the entry of such an individual in the Register,

the authority may require that person to provide it with the information.

(3) It shall be the duty of a person who—
   (a) is required to provide information under this section, and
   (b) has the information in his possession, to comply with the requirement within whatever period is specified in the requirement.

(4) A requirement may be imposed under this section on any person specified for the purposes of this section in an order made by the Secretary of State.

(5) The persons who may be specified in such an order include—
   (a) Ministers of the Crown;
   (b) government departments;
   (c) a Northern Ireland department;
   (d) the National Assembly for Wales;
   (e) any other person who carries out functions conferred by or under an enactment that fall to be carried out on behalf of the Crown.

(6) The power of the Secretary of State to make an order specifying a person as a person on whom a requirement may be imposed under this section includes power to provide—
   (a) that his duty to provide the information that he is required to provide is owed to the person imposing it; and
   (b) that the duty is enforceable in civil proceedings—
      (i) for an injunction;
      (ii) for specific performance of a statutory duty under section 45 of the Court of Session Act 1988; or
      (iii) for any other appropriate remedy or relief.

(7) The Secretary of State may, in such cases (if any) as he thinks fit, make payments to a person providing information in accordance with this section in respect of the provision of the information.

(8) The Secretary of State must not make an order containing (with or without other provision) any provision that he is authorised to make by this section unless a draft of the order has been laid before Parliament and approved by a resolution of each House.

10 Notification of changes affecting accuracy of Register

(1) An individual to whom an ID card has been issued must notify the Secretary of State about—
   (a) every prescribed change of circumstances affecting the information recorded about him in the Register; and
   (b) every error in that information of which he is aware.

(2) A notification for the purposes of this section must be given—
   (a) in the prescribed manner; and
   (b) within the prescribed period after the change of circumstances occurs or the individual in question becomes aware of the error.

(3) Where an individual has given a notification for the purposes of this section, the Secretary of State may require him to do such one or more of the things falling within subsection

(4) as the Secretary of State thinks fit for the purpose of—
   (a) verifying the information that may be entered in the Register about that individual in consequence of the notified change or for the purpose of correcting the error; or
   (b) otherwise ensuring that there is a complete, up-to-date and accurate entry about that individual in the Register.

(4) The things that an individual may be required to do under subsection (3) are—
   (a) to attend at an agreed place and time or (in the absence of agreement) at a specified place and time;

        (b) to allow his fingerprints, and other biometric information about himself, to be taken and recorded;
        (c) to allow himself to be photographed;
        (d) otherwise to provide such information as may be required by the Secretary of State.
    (5) Regulations under this section must not require an individual to provide information to another person unless it is information required by the Secretary of State for the statutory purposes.
    (6) The power of the Secretary of State to make regulations containing (with or without other provision) any provision that he is authorised to make by this section is exercisable, on the first occasion on which regulations are made under this section, only if a draft of the regulations has been laid before Parliament and approved by a resolution of each House.
    (7) An individual who contravenes a requirement imposed on him by or under this section shall be liable to a civil penalty not exceeding £1,000.

11 Invalidity and surrender of ID cards
    (1) Regulations may require an individual to whom an ID card has been issued to notify the Secretary of State, and such other persons as may be prescribed, if he knows or has reason to suspect that the card has been—
        (a) lost;
        (b) stolen;
        (c) damaged;
        (d) tampered with; or
        (e) destroyed.
    (2) The Secretary of State may cancel an ID card if it appears to him—
        (a) that the card was issued in reliance on inaccurate or incomplete information;
        (b) that the card has been lost, stolen, damaged, tampered with or destroyed;
        (c) that there has been a modification of information recorded in the entry in the Register of the holder of the card;
        (d) that another change of circumstances requires a modification of information recorded in or on the card; or
        (e) that it is an ID card of a description of cards that the Secretary of State has decided should be re-issued.
    (3) A person who is knowingly in possession of an ID card without either—
        (a) the lawful authority of the individual to whom it was issued, or
        (b) the permission of the Secretary of State,
        must surrender the card as soon as it is practicable to do so.
    (4) Where it appears to the Secretary of State that a person is in possession of—
        (a) an ID card issued to another,
        (b) an ID card that has expired or been cancelled or is otherwise invalid,
        (c) an ID card that has not yet been cancelled but is of a description of cards that the Secretary of State has decided should be re-issued, or
        (d) an ID card that is in that person's possession in consequence of a contravention of a relevant requirement,
        the Secretary of State may require that person to surrender the card within such period as he may specify.
    (5) Where an ID card has to be surrendered under subsection (3) or (4), it must be surrendered—
        (a) to the Secretary of State; or
        (b) in the case of a card issued by a designated documents authority, either to the Secretary of State or to that authority.
    (6) A person who contravenes a requirement imposed by or under—
        (a) any regulations under subsection (1), or
        (b) subsection (3) or (4),
        shall be liable to a civil penalty not exceeding £1,000.
    (7) In this section—

(a) references to a card having been damaged include references to anything in or on it being, or having become, unreadable or otherwise unusable; and
(b) references to a card having been tampered with include references to information in or on it having been modified for an unlawful purpose, or copied or otherwise extracted for such a purpose.

(8) In this section "relevant requirement" means a requirement to surrender or otherwise to deliver an ID card to the Secretary of State, or to another, which is imposed—
(a) by virtue of any order under section 39, or
(b) by any enactment relating to the surrender of any other document.

Provision of information from Register for verification purposes etc.

12 Provision of information for verification or otherwise with consent

(1) The Secretary of State may provide a person with information recorded in an individual's entry in the Register if—
(a) an application for the provision of the information to that person is made by or with the authority of that individual; or
(b) that individual otherwise consents to the provision of that information to that person.

(2) The only information about an individual that may be provided to a person under this section is—
(a) information about the individual falling within paragraph 1, 3 or 4 of Schedule 1 (name, date and place of birth, gender and addresses, residential status, identifying numbers and validity of identifying documents);
(b) the information contained in any photograph of the individual recorded in the Register;
(c) the information about the individual's signature that is so recorded;
(d) information about whether an ID card issued to the individual is in force and, if not, why not;
(e) information which, by virtue of section 3(3), is recorded in the Register at the individual's request;
(f) the questions recorded by virtue of paragraph 8 of Schedule 1 for use for the purposes of applications for information about the individual;
(g) information confined to the grant or refusal of confirmation that information falling within subsection (3) that has been submitted to the Secretary of State coincides with information so falling that is recorded in the individual's entry in the Register; and
(h) information confined to the grant or refusal of confirmation that the individual's entry in the Register does not contain information of a particular description falling within that subsection.

(3) The information falling within this subsection is—
(a) information comprised in a fingerprint;
(b) other biometric information;
(c) the number to be used for the purposes of applications for information about the individual in question;
(d) the password or other code to be so used; and
(e) the answers to the questions to be so used.

(4) The Secretary of State may—
(a) by order modify subsections (2) and (3); and
(b) by regulations impose restrictions in addition to those contained in this section on the information that may be provided to a person under this section.

(5) The power of the Secretary of State by order to modify subsections (2) and (3) does not include—
(a) power to omit subsection (2); or
(b) power to add information falling within paragraph 9 of Schedule 1 to either of those subsections.

(6) The Secretary of State may also by regulations make provision as to—
(a) how an authority or consent for the purposes of subsection (1) is to be given;

(b) the persons by whom, and the circumstances in which, an application for those purposes may be made; and
(c) how such an application is to be made.

(7) The Secretary of State may by regulations make it a condition of the provision of information under this section—
(a) that the person to whom it is provided has registered prescribed particulars about himself with the Secretary of State;
(b) that that person and the applicant for the information (where different) are for the time being approved by the Secretary of State in the prescribed manner; and
(c) that apparatus used for the purposes of the application, and apparatus that it is proposed to use for the receipt and storage of the information, is for the time being approved in the prescribed manner by the person specified in or determined under the regulations.

(8) The power of the Secretary of State under this section to provide information about an individual to another person is exercisable only where the provision of the information is subject to the satisfaction in relation to that other person of conditions imposed under subsection (7)(a) and (b).

(9) The Secretary of State must not make an order containing (with or without other provision) any provision that he is authorised to make by subsection (4)(a) unless a draft of the order has been laid before Parliament and approved by a resolution of each House.

(10) The restrictions imposed by or under this section on the information that may be provided to a person do not affect any right apart from this Act for an individual to be provided with information about the contents of his entry in the Register.

Required identity checks

13 Power to make public services conditional on identity checks

(1) Regulations may make provision allowing or requiring a person who provides a public service to make it a condition of providing the service to an individual that the individual produces—
(a) an ID card;
(b) other evidence of registrable facts about himself; or
(c) both.

(2) Regulations under this section may not allow or require the imposition of a condition on—
(a) the entitlement of an individual to receive a payment under or in accordance with any enactment, or
(b) the provision of any public service that has to be provided free of charge,

except in cases where the individual is of a description of individuals who are subject to compulsory registration.

(3) Nothing in this section authorises the making of regulations the effect of which would be to require an individual—
(a) to carry an ID card with him at all times; or
(b) to produce such a card otherwise than for purposes connected with an application by him for the provision of a public service, or with the provision of a public service for which he has applied.

15 Power to provide for checks on the Register

(1) The Secretary of State may by regulations make provision authorising a person providing a public service in respect of which—
(a) a condition is imposed under section 13, or
(b) a condition for the production of an ID card, or of evidence of registrable facts, or both, is imposed by or under any other enactment,

to be provided with information recorded in the Register that he requires for the purpose of ascertaining or verifying registrable facts about an individual who has applied for the provision of the service.

. . .

16   Prohibition on requirements to produce identity cards

(1) It shall be unlawful to make it a condition of doing anything in relation to an individual that the individual—
   (a) makes an application under section 12(1) for the provision to him of information recorded in his entry in the Register;
   (b) exercises the right conferred by section 7 of the Data Protection Act 1998 to obtain information recorded in his entry in the Register; or
   (c) provides a person with information about what is recorded in his entry in the Register.

(2) It shall also be unlawful in cases not falling within subsection (3) for any person—
   (a) to make it a condition of doing anything in relation to an individual that the individual makes an application, or gives an authority or consent, for the purposes of section 12(1) in order to secure the provision to another person of information recorded in the individual's entry in the Register;
   (b) to make it a condition of doing anything in relation to an individual that the individual establishes his identity by the production of an ID card; or
   (c) otherwise to impose a requirement on an individual to produce such a card.

. . .

Other purposes for which registered information can be provided

17   Public authorities etc.

(1) The Secretary of State may, without the individual's consent, provide a person with information recorded in an individual's entry in the Register if—
   (a) the provision of the information is authorised by this section; and
   (b) there is compliance with any requirements imposed by or under section 21 in relation to the provision of the information.

(2) The provision of information is authorised by this section where it is—
   (a) the provision of information to the Director-General of the Security Service for purposes connected with the carrying out of any of that Service's functions;
   (b) the provision of information to the Chief of the Secret Intelligence Service for purposes connected with the carrying out of any of that Service's functions;
   (c) the provision of information to the Director of the Government Communications Headquarters for purposes connected with the carrying out of any of the functions of GCHQ; or
   (d) the provision of information to the Director General of the Serious Organised Crime Agency for purposes connected with the carrying out of any of that Agency's functions.

(3) The provision of information not falling within paragraph 9 of Schedule 1 is authorised by this section where the information is provided to a chief officer of police—
   (a) in the interests of national security;
   (b) for purposes connected with the prevention or detection of crime; or
   (c) for other purposes specified by order made by the Secretary of State.

(4) The provision of information not falling within paragraph 9 of Schedule 1 is authorised by this section where the information is provided to the Commissioners for Her Majesty's Revenue and Customs—
   (a) in the interests of national security;
   (b) for purposes connected with the prevention or detection of crime;
   (c) for purposes connected with the prevention, detection or investigation of conduct in respect of which the Commissioners have power to impose penalties, or with the imposition of such penalties;
   (d) for the purpose of facilitating the checking of information provided to the Commissioners in connection with anything under their care and management, or with any other matter in relation to which the Commissioners have duties under any enactment;

(e) for purposes connected with any of the functions of the Commissioners in relation to national insurance contributions or national insurance numbers; or
(f) for other purposes specified by order made by the Secretary of State.

(5) The provision of information not falling within paragraph 9 of Schedule 1 is authorised by this section where the information is provided—
 (a) to a prescribed government department, or
 (b) to a prescribed Northern Ireland department,
 for purposes connected with the carrying out of any prescribed functions of that department or of a Minister in charge of it.

(6) The provision of information to a designated documents authority is authorised by this section where the information is provided for purposes connected with the exercise or performance by the authority of—
 (a) any of its powers or duties by virtue of this Act; or
 (b) any of its other powers or duties in relation to the issue or modification of designated documents.

(7) The powers of the Secretary of State by virtue of this section to make an order or regulations authorising the provision of information to a person are exercisable for the purposes only of authorising the provision of information in circumstances in which its provision to the person in question is necessary in the public interest.

(8) The Secretary of State must not make an order or regulations containing (with or without other provision) any provision that he is authorised to make under this section unless a draft of the order or regulations has been laid before Parliament and approved by a resolution of each House.

(9) In this section—
 "chief officer of police" means—
 (a) the chief officer of police of a police force maintained for a police area in England and Wales;
 (b) the chief constable of a police force maintained under the Police (Scotland) Act 1967;
 (c) the Chief Constable of the Police Service of Northern Ireland;
 (d) the Chief Constable of the Ministry of Defence Police;
 (e) the Chief Constable of the Civil Nuclear Constabulary;
 (f) the Chief Constable of the British Transport Police;
 (g) the chief officer of the States of Jersey Police Force;
 (h) the chief officer of the salaried police force of the Island of Guernsey; or
 (i) the Chief Constable of the Isle of Man Constabulary;
 "GCHQ" has the same meaning as in the Intelligence Services Act 1994.

(10) Nothing in this section is to be construed as restricting any power to disclose information that exists apart from this section.

18 Prevention and detection of crime

(1) The Secretary of State may, without the individual's consent, provide a person with information recorded in an individual's entry in the Register if—
 (a) the provision of the information is authorised by this section; and
 (b) there is compliance with any requirements imposed by or under section 21 in relation to the provision of the information.

(2) The provision to a person of information not falling within paragraph 9 of Schedule 1 is authorised by this section (so far as it is not otherwise authorised by section 17) if the information is provided for any of the purposes specified in section 17(2)(a) to (d) of the Anti-terrorism, Crime and Security Act 2001 (criminal proceedings and investigations).

(3) Section 18 of the Anti-terrorism, Crime and Security Act 2001 (restriction on disclosure of information for overseas purposes) shall have effect in relation to the provision to a person of information by virtue of subsection (2) as it applies in relation to a disclosure of information in exercise of a power to which section 17 of that Act applies.

(4) The provision of information falling within paragraph 9 of Schedule 1 is authorised by this section if it is provided—

(a) to a person to whom information may be provided by virtue of any of subsections (3) to (5) of section 17 or is made as mentioned in subsection (2) of this section; and (b) for purposes connected with the prevention or detection of serious crime.

19 Correcting inaccurate or incomplete information

(1) This section applies where—
   (a) information about an individual has been provided for verification purposes to the Secretary of State or to a designated documents authority; and
   (b) it appears to the Secretary of State that the information was inaccurate or incomplete in one or more particulars.
(2) The Secretary of State may, without the individual's consent, provide the person who provided the inaccurate or incomplete information with information about—
   (a) the respects in which it is inaccurate or incomplete; and
   (b) what is in fact recorded in that individual's entry in respect of the matters to which the inaccurate or incomplete information related.
(3) The provision of information to a person under this section is subject to compliance with any requirements imposed by or under section 21 in relation to its provision.
(4) The reference in this section to providing information about an individual for verification purposes is a reference to providing information about that individual which is required (whether under section 9 or otherwise) or intended to be used by the Secretary of State or a designated documents authority for verifying—
   (a) something recorded in that individual's entry in the Register,
   (b) something provided to the Secretary of State or a designated documents authority for the purpose of being recorded in an entry about that individual in the Register, or
   (c) something otherwise available to the Secretary of State to be so recorded.

21 Rules for providing information without individual's consent

(1) Under sections 17 to 20 the Secretary of State may provide a person with information within paragraph 2 of Schedule 1 only if he is satisfied that it would not have been reasonably practicable for the person to whom the information is provided to have obtained the information by other means.
(2) The Secretary of State may by regulations make provision—
   (a) imposing requirements that must be satisfied before information is provided under any of sections 17 to 20; and
   (b) restricting the persons who may be authorised to act on his behalf for or in connection with the provision of information under any of those sections.
(3) Those regulations may include—
   (a) provision requiring a person to be provided with information only where an application for it has been made by or on behalf of that person;
   (b) provision specifying or describing the persons who are entitled to make applications for the provision of information to a person; and
   (c) provision imposing other requirements as to the manner in which such applications must be made.
(4) The Secretary of State may by regulations make it a condition of providing information to a person—
   (a) that that person (where not specified in sections 17 to 20) and the applicant for the information (where different) are for the time being approved by the Secretary of State in the prescribed manner; and
   (b) that apparatus used for the purposes of the application, and apparatus that it is proposed to use for the receipt and storage of the information, is for the time being approved in the prescribed manner by the person specified in or determined under the regulations.
(5) The Secretary of State may also by regulations provide that information that may be provided to a person under any of sections 17 to 20 may be provided instead to another person who—

(a) is authorised by that person to be a recipient of information provided under that section;
(b) holds such office, rank or position as may be specified in the regulations; and
(c) is under the direction or control of that person, or is otherwise answerable or subordinate to him, in respect of any of his duties as a person holding that office, rank or position.

(6) A power of the Secretary of State under any of sections 17 to 20 to provide information about an individual to another person is exercisable only where the provision of the information is subject to the satisfaction in relation to that other person of conditions imposed under subsection (4)(a).

(7) The Secretary of State must not make regulations containing (with or without other provision) any provision that he is authorised to make by this section unless a draft of the regulations has been laid before Parliament and approved by a resolution of each House.

Supervision of operation of Act

22 Appointment of National Identity Scheme Commissioner

(1) The Secretary of State must appoint a Commissioner to be known as the National Identity Scheme Commissioner.

(2) It shall be the function of the Commissioner (subject to subsection (4)) to keep under review—
(a) the arrangements for the time being maintained by the Secretary of State for the purposes of his functions under this Act or the subordinate legislation made under it;
(b) the arrangements for the time being maintained by designated documents authorities for the purposes of their functions under this Act or that subordinate legislation;
(c) the arrangements made, by persons to whom information may be provided, for obtaining the information available to them under this Act or that subordinate legislation and for recording and using it; and
(d) the uses to which ID cards are being put.

(3) Where the Commissioner reviews any arrangements in accordance with subsection (2), his review must include, in particular, a review of the extent to which the arrangements make appropriate provision—
(a) for securing the confidentiality and integrity of information recorded in the Register; and
(b) for dealing with complaints made to the Secretary of State or a designated documents authority about the carrying out of the functions mentioned in that subsection.

(4) The matters to be kept under review by the Commissioner do not include—
(a) the exercise of powers which under this Act are exercisable by statutory instrument or by statutory rule for the purposes of the Statutory Rules (Northern Ireland) Order 1979;
(b) appeals against civil penalties;
(c) the operation of so much of this Act or of any subordinate legislation as imposes or relates to criminal offences;
(d) the provision of information to the Director-General of the Security Service, the Chief of the Secret Intelligence Service or the Director of the Government Communications Headquarters;
(e) the provision to another member of the intelligence services, in accordance with regulations under section 21(5), of information that may be provided to that Director-General, Chief or Director;
(f) the exercise by the Secretary of State of his powers under section 38; or
(g) arrangements made for the purposes of anything mentioned in paragraphs (a) to (f).

(5) It shall be the duty of every official of the Secretary of State's department to provide the Commissioner with all such information (including information recorded in the Register) as he may require for the purpose of carrying out his functions under this Act.

(6) The Commissioner is to hold office in accordance with the terms of his appointment; and there shall be paid to him out of money provided by Parliament such allowances as the Treasury may determine.

(7) The Secretary of State—
 (a) after consultation with the Commissioner, and
 (b) subject to the approval of the Treasury as to numbers,
 must provide the Commissioner with such staff as the Secretary of State considers necessary for the carrying out of the Commissioner's functions.

(8) In Part 6 of Schedule 1 to the Freedom of Information Act 2000 (public authorities for the purposes of that Act), at the appropriate place, insert—
 "The National Identity Scheme Commissioner."

(9) In this section "intelligence service" has the same meaning as in the Regulation of Investigatory Powers Act 2000.

Offences

25 Possession of false identity documents etc.

(1) It is an offence for a person with the requisite intention to have in his possession or under his control—
 (a) an identity document that is false and that he knows or believes to be false;
 (b) an identity document that was improperly obtained and that he knows or believes to have been improperly obtained; or
 (c) an identity document that relates to someone else.

(2) The requisite intention for the purposes of subsection (1) is—
 (a) the intention of using the document for establishing registrable facts about himself; or
 (b) the intention of allowing or inducing another to use it for establishing, ascertaining or verifying registrable facts about himself or about any other person (with the exception, in the case of a document within paragraph (c) of that subsection, of the individual to whom it relates).

(3) It is an offence for a person with the requisite intention to make, or to have in his possession or under his control—
 (a) any apparatus which, to his knowledge, is or has been specially designed or adapted for the making of false identity documents; or
 (b) any article or material which, to his knowledge, is or has been specially designed or adapted to be used in the making of false identity documents.

(4) The requisite intention for the purposes of subsection (3) is the intention—
 (a) that he or another will make a false identity document; and
 (b) that the document will be used by somebody for establishing, ascertaining or verifying registrable facts about a person.

(5) It is an offence for a person to have in his possession or under his control, without reasonable excuse—
 (a) an identity document that is false;
 (b) an identity document that was improperly obtained;
 (c) an identity document that relates to someone else; or
 (d) any apparatus, article or material which, to his knowledge, is or has been specially designed or adapted for the making of false identity documents or to be used in the making of such documents.

(6) A person guilty of an offence under subsection (1) or (3) shall be liable, on conviction on indictment, to imprisonment for a term not exceeding ten years or to a fine, or to both.

(7) A person guilty of an offence under subsection (5) shall be liable—
 (a) on conviction on indictment, to imprisonment for a term not exceeding two years or to a fine, or to both;
 (b) on summary conviction in England and Wales, to imprisonment for a term not exceeding twelve months or to a fine not exceeding the statutory maximum, or to both;

(c) on summary conviction in Scotland or Northern Ireland, to imprisonment for a term not exceeding six months or to a fine not exceeding the statutory maximum, or to both;

but, in relation to an offence committed before the commencement of section 154(1)of the Criminal Justice Act 2003, the reference in paragraph (b) to twelve months is to be read as a reference to six months.

(8) For the purposes of this section—
    (a) an identity document is false only if it is false within the meaning of Part 1 of the Forgery and Counterfeiting Act 1981 (see section 9(1) of that Act); and
    (b) an identity document was improperly obtained if false information was provided, in or in connection with the application for its issue or an application for its modification, to the person who issued it or (as the case may be) to a person entitled to modify it;
and references to the making of a false identity document include references to the modification of an identity document so that it becomes false.

(9) Subsection (8)(a) does not apply in the application of this section to Scotland.

(10) In this section "identity document" has the meaning given by section 26.

26 Identity documents for the purposes of s. 25

(1) In section 25 "identity document" means any document that is, or purports to be—
    (a) an ID card;
    (b) a designated document;
    (c) an immigration document;
    (d) a United Kingdom passport (within the meaning of the Immigration Act 1971);
    (e) a passport issued by or on behalf of the authorities of a country or territory outside the United Kingdom or by or on behalf of an international organisation;
    (f) a document that can be used (in some or all circumstances) instead of a passport;
    (g) a UK driving licence; or
    (h) a driving licence issued by or on behalf of the authorities of a country or territory outside the United Kingdom.

(2) In subsection (1) "immigration document" means—
    (a) a document used for confirming the right of a person under the Community Treaties in respect of entry or residence in the United Kingdom;
    (b) a document which is given in exercise of immigration functions and records information about leave granted to a person to enter or to remain in the United Kingdom; or
    (c) a registration card (within the meaning of section 26A of the Immigration Act 1971);
and in paragraph (b) "immigration functions" means functions under the Immigration Acts (within the meaning of the Asylum and Immigration (Treatment of Claimants, etc.) Act 2004).

(3) In that subsection "UK driving licence" means—
    (a) a licence to drive a motor vehicle granted under Part 3 of the Road Traffic Act 1988; or
    (b) a licence to drive a motor vehicle granted under Part 2 of the Road Traffic (Northern Ireland) Order 1981.

(4) The Secretary of State may by order modify the list of documents in subsection (1).

(5) The Secretary of State must not make an order containing (with or without other provision) any provision that he is authorised to make by subsection (4) unless a draft of the order has been laid before Parliament and approved by a resolution of each House.

27 Unauthorised disclosure of information

(1) A person is guilty of an offence if, without lawful authority—
    (a) he provides any person with information that he is required to keep confidential; or
    (b) he otherwise makes a disclosure of any such information.

(2) For the purposes of this section a person is required to keep information confidential if it is information that is or has become available to him by reason of his holding an office or employment the duties of which relate, in whole or in part, to—
    (a) the establishment or maintenance of the Register;

(b) the issue, manufacture, modification, cancellation or surrender of ID cards; or
(c) the carrying out of the Commissioner's functions.
(3) For the purposes of this section information is provided or otherwise disclosed with lawful authority if, and only if the provision or other disclosure of the information—
   (a) is authorised by or under this Act or another enactment;
   (b) is in pursuance of an order or direction of a court or of a tribunal established by or under any enactment;
   (c) is in pursuance of a Community obligation; or
   (d) is for the purposes of the performance of the duties of an office or employment of the sort mentioned in subsection (2).
(4) It is a defence for a person charged with an offence under this section to show that, at the time of the alleged offence, he believed, on reasonable grounds, that he had lawful authority to provide the information or to make the other disclosure in question.
(5) A person guilty of an offence under this section shall be liable, on conviction on indictment, to imprisonment for a term not exceeding two years or to a fine, or to both.

28 Providing false information

(1) A person is guilty of an offence if, in circumstances falling within subsection (2), he provides false information to any person—
   (a) for the purpose of securing the making or modification of an entry in the Register;
   (b) in confirming (with or without changes) the contents of an entry in the Register; or
   (c) for the purpose of obtaining for himself or another the issue or modification of an ID card.
(2) Those circumstances are that, at the time of the provision of the information he—
   (a) knows or believes the information to be false; or
   (b) is reckless as to whether or not it is false.
(3) A person guilty of an offence under this section shall be liable—
   (a) on conviction on indictment, to imprisonment for a term not exceeding two years or to a fine, or to both;
   (b) on summary conviction in England and Wales, to imprisonment for a term not exceeding twelve months or to a fine not exceeding the statutory maximum, or to both;
   (c) on summary conviction in Scotland or Northern Ireland, to imprisonment for a term not exceeding six months or to a fine not exceeding the statutory maximum, or to both;
but, in relation to an offence committed before the commencement of section 154(1) of the Criminal Justice Act 2003, the reference in paragraph (b) to twelve months is to be read as a reference to six months.

29 Tampering with the Register etc.

(1) A person is guilty of an offence under this section if—
   (a) he engages in any conduct that causes an unauthorised modification of information recorded in the Register; and
   (b) at the time when he engages in the conduct, he has the requisite intent.
(2) For the purposes of this section a person has the requisite intent if he—
   (a) intends to cause a modification of information recorded in the Register; or
   (b) is reckless as to whether or not his conduct will cause such a modification.
(3) For the purposes of this section the cases in which conduct causes a modification of information recorded in the Register include—
   (a) where it contributes to a modification of such information; and
   (b) where it makes it more difficult or impossible for such information to be retrieved in a legible form from a computer on which it is stored by the Secretary of State, or contributes to making that more difficult or impossible.
(4) It is immaterial for the purposes of this section—
   (a) whether the conduct constituting the offence, or any of it, took place in the United Kingdom; or

(b) in the case of conduct outside the United Kingdom, whether it is conduct of a British citizen.

(5) For the purposes of this section a modification is unauthorised, in relation to the person whose conduct causes it, if—
 (a) he is not himself entitled to determine if the modification may be made; and
 (b) he does not have a consent to the modification from a person who is so entitled.

(6) In proceedings against a person for an offence under this section in respect of conduct causing a modification of information recorded in the Register it is to be a defence for that person to show that, at the time of the conduct, he believed, on reasonable grounds—
 (a) that he was a person entitled to determine if that modification might be made; or
 (b) that consent to the modification had been given by a person so entitled.

(7) A person guilty of an offence under this section shall be liable-
 (a) on conviction on indictment, to imprisonment for a term not exceeding ten years or to a fine, or to both;
 (b) on summary conviction in England and Wales, to imprisonment for a term not exceeding twelve months or to a fine not exceeding the statutory maximum, or to both;
 (c) on summary conviction in Scotland or Northern Ireland, to imprisonment for a term not exceeding six months or to a fine not exceeding the statutory maximum, or to both;
 but, in relation to an offence committed before the commencement of section 154(1) of the Criminal Justice Act 2003, the reference in paragraph (b) to twelve months is to be read as a reference to six months.

(8) In the case of an offence by virtue of this section in respect of conduct wholly or partly outside the United Kingdom—
 (a) proceedings for the offence may be taken at any place in the United Kingdom; and
 (b) the offence may for all incidental purposes be treated as having been committed at any such place.

(9) In this section—
"conduct" includes acts and omissions; and
"modification" includes a temporary modification.

Civil penalties

31 Imposition of civil penalties

(1) This section applies where the Secretary of State is satisfied that a person ("the defaulter") is a person who is liable under this Act to a civil penalty not exceeding a specified amount.

(2) The Secretary of State may, by a notice given to the defaulter in the prescribed manner, impose on him a penalty of such amount, not exceeding the specified amount, as the Secretary of State thinks fit.

(3) A notice imposing such a penalty must—
 (a) set out the Secretary of State's reasons for deciding that the defaulter is liable to a penalty;
 (b) state the amount of the penalty that is being imposed;
 (c) specify a date before which the penalty must be paid to the Secretary of State;
 (d) describe how payment may be made;
 (e) explain the steps that the defaulter may take if he objects to the penalty; and
 (f) set out and explain the powers of the Secretary of State to enforce the penalty.

(4) The date for the payment of a penalty must be not less than 14 days after the giving of the notice imposing it.

(5) A penalty imposed in accordance with this section—
 (a) must be paid to the Secretary of State in a manner described in the notice imposing it; and
 (b) if not so paid by the specified date, is to be recoverable by him accordingly.

(6) In proceedings for recovery of a penalty so imposed no question may be raised as to—
 (a) whether the defaulter was liable to the penalty;
 (b) whether the imposition of the penalty was unreasonable; or

(c) the amount of the penalty.

(7) Sums received by the Secretary of State in respect of penalties imposed in accordance with this section must be paid into the Consolidated Fund.

32 Objection to penalty

(1) A person to whom a notice under section 31 has been given may give notice to the Secretary of State that he objects to the penalty on one or more of the following grounds—
   (a) that he is not liable to it;
   (b) that the circumstances of the contravention in respect of which he is liable make the imposition of a penalty unreasonable;
   (c) that the amount of the penalty is too high.

...

33 Appeals against penalties

(1) A person on whom a penalty has been imposed under section 31 may appeal to the court on one or more of the following grounds—
   (a) that he is not liable to it;
   (b) that the circumstances of the contravention in respect of which he is liable make the imposition of a penalty unreasonable;
   (c) that the amount of the penalty is too high.

...

35 Fees in respect of functions carried out under Act

(1) The Secretary of State may by regulations impose fees, of such amounts as he thinks fit, to be paid to him in respect of any one or more of the following—
   (a) applications to him for entries to be made in the Register, for the modification of entries or for the issue of ID cards;
   (b) the making or modification of entries in the Register;
   (c) the issue of ID cards;
   (d) applications for the provision of information contained in entries in the Register;
   (e) the provision of such information;
   (f) applications for confirmation that information supplied coincides with information recorded in the Register;
   (g) the issue or refusal of such confirmations;
   (h) applications for the approval of a person or of apparatus in accordance with any regulations under this Act;
   (i) the grant of such approvals.

...

37 Report to Parliament about likely costs of ID cards scheme

(1) Before the end of the six months beginning with the day on which this Act is passed, the Secretary of State must prepare and lay before Parliament a report setting out his estimate of the public expenditure likely to be incurred on the ID cards scheme during the ten years beginning with the laying of the report.

(2) Before the end of every six months beginning with the laying of a report under this section, the Secretary of State must prepare and lay before Parliament a further report setting out his estimate of the public expenditure likely to be incurred on the ID cards scheme during the ten years beginning with the end of those six months.

(3) References in this section, in relation to any period of ten years, to the public expenditure likely to be incurred on the ID cards scheme are references to the expenditure likely to be incurred over that period by the Secretary of State and designated documents authorities on—
   (a) the establishment and maintenance of the Register;
   (b) the issue, modification, renewal, replacement, re-issue and surrender of ID cards;
   (c) the provision to persons by the Secretary of State of information recorded in individuals' entries in the Register.

(4) If it appears to the Secretary of State that it would be prejudicial to securing the best value from the use of public money to publish any matter by including it in his next report under this section, he may exclude that matter from that report.

SCHEDULES

SCHEDULE 1

Section 3

INFORMATION THAT MAY BE RECORDED IN REGISTER

Personal information

1. The following may be recorded in an individual's entry in the Register—
   (a) his full name;
   (b) other names by which he is or has been known;
   (c) his date of birth;
   (d) his place of birth;
   (e) his gender;
   (f) the address of his principal place of residence in the United Kingdom;
   (g) the address of every other place in the United Kingdom or elsewhere where he has a place of residence.

Identifying information

2. The following may be recorded in an individual's entry in the Register—
   (a) a photograph of his head and shoulders (showing the features of the face);
   (b) his signature;
   (c) his fingerprints;
   (d) other biometric information about him.

Residential status

3. The following may be recorded in an individual's entry in the Register—
   (a) his nationality;
   (b) his entitlement to remain in the United Kingdom;
   (c) where that entitlement derives from a grant of leave to enter or remain in the United Kingdom, the terms and conditions of that leave.

Personal reference numbers etc.

4. (1) The following may be recorded in an individual's entry in the Register—
   (a) his National Identity Registration Number;
   (b) the number of any ID card issued to him;
   (c) any national insurance number allocated to him;
   (d) the number of any immigration document relating to him;
   (e) the number of any United Kingdom passport (within the meaning of the Immigration Act 1971) that has been issued to him;
   (f) the number of any passport issued to him by or on behalf of the authorities of a country or territory outside the United Kingdom or by or on behalf of an international organisation;
   (g) the number of any document that can be used by him (in some or all circumstances) instead of a passport;
   (h) the number of any identity card issued to him by the authorities of a country or territory outside the United Kingdom;
   (i) any reference number allocated to him by the Secretary of State in connection with an application made by him for permission to enter or to remain in the United Kingdom;
   (j) the number of any work permit (within the meaning of the Immigration Act 1971) relating to him;
   (k) any driver number given to him by a driving licence;
   (l) the number of any designated document which is held by him and is a document the number of which does not fall within any of the preceding sub-paragraphs;

(m) the date of expiry or period of validity of a document the number of which is recorded by virtue of this paragraph.
(2) In this paragraph "immigration document" means—
  (a) a document used for confirming the right of a person under the Community Treaties in respect of entry or residence in the United Kingdom;
  (b) a document which is given in exercise of immigration functions and records information about leave granted to a person to enter or to remain in the United Kingdom; or
  (c) a registration card (within the meaning of section 26A of the Immigration Act 1971);
  and in paragraph (b) "immigration functions" means functions under the Immigration Acts (within the meaning of the Asylum and Immigration (Treatment of Claimants, etc.) Act 2004).
(3) In this paragraph "driving licence" means—
  (a) a licence to drive a motor vehicle granted under Part 3 of the Road Traffic Act 1988; or
  (b) a licence to drive a motor vehicle granted under Part 2 of the Road Traffic (Northern Ireland) Order 1981.

...

GOVERNMENT OF WALES ACT 2006
(2006 c. 32)

An Act to make provision about the government of Wales. [25 July 2006]

PART 1

NATIONAL ASSEMBLY FOR WALES

The Assembly

1 **The Assembly**
(1) There is to be an Assembly for Wales to be known as the National Assembly for Wales or Cynulliad Cenedlaethol Cymru (referred to in this Act as "the Assembly").
(2) The Assembly is to consist of—
  (a) one member for each Assembly constituency (referred to in this Act as "Assembly constituency members"), and
  (b) members for each Assembly electoral region (referred to in this Act as "Assembly regional members").
...

2 **Assembly constituencies and electoral regions**
(1) The Assembly constituencies are the parliamentary constituencies in Wales (as specified in the Parliamentary Constituencies and Assembly Electoral Regions (Wales) Order 2006).
(2) There are five Assembly electoral regions.
(3) The Assembly electoral regions are as specified in the Parliamentary Constituencies and Assembly Electoral Regions (Wales) Order 2006.
(4) There are four seats for each Assembly electoral region.
...

General elections

3 **Ordinary general elections**
(1) The poll at an ordinary general election is to be held on the first Thursday in May in the fourth calendar year following that in which the previous ordinary general election was held, unless provision is made for the day of the poll by an order under section 4.
(2) If the poll is to be held on the first Thursday in May, the Assembly—
  (a) is dissolved by virtue of this section at the beginning of the minimum period which ends with that day, and

(b) must meet within the period of seven days beginning immediately after the day of the poll.

(3) In subsection (2) "the minimum period" means the period determined in accordance with an order under section 13.

. . .

5 Extraordinary general elections

(1) The Secretary of State must propose a day for the holding of a poll at an extraordinary general election if subsection (2) or (3) applies.

(2) This subsection applies if—
  (a) the Assembly resolves that it should be dissolved, and
  (b) the resolution of the Assembly is passed on a vote in which the number of Assembly members voting in favour of it is not less than two-thirds of the total number of Assembly seats.

(3) This subsection applies if any period during which the Assembly is required under section 47 to nominate an Assembly member for appointment as the First Minister ends without such a nomination being made.

6 Voting at general elections

(1) Each person entitled to vote at a general election in an Assembly constituency has two votes.

(2) One (referred to in this Act as a "constituency vote") is a vote which may be given for a candidate to be the Assembly constituency member for the Assembly constituency.

(3) The other (referred to in this Act as an "electoral region vote") is a vote which may be given for—
  (a) a registered political party which has submitted a list of candidates to be Assembly regional members for the Assembly electoral region in which the Assembly constituency is included, or
  (b) an individual who is a candidate to be an Assembly regional member for that Assembly electoral region.

(4) The Assembly constituency member for the Assembly constituency is to be returned under the simple majority system.

(5) The Assembly regional members for the Assembly electoral region are to be returned under the additional member system of proportional representation provided for in this Part.

(6) In this Act "registered political party" means a party registered under Part 2 of the Political Parties, Elections and Referendums Act 2000.

7 Candidates at general elections

(1) At a general election a person may not be a candidate to be the Assembly constituency member for more than one Assembly constituency.

(2) Any registered political party may submit a list of candidates for return as Assembly regional members for a particular Assembly electoral region at a general election.

(3) The list must be submitted to the regional returning officer.

(4) The list must not include more than twelve persons (but may include only one).

(5) The list must not include a person—
  (a) who is included on any other list submitted for the Assembly electoral region or any list submitted for another Assembly electoral region,
  (b) who is an individual candidate to be an Assembly regional member for the Assembly electoral region or another Assembly electoral region, or
  (c) who is a candidate to be the Assembly constituency member for an Assembly constituency.

(6) A person may not be an individual candidate to be an Assembly regional member for the Assembly electoral region if that person is—
  (a) included on a list submitted by a registered political party for the Assembly electoral region or another Assembly electoral region,

(b) an individual candidate to be an Assembly regional member for another Assembly electoral region, or
(c) a candidate to be the Assembly constituency member for an Assembly constituency.

(7) In this Act "regional returning officer", in relation to an Assembly electoral region, means the person designated as the regional returning officer for the Assembly electoral region in accordance with an order under section 13.

8 Calculation of electoral region figures

(1) This section and section 9 are about the return of Assembly regional members for an electoral region at a general election.

(2) The person who is to be returned as the Assembly constituency member for each Assembly constituency in the Assembly electoral region is to be determined before it is determined who are to be returned as the Assembly regional members for the Assembly electoral region.

(3) For each registered political party by which a list of candidates has been submitted for the Assembly electoral region—
    (a) there is to be added together the number of electoral region votes given for the party in the Assembly constituencies included in the Assembly electoral region, and
    (b) the number arrived at under paragraph (a) is then to be divided by the aggregate of one and the number of candidates of the party returned as Assembly constituency members for any of those Assembly constituencies.

(4) For each individual candidate to be an Assembly regional member for the Assembly electoral region there is to be added together the number of electoral region votes given for the candidate in the Assembly constituencies included in the Assembly electoral region.

(5) The number arrived at—
    (a) in the case of a registered political party, under subsection (3)(b), or
    (b) in the case of an individual candidate, under subsection (4),
    is referred to in this Act as the electoral region figure for that party or individual candidate.

9 Allocation of seats to electoral region members

(1) The first seat for the Assembly electoral region is to be allocated to the party or individual candidate with the highest electoral region figure.

(2) The second and subsequent seats for the Assembly electoral region are to be allocated to the party or individual candidate with the highest electoral region figure after any recalculation required by subsection (3) has been carried out.

(3) This subsection requires a recalculation under paragraph (b) of section 8(3) in relation to a party—
    (a) for the first application of subsection (2), if the application of subsection (1) resulted in the allocation of an Assembly seat to the party, or
    (b) for any subsequent application of subsection (2), if the previous application of that subsection did so,
    and a recalculation is to be carried out after adding one to the aggregate mentioned in that paragraph.

(4) An individual candidate already returned as an Assembly regional member is to be disregarded.

(5) Seats for the Assembly electoral region which are allocated to a party are to be filled by the persons on the party's list in the order in which they appear on the list.

(6) Once a party's list has been exhausted by the return of persons included on it as Assembly regional members by the previous application of subsection (1) or (2), the party is to be disregarded.

(7) If (on the application of subsection (1) or any application of subsection (2)) the highest electoral region figure is the electoral region figure of two or more parties or individual candidates, the subsection applies to each of them.

(8) However, if subsection (7) would mean that more than the full number of seats for the Assembly electoral region were allocated, subsection (1) or (2) does not apply until—

(a) a recalculation has been carried out under section 8(3)(b) after adding one to the number of votes given for each party with that electoral region figure, and
(b) one has been added to the number of votes given for each individual candidate with that electoral region figure.

(9) If, after that, the highest electoral region figure is still the electoral region figure of two or more parties or individual candidates, the regional returning officer must decide between them by lots.

Vacancies

10 Constituency vacancies

(1) This section applies if the seat of an Assembly constituency member returned for an Assembly constituency is vacant.
(2) Subject to subsection (7), an election must be held in the Assembly constituency to fill the vacancy.
(3) At the election, each person entitled to vote only has a constituency vote; and the Assembly constituency member for the Assembly constituency is to be returned under the simple majority system.
(4) The date of the poll at the election must be fixed by the Presiding Officer.
(5) The date must fall within the period of three months beginning with the occurrence of the vacancy.
(6) But if the vacancy does not come to the Presiding Officer's notice within the period of one month beginning with its occurrence, the date must fall within the period of three months beginning when it does come to the Presiding Officer's notice.
(7) The election must not be held if it appears to the Presiding Officer that the latest date which may be fixed for the poll would fall within the period of three months ending with the day on which the poll at the next ordinary general election would be held (disregarding section 4).
(8) The standing orders must make provision for determining the date on which a vacancy occurs for the purposes of this section.
(9) A person may not be a candidate in an election to fill a vacancy if the person is—
(a) an Assembly member, or
(b) a candidate in another such election.

11 Electoral region vacancies

(1) This section applies if the seat of an Assembly regional member returned for an Assembly electoral region is vacant.
(2) If the Assembly regional member was returned (under section 9 or this section) from the list of a registered political party, the regional returning officer must notify to the Presiding Officer the name of the person who is to fill the vacancy.
(3) A person's name may only be so notified if the person—
(a) is included on the list submitted by the registered political party for the last general election,
(b) is willing to serve as an Assembly regional member for the Assembly electoral region, and
(c) is not a person to whom subsection (4) applies.
(4) This subsection applies to a person if—
(a) the person is not a member of the registered political party, and
(b) the registered political party gives notice to the regional returning officer that the person's name is not to be notified to the Presiding Officer as the name of the person who is to fill the vacancy.
(5) But if there is more than one person who satisfies the conditions in subsection (3), the regional returning officer may only notify the name of whichever of them was the higher, or the highest, on that list.

(6) A person whose name is notified under subsection (2) is to be treated as having been declared to be returned as an Assembly regional member for the Assembly electoral region on the day on which notification of the person's name is received by the Presiding Officer.

(7) The seat remains vacant until the next general election—
   (a) if the Assembly regional member was returned as an individual candidate, or
   (b) if that Assembly regional member was returned from the list of a registered political party but there is no-one who satisfies the conditions in subsection (3).

(8) For the purposes of this section, a person included on the list submitted by a registered political party for the last general election who—
   (a) was returned as an Assembly regional member under section 9 at that election (even if the return was void),
   (b) has subsequently been a candidate in an election held under section 10 (whether or not returned), or
   (c) has subsequently been returned under this section (even if the return was void),
   is treated on and after the return of the person, or of the successful candidate at the election, as not having been included on the list.

Franchise and conduct of elections

13 Power to make provision about elections etc.

(1) The Secretary of State may by order make provision as to—
   (a) the conduct of elections for the return of Assembly members,
   (b) the questioning of an election for the return of Assembly members and the consequences of irregularities, and
   (c) the return of an Assembly member otherwise than at an election.

...

Duration of membership

14 Term of office of Assembly members

The term of office of an Assembly member—
(a) begins when the Assembly member is declared to be returned, and
(b) ends with the dissolution of the Assembly.

Disqualification

16 Disqualification from being Assembly member

(1) A person is disqualified from being an Assembly member if that person—
   (a) is disqualified from being a member of the House of Commons under paragraphs (a) to (e) of section 1(1) of the House of Commons Disqualification Act 1975 (c. 24) (judges, civil servants, members of the armed forces, members of police forces and members of foreign legislatures),
   (b) holds any of the offices for the time being designated by Order in Council as offices disqualifying persons from being Assembly members,
   (c) holds the office of Auditor General,
   (d) holds the office of Public Services Ombudsman for Wales, or
   (e) is employed as a member of the staff of the Assembly.

(2) Subject to section 17(1) and (2), a person is also disqualified from being an Assembly member if that person is disqualified otherwise than under the House of Commons Disqualification Act 1975 (c. 24) (either generally or in relation to a particular constituency) from being a member of the House of Commons or from sitting and voting in it.

(3) For the purposes of subsection (2) the references to the Republic of Ireland in section 1 of the Representation of the People Act 1981 (c. 34) (disqualification of offenders detained in, or unlawfully at large from detention in, the British Islands or the Republic of Ireland) are to be treated as references to any member State (other than the United Kingdom).

(4) A person who holds office as lord-lieutenant, lieutenant or high sheriff of any area in Wales is disqualified from being an Assembly member for any Assembly constituency or Assembly electoral region wholly or partly included in that area.

...

17 Exceptions and relief from disqualification

(1) A person is not disqualified from being an Assembly member merely because that person is—
   (a) a peer (whether of the United Kingdom, Great Britain, England or Scotland), or
   (b) a Lord Spiritual.
(2) A citizen of the European Union who is resident in the United Kingdom is not disqualified from being an Assembly member merely because of section 3 of the Act of Settlement (disqualification of certain persons born outside United Kingdom).

...

26 Clerk of Assembly

(1) The Assembly Commission must appoint a person to be the Clerk of the Assembly (referred to in this Act as "the Clerk").

...

Committees

28 Committees and sub-committees

(1) The standing orders may provide—
   (a) for the appointment of committees of the Assembly, and
   (b) for such committees to have power to appoint sub-committees.
(2) The members of a committee of the Assembly, or of a sub-committee of such a committee, may not include anyone who is not an Assembly member.

...

Proceedings etc.

31 Standing orders

(1) Assembly proceedings are to be regulated by standing orders (referred to in this Act as "the standing orders").

...

32 Participation by UK Ministers etc.

(1) The Secretary of State for Wales is entitled to participate in proceedings of the Assembly but not to vote.

...

33 Consultation about UK Government's legislative programme

(1) As soon as is reasonably practicable after the beginning of each session of Parliament, the Secretary of State for Wales must undertake with the Assembly such consultation about the UK Government's legislative programme for the session as appears to the Secretary of State to be appropriate.
(2) The consultation in relation to the UK Government's legislative programme for a session must include participating in proceedings of the Assembly relating to it on at least one occasion.
(3) For this purpose the UK Government's legislative programme for a session of Parliament consists of the bills which, at the beginning of the session, are intended to be introduced into either House of Parliament during the session by a Minister of the Crown.

...

(5) This section does not require the undertaking of consultation with the Assembly about a bill if it appears to the Secretary of State for Wales that there are considerations relating to the bill that make such consultation inappropriate.

34 Participation by Counsel General

(1) If not an Assembly member the Counsel General may participate in Assembly proceedings to the extent permitted by the standing orders, but may not vote.

...

35 Equality of treatment

(1) The Assembly must, in the conduct of Assembly proceedings, give effect, so far as is both appropriate in the circumstances and reasonably practicable, to the principle that the English and Welsh languages should be treated on a basis of equality.

...

36 Integrity

(1) The standing orders must include provision—
   (a) for a register of interests of Assembly members, and
   (b) for the register to be published and made available for public inspection.
(2) The standing orders must require Assembly members to register in the register of interests registrable interests, as defined for the purposes of this subsection.
(3) The standing orders must require any Assembly member who has—
   (a) a financial interest, as defined for the purposes of this subsection, or
   (b) any other interest, or an interest of any other kind, as so defined,
   in any matter to declare that interest before taking part in Assembly proceedings relating to that matter.
(4) The standing orders may include provision for preventing or restricting the participation in any Assembly proceedings of an Assembly member who has an interest within subsection (2) or (3) in any matter to which the proceedings relate.
(5) The standing orders must include provision prohibiting an Assembly member from—
   (a) advocating or initiating any cause or matter on behalf of any person, by any means specified in the standing orders, in consideration of any payment or benefit in kind of a description so specified, or
   (b) urging, in consideration of any such payment or benefit in kind, any other Assembly member to advocate or initiate any cause or matter on behalf of any person by any such means.
(6) The standing orders must include provision about (or for the making of a code or protocol about) the different roles and responsibilities of Assembly constituency members and Assembly regional members; and—
   (a) Assembly constituency members must not describe themselves in a manner which suggests that they are Assembly regional members, and
   (b) Assembly regional members must not describe themselves in a manner which suggests that they are Assembly constituency members.
(7) An Assembly member who—
   (a) takes part in Assembly proceedings without having complied with, or in contravention of, any provision included in the standing orders in pursuance of subsections (2) to (4), or
   (b) contravenes any provision included in the standing orders in pursuance of subsection (5),
   commits an offence.
(8) A person guilty of an offence under subsection (7) is liable on summary conviction to a fine not exceeding level 5 on the standard scale.
(9) A prosecution for an offence under subsection (7) cannot be instituted except by or with the consent of the Director of Public Prosecutions.
(10) The validity of any Assembly proceedings is not affected by any contravention or failure to comply with any provision included in the standing orders in pursuance of this section.
(11) In this section—
   (a) references to an Assembly member (apart from those in subsection (6)) include the Counsel General, if not an Assembly member, and
   (b) "financial interest" includes a benefit in kind.

PART 2
WELSH ASSEMBLY GOVERNMENT

Government

45 Welsh Assembly Government
(1) There is to be a Welsh Assembly Government, or Llywodraeth Cynulliad Cymru, whose members are—
   (a) the First Minister or Prif Weinidog (see sections 46 and 47),
   (b) the Welsh Ministers, or Gweinidogion Cymru, appointed under section 48,
   (c) the Counsel General to the Welsh Assembly Government or Cwnsler Cyffredinol i Lywodraeth Cynulliad Cymru (see section 49) (referred to in this Act as "the Counsel General"), and
   (d) the Deputy Welsh Ministers or Dirprwy Weinidogion Cymru (see section 50).
(2) In this Act and in any other enactment or instrument the First Minister and the Welsh Ministers appointed under section 48 are referred to collectively as the Welsh Ministers.

Ministers, staff etc.

46 The First Minister
(1) The First Minister is to be appointed by Her Majesty after nomination in accordance with section 47.
(2) The First Minister holds office at Her Majesty's pleasure.
(3) The First Minister may at any time tender resignation to Her Majesty and ceases to hold office as First Minister when it is accepted.
. . .
(5) The functions of the First Minister are exercisable by a person designated by the Presiding Officer if—
   (a) the office of the First Minister is vacant,
   (b) the First Minister is for any reason unable to act, or
   (c) the First Minister has ceased to be an Assembly member.
. . .
(8) If a person is designated to exercise the functions of the First Minister, the designation continues to have effect even if the Assembly is dissolved.

47 Choice of First Minister
(1) If one of the following events occurs, the Assembly must, before the end of the relevant period, nominate an Assembly member for appointment as First Minister.
(2) The events are—
   (a) the holding of a poll at a general election,
   (b) the Assembly resolving that the Welsh Ministers no longer enjoy the confidence of the Assembly,
   (c) the First Minister tendering resignation to Her Majesty,
   (d) the First Minister dying or becoming permanently unable to act and to tender resignation, and
   (e) the First Minister ceasing to be an Assembly member otherwise than by reason of a dissolution.
(3) The relevant period is the period of 28 days beginning with the day on which the event occurs; . . .
(4) The Presiding Officer must recommend to Her Majesty the appointment of the person nominated by the Assembly under subsection (1).

48 Welsh Ministers
(1) The First Minister may, with the approval of Her Majesty, appoint Welsh Ministers from among the Assembly members.
(2) A Welsh Minister appointed under this section holds office at Her Majesty's pleasure.

(3) A Welsh Minister appointed under this section may be removed from office by the First Minister.

...

49 Counsel General

(1) The Counsel General is to be appointed by Her Majesty on the recommendation of the First Minister.

...

50 Deputy Welsh Ministers

(1) The First Minister may, with the approval of Her Majesty, appoint Deputy Welsh Ministers from among the Assembly members to assist the First Minister, a Welsh Minister appointed under section 48 or the Counsel General in the exercise of functions.

...

51 Limit on number of Ministers

(1) No more than twelve persons are to hold a relevant Welsh Ministerial office at any time.

(2) A relevant Welsh Ministerial office means the office of Welsh Minister appointed under section 48 or the office of Deputy Welsh Minister.

52 Staff

(1) The Welsh Ministers may appoint persons to be members of the staff of the Welsh Assembly Government.

(2) Service as a member of the staff of the Welsh Assembly Government is service in the Home Civil Service.

...

Functions

56 Introduction

(1) The persons to whom this section applies have the functions conferred or imposed on them by or by virtue of this Act or any other enactment or prerogative instrument.

(2) This section applies to the Welsh Ministers, the First Minister and the Counsel General.

57 Exercise of functions

(1) Functions may be conferred or imposed on the Welsh Ministers by that name.

(2) Functions of the Welsh Ministers, the First Minister and the Counsel General are exercisable on behalf of Her Majesty.

...

(4) Any act or omission of, or in relation to, the First Minister or any of the Welsh Ministers appointed under section 48 is to be treated as an act or omission of, or in relation to, each of them.

(5) But subsection (4) does not apply in relation to the exercise of functions conferred or imposed on the First Minister alone.

...

58 Transfer of Ministerial functions

(1) Her Majesty may by Order in Council—

(a) provide for the transfer to the Welsh Ministers, the First Minister or the Counsel General of any function so far as exercisable by a Minister of the Crown in relation to Wales,

(b) direct that any function so far as so exercisable is to be exercisable by the Welsh Ministers, the First Minister or the Counsel General concurrently with the Minister of the Crown, or

(c) direct that any function so far as exercisable by a Minister of the Crown in relation to Wales is to be exercisable by the Minister of the Crown only with the agreement of, or after consultation with, the Welsh Ministers, the First Minister or the Counsel General.

...

59 Implementation of Community law
(1) The power to designate a Minister of the Crown or government department under section 2(2) of the European Communities Act 1972 (c. 68) may be exercised to designate the Welsh Ministers.
...

60 Promotion etc. of well-being
(1) The Welsh Ministers may do anything which they consider appropriate to achieve any one or more of the following objects—
 (a) the promotion or improvement of the economic well-being of Wales,
 (b) the promotion or improvement of the social well-being of Wales, and
 (c) the promotion or improvement of the environmental well-being of Wales.
(2) The power under subsection (1) may be exercised in relation to or for the benefit of—
 (a) the whole or any part of Wales, or
 (b) all or any persons resident or present in Wales.
(3) The power under subsection (1) includes power to do anything in relation to or for the benefit of any area outside Wales, or all or any persons resident or present anywhere outside Wales, if the Welsh Ministers consider that it is likely to achieve one or more of the objects in that subsection.
(4) The power under subsection (1) includes power—
 (a) to enter into arrangements or agreements with any person,
 (b) to co-operate with, or facilitate or co-ordinate the activities of, any person,
 (c) to exercise on behalf of any person any functions of that person, and
 (d) to provide staff, goods, services or accommodation to any person.

61 Support of culture etc.
 (a) archaeological remains in Wales,
 (b) ancient monuments in Wales,
 (c) buildings and places of historical or architectural interest in Wales,
 (d) historic wrecks in Wales,
 (e) arts and crafts relating to Wales,
 (f) museums and galleries in Wales,
 (g) libraries in Wales,
 (h) archives and historical records relating to Wales,
 (i) cultural activities and projects relating to Wales,
 (j) sport and recreational activities relating to Wales, and
 (k) the Welsh language.

62 Representations about matters affecting Wales
The Welsh Ministers, the First Minister and the Counsel General may make appropriate representations about any matter affecting Wales.

63 Consultation about cross-border bodies
(1) A Minister of the Crown must consult the Welsh Ministers—
 (a) before exercising any function which relates to the appointment or removal of a relevant cross-border body,
 (b) before exercising any function which relates to the appointment or removal of any member or office-holder of a relevant cross-border body, other than one who is not concerned in the functions or activities which the body exercises or carries on in or with respect to Wales, and
 (c) before exercising, in relation to a relevant cross-border body, any function the exercise of which might affect Wales in relation to any matter as respects which functions are exercisable by the Welsh Ministers.
...

64 Polls for ascertaining views of the public

(1) The Welsh Ministers may hold a poll in an area consisting of Wales or any part (or parts) of Wales for the purpose of ascertaining the views of those polled about whether or how any of the functions of the Welsh Ministers (other than that under section 62) should be exercised.

(2) The persons entitled to vote in a poll under this section are those who—
   (a) would be entitled to vote as electors at a local government election in an electoral area wholly or partly included in the area in which the poll is held, and
   (b) are registered in the register of local government electors at an address within the area in which the poll is held.

...

65 Private bills

(1) The Welsh Ministers may promote private bills in Parliament and may oppose any private bill in Parliament.

...

"Inclusive" approach to exercise of functions

72 Partnership Council

(1) The Welsh Ministers must establish and maintain a body to be known as the Partnership Council for Wales or Cyngor Partneriaeth Cymru ("the Partnership Council").

(2) The Partnership Council is to consist of members appointed by the Welsh Ministers from among—
   (a) the Welsh Ministers,
   (b) the Deputy Welsh Ministers, and
   (c) the members of local authorities in Wales.

(3) Before appointing members of the Partnership Council under subsection (2)(c), the Welsh Ministers must consult such associations of local authorities in Wales as they consider appropriate.

(4) The Partnership Council may—
   (a) give advice to the Welsh Ministers about matters affecting the exercise of any of their functions,
   (b) make representations to the Welsh Ministers about any matters affecting, or of concern to, those involved in local government in Wales, and
   (c) give advice to those involved in local government in Wales.

...

73 Local government scheme

(1) The Welsh Ministers must make a scheme ("the local government scheme") setting out how they propose, in the exercise of their functions, to sustain and promote local government in Wales.

(2) The Welsh Ministers—
   (a) must keep the local government scheme under review, and
   (b) may from time to time remake or revise it.

(3) In determining the provision to be included in the local government scheme, the Welsh Ministers must have regard to any advice which has been given, and to any representations which have been made, to them by the Partnership Council.

...

74 Voluntary sector scheme

(1) The Welsh Ministers must make a scheme ("the voluntary sector scheme") setting out how they propose, in the exercise of their functions, to promote the interests of relevant voluntary organisations.

...

75 Business scheme
(1) The Welsh Ministers must make a scheme ("the business scheme") setting out how they propose, in the exercise of their functions, to take account of the interests of business.
...

78 The Welsh language
(1) The Welsh Ministers must adopt a strategy ("the Welsh language strategy") setting out how they propose to promote and facilitate the use of the Welsh language.
(2) The Welsh Ministers must adopt a scheme ("the Welsh language scheme") specifying measures which they propose to take, for the purpose mentioned in subsection (3), as to the use of the Welsh language in connection with the provision of services to the public in Wales by them, or by others who—
  (a) are acting as servants or agents of the Crown, or
  (b) are public bodies (within the meaning of Part 2 of the Welsh Language Act 1993).
(3) The purpose referred to in subsection (2) is that of giving effect, so far as is both appropriate in the circumstances and reasonably practicable, to the principle that in the conduct of public business in Wales the English and Welsh languages should be treated on a basis of equality.
(4) The Welsh Ministers—
  (a) must keep under review both the Welsh language strategy and the Welsh language scheme, and
  (b) may from time to time adopt a new strategy or scheme or revise them.
(5) Before adopting or revising a strategy or scheme, the Welsh Ministers must consult such persons as they consider appropriate.
(6) The Welsh Ministers must publish the Welsh language strategy and the Welsh language scheme when they first adopt it and—
  (a) if they adopt a new strategy or scheme they must publish it, and
  (b) if they revise the Welsh language strategy or the Welsh language scheme (rather than adopting a new strategy or scheme) they must publish either the revisions or the strategy or scheme as revised (as they consider appropriate).
(7) If the Welsh Ministers publish a strategy or scheme, or revisions, under subsection (6) they must lay a copy of the strategy or scheme, or revisions, before the Assembly.
(8) After each financial year the Welsh Ministers must publish a report of—
  (a) how the proposals set out in the Welsh language strategy were implemented in that financial year and how effective their implementation has been in promoting and facilitating the use of the Welsh language, and
  (b) how the proposals set out in the Welsh language scheme were implemented in that financial year,
  and must lay a copy of the report before the Assembly.

79 Sustainable development
(1) The Welsh Ministers must make a scheme ("the sustainable development scheme") setting out how they propose, in the exercise of their functions, to promote sustainable development.
...

Community law, human rights and international obligations etc.

80 Community law
(1) A community obligation of the United Kingdom is also an obligation of the Welsh Ministers if and to the extent that the obligation could be implemented (or enabled to be implemented) or complied with by the exercise by the Welsh Ministers of any of their functions.
(2) Subsection (1) does not apply in the case of a Community obligation of the United Kingdom if—
  (a) it is an obligation to achieve a result defined by reference to a quantity (whether expressed as an amount, proportion or ratio or otherwise), and

(b) the quantity relates to the United Kingdom (or to an area including the United Kingdom or to an area consisting of a part of the United Kingdom which includes the whole or part of Wales).

(3) But if such a Community obligation could (to any extent) be implemented (or enabled to be implemented) or complied with by the exercise by the Welsh Ministers of any of their functions, a Minister of the Crown may by order provide for the achievement by the Welsh Ministers (in the exercise of their functions) of so much of the result to be achieved under the Community obligation as is specified in the order.

...

(7) Where an order under subsection (3) is in force in relation to a Community obligation, to the extent that the Community obligation involves achieving what is specified in the order it is also an obligation of the Welsh Ministers (enforceable as if it were an obligation of the Welsh Ministers under subsection (1)).

(8) The Welsh Ministers have no power—
 (a) to make, confirm or approve any subordinate legislation, or
 (b) to do any other act,
 so far as the subordinate legislation or act is incompatible with Community law or an obligation under subsection (7).

...

81 Human rights

(1) The Welsh Ministers have no power—
 (a) to make, confirm or approve any subordinate legislation, or
 (b) to do any other act,
 so far as the subordinate legislation or act is incompatible with any of the Convention rights.

(2) Subsection (1) does not enable a person—
 (a) to bring any proceedings in a court or tribunal, or
 (b) to rely on any of the Convention rights in any such proceedings,
 in respect of an act unless that person would be a victim for the purposes of Article 34 of the Convention if proceedings were brought in the European Court of Human Rights in respect of that act.

(3) Subsection (2) does not apply to the Attorney General, the Counsel General, the Advocate General for Scotland or the Advocate General for Northern Ireland.

(4) Subsection (1)—
 (a) does not apply to an act which, by virtue of subsection (2) of section 6 of the Human Rights Act 1998, is not unlawful under subsection (1) of that section, and
 (b) does not enable a court or tribunal to award in respect of any act any damages which it could not award on finding the act unlawful under that subsection.

...

(6) In subsection (2) "the Convention" has the same meaning as in the Human Rights Act 1998.

82 International obligations etc.

(1) If the Secretary of State considers that any action proposed to be taken by the Welsh Ministers would be incompatible with any international obligation, the Secretary of State may by order direct that the proposed action is not to be taken.

...

90 Documents

(1) A document is validly executed by the Welsh Ministers if it is executed by the First Minister or any Welsh Minister appointed under section 48.

(2) The application of the seal of the Welsh Ministers is to be authenticated by the First Minister, any Welsh Minister appointed under section 48 or any person authorised by the Welsh Ministers (whether generally or specifically) for that purpose.

(3) A document purporting to be—
 (a) duly executed under the seal of the Welsh Ministers, or
 (b) signed on behalf of the Welsh Ministers,

is to be received in evidence and, unless the contrary is proved, is to be taken to be so executed or signed.

...

PART 3
ASSEMBLY MEASURES

Power

93 Assembly Measures

(1) The Assembly may make laws, to be known as Measures of the National Assembly for Wales or Mesurau Cynulliad Cenedlaethol Cymru (referred to in this Act as "Assembly Measures").

(2) A proposed Assembly Measure is enacted by being passed by the Assembly and approved by Her Majesty in Council.

(3) The validity of an Assembly Measure is not affected by any invalidity in the Assembly proceedings leading to its enactment.

(4) Every Assembly Measure is to be judicially noticed.

(5) This Part does not affect the power of the Parliament of the United Kingdom to make laws for Wales.

94 Legislative competence

(1) Subject to the provisions of this Part, an Assembly Measure may make any provision that could be made by an Act of Parliament.

(2) An Assembly Measure is not law so far as any provision of the Assembly Measure is outside the Assembly's legislative competence.

(3) A provision of an Assembly Measure is within the Assembly's legislative competence only if it falls within subsection (4) or (5).

(4) A provision of an Assembly Measure falls within this subsection if—
   (a) it relates to one or more of the matters specified in Part 1 of Schedule 5, and
   (b) it neither applies otherwise than in relation to Wales nor confers, imposes, modifies or removes (or gives power to confer, impose, modify or remove) functions exercisable otherwise than in relation to Wales.

(5) A provision of an Assembly Measure falls within this subsection if—
   (a) it provides for the enforcement of a provision (of that or any other Assembly Measure) which falls within subsection (4) or it is otherwise appropriate for making such a provision effective, or
   (b) it is otherwise incidental to, or consequential on, such a provision.

(6) But a provision which falls within subsection (4) or (5) is outside the Assembly's legislative competence if—
   (a) it breaches any of the restrictions in Part 2 of Schedule 5, having regard to any exception in Part 3 of that Schedule from those restrictions,
   (b) it extends otherwise than only to England and Wales, or
   (c) it is incompatible with the Convention rights or with Community law.

(7) For the purposes of this section the question whether a provision of an Assembly Measure relates to one or more of the matters specified in Part 1 of Schedule 5 is to be determined by reference to the purpose of the provision, having regard (among other things) to its effect in all the circumstances.

95 Legislative competence: supplementary

(1) Her Majesty may by Order in Council—
   (a) amend Part 1 of Schedule 5 to add a matter which relates to one or more of the fields listed in that Part, or to vary or remove any matter,
   (b) amend that Part to add a new field or to vary or remove any field, or
   (c) amend Part 2 or 3 of that Schedule.

(2) An Order in Council under this section does not have effect to amend Part 1 of Schedule 5 by adding a field if, at the time when the amendment comes into force, no functions in the field are exercisable by the Welsh Ministers, the First Minister or the Counsel General.

(3) An Order in Council under this section may make such modifications of—
   (a) any enactment (including any enactment comprised in or made under this Act) or prerogative instrument, or
   (b) any other instrument or document,
   as Her Majesty considers appropriate in connection with the provision made by the Order in Council.

(4) An Order in Council under this section may make provision having retrospective effect.

(5) No recommendation is to be made to Her Majesty in Council to make an Order in Council under this section unless a draft of the statutory instrument containing the Order in Council—
   (a) has been laid before, and approved by a resolution of, the Assembly, and
   (b) having been so approved, has been laid before, and approved by a resolution of, each House of Parliament.

(6) As soon as is reasonably practicable after the draft of an Order in Council under this section has been approved by a resolution of the Assembly, the First Minister must ensure that—
   (a) notice in writing of the resolution, and
   (b) a copy of the draft,
   is sent to the Secretary of State.

(7) The Secretary of State must, before the end of the period of 60 days beginning immediately after the day on which notice of the Assembly's resolution is received, either—
   (a) lay the draft before each House of Parliament, or
   (b) give notice in writing to the First Minister of the Secretary of State's refusal to do so and the reasons for that refusal.

(8) As soon as is reasonably practicable after the First Minister receives notice of the Secretary of State's refusal to lay the draft before each House of Parliament and the reasons for that refusal—
   (a) the First Minister must lay a copy of the notice before the Assembly, and
   (b) the Assembly must ensure that it is published.

(9) In reckoning the period of 60 days mentioned in subsection (7) no account is to be taken of any period during which Parliament is dissolved or prorogued or both Houses are adjourned for more than four days.

(10) The amendment of Schedule 5 by an Order in Council under this section does not affect—
   (a) the validity of an Assembly Measure passed before the amendment comes into force, or
   (b) the previous or continuing operation of such an Assembly Measure.

96 Scrutiny of proposed Orders in Council

The Counsel General or the Attorney General may refer to the Judicial Committee of the Privy Council for decision the question whether a matter which a proposed Order in Council under section 95 proposes to add to Part 1 of Schedule 5 relates to a field listed in that Part.

Procedure

97 Introduction of proposed Assembly Measures

(1) A proposed Assembly Measure may, subject to the standing orders, be introduced in the Assembly—
   (a) by the First Minister, any Welsh Minister appointed under section 48, any Deputy Welsh Minister or the Counsel General, or
   (b) by any other Assembly member.

(2) The person in charge of a proposed Assembly Measure must, on or before the introduction of the proposed Assembly Measure, state that, in that person's view, its provisions would be within the Assembly's legislative competence.

(3) The Presiding Officer must, on or before the introduction of a proposed Assembly Measure in the Assembly—
  (a) decide whether or not, in the view of the Presiding Officer, the provisions of the proposed Assembly Measure would be within the Assembly's legislative competence, and
  (b) state that decision.
(4) A statement under this section must be made in both English and Welsh; but, subject to that, the form of the statement and the manner in which it is to be made are to be determined under the standing orders.
(5) The standing orders—
  (a) may provide for a statement under this section to be published, and
  (b) if they do so, must provide for it to be published in both English and Welsh.

98 Proceedings on proposed Assembly Measures

(1) The standing orders must include provision—
  (a) for general debate on a proposed Assembly Measure with an opportunity for Assembly members to vote on its general principles,
  (b) for the consideration of, and an opportunity for Assembly members to vote on, the details of a proposed Assembly Measure, and
  (c) for a final stage at which a proposed Assembly Measure can be passed or rejected.
(2) Subsection (1) does not prevent the standing orders making provision to enable the Assembly to expedite proceedings in relation to a particular proposed Assembly Measure.
(3) The standing orders may make provision different from that required by subsection (1) for the procedure applicable to proposed Assembly Measures of any of the following kinds—
  (a) proposed Assembly Measures which restate the law,
  (b) proposed Assembly Measures which repeal or revoke spent enactments, and
  (c) private proposed Assembly Measures.
(4) The standing orders must include provision for securing that the Assembly may only pass a proposed Assembly Measure containing provisions which would, if contained in a Bill for an Act of Parliament, require the consent of Her Majesty or the Duke of Cornwall if such consent has been signified in accordance with the standing orders.
(5) The standing orders must include provision for securing that the Assembly may only pass a proposed Assembly Measure if the text of the proposed Assembly Measure is in both English and Welsh, unless the circumstances are such as are specified by the standing orders as any in which the text need not be in both languages.

...

99 Scrutiny of proposed Assembly Measures by the Judicial Committee of the Privy Council

(1) The Counsel General or the Attorney General may refer the question whether a proposed Assembly Measure, or any provision of a proposed Assembly Measure, would be within the Assembly's legislative competence to the Judicial Committee of the Privy Council for decision.

...

100 ECJ references

(1) This section applies where—
  (a) a reference has been made in relation to a proposed Assembly Measure under section 99,
  (b) a reference for a preliminary European Court ruling has been made by the Judicial Committee of the Privy Council in connection with that reference, and
  (c) neither of those references has been decided or otherwise disposed of.
(2) If the Assembly resolves that it wishes to reconsider the proposed Assembly Measure—
  (a) the Clerk must notify the Counsel General and the Attorney General of that fact, and
  (b) the person who made the reference in relation to the proposed Assembly Measure under section 99 must request the withdrawal of the reference.

101 Power to intervene in certain cases
(1) This section applies if a proposed Assembly Measure contains provisions which the Secretary of State has reasonable grounds to believe—
   (a) would have an adverse effect on any matter which is not specified in Part 1 of Schedule 5,
   (b) might have a serious adverse impact on water resources in England, water supply in England or the quality of water in England,
   (c) would have an adverse effect on the operation of the law as it applies in England, or
   (d) would be incompatible with any international obligation or the interests of defence or national security.
(2) The Secretary of State may make an order prohibiting the Clerk from submitting the proposed Assembly Measure for approval by Her Majesty in Council.
...

102 Approval of proposed Assembly Measures
(1) It is for the Clerk to submit proposed Assembly Measures for approval by Her Majesty in Council.
...

PART 4
ACTS OF THE ASSEMBLY

Referendum

103 Referendum about commencement of Assembly Act provisions
   (1) Her Majesty may by Order in Council cause a referendum to be held throughout Wales about whether the Assembly Act provisions should come into force.
   (2) If the majority of the voters in a referendum held by virtue of subsection (1) vote in favour of the Assembly Act provisions coming into force, the Assembly Act provisions are to come into force in accordance with section 105.
...

106 Effect on Measures of commencement of Assembly Act provisions
   (1) Part 3 ceases to have effect on the day on which the Assembly Act provisions come into force.
   (2) But that does not affect the continuing operation on and after that day of any Assembly Measure enacted before that day.

Power

107 Acts of the Assembly
   (1) The Assembly may make laws, to be known as Acts of the National Assembly for Wales or Deddfau Cynulliad Cenedlaethol Cymru (referred to in this Act as "Acts of the Assembly").
   (2) Proposed Acts of the Assembly are to be known as Bills; and a Bill becomes an Act of the Assembly when it has been passed by the Assembly and has received Royal Assent.
...

108 Legislative competence
   (1) Subject to the provisions of this Part, an Act of the Assembly may make any provision that could be made by an Act of Parliament.
   (2) An Act of the Assembly is not law so far as any provision of the Act is outside the Assembly's legislative competence.
   (3) A provision of an Act of the Assembly is within the Assembly's legislative competence only if it falls within subsection (4) or (5).
   (4) A provision of an Act of the Assembly falls within this subsection if—
      (a) it relates to one or more of the subjects listed under any of the headings in Part 1 of Schedule 7 and does not fall within any of the exceptions specified in that Part of that Schedule (whether or not under that heading or any of those headings), and

(b) it neither applies otherwise than in relation to Wales nor confers, imposes, modifies or removes (or gives power to confer, impose, modify or remove) functions exercisable otherwise than in relation to Wales.

(5) A provision of an Act of the Assembly falls within this subsection if—
   (a) it provides for the enforcement of a provision (of that or any other Act of the Assembly) which falls within subsection (4) or a provision of an Assembly Measure or it is otherwise appropriate for making such a provision effective, or
   (b) it is otherwise incidental to, or consequential on, such a provision.

(6) But a provision which falls within subsection (4) or (5) is outside the Assembly's legislative competence if—
   (a) it breaches any of the restrictions in Part 2 of Schedule 7, having regard to any exception in Part 3 of that Schedule from those restrictions,
   (b) it extends otherwise than only to England and Wales, or
   (c) it is incompatible with the Convention rights or with Community law.

(7) For the purposes of this section the question whether a provision of an Act of the Assembly relates to one or more of the subjects listed in Part 1 of Schedule 7 (or falls within any of the exceptions specified in that Part of that Schedule) is to be determined by reference to the purpose of the provision, having regard (among other things) to its effect in all the circumstances.

PART 6
MISCELLANEOUS AND SUPPLEMENTARY

Welsh public records

146 Status of Welsh public records

(1) Welsh public records are not public records for the purposes of the Public Records Act 1958.

(2) But that Act has effect in relation to Welsh public records (as if they were public records for the purpose of that Act) until an order under section 147 imposes a duty to preserve them on the Welsh Ministers (or a member of the staff of the Welsh Assembly Government).

(3) Subsection (2) applies to Welsh public records whether or not, apart from subsection (1), they would be public records for the purposes of the Public Records Act 1958.

156 English and Welsh texts of legislation

(1) The English and Welsh texts of—
   (a) any Assembly Measure or Act of the Assembly which is in both English and Welsh when it is enacted, or
   (b) any subordinate legislation which is in both English and Welsh when it is made,
   are to be treated for all purposes as being of equal standing.

POLICE AND JUSTICE ACT 2006
(2006, c. 48)

An Act to establish a National Policing Improvement Agency. [8 November 2006]

PART 1
POLICE REFORM

National Policing Improvement Agency

1 National Policing Improvement Agency

(1) There is to be a body corporate to be known as the National Policing Improvement Agency.

(2) The following are abolished—
   (a) the Central Police Training and Development Authority;
   (b) the Police Information Technology Organisation.

(3) Schedule 1 (further provision about the National Policing Improvement Agency, and related amendments) has effect.

PART 3
CRIME AND ANTI-SOCIAL BEHAVIOUR

Crime and disorder

19 *Local authority scrutiny of crime and disorder matters*

(1) Every local authority shall ensure that it has a committee (the "crime and disorder committee") with power—
  (a) to review or scrutinise decisions made, or other action taken, in connection with the discharge by the responsible authorities of their crime and disorder functions;
  (b) to make reports or recommendations to the local authority with respect to the discharge of those functions.
  "The responsible authorities" means the bodies and persons who are responsible authorities within the meaning given by section 5 of the Crime and Disorder Act 1998 (authorities responsible for crime and disorder strategies) in relation to the local authority's area.

(2) Where by virtue of subsection (1)(b) the crime and disorder committee makes a report or recommendations it shall provide a copy—
  (a) to each of the responsible authorities, and
  (b) to each of the persons with whom, and bodies with which, the responsible authorities have a duty to co-operate under section 5(2) of the Crime and Disorder Act 1998 ("the co-operating persons and bodies").

(3) Where a member of a local authority ("the councillor") is asked to consider a local crime and disorder matter by a person who lives or works in the area that the councillor represents—
  (a) the councillor shall consider the matter and respond to the person who asked him to consider it, indicating what (if any) action he proposes to take;
  (b) the councillor may refer the matter to the crime and disorder committee.
  In this subsection and subsections (4) to (6) "local authority" does not include the county council for an area for which there are district councils.

(4) Where a member of a local authority operating executive arrangements declines to refer a matter to the crime and disorder committee under subsection (3)(b), the person who asked him to consider it may refer the matter to the executive of that authority.

(5) Where a matter is referred under subsection (4) to the executive of a local authority—
  (a) the executive shall consider the matter and respond to the person who referred the matter to it, indicating what (if any) action it proposes to take;
  (b) the executive may refer the matter to the crime and disorder committee.

(6) The crime and disorder committee shall consider any local crime and disorder matter—
  (a) referred to it by a member of the local authority in question (whether under subsection (3)(b) or not), or
  (b) referred to it under subsection (5),
  and may make a report or recommendations to the local authority with respect to it.

(7) Where the crime and disorder committee makes a report or recommendations under subsection (6) it shall provide a copy to such of the responsible authorities and to such of the co-operating persons and bodies as it thinks appropriate.

(8) An authority, person or body to which a copy of a report or recommendations is provided under subsection (2) or (7) shall—
  (a) consider the report or recommendations;
  (b) respond to the crime and disorder committee indicating what (if any) action it proposes to take;
  (c) have regard to the report or recommendations in exercising its functions.

(9) In the case of a local authority operating executive arrangements—

(a) the crime and disorder committee is to be an overview and scrutiny committee of the authority (within the meaning of Part 2 of the Local Government Act 2000);

(b) a reference in subsection (1)(b) or (6) to making a report or recommendations to the local authority is to be read as a reference to making a report or recommendations to the local authority or the executive.

(10) Schedule 8 (which makes further provision about the crime and disorder committees of local authorities not operating executive arrangements, made up of provision corresponding to that made by section 21 of the Local Government Act 2000 and particular provision for the City of London) has effect.

(11) In this section—

"crime and disorder functions" means functions conferred by or under section 6 of the Crime and Disorder Act 1998 (formulation and implementation of crime and disorder strategies);

"electoral area" has the meaning given by section 203(1) of the Representation of the People Act 1983;

"executive arrangements" means executive arrangements under Part 2 of the Local Government Act 2000;

"local authority" means—

(a) in relation to England, a county council, a district council, a London borough council, the Common Council of the City of London or the Council of the Isles of Scilly;

(b) in relation to Wales, a county council or a county borough council;

"local crime and disorder matter", in relation to a member of a local authority, means a matter concerning—

(a) crime and disorder (including in particular forms of crime and disorder that involve anti-social behaviour or other behaviour adversely affecting the local environment) in the area represented by the member, or

(b) the misuse of drugs, alcohol and other substances in that area.

20 Guidance and regulations regarding crime and disorder matters

(1) The Secretary of State may issue guidance to—
    (a) local authorities in England,
    (b) members of those authorities, and
    (c) crime and disorder committees of those authorities,
    with regard to the exercise of their functions under or by virtue of section 19.

(2) The National Assembly for Wales, after consulting the Secretary of State, may issue guidance to—
    (a) local authorities in Wales,
    (b) members of those authorities, and
    (c) crime and disorder committees of those authorities,
    with regard to the exercise of their functions under or by virtue of section 19.

(3) The Secretary of State may by regulations make provision supplementing that made by section 19 in relation to local authorities in England.

(4) The Secretary of State, after consulting the National Assembly for Wales, may by regulations make provision supplementing that made by section 19 in relation to local authorities in Wales.

(5) Regulations under subsection (3) or (4) may in particular make provision—
    (a) as to the co-opting of additional members to serve on the crime and disorder committee of a local authority;
    (b) as to the frequency with which the power mentioned in section 19(1)(a) is to be exercised;
    (c) requiring information to be provided to the crime and disorder committee by the responsible authorities and the co-operating persons and bodies;
    (d) imposing restrictions on the provision of information to the crime and disorder committee by the responsible authorities and the co-operating persons and bodies;

(e) requiring officers or employees of the responsible authorities and the co-operating persons and bodies to attend before the crime and disorder committee to answer questions;

(f) specifying how a person is to refer a matter to a member of a local authority, or to the executive of a local authority, under section 19(3) or (4);

(g) specifying the periods within which—
  (i) a member of a local authority is to deal with a request under section 19(3);
  (ii) the executive of a local authority is to deal with a matter referred under section 19(4);
  (iii) the crime and disorder committee is to deal with a matter referred as mentioned in section 19(6);
  (iv) the responsible authorities and the co-operating persons and bodies are to consider and respond to a report or recommendations made under or by virtue of section 19.

(6A) . . .

(6) Regulations made by virtue of subsection (5)(a) may provide for a person co-opted to serve as a member of a crime and disorder committee to have the same entitlement to vote as any other member.

(7) In this section "local authority", "crime and disorder committee", "responsible authorities" and "co-operating persons and bodies" have the same meaning as in section 19.

Section 1

SCHEDULE 1
NATIONAL POLICING IMPROVEMENT AGENCY

PART 1
OBJECTS AND POWERS

The Agency's objects

1. The objects of the Agency are—
   (a) the identification, development and promulgation of good practice in policing;
   (b) the provision to listed police forces of expert advice about, and expert assistance in connection with, operational and other policing matters;
   (c) the identification and assessment of—
     (i) opportunities for, and
     (ii) threats to,
     police forces within the meaning given by section 101 of the Police Act 1996 (police forces for police areas in England and Wales), and the making of recommendations to the Secretary of State in the light of its assessment of any opportunities and threats;
   (d) the international sharing of understanding of policing issues;
   (e) the provision of support to listed police forces in connection with—
     (i) information technology,
     (ii) the procurement of goods, other property and services, and
     (iii) training and other personnel matters;
   (ea) the carrying out of its functions under section 3 of the Proceeds of Crime Act 2002 (accreditation and training of financial investigators);
   (f) the doing of all such other things as are incidental or conducive to the attainment of any of the objects mentioned in paragraphs (a) to (ea).

The Agency's principal power

2. (1) The Agency may do anything it considers appropriate for the attainment of its objects, subject to sub-paragraphs (4) and (5).
   (2) In exercise of the power under sub-paragraph (1), the Agency—
     (a) for the purpose of providing such support to listed police forces as is mentioned in paragraph 1(e)—
       (i) may carry on activities itself with a view to forces making use of what is pro-

vided through the carrying-on of the activities,
 (ii) may support forces in their carrying-on of activities themselves, and
 (iii) may support forces in any other way the Agency considers appropriate; and
 (b) may (subject to sub-paragraph (4)) accept gifts, and loans, of money and other property.

(3) The terms on which the Agency accepts a gift or loan of money or other property may (in particular) include provision for the commercial sponsorship of any activity of the Agency.

(4) The Agency may borrow money or other property only with the consent of the Secretary of State.

. . .

Annual plans

5. (1) Before the beginning of each financial year the Agency must prepare a plan setting out how it intends during that year to exercise its powers.

(2) The plan for a financial year ("the plan") must state—
 (a) any priorities that the Agency has determined for that year,
 (b) any current strategic priorities determined by the Secretary of State under paragraph 6,
 (c) any current performance targets established by the Agency, and
 (d) the financial resources that are expected to be available to the Agency for that year.

(3) Priorities within sub-paragraph (2)(a)—
 (a) may relate to matters to which strategic priorities determined under paragraph 6 also relate, or
 (b) may relate to other matters,
but in any event must be so framed as to be consistent with strategic priorities determined under that paragraph.

(4) The plan must state, in relation to each priority within sub-paragraph (2)(a) or (b), how the Agency intends to give effect to that priority.

(5) The Agency must arrange for the plan to be published in such manner as it considers appropriate.

(6) The Agency must send a copy of the plan to—
 (a) the Secretary of State,
 (b) the police authority for each police area in England and Wales,
 (c) the chief officer of police of each police force in England and Wales, and
 (d) such other persons as the Agency considers appropriate.

(7) Before finalising the plan, the Agency must consult—
 (a) the Secretary of State,
 (b) the Association of Police Authorities,
 (c) the Association of Chief Police Officers, and
 (d) such other persons as the Agency considers appropriate.

Strategic priorities

6. (1) The Secretary of State may determine strategic priorities for the Agency.

(2) Before determining any such priorities the Secretary of State must consult—
 (a) the Agency,
 (b) the Association of Chief Police Officers, and
 (c) the Association of Police Authorities.

(3) Sub-paragraph (2)(b) and (c) do not apply in relation to strategic priorities for the Agency so far as the priorities relate—
 (a) to the doing of things by the Agency in relation to any of the persons mentioned in sub-paragraph (4) in exercise of its power under paragraph 2(1), or
 (b) to the doing of things by the Agency in exercise of that power that may or will affect what it may do in relation to any of those persons in future exercise of that power,
but before determining any such priorities so far as so relating, the Secretary of State must consult the Scottish Ministers.

(4) Those persons are—

(a) a police force maintained under or by virtue of section 1 of the Police (Scotland) Act 1967,
(b) cadets under the control of the chief constable of such a force,
(c) persons employed for the purposes of such a force,
(d) the Scottish Police Services Authority, and
(e) any institution, organisation or other body established and maintained by that Authority.

(4A) ...

(5) The Secretary of State must arrange for any priorities determined under this paragraph to be published in such manner as he considers appropriate.

PART 2
MEMBERSHIP ETC

Chairman and other members

7. (1) The Agency is to consist of—
   (a) a chairman appointed by the Secretary of State,
   (b) the chief executive of the Agency, and
   (c) other members appointed by the Secretary of State.
   (2) Before appointing the chairman of the Agency, the Secretary of State must consult—
   (a) the Association of Police Authorities, and
   (b) the Association of Chief Police Officers.
   (3) The Secretary of State may not appoint a person to be chairman of the Agency for more than five years at a time.
   (4) The Secretary of State must exercise his power under sub-paragraph (1)(c) to ensure that at all times the members appointed under that provision include—
   (a) at least one member nominated by the Association of Police Authorities,
   (b) at least one member nominated by the Association of Chief Police Officers, and
   (c) at least one member of Her Majesty's Home Civil Service.
   (5) The Secretary of State may not under sub-paragraph (1)(c) appoint a person to be a member of the Agency for more than five years at a time.
   (6) In this Part of this Schedule "appointed member" means—
   (a) the chairman of the Agency, or
   (b) a member appointed under sub-paragraph (1)(c).

Tenure

8. Subject to paragraphs 9 and 10, an appointed member of the Agency shall hold and vacate office in accordance with the terms of his appointment.
9. An appointed member may resign by giving written notice to the Secretary of State.
10. The Secretary of State may remove a person from office as an appointed member if the Secretary of State is satisfied that—
    (a) the person has been absent from meetings of the Agency, without its permission, for a period longer than four months,
    (b) the person has been convicted of an offence in the British Islands or elsewhere,
    (c) a bankruptcy order has been made against the person, or the person's estate has been sequestrated, or the person has made a composition or arrangement with, or granted a trust deed for, his creditors,
    (d) the person has failed to comply with the terms of his appointment, or
    (e) the person is unable or unfit to carry out his functions.

Re-appointment

11. Previous service as an appointed member of the Agency does not affect a person's eligibility for re-appointment.

PART 3
ACCOUNTABILITY AND SUPERVISION

Annual reports

28. (1) As soon as possible after the end of each financial year the Agency must prepare a report on the carrying out of its functions during that year.
    (2) The report for a financial year ("the report") must include an assessment of the extent to which the annual plan for that year under paragraph 5 has been carried out.
    (3) The Agency must arrange for the report to be published in such manner as it considers appropriate.
    (4) The Agency must send a copy of the report to—
        (a) the Secretary of State,
        (b) the police authority for each police area in England and Wales,
        (c) the chief officer of police of each police force in England and Wales, and
        (d) such other persons as the Agency considers appropriate.
    (5) The Secretary of State must lay a copy of the report before each House of Parliament.

Reports to Secretary of State

29. (1) The Secretary of State may require the Agency to submit a report to him on specified matters—
        (a) connected with the carrying out of its functions, or
        (b) otherwise connected with any of its activities.
    (2) A report under sub-paragraph (1) must be in such form as the Secretary of State may specify.
    (3) The Secretary of State may arrange, or require the Agency to arrange, for a report under this paragraph to be published in such manner as he considers appropriate.

...

Inspections

30. (1) The Secretary of State may require Her Majesty's Chief Inspector of Constabulary to inspect, and report on, the efficiency and effectiveness of the Agency.
    (2) A requirement under sub-paragraph (1) may be general or relate to a particular matter.

...

TRIBUNALS, COURTS AND ENFORCEMENT ACT 2007
(2007, c. 15)

An Act to make provision about tribunals and inquiries; to establish an Administrative Justice and Tribunals Council; to amend the law relating to judicial appointments and appointments to the Law Commission; to amend the law relating to the enforcement of judgments and debts; to make further provision about the management and relief of debt; to make provision protecting cultural objects from seizure or forfeiture in certain circumstances; to amend the law relating to the taking of possession of land affected by compulsory purchase; to alter the powers of the High Court in judicial review applications; and for connected purposes. [19 July 2007]

PART 1
TRIBUNALS AND INQUIRIES

CHAPTER 1
TRIBUNAL JUDICIARY: INDEPENDENCE AND SENIOR PRESIDENT

2 Senior President of Tribunals

(1) Her Majesty may, on the recommendation of the Lord Chancellor, appoint a person to the office of Senior President of Tribunals.

(2) Schedule 1 makes further provision about the Senior President of Tribunals and about recommendations for appointment under subsection (1).

(3) A holder of the office of Senior President of Tribunals must, in carrying out the functions of that office, have regard to—
    (a) the need for tribunals to be accessible,
    (b) the need for proceedings before tribunals—
        (i) to be fair, and
        (ii) to be handled quickly and efficiently,
    (c) the need for members of tribunals to be experts in the subject-matter of, or the law to be applied in, cases in which they decide matters, and
    (d) the need to develop innovative methods of resolving disputes that are of a type that may be brought before tribunals.
(4) In subsection (3) "tribunals" means—
    (a) the First-tier Tribunal,
    (b) the Upper Tribunal,
    (c) employment tribunals,
    (d) the Employment Appeal Tribunal, and
    (e) the Asylum and Immigration Tribunal.

CHAPTER 2

FIRST-TIER TRIBUNAL AND UPPER TRIBUNAL

Establishment

3 **The First-tier Tribunal and the Upper Tribunal**

(1) There is to be a tribunal, known as the First-tier Tribunal, for the purpose of exercising the functions conferred on it under or by virtue of this Act or any other Act.
(2) There is to be a tribunal, known as the Upper Tribunal, for the purpose of exercising the functions conferred on it under or by virtue of this Act or any other Act.
(3) Each of the First-tier Tribunal, and the Upper Tribunal, is to consist of its judges and other members.
(4) The Senior President of Tribunals is to preside over both of the First-tier Tribunal and the Upper Tribunal.
(5) The Upper Tribunal is to be a superior court of record.

Members and composition of tribunals

4 **Judges and other members of the First-tier Tribunal**

(1) A person is a judge of the First-tier Tribunal if the person—
    (a) is a judge of the First-tier Tribunal by virtue of appointment under paragraph 1(1) of Schedule 2,
    (b) is a transferred-in judge of the First-tier Tribunal (see section 31(2)),
    (c) is a judge of the Upper Tribunal,
    (d) is a member of the Asylum and Immigration Tribunal appointed under paragraph 2(1)(a) to (d) of Schedule 4 to the Nationality, Immigration and Asylum Act 2002 (legally qualified members) and is not a judge of the Upper Tribunal, or
    (e) is a member of a panel of chairmen of employment tribunals.
(2) A person is also a judge of the First-tier Tribunal, but only as regards functions of the tribunal in relation to appeals such as are mentioned in subsection (1) of section 5 of the Criminal Injuries Compensation Act 1995, if the person is an adjudicator appointed under that section by the Scottish Ministers.
(3) A person is one of the other members of the First-tier Tribunal if the person—
    (a) is a member of the First-tier Tribunal by virtue of appointment under paragraph 2(1) of Schedule 2,
    (b) is a transferred-in other member of the First-tier Tribunal (see section 31(2)),
    (c) is one of the other members of the Upper Tribunal, or
    (d) is a member of a panel of members of employment tribunals that is not a panel of chairmen of employment tribunals.
(4) Schedule 2—

contains provision for the appointment of persons to be judges or other members of the First-tier Tribunal, and

makes further provision in connection with judges and other members of the First-tier Tribunal.

5 Judges and other members of the Upper Tribunal

(1) A person is a judge of the Upper Tribunal if the person—
   (a) is the Senior President of Tribunals,
   (b) is a judge of the Upper Tribunal by virtue of appointment under paragraph 1(1) of Schedule 3,
   (c) is a transferred-in judge of the Upper Tribunal (see section 31(2)),
   (d) is a member of the Asylum and Immigration Tribunal appointed under paragraph 2(1)(a) to (d) of Schedule 4 to the Nationality, Immigration and Asylum Act 2002 (legally qualified members) who—
      (i) is the President or a Deputy President of that tribunal, or
      (ii) has the title Senior Immigration Judge but is neither the President nor a Deputy President of that tribunal,
   (e) is the Chief Social Security Commissioner, or any other Social Security Commissioner, appointed under section 50(1) of the Social Security Administration (Northern Ireland) Act 1992,
   (f) is a Social Security Commissioner appointed under section 50(2) of that Act (deputy Commissioners),
   (g) is within section 6(1),
   (h) is a deputy judge of the Upper Tribunal (whether under paragraph 7 of Schedule 3 or under section 31(2)), or
   (i) is a Chamber President or a Deputy Chamber President, whether of a chamber of the Upper Tribunal or of a chamber of the First-tier Tribunal, and does not fall within any of paragraphs (a) to (h).

(2) A person is one of the other members of the Upper Tribunal if the person—
   (a) is a member of the Upper Tribunal by virtue of appointment under paragraph 2(1) of Schedule 3,
   (b) is a transferred-in other member of the Upper Tribunal (see section 31(2)),
   (c) is a member of the Employment Appeal Tribunal appointed under section 22(1)(c) of the Employment Tribunals Act 1996, or
   (d) is a member of the Asylum and Immigration Tribunal appointed under paragraph 2(1)(e) of Schedule 4 to the Nationality, Immigration and Asylum Act 2002 (members other than "legally qualified members").

(3) Schedule 3—

contains provision for the appointment of persons to be judges (including deputy judges), or other members, of the Upper Tribunal, and

makes further provision in connection with judges and other members of the Upper Tribunal.

6 Certain judges who are also judges of First-tier Tribunal and Upper Tribunal

(1) A person is within this subsection (and so, by virtue of sections 4(1)(c) and 5(1)(g), is a judge of the First-tier Tribunal and of the Upper Tribunal) if the person—
   (a) is an ordinary judge of the Court of Appeal in England and Wales (including the vice-president, if any, of either division of that Court),
   (b) is a Lord Justice of Appeal in Northern Ireland,
   (c) is a judge of the Court of Session,
   (d) is a puisne judge of the High Court in England and Wales or Northern Ireland,
   (e) is a circuit judge,
   (f) is a sheriff in Scotland,
   (g) is a county court judge in Northern Ireland,
   (h) is a district judge in England and Wales or Northern Ireland, or
   (i) is a District Judge (Magistrates' Courts).

(2) References in subsection (1)(c) to (i) to office-holders do not include deputies or temporary office-holders.

7 Chambers: jurisdiction and Presidents

(1) The Lord Chancellor may, with the concurrence of the Senior President of Tribunals, by order make provision for the organisation of each of the First-tier Tribunal and the Upper Tribunal into a number of chambers.

(2) There is—
   (a) for each chamber of the First-tier Tribunal, and
   (b) for each chamber of the Upper Tribunal,
   to be a person, or two persons, to preside over that chamber.

(3) A person may not at any particular time preside over more than one chamber of the First-tier Tribunal and may not at any particular time preside over more than one chamber of the Upper Tribunal (but may at the same time preside over one chamber of the First-tier Tribunal and over one chamber of the Upper Tribunal).

(4) A person appointed under this section to preside over a chamber is to be known as a Chamber President.

(5) Where two persons are appointed under this section to preside over the same chamber, any reference in an enactment to the Chamber President of the chamber is a reference to a person appointed under this section to preside over the chamber.

(6) The Senior President of Tribunals may (consistently with subsections (2) and (3)) appoint a person who is the Chamber President of a chamber to preside instead, or to preside also, over another chamber.

(7) The Lord Chancellor may (consistently with subsections (2) and (3)) appoint a person who is not a Chamber President to preside over a chamber.

(8) Schedule 4 (eligibility for appointment under subsection (7), appointment of Deputy Chamber Presidents and Acting Chamber Presidents, assignment of judges and other members of the First-tier Tribunal and Upper Tribunal, and further provision about Chamber Presidents and chambers) has effect.

(9) Each of the Lord Chancellor and the Senior President of Tribunals may, with the concurrence of the other, by order—
   (a) make provision for the allocation of the First-tier Tribunal's functions between its chambers;
   (b) make provision for the allocation of the Upper Tribunal's functions between its chambers;
   (c) amend or revoke any order made under this subsection.

8 Senior President of Tribunals: power to delegate

(1) The Senior President of Tribunals may delegate any function he has in his capacity as Senior President of Tribunals—
   (a) to any judge, or other member, of the Upper Tribunal or First-tier Tribunal;
   (b) to staff appointed under section 40(1).

(2) Subsection (1) does not apply to functions of the Senior President of Tribunals under section 7(9).

(3) A delegation under subsection (1) is not revoked by the delegator's becoming incapacitated.

(4) Any delegation under subsection (1) that is in force immediately before a person ceases to be Senior President of Tribunals continues in force until varied or revoked by a subsequent holder of the office of Senior President of Tribunals.

(5) The delegation under this section of a function shall not prevent the exercise of the function by the Senior President of Tribunals.

Review of decisions and appeals

9 Review of decision of First-tier Tribunal

(1) The First-tier Tribunal may review a decision made by it on a matter in a case, other than a decision that is an excluded decision for the purposes of section 11(1) (but see subsection (9)).

(2) The First-tier Tribunal's power under subsection (1) in relation to a decision is exercisable—
   (a) of its own initiative, or
   (b) on application by a person who for the purposes of section 11(2) has a right of appeal in respect of the decision.
(3) Tribunal Procedure Rules may—
   (a) provide that the First-tier Tribunal may not under subsection (1) review (whether of its own initiative or on application under subsection (2)(b)) a decision of a description specified for the purposes of this paragraph in Tribunal Procedure Rules;
   (b) provide that the First-tier Tribunal's power under subsection (1) to review a decision of a description specified for the purposes of this paragraph in Tribunal Procedure Rules is exercisable only of the tribunal's own initiative;
   (c) provide that an application under subsection (2)(b) that is of a description specified for the purposes of this paragraph in Tribunal Procedure Rules may be made only on grounds specified for the purposes of this paragraph in Tribunal Procedure Rules;
   (d) provide, in relation to a decision of a description specified for the purposes of this paragraph in Tribunal Procedure Rules, that the First-tier Tribunal's power under subsection (1) to review the decision of its own initiative is exercisable only on grounds specified for the purposes of this paragraph in Tribunal Procedure Rules.
(4) Where the First-tier Tribunal has under subsection (1) reviewed a decision, the First-tier Tribunal may in the light of the review do any of the following—
   (a) correct accidental errors in the decision or in a record of the decision;
   (b) amend reasons given for the decision;
   (c) set the decision aside.
(5) Where under subsection (4)(c) the First-tier Tribunal sets a decision aside, the First-tier Tribunal must either—
   (a) re-decide the matter concerned, or
   (b) refer that matter to the Upper Tribunal.
(6) Where a matter is referred to the Upper Tribunal under subsection (5)(b), the Upper Tribunal must re-decide the matter.
(7) Where the Upper Tribunal is under subsection (6) re-deciding a matter, it may make any decision which the First-tier Tribunal could make if the First-tier Tribunal were re-deciding the matter.
(8) Where a tribunal is acting under subsection (5)(a) or (6), it may make such findings of fact as it considers appropriate.
(9) This section has effect as if a decision under subsection (4)(c) to set aside an earlier decision were not an excluded decision for the purposes of section 11(1), but the First-tier Tribunal's only power in the light of a review under subsection (1) of a decision under subsection (4)(c) is the power under subsection (4)(a).
(10) A decision of the First-tier Tribunal may not be reviewed under subsection (1) more than once, and once the First-tier Tribunal has decided that an earlier decision should not be reviewed under subsection (1) it may not then decide to review that earlier decision under that subsection.
(11) Where under this section a decision is set aside and the matter concerned is then re-decided, the decision set aside and the decision made in re-deciding the matter are for the purposes of subsection (10) to be taken to be different decisions.

10 Review of decision of Upper Tribunal

(1) The Upper Tribunal may review a decision made by it on a matter in a case, other than a decision that is an excluded decision for the purposes of section 13(1) (but see subsection (7)).
(2) The Upper Tribunal's power under subsection (1) in relation to a decision is exercisable—
   (a) of its own initiative, or
   (b) on application by a person who for the purposes of section 13(2) has a right of appeal in respect of the decision.

(3) Tribunal Procedure Rules may—
  (a) provide that the Upper Tribunal may not under subsection (1) review (whether of its own initiative or on application under subsection (2)(b)) a decision of a description specified for the purposes of this paragraph in Tribunal Procedure Rules;
  (b) provide that the Upper Tribunal's power under subsection (1) to review a decision of a description specified for the purposes of this paragraph in Tribunal Procedure Rules is exercisable only of the tribunal's own initiative;
  (c) provide that an application under subsection (2)(b) that is of a description specified for the purposes of this paragraph in Tribunal Procedure Rules may be made only on grounds specified for the purposes of this paragraph in Tribunal Procedure Rules;
  (d) provide, in relation to a decision of a description specified for the purposes of this paragraph in Tribunal Procedure Rules, that the Upper Tribunal's power under subsection (1) to review the decision of its own initiative is exercisable only on grounds specified for the purposes of this paragraph in Tribunal Procedure Rules.
(4) Where the Upper Tribunal has under subsection (1) reviewed a decision, the Upper Tribunal may in the light of the review do any of the following—
  (a) correct accidental errors in the decision or in a record of the decision;
  (b) amend reasons given for the decision;
  (c) set the decision aside.
(5) Where under subsection (4)(c) the Upper Tribunal sets a decision aside, the Upper Tribunal must re-decide the matter concerned.
(6) Where the Upper Tribunal is acting under subsection (5), it may make such findings of fact as it considers appropriate.
(7) This section has effect as if a decision under subsection (4)(c) to set aside an earlier decision were not an excluded decision for the purposes of section 13(1), but the Upper Tribunal's only power in the light of a review under subsection (1) of a decision under subsection (4)(c) is the power under subsection (4)(a).
(8) A decision of the Upper Tribunal may not be reviewed under subsection (1) more than once, and once the Upper Tribunal has decided that an earlier decision should not be reviewed under subsection (1) it may not then decide to review that earlier decision under that subsection.
(9) Where under this section a decision is set aside and the matter concerned is then re-decided, the decision set aside and the decision made in re-deciding the matter are for the purposes of subsection (8) to be taken to be different decisions.

11 Right to appeal to Upper Tribunal

(1) For the purposes of subsection (2), the reference to a right of appeal is to a right to appeal to the Upper Tribunal on any point of law arising from a decision made by the First-tier Tribunal other than an excluded decision.
(2) Any party to a case has a right of appeal, subject to subsection (8).
(3) That right may be exercised only with permission (or, in Northern Ireland, leave).
(4) Permission (or leave) may be given by—
  (a) the First-tier Tribunal, or
  (b) the Upper Tribunal,
  on an application by the party.
(5) For the purposes of subsection (1), an "excluded decision" is—
  (a) any decision of the First-tier Tribunal on an appeal made in exercise of a right conferred by the Criminal Injuries Compensation Scheme in compliance with section 5(1)(a) of the Criminal Injuries Compensation Act 1995 (appeals against decisions on reviews),
  (b) any decision of the First-tier Tribunal on an appeal under section 28(4) or (6) of the Data Protection Act 1998 (appeals against national security certificate),
  (c) any decision of the First-tier Tribunal on an appeal under section 60(1) or (4) of the Freedom of Information Act 2000 (appeals against national security certificate),
  (d) a decision of the First-tier Tribunal under section 9—

(i) to review, or not to review, an earlier decision of the tribunal,
(ii) to take no action, or not to take any particular action, in the light of a review of an earlier decision of the tribunal,
(iii) to set aside an earlier decision of the tribunal, or
(iv) to refer, or not to refer, a matter to the Upper Tribunal,

(e) a decision of the First-tier Tribunal that is set aside under section 9 (including a decision set aside after proceedings on an appeal under this section have been begun), or

(f) any decision of the First-tier Tribunal that is of a description specified in an order made by the Lord Chancellor.

(6) A description may be specified under subsection (5)(f) only if—
(a) in the case of a decision of that description, there is a right to appeal to a court, the Upper Tribunal or any other tribunal from the decision and that right is, or includes, something other than a right (however expressed) to appeal on any point of law arising from the decision, or
(b) decisions of that description are made in carrying out a function transferred under section 30 and prior to the transfer of the function under section 30(1) there was no right to appeal from decisions of that description.

(7) Where—
(a) an order under subsection (5)(f) specifies a description of decisions, and
(b) decisions of that description are made in carrying out a function transferred under section 30,
the order must be framed so as to come into force no later than the time when the transfer under section 30 of the function takes effect (but power to revoke the order continues to be exercisable after that time, and power to amend the order continues to be exercisable after that time for the purpose of narrowing the description for the time being specified).

(8) The Lord Chancellor may by order make provision for a person to be treated as being, or to be treated as not being, a party to a case for the purposes of subsection (2).

12 Proceedings on appeal to Upper Tribunal

(1) Subsection (2) applies if the Upper Tribunal, in deciding an appeal under section 11, finds that the making of the decision concerned involved the making of an error on a point of law.

(2) The Upper Tribunal—
(a) may (but need not) set aside the decision of the First-tier Tribunal, and
(b) if it does, must either—
(i) remit the case to the First-tier Tribunal with directions for its reconsideration, or
(ii) re-make the decision.

(3) In acting under subsection (2)(b)(i), the Upper Tribunal may also—
(a) direct that the members of the First-tier Tribunal who are chosen to reconsider the case are not to be the same as those who made the decision that has been set aside;
(b) give procedural directions in connection with the reconsideration of the case by the First-tier Tribunal.

(4) In acting under subsection (2)(b)(ii), the Upper Tribunal—
(a) may make any decision which the First-tier Tribunal could make if the First-tier Tribunal were re-making the decision, and
(b) may make such findings of fact as it considers appropriate.

13 Right to appeal to Court of Appeal etc.

(1) For the purposes of subsection (2), the reference to a right of appeal is to a right to appeal to the relevant appellate court on any point of law arising from a decision made by the Upper Tribunal other than an excluded decision.

(2) Any party to a case has a right of appeal, subject to subsection (14).

(3) That right may be exercised only with permission (or, in Northern Ireland, leave).

(4) Permission (or leave) may be given by—

(a) the Upper Tribunal, or
(b) the relevant appellate court,
on an application by the party.

(5) An application may be made under subsection (4) to the relevant appellate court only if permission (or leave) has been refused by the Upper Tribunal.

(6) The Lord Chancellor may, as respects an application under subsection (4) that falls within subsection (7) and for which the relevant appellate court is the Court of Appeal in England and Wales or the Court of Appeal in Northern Ireland, by order make provision for permission (or leave) not to be granted on the application unless the Upper Tribunal or (as the case may be) the relevant appellate court considers—
   (a) that the proposed appeal would raise some important point of principle or practice, or
   (b) that there is some other compelling reason for the relevant appellate court to hear the appeal.

(7) An application falls within this subsection if the application is for permission (or leave) to appeal from any decision of the Upper Tribunal on an appeal under section 11.

(8) For the purposes of subsection (1), an "excluded decision" is—
   (a) any decision of the Upper Tribunal on an appeal under section 28(4) or (6) of the Data Protection Act 1998 (appeals against national security certificate),
   (b) any decision of the Upper Tribunal on an appeal under section 60(1) or (4) of the Freedom of Information Act 2000 (appeals against national security certificate),
   (c) any decision of the Upper Tribunal on an application under section 11(4)(b) (application for permission or leave to appeal),
   (d) a decision of the Upper Tribunal under section 10—
      (i) to review, or not to review, an earlier decision of the tribunal,
      (ii) to take no action, or not to take any particular action, in the light of a review of an earlier decision of the tribunal, or
      (iii) to set aside an earlier decision of the tribunal,
   (e) a decision of the Upper Tribunal that is set aside under section 10 (including a decision set aside after proceedings on an appeal under this section have been begun), or
   (f) any decision of the Upper Tribunal that is of a description specified in an order made by the Lord Chancellor.

(9) A description may be specified under subsection (8)(f) only if—
   (a) in the case of a decision of that description, there is a right to appeal to a court from the decision and that right is, or includes, something other than a right (however expressed) to appeal on any point of law arising from the decision, or
   (b) decisions of that description are made in carrying out a function transferred under section 30 and prior to the transfer of the function under section 30(1) there was no right to appeal from decisions of that description.

(10) Where—
   (a) an order under subsection (8)(f) specifies a description of decisions, and
   (b) decisions of that description are made in carrying out a function transferred under section 30,
   the order must be framed so as to come into force no later than the time when the transfer under section 30 of the function takes effect (but power to revoke the order continues to be exercisable after that time, and power to amend the order continues to be exercisable after that time for the purpose of narrowing the description for the time being specified).

(11) Before the Upper Tribunal decides an application made to it under subsection (4), the Upper Tribunal must specify the court that is to be the relevant appellate court as respects the proposed appeal.

(12) The court to be specified under subsection (11) in relation to a proposed appeal is whichever of the following courts appears to the Upper Tribunal to be the most appropriate—
   (a) the Court of Appeal in England and Wales;

(b) the Court of Session;
(c) the Court of Appeal in Northern Ireland.
(13) In this section except subsection (11), "the relevant appellate court", as respects an appeal, means the court specified as respects that appeal by the Upper Tribunal under subsection (11).
(14) The Lord Chancellor may by order make provision for a person to be treated as being, or to be treated as not being, a party to a case for the purposes of subsection (2).
(15) Rules of court may make provision as to the time within which an application under subsection (4) to the relevant appellate court must be made.

14 Proceedings on appeal to Court of Appeal etc.

(1) Subsection (2) applies if the relevant appellate court, in deciding an appeal under section 13, finds that the making of the decision concerned involved the making of an error on a point of law.
(2) The relevant appellate court—
　(a) may (but need not) set aside the decision of the Upper Tribunal, and
　(b) if it does, must either—
　　(i) remit the case to the Upper Tribunal or, where the decision of the Upper Tribunal was on an appeal or reference from another tribunal or some other person, to the Upper Tribunal or that other tribunal or person, with directions for its reconsideration, or
　　(ii) re-make the decision.
(3) In acting under subsection (2)(b)(i), the relevant appellate court may also—
　(a) direct that the persons who are chosen to reconsider the case are not to be the same as those who—
　　(i) where the case is remitted to the Upper Tribunal, made the decision of the Upper Tribunal that has been set aside, or
　　(ii) where the case is remitted to another tribunal or person, made the decision in respect of which the appeal or reference to the Upper Tribunal was made;
　(b) give procedural directions in connection with the reconsideration of the case by the Upper Tribunal or other tribunal or person.
(4) In acting under subsection (2)(b)(ii), the relevant appellate court—
　(a) may make any decision which the Upper Tribunal could make if the Upper Tribunal were re-making the decision or (as the case may be) which the other tribunal or person could make if that other tribunal or person were re-making the decision, and
　(b) may make such findings of fact as it considers appropriate.
(5) Where—
　(a) under subsection (2)(b)(i) the relevant appellate court remits a case to the Upper Tribunal, and
　(b) the decision set aside under subsection (2)(a) was made by the Upper Tribunal on an appeal or reference from another tribunal or some other person,
the Upper Tribunal may (instead of reconsidering the case itself) remit the case to that other tribunal or person, with the directions given by the relevant appellate court for its reconsideration.
(6) In acting under subsection (5), the Upper Tribunal may also—
　(a) direct that the persons who are chosen to reconsider the case are not to be the same as those who made the decision in respect of which the appeal or reference to the Upper Tribunal was made;
　(b) give procedural directions in connection with the reconsideration of the case by the other tribunal or person.
(7) In this section "the relevant appellate court", as respects an appeal under section 13, means the court specified as respects that appeal by the Upper Tribunal under section 13(11).

"Judicial review"

15 Upper Tribunal's "judicial review" jurisdiction

(1) The Upper Tribunal has power, in cases arising under the law of England and Wales or under the law of Northern Ireland, to grant the following kinds of relief—
    (a) a mandatory order;
    (b) a prohibiting order;
    (c) a quashing order;
    (d) a declaration;
    (e) an injunction.

(2) The power under subsection (1) may be exercised by the Upper Tribunal if—
    (a) certain conditions are met (see section 18), or
    (b) the tribunal is authorised to proceed even though not all of those conditions are met (see section 19(3) and (4)).

(3) Relief under subsection (1) granted by the Upper Tribunal—
    (a) has the same effect as the corresponding relief granted by the High Court on an application for judicial review, and
    (b) is enforceable as if it were relief granted by the High Court on an application for judicial review.

(4) In deciding whether to grant relief under subsection (1)(a), (b) or (c), the Upper Tribunal must apply the principles that the High Court would apply in deciding whether to grant that relief on an application for judicial review.

(5) In deciding whether to grant relief under subsection (1)(d) or (e), the Upper Tribunal must—
    (a) in cases arising under the law of England and Wales apply the principles that the High Court would apply in deciding whether to grant that relief under section 31(2) of the Supreme Court Act 1981 (c. 54) on an application for judicial review, and
    (b) in cases arising under the law of Northern Ireland apply the principles that the High Court would apply in deciding whether to grant that relief on an application for judicial review.

(6) For the purposes of the application of subsection (3)(a) in relation to cases arising under the law of Northern Ireland—
    (a) a mandatory order under subsection (1)(a) shall be taken to correspond to an order of mandamus,
    (b) a prohibiting order under subsection (1)(b) shall be taken to correspond to an order of prohibition, and
    (c) a quashing order under subsection (1)(c) shall be taken to correspond to an order of certiorari.

16 Application for relief under section 15(1)

(1) This section applies in relation to an application to the Upper Tribunal for relief under section 15(1).

(2) The application may be made only if permission (or, in a case arising under the law of Northern Ireland, leave) to make it has been obtained from the tribunal.

(3) The tribunal may not grant permission (or leave) to make the application unless it considers that the applicant has a sufficient interest in the matter to which the application relates.

(4) Subsection (5) applies where the tribunal considers—
    (a) that there has been undue delay in making the application, and
    (b) that granting the relief sought on the application would be likely to cause substantial hardship to, or substantially prejudice the rights of, any person or would be detrimental to good administration.

(5) The tribunal may—
    (a) refuse to grant permission (or leave) for the making of the application;
    (b) refuse to grant any relief sought on the application.

(6) The tribunal may award to the applicant damages, restitution or the recovery of a sum due if—
  (a) the application includes a claim for such an award arising from any matter to which the application relates, and
  (b) the tribunal is satisfied that such an award would have been made by the High Court if the claim had been made in an action begun in the High Court by the applicant at the time of making the application.
(7) An award under subsection (6) may be enforced as if it were an award of the High Court.
(8) Where—
  (a) the tribunal refuses to grant permission (or leave) to apply for relief under section 15(1),
  (b) the applicant appeals against that refusal, and
  (c) the Court of Appeal grants the permission (or leave),
  the Court of Appeal may go on to decide the application for relief under section 15(1).
(9) Subsections (4) and (5) do not prevent Tribunal Procedure Rules from limiting the time within which applications may be made.

17 Quashing orders under section 15(1): supplementary provision

(1) If the Upper Tribunal makes a quashing order under section 15(1)(c) in respect of a decision, it may in addition—
  (a) remit the matter concerned to the court, tribunal or authority that made the decision, with a direction to reconsider the matter and reach a decision in accordance with the findings of the Upper Tribunal, or
  (b) substitute its own decision for the decision in question.
(2) The power conferred by subsection (1)(b) is exercisable only if—
  (a) the decision in question was made by a court or tribunal,
  (b) the decision is quashed on the ground that there has been an error of law, and
  (c) without the error, there would have been only one decision that the court or tribunal could have reached.
(3) Unless the Upper Tribunal otherwise directs, a decision substituted by it under subsection (1)(b) has effect as if it were a decision of the relevant court or tribunal.

18 Limits of jurisdiction under section 15(1)

(1) This section applies where an application made to the Upper Tribunal seeks (whether or not alone)—
  (a) relief under section 15(1), or
  (b) permission (or, in a case arising under the law of Northern Ireland, leave) to apply for relief under section 15(1).
(2) If Conditions 1 to 4 are met, the tribunal has the function of deciding the application.
(3) If the tribunal does not have the function of deciding the application, it must by order transfer the application to the High Court.
(4) Condition 1 is that the application does not seek anything other than—
  (a) relief under section 15(1);
  (b) permission (or, in a case arising under the law of Northern Ireland, leave) to apply for relief under section 15(1);
  (c) an award under section 16(6);
  (d) interest;
  (e) costs.
(5) Condition 2 is that the application does not call into question anything done by the Crown Court.
(6) Condition 3 is that the application falls within a class specified for the purposes of this subsection in a direction given in accordance with Part 1 of Schedule 2 to the Constitutional Reform Act 2005 (c. 4).
(7) The power to give directions under subsection (6) includes—
  (a) power to vary or revoke directions made in exercise of the power, and

(b) power to make different provision for different purposes.
(8) Condition 4 is that the judge presiding at the hearing of the application is either—
  (a) a judge of the High Court or the Court of Appeal in England and Wales or Northern Ireland, or a judge of the Court of Session, or
  (b) such other persons as may be agreed from time to time between the Lord Chief Justice, the Lord President, or the Lord Chief Justice of Northern Ireland, as the case may be, and the Senior President of Tribunals.
(9) Where the application is transferred to the High Court under subsection (3)—
  (a) the application is to be treated for all purposes as if it—
    (i) had been made to the High Court, and
    (ii) sought things corresponding to those sought from the tribunal, and
  (b) any steps taken, permission (or leave) given or orders made by the tribunal in relation to the application are to be treated as taken, given or made by the High Court.
(10) Rules of court may make provision for the purpose of supplementing subsection (9).
(11) The provision that may be made by Tribunal Procedure Rules about amendment of an application for relief under section 15(1) includes, in particular, provision about amendments that would cause the application to become transferrable under subsection (3).
(12) For the purposes of subsection (9)(a)(ii), in relation to an application transferred to the High Court in Northern Ireland—
  (a) an order of mandamus shall be taken to correspond to a mandatory order under section 15(1)(a),
  (b) an order of prohibition shall be taken to correspond to a prohibiting order under section 15(1)(b), and
  (c) an order of certiorari shall be taken to correspond to a quashing order under section 15(1)(c).

Miscellaneous

22 Tribunal Procedure Rules
(1) There are to be rules, to be called "Tribunal Procedure Rules", governing—
  (a) the practice and procedure to be followed in the First-tier Tribunal, and
  (b) the practice and procedure to be followed in the Upper Tribunal.
(2) Tribunal Procedure Rules are to be made by the Tribunal Procedure Committee.
(3) In Schedule 5—
Part 1 makes further provision about the content of Tribunal Procedure Rules,
Part 2 makes provision about the membership of the Tribunal Procedure Committee,
Part 3 makes provision about the making of Tribunal Procedure Rules by the Committee, and
Part 4 confers power to amend legislation in connection with Tribunal Procedure Rules.
(4) Power to make Tribunal Procedure Rules is to be exercised with a view to securing—
  (a) that, in proceedings before the First-tier Tribunal and Upper Tribunal, justice is done,
  (b) that the tribunal system is accessible and fair,
  (c) that proceedings before the First-tier Tribunal or Upper Tribunal are handled quickly and efficiently,
  (d) that the rules are both simple and simply expressed, and
  (e) that the rules where appropriate confer on members of the First-tier Tribunal, or Upper Tribunal, responsibility for ensuring that proceedings before the tribunal are handled quickly and efficiently.
(5) In subsection (4)(b) "the tribunal system" means the system for deciding matters within the jurisdiction of the First-tier Tribunal or the Upper Tribunal.

24 *Mediation*
(1) A person exercising power to make Tribunal Procedure Rules or give practice directions must, when making provision in relation to mediation, have regard to the following principles—

(a) mediation of matters in dispute between parties to proceedings is to take place only by agreement between those parties;
(b) where parties to proceedings fail to mediate, or where mediation between parties to proceedings fails to resolve disputed matters, the failure is not to affect the outcome of the proceedings.
(2) Practice directions may provide for members to act as mediators in relation to disputed matters in a case that is the subject of proceedings.
(3) The provision that may be made by virtue of subsection (2) includes provision for a member to act as a mediator in relation to disputed matters in a case even though the member has been chosen to decide matters in the case.
(4) Once a member has begun to act as a mediator in relation to a disputed matter in a case that is the subject of proceedings, the member may decide matters in the case only with the consent of the parties.
(5) Staff appointed under section 40(1) may, subject to their terms of appointment, act as mediators in relation to disputed matters in a case that is the subject of proceedings.
(6) In this section—
"member" means a judge or other member of the First-tier Tribunal or a judge or other member of the Upper Tribunal;
"practice direction" means a direction under section 23(1) or (2);
"proceedings" means proceedings before the First-tier Tribunal or proceedings before the Upper Tribunal.

SERIOUS CRIME ACT 2007
(2007, c. 27)

An Act to make provision about serious crime prevention orders; to create offences in respect of the encouragement or assistance of crime; to enable information to be shared or processed to prevent fraud or for purposes relating to proceeds of crime; to enable data matching to be conducted both in relation to fraud and for other purposes; to transfer functions of the Director of the Assets Recovery Agency to the Serious Organised Crime Agency and other persons and to make further provision in connection with the abolition of the Agency and the office of Director; to amend the Proceeds of Crime Act 2002 in relation to certain investigations and in relation to accredited financial investigators, management receivers and enforcement receivers, cash recovery proceedings and search warrants; to extend stop and search powers in connection with incidents involving serious violence; to make amendments relating to Her Majesty's Revenue and Customs in connection with the regulation of investigatory powers; and for connected purposes. [30 October 2007]

PART 1
SERIOUS CRIME PREVENTION ORDERS

General

1 Serious crime prevention orders
(1) The High Court in England and Wales may make an order if—
(a) it is satisfied that a person has been involved in serious crime (whether in England and Wales or elsewhere); and
(b) it has reasonable grounds to believe that the order would protect the public by preventing, restricting or disrupting involvement by the person in serious crime in England and Wales.
(2) The High Court in Northern Ireland may make an order if—
(a) it is satisfied that a person has been involved in serious crime (whether in Northern Ireland or elsewhere); and
(b) it has reasonable grounds to believe that the order would protect the public by preventing, restricting or disrupting involvement by the person in serious crime in Northern Ireland.

(3) An order under this section may contain—
   (a) such prohibitions, restrictions or requirements; and
   (b) such other terms;
   as the court considers appropriate for the purpose of protecting the public by preventing, restricting or disrupting involvement by the person concerned in serious crime in England and Wales or (as the case may be) Northern Ireland.
(4) The powers of the court in respect of an order under this section are subject to sections 6 to 15 (safeguards).
(5) In this Part "serious crime prevention order" means—
   (a) an order under this section; or
   (b) an order under section 19 (corresponding order of the Crown Court on conviction).
(6) For the purposes of this Part references to the person who is the subject of a serious crime prevention order are references to the person against whom the public are to be protected.

2 Involvement in serious crime: England and Wales orders

(1) For the purposes of this Part, a person has been involved in serious crime in England and Wales if he—
   (a) has committed a serious offence in England and Wales;
   (b) has facilitated the commission by another person of a serious offence in England and Wales; or
   (c) has conducted himself in a way that was likely to facilitate the commission by himself or another person of a serious offence in England and Wales (whether or not such an offence was committed).
(2) In this Part "a serious offence in England and Wales" means an offence under the law of England and Wales which, at the time when the court is considering the application or matter in question—
   (a) is specified, or falls within a description specified, in Part 1 of Schedule 1; or
   (b) is one which, in the particular circumstances of the case, the court considers to be sufficiently serious to be treated for the purposes of the application or matter as if it were so specified.
(3) For the purposes of this Part, involvement in serious crime in England and Wales is any one or more of the following—
   (a) the commission of a serious offence in England and Wales;
   (b) conduct which facilitates the commission by another person of a serious offence in England and Wales;
   (c) conduct which is likely to facilitate the commission, by the person whose conduct it is or another person, of a serious offence in England and Wales (whether or not such an offence is committed).
(4) For the purposes of section 1(1)(a), a person has been involved in serious crime elsewhere than in England and Wales if he—
   (a) has committed a serious offence in a country outside England and Wales;
   (b) has facilitated the commission by another person of a serious offence in a country outside England and Wales; or
   (c) has conducted himself in a way that was likely to facilitate the commission by himself or another person of a serious offence in a country outside England and Wales (whether or not such an offence was committed).
(5) In subsection (4) "a serious offence in a country outside England and Wales" means an offence under the law of a country outside England and Wales which, at the time when the court is considering the application or matter in question—
   (a) would be an offence under the law of England and Wales if committed in or as regards England and Wales; and
   (b) either—
      (i) would be an offence which is specified, or falls within a description specified, in Part 1 of Schedule 1 if committed in or as regards England and Wales; or

(ii) is conduct which, in the particular circumstances of the case, the court considers to be sufficiently serious to be treated for the purposes of the application or matter as if it meets the test in sub-paragraph (i).

(6) The test in subsection (4) is to be used instead of the test in section 3(1) in deciding for the purposes of section 1(1)(a) whether a person has been involved in serious crime in Northern Ireland.

(7) An act punishable under the law of a country outside the United Kingdom constitutes an offence under that law for the purposes of subsection (5), however it is described in that law.

3 Involvement in serious crime: Northern Ireland orders

(1) For the purposes of this Part, a person has been involved in serious crime in Northern Ireland if he—
   (a) has committed a serious offence in Northern Ireland;
   (b) has facilitated the commission by another person of a serious offence in Northern Ireland; or
   (c) has conducted himself in a way that was likely to facilitate the commission by himself or another person of a serious offence in Northern Ireland (whether or not such an offence was committed).

(2) In this Part "a serious offence in Northern Ireland" means an offence under the law of Northern Ireland which, at the time when the court is considering the application or matter in question—
   (a) is specified, or falls within a description specified, in Part 2 of Schedule 1; or
   (b) is one which, in the particular circumstances of the case, the court considers to be sufficiently serious to be treated for the purposes of the application or matter as if it were so specified.

(3) For the purposes of this Part, involvement in serious crime in Northern Ireland is any one or more of the following—
   (a) the commission of a serious offence in Northern Ireland;
   (b) conduct which facilitates the commission by another person of a serious offence in Northern Ireland;
   (c) conduct which is likely to facilitate the commission, by the person whose conduct it is or another person, of a serious offence in Northern Ireland (whether or not such an offence is committed).

(4) For the purposes of section 1(2)(a), a person has been involved in serious crime elsewhere than in Northern Ireland if he—
   (a) has committed a serious offence in a country outside Northern Ireland;
   (b) has facilitated the commission by another person of a serious offence in a country outside Northern Ireland; or
   (c) has conducted himself in a way that was likely to facilitate the commission by himself or another person of a serious offence in a country outside Northern Ireland (whether or not such an offence was committed).

(5) In subsection (4) "a serious offence in a country outside Northern Ireland" means an offence under the law of a country outside Northern Ireland which, at the time when the court is considering the application or matter in question—
   (a) would be an offence under the law of Northern Ireland if committed in or as regards Northern Ireland; and
   (b) either—
      (i) would be an offence which is specified, or falls within a description specified, in Part 2 of Schedule 1 if committed in or as regards Northern Ireland; or
      (ii) is conduct which, in the particular circumstances of the case, the court considers to be sufficiently serious to be treated for the purposes of the application or matter as if it meets the test in sub-paragraph (i).

(6) The test in subsection (4) is to be used instead of the test in section 2(1) in deciding for the purposes of section 1(2)(a) whether a person has been involved in serious crime in England and Wales.

(7) An act punishable under the law of a country outside the United Kingdom constitutes an offence under that law for the purposes of subsection (5), however it is described in that law.

4 Involvement in serious crime: supplementary

(1) In considering for the purposes of this Part whether a person has committed a serious offence—
 (a) the court must decide that the person has committed the offence if—
  (i) he has been convicted of the offence; and
  (ii) the conviction has not been quashed on appeal nor has the person been pardoned of the offence; but
 (b) the court must not otherwise decide that the person has committed the offence.
(2) In deciding for the purposes of this Part whether a person ("the respondent") facilitates the commission by another person of a serious offence, the court must ignore—
 (a) any act that the respondent can show to be reasonable in the circumstances; and
 (b) subject to this, his intentions, or any other aspect of his mental state, at the time.
(3) In deciding for the purposes of this Part whether a person ("the respondent") conducts himself in a way that is likely to facilitate the commission by himself or another person of a serious offence (whether or not such an offence is committed), the court must ignore—
 (a) any act that the respondent can show to be reasonable in the circumstances; and
 (b) subject to this, his intentions, or any other aspect of his mental state, at the time.
(4) The Secretary of State may by order amend Schedule 1.

5 Type of provision that may be made by orders

(1) This section contains examples of the type of provision that may be made by a serious crime prevention order but it does not limit the type of provision that may be made by such an order.
(2) Examples of prohibitions, restrictions or requirements that may be imposed by serious crime prevention orders in England and Wales or Northern Ireland include prohibitions, restrictions or requirements in relation to places other than England and Wales or (as the case may be) Northern Ireland.
(3) Examples of prohibitions, restrictions or requirements that may be imposed on individuals (including partners in a partnership) by serious crime prevention orders include prohibitions or restrictions on, or requirements in relation to—
 (a) an individual's financial, property or business dealings or holdings;
 (b) an individual's working arrangements;
 (c) the means by which an individual communicates or associates with others, or the persons with whom he communicates or associates;
 (d) the premises to which an individual has access;
 (e) the use of any premises or item by an individual;
 (f) an individual's travel (whether within the United Kingdom, between the United Kingdom and other places or otherwise).
(4) Examples of prohibitions, restrictions or requirements that may be imposed on bodies corporate, partnerships and unincorporated associations by serious crime prevention orders include prohibitions or restrictions on, or requirements in relation to—
 (a) financial, property or business dealings or holdings of such persons;
 (b) the types of agreements to which such persons may be a party;
 (c) the provision of goods or services by such persons;
 (d) the premises to which such persons have access;
 (e) the use of any premises or item by such persons;
 (f) the employment of staff by such persons.
(5) Examples of requirements that may be imposed on any persons by serious crime prevention orders include—
 (a) a requirement on a person to answer questions, or provide information, specified or described in an order—
  (i) at a time, within a period or at a frequency;

        (ii) at a place;
        (iii) in a form and manner; and
        (iv) to a law enforcement officer or description of law enforcement officer;
        notified to the person by a law enforcement officer specified or described in the order;
    (b) a requirement on a person to produce documents specified or described in an order—
        (i) at a time, within a period or at a frequency;
        (ii) at a place;
        (iii) in a manner; and
        (iv) to a law enforcement officer or description of law enforcement officer;
        notified to the person by a law enforcement officer specified or described in the order.
(6) The prohibitions, restrictions or requirements that may be imposed on individuals by serious crime prevention orders include prohibitions, restrictions or requirements in relation to an individual's private dwelling (including, for example, prohibitions or restrictions on, or requirements in relation to, where an individual may reside).
(7) In this Part—
"document" means anything in which information of any description is recorded (whether or not in legible form);
"a law enforcement officer" means—
    (a) a constable;
    (b) a member of the staff of the Serious Organised Crime Agency who is for the time being designated under section 43 of the Serious Organised Crime and Police Act 2005;
    (c) an officer of Revenue and Customs; or
    (d) a member of the Serious Fraud Office; and
"premises" includes any land, vehicle, vessel, aircraft or hovercraft.
(8) Any reference in this Part to the production of documents is, in the case of a document which contains information recorded otherwise than in legible form, a reference to the production of a copy of the information in legible form.

Extension of jurisdiction to Crown Court

19 Orders by Crown Court on conviction

(1) Subsection (2) applies where the Crown Court in England and Wales is dealing with a person who—
    (a) has been convicted by or before a magistrates' court of having committed a serious offence in England and Wales and has been committed to the Crown Court to be dealt with; or
    (b) has been convicted by or before the Crown Court of having committed a serious offence in England and Wales.
(2) The Crown Court may, in addition to dealing with the person in relation to the offence, make an order if it has reasonable grounds to believe that the order would protect the public by preventing, restricting or disrupting involvement by the person in serious crime in England and Wales.
(3) Subsection (4) applies where the Crown Court in Northern Ireland is dealing with a person who has been convicted by or before the Crown Court of having committed a serious offence in Northern Ireland.
(4) The Crown Court may, in addition to dealing with the person in relation to the offence, make an order if it has reasonable grounds to believe that the order would protect the public by preventing, restricting or disrupting involvement by the person in serious crime in Northern Ireland.
(5) An order under this section may contain—
    (a) such prohibitions, restrictions or requirements; and
    (b) such other terms;

as the court considers appropriate for the purpose of protecting the public by preventing, restricting or disrupting involvement by the person concerned in serious crime in England and Wales or (as the case may be) Northern Ireland.

(6) The powers of the court in respect of an order under this section are subject to sections 6 to 15 (safeguards).

(7) An order must not be made under this section except—
- (a) in addition to a sentence imposed in respect of the offence concerned; or
- (b) in addition to an order discharging the person conditionally.

(8) An order under this section is also called a serious crime prevention order.

UK BORDERS ACT 2007
(2007, c. 30)

An Act to make provision about immigration and asylum; and for connected purposes.

[30 October 2007]

Detention at ports

1 Designated immigration officers

(1) The Secretary of State may designate immigration officers for the purposes of section 2.

(2) The Secretary of State may designate only officers who the Secretary of State thinks are—
- (a) fit and proper for the purpose, and
- (b) suitably trained.

(3) A designation—
- (a) may be permanent or for a specified period, and
- (b) may (in either case) be revoked.

2 Detention

(1) A designated immigration officer at a port in England, Wales or Northern Ireland may detain an individual if the immigration officer thinks that the individual—
- (a) may be liable to arrest by a constable under section 24(1), (2) or (3) of the Police and Criminal Evidence Act 1984 or Article 26(1), (2) or (3) of the Police and Criminal Evidence (Northern Ireland) Order 1989, or
- (b) is subject to a warrant for arrest.

(2) A designated immigration officer who detains an individual—
- (a) must arrange for a constable to attend as soon as is reasonably practicable,
- (b) may search the individual for, and retain, anything that might be used to assist escape or to cause physical injury to the individual or another person,
- (c) must retain anything found on a search which the immigration officer thinks may be evidence of the commission of an offence, and
- (d) must, when the constable arrives, deliver to the constable the individual and anything retained on a search.

(3) An individual may not be detained under this section for longer than three hours.

(4) A designated immigration officer may use reasonable force for the purpose of exercising a power under this section.

(5) Where an individual whom a designated immigration officer has detained or attempted to detain under this section leaves the port, a designated immigration officer may—
- (a) pursue the individual, and
- (b) return the individual to the port.

(6) Detention under this section shall be treated as detention under the Immigration Act 1971 for the purposes of Part 8 of the Immigration and Asylum Act 1999 (detained persons).

POLICE AND CRIMINAL EVIDENCE ACT 1984
CODE A

CODE OF PRACTICE FOR THE EXERCISE BY:

POLICE OFFICERS OF STATUTORY POWERS OF STOP AND SEARCH

POLICE OFFICERS AND POLICE STAFF OF REQUIREMENTS TO RECORD PUBLIC ENCOUNTERS

Commencement - Transitional Arrangements

This code appplies to any search by a police officer and the requirement to record public encounters taking place after midnight on 31 January 2008.

General

This code of practice must be readily available at all police stations for consultation by police officers, police staff, detained persons and members of the public.

The notes for guidance included are not provisions of this code, but are guidance to police officers and others about its application and interpretation. Provisions in the annexes to the code are provisions of this code.

This code governs the exercise by police officers of statutory powers to search a person or a vehicle without first making an arrest. The main stop and search powers to which this code applies are set out in Annex A, but that list should not be regarded as definitive. [See *Note 1*] In addition, it covers requirements on police officers and police staff to record encounters not governed by statutory powers.This code does not apply to:

(a) the powers of stop and search under;
  (i) Aviation Security Act 1982, section 27(2);
  (ii) Police and Criminal Evidence Act 1984, section 6(1) (which relates specifically to powers of constables employed by statutory undertakers on the premises of the statutory undertakers).
(b) searches carried out for the purposes of examination under Schedule 7 to the (b) Terrorism Act 2000 and to which the Code of Practice issued under paragraph 6 of Schedule 14 to the Terrorism Act 2000 applies.

1 Principles governing stop and search 1

1.1 Powers to stop and search must be used fairly, responsibly, with respect for people being searched and without unlawful discrimination. The Race Relations (Amendment) Act 2000 makes it unlawful for police officers to discriminate on the grounds of race, colour, ethnic origin, nationality or national origins when using their powers.

1.2 The intrusion on the liberty of the person stopped or searched must be brief and detention for the purposes of a search must take place at or near the location of the stop.

1.3 If these fundamental principles are not observed the use of powers to stop and search may be drawn into question. Failure to use the powers in the proper manner reduces their effectiveness. Stop and search can play an important role in the detection and prevention of crime, and using the powers fairly makes them more effective.

1.4 The primary purpose of stop and search powers is to enable officers to allay or confirm suspicions about individuals without exercising their power of arrest. Officers may be required to justify the use or authorisation of such powers, in relation both to individual searches and the overall pattern of their activity in this regard, to their supervisory officers or in court. Any misuse of the powers is likely to be harmful to policing and lead to mistrust of the police. Officers must also be able to explain their actions to the member of the public searched. The misuse of these powers can lead to disciplinary action.

1.5 An officer must not search a person, even with his or her consent, where no power to search is applicable. Even where a person is prepared to submit to a search voluntarily, the person must not be searched unless the necessary legal power exists, and the search must be in accordance with the relevant power and the provisions of this Code. The only exception, where an officer does not require a specific power, applies to searches of persons entering sports grounds or other premises carried out with their consent given as a condition of entry.

2 Explanation of powers to stop and search

2.1 This code applies to powers of stop and search as follows:
    (a) powers which require reasonable grounds for suspicion, before they may be exercised; that articles unlawfully obtained or possessed are being carried, or under Section 43 of the Terrorism Act 2000 that a person is a terrorist;
    (b) authorised under section 60 of the Criminal Justice and Public Order Act 1994, based upon a reasonable belief that incidents involving serious violence may take place or that people are carrying dangerous instruments or offensive weapons within any locality in the police area;
    (c) authorised under section 44(1) and (2) of the Terrorism Act 2000 based upon a consideration that the exercise of one or both powers is expedient for the prevention of acts of terrorism;
    (d) powers to search a person who has not been arrested in the exercise of a power to search premises (see Code B paragraph 2.4).

Searches requiring reasonable grounds for suspicion

2.2 Reasonable grounds for suspicion depend on the circumstances in each case. There must be an objective basis for that suspicion based on facts, information, and/or intelligence which are relevant to the likelihood of finding an article of a certain kind or, in the case of searches under section 43 of the Terrorism Act 2000, to the likelihood that the person is a terrorist. Reasonable suspicion can never be supported on the basis of personal factors alone without reliable supporting intelligence or information or some specific behaviour by the person concerned. For example, a person's race, age, appearance, or the fact that the person is known to have a previous conviction, cannot be used alone or in combination with each other as the reason for searching that person. Reasonable suspicion cannot be based on generalisations or stereotypical images of certain groups or categories of people as more likely to be involved in criminal activity. A person's religion cannot be considered as reasonable grounds for suspicion and should never be considered as a reason to stop or stop and search an individual.

2.3 Reasonable suspicion can sometimes exist without specific information or intelligence and on the basis of some level of generalisation stemming from the behaviour of a person. For example, if an officer encounters someone on the street at night who is obviously trying to hide something, the officer may (depending on the other surrounding circumstances) base such suspicion on the fact that this kind of behaviour is often linked to stolen or prohibited articles being carried. Similarly, for the purposes of section 43 of the Terrorism Act 2000, suspicion that a person is a terrorist may arise from the person's behaviour at or near a location which has been identified as a potential target for terrorists.

2.4 However, reasonable suspicion should normally be linked to accurate and current intelligence or information, such as information describing an article being carried, a suspected offender, or a person who has been seen carrying a type of article known to have been stolen recently from premises in the area. Searches based on accurate and current intelligence or information are more likely to be effective. Targeting searches in a particular area at specified crime problems increases their effectiveness and minimises inconvenience to law-abiding members of the public. It also helps in justifying the use of searches both to those who are searched and to the public. This does not however prevent stop and search powers being exercised in other locations where such powers may be exercised and reasonable suspicion exists.

2.5 Searches are more likely to be effective, legitimate, and secure public confidence when reasonable suspicion is based on a range of factors. The overall use of these powers is more likely to be effective when up to date and accurate intelligence or information is communicated to officers and they are well-informed about local crime patterns.

2.6 Where there is reliable information or intelligence that members of a group or gang habitually carry knives unlawfully or weapons or controlled drugs, and wear a distinctive item of clothing or other means of identification to indicate their membership of the group or gang, that distinctive item of clothing or other means of identification may provide reasonable grounds to stop and search a person. [See Note 9]

2.7 A police officer may have reasonable grounds to suspect that a person is in innocent possession of a stolen or prohibited article or other item for which he or she is empowered to search. In that case the officer may stop and search the person even though there would be no power of arrest.

2.8 Under section 43(1) of the Terrorism Act 2000 a constable may stop and search a person whom the officer reasonably suspects to be a terrorist to discover whether the person is in possession of anything which may constitute evidence that the person is a terrorist. These searches may only be carried out by an officer of the same sex as the person searched.

2.9 An officer who has reasonable grounds for suspicion may detain the person concerned in order to carry out a search. Before carrying out a search the officer may ask questions about the person's behaviour or presence in circumstances which gave rise to the suspicion. As a result of questioning the detained person, the reasonable grounds for suspicion necessary to detain that person may be confirmed or, because of a satisfactory explanation, be eliminated. [See *Notes 2 and 3*] Questioning may also reveal reasonable grounds to suspect the possession of a different kind of unlawful article from that originally suspected. Reasonable grounds for suspicion however cannot be provided retrospectively by such questioning during a person's detention or by refusal to answer any questions put.

2.10 If, as a result of questioning before a search, or other circumstances which come to the attention of the officer, there cease to be reasonable grounds for suspecting that an article is being carried of a kind for which there is a power to stop and search, no search may take place. [See *Note 3*] In the absence of any other lawful power to detain, the person is free to leave at will and must be so informed.

2.11 There is no power to stop or detain a person in order to find grounds for a search. Police officers have many encounters with members of the public which do not involve detaining people against their will. If reasonable grounds for suspicion emerge during such an encounter, the officer may search the person, even though no grounds existed when the encounter began. If an officer is detaining someone for the purpose of a search, he or she should inform the person as soon as detention begins.

Searches authorised under section 60 of the Criminal Justice and Public Order Act 1994

2.12 Authority for a constable in uniform to stop and search under section 60 of the Criminal Justice and Public Order Act 1994 may be given if the authorising officer reasonably believes:
(a) that incidents involving serious violence may take place in any locality in the officer's police area, and it is expedient to use these powers to prevent their occurrence, or
(b) that persons are carrying dangerous instruments or offensive weapons without good reason in any locality in the officer's police area.

2.13 An authorisation under section 60 may only be given by an officer of the rank of inspector or above, in writing, specifying the grounds on which it was given, the locality in which the powers may be exercised and the period of time for which they are in force. The period authorised shall be no longer than appears reasonably necessary to prevent, or seek to prevent incidents of serious violence, or to deal with the problem of carrying dangerous instruments or offensive weapons. It may not exceed 24 hours. [See *Notes 10-13*]

2.14 If an inspector gives an authorisation, he or she must, as soon as practicable, inform an officer of or above the rank of superintendent. This officer may direct that the authorisation shall be extended for a further 24 hours, if violence or the carrying of dangerous instruments or offensive weapons has occurred, or is suspected to have occurred, and the continued use of the powers is considered necessary to prevent or deal with further such activity. That direction must also be given in writing at the time or as soon as practicable afterwards. [See *Note 12*]

Powers to require removal of face coverings

2.15 Section 60AA of the Criminal Justice and Public Order Act 1994 also provides a power to demand the removal of disguises. The officer exercising the power must reasonably believe that someone is wearing an item wholly or mainly for the purpose of concealing identity. There is also a power to seize such items where the officer believes that a person intends to wear them for this purpose. There is no power to stop and search for disguises. An officer may seize any such item which is discovered when exercising a power of search for something else, or which is being carried, and which the officer reasonably believes is intended to be used for concealing anyone's identity. This power can only be used if an authorisation under section 60 or an authorisation under section 60AA is in force.

2.16 Authority for a constable in uniform to require the removal of disguises and to seize them under section 60AA may be given if the authorising officer reasonably believes that activities may take place in any locality in the officer's police area that are likely to involve the commission of offences and it is expedient to use these powers to prevent or control these activities.

2.17 An authorisation under section 60AA may only be given by an officer of the rank of inspector or above, in writing, specifying the grounds on which it was given, the locality in which the powers may be exercised and the period of time for which they are in force. The period authorised shall be no longer than appears reasonably necessary to prevent, or seek to prevent the commission of offences. It may not exceed 24 hours. [See *Notes 10-13*]

2.18 If an inspector gives an authorisation, he or she must, as soon as practicable, inform an officer of or above the rank of superintendent. This officer may direct that the authorisation shall be extended for a further 24 hours, if crimes have been committed, or is suspected to have been committed, and the continued use of the powers is considered necessary to prevent or deal with further such activity. This direction must also be given in writing at the time or as soon as practicable afterwards. [See *Note 12*]

Searches authorised under section 44 of the Terrorism Act 2000

2.19 An officer of the rank of assistant chief constable (or equivalent) or above, may give authority for the following powers of stop and search under section 44 of the Terrorism Act 2000 to be exercised in the whole or part of his or her police area if the officer considers it is expedient for the prevention of acts of terrorism:
 (a) under section 44(1) of the Terrorism Act 2000, to give a constable in uniform power to stop and search any vehicle, its driver, any passenger in the vehicle and anything in or on the vehicle or carried by the driver or any passenger; and
 (b) under section 44(2) of the Terrorism Act 2000, to give a constable in uniform power to stop and search any pedestrian and anything carried by the pedestrian.
 An authorisation under section 44(1) may be combined with one under section 44(2).

2.20 If an authorisation is given orally at first, it must be confirmed in writing by the officer who gave it as soon as reasonably practicable.

2.21 When giving an authorisation, the officer must specify the geographical area in which the power may be used, and the time and date that the authorisation ends (up to a maximum of 28 days from the time the authorisation was given). [See *Notes 12* and *13*]

2.22 The officer giving an authorisation under section 44(1) or (2) must cause the Secretary of State to be informed, as soon as reasonably practicable, that such an authorisation has been given. An authorisation which is not confirmed by the Secretary of State within 48 hours of its having been given, shall have effect up until the end of that 48 hour period or the end of the period specified in the authorisation (whichever is the earlier). [See *Note 14*]

2.23 Following notification of the authorisation, the Secretary of State may:
 (i) cancel the authorisation with immediate effect or with effect from such other time as he or she may direct;
 (ii) confirm it but for a shorter period than that specified in the authorisation; or
 (iii) confirm the authorisation as given.

2.24 When an authorisation under section 44 is given, a constable in uniform may exercise the powers:
 (a) only for the purpose of searching for articles of a kind which could be used in connection with terrorism (see paragraph 2.25);
 (b) whether or not there are any grounds for suspecting the presence of such articles.

2.24A When a Community Support Officer on duty and in uniform has been conferred powers under Section 44 of the Terrorism Act 2000 by a Chief Officer of their force, the exercise of this power must comply with the requirements of this Code of Practice, including the recording requirements.

2.25 The selection of persons stopped under section 44 of Terrorism Act 2000 should reflect an objective assessment of the threat posed by the various terrorist groups active in Great Britain.

The powers must not be used to stop and search for reasons unconnected with terrorism. Officers must take particular care not to discriminate against members of minority ethnic groups in the exercise of these powers. There may be circumstances, however, where it is appropriate for officers to take account of a person's ethnic origin in selecting persons to be stopped in response to a specific terrorist threat (for example, some international terrorist groups are associated with particular ethnic identities). [See *Notes 12* and *13*]

2.26 The powers under sections 43 and 44 of the Terrorism Act 2000 allow a constable to search only for articles which could be used for terrorist purposes. However, this would not prevent a search being carried out under other powers if, in the course of exercising these powers, the officer formed reasonable grounds for suspicion.

Powers to search in the exercise of a power to search premises

2.27 The following powers to search premises also authorise the search of a person, not under arrest, who is found on the premises during the course of the search:
(a) section 139B of the Criminal Justice Act 1988 under which a constable may enter school premises and search the premises and any person on those premises for any bladed or pointed article or offensive weapon; and
(b) under a warrant issued under section 23(3) of the Misuse of Drugs Act 1971 to search premises for drugs or documents but only if the warrant specifically authorises the search of persons found on the premises.

2.28 Before the power under section 139B of the Criminal Justice Act 1988 may be exercised, the constable must have reasonable grounds to believe that an offence under section 139A of the Criminal Justice Act 1988 (having a bladed or pointed article or offensive weapon on school premises) has been or is being committed. A warrant to search premises and persons found therein may be issued under section 23(3) of the Misuse of Drugs Act 1971 if there are reasonable grounds to suspect that controlled drugs or certain documents are in the possession of a person on the premises.

2.29 The powers in paragraph 2.27(a) or (b) do not require prior specific grounds to suspect that the person to be searched is in possession of an item for which there is an existing power to search. However, it is still necessary to ensure that the selection and treatment of those searched under these powers is based upon objective factors connected with the search of the premises, and not upon personal prejudice.

3 Conduct of searches

3.1 All stops and searches must be carried out with courtesy, consideration and respect for the person concerned. This has a significant impact on public confidence in the police. Every reasonable effort must be made to minimise the embarrassment that a person being searched may experience. [See *Note 4*]

3.2 The co-operation of the person to be searched must be sought in every case, even if the person initially objects to the search. A forcible search may be made only if it has been established that the person is unwilling to co-operate or resists. Reasonable force may be used as a last resort if necessary to conduct a search or to detain a person or vehicle for the purposes of a search.

3.3 The length of time for which a person or vehicle may be detained must be reasonable and kept to a minimum. Where the exercise of the power requires reasonable suspicion, the thoroughness and extent of a search must depend on what is suspected of being carried, and by whom. If the suspicion relates to a particular article which is seen to be slipped into a person's pocket, then, in the absence of other grounds for suspicion or an opportunity for the article to be moved elsewhere, the search must be confined to that pocket. In the case of a small article which can readily be concealed, such as a drug, and which might be concealed anywhere on the person, a more extensive search may be necessary. In the case of searches mentioned in paragraph 2.1(b), (c), and (d), which do not require reasonable grounds for suspicion, officers may make any reasonable search to look for items for which they are empowered to search. [See *Note 5*]

3.4 The search must be carried out at or near the place where the person or vehicle was first detained. [See *Note 6*]

3.5 There is no power to require a person to remove any clothing in public other than an outer coat, jacket or gloves except under section 45(3) of the Terrorism Act 2000 (which empowers a constable conducting a search under section 44(1) or 44(2) of that Act to require a person to remove headgear and footwear in public) and under section 60AA of the Criminal Justice and Public Order Act 1994 (which empowers a constable to require a person to remove any item worn to conceal identity). [See *Notes 4* and *6*] A search in public of a person's clothing which has not been removed must be restricted to superficial examination of outer garments. This does not, however, prevent an officer from placing his or her hand inside the pockets of the outer clothing, or feeling round the inside of collars, socks and shoes if this is reasonably necessary in the circumstances to look for the object of the search or to remove and examine any item reasonably suspected to be the object of the search. For the same reasons, subject to the restrictions on the removal of headgear, a person's hair may also be searched in public (see paragraphs 3.1 and 3.3).

3.6 Where on reasonable grounds it is considered necessary to conduct a more thorough search (e.g. by requiring a person to take off a T-shirt), this must be done out of public view, for example, in a police van unless paragraph 3.7 applies, or police station if there is one nearby. [See *Note 6*] Any search involving the removal of more than an outer coat, jacket, gloves, headgear or footwear, or any other item concealing identity, may only be made by an officer of the same sex as the person searched and may not be made in the presence of anyone of the opposite sex unless the person being searched specifically requests it. [See *Notes 4, 7* and *8*]

3.7 Searches involving exposure of intimate parts of the body must not be conducted as a routine extension of a less thorough search, simply because nothing is found in the course of the initial search. Searches involving exposure of intimate parts of the body may be carried out only at a nearby police station or other nearby location which is out of public view (but not a police vehicle). These searches must be conducted in accordance with paragraph 11 of Annex A to Code C except that an intimate search mentioned in paragraph 11(f) of Annex A to Code C may not be authorised or carried out under any stop and search powers. The other provisions of Code C do not apply to the conduct and recording of searches of persons detained at police stations in the exercise of stop and search powers. [See *Note 7*]

Steps to be taken prior to a search

3.8 Before any search of a detained person or attended vehicle takes place the officer must take reasonable steps to give the person to be searched or in charge of the vehicle the following information:
  (a) that they are being detained for the purposes of a search
  (b) the officer's name (except in the case of enquiries linked to the investigation of terrorism, or otherwise where the officer reasonably believes that giving his or her name might put him or her in danger, in which case a warrant or other identification number shall be given) and the name of the police station to which the officer is attached;
  (c) the legal search power which is being exercised; and
  (d) a clear explanation of:
    (i) the purpose of the search in terms of the article or articles for which there is a power to search; and
    (ii) in the case of powers requiring reasonable suspicion (see paragraph 2.1(a)), the grounds for that suspicion; or
    (iii) in the case of powers which do not require reasonable suspicion (see paragraph 2.1(b), and (c)), the nature of the power and of any necessary authorisation and the fact that it has been given.

3.9 Officers not in uniform must show their warrant cards. Stops and searches under the powers mentioned in paragraphs 2.1(b), and (c) may be undertaken only by a constable in uniform.

3.10 Before the search takes place the officer must inform the person (or the owner or person in charge of the vehicle that is to be searched) of his or her entitlement to a copy of the record of the search, including his entitlement to a record of the search if an application is made within 12 months, if it is wholly impracticable to make a record at the time. If a record is not made at the time the person should also be told how a copy can be obtained (see section 4). The person should also be given information about police powers to stop and search and the individual's rights in these circumstances.

3.11 If the person to be searched, or in charge of a vehicle to be searched, does not appear to understand what is being said, or there is any doubt about the person's ability to understand English, the officer must take reasonable steps to bring information regarding the person's rights and any relevant provisions of this Code to his or her attention. If the person is deaf or cannot understand English and is accompanied by someone, then the officer must try to establish whether that person can interpret or otherwise help the officer to give the required information.

4 Recording requirements

4.1 An officer who has carried out a search in the exercise of any power to which this Code applies, must make a record of it at the time, unless there are exceptional circumstances which would make this wholly impracticable (e.g. in situations involving public disorder or when the officer's presence is urgently required elsewhere). If a record is not made at the time, the officer must do so as soon as practicable afterwards. There may be situations in which it is not practicable to obtain the information necessary to complete a record, but the officer should make every reasonable effort to do so. [See *Note 21*.]

4.2 A copy of a record made at the time must be given immediately to the person who has been searched. The officer must ask for the name, address and date of birth of the person searched, but there is no obligation on a person to provide these details and no power of detention if the person is unwilling to do so.

4.3 The following information must always be included in the record of a search even if the person does not wish to provide any personal details:
   (i) the name of the person searched, or (if it is withheld) a description;
   (ii) a note of the person's self-defined ethnic background; [See *Note 18*]
   (iii) when a vehicle is searched, its registration number; [See *Note 16*]
   (iv) the date, time, and place that the person or vehicle was first detained;
   (v) the date, time and place the person or vehicle was searched (if different from (iv));
   (vi) the purpose of the search;
   (vii) the grounds for making it, or in the case of those searches mentioned in paragraph 2.1(b) and (c), the nature of the power and of any necessary authorisation and the fact that it has been given; [See *Note 17*]
   (viii) its outcome (e.g. arrest or no further action);
   (ix) a note of any injury or damage to property resulting from it;
   (x) subject to paragraph 3.8(b), the identity of the officer making the search. [See *Note 15*]

4.4 Nothing in paragraph 4.3 (x) or 4.10A requires the names of police officers to be shown on the search record or any other record required to be made under this code in the case of enquiries linked to the investigation of terrorism or otherwise where an officer reasonably believes that recording names might endanger the officers. In such cases the record must show the officers' warrant or other identification number and duty station.

4.5 A record is required for each person and each vehicle searched. However, if a person is in a vehicle and both are searched, and the object and grounds of the search are the same, only one record need be completed. If more than one person in a vehicle is searched, separate records for each search of a person must be made. If only a vehicle is searched, the name of the driver and his or her self-defined ethnic background must be recorded, unless the vehicle is unattended.

4.6 The record of the grounds for making a search must, briefly but informatively, explain the reason for suspecting the person concerned, by reference to the person's behaviour and/or other circumstances.

4.7 Where officers detain an individual with a view to performing a search, but the search is not carried out due to the grounds for suspicion being eliminated as a result of questioning the person detained, a record must still be made in accordance with the procedure outlined in Paragraph 4.12.

4.8 After searching an unattended vehicle, or anything in or on it, an officer must leave a notice in it (or on it, if things on it have been searched without opening it) recording the fact that it has been searched.

4.9 The notice must include the name of the police station to which the officer concerned is attached and state where a copy of the record of the search may be obtained and where any application for compensation should be directed.

4.10 The vehicle must if practicable be left secure.

4.10A When an officer makes a record of the stop electronically and is unable to produce a copy of the form at the time, the officer must explain how the person can obtain a full copy of the record of the stop or search and give the person a receipt which contains:
- a unique reference number and guidance on how to obtain a full copy of the stop or search;
- the name of the officer who carried out the stop or search (unless paragraph 4.4 applies); and
- the power used to stop and search them. [See *Note 21*]

Recording of encounters not governed by Statutory Powers

4.11 Not used.

4.12 When an officer requests a person in a public place to account for themselves, i.e. their actions, behaviour, presence in an area or possession of anything, a record of the encounter must be completed at the time and a copy given to the person who has been questioned. The record must identify the name of the officer who has made the stop and conducted the encounter. This does not apply under the exceptional circumstances outlined in paragraph 4.1 of this code.

4.13 This requirement does not apply to general conversations such as when giving directions to a place, or when seeking witnesses. It also does not include occasions on which an officer is seeking general information or questioning people to establish background to incidents which have required officers to intervene to keep the peace or resolve a dispute.

4.14 A separate record need not be completed when:
- stopping a person in a vehicle when an HORT/1 form, a Vehicle Defect Rectification Scheme Notice, or aFixed Penalty Notice is issued. It also does not apply when a specimen of breath is required under Section 6 of the Road Traffic Act 1988.
- stopping a person when a Penalty Notice is issued for an offence.

4.15 Officers must inform the person of their entitlement to a copy of a record of the encounter.

4.16 The provisions of paragraph 4.4 of this code apply equally when the encounters described in 4.12 and 4.13 are recorded.

4.17 The following information must be included in the record
  (i) the date, time and place of the encounter;
  (ii) if the person is in a vehicle, the registration number;
  (iii) the reason why the officer questioned that person; [See *Note 17*]
  (iv) a note of the person's self-defined ethnic background; [See *Note 18*]
  (v) the outcome of the encounter.

4.18 There is no power to require the person questioned to provide personal details. If a person refuses to give their self-defined ethnic background, a form must still be completed, which includes a description of the person's ethnic background. [See *Note 18*]

4.19 A record of an encounter must always be made when the criteria set out in 4.12 have been met. If the criteria are not met but the person requests a record, the officer should provide a copy of the form but record on it that the encounter did not meet the criteria. The officer can refuse to issue the form if he or she reasonably believes that the purpose of the request is deliberately aimed at frustrating or delaying legitimate police activity. [See *Note 20*]

4.20 All references to officers in this section include police staff designated as Community Support Officers under section 38 of the Police Reform Act 2002.

5 Monitoring and supervising the use of stop and search powers

5.1 Supervising officers must monitor the use of stop and search powers and should consider in particular whether there is any evidence that they are being exercised on the basis of stereotyped images or inappropriate generalisations. Supervising officers should satisfy themselves that the practice of officers under their supervision in stopping, searching and recording is fully in accordance with this Code. Supervisors must also examine whether the records reveal any trends or patterns which give cause for concern, and if so take appropriate action to address this

5.2 Senior officers with area or force-wide responsibilities must also monitor the broader use of stop and search powers and, where necessary, take action at the relevant level.

5.3 Supervision and monitoring must be supported by the compilation of comprehensive statistical records of stops and searches at force, area and local level. Any apparently disproportionate use of the powers by particular officers or groups of officers or in relation to specific sections of the community should be identified and investigated.

5.4 In order to promote public confidence in the use of the powers, forces in consultation with police authorities must make arrangements for the records to be scrutinised by representatives of the community, and to explain the use of the powers at a local level. [See Note 19].

Notes for guidance

Officers exercising stop and search powers

1   *This code does not affect the ability of an officer to speak to or question a person in the ordinary course of the officer's duties without detaining the person or exercising any element of compulsion. It is not the purpose of the code to prohibit such encounters between the police and the community with the co-operation of the person concerned and neither does it affect the principle that all citizens have a duty to help police officers to prevent crime and discover offenders. This is a civic rather than a legal duty; but when a police officer is trying to discover whether, or by whom, an offence has been committed he or she may question any person from whom useful information might be obtained, subject to the restrictions imposed by Code C. A person's unwillingness to reply does not alter this entitlement, but in the absence of a power to arrest, or to detain in order to search, the person is free to leave at will and cannot be compelled to remain with the officer.*

2   *In some circumstances preparatory questioning may be unnecessary, but in general a brief conversation or exchange will be desirable not only as a means of avoiding unsuccessful searches, but to explain the grounds for the stop/search, to gain cooperation and reduce any tension there might be surrounding the stop/search.*

3   *Where a person is lawfully detained for the purpose of a search, but no search in the event takes place, the detention will not thereby have been rendered unlawful.*

4   *Many people customarily cover their heads or faces for religious reasons – for example, Muslim women, Sikh men, Sikh or Hindu women, or Rastarfarian men or women. A police officer cannot order the removal of a head or face covering except where there is reason to believe that the item is being worn by the individual wholly or mainly for the purpose of disguising identity, not simply because it disguises identity. Where there may be religious sensitivities about ordering the removal of such an item, the officer should permit the item to be removed out of public view. Where practicable, the item should be removed in the presence of an officer of the same sex as the person and out of sight of anyone of the opposite sex.*

5   *A search of a person in public should be completed as soon as possible.*

6   *A person may be detained under a stop and search power at a place other than where the person was first detained, only if that place, be it a police station or elsewhere, is nearby. Such a place should be located within a reasonable travelling distance using whatever mode of travel (on foot or by car) is appropriate. This applies to all searches under stop and search powers, whether or not they involve the removal of clothing or exposure of intimate parts of the body (see paragraphs 3.6 and 3.7) or take place in or out of public view. It means, for example, that a search under the stop and search power in section 23 of the Misuse of Drugs Act 1971 which involves the*

compulsory removal of more than a person's outer coat, jacket or gloves cannot be carried out unless a place which is both nearby the place they were first detained and out of public view, is available. If a search involves exposure of intimate parts of the body and a police station is not nearby, particular care must be taken to ensure that the location is suitable in that it enables the search to be conducted in accordance with the requirements of paragraph 11 of Annex A to Code C.

7 *A search in the street itself should be regarded as being in public for the purposes of paragraphs 3.6 and 3.7 above, even though it may be empty at the time a search begins. Although there is no power to require a person to do so, there is nothing to prevent an officer from asking a person voluntarily to remove more than an outer coat, jacket or gloves (and headgear or footwear under section 45(3) of the Terrorism Act 2000) in public.*

8 *Where there may be religious sensitivities about asking someone to remove headgear using a power under section 45(3) of the Terrorism Act 2000, the police officer should offer to carry out the search out of public view (for example, in a police van or police station if there is one nearby).*

9 *Other means of identification might include jewellery, insignias, tattoos or other features which are known to identify members of the particular gang or group.*

Authorising officers

10 *The powers under section 60 are separate from and additional to the normal stop and search powers which require reasonable grounds to suspect an individual of carrying an offensive weapon (or other article). Their overall purpose is to prevent serious violence and the widespread carrying of weapons which might lead to persons being seriously injured by disarming potential offenders in circumstances where other powers would not be sufficient. They should not therefore be used to replace or circumvent the normal powers for dealing with routine crime problems. The purpose of the powers under section 60AA is to prevent those involved in intimidatory or violent protests using face coverings to disguise identity.*

11 *Authorisations under section 60 require a reasonable belief on the part of the authorising officer. This must have an objective basis, for example: intelligence or relevant information such as a history of antagonism and violence between particular groups; previous incidents of violence at, or connected with, particular events or locations; a significant increase in knife-point robberies in a limited area; reports that individuals are regularly carrying weapons in a particular locality; or in the case of section 60AA previous incidents of crimes being committed while wearing face coverings to conceal identity.*

12 *It is for the authorising officer to determine the period of time during which the powers mentioned in paragraph 2.1 (b) and (c) may be exercised. The officer should set the minimum period he or she considers necessary to deal with the risk of violence, the carrying of knives or offensive weapons, or terrorism. A direction to extend the period authorised under the powers mentioned in paragraph 2.1(b) may be given only once. Thereafter further use of the powers requires a new authorisation. There is no provision to extend an authorisation of the powers mentioned in paragraph 2.1(c); further use of the powers requires a new authorisation.*

13 *It is for the authorising officer to determine the geographical area in which the use of the powers is to be authorised. In doing so the officer may wish to take into account factors such as the nature and venue of the anticipated incident, the number of people who may be in the immediate area of any possible incident, their access to surrounding areas and the anticipated level of violence. The officer should not set a geographical area which is wider than that he or she believes necessary for the purpose of preventing anticipated violence, the carrying of knives or offensive weapons, acts of terrorism, or, in the case of section 60AA, the prevention of commission of offences. It is particularly important to ensure that constables exercising such powers are fully aware of where they may be used. If the area specified is smaller than the whole force area, the officer giving the authorisation should specify either the streets which form the boundary of the area or a divisional boundary within the force area. If the power is to be used in response to a threat or incident that straddles police force areas, an officer from each of the forces concerned will need to give an authorisation.*

14 *An officer who has authorised the use of powers under section 44 of the Terrorism Act 2000 must take immediate steps to send a copy of the authorisation to the National Joint Unit, Metropolitan*

Police Special Branch, who will forward it to the Secretary of State. The Secretary of State should be informed of the reasons for the authorisation. The National Joint Unit will inform the force concerned, within 48 hours of the authorisation being made, whether the Secretary of State has confirmed or cancelled or altered the authorisation.

Recording

15 *Where a stop and search is conducted by more than one officer the identity of all the officers engaged in the search must be recorded on the record. Nothing prevents an officer who is present but not directly involved in searching from completing the record during the course of the encounter.*

16 *Where a vehicle has not been allocated a registration number (e.g. a rally car or a trials motorbike) that part of the requirement under 4.3(iii) does not apply.*

17 *It is important for monitoring purposes to specify whether the authority for exercising a stop and search power was given under section 60 of the Criminal Justice and Public Order Act 1994, or under section 44(1) or 44(2) of the Terrorism Act 2000.*

18 *Officers should record the self-defined ethnicity of every person stopped according to the categories used in the 2001 census question listed in Annex B. Respondents should be asked to select one of the five main categories representing broad ethnic groups and then a more specific cultural background from within this group. The ethnic classification should be coded for recording purposes using the coding system in Annex B. An additional "Not stated" box is available but should not be offered to respondents explicitly. Officers should be aware and explain to members of the public, especially where concerns are raised, that this information is required to obtain a true picture of stop and search activity and to help improve ethnic monitoring, tackle discriminatory practice, and promote effective use of the powers. If the person gives what appears to the officer to be an "incorrect" answer (e.g. a person who appears to be white states that they are black), the officer should record the response that has been given. Officers should also record their own perception of the ethnic background of every person stopped and this must be done by using the PNC/Phoenix classification system. If the "Not stated" category is used the reason for this must be recorded on the form.*

19 *Arrangements for public scrutiny of records should take account of the right to confidentiality of those stopped and searched. Anonymised forms and/or statistics generated from records should be the focus of the examinations by members of the public.*

20 *Where an officer engages in conversation which is not pertinent to the actions or whereabouts of the individual (e.g. does not relate to why the person is there, what they are doing or where they have been or are going) then issuing a form would not meet the criteria set out in paragraph 4.12. Situations designed to impede police activity may arise, for example, in public order situations where individuals engage in dialogue with the officer but the officer does not initiate or engage in contact about the person's individual circumstances.*

21 *In situations where it is not practicable to provide a written record of the stop or stop and search at that time, the officer should consider providing the person with details of the station to which the person may attend for a record. This may take the form of a simple business card, adding the date of the stop or stop and search.*

Definition of Offensive Weapon

22 *'Offensive weapon' is defined as any article made or adapted for use for causing injury to the person, or intended by the person having it with him for such use or by someone else. There are three categories of offensive weapons: those made for causing injury to the person; those adapted for such a purpose; and those not so made or adapted, but carried with the intention of causing injury to the person. A firearm, as defined by section 57 of the Firearms Act 1968, would fall within the definition of offensive weapon if any of the criteria above.*

POLICE AND CRIMINAL EVIDENCE ACT 1984 CODE C

CODE OF PRACTICE FOR THE DETENTION, TREATMENT AND QUESTIONING OF PERSONS BY POLICE OFFICERS

Commencement — Transitional Arrangements

This Code applies to people in police detention after midnight on 31 January 2008, notwithstanding that their period of detention may have commenced before that time.

1 General

1.1 All persons in custody must be dealt with expeditiously, and released as soon as the need for detention no longer applies.

1.1A A custody officer must perform the functions in this Code as soon as practicable. A custody officer will not be in breach of this Code if delay is justifiable and reasonable steps are taken to prevent unnecessary delay. The custody record shall show when a delay has occurred and the reason. See *Note 1H*

1.2 This Code of Practice must be readily available at all police stations for consultation by:
- police officers
- police staff
- detained persons
- members of the public.

1.3 The provisions of this Code:
- include the *Annexes*
- do not include the *Notes for Guidance*.

1.4 If an officer has any suspicion, or is told in good faith, that a person of any age may be mentally disordered or otherwise mentally vulnerable, in the absence of clear evidence to dispel that suspicion, the person shall be treated as such for the purposes of this Code. See *Note 1G*

1.5 If anyone appears to be under 17, they shall be treated as a juvenile for the purposes of this Code in the absence of clear evidence that they are older.

1.6 If a person appears to be blind, seriously visually impaired, deaf, unable to read or speak or has difficulty orally because of a speech impediment, they shall be treated as such for the purposes of this Code in the absence of clear evidence to the contrary.

1.7 "The appropriate adult" means, in the case of a:
    (a) juvenile:
        (i) the parent, guardian or, if the juvenile is in local authority or voluntary organisation care, or is otherwise being looked after under the Children Act 1989, a person representing that authority or organisation;
        (ii) a social worker of a local authority;
        (iii) failing these, some other responsible adult aged 18 or over who is not a police officer or employed by the police.
    (b) person who is mentally disordered or mentally vulnerable: See *Note 1D*
        (iv) a relative, guardian or other person responsible for their care or custody;
        (v) someone experienced in dealing with mentally disordered or mentally vulnerable people but who is not a police officer or employed by the police;
        (vi) failing these, some other responsible adult aged 18 or over who is not a police officer or employed by the police.

1.8 If this Code requires a person be given certain information, they do not have to be given it if at the time they are incapable of understanding what is said, are violent or may become violent or in urgent need of medical attention, but they must be given it as soon as practicable.

1.9 References to a custody officer include any:
- police officer; or
- designated staff custody officer acting in the exercise or performance of the powers and duties conferred or imposed on them by their designation,

performing the functions of a custody officer. See *Note 1J*.
1.9A When this Code requires the prior authority or agreement of an officer of at least inspector or superintendent rank, that authority may be given by a sergeant or chief inspector authorised to perform the functions of the higher rank under the Police and Criminal Evidence Act 1984 (PACE), section 107.
1.10 Subject to *paragraph 1.12*, this Code applies to people in custody at police stations in England and Wales, whether or not they have been arrested, and to those removed to a police station as a place of safety under the Mental Health Act 1983, sections 135 and 136. *Section 15* applies solely to people in police detention, e.g. those brought to a police station under arrest or arrested at a police station for an offence after going there voluntarily.
1.11 People detained under the Terrorism Act 2000, Schedule 8 and section 41 and other provisions of that Act are not subject to any part of this Code. Such persons are subject to the Code of Practice for detention, treatment and questioning of persons by police officers detained under that Act.
1.12 This Code's provisions do not apply to people in custody:
(i) arrested on warrants issued in Scotland by officers under the Criminal Justice and Public Order Act 1994, section 136(2), or arrested or detained without warrant by officers from a police force in Scotland under section 137(2). In these cases, police powers and duties and the person's rights and entitlements whilst at a police station in England or Wales are the same as those in Scotland;
(ii) arrested under the Immigration and Asylum Act 1999, section 142(3) in order to have their fingerprints taken;
(iii) whose detention is authorised by an immigration officer under the Immigration Act 1971;
(iv) who are convicted or remanded prisoners held in police cells on behalf of the Prison Service under the Imprisonment (Temporary Provisions) Act 1980;
(v) not used
(vi) detained for searches under stop and search powers except as required by Code A.
The provisions on conditions of detention and treatment in *sections 8* and *9* must be considered as the minimum standards of treatment for such detainees.
1.13 In this Code:
(a) 'designated person' means a person other than a police officer, designated under the Police Reform Act 2002, Part 4 who has specified powers and duties of police officers conferred or imposed on them;
(b) reference to a police officer includes a designated person acting in the exercise or performance of the powers and duties conferred or imposed on them by their designation.
1.14 Designated persons are entitled to use reasonable force as follows:
(a) when exercising a power conferred on them which allows a police officer exercising that power to use reasonable force, a designated person has the same entitlement to use force; and
(b) at other times when carrying out duties conferred or imposed on them that also entitle them to use reasonable force, for example:
- when at a police station carrying out the duty to keep detainees for whom they are responsible under control and to assist any other police officer or designated person to keep any detainee under control and to prevent their escape.
- when securing, or assisting any other police officer or designated person in securing, the detention of a person at a police station.
- when escorting, or assisting any other police officer or designated person in escorting, a detainee within a police station.
- for the purpose of saving life or limb; or
- preventing serious damage to property.
1.15 Nothing in this Code prevents the custody officer, or other officer given custody of the detainee, from allowing police staff who are not designated persons to carry out individual

procedures or tasks at the police station if the law allows. However, the officer remains responsible for making sure the procedures and tasks are carried out correctly in accordance with the Codes of Practice. Any such person must be:

(a) a person employed by a police authority maintaining a police force and under the control and direction of the Chief Officer of that force;

(b) employed by a person with whom a police authority has a contract for the provision of services relating to persons arrested or otherwise in custody.

1.16 Designated persons and other police staff must have regard to any relevant provisions of the Codes of Practice.

1.17 References to pocket books include any official report book issued to police officers or other police staff.

2 Custody records

2.1A When a person is brought to a police station:
- under arrest
- is arrested at the police station having attended there voluntarily or
- attends a police station to answer bail

they should be brought before the custody officer as soon as practicable after their arrival at the station or, if appropriate, following arrest after attending the police station voluntarily. This applies to designated and non-designated police stations. A person is deemed to be "at a police station" for these purposes if they are within the boundary of any building or enclosed yard which forms part of that police station.

2.1 A separate custody record must be opened as soon as practicable for each person brought to a police station under arrest or arrested at the station having gone there voluntarily or attending a police station in answer to street bail. All information recorded under this Code must be recorded as soon as practicable in the custody record unless otherwise specified. Any audio or video recording made in the custody area is not part of the custody record.

2.2 If any action requires the authority of an officer of a specified rank, subject to *paragraph 2.6A*, their name and rank must be noted in the custody record.

2.3 The custody officer is responsible for the custody record's accuracy and completeness and for making sure the record or copy of the record accompanies a detainee if they are transferred to another police station. The record shall show the:
- time and reason for transfer;
- time a person is released from detention.

2.4 A solicitor or appropriate adult must be permitted to consult a detainee's custody record as soon as practicable after their arrival at the station and at any other time whilst the person is detained. Arrangements for this access must be agreed with the custody officer and may not unreasonably interfere with the custody officer's duties.

2.4A When a detainee leaves police detention or is taken before a court they, their legal representative or appropriate adult shall be given, on request, a copy of the custody record as soon as practicable. This entitlement lasts for 12 months after release.

2.5 The detainee, appropriate adult or legal representative shall be permitted to inspect the original custody record after the detainee has left police detention provided they give reasonable notice of their request. Any such inspection shall be noted in the custody record.

2.6 Subject to *paragraph 2.6A*, all entries in custody records must be timed and signed by the maker. Records entered on computer shall be timed and contain the operator's identification.

2.6A Nothing in this Code requires the identity of officers or other police staff to be recorded or disclosed:
(a) not used;
(b) if the officer or police staff reasonably believe recording or disclosing their name might put them in danger.

In these cases, they shall use their warrant or other identification numbers and the name of their police station. See *Note 2A*

2.7 The fact and time of any detainee's refusal to sign a custody record, when asked in accordance with this Code, must be recorded.

3 Initial action

(a) Detained persons – normal procedure

3.1 When a person is brought to a police station under arrest or arrested at the station having gone there voluntarily, the custody officer must make sure the person is told clearly about the following continuing rights which may be exercised at any stage during the period in custody:
   (i) the right to have someone informed of their arrest as in *section 5*;
   (ii) the right to consult privately with a solicitor and that free independent legal advice is available;
   (iii) the right to consult these Codes of Practice. See *Note 3D*

3.2 The detainee must also be given:
   - a written notice setting out:
     – the above three rights;
     – the arrangements for obtaining legal advice;
     – the right to a copy of the custody record as in *paragraph 2.4A*;
     – the caution in the terms prescribed in section 10.
   - an additional written notice briefly setting out their entitlements while in custody, see *Notes 3A* and *3B*.

   Note: The detainee shall be asked to sign the custody record to acknowledge receipt of these notices. Any refusal must be recorded on the custody record.

3.3 A citizen of an independent Commonwealth country or a national of a foreign country, including the Republic of Ireland, must be informed as soon as practicable about their rights of communication with their High Commission, Embassy or Consulate. See *section 7*

3.4 The custody officer shall:
   - record the offence(s) that the detainee has been arrested for and the reason(s) for the arrest on the custody record. See *paragraph 10.3* and *Code G paragraphs 2.2* and *4.3*.
   - note on the custody record any comment the detainee makes in relation to the arresting officer's account but shall not invite comment. If the arresting officer is not physically present when the detainee is brought to a police station, the arresting officer's account must be made available to the custody officer remotely or by a third party on the arresting officer's behalf. If the custody officer authorises a person's detention the detainee must be informed of the grounds as soon as practicable and before they are questioned about any offence;
   - note any comment the detainee makes in respect of the decision to detain them but shall not invite comment;
   - not put specific questions to the detainee regarding their involvement in any offence, nor in respect of any comments they may make in response to the arresting officer's account or the decision to place them in detention. Such an exchange is likely to constitute an interview as in *paragraph 11.1A* and require the associated safeguards in section 11.

   See *paragraph 11.13* in respect of unsolicited comments. 3.5 The custody officer shall:
   (a) ask the detainee, whether at this time, they:
       (i) would like legal advice, see *paragraph 6.5*;
       (iii) want someone informed of their detention, see *section 5*;
   (b) ask the detainee to sign the custody record to confirm their decisions in respect of (a);
   (c) determine whether the detainee:
       (iii) is, or might be, in need of medical treatment or attention, see *section 9*;
       (iv) requires:
           - an appropriate adult;
           - help to check documentation;
           - an interpreter;
   (d) record the decision in respect of (c).

3.6 When determining these needs the custody officer is responsible for initiating an assessment to consider whether the detainee is likely to present specific risks to custody staff or themselves. Such assessments should always include a check on the Police National Computer, to be carried out as soon as practicable, to identify any risks highlighted in relation to the detainee. Although such assessments are primarily the custody officer's responsibility, it may be necessary for them to consult and involve others, e.g. the arresting officer or an appropriate health care professional, see *paragraph 9.13*. Reasons for delaying the initiation or completion of the assessment must be recorded.

3.7 Chief Officers should ensure that arrangements for proper and effective risk assessments required by *paragraph 3.6* are implemented in respect of all detainees at police stations in their area.

3.8 Risk assessments must follow a structured process which clearly defines the categories of risk to be considered and the results must be incorporated in the detainee's custody record. The custody officer is responsible for making sure those responsible for the detainee's custody are appropriately briefed about the risks. If no specific risks are identified by the assessment, that should be noted in the custody record. See *Note 3E* and *paragraph 9.14*

3.9 The custody officer is responsible for implementing the response to any specific risk assessment, e.g.:
- reducing opportunities for self harm;
- calling a health care professional;
- increasing levels of monitoring or observation.

3.10 Risk assessment is an ongoing process and assessments must always be subject to review if circumstances change.

3.11 If video cameras are installed in the custody area, notices shall be prominently displayed showing cameras are in use. Any request to have video cameras switched off shall be refused.

(b) *Detained persons – special groups*

3.12 If the detainee appears deaf or there is doubt about their hearing or speaking ability or ability to understand English, and the custody officer cannot establish effective communication, the custody officer must, as soon as practicable, call an interpreter for assistance in the action under *paragraphs 3.1–3.5*. See *section 13*

3.13 If the detainee is a juvenile, the custody officer must, if it is practicable, ascertain the identity of a person responsible for their welfare. That person:
- may be:
  - the parent or guardian;
  - if the juvenile is in local authority or voluntary organisation care, or is otherwise being looked after under the Children Act 1989, a person appointed by that authority or organisation to have responsibility for the juvenile's welfare;
  - any other person who has, for the time being, assumed responsibility for the juvenile's welfare.
- must be informed as soon as practicable that the juvenile has been arrested, why they have been arrested and where they are detained. This right is in addition to the juvenile's right in *section 5* not to be held incommunicado. See *Note 3C*

3.14 If a juvenile is known to be subject to a court order under which a person or organisation is given any degree of statutory responsibility to supervise or otherwise monitor them, reasonable steps must also be taken to notify that person or organisation (the 'responsible officer'). The responsible officer will normally be a member of a Youth Offending Team, except for a curfew order which involves electronic monitoring when the contractor providing the monitoring will normally be the responsible officer.

3.15 If the detainee is a juvenile, mentally disordered or otherwise mentally vulnerable, the custody officer must, as soon as practicable:
- inform the appropriate adult, who in the case of a juvenile may or may not be a person responsible for their welfare, as in *paragraph 3.13*, of:
  - the grounds for their detention;
  - their whereabouts.
- ask the adult to come to the police station to see the detainee.

3.16 It is imperative that a mentally disordered or otherwise mentally vulnerable person, detained under the Mental Health Act 1983, section 136, be assessed as soon as possible. If that assessment is to take place at the police station, an approved social worker and a registered medical practitioner shall be called to the station as soon as possible in order to interview and examine the detainee. Once the detainee has been interviewed, examined and suitable arrangements made for their treatment or care, they can no longer be detained under section 136. A detainee must be immediately discharged from detention under section 136 if a registered medical practitioner, having examined them, concludes they are not mentally disordered within the meaning of the Act.

3.17 If the appropriate adult is:
- already at the police station, the provisions of *paragraphs 3.1* to *3.5* must be complied with in the appropriate adult's presence;
- not at the station when these provisions are complied with, they must be complied with again in the presence of the appropriate adult when they arrive.

3.18 The detainee shall be advised that:
- the duties of the appropriate adult include giving advice and assistance;
- they can consult privately with the appropriate adult at any time.

3.19 If the detainee, or appropriate adult on the detainee's behalf, asks for a solicitor to be called to give legal advice, the provisions of *section 6* apply.

3.20 If the detainee is blind, seriously visually impaired or unable to read, the custody officer shall make sure their solicitor, relative, appropriate adult or some other person likely to take an interest in them and not involved in the investigation is available to help check any documentation. When this Code requires written consent or signing the person assisting may be asked to sign instead, if the detainee prefers. This paragraph does not require an appropriate adult to be called solely to assist in checking and signing documentation for a person who is not a juvenile, or mentally disordered or otherwise mentally vulnerable (see *paragraph 3.15*).

(c) *Persons attending a police station voluntarily*

3.21 Anybody attending a police station voluntarily to assist with an investigation may leave at will unless arrested. See *Note 1K*. If it is decided they shall not be allowed to leave, they must be informed at once that they are under arrest and brought before the custody officer, who is responsible for making sure they are notified of their rights in the same way as other detainees. If they are not arrested but are cautioned as in *section 10*, the person who gives the caution must, at the same time, inform them they are not under arrest, they are not obliged to remain at the station but if they remain at the station they may obtain free and independent legal advice if they want. They shall be told the right to legal advice includes the right to speak with a solicitor on the telephone and be asked if they want to do so.

3.22 If a person attending the police station voluntarily asks about their entitlement to legal advice, they shall be given a copy of the notice explaining the arrangements for obtaining legal advice. See *paragraph 3.2*

(d) *Documentation*

3.23 The grounds for a person's detention shall be recorded, in the person's presence if practicable.

3.24 Action taken under *paragraphs 3.12* to *3.20* shall be recorded.

(e) *Persons answering street bail*

3.25 When a person is answering street bail, the custody officer should link any documentation held in relation to arrest with the custody record. Any further action shall be recorded on the custody record in accordance with paragraphs 3.23 and 3.24 above.

4 Detainee's property

(a) *Action*

4.1 The custody officer is responsible for:
    (a) ascertaining what property a detainee:
        (i) has with them when they come to the police station, whether on:
- arrest or re-detention on answering to bail;

- commitment to prison custody on the order or sentence of a court;
- lodgement at the police station with a view to their production in court from prison custody;
- transfer from detention at another station or hospital;
- detention under the Mental Health Act 1983, section 135 or 136;
- remand into police custody on the authority of a court

  (ii) might have acquired for an unlawful or harmful purpose while in custody;

(b) the safekeeping of any property taken from a detainee which remains at the police station.

The custody officer may search the detainee or authorise their being searched to the extent they consider necessary, provided a search of intimate parts of the body or involving the removal of more than outer clothing is only made as in *Annex A*. A search may only be carried out by an officer of the same sex as the detainee. See *Note 4A*

4.2 Detainees may retain clothing and personal effects at their own risk unless the custody officer considers they may use them to cause harm to themselves or others, interfere with evidence, damage property, effect an escape or they are needed as evidence. In this event the custody officer may withhold such articles as they consider necessary and must tell the detainee why.

4.3 Personal effects are those items a detainee may lawfully need, use or refer to while in detention but do not include cash and other items of value.

(b) Documentation

4.4 It is a matter for the custody officer to determine whether a record should be made of the property a detained person has with him or had taken from him on arrest. Any record made is not required to be kept as part of the custody record but the custody record should be noted as to where such a record exists. Whenever a record is made the detainee shall be allowed to check and sign the record of property as correct. Any refusal to sign shall be recorded.

4.5 If a detainee is not allowed to keep any article of clothing or personal effects, the reason must be recorded.

Notes for guidance

4A *PACE, Section 54(1) and paragraph 4.1 require a detainee to be searched when it is clear the custody officer will have continuing duties in relation to that detainee or when that detainee's behaviour or offence makes an inventory appropriate. They do not require every detainee to be searched, e.g. if it is clear a person will only be detained for a short period and is not to be placed in a cell, the custody officer may decide not to search them. In such a case the custody record will be endorsed 'not searched', paragraph 4.4 will not apply, and the detainee will be invited to sign the entry. If the detainee refuses, the custody officer will be obliged to ascertain what property they have in accordance with paragraph 4.1.*

. . .

5 Right not to be held incommunicado (a) Action

5.1 Any person arrested and held in custody at a police station or other premises may, on request, have one person known to them or likely to take an interest in their welfare informed at public expense of their whereabouts as soon as practicable. If the person cannot be contacted the detainee may choose up to two alternatives. If they cannot be contacted, the person in charge of detention or the investigation has discretion to allow further attempts until the information has been conveyed. See *Notes 5C* and *5D*

5.2 The exercise of the above right in respect of each person nominated may be delayed only in accordance with *Annex B*.

5.3 The above right may be exercised each time a detainee is taken to another police station.

5.4 The detainee may receive visits at the custody officer's discretion. See *Note 5B*

5.5 If a friend, relative or person with an interest in the detainee's welfare enquires about their whereabouts, this information shall be given if the suspect agrees and *Annex B* does not apply. See *Note 5D*

5.6 The detainee shall be given writing materials, on request, and allowed to telephone one person for a reasonable time, see *Notes 5A* and *5E*. Either or both these privileges may be denied or delayed if an officer of inspector rank or above considers sending a letter or making a telephone call may result in any of the consequences in:
    (a) *Annex B paragraphs 1* and *2* and the person is detained in connection with an indictable offence;
    (b) *Not used*
Nothing in this paragraph permits the restriction or denial of the rights in *paragraphs 5.1* and *6.1*.

5.7 Before any letter or message is sent, or telephone call made, the detainee shall be informed that what they say in any letter, call or message (other than in a communication to a solicitor) may be read or listened to and may be given in evidence. A telephone call may be terminated if it is being abused. The costs can be at public expense at the custody officer's discretion.

5.7A Any delay or denial of the rights in this section should be proportionate and should last no longer than necessary.

(b) **Documentation**

5.8 A record must be kept of any:
    (a) request made under this section and the action taken;
    (b) letters, messages or telephone calls made or received or visit received;
    (c) refusal by the detainee to have information about them given to an outside enquirer. The detainee must be asked to countersign the record accordingly and any refusal recorded.

6 Right to legal advice

(a) **Action**

6.1 Unless *Annex B* applies, all detainees must be informed that they may at any time consult and communicate privately with a solicitor, whether in person, in writing or by telephone, and that free independent legal advice is available. See *paragraph 3.1*, *Note 6B, 6B1, 6B2* and *Note 6J*

6.2 Not Used

6.3 A poster advertising the right to legal advice must be prominently displayed in the charging area of every police station. See *Note 6H*

6.4 No police officer should, at any time, do or say anything with the intention of dissuading a detainee from obtaining legal advice.

6.5 The exercise of the right of access to legal advice may be delayed only as in Annex B. Whenever legal advice is requested, and unless Annex B applies, the custody officer must act without delay to secure the provision of such advice. If, on being informed or reminded of this right, the detainee declines to speak to a solicitor in person, the officer should point out that the right includes the right to speak with a solicitor on the telephone. If the detainee continues to waive this right the officer should ask them why and any reasons should be recorded on the custody record or the interview record as appropriate. Reminders of the right to legal advice must be given as in paragraphs *3.5, 11.2, 15.4, 16.4, 2B of Annex A, 3 of Annex K* and *16.5* and Code D, *paragraphs 3.17(ii)* and *6.3*. Once it is clear a detainee does not want to speak to a solicitor in person or by telephone they should cease to be asked their reasons. See *Note 6K*

6.5A In the case of a juvenile, an appropriate adult should consider whether legal advice from a solicitor is required. If the juvenile indicates that they do not want legal advice, the appropriate adult has the right to ask for a solicitor to attend if this would be in the best interests of the person. However, the detained person cannot be forced to see the solicitor if he is adamant that he does not wish to do so.

6.6 A detainee who wants legal advice may not be interviewed or continue to be interviewed until they have received such advice unless:

(a) *Annex B* applies, when the restriction on drawing adverse inferences from silence in *Annex C* will apply because the detainee is not allowed an opportunity to consult a solicitor; or

(b) an officer of superintendent rank or above has reasonable grounds for believing that:
   (i) the consequent delay might:
   - lead to interference with, or harm to, evidence connected with an offence;
   - lead to interference with, or physical harm to, other people;
   - lead to serious loss of, or damage to, property;
   - lead to alerting other people suspected of having committed an offence but not yet arrested for it;
   - hinder the recovery of property obtained in consequence of the commission of an offence.
   (ii) when a solicitor, including a duty solicitor, has been contacted and has agreed to attend, awaiting their arrival would cause unreasonable delay to the process of investigation.
   Note: In these cases the restriction on drawing adverse inferences from silence in *Annex C* will apply because the detainee is not allowed an opportunity to consult a solicitor.

(c) the solicitor the detainee has nominated or selected from a list:
   (i) cannot be contacted;
   (ii) has previously indicated they do not wish to be contacted; or
   (iii) having been contacted, has declined to attend; and
   the detainee has been advised of the Duty Solicitor Scheme but has declined to ask for the duty solicitor.
   In these circumstances the interview may be started or continued without further delay provided an officer of inspector rank or above has agreed to the interview proceeding.
   Note: The restriction on drawing adverse inferences from silence in Annex C will not apply because the detainee is allowed an opportunity to consult the duty solicitor;

(d) the detainee changes their mind, about wanting legal advice.
   In these circumstances the interview may be started or continued without delay provided that:
   (i) the detainee agrees to do so , in writing or on the interview record made in accordance with Code E or F; and
   (ii) an officer of inspector rank or above has inquired about the detainee's reasons for their change of mind and gives authority for the interview to proceed.
   Confirmation of the detainee's agreement, their change of mind, the reasons for it if given and, subject to *paragraph 2.6A*, the name of the authorising officer shall be recorded in the written interview record or the interview record made in accordance with Code E or F. See *Note 6I*. Note: In these circumstances the restriction on drawing adverse inferences from silence in *Annex C* will not apply because the detainee is allowed an opportunity to consult a solicitor if they wish.

6.7 If *paragraph 6.6(b)(i)* applies, once sufficient information has been obtained to avert the risk, questioning must cease until the detainee has received legal advice unless *paragraph 6.6(a), (b)(ii), (c)* or *(d)* applies.

6.8 A detainee who has been permitted to consult a solicitor shall be entitled on request to have the solicitor present when they are interviewed unless one of the exceptions in *paragraph 6.6* applies.

6.9 The solicitor may only be required to leave the interview if their conduct is such that the interviewer is unable properly to put questions to the suspect. See *Notes 6D* and *6E*

6.10 If the interviewer considers a solicitor is acting in such a way, they will stop the interview and consult an officer not below superintendent rank, if one is readily available, and otherwise an officer not below inspector rank not connected with the investigation. After speaking to the solicitor, the officer consulted will decide if the interview should continue in the presence of that solicitor. If they decide it should not, the suspect will be given the opportunity to consult another solicitor before the interview continues and that solicitor given an opportunity to be present at the interview. See *Note 6E*

6.11 The removal of a solicitor from an interview is a serious step and, if it occurs, the officer of superintendent rank or above who took the decision will consider if the incident should be reported to the Law Society. If the decision to remove the solicitor has been taken by an officer below superintendent rank, the facts must be reported to an officer of superintendent rank or above who will similarly consider whether a report to the Law Society would be appropriate. When the solicitor concerned is a duty solicitor, the report should be both to the Law Society and to the Legal Services Commission.

6.12 'Solicitor' in this Code means:
- a solicitor who holds a current practising certificate
- an accredited or probationary representative included on the register of representatives maintained by the Legal Services Commission.

6.12A An accredited or probationary representative sent to provide advice by, and on behalf of, a solicitor shall be admitted to the police station for this purpose unless an officer of inspector rank or above considers such a visit will hinder the investigation and directs otherwise. Hindering the investigation does not include giving proper legal advice to a detainee as in *Note 6D*. Once admitted to the police station, *paragraphs 6.6* to *6.10* apply.

6.13 In exercising their discretion under paragraph 6.12A, the officer should take into account in particular:
- whether:
  - the identity and status of an accredited or probationary representative have been satisfactorily established;
  - they are of suitable character to provide legal advice, e.g. a person with a criminal record is unlikely to be suitable unless the conviction was for a minor offence and not recent.
- any other matters in any written letter of authorisation provided by the solicitor on whose behalf the person is attending the police station. See *Note 6F*

6.14 If the inspector refuses access to an accredited or probationary representative or a decision is taken that such a person should not be permitted to remain at an interview, the inspector must notify the solicitor on whose behalf the representative was acting and give them an opportunity to make alternative arrangements. The detainee must be informed and the custody record noted.

6.15 If a solicitor arrives at the station to see a particular person, that person must, unless *Annex B* applies, be so informed whether or not they are being interviewed and asked if they would like to see the solicitor. This applies even if the detainee has declined legal advice or, having requested it, subsequently agreed to be interviewed without receiving advice. The solicitor's attendance and the detainee's decision must be noted in the custody record.

(b) *Documentation*

6.16 Any request for legal advice and the action taken shall be recorded.

6.17 A record shall be made in the interview record if a detainee asks for legal advice and an interview is begun either in the absence of a solicitor or their representative, or they have been required to leave an interview.

...

8 Conditions of detention

(a) *Action*

8.1 So far as it is practicable, not more than one detainee should be detained in each cell.

8.2 Cells in use must be adequately heated, cleaned and ventilated. They must be adequately lit, subject to such dimming as is compatible with safety and security to allow people detained overnight to sleep. No additional restraints shall be used within a locked cell unless absolutely necessary and then only restraint equipment, approved for use in that force by the Chief Officer, which is reasonable and necessary in the circumstances having regard to the detainee's demeanour and with a view to ensuring their safety and the safety of others. If a detainee is deaf, mentally disordered or otherwise mentally vulnerable, particular care must be taken when deciding whether to use any form of approved restraints.

8.3 Blankets, mattresses, pillows and other bedding supplied shall be of a reasonable standard and in a clean and sanitary condition. See *Note 8A*

8.4 Access to toilet and washing facilities must be provided.

8.5 If it is necessary to remove a detainee's clothes for the purposes of investigation, for hygiene, health reasons or cleaning, replacement clothing of a reasonable standard of comfort and cleanliness shall be provided. A detainee may not be interviewed unless adequate clothing has been offered.

8.6 At least two light meals and one main meal should be offered in any 24 hour period. See *Note 8B*. Drinks should be provided at meal times and upon reasonable request between meals. Whenever necessary, advice shall be sought from the appropriate health care professional, see Note 9A, on medical and dietary matters. As far as practicable, meals provided shall offer a varied diet and meet any specific dietary needs or religious beliefs the detainee may have. The detainee may, at the custody officer's discretion, have meals supplied by their family or friends at their expense. See *Note 8A*

8.7 Brief outdoor exercise shall be offered daily if practicable.

8.8 A juvenile shall not be placed in a police cell unless no other secure accommodation is available and the custody officer considers it is not practicable to supervise them if they are not placed in a cell or that a cell provides more comfortable accommodation than other secure accommodation in the station. A juvenile may not be placed in a cell with a detained adult.

...

9 Care and treatment of detained persons

(a) *General*

...

9.3 Detainees should be visited at least every hour. If no reasonably foreseeable risk was identified in a risk assessment, see *paragraphs 3.6–3.10*, there is no need to wake a sleeping detainee. Those suspected of being intoxicated through drink or drugs or having swallowed drugs, see *Note 9CA*, or whose level of consciousness causes concern must, subject to any clinical directions given by the appropriate health care professional, see *paragraph 9.13*:
- be visited and roused at least every half hour
- have their condition assessed as in *Annex H*
- and clinical treatment arranged if appropriate See *Notes 9B, 9C* and *9H*

...

10 Cautions

(a) *When a caution must be given*

10.1 A person whom there are grounds to suspect of an offence, see *Note 10A*, must be cautioned before any questions about an offence, or further questions if the answers provide the grounds for suspicion, are put to them if either the suspect's answers or silence, (i.e. failure or refusal to answer or answer satisfactorily) may be given in evidence to a court in a prosecution. A person need not be cautioned if questions are for other necessary purposes, e.g.:
(a) solely to establish their identity or ownership of any vehicle;
(b) to obtain information in accordance with any relevant statutory requirement, see *paragraph 10.9*;
(c) in furtherance of the proper and effective conduct of a search, e.g. to determine the need to search in the exercise of powers of stop and search or to seek cooperation while carrying out a search;
(d) to seek verification of a written record as in *paragraph 11.13*;
(e) Not used

10.2 Whenever a person not under arrest is initially cautioned, or reminded they are under caution, that person must at the same time be told they are not under arrest and are free to leave if they want to. See *Note 10C*

...

(b) *Terms of the cautions*

10.5 The caution which must be given on:
   (a) arrest;
   (b) all other occasions before a person is charged or informed they may be prosecuted, see *section 16*,

should, unless the restriction on drawing adverse inferences from silence applies, see *Annex C*, be in the following terms:

"You do not have to say anything. But it may harm your defence if you do not mention when questioned something which you later rely on in Court. Anything you do say may be given in evidence."

Where the use of the Welsh Language is appropriate, a constable may provide the caution directly in Welsh in the following terms:

"Does dim rhaid i chi ddweud dim byd. Ond gall niweidio eich amddiffyniad os na fyddwch chi'n sôn, wrth gael eich holi, am rywbeth y byddwch chi'n dibynnu arno nes ymlaen yn y Llys. Gall unrhyw beth yr ydych yn ei ddweud gael ei roi fel tystiolaeth."

(c) *Special warnings under the Criminal Justice and Public Order Act 1994, sections 36 and 37*

10.10 When a suspect interviewed at a police station or authorised place of detention after arrest fails or refuses to answer certain questions, or to answer satisfactorily, after due warning, see *Note 10F*, a court or jury may draw such inferences as appear proper under the Criminal Justice and Public Order Act 1994, sections 36 and 37. Such inferences may only be drawn when:
   (a) the restriction on drawing adverse inferences from silence, see *Annex C*, does not apply; and
   (b) the suspect is arrested by a constable and fails or refuses to account for any objects, marks or substances, or marks on such objects found:
   - on their person;
   - in or on their clothing or footwear;
   - otherwise in their possession; or
   - in the place they were arrested;
   (c) the arrested suspect was found by a constable at a place at or about the time the offence for which that officer has arrested them is alleged to have been committed, and the suspect fails or refuses to account for their presence there.

When the restriction on drawing adverse inferences from silence applies, the suspect may still be asked to account for any of the matters in (b) or (c) but the special warning described in *paragraph 10.11* will not apply and must not be given.

10.11 For an inference to be drawn when a suspect fails or refuses to answer a question about one of these matters or to answer it satisfactorily, the suspect must first be told in ordinary language:
   (a) what offence is being investigated;
   (b) what fact they are being asked to account for;
   (c) this fact may be due to them taking part in the commission of the offence;
   (d) a court may draw a proper inference if they fail or refuse to account for this fact;
   (e) a record is being made of the interview and it may be given in evidence if they are brought to trial.

...

11 Interviews – general

(a) *Action*

11.1A An interview is the questioning of a person regarding their involvement or suspected involvement in a criminal offence or offences which, under *paragraph 10.1*, must be carried out under caution. Whenever a person is interviewed they must be informed of the nature of the offence, or further offence. Procedures under the Road Traffic Act 1988, section 7 or the Transport and Works Act 1992, section 31 do not constitute interviewing for the purpose of this Code.

11.1 Following a decision to arrest a suspect, they must not be interviewed about the relevant offence except at a police station or other authorised place of detention, unless the consequent delay would be likely to:
 (a) lead to:
  - interference with, or harm to, evidence connected with an offence;
  - interference with, or physical harm to, other people; or
  - serious loss of, or damage to, property;
 (b) lead to alerting other people suspected of committing an offence but not yet arrested for it; or
 (c) hinder the recovery of property obtained in consequence of the commission of an offence.

Interviewing in any of these circumstances shall cease once the relevant risk has been averted or the necessary questions have been put in order to attempt to avert that risk.

11.2 Immediately prior to the commencement or re-commencement of any interview at a police station or other authorised place of detention, the interviewer should remind the suspect of their entitlement to free legal advice and that the interview can be delayed for legal advice to be obtained, unless one of the exceptions in *paragraph 6.6* applies. It is the interviewer's responsibility to make sure all reminders are recorded in the interview record.

11.3 Not Used

11.4 At the beginning of an interview the interviewer, after cautioning the suspect, see *section 10*, shall put to them any significant statement or silence which occurred in the presence and hearing of a police officer or other police staff before the start of the interview and which have not been put to the suspect in the course of a previous interview. See *Note 11A*. The interviewer shall ask the suspect whether they confirm or deny that earlier statement or silence and if they want to add anything.

11.4A A significant statement is one which appears capable of being used in evidence against the suspect, in particular a direct admission of guilt. A significant silence is a failure or refusal to answer a question or answer satisfactorily when under caution, which might, allowing for the restriction on drawing adverse inferences from silence, see *Annex C*, give rise to an inference under the Criminal Justice and Public Order Act 1994, Part III.

11.5 No interviewer may try to obtain answers or elicit a statement by the use of oppression. Except as in *paragraph 10.9*, no interviewer shall indicate, except to answer a direct question, what action will be taken by the police if the person being questioned answers questions, makes a statement or refuses to do either. If the person asks directly what action will be taken if they answer questions, make a statement or refuse to do either, the interviewer may inform them what action the police propose to take provided that action is itself proper and warranted.

11.6 The interview or further interview of a person about an offence with which that person has not been charged or for which they have not been informed they may be prosecuted, must cease when:
 (a) the officer in charge of the investigation is satisfied all the questions they consider relevant to obtaining accurate and reliable information about the offence have been put to the suspect, this includes allowing the suspect an opportunity to give an innocent explanation and asking questions to test if the explanation is accurate and reliable, e.g. to clear up ambiguities or clarify what the suspect said;
 (b) the officer in charge of the investigation has taken account of any other available evidence; and
 (c) the officer in charge of the investigation, or in the case of a detained suspect, the custody officer, see *paragraph 16.1*, reasonably believes there is sufficient evidence to provide a realistic prospect of conviction for that offence. See *Note 11B*

This paragraph does not prevent officers in revenue cases or acting under the confiscation provisions of the Criminal Justice Act 1988 or the Drug Trafficking Act 1994 from inviting suspects to complete a formal question and answer record after the interview is concluded.

(b) *Interview records*

11.7 (a) An accurate record must be made of each interview, whether or not the interview takes place at a police station

. . .

. . .

POLICE AND CRIMINAL EVIDENCE ACT 1984
CODE G

CODE OF PRACTICE FOR THE STATUTORY POWER OF ARREST BY POLICE OFFICERS

Commencement

This Code applies to any arrest made by a police officer after midnight on 31 December 2005

1 **Introduction**

1.1 This Code of Practice deals with statutory power of police to arrest persons suspected of involvement in a criminal offence.

1.2 The right to liberty is a key principle of the Human Rights Act 1998. The exercise of the power of arrest represents an obvious and significant interference with that right.

1.3 The use of the power must be fully justified and officers exercising the power should consider if the necessary objectives can be met by other, less intrusive means. Arrest must never be used simply because it can be used. Absence of justification for exercising the powers of arrest may lead to challenges should the case proceed to court. When the power of arrest is exercised it is essential that it is exercised in a nondiscriminatory and proportionate manner.

1.4 Section 24 of the Police and Criminal Evidence Act 1984 (as substituted by section 110 of the Serious Organised Crime and Police Act 2005) provides the statutory power of arrest. If the provisions of the Act and this Code are not observed, both the arrest and the conduct of any subsequent investigation may be open to question.

1.5 This code of practice must be readily available at all police stations for consultation by police officers and police staff, detained persons and members of the public.

1.6 The notes for guidance are not provisions of this code.

2 **Elements of Arrest under section 24 PACE**

2.1 A lawful arrest requires two elements:

A person's involvement or suspected involvement or attempted involvement in the commission of a criminal offence;

AND

Reasonable grounds for believing that the person's arrest is necessary.

2.2 Arresting officers are required to inform the person arrested that they have been arrested, even if this fact is obvious, and of the relevant circumstances of the arrest in relation to both elements and to inform the custody officer of these on arrival at the police station. See Code C paragraph 3.4.

Involvement in the commission of an offence'

2.3 A constable may arrest without warrant in relation to any offence, except for the single exception listed in Note for Guidance 1. A constable may arrest anyone:

- who is about to commit an offence or is in the act of committing an offence
- whom the officer has reasonable grounds for suspecting is about to commit an offence or to be committing an offence
- whom the officer has reasonable grounds to suspect of being guilty of an offence which he or she has reasonable grounds for suspecting has been committed

- anyone who is guilty of an offence which has been committed or anyone whom the officer has reasonable grounds for suspecting to be guilty of that offence.

Necessity criteria

2.4 The power of arrest is only exercisable if the constable has reasonable grounds for believing that it is necessary to arrest the person. The criteria for what may constitute necessity are set out in paragraph 2.9. It remains an operational decision at the discretion of the arresting officer as to:
- what action he or she may take at the point of contact with the individual;
- the necessity criterion or criteria (if any) which applies to the individual; and
- whether to arrest, report for summons, grant street bail, issue a fixed penalty notice or take any other action that is open to the officer.

2.5 In applying the criteria, the arresting officer has to be satisfied that at least one of the reasons supporting the need for arrest is satisfied.

2.6 Extending the power of arrest to all offences provides a constable with the ability to use that power to deal with any situation. However applying the necessity criteria requires the constable to examine and justify the reason or reasons why a person needs to be taken to a police station for the custody officer to decide whether the person should be placed in police detention.

2.7 The criteria below are set out in section 24 of PACE as substituted by section 110 of the Serious Organised Crime and Police Act 2005. The criteria are exhaustive. However, the circumstances that may satisfy those criteria remain a matter for the operational discretion of individual officers. Some examples are given below of what those circumstances may be.

2.8 In considering the individual circumstances, the constable must take into account the situation of the victim, the nature of the offence, the circumstances of the suspect and the needs of the investigative process.

2.9 The criteria are that the arrest is necessary:
(a) to enable the name of the person in question to be ascertained (in the case where the constable does not know, and cannot readily ascertain, the person's name, or has reasonable grounds for doubting whether a name given by the person as his name is his real name)
(b) correspondingly as regards the person's address
an address is a satisfactory address for service of summons if the person will be at it for a sufficiently long period for it to be possible to serve him or her with a summons; or, that some other person at that address specified by the person will accept service of the summons on their behalf.
(c) to prevent the person in question—
  (i) causing physical injury to himself or any other person;
  (ii) suffering physical injury;
  (iii) causing loss or damage to property;
  (iv) committing an offence against public decency (only applies where members of the public going about their normal business cannot reasonably be expected to avoid the person in question); or
  (v) causing an unlawful obstruction of the highway;
(d) to protect a child or other vulnerable person from the person in question
(e) to allow the prompt and effective investigation of the offence or of the conduct of the person in question.
This may include cases such as:
  (i) Where there are reasonable grounds to believe that the person:
    - has made false statements;
    - has made statements which cannot be readily verified;
    - has presented false evidence;
    - may steal or destroy evidence;
    - may make contact with co-suspects or conspirators;
    - may intimidate or threaten or make contact with witnesses;
    - where it is necessary to obtain evidence by questioning; or
  (ii) when considering arrest in connection with an indictable offence, there is a need to:
    - enter and search any premises occupied or controlled by a person

- search the person
- prevent contact with others
- take fingerprints, footwear impressions, samples or photographs of the suspect

(iii) ensuring compliance with statutory drug testing requirements.

(f) to prevent any prosecution for the offence from being hindered by the disappearance of the person in question.

This may arise if there are reasonable grounds for believing that
- if the person is not arrested he or she will fail to attend court
- street bail after arrest would be insufficient to deter the suspect from trying to evade prosecution

3 Information to be given on Arrest

(a) Cautions - when a caution must be given (taken from Code C section 10) (a)

3.1 A person whom there are grounds to suspect of an offence (see *Note 2*) must be cautioned before any questions about an offence, or further questions if the answers provide the grounds for suspicion, are put to them if either the suspect's answers or silence, (i.e. failure or refusal to answer or answer satisfactorily) may be given in evidence to a court in a prosecution. A person need not be cautioned if questions are for other necessary purposes e.g.:
   (a) solely to establish their identity or ownership of any vehicle;
   (b) to obtain information in accordance with any relevant statutory requirement;
   (c) in furtherance of the proper and effective conduct of a search, e.g. to determine the need to search in the exercise of powers of stop and search or to seek cooperation while carrying out a search;
   (d) to seek verification of a written record as in *Code C paragraph 11.13*;
   (e) when examining a person in accordance with the Terrorism Act 2000, Schedule 7 and the Code of Practice for Examining Officers issued under that Act, Schedule 14, paragraph 6.

3.2 Whenever a person not under arrest is initially cautioned, or reminded they are under caution, that person must at the same time be told they are not under arrest and are free to leave if they want to.

3.3 A person who is arrested, or further arrested, must be informed at the time, or as soon as practicable thereafter, that they are under arrest and the grounds for their arrest, see *Note 3*.

3.4 A person who is arrested, or further arrested, must also be cautioned unless:
   (a) it is impracticable to do so by reason of their condition or behaviour at the time;
   (b) they have already been cautioned immediately prior to arrest as in *paragraph 3.1*.
   (c) Terms of the caution (Taken from Code C section 10)

3.5 The caution, which must be given on arrest, should be in the following terms:
"You do not have to say anything. But it may harm your defence if you do not mention when questioned something which you later rely on in Court. Anything you do say may be given in evidence."
See *Note 5*

3.6 Minor deviations from the words of any caution given in accordance with this Code do not constitute a breach of this Code, provided the sense of the relevant caution is preserved. See *Note 6*

3.7 When, despite being cautioned, a person fails to co-operate or to answer particular questions which may affect their immediate treatment, the person should be informed of any relevant consequences and that those consequences are not affected by the caution. Examples are when a person's refusal to provide:
- their name and address when charged may make them liable to detention;
- particulars and information in accordance with a statutory requirement, e.g. under the Road Traffic Act 1988, may amount to an offence or may make the person liable to a further arrest.

4 Records of Arrest

(a) General

4.1 The arresting officer is required to record in his pocket book or by other methods used for recording information:
- the nature and circumstances of the offence leading to the arrest
- the reason or reasons why arrest was necessary
- the giving of the caution
- anything said by the person at the time of arrest

4.2 Such a record should be made at the time of the arrest unless impracticable to do. If not made at that time, the record should then be completed as soon as possible thereafter.

4.3 On arrival at the police station, the custody officer shall open the custody record (see paragraph 1.1A and section 2 of Code C). The information given by the arresting officer on the circumstances and reason or reasons for arrest shall be recorded as part of the custody record. Alternatively, a copy of the record made by the officer in accordance with paragraph 4.1 above shall be attached as part of the custody record. See *paragraph 2.2* and *Code C paragraphs 3.4 and 10.3*.

4.4 The custody record will serve as a record of the arrest. Copies of the custody record will be provided in accordance with paragraphs 2.4 and 2.4A of Code C and access for inspection of the original record in accordance with paragraph 2.5 of Code C.

(b) Interviews and arrests

4.5 Records of interview, significant statements or silences will be treated in the same way as set out in sections 10 and 11 of Code C and in Code E (tape recording of interviews).

Notes for guidance

1. The powers of arrest for offences under sections 4(1) and 5(1) of the Criminal Law Act 1967 require that the offences to which they relate must carry a sentence fixed by law or one in which a first time offender aged 18 or over could be sentenced to 5 years or more imprisonment

2. There must be some reasonable, objective grounds for the suspicion, based on known facts or information which are relevant to the likelihood the offence has been committed and the person to be questioned committed it.

3. An arrested person must be given sufficient information to enable them to understand they have been deprived of their liberty and the reason they have been arrested, e.g. when a person is arrested on suspicion of committing an offence they must be informed of the suspected offence's nature, when and where it was committed. The suspect must also be informed of the reason or reasons why arrest is considered necessary. Vague or technical language should be avoided.

4. Nothing in this Code requires a caution to be given or repeated when informing a person not under arrest they may be prosecuted for an offence. However, a court will not be able to draw any inferences under the Criminal Justice and Public Order Act 1994, section 34, if the person was not cautioned.

5. If it appears a person does not understand the caution, the people giving it should explain it in their own words.

6. The powers available to an officer as the result of an arrest – for example, entry and search of premises, holding a person incommunicado, setting up road blocks – are only available in respect of indictable offences and are subject to the specific requirements on authorisation as set out in the 1984 Act and relevant PACE Code of Practice.

CIVIL PROCEDURE RULES 1998, PART 54

I JUDICIAL REVIEW

54.1 Scope and interpretation

(1) This Section of this Part contains rules about judicial review.

(2) In this Section—
  (a) a 'claim for judicial review' means a claim to review the lawfulness of—
    (i) an enactment; or
    (ii) a decision, action or failure to act in relation to the exercise of a public function.
  (b)-(d)…
  (e) 'the judicial review procedure' means the Part 8 procedure as modified by this Section;
  (f) 'interested party' means any person (other than the claimant and defendant) who is directly affected by the claim; and
  (g) 'court' means the High Court, unless otherwise stated.

(Rule 8.1(6)(b) provides that a rule or practice direction may, in relation to a specified type of proceedings, disapply or modify any of the rules set out in Part 8 as they apply to those proceedings)

54.2 When this Section must be used

The judicial review procedure must be used in a claim for judicial review where the claimant is seeking—
(a) a mandatory order;
(b) a prohibiting order;
(c) a quashing order; or
(d) an injunction under section 30 of the Supreme Court Act 1981 (restraining a person from acting in any office in which he is not entitled to act).

54.3 When this Section may be used

(1) The judicial review procedure may be used in a claim for judicial review where the claimant is seeking—
  (a) a declaration; or
  (b) an injunction.

(Section 31(2) of the Supreme Court Act 1981 sets out the circumstances in which the court may grant a declaration or injunction in a claim for judicial review)

(Where the claimant is seeking a declaration or injunction in addition to one of the remedies listed in rule 54.2, the judicial review procedure must be used)

(2) A claim for judicial review may include a claim for damages, restitution or the recovery of a sum due but may not seek such a remedy alone.

(Section 31(4) of the Supreme Court Act sets out the circumstances in which the court may award damages, restitution or the recovery of a sum due on a claim for judicial review)

54.4 Permission required

The court's permission to proceed is required in a claim for judicial review whether started under this Section or transferred to the Administrative Court.

54.5 Time limit for filing claim form

(1) The claim form must be filed—
  (a) promptly; and
  (b) in any event not later than 3 months after the grounds to make the claim first arose.

(2) The time limit in this rule may not be extended by agreement between the parties.

(3) This rule does not apply when any other enactment specifies a shorter time limit for making the claim for judicial review.

54.6 Claim form

(1) In addition to the matters set out in rule 8.2 (contents of the claim form) the claimant must also state—

(a) the name and address of any person he considers to be an interested party;
(b) that he is requesting permission to proceed with a claim for judicial review; and
(c) any remedy (including any interim remedy) he is claiming.
(Part 25 sets out how to apply for an interim remedy)
(2) The claim form must be accompanied by the documents required by the relevant practice direction.

54.7 Service of claim form
The claim form must be served on—
(a) the defendant; and
(b) unless the court otherwise directs, any person the claimant considers to be an interested party,
within 7 days after the date of issue.

54.8 Acknowledgment of service
(1) Any person served with the claim form who wishes to take part in the judicial review must file an acknowledgment of service in the relevant practice form in accordance with the following provisions of this rule.
(2) Any acknowledgment of service must be—
(a) filed not more than 21 days after service of the claim form; and
(b) served on—
(i) the claimant; and
(ii) subject to any direction under rule 54.7(b), any other person named in the claim form,
as soon as practicable and, in any event, not later than 7 days after it is filed.
(3) The time limits under this rule may not be extended by agreement between the parties.
(4) The acknowledgment of service—
(a) must—
(i) where the person filing it intends to contest the claim, set out a summary of his grounds for doing so; and
(ii) state the name and address of any person the person filing it considers to be an interested party; and
(b) may include or be accompanied by an application for directions.
(5) Rule 10.3(2) does not apply.

54.9 Failure to file acknowledgment of service
(1) Where a person served with the claim form has failed to file an acknowledgment of service in accordance with rule 54.8, he—
(a) may not take part in a hearing to decide whether permission should be given unless the court allows him to do so; but
(b) provided he complies with rule 54.14 or any other direction of the court regarding the filing and service of—
(i) detailed grounds for contesting the claim or supporting it on additional grounds; and
(ii) any written evidence,
may take part in the hearing of the judicial review.
(2) Where that person takes part in the hearing of the judicial review, the court may take his failure to file an acknowledgment of service into account when deciding what order to make about costs.
(3) Rule 8.4 does not apply.

54.10 Permission given
(1) Where permission to proceed is given the court may also give directions.
(2) Directions under paragraph (1) may include a stay of proceedings to which the claim relates.
(Rule 3.7 provides a sanction for the non-payment of the fee payable when permission to proceed has been given)

54.11 Service of order giving or refusing permission
The court will serve—
(a) the order giving or refusing permission; and
(b) any directions,
on—
  (i) the claimant;
  (ii) the defendant; and
  (iii) any other person who filed an acknowledgment of service.

54.12 Permission decision without a hearing
(1) This rule applies where the court, without a hearing—
  (a) refuses permission to proceed; or
  (b) gives permission to proceed—
    (i) subject to conditions; or
    (ii) on certain grounds only.
(2) The court will serve its reasons for making the decision when it serves the order giving or refusing permission in accordance with rule 54.11.
(3) The claimant may not appeal but may request the decision to be reconsidered at a hearing.
(4) A request under paragraph (3) must be filed within 7 days after service of the reasons under paragraph (2).
(5) The claimant, defendant and any other person who has filed an acknowledgment of service will be given at least 2 days' notice of the hearing date.

54.13 Defendant etc. may not apply to set aside
Neither the defendant nor any other person served with the claim form may apply to set aside an order giving permission to proceed.

54.14 Response
(1) A defendant and any other person served with the claim form who wishes to contest the claim or support it on additional grounds must file and serve—
  (a) detailed grounds for contesting the claim or supporting it on additional grounds; and
  (b) any written evidence,
within 35 days after service of the order giving permission.
(2) The following rules do not apply—
  (a) rule 8.5 (3) and 8.5 (4)(defendant to file and serve written evidence at the same time as acknowledgment of service); and
  (b) rule 8.5 (5) and 8.5(6) (claimant to file and serve any reply within 14 days).

54.15 Where claimant seeks to rely on additional grounds
The court's permission is required if a claimant seeks to rely on grounds other than those for which he has been given permission to proceed.

54.16 Evidence
(1) Rule 8.6 (1) does not apply.
(2) No written evidence may be relied on unless—
  (a) it has been served in accordance with any—
    (i) rule under this Section; or
    (ii) direction of the court; or
  (b) the court gives permission.

54.17 Court's powers to hear any person
(1) Any person may apply for permission—
  (a) to file evidence; or
  (b) make representations at the hearing of the judicial review.
(2) An application under paragraph (1) should be made promptly.

54.18 Judicial review may be decided without a hearing
The court may decide the claim for judicial review without a hearing where all the parties agree.

54.19 Court's powers in respect of quashing orders
(1) This rule applies where the court makes a quashing order in respect of the decision to which the claim relates.
(2) The court may—
    (a) (i) remit the matter to the decision-maker; and
        (ii) direct it to reconsider the matter and reach a decision in accordance with the judgment of the court; or
    (b) in so far as any enactment permits, substitute its own decision for the decision to which the claim relates.
(Section 31 of the Supreme Court Act 1981 enables the High Court, subject to certain conditions, to substitute its own decision for the decision in question.)

54.20 Transfer
The court may
(a) order a claim to continue as if it had not been started under this Section; and
(b) where it does so, give directions about the future management of the claim.
(Part 30 (transfer) applies to transfers to and from the Administrative Court)

CIVIL PROCEDURE RULES 1998, PD 54

The Court
2.1 Part 54 claims for judicial review are dealt with in the Administrative Court.
2.2 Where the claim is proceeding in the Administrative Court in London, documents must be filed at the Administrative Court Office, the Royal Courts of Justice, Strand, London, WC2A 2LL.
2.3 Where the claim is proceeding in the Administrative Court in Wales (see paragraph 3.1), documents must be filed at the Civil Justice Centre, 2 Park Street, Cardiff, CF10 1ET.

Urgent applications

2.4 Where urgency makes it necessary for the claim for judicial review to be made outside London or Cardiff, the Administrative Court Office in London should be consulted (if necessary, by telephone) prior to filing the claim form.

Rule 54.5 – Time limit for filing claim form

4.1 Where the claim is for a quashing order in respect of a judgment, order or conviction, the date when the grounds to make the claim first arose, for the purposes of rule 54.5(1)(b), is the date of that judgment, order or conviction.

Rule 54.6 – claim form

Interested parties

5.1 Where the claim for judicial review relates to proceedings in a court or tribunal, any other parties to those proceedings must be named in the claim form as interested parties under rule 54.6(1)(a) (and therefore served with the claim form under rule 54.7(b)).
5.2 For example, in a claim by a defendant in a criminal case in the Magistrates or Crown Court for judicial review of a decision in that case, the prosecution must always be named as an interested party.

Human rights

5.3 Where the claimant is seeking to raise any issue under the Human Rights Act 1998, or seeks a remedy available under that Act, the claim form must include the information required by paragraph 15 of the practice direction supplementing Part 16.

Devolution issues

5.4 Where the claimant intends to raise a devolution issue, the claim form must:
    (1) specify that the applicant wishes to raise a devolution issue and identify the relevant provisions of the Government of Wales Act 1998, the Northern Ireland Act 1998 or the Scotland Act 1998; and
    (2) contain a summary of the facts, circumstances and points of law on the basis of which it is alleged that a devolution issue arises.

5.5 In this practice direction 'devolution issue' has the same meaning as in paragraph 1, schedule 8 to the Government of Wales Act 1998; paragraph 1, schedule 10 to the Northern Ireland Act 1998; and paragraph 1, schedule 6 of the Scotland Act 1998.

Claim form

5.6 The claim form must include or be accompanied by—
    (1) a detailed statement of the claimant's grounds for bringing the claim for judicial review;
    (2) a statement of the facts relied on;
    (3) any application to extend the time limit for filing the claim form;
    (4) any application for directions.

5.7 In addition, the claim form must be accompanied by
    (1) any written evidence in support of the claim or application to extend time;
    (2) a copy of any order that the claimant seeks to have quashed;
    (3) where the claim for judicial review relates to a decision of a court or tribunal, an approved copy of the reasons for reaching that decision;
    (4) copies of any documents on which the claimant proposes to rely;
    (5) copies of any relevant statutory material; and
    (6) a list of essential documents for advance reading by the court (with page references to the passages relied on).

5.8 Where it is not possible to file all the above documents, the claimant must indicate which documents have not been filed and the reasons why they are not currently available.

Bundle of documents

5.9 The claimant must file two copies of a paginated and indexed bundle containing all the documents referred to in paragraphs 5.6 and 5.7.

5.10 Attention is drawn to rules 8.5(1) and 8.5(7).

Rule 54.7 – service of claim form

6.1 Except as required by rules 54.11 or 54.12(2), the Administrative Court will not serve documents and service must be effected by the parties.

Rule 54.8 – acknowledgment of service

7.1 Attention is drawn to rule 8.3(2) and the relevant practice direction and to rule 10.5.

Rule 54.10 – permission given

Directions

8.1 Case management directions under rule 54.10(1) may include directions about serving the claim form and any evidence on other persons.

8.2 Where a claim is made under the Human Rights Act 1998, a direction may be made for giving notice to the Crown or joining the Crown as a party. Attention is drawn to rule 19.4A and paragraph 6 of the Practice Direction supplementing Section I of Part 19.

8.3 A direction may be made for the hearing of the claim for judicial review to be held outside London or Cardiff. Before making any such direction the judge will consult the judge in charge of the Administrative Court as to its feasibility.

Permission without a hearing

8.4 The court will generally, in the first instance, consider the question of permission without a hearing.

Permission hearing

8.5 Neither the defendant nor any other interested party need attend a hearing on the question of permission unless the court directs otherwise.

8.6 Where the defendant or any party does attend a hearing, the court will not generally make an order for costs against the claimant.

Rule 54.11 – service of order giving or refusing permission

9.1 An order refusing permission or giving it subject to conditions or on certain grounds only must set out or be accompanied by the court's reasons for coming to that decision.

Rule 54.14 – response

10.1 Where the party filing the detailed grounds intends to rely on documents not already filed, he must file a paginated bundle of those documents when he files the detailed grounds.

Rule 54.15 – where claimant seeks to rely on additional grounds

11.1 Where the claimant intends to apply to rely on additional grounds at the hearing of the claim for judicial review, he must give notice to the court and to any other person served with the claim form no later than 7 clear days before the hearing (or the warned date where appropriate).

Rule 54.16 – evidence

12.1 Disclosure is not required unless the court orders otherwise.

Rule 54.17 – court's powers to hear any person

13.1 Where all the parties consent, the court may deal with an application under rule 54.17 without a hearing.

13.2 Where the court gives permission for a person to file evidence or make representations at the hearing of the claim for judicial review, it may do so on conditions and may give case management directions.

13.3 An application for permission should be made by letter to the Administrative Court office, identifying the claim, explaining who the applicant is and indicating why and in what form the applicant wants to participate in the hearing.

13.4 If the applicant is seeking a prospective order as to costs, the letter should say what kind of order and on what grounds.

13.5 Applications to intervene must be made at the earliest reasonable opportunity, since it will usually be essential not to delay the hearing.

Rule 54.20 – transfer

14.1 Attention is drawn to rule 30.5.

14.2 In deciding whether a claim is suitable for transfer to the Administrative Court, the court will consider whether it raises issues of public law to which Part 54 should apply.

Skeleton arguments

15.1 The claimant must file and serve a skeleton argument not less than 21 working days before the date of the hearing of the judicial review (or the warned date).

15.2 The defendant and any other party wishing to make representations at the hearing of the judicial review must file and serve a skeleton argument not less than 14 working days before the date of the hearing of the judicial review (or the warned date).

15.3 Skeleton arguments must contain:
   (1) a time estimate for the complete hearing, including delivery of judgment;
   (2) a list of issues;
   (3) a list of the legal points to be taken (together with any relevant authorities with page references to the passages relied on);
   (4) a chronology of events (with page references to the bundle of documents (see paragraph 16.1);
   (5) a list of essential documents for the advance reading of the court (with page references to the passages relied on) (if different from that filed with the claim form) and a time estimate for that reading; and

(6) a list of persons referred to.

Bundle of documents to be filed

16.1 The claimant must file a paginated and indexed bundle of all relevant documents required for the hearing of the judicial review when he files his skeleton argument.

16.2 The bundle must also include those documents required by the defendant and any other party who is to make representations at the hearing.

Agreed final order

17.1 If the parties agree about the final order to be made in a claim for judicial review, the claimant must file at the court a document (with 2 copies) signed by all the parties setting out the terms of the proposed agreed order together with a short statement of the matters relied on as justifying the proposed agreed order and copies of any authorities or statutory provisions relied on.

17.2 The court will consider the documents referred to in paragraph 17.1 and will make the order if satisfied that the order should be made.

17.3 If the court is not satisfied that the order should be made, a hearing date will be set.

17.4 Where the agreement relates to an order for costs only, the parties need only file a document signed by all the parties setting out the terms of the proposed order.

CONVENTION FOR THE PROTECTION OF HUMAN RIGHTS AND FUNDAMENTAL FREEDOMS AS AMENDED BY PROTOCOL NO. 11

Rome, 4.XI.1950

The governments signatory hereto, being members of the Council of Europe,

Considering the Universal Declaration of Human Rights proclaimed by the General Assembly of the United Nations on 10th December 1948;

Considering that this Declaration aims at securing the universal and effective recognition and observance of the Rights therein declared;

Considering that the aim of the Council of Europe is the achievement of greater unity between its members and that one of the methods by which that aim is to be pursued is the maintenance and further realisation of human rights and fundamental freedoms;

Reaffirming their profound belief in those fundamental freedoms which are the foundation of justice and peace in the world and are best maintained on the one hand by an effective political democracy and on the other by a common understanding and observance of the human rights upon which they depend;

Being resolved, as the governments of European countries which are like-minded and have a common heritage of political traditions, ideals, freedom and the rule of law, to take the first steps for the collective enforcement of certain of the rights stated in the Universal Declaration,

Have agreed as follows:

Article 1 – Obligation to respect human rights

The High Contracting Parties shall secure to everyone within their jurisdiction the rights and freedoms defined in Section I of this Convention.

SECTION I – RIGHTS AND FREEDOMS

Article 2 – Right to life

1 Everyone's right to life shall be protected by law. No one shall be deprived of his life intentionally save in the execution of a sentence of a court following his conviction of a crime for which this penalty is provided by law.
2 Deprivation of life shall not be regarded as inflicted in contravention of this article when it results from the use of force which is no more than absolutely necessary:
    a   in defence of any person from unlawful violence;
    b   in order to effect a lawful arrest or to prevent the escape of a person lawfully detained;
    c   in action lawfully taken for the purpose of quelling a riot or insurrection.

Article 3 – Prohibition of torture

No one shall be subjected to torture or to inhuman or degrading treatment or punishment.

Article 4 – Prohibition of slavery and forced labour

1 No one shall be held in slavery or servitude.
2 No one shall be required to perform forced or compulsory labour.
3 For the purpose of this article the term "forced or compulsory labour" shall not include:
    a   any work required to be done in the ordinary course of detention imposed according to the provisions of Article 5 of this Convention or during conditional release from such detention;
    b   any service of a military character or, in case of conscientious objectors in countries where they are recognised, service exacted instead of compulsory military service;
    c   any service exacted in case of an emergency or calamity threatening the life or well-being of the community;
    d   any work or service which forms part of normal civic obligations.

Article 5 – Right to liberty and security

1 Everyone has the right to liberty and security of person. No one shall be deprived of his liberty save in the following cases and in accordance with a procedure prescribed by law:
    a   the lawful detention of a person after conviction by a competent court;
    b   the lawful arrest or detention of a person for non-compliance with the lawful order of a court or in order to secure the fulfilment of any obligation prescribed by law;

	c	the lawful arrest or detention of a person effected for the purpose of bringing him before the competent legal authority on reasonable suspicion of having committed an offence or when it is reasonably considered necessary to prevent his committing an offence or fleeing after having done so;
	d	the detention of a minor by lawful order for the purpose of educational supervision or his lawful detention for the purpose of bringing him before the competent legal authority;
	e	the lawful detention of persons for the prevention of the spreading of infectious diseases, of persons of unsound mind, alcoholics or drug addicts or vagrants;
	f	the lawful arrest or detention of a person to prevent his effecting an unauthorised entry into the country or of a person against whom action is being taken with a view to deportation or extradition.
2		Everyone who is arrested shall be informed promptly, in a language which he understands, of the reasons for his arrest and of any charge against him.
3		Everyone arrested or detained in accordance with the provisions of paragraph 1.c of this article shall be brought promptly before a judge or other officer authorised by law to exercise judicial power and shall be entitled to trial within a reasonable time or to release pending trial. Release may be conditioned by guarantees to appear for trial.
4		Everyone who is deprived of his liberty by arrest or detention shall be entitled to take proceedings by which the lawfulness of his detention shall be decided speedily by a court and his release ordered if the detention is not lawful.
5		Everyone who has been the victim of arrest or detention in contravention of the provisions of this article shall have an enforceable right to compensation.

Article 6 – Right to a fair trial

1 In the determination of his civil rights and obligations or of any criminal charge against him, everyone is entitled to a fair and public hearing within a reasonable time by an independent and impartial tribunal established by law. Judgment shall be pronounced publicly but the press and public may be excluded from all or part of the trial in the interests of morals, public order or national security in a democratic society, where the interests of juveniles or the protection of the private life of the parties so require, or to the extent strictly necessary in the opinion of the court in special circumstances where publicity would prejudice the interests of justice.

2 Everyone charged with a criminal offence shall be presumed innocent until proved guilty according to law.

3 Everyone charged with a criminal offence has the following minimum rights:
- a to be informed promptly, in a language which he understands and in detail, of the nature and cause of the accusation against him;
- b to have adequate time and facilities for the preparation of his defence;
- c to defend himself in person or through legal assistance of his own choosing or, if he has not sufficient means to pay for legal assistance, to be given it free when the interests of justice so require;
- d to examine or have examined witnesses against him and to obtain the attendance and examination of witnesses on his behalf under the same conditions as witnesses against him;
- e to have the free assistance of an interpreter if he cannot understand or speak the language used in court.

Article 7 – No punishment without law

1 No one shall be held guilty of any criminal offence on account of any act or omission which did not constitute a criminal offence under national or international law at the time when it was committed. Nor shall a heavier penalty be imposed than the one that was applicable at the time the criminal offence was committed.

2 This article shall not prejudice the trial and punishment of any person for any act or omission which, at the time when it was committed, was criminal according to the general principles of law recognised by civilised nations.

Article 8 – Right to respect for private and family life

1 Everyone has the right to respect for his private and family life, his home and his correspondence.

2   There shall be no interference by a public authority with the exercise of this right except such as is in accordance with the law and is necessary in a democratic society in the interests of national security, public safety or the economic well-being of the country, for the prevention of disorder or crime, for the protection of health or morals, or for the protection of the rights and freedoms of others.

Article 9 – Freedom of thought, conscience and religion

1   Everyone has the right to freedom of thought, conscience and religion; this right includes freedom to change his religion or belief and freedom, either alone or in community with others and in public or private, to manifest his religion or belief, in worship, teaching, practice and observance.
2   Freedom to manifest one's religion or beliefs shall be subject only to such limitations as are prescribed by law and are necessary in a democratic society in the interests of public safety, for the protection of public order, health or morals, or for the protection of the rights and freedoms of others.

Article 10 – Freedom of expression

1   Everyone has the right to freedom of expression. This right shall include freedom to hold opinions and to receive and impart information and ideas without interference by public authority and regardless of frontiers. This article shall not prevent States from requiring the licensing of broadcasting, television or cinema enterprises.
2   The exercise of these freedoms, since it carries with it duties and responsibilities, may be subject to such formalities, conditions, restrictions or penalties as are prescribed by law and are necessary in a democratic society, in the interests of national security, territorial integrity or public safety, for the prevention of disorder or crime, for the protection of health or morals, for the protection of the reputation or rights of others, for preventing the disclosure of information received in confidence, or for maintaining the authority and impartiality of the judiciary.

Article 11 – Freedom of assembly and association

1   Everyone has the right to freedom of peaceful assembly and to freedom of association with others, including the right to form and to join trade unions for the protection of his interests.
2   No restrictions shall be placed on the exercise of these rights other than such as are prescribed by law and are necessary in a democratic society in the interests of national security or public safety, for the prevention of disorder or crime, for the protection of health or morals or for the protection of the rights and freedoms of others. This article shall not prevent the imposition of lawful restrictions on the exercise of these rights by members of the armed forces, of the police or of the administration of the State.

Article 12 – Right to marry

Men and women of marriageable age have the right to marry and to found a family, according to the national laws governing the exercise of this right.

Article 13 – Right to an effective remedy

Everyone whose rights and freedoms as set forth in this Convention are violated shall have an effective remedy before a national authority notwithstanding that the violation has been committed by persons acting in an official capacity.

Article 14 – Prohibition of discrimination

The enjoyment of the rights and freedoms set forth in this Convention shall be secured without discrimination on any ground such as sex, race, colour, language, religion, political or other opinion, national or social origin, association with a national minority, property, birth or other status.

Article 15 – Derogation in time of emergency

1   In time of war or other public emergency threatening the life of the nation any High Contracting Party may take measures derogating from its obligations under this Convention to the extent strictly required by the exigencies of the situation, provided that such measures are not inconsistent with its other obligations under international law.
2   No derogation from Article 2, except in respect of deaths resulting from lawful acts of war, or from Articles 3, 4 (paragraph 1) and 7 shall be made under this provision.

3   Any High Contracting Party availing itself of this right of derogation shall keep the Secretary General of the Council of Europe fully informed of the measures which it has taken and the reasons therefor. It shall also inform the Secretary General of the Council of Europe when such measures have ceased to operate and the provisions of the Convention are again being fully executed.

SECTION II – EUROPEAN COURT OF HUMAN RIGHTS

Article 19 – Establishment of the Court

To ensure the observance of the engagements undertaken by the High Contracting Parties in the Convention and the Protocols thereto, there shall be set up a European Court of Human Rights, hereinafter referred to as "the Court". It shall function on a permanent basis.

Article 20 – Number of judges

The Court shall consist of a number of judges equal to that of the High Contracting Parties.

Article 21 – Criteria for office

1   The judges shall be of high moral character and must either possess the qualifications required for appointment to high judicial office or be jurisconsults of recognised competence.
2   The judges shall sit on the Court in their individual capacity.
3   During their term of office the judges shall not engage in any activity which is incompatible with their independence, impartiality or with the demands of a full-time office; all questions arising from the application of this paragraph shall be decided by the Court.

Article 22 – Election of judges

1   The judges shall be elected by the Parliamentary Assembly with respect to each High Contracting Party by a majority of votes cast from a list of three candidates nominated by the High Contracting Party.
2   The same procedure shall be followed to complete the Court in the event of the accession of new High Contracting Parties and in filling casual vacancies.

Article 23 – Terms of office

1   The judges shall be elected for a period of six years. They may be re-elected. However, the terms of office of one-half of the judges elected at the first election shall expire at the end of three years.
2   The judges whose terms of office are to expire at the end of the initial period of three years shall be chosen by lot by the Secretary General of the Council of Europe immediately after their election.
3   In order to ensure that, as far as possible, the terms of office of one-half of the judges are renewed every three years, the Parliamentary Assembly may decide, before proceeding to any subsequent election, that the term or terms of office of one or more judges to be elected shall be for a period other than six years but not more than nine and not less than three years.
4   In cases where more than one term of office is involved and where the Parliamentary Assembly applies the preceding paragraph, the allocation of the terms of office shall be effected by a drawing of lots by the Secretary General of the Council of Europe immediately after the election.
5   A judge elected to replace a judge whose term of office has not expired shall hold office for the remainder of his predecessor's term.
6   The terms of office of judges shall expire when they reach the age of 70.
7   The judges shall hold office until replaced. They shall, however, continue to deal with such cases as they already have under consideration.

Article 24 – Dismissal

No judge may be dismissed from his office unless the other judges decide by a majority of two-thirds that he has ceased to fulfil the required conditions.

Article 25 – Registry and legal secretaries

The Court shall have a registry, the functions and organisation of which shall be laid down in the rules of the Court. The Court shall be assisted by legal secretaries.

Article 26 – Plenary Court

The plenary Court shall

a   elect its President and one or two Vice-Presidents for a period of three years; they may be re-elected;
b   set up Chambers, constituted for a fixed period of time;
c   elect the Presidents of the Chambers of the Court; they may be re-elected;
d   adopt the rules of the Court, and
e   elect the Registrar and one or more Deputy Registrars.

Article 27 – Committees, Chambers and Grand Chamber

1   To consider cases brought before it, the Court shall sit in committees of three judges, in Chambers of seven judges and in a Grand Chamber of seventeen judges. The Court's Chambers shall set up committees for a fixed period of time.
2   There shall sit as an ex officio member of the Chamber and the Grand Chamber the judge elected in respect of the State Party concerned or, if there is none or if he is unable to sit, a person of its choice who shall sit in the capacity of judge.
3   The Grand Chamber shall also include the President of the Court, the Vice-Presidents, the Presidents of the Chambers and other judges chosen in accordance with the rules of the Court. When a case is referred to the Grand Chamber under Article 43, no judge from the Chamber which rendered the judgment shall sit in the Grand Chamber, with the exception of the President of the Chamber and the judge who sat in respect of the State Party concerned.

Article 28 – Declarations of inadmissibility by committees

A committee may, by a unanimous vote, declare inadmissible or strike out of its list of cases an application submitted under Article 34 where such a decision can be taken without further examination. The decision shall be final.

Article 29 – Decisions by Chambers on admissibility and merits

1   If no decision is taken under Article 28, a Chamber shall decide on the admissibility and merits of individual applications submitted under Article 34.
2   A Chamber shall decide on the admissibility and merits of inter-State applications submitted under Article 33.
3   The decision on admissibility shall be taken separately unless the Court, in exceptional cases, decides otherwise.

Article 30 – Relinquishment of jurisdiction to the Grand Chamber

Where a case pending before a Chamber raises a serious question affecting the interpretation of the Convention or the protocols thereto, or where the resolution of a question before the Chamber might have a result inconsistent with a judgment previously delivered by the Court, the Chamber may, at any time before it has rendered its judgment, relinquish jurisdiction in favour of the Grand Chamber, unless one of the parties to the case objects.

Article 31 – Powers of the Grand Chamber

The Grand Chamber shall

a   determine applications submitted either under Article 33 or Article 34 when a Chamber has relinquished jurisdiction under Article 30 or when the case has been referred to it under Article 43; and
b   consider requests for advisory opinions submitted under Article 47.

Article 32 – Jurisdiction of the Court

1   The jurisdiction of the Court shall extend to all matters concerning the interpretation and application of the Convention and the protocols thereto which are referred to it as provided in Articles 33, 34 and 47.
2   In the event of dispute as to whether the Court has jurisdiction, the Court shall decide.

Article 33 – Inter-State cases

Any High Contracting Party may refer to the Court any alleged breach of the provisions of the Convention and the protocols thereto by another High Contracting Party.

Article 34 – Individual applications

The Court may receive applications from any person, non-governmental organisation or group of individuals claiming to be the victim of a violation by one of the High Contracting Parties of the rights set forth in the Convention or the protocols thereto. The High Contracting Parties undertake not to hinder in any way the effective exercise of this right.

Article 35 – Admissibility criteria

1 The Court may only deal with the matter after all domestic remedies have been exhausted, according to the generally recognised rules of international law, and within a period of six months from the date on which the final decision was taken.
2 The Court shall not deal with any application submitted under Article 34 that
   a is anonymous; or
   b is substantially the same as a matter that has already been examined by the Court or has already been submitted to another procedure of international investigation or settlement and contains no relevant new information.
3 The Court shall declare inadmissible any individual application submitted under Article 34 which it considers incompatible with the provisions of the Convention or the protocols thereto, manifestly ill-founded, or an abuse of the right of application.
4 The Court shall reject any application which it considers inadmissible under this Article. It may do so at any stage of the proceedings.

Article 36 – Third party intervention

1 In all cases before a Chamber or the Grand Chamber, a High Contracting Party one of whose nationals is an applicant shall have the right to submit written comments and to take part in hearings.
2 The President of the Court may, in the interest of the proper administration of justice, invite any High Contracting Party which is not a party to the proceedings or any person concerned who is not the applicant to submit written comments or take part in hearings.

Article 37 – Striking out applications

1 The Court may at any stage of the proceedings decide to strike an application out of its list of cases where the circumstances lead to the conclusion that
   a the applicant does not intend to pursue his application; or
   b the matter has been resolved; or
   c for any other reason established by the Court, it is no longer justified to continue the examination of the application.
However, the Court shall continue the examination of the application if respect for human rights as defined in the Convention and the protocols thereto so requires.
2 The Court may decide to restore an application to its list of cases if it considers that the circumstances justify such a course.

Article 38 – Examination of the case and friendly settlement proceedings

1 If the Court declares the application admissible, it shall
   a pursue the examination of the case, together with the representatives of the parties, and if need be, undertake an investigation, for the effective conduct of which the States concerned shall furnish all necessary facilities;
   b place itself at the disposal of the parties concerned with a view to securing a friendly settlement of the matter on the basis of respect for human rights as defined in the Convention and the protocols thereto.
2 Proceedings conducted under paragraph 1.b shall be confidential.

Article 39 – Finding of a friendly settlement
If a friendly settlement is effected, the Court shall strike the case out of its list by means of a decision which shall be confined to a brief statement of the facts and of the solution reached.

Article 40 – Public hearings and access to documents
1 Hearings shall be in public unless the Court in exceptional circumstances decides otherwise.
2 Documents deposited with the Registrar shall be accessible to the public unless the President of the Court decides otherwise.

Article 41 – Just satisfaction
If the Court finds that there has been a violation of the Convention or the protocols thereto, and if the internal law of the High Contracting Party concerned allows only partial reparation to be made, the Court shall, if necessary, afford just satisfaction to the injured party.

Article 42 – Judgments of Chambers
Judgments of Chambers shall become final in accordance with the provisions of Article 44, paragraph 2.

Article 43 – Referral to the Grand Chamber
1 Within a period of three months from the date of the judgment of the Chamber, any party to the case may, in exceptional cases, request that the case be referred to the Grand Chamber.
2 A panel of five judges of the Grand Chamber shall accept the request if the case raises a serious question affecting the interpretation or application of the Convention or the protocols thereto, or a serious issue of general importance.
3 If the panel accepts the request, the Grand Chamber shall decide the case by means of a judgment.

Article 44 – Final judgments
1 The judgment of the Grand Chamber shall be final.
2 The judgment of a Chamber shall become final
   a when the parties declare that they will not request that the case be referred to the Grand Chamber; or
   b three months after the date of the judgment, if reference of the case to the Grand Chamber has not been requested; or
   c when the panel of the Grand Chamber rejects the request to refer under Article 43.
3 The final judgment shall be published.

Article 45 – Reasons for judgments and decisions
1 Reasons shall be given for judgments as well as for decisions declaring applications admissible or inadmissible.
2 If a judgment does not represent, in whole or in part, the unanimous opinion of the judges, any judge shall be entitled to deliver a separate opinion.

Article 46 – Binding force and execution of judgments
1 The High Contracting Parties undertake to abide by the final judgment of the Court in any case to which they are parties.
2 The final judgment of the Court shall be transmitted to the Committee of Ministers, which shall supervise its execution.

Article 53 – Safeguard for existing human rights
Nothing in this Convention shall be construed as limiting or derogating from any of the human rights and fundamental freedoms which may be ensured under the laws of any High Contracting Party or under any other agreement to which it is a Party.

Protocol to the Convention for the Protection of Human Rights and Fundamental Freedoms

Paris, 20.III.1952

Article 1 – Protection of property
Every natural or legal person is entitled to the peaceful enjoyment of his possessions. No one shall be deprived of his possessions except in the public interest and subject to the conditions provided for by law and by the general principles of international law.

The preceding provisions shall not, however, in any way impair the right of a State to enforce such laws as it deems necessary to control the use of property in accordance with the general interest or to secure the payment of taxes or other contributions or penalties.

Article 2 – Right to education
No person shall be denied the right to education. In the exercise of any functions which it assumes in relation to education and to teaching, the State shall respect the right of parents to ensure such education and teaching in conformity with their own religious and philosophical convictions.

Article 3 – Right to free elections
The High Contracting Parties undertake to hold free elections at reasonable intervals by secret ballot, under conditions which will ensure the free expression of the opinion of the people in the choice of the legislature.

Protocol No. 6 to the Convention for the Protection of Human Rights and Fundamental Freedoms concerning the abolition of the death penalty

Strasbourg, 28.IV.1983

Article 1 – Abolition of the death penalty
The death penalty shall be abolished. No-one shall be condemned to such penalty or executed.

Article 2 – Death penalty in time of war
A State may make provision in its law for the death penalty in respect of acts committed in time of war or of imminent threat of war; such penalty shall be applied only in the instances laid down in the law and in accordance with its provisions. The State shall communicate to the Secretary General of the Council of Europe the relevant provisions of that law.

INDEX

Act of Settlement (1700) — *6–8*
Anti-social Behaviour Act 2003
 ss 30-32, 36 — *244–246*
Anti-terrorism, Crime and Security Act 2001
 ss 1, 4, 5, 10 — *223–224*

Bill of Rights (1688) — *2–5*

Civil Procedure Rules 1998
 Part 54, PD 54 — *383–389*
Constitutional Reform Act 2005
 ss 1-3, 5, 7, 8, 14, 15, 18, 23-31, 33, 34, 41, 61-65, 67, 70, 71, Sch 12 — *258–265*
Crime and Disorder Act 1998
 ss 1, 4, 11, 13-15, 28-32, 34, 36 — *151–156*
Criminal Justice Act 2003
 ss 29, 30 — *246–248*
Criminal Justice and Police Act 2001
 ss 50-56, 58, 59, 61, 63 — *216–223*
Criminal Justice and Public Order Act 1994
 ss 34-37, 60-64 — *119–125*
Crown Proceedings Act 1947
 ss 1, 2, 4, 11, 17, 21, 40 — *19–22*

Equality Act 2006
 ss 1, 3, 4, 8-11, 13, 20 — *281–284*
European Communities Act 1972
 ss 1-3 — *31–32*
European Convention for the Protection of Human Rights and Fundamental Freedoms
 Arts 1-15, 19-46, 53, Protocol 1, Arts 1-3, Protocol 6, Arts 1, 2 — *390–397*

Freedom of Information Act 2000
 ss 1-3, 6, 8-12, 14, 16-24, 26-45, 47, 49, 50 — *192–205*

Government of Wales Act 2006
 ss 1-3, 5-11, 13, 14, 16, 17, 26, 28, 31-36, 45-52, 56-65, 72-75, 78-82, 90, 93-103, 106-108, 146, 156 — *314–331*

Highways Act 1980
 s 137 — *48*
House of Commons Disqualification Act 1975
 ss 1, 2, 5-8, Sch 2 — *45–47*

House of Commons (Removal of Clergy Disqualification) Act 2001
 ss 1 — *215–216*
House of Lords Act 1999
 ss 1-3, 6 — *191–192*
Human Rights Act 1998
 ss 1-16, 19, 20, Sch 2 — *156–163*

Identity Cards Act 2006
 ss 1-3, 5-13, 15-19, 21, 22, 25-29, 31-33, 35, 37, Sch 1 — *294–314*
Intelligence Services Act 1994
 ss 1–6, 10, 11 — *115–118*

Life Peerages Act 1958
 s 1 — *22*
Local Government Act 1972
 ss 100A-100E, 100G, 101, 111, 112, 222, 235, Sch 12A — *33–38*
Local Government Act 1974
 ss 23, 26, 26A, 28-31, 34, Sch 5 — *38–45*

Magna Carta (1215) — *1–2*
Ministerial and Other Salaries Act 1975
 ss 1, 2, 4 — *47–48*

Northern Ireland Act 1998
 ss 1, 5-7, 9-11, 13, 14, 16A-18, 20, 22-26, 39-43, 68-71, 80, 83 — *181–191*
Obscene Publications Act 1959
 ss 1-4 — *22–24*
Official Secrets Act 1911
 ss 1, 3, 8-10 — *11–12*
Official Secrets Act 1920
 ss 1, 6 — *14–15*
Official Secrets Act 1989
 ss 1-10, 12, 13 — *105–111*

Parliament Act 1911
 ss 1-7 — *12–14*
Parliamentary Commissioner Act 1967
 ss 1, 3-10, 12, Sch 3 — *24–31*
Parliamentary Papers Act 1840
 ss 1-4 — *10*
Police Act 1996
 ss 1-6ZC, 9A-14, 20, 22, 25, 29, 30, 32, 36, 37A-44, 46, 50, 54, 55, 59, 60, 64, 84, 85, 88-91, 93, 96, 126-145, Schs 2, 2A, 4 — *126–145*
Police Act 1997
 ss 93, 95-100, 103, 104, 107 — *146–151*

Police and Criminal Evidence Act 1984
  ss 1-4, 8-24A, 26, 28-30B, 30CA, 30D-32,
    34-47, 53-56, 58, 60-63, 63B-67, 76-78,
    82, 117, Sch 1 *53–94*
Police and Criminal Evidence Act 1984
  Code A
    paras 1-5, Notes *355–365*
Police and Criminal Evidence Act 1984
  Code C
    paras 1-6, 8-11 *366–379*
Police and Criminal Evidence Act 1984
  Code G
    paras 1, 3, 4, Notes *379–382*
Police and Justice Act 2006
  ss 1, 19, 20, Sch 1 *331–337*
Police Reform Act 2002
  ss 9-15, 17-22, 29, 38-40, 41A, 42,
    46, 47, 50, 51, 59, 60 *224–244*
Prevention of Terrorism Act 2005
  ss 1-5, 7-11, 13, 14 *248–257*
Public Order Act 1936
  ss 1, 2 *16–17*
Public Order Act 1986
  ss 1-9, 11-24, 26, 27, 40 *94–104*

Scotland Act 1998
  ss 1, 2, 5-8, 11, 13-16, 19, 22, 28-33, 36,
    37, 39-48, 53, 54, 57, 91, 98-102,
    107, Schs 4, 5, 6 *163–181*

Security Service Act 1989
  ss 1, 2 *112*
Serious Crime Act 2007
  ss 1-5, 19 *349–354*
Serious Organised Crime and Police
  Act 2005
  ss 1-3, 5, 7-9, 11, 21, 32-37, 41, 60-67,
    69, 112, 128, 131-138 *265–281*
Statute of Westminster 1931
  ss 1-4 *15–16*
Statutory Instruments Act 1946
  ss 1-6 *17–19*
Supreme Court [Senior Courts] Act 1981
  ss 1-4, 8, 10-12, 19, 29, 31 *48–53*

Terrorism Act 2000
  ss 1, 3-6, 11-13, 15, 19, 22, 23, 40-43,
    59, 62, 114, 116, Schs 2, 3, 6 *205–215*
Terrorism Act 2006
  ss 1-11, 17-20 *284–294*
Tribunals, Courts and Enforcement Act 2007
  ss 2-18, 22, 24 *337–349*
Tribunals and Inquiries Act 1992
  ss 10-12 *113–114*

UK Borders Act 2007
  ss 1, 2 *354*
Union with Scotland Act 1706
  Arts I-IIII, VI, XVIII, XXV *8–9*